SHAKSPERE'S PREDECESSORS

SHAKSPERE'S PREDECESSORS IN THE ENGLISH DRAMA

BY JOHN ADDINGTON SYMONDS

GREENWOOD PRESS, PUBLISHERS
NEW YORK

Originally published in 1924
by John Murray

First Greenwood Reprinting, 1969

Library of Congress Catalogue Card Number 69-14105

SBN 8371-1154-4

PRINTED IN UNITED STATES OF AMERICA

TO

MY NEPHEW

JOHN Sᵀ LOE STRACHEY

I DEDICATE THESE STUDIES

RESUMED AND CONTINUED AT HIS REQUEST

PREFACE

BETWEEN the years 1862 and 1865 I undertook a History of the Drama in England during the reigns of Elizabeth, James I., and Charles I. With this object in view I composed a series of essays, embracing the chief points in that history, and discussing the leading playwrights from the period of the Miracles down to that of Shirley. Having so far advanced toward the completion of this plan, I laid my manuscripts aside, discouraged partly by ill-health, partly by a conviction that the subject was beyond the scope and judgment of a literary beginner.

These early studies I have now resumed. The present volume is the first instalment of a critical inquiry into the conditions of the English Drama, based upon work which I began some twenty years ago, but which has been entirely re-handled and revised.

In the space of those twenty years the origins and evolution of our Drama have been amply treated and diligently explored by more than one distinguished and by many competent writers. Professor A. W. Ward's 'History of English Dramatic Literature' supplies what was conspicuous by its absence from our libraries in 1862, namely, a comprehensive and excellently balanced survey of the works of the chief dramatists. The New Shakspere Society has instituted an original method of inquiry into questions of text, chronology and authorship. Mr. Swinburne, Professor Dowden, and Mr. Gosse have published monographs of fine critical and æsthetic quality. Mr. W. C. Hazlitt, Mr. Churton Collins, Mr. A. H. Bullen, and the late Richard Simpson—to mention only a few prominent names—have enriched our stores of accessible documents with plays reprinted from rare copies or published for the first time from MS. Professor Arber and Dr. Grosart have placed at the student's disposition masses of useful materials, extracted from sources inaccessible to the general reader, and edited with unimpeachable accuracy. American scholarship, meanwhile, has not been altogether idle in this field; while German criticism has been voluminously prolific.

To mention all the men of distinction whose varied labours have aided the student of Elizabethan Dramatic Literature during the last twenty years, would involve too long a catalogue of names and publications.

I may well feel diffidence in bringing forth my own studies to the light of day, after this computation of recent and still active workers on the subject. Elizabethan Dramatic Literature is a well-defined speciality, important enough to occupy a man's life-labours. I cannot pretend to be a specialist in this department;

nor have I sought to write for specialists. It has been my intention to bring the history of the English Drama within the sphere of popular treatment; not shrinking from the discussion of topics which are only too familiar to special students; combining exposition with criticism; and endeavouring to fix attention on the main points of literary evolution.

I have only to add in conclusion that the present volume has been produced under the disadvantageous conditions of continued residence in the High Alps, at a distance from all libraries except my own. But for the generous and disinterested assistance rendered me by Mr. A. H. BULLEN, I should almost dread to print a work of this nature, composed in such unfavourable circumstances. To this gentleman, so well known by his edition of Day's works and by his series of Old Plays in course of publication, my warmest thanks are due for reading each sheet as it passed through the press, and for making most valuable suggestions and corrections, which give me confidence in the comparative accuracy of my statements.

DAVOS PLATZ: *Nov.* 9, 1888.

CONTENTS

CHAPTER I

INTRODUCTORY

CHAPTER II

THE NATION AND THE DRAMA

CHAPTER III

MIRACLE PLAYS

I. Emergence of the Drama from the Mystery—Ecclesiastical
Condemnation of Theatres and Players—Obscure Survival of
Mimes from Pagan Times—Their Place in Medieval Society.
—II. Hroswitha—Liturgical Drama.—III. Transition to the
Mystery or Miracle Play—Ludi—Italian *Sacre Rappresen-
tazioni*—Spanish *Auto*—French *Mystère*—English Miracle.—
IV. Passage of the Miracle from the Clergy to the People—
From Latin to the Vulgar Tongue—Gradual Emergence of
Secular Drama.—V. Three English Cycles—Origin of the
Chester Plays—Of the Coventry Plays—Differences between
the Three Sets—Other Places famous for Sacred Plays.—VI.
Methods of Representation—Pageant—Procession—Italian,
French, and Spanish Peculiarities—The Guilds—Cost of the
Show—Concourse of People—Stage Effects and Properties.—
VII. Relation of the Miracle to Medieval Art—Materialistic
Realism—Place in the Cathedral—Effect upon the Audience.

CHAPTER IV

MORAL PLAYS

CHAPTER V

THE RISE OF COMEDY

CHAPTER VI

THE RISE OF TRAGEDY

CHAPTER VII

TRIUMPH OF THE ROMANTIC DRAMA

CHAPTER VIII

THEATRES, PLAYWRIGHTS, ACTORS, AND PLAYGOERS

CHAPTER IX

MASQUES AT COURT

CHAPTER X

ENGLISH HISTORY

CHAPTER XI

DOMESTIC TRAGEDY

CHAPTER XII

TRAGEDY OF BLOOD

CHAPTER XIII

JOHN LYLY

CHAPTER XIV

GREENE, PEELE, NASH, AND LODGE

CHAPTER XV

MARLOWE

SHAKSPERE'S PREDECESSORS

CHAPTER I

INTRODUCTORY

Method of Inquiry—Chronological Limits—Unity of the Subject.—
II. Three Stages in Evolution of the Drama—Stage of Preparation
and Formation—Closed by Marlowe—Stage of perfectly developed
Type—Character of Shakspere's Art—Jonson and Fletcher—Stage of
Gradual Decline.—III. The Law of Artistic Evolution—Illustrations
from Gothic Architecture, Greek Drama, Italian Painting.—IV. The
Problem for Criticism—In Biography—In History—Shakspere
personifies English Genius in his Century—Criticism has to demon-
strate this.—V. Chronology is scarcely helpful—Complexity of the
Subject—Imperfection of our Drama as a Work of Art—Abundance
of Materials for Studying all Three Stages—Unique Richness of our
Dramatic Literature.—VI. Shakspere's Relation to his Age—To
his Predecessors—To his Successors.—VII. Double Direction of
English Literary Art—Jonson, Milton, Dryden, Pope—Spirit of the
Elizabethan Epoch.—VIII. The Elizabethan Inspiration is ex-
hausted in the Reign of Charles I.—Dramatists of the Restoration
—Rise of the Novel—Place of Novelists in the Victorian Age.

I

In attempting a survey of one of the great periods of literary
history, the critic is met with a problem, upon his conception
and solution of which will depend both method and distribution of material. This initial difficulty may be stated in the
form of questions. What central point of view can be
adopted? How shall the order of inquiry be determined?
Do the phenomena to be considered suggest some natural
classification; or must the semblance of a system be introduced by means of artificial manipulation?

This difficulty makes itself fully felt in dealing with what we call Elizabethan Drama. The subject is at once one of the largest and the narrowest, of the most simple and the most complex. It ranks among the largest, because it involves a wide and varied survey of human experience; among the narrowest, because it is confined to a brief space of time and to a single nation; among the most simple, because the nation which produced that Drama was insulated and independent of foreign interference; among the most complex, because the English people at that epoch exhibited the whole of its exuberant life together with an important stage of European culture in its theatre.

Confined within the strictest chronological limits (1580-1630), the period embraced by such a study does not exceed fifty years. Very little therefore of assistance to the critical method can be expected from the mere observation of development in time. Yet the ruling instinct of the present century demands, and in my opinion demands rightly, some demonstration of a process in the facts collected and presented by a student to the public. It is both unphilosophical and uninteresting to bind up notices, reviews, and criticisms of a score or two of dramatists; as though these writers had sprung, each unaided by the other, into the pale light of history; as though they did not acknowledge one law, controlling the noblest no less than the meanest; as though their work, surveyed in its entirety, were not obedient to some spirit, regulating and determining each portion of the whole.

We are bound to discover links of connection between man and man, ruling principles by which all were governed, common qualities of national character conspicuous throughout the series, before we have the right to style the result of our studies anything better than a bundle of literary essays. It is even incumbent upon us to do more than this. In spite of narrow chronological limitations, it is our duty to show that the subject we have undertaken has a beginning, a middle, and an ending in the category of time, and that the completion of the process was inherent in its earliest, embryonic stages.

II

In the history of the English Drama during the reigns of Elizabeth and James, the conditions which render a well-ordered inquiry possible were sufficiently realised. Whatever method the critic may decide on, this at least he must both recognise and bear in view. He has to deal with a growth of poetry, shooting complete in stem and foliage and blossom, with extraordinary force and exuberant fertility, in a space of time almost unparalleled for brevity. The unity of his subject, the organic interdependence of its several parts, is what he has to keep before his mind.

Three stages may be marked in the short but vigorous evolution of our dramatic literature. The first and longest is the stage of preparation and of tentative endeavour. In the second maturity is reached ; the type is fixed by one great master, perfected and presented to the world in unapproachable magnificence by one immeasurably greater. The third is a stage of decadence and dissipation ; the type, brought previously to perfection, suffers from attempts to vary or refine upon it.

In the first stage we trace the efforts of our national genius to form for itself, instinctively, almost unconsciously, its own peculiar language of expression. Various influences are brought to bear upon the people at this epoch—through the religious conflicts of the Reformation, through the revival of classical learning, in the definition of English nationality against the powers of Spain and Rome, in the contact with Italian culture. England had not fashioned her own forms of art before the literatures of other and widely different races were held up for emulative admiration to our students. There was a danger lest invention should be crushed by imitation at the outset. Pedantic rules, borrowed from Aristotelian commentators and the apes of Seneca, were imposed by learned critics on the playwright. And no sooner had this peril been avoided, than another threatened. It seemed for a moment as though our theatre might be prostituted to purposes of political satire, diverted from its proper function of artistic presentation, and finally suppressed as a seditious engine. Meanwhile, a powerful body in the State, headed by the Puritans, but recruited from all classes of order-loving citizens, regarded the theatre with suspicion and dislike.

The native genius of the English people, though menaced by these divers dangers, was so vigorous, the race itself was so isolated and so full of a robust tempestuous vitality, the language was so copious and vivid in its spoken strength, the poetic impulse was so powerful, that all efforts to domesticate alien styles, all inducements to degrade or scurrilise the theatre, all factious opposition to the will and pleasure of the people, ended in the assimilation of congenial and the rejection of repugnant elements. The style of England, the expression of our race in a specific form of art, grew steadily, instinctively, spontaneously, by evolution from within.

From this first period, which embraces the Miracles, Moralities, and Interludes, the earliest comedies of common manners, the classical experiments of Sackville and Norton, Hughes, Gascoigne, Edwards, and their satellites, the euphuistic phantasies of Lyly, the melodramas of Kyd, Greene, and Peele, together with the first rude history-plays and realistic tragedies of daily life, emerges Marlowe. Marlowe is the dramatist under whose hand the type, as it is destined to endure and triumph, takes form, becomes a thing of power and beauty. Marlowe closes the first, inaugurates the second period.

Over the second period Shakspere reigns paramount; perhaps we ought to say, he reigns alone; although a Titan so robust as Jonson stands at his right hand, with claims to sovereignty, and large scope in the future for the proclamation of his title. We, however, who regard the evolution of the Drama from the vantage-ground of time, see that in Shakspere the art of sixteenth-century England was completed and accomplished. It had imbibed all elements it needed for its growth; comic humour, lyrical loveliness, the tragic earnestness and intense reality of English imagination, classical story and Italian romance, the phantasmagoric brilliancy of shows at Court, the gust of fresh life breathed into the spirit of a haughty and heroic nation by the conflicts and the triumphs of a recent past. The point about Shakspere's art is that it *is* Art, mature, self-conscious, working upon given methods to a single aim. Those methods, the external forms, of Shakspere's drama had been determined for him by his predecessors. That aim, the one aim of true dramatic art, the aim which he alone triumphantly achieved, was the presentation of human character in action. To this artistic end all elements, however various, however wonderfully blent, however used and scattered with the profuse prodigality of an unrivalled genius, are impartially subordinated. In order to illustrate the single-hearted sincerity of Shakspere as an artist, it is only needful to observe the exclusion of religious comment, of marked political intention, of deliberate moralising, from works so full of opportunities for their display, and in an age when the very foundations of opinion had been stirred, when Europe was convulsed with wars and schisms, when speculative philosophy was essaying fresh Icarian flights over the whole range of human experience. True to his vocation, Shakspere never permitted these ferments of the time to distract him from the poet's task, although he found in them a source of intellectual stimulus and moral insight, an atmosphere of mental energy, which makes his plays the school of human nature for all time.

Shakspere realised the previous efforts of the English genius to form a Drama, and perfected the type in his imperishable masterpieces. With him, in the second period, but after a wide interval, we have to rank Ben Jonson, who adapted the classical bias of the earlier stage to England's now developed art, and Fletcher, through whom the romantic motives borrowed from Italian and Spanish sources found new and luminous expression. In the third period we meet a host of valiant playwrights, led by Webster, Ford, Massinger, Shirley: none of them mean men. Yet these are influenced and circumscribed by their commanding predecessors ; limited in their resources by the exhaustion of more salient subjects ;

incapable of reforming the type upon a different conception of
dramatic art; forced to affect novelty and to stimulate the
jaded sensibilities of a sated audience by means of ingenious
extravagances, by the invention of strained incidents, by
curious combinations, far-sought fables, monstrosities, and
tangled plots. After them the type dies down into inanities
and laboured incoherent imitations.

III

This evolution of our Drama through three broadly marked
stages follows the law of growth which may be traced in all
continuous products of the human spirit. A close parallel is
afforded by the familiar periods of medieval architecture;
which in all countries of Europe emerged from Romanesque
into Pointed Gothic, the latter style passing through stages of
early purity, decorative richness, and efflorescent decadence.
Greek dramatic art, obeying the same rule of triple progres-
sion, took its origin in religious mysteries and rites of Dionysus;
assumed shape at the hands of Thespis and Susarion, Phrynichus
and Cratinus; received accomplished form in the master-
works of Æschylus, Sophocles, Euripides, and Aristophanes;
broke up into the tragedy of Agathon, Chæremon, Moschion,
the middle Comedy of Plato and Antiphanes, the new Comedy
of Menander and Philemon. In dealing with the later stages
of the Attic Drama, it is, however, more proper to speak of
divergences from the primitive stock than of absolute decadence. While we have good reason to believe that Tragedy
declined after the age of Agathon, owing to the same cause
which led to its decline in England—inability to alter or to
vary an established type; the Comedy of Menander indicated
no such exhaustion of the soil, no diminution of creative
vigour. It was a new form, corresponding to altered conditions of Greek life; and in this respect it might be compared
to our own Comedy of the Restoration.

To multiply instances would be superfluous. Yet I am
loth to omit the illustration of this law of artistic development, which is furnished by Italian painting. Emerging

from Byzantine or Romanesque tradition, painting traverses
the stage of Giotto and the Giottesque schools; produces
almost simultaneously in several provinces of Italy the intermediate art of Ghirlandajo and Bellini, of Mantegna and
Signorelli, of Lippi and Perugino; concentrates its force in
Raphael, Da Vinci, Michelangelo, Correggio, Titian; then, as
though its inner source of life had been exhausted, breaks off
into extravagance, debility, and facile formalism in the works
of Giulio Romano, Perino del Vaga, Giorgio Vasari, Pietro
da Cortona, the younger Caliari and Robusti, and countless
hosts of academical revivalists and imitators. The slovenly
and empty performance of those epigoni to the true heroes of
Italian painting, in which, however, the tradition of a mighty
style yet lingers, may not inaptly be paralleled by the loose and
hasty plays of men like Davenant and Crowne, by their dis-
located plots and conventional characters, by their blurred
and sketchy treatment of old motives, and by the break-down
of dramatic blank verse into a chaos of rhythmic incoherences.

Reverting once more to Gothic architecture, we notice
precisely the same enervation and extravagance, the same
facility of execution combined with the same formalism and
fatuity, the same straining after novelty through an exhausted
method, effects of over-ripeness and irresistible decay, in the
flamboyance of French window-traceries, the sprawling casements and splayed ogees of expiring Perpendicular in
England.

IV

The critic, whether he be dealing with the English or the
Attic Drama, with Gothic Architecture or Italian Painting,
has to aim at seizing the essential nature of the product laid
before him, at fixing on the culminating point in the development he traces, observing the gradual approaches toward
maturity, and explaining the inevitable decadence by causes
sought for in the matter of his theme. With this in view,
the analogy between history and biography, between national
genius in one of its decisive epochs and individual genius in

one of the world's heroes, is not to be contemned, provided
we apply it with the freedom of a metaphor. There is
nothing good, beautiful, or strong upon our planet, no
religion and no empire, no phase of polity or form of art,
however the idea of it may survive inviolable in the memory
of ages, however its essential truth and spirit may abide
beyond the reach of change and time, but in its actual
historic manifestation is subject, like a human being, to birth,
development, decay, and dissolution.

> All the flowers of the spring
> Meet to perfume our burying :
> These have but their growing prime ;
> And man does flourish but his time :
> Survey our progress from our birth ;
> We are set, we grow, we turn to earth.

Such reflections seem trite enough. But they have a point
which either the carelessness of the observer or the pride of
man is apt to overlook. Why, it is often asked, should such
a process of the arts as that displayed in Italy not have continued through further phases and a richer growth? Why
should a State like Venice have decayed? Why should Ford
and Massinger have only led to Davenant and Crowne? The
answer is that each particular polity, each specific form of art,
has, like a plant or like a man, its destined evolution from
a germ, its given stock of energy, its limited supply of vital
force. To unfold and to exhibit its potential faculties, is all
that each can do. Granted favouring circumstances and no
thwarting influence, it will pass through the phases of adolescence, maturity, and old age. But it cannot alter its type.
It has no power at a certain moment of its growth to turn
aside and make itself a different thing. It cannot prolong
existence on an altered track, or attain to perpetuity by successive metamorphoses.

Criticism seeks the individuality imprisoned in the germ,
exhibited in the growth, exhausted in the season of decline.
Critical biography sets itself to find the man himself, what
made him operative, what hampered him in action, what,
after all the injuries of chance and age, survives of him im-

perishable in the world of thoughts and things. Critical history seeks the potency of an epoch, of a nation, of an empire, of a faith ; discriminates adventitious circumstance ; allows for retardation, accident, and partial failure ; discerns efficient factors ; concentrates attention on specific qualities ; traces the germ, the growth, the efflorescence, and the dwindling of a complex organism through the lives which worked instinctively in sympathy for its effectuation.

What differentiates biography and history in the sphere of criticism is, that the former deals with individuality manifested in a person, the latter with individuality, no less complete although more complicated, in a series and a company of persons. The former aims at demonstrating the unity of one man's work, subject to influences which make or mar it ; the latter exhibits the unity of a work composed of the works of many men, subject to influences wider and more intricate which make or mar it. In the one case, criticism has to answer how the man did what he lived to do ; in the other, how those many men contributed to what remains for survey as the single product of their several co-operative lives.

Applying these considerations to the subject of our study, it is not difficult to see that in Shakspere we have the culmination of dramatic art in England. To explain how Shakspere became possible, to show how he articulated what the nation struggled to express, to demonstrate how he necessitated a decline, is the critic's task. The individuality of the Elizabethan Drama is personified in Shakspere ; and such a study as I have undertaken is a contribution toward his better understanding, and through that to a perception of the age and race which he expounded to the world.

V

The succession in time of the stages I have tried to indicate must not be insisted on too harshly. These stages are observable at a distance better than on close inspection. The works by which we mark them, overlap and interpenetrate. Phenomena present themselves, defying the strictest systematic treatment, and seeming to contradict well-grounded generalisations. We are dealing with an organism compact of many organisms ; and just as in the intellectual development of a person it often happens that thoughts of middle life precede maturity, while youthful fancies blossom on the verge of age, so here we find a poet of the prime surviving in the decadence, and verses written in the morning of the art anticipating its late afternoon. The rapidity with which the changes in our drama were accomplished introduces some confusion. We are sometimes at a loss whether to maintain the chronological or the ideal sequence, whether to treat our subject according to the order of time or according to the laws of artistic structure. Some authors stretch far out beyond their temporal limit toward the coming group; others lag behind, and by their style perpetuate the past. Another sort seem to stand alone, perplexing classification, refusing to take their place in any one of the groups which criticism studies to compose.

Lastly, like every other product of the modern world, there is nothing simple in the subject. Various forces combined to start the Drama in London. Various influences determined its development. For the English people it embodied a whole European phase of thought and feeling. It was for them the mirror of the sixteenth century, the compendium of all that the Renaissance had brought to light. It meant for England the recovery of Greek and Latin culture, the emancipation of the mind from medieval bondage, the emergence of the human spirit in its freedom. It meant newly discovered heavens, a larger earth, sail-swept oceans, awakened continents beyond Atlantic seas. It meant the pulse of now ascendant and puissant heart-blood through a people conscious of their unity and strength, the puberty and adolescence of a race which in its manhood was destined to give social freedom to the world. For England the Drama supplied a form commensurate with the great interests and mighty stirrings of that age. Into all these things it poured the spirit of that art which only was our own—the soul of poetry. Sculpture and painting we had none. Music lay yet in the cradle, awaiting the touch of Italy upon her strings, the touch of Germany upon her keys. But poetry, the metaphysic of all arts, was ours. And poetry, using the drama for a vehicle, conveyed to English minds what Italy, great mother of renascent Europe, had with all her arts, with all her industries and sciences, made manifest. On man, as on the proper appanage of English thought, our poets, like a flight of eagles, swooped. Man was their quarry; and in the sphere of man's mixed nature there is nothing, save its baser parts, its carrion, unportrayed by them.

Reviewing this unique achievement of our literary genius, the critic is puzzled not only by its complexity, but also by its incompleteness as a work of art. The Drama in England has no Attic purity of outline, no statuesque definition of form, no unimpeachable perfection of detail. The total effect of those accumulated plays might be compared to that of a painted window or a piece of tapestry, where the colour and assembled forms convey an ineffaceable impression, but which, when we examine the whole work more closely, seems to consist of hues laid side by side without a harmonising medium. The greatness of the material presented to our study lies less in the parts than in the mass, less in particular achievements than in the spirit which sustains and animates the whole. It is the volume and variety of this dramatic literature, poured forth with almost incoherent volubility by a crowd of poets, jostling together in the storm and stress of an instinctive impulse to express one cardinal conception of their art, each striving, after his own fashion, to grapple with a problem suggested by the temper of their race and age:— it is the multitude of fellow-workers, and the bulk of work produced in concert, that impress the mind; the unity not of a simple and coherent thing of beauty, but of an intricate and many-membered organism, striving after self-accomplishment, and reaching that accomplishment in Shakspere's art, which enthrals attention. Our dramatists produced very few plays which deserve the name of masterpiece. Yet, taken altogether, their works, although so different in quality and so uneven in execution, make up one vast and monumental edifice. The right point of view, therefore, for regarding them, is that from which in music we contemplate a symphony or chorus, or in painting judge the frescoed decoration of a hall, or in philosophy observe the genesis of an idea evolved by kindred and competing thinkers, or in architecture approach some huge cathedral of the Middle Ages.

Surveyed in its totality, the Elizabethan Drama is so complex in its animating motives, so imperfect in its details, that it may well seem to defy analysis. And yet it has the internal coherence of a real, a spiritual unity. It furnishes a rare specimen of literary evolution circumscribed within well-defined limits of time and place, confined to the conditions of a single nation at a certain moment of its growth. We are furthermore fortunate in possessing copious remains of its chief monuments illustrative of each successive stage. In spite of the Great Fire, in spite of Warburton's Cook, in spite of the indifference of two succeeding centuries, our stores of plays are abundant and amply representative. Through these we trace the seed sown in the Miracles and Interludes. We watch the root struck and the plant emerging in the fertile soil of the metropolis. We analyse the several elements which it rejected as unnecessary to its growth, and those which it assimilated. We pluck the flower and fruitage of its prime. We follow it to its decay, fading, and finally cut off by frost. There is no similar instance of uninterrupted progress in the dramatic art. Through lack of documentary evidence, the origins of the Athenian Drama are obscure. From the Dithyrambic and the Thespian age no remnants have survived. Our knowledge of the playwrights who competed with Sophocles is fragmentary and vague. The successors of Euripides owe their shadowy fame to a few dim notices, a poor collection of imperfect extracts.

VI

It is not here the place to treat in detail of those intimate connections which may be traced between the many writers for our theatre. Suffice it to say that Shakspere forms a

focus for all the rays of light which had emerged before his
time, and that after him these rays were once more decom-
posed and scattered over a wide area. Thus at least we may
regard the matter from our present point of survey. Yet
during Shakspere's lifetime his predominance was by no
means so obvious. To explain the defect of intelligence in
Shakspere's contemporaries, to understand why they chose
epithets like 'mellifluous,' 'sweet,' and 'gentle,' to describe
the author of 'King Lear,' 'Othello,' and 'Troilus and
Cressida'; why they praised his 'right happy and copious
industry' instead of dwelling on his interchange of tragic
force and fanciful inventiveness; why the misconception of
his now acknowledged place in literature extended even to
Milton and to Dryden, will remain perhaps for ever impossible
to every student of those times. But this intellectual
obtuseness is itself instructive, when we regard Shakspere as
the creature, not as the creator, of a widely diffused movement
in the spirit of the nation, of which all his contemporaries
were dimly conscious. They felt that behind him, as behind
themselves, dwelt a motive force superior to all of them.
Instead, then, of comparing him, as some have done, to the
central orb of a solar system, from whom the planetary
bodies take their light, it would be more correct to say that
the fire of the age which burns in him so intensely, burned
in them also, more dimly, but independently of him. He
represents the English dramatic genius in its fulness. The
subordinate playwrights bring into prominence minor qualities
and special aspects of that genius. Men like Webster and
Heywood, Jonson and Ford, Fletcher and Shirley, have an
existence in literature outside Shakspere, and are only in
an indirect sense satellites and vassals. Could Shakspere's
works be obliterated from man's memory, they would still
sustain the honours of the English stage with decent
splendour. Still it is only when Shakspere shines among
them, highest, purest, brightest of that brotherhood, that the
real radiance of his epoch is discernible—that the real value
and meaning of their work become apparent.

The more we study Shakspere in relation to his predecessors, the more obliged are we to reverse Dryden's famous dictum that he 'found not, but created first the stage.' The fact is, that he found dramatic form already fixed. When he began to work among the London playwrights, the Romantic Drama in its several species—Comedy, Italian Novella, Roman History, English Chronicle, Masque, Domestic Tragedy, Melodrama—had achieved its triumph over the Classical Drama of the scholars. Rhyme had been discarded, and blank verse adopted as the proper vehicle of dramatic expression. Shakspere's greatness consisted in bringing the type established by his predecessors to artistic ripeness, not in creating a new type. It may even be doubted whether Shakspere was born to be a playwright—whether it was not rather circumstance which led him to assume his place as coryphæus to the choir of dramatists. The defects of the Romantic form were accepted by him with easy acquiescence, nor did he aim at altering that form in any essential particular. He dealt with English Drama as he dealt with the materials of his plays; following an outline traced already, but glorifying each particular of style and matter; breathing into the clay-figures of a tale his own creator's breath of life, enlarging prescribed incident and vivifying suggested thought with the art of an unrivalled poet-rhetorician, raising the verse invented for him to its highest potency and beauty with inexhaustible resource and tact incomparable in the use of language.

At the same time, the more we study Shakspere in his own works, the more do we perceive that his predecessors, no less than his successors, exist for him; that without him English dramatic art would be but second rate; that he is the keystone of the arch, the justifier and interpreter of his time's striving impulses. The forms he employs are the forms he found in common usage among his fellow-craftsmen. But his method of employing them is so vastly superior, the quality of his work is so incommensurable by any standard we apply to the best of theirs, that we cannot help regarding the plays of Shakspere as not exactly different in kind, but diverse in inspiration. Without those predecessors, Shakspere would certainly not have been what he is. But having him, we might well afford to lose them. Without those successors, we should still miss much that lay implicit in the art of Shakspere. But having him, we could well dispense with them. His predecessors lead up to him, and help us to explain his method. His successors supplement his work, illustrating the breadth and length and depth and versatility of English poetry in that prolific age.

It is this twofold point of view from which Shakspere must be studied in connection with the minor dramatists, which gives them value. It appears that a whole nation laboured in those fifty years' activity to give the world one Shakspere; but it is no less manifest that Shakspere did not stand alone, without support and without lineage. He and his fellow playwrights are interdependent, mutually illustrative; and their aggregated performance is the expression of a nation's spirit.

VII

That the English genius for art has followed two directions, appears from the revolution in literature which prevailed from the Restoration to the end of the eighteenth century. Shakspere represents the one type, which preponderated in the reigns of Elizabeth and the first two Stuarts. Ben Jonson represents the other, less popular during the golden age of the Drama, but destined to assert itself after the Civil Wars. Jonson was a learned, and aimed at being a correct, poet. He formed a conception of poetry as the proper instrument of moral education, to which he gave clear utterance in his prose essays, and which was afterwards advocated by Milton. He taught the propriety of observing rules and precedents in art. Under the dictatorships of Dryden and Pope this subordination of fancy to canons of prescribed taste and sense was accepted as a law. The principles for which Jonson waged his manful but unsuccessful warfare triumphed. The men who adopted those principles and insured their victory were of like calibre and quality with Jonson—Titans, as the case has been well put, rather than Olympians.

The object of these remarks is to point out that the Elizabethan Drama contained within itself, in the work of our second greatest playwright, the germ of a new type of art, which only flourished at a later period. The critic must not neglect the difference between Jonson's method and that of his contemporaries, while at the same time he shows to what extent Jonson submitted to the spirit that controlled his age. What that spirit was, cannot in this place be described.

Its analysis may more fitly be reserved for the conclusion of these studies. Yet some broad points can here be briefly indicated. It was a spirit of civil and religious freedom, in the interval between discomfited Romanism and Puritan victory; a spirit of nationality mature and conscious, perplexed as yet by no deeply reaching political discords such as those which later on confused the hierarchy of classes and imperilled the monarchical principle. It was a spirit in which loyalty to the person of the sovereign was at one with the sense of national independence. A powerful grasp on the realities of life was then compatible with romantic fancy and imaginative fervour. The solid earth supported the poet; but while he never quitted this firm standing-ground, he held a wand which at a touch transmuted things of fact into the airy substance of a vision. Contempt for studied purity of style and for the artificial delicacies of sentiment was combined with extraordinary vigour and vividness in the use of language, running riot often in extravagance and verbose eccentricity, and also with the most sensitive perception of emotional gradations, the most hyperbolical enthusiasms. The moral sense was sound and homely; insight into character acute; aptitude for observing and portraying psychological peculiarities, unrivalled in its elasticity and ease. These are some of the distinctive qualities shared in common by our playwrights. It should also be added that their intolerance of rules, indifference to literary fame, and haste of composition exposed them all, with one or two illustrious exceptions, to artistic incompleteness.

VIII

This chapter in our literature properly closes with the fall of Charles I. from power. The inspiration of Marlowe and Shakspere, the true Elizabethan impulse, had worn itself out. Judging by the latest products of the Caroline age, I cannot resist the belief that even had the Puritans not dealt a death-blow to the stage, that impulse could scarcely have yielded another succession of really vital works.

After the Restoration, Dryden and Otway, Congreve, Wycherley, Farquhar, and Vanbrugh partly refined upon some comic and tragic motives, suggested by the latest of their predecessors, and partly succeeded in creating a novel style in sympathy with altered social customs. No one will dispute the piquancy of Congreve's dialogue, the effectiveness of the domestic scenes from town and country life depicted on that glittering theatre. Yet this brilliant group of play-wrights stands apart; isolated by differences of thought and sentiment, method and language, from their Elizabethan predecessors; hardly less isolated from their few worthy successors of the Georgian age.

Far more significant than the vamped-up dramas of the eighteenth century are the novels which now take their rise, and which preserve the old dramatic genius of the English in an altered form. Our time, which offers so many parallels to that of Elizabeth, shows its literary character in no point more distinctively than in its cultivation of prose romance. Instead of dramas written to be acted, we have novels written to be read. These are produced in such profusion, with such spontaneous and untutored licence, so various in quality and yet upon the whole so excellent, that the Victorian period vindicates the survival of that dramatic aptitude which glorified the period of Elizabeth.

CHAPTER II

THE NATION AND THE DRAMA

I

AT all periods of history the stage has been a mirror of the
age and race in which it has arisen. Dramatic poets more
than any other artists reproduce the life of men around them ;
exhibiting their aims, hopes, wishes, aspirations, passions, in

an abstract more intensely coloured than the diffuse facts of daily experience. It is the function of all artistic genius to interpret human nature to itself, and to leave in abiding form a record of past ages to posterity ; but more especially of the dramatic genius, which rules for its domain the manners, actions, destinies of men. The result attained by a great drama in those few ages and among those rare races which can boast this highest growth of art, is twofold. On the one hand it shows 'the very age and body of the time his form and pressure ; ' it is strictly local, national, true to the epoch of its origin. But it is more than this ; it is on the other hand a glass held up to nature, reflecting what is permanent in man beneath the customs and costumes, the creeds and polities, of any age or nation.

These remarks, though obvious enough, contain a truth which must not be neglected on the threshold of our inquiry into the origins of the English Drama. If it be granted that other theatres—the Greek, the Spanish, and the French—each of which embalms for us the spirit of a great people at one period of the world's development, are at the same time by their revelation of man's nature permanent and universal, this may be claimed in even a stricter sense for the English. Never since the birth of the dramatic art in Greece has any theatre displayed a genius so local and spontaneously popular, so thoroughly representative of the century in which it sprang to power, so national in tone and character. Yet none has been more universal by right of insight into the essential qualities of human nature, by right of sympathy with every phase of human feeling, by right of meditation upon all the problems which have vexed the human spirit ; none is more permanent by right of artistic potency and beauty, accumulated learning, manifold experience, variety of presentation, commanding interest, and inexhaustible fertility of motives.

We are led to ask how our Drama came to be in this high sense both national and universal ; how our playwrights, working for their age and race, achieved the artistic triumph of presenting to the world an abstract picture of humanity so complex and so perfect. Questions like these can never be completely answered. There remains always something inscrutable in the spontaneous efforts of a nation finely touched to a fine issue. Yet some considerations will help us to understand, if not to explain, the problem. And, in the first place, it may be repeated that the intellectual movement, to which we give the name of Renaissance, expressed itself in England mainly through the Drama. Other races in that era of quickened activity, when modern man regained the consciousness of his own strength and goodliness after centuries of mental stagnation and social depression, threw their energies into the plastic arts and scholarship. The English found a similar outlet for their pent-up forces in the Drama. The arts and literature of Greece and Rome had been revealed by Italy to Europe. Humanism had placed the present once more in a vital relation to the past. The navies of Portugal and Spain had discovered new continents beyond the ocean ; the merchants of Venice and Genoa had explored the farthest East. Copernicus had revolutionised astronomy, and the telescope was revealing fresh worlds beyond the sun.

The Bible had been rescued from the mortmain of the Church ; scholars studied it in the language of its authors, and the people read it in their own tongue. In this rapid development of art, literature, science, and discovery the English had hitherto taken but little part. But they were ready to reap what other men had sown. Unfatigued by the labours of the pioneer, unsophisticated by the pedantries and sophistries of the schools, in the freshness of their youth and vigour, they surveyed the world unfolded to them. For more than half a century they freely enjoyed the splendour of this spectacle, until the struggle for political and religious liberty replunged them in the hard realities of life. During that eventful period of spiritual disengagement from absorbing cares, the race was fully conscious of its national importance. It had shaken off the shackles of oppressive feudalism, the trammels of ecclesiastical tyranny. It had not yet passed under the Puritan yoke, or felt the encroachments of despotic monarchy. It was justly proud of the Virgin Queen, with whose idealised personality the people identified their newly acquired sense of greatness. During those fortunate years, the nation, which was destined to expend its vigour in civil struggles and constitutional reforms between 1642 and 1689, and then to begin that strenuous career of colonisation and conquest in both hemispheres, devoted its best mental energy to self-expression in one field of literature. The pageant of renascent humanity to which the English were invited by Italians, Spaniards, and Frenchmen, our predecessors in the arts and studies of two centuries, stimulated the poets of the race to their dramatic triumphs. What in those fifty years they saw with the clairvoyant eyes of artists, the poets wrote. And what they wrote, remains imperishable. It is the portrait of their age, the portrait of an age in which humanity stood self-revealed, a miracle and marvel to its own admiring curiosity.

II

England was in a state of transition when the Drama came to perfection. That was one of those rare periods when the past and the future are both coloured by imagination, and both shed a glory on the present. The medieval order was in dissolution ; the modern order was in process of formation. Yet the old state of things had not faded from memory and usage ; the new had not assumed despotic sway. Men stood then, as it were, between two dreams—a dream of the past, thronged with sinister and splendid reminiscences ; a dream of the future, bright with unlimited aspirations and indefinite hopes. Neither the retreating forces of the Middle Ages nor the advancing forces of the modern era pressed upon them with the iron weight of actuality. The brutalities of feudalism had been softened ; but the chivalrous sentiment remained to inspire the Surreys and the Sidneys of a milder epoch—its high enthusiasm and religious zeal, its devotion to women, its ideal of the knightly character, its cheerful endurance of hardship, its brave reliance on a righteous cause. The Papacy, after successive revolutions of opinion, had become odious to the large majority of the nation ; but

Protestantism had not yet condensed into a compact body of sectarian doctrines. The best work of our dramatists, so far from reticent, so comprehensive as it is, reveals no theological orthodoxy, no polemical antagonism to dogmatic creeds. The poet, whether he sounds the depths of sceptical despair or soars aloft on wings of aspiration, appeals less to religious principle than to human emotion, to doubts and hopes instinctive in the breast of man. It is as though in this transition state of thought, humanity were left alone, surveying with clear eyes the universe, sustained by its own adolescent fearlessness and strength. The fields, again, of wealth, discovery, and science, over which we plod with measured and methodic footsteps, spread before those men like a fairyland of palaces and groves, teeming with strange adventures, offering rich harvests of heroic deeds. To the New World Raleigh sailed with the courage of a Paladin, the boyishness of Astolf mounted on his hippogriff. He little dreamed what unromantic scenes of modern life, what monotonous migrations of innumerable settlers, he inaugurated on the shores of El Dorado. The Old World was hardly less a land of wonders. When Faustus clasped Helen in a vision ; when Miramont protested :

> Though I can speak no Greek, I love the sound on 't ;
> It goes so thundering as it conjured devils :

both characters expressed the spirit of an age when scholarship was a romantic passion. Even the pioneers of science in the seventeenth century were poets. Bruno compares himself upon his philosophic flight to Icarus. Bacon founds the inductive method upon metaphors—Idola Specûs, Vindemia Inductionis. Galileo, to his English contemporaries, is ' the Italian star-wright.'

III

The genius of youthfulness, renascent, not new-born, was dominant in that age. Adam stepped forth again in Eden, gazed with bold eyes upon the earth and stars, felt himself master there, plucked fruit from the forbidden tree. But though still young, though 'bright as at creation's day,' this now rejuvenescent Adam had six thousand centuries of conscious life, how many countless centuries of dim unconscious life, behind him! Not the material world alone, not the world of his unquenchable self alone, not the world of inscrutable futurity alone, but, in addition to all this, a ruinous world of his own works awaiting reconstruction lay around him. The nations moved 'immersed in rich foreshadowings' of the future, amid the dust of creeds and empires, which crumbled like 'the wrecks of a dissolving dream.' Refreshed with sleep, the giant of the modern age rose up strong to shatter and create. Thought and action were no longer to be fettered. Instead of tradition and prescription, passion and instinct ruled the hour. Every nerve was sensitive to pleasure bordering on pain, and pain that lost itself in ecstasy. Men saw and coveted and grasped at their desire. If they hated, they slew. If they loved and could not win, again they slew. If they climbed to the height of their ambition and fell toppling down, they died with smiles upon their lips like Marlowe's Mortimer:

> Weep not for Mortimer,
> That scorns the world, and, as a traveller
> Goes to discover countries yet unknown.

Turbulence, not the turbulence of a medieval barony, but the turbulence of artists, lovers, pleasure-seekers, aspirants after pomp and spiritual empire, ruffled the ocean of existence. The characters of men were harshly marked, and separated by abrupt distinctions. They had not been rubbed down by contact and culture into uniformity. Not conformity to established laws of taste, but eccentricity betokening emergence of the inner self, denoted breeding. To adopt foreign fashions, to cut the beard into fantastic shapes, to flourish in parti-coloured garments, to coin new oaths, to affect a style of speech and manner at variance with one's neighbours, passed for manliness. Everyone lived in his own humour then, and openly avowed his tastes. You might distinguish the inhabitants of different countries, the artisans of different crafts, the professors of different sciences—the lawyer, the physician, the courtier, or the churchman—by their clothes, their gait, their language. Instead of curbing passions or concealing appetites, men gloried in their exercise. They veiled nothing which savoured of virility; and even conversation lacked the reserve of decency which civilised society throws over it.

IV

Benvenuto Cellini, in his autobiography, presents a graphic picture of the times ; and what we know of life in other European countries at that epoch justifies us in taking that picture as fairly typical. He and the Italians of his century killed their rivals in the streets by day ; they girded on their daggers when they went into a court of justice ; they sickened to the death with disappointed vengeance or unhappy love ; they dragged a faithless mistress by the hair about their rooms ; they murdered an adulterous wife with their own hands, and hired assassins to pursue her paramour ; lying for months in prison, unaccused or uncondemned, in daily dread of poison, they read the Bible and the sermons of Savonarola, and made their dungeons echo with psalm-singing ; they broke their fetters, dropped from castle walls, swam moats and rivers, dreamed that angels had been sent to rescue them ; they carved Madonna and Adonis on the self-same shrine, paying indiscriminate devotion to Ganymede and Aphrodite ; they confused the mythology of Olympus with the mysteries of Sinai and Calvary, the oracles of necromancers with the voice of prophets, the authority of pagan poets with the inspiration of Isaiah and S. Paul ; they prayed in one breath for vengeance on their enemies, for favour with the women whom they loved, for succour in their homicidal acts, for Paradise in the life to come ; they flung defiance at popes, and trembled for absolution before a barefoot friar ; they watched salamanders playing in flames, saw aureoles of light reflected from their heads upon the morning dew, turned dross to gold with alchemists, raised spirits in the ruins of deserted amphitheatres ; they passed men dying on the road, and durst not pity them, because a cardinal had left them there to perish ; they took the Sacrament from hands of prelates whom they had guarded with drawn swords at doors of infamy and riot. The wildest passions, the grossest superstitions, the most fervent faith, the coldest cynicism, the gravest learning, the darkest lusts, the most delicate sense of beauty, met in the same persons, and were fused into one wayward glittering humanity. Ficino, who revealed Plato to Europe, pondered on the occult virtue of amulets. Cardan, a pioneer of physical science, wrote volumes of predictions gathered from the buzzings of a wasp, and died in order to fulfil his horoscope. Bembo, a prince of the Church, warned hopeful scholars against reading the Bible lest they should contaminate their style. Aretino, the byword of obscenity and impudence, penned lives of saints, and won the praise of women like Vittoria Colonna. A pope, to please the Sultan, poisoned a Turkish prince, and was rewarded by the present of Christ's seamless coat. A Duke of Urbino poignarded a cardinal in the streets of Bologna. Alexander VI. regaled his daughter in the Vatican with naked ballets, and dragged the young lord of Faenza, before killing him, through outrages for which there is no language. Every student of Renaissance Italy and France can multiply these instances. It is enough to have suggested how, and with what salience of unmasked appetite, the springs of life were opened in that age of splendour ; how the most heterogeneous elements of character and the most incongruous motives of action displayed themselves in a carnival medley of intensely vivid life.

V

What distinguished the English at this epoch from the nations of the South was not refinement of manners, sobriety, or self-control. On the contrary, they retained an unenviable character for more than common savagery. Cellini speaks of them as *questi diavoli—quelle bestie di quegli Inglesi.*

Erasmus describes the filth of their houses, and the sick-
nesses engendered in their cities by bad ventilation. What
rendered the people superior to Italians and Spaniards was
the firmness of their moral fibre, the sweetness of their
humanity, a more masculine temper, less vitiated instincts
and sophisticated intellects, a law-abiding and religious conscience, contempt for treachery and baseness, intolerance of
political or ecclesiastical despotism combined with fervent
love of home and country. They were coarse, but not
vicious; pleasure-loving, but not licentious; violent, but not
cruel; luxurious, but not effeminate. Machiavelli was a
name of loathing to them. Sidney, Essex, Raleigh, More,
and Drake were popular heroes; and whatever may be
thought of these men, they certainly counted no Marquis of
Pescara, no Duke of Valentino, no Malatesta Baglioni, no
Cosimo de' Medici among them. The Southern European
type betrayed itself but faintly in politicians like Thomas
Cromwell and Robert Dudley.

The English then, as now, were great travellers. Young
men, not merely of the noble classes, visited the South and
returned with the arts, accomplishments, and follies of Italian
capitals. A frequent theme for satire was the incongruity of
fashions displayed in the dress of travelled dandies, their language mixed of all the dialects of Europe, their aptitude for
foreign dissipations. 'We have robbed Greece of gluttony,'
writes Stephen Gosson, 'Italy of wantonness, Spain of pride,
France of deceit, and Dutchland of quaffing.' Nash ascribes
the notable increase of drunkenness to habits contracted by
the soldiers in their Flemish campaigns. Ascham attributes
the new-fangled lewdness of the youth to their sojourn in
Venice. But these affectations of foreign vices were only a
varnish on the surface of society. The core of the nation
remained sound and wholesome. Nor was the culture which
the English borrowed from less unsophisticated nations more
than superficial. The incidents of Court gossip show how
savage was the life beneath. Queen Elizabeth spat, in the
presence of her nobles, at a gentleman who had displeased
her; struck Essex on the cheek; drove Burleigh blubbering

from her apartment. Laws in merry England were executed with uncompromising severity. Every township had its gallows; every village its stocks, whipping-post, and pillory. Here and there, heretics were burned upon the market-place; and the block upon Tower Hill was seldom dry. Sir Henry Sidney, sent to quell the Irish rebels, 'put man, woman, and child to the sword,' after reading the Queen's proclamation. His officers balanced the amusements of pillage or 'having some killing,' with a preference for the latter sport when they felt themselves in humour for the chase. Witches and the belief in witches increased; it was a common village pastime to drown old women in the ponds, or to rack and prick them till they made confession of impossible crimes. A coarse freedom prevailed in hock-tide festivals and rustic revels. Lords of Misrule led forth their motley train; girls went a-maying with their lovers to the woods at night; Feasts of Asses and of Fools profaned the sanctuaries; Christmas perpetuated rites of Woden and of Freya; harvest brought back the pagan deities of animal enjoyment. Men and women who read Plato, or discussed the elegancies of Petrarch, suffered brutal practical jokes, relished the obscenities of jesters, used the grossest language of the people. Carrying farms and acres on their backs in the shape of costly silks and laces, they lay upon rushes filthy with the vomit of old banquets. Glittering in suits of gilt and jewelled mail, they jostled with town-porters in the stench of the bear-gardens, or the bloody bull-pit. The Church itself was not respected. The nave of old S. Paul's became a rendezvous for thieves and prostitutes. Fine gentlemen paid fees for the privilege of clanking up and down its aisles in service-time. Dancers and masquers, crowding from the streets outside in all their frippery, would take the Sacrament and then run out to recommence their revels. Men were Papists and Protestants according to the time of day; hearing Mass in the morning and sermon in the afternoon, and winding up their Sunday with a farce in some inn-yard. It is difficult, even by noting an infinity of such characteristics, to paint the many-coloured incongruities of England at that epoch. Yet in the midst of

this confusion rose cavaliers like Sidney, philosophers like
Bacon, poets like Spenser; men in whom all that is pure,
elevated, subtle, tender, strong, wise, delicate, and learned in
our modern civilisation displayed itself. And the masses of
the people were still in harmony with these high strains.
They formed the audience of Shakspere. They wept for
Desdemona, adored Imogen, listened with Jessica to music
in the moonlight at Belmont, wandered with Rosalind
through woodland glades of Arden.

VI

Such was the society of which our theatre became the
mirror. The splendour and ideal beauty of the world which
it presented, in contrast with the semi-barbarism from which
society was then emerging, added imaginative charm to scenic
pageants, and raised the fancy of the playwrights to the
heavens of poetry. This contrast converted dramatic art into
a vivid dream, a golden intuition, a glowing anticipation of
man's highest possibilities. The poets were Prosperos. In
the dark and unpaved streets of London visions came to them
of Florence or Verona, bright with palaces and lucid with
perpetual sunlight. The energetic passions which they
found in their own breasts and everywhere among the men
around them, attained to tragic grandeur in their imaginations. They translated the crude violence, the fanciful eccentricities, the wayward humours of the day, into animated
types; and because they kept touch with human nature,
their transcripts from the life of their own time are indestructible.

The form assumed by the Drama in England was not
accidental; nor was the triumph of the Romantic over the
Classic type of art attained without a vigorous struggle.
Scholars at the University and purists at the Court, Sidney
by his precepts and Sackville by his practice, the translators
of Seneca and the imitators of Italian poets, Ben Jonson's
learning and Bacon's authority, were unable to force upon the
genius of the people a style alien to the spirit of the times

and of the race. Between the age of Pericles and the sixteenth century of our era, the stream of time had swept mightily and gathered volume, bearing down upon its tide the full development of Greek philosophy and Roman law, the rise and fall of Greek and Roman Empires, the birth and progress of Christianity and Islam, the irruption of Teutonic tribes into the community of civilised races, the growth of modern nationalities and modern tongues, the formation and decay of feudalism, the theology of Alexandria, Byzantium, and Paris, the theocratic despotism of the Papal See, the intellectual stagnation of the Dark Ages, the mental ferment of the Middle Ages, the revival of scholarship, philosophy, and art in Southern Europe, and, last of all, the revolution which shook Papal Rome and freed the energies of man. How was it possible, after these vital changes in the substance, composition, and direction of the human spirit, that a Drama, representative of the new world, should be built upon the lines of Greek or Græco-Roman precedents? In Italy, under the oppressive weight of humanism, such a revival of the antique forms had been attempted—with what feeble results all students of Italian tragedy are well aware.[1] The instinct of the English, who were destined to resuscitate the Drama, rejected that tame formalism. They worked at first without rule or method. Their earliest efforts were mere gropings, tentative endeavours, studies of untaught craftsmen seeking after style. But they adhered closely to the life before their eyes; and their ill-digested scenes brought nature piecemeal on the stage. The justice of this method was triumphantly demonstrated by Shakspere; as the justice of the method of Pisano and Giotto was demonstrated by Michelangelo and Raffaello. Neither Italian painting nor English poetry can be called a silver-age revival of antique art; because in neither of these products did the modern mind start from imitation, but initiated and completed a new process of its own.

The Romantic Drama is of necessity deficient in statuesque repose and classic unity of design. It obeys specific laws of

---

[1] See my *Renaissance in Italy*, vol. v. chap. ii.

vehement activity and wayward beauty; while the discords
and the imperfections of the type are such as only genius of
the highest order can reduce to harmony. Aiming at the
manifestation of human life as a complex whole, with all its
multiformity of elements impartially considered and presented,
our playwrights seized on every salient motive in the sphere
of man's experience. They rifled the stores of history and
learning with indiscriminate rapacity. The heterogeneous
booty of their raids, the ore and dross of their discovery,
passed through a furnace in their brains, took form from
their invention. In no sense can these men be arraigned for
plagiarism or for imitation, although they made free use of
all that had been published in the past.[1] The Renaissance
lent them, not its pedantic humanism, but the deep colouring,
the pulse of energy, the pomp and pride and passion of its
glowing youth. From Italy they drew romance and sensuous
beauty—the names of Venice and Amalfi and Verona—the
lust of lust, the concentrated malice of that Southern Circe.
In Spain they delved a mine of murders, treasons, duels,
intrigues, persecutions, and ancestral guilt. Plutarch taught
them deeds of citizens, heroic lives, and civic virtues. The
Elegists and Ovid were for them the fountain-head of mythic
fables. From sagas of the North and annals of Old England
they borrowed the substance of 'King Lear,' 'Bonduca,'
'Hamlet.' From the chronicles of recent history they
quarried tragedies of Tudors and Plantagenets. The law-
courts gave them motives for domestic drama. The streets
and taverns, homes and houses of debauch, in London
furnished them with comic scenes. Nor did these materials,
in spite of their incongruous variety, confuse the minds which
they enriched. Our dramatists inspired with living energy
each character of myth, romance, experience, or story.
Anachronisms, ignorance, credulity, abound upon their pages.

[1] As early as 1580, Stephen Gosson wrote in his *Plays Confuted in
Five Actions*: 'I may boldly say it because I have seen it, that the
*Palace of Pleasure, The Golden Ass, The Æthiopian History, Amadis of
France, The Round Table*, bawdy comedies in Latin, French, Italian, and
Spanish, have been thoroughly ransacked to furnish the playhouses in
London.' (Roxburgh Library, *The English Drama and Stage*, p. 188.)

Criticism had not yet begun its reign. Legend was still mistaken for fact. The tale of 'Cymbeline' seemed to Shakspere almost as historical as that of 'Henry V.' Yet, feeling the reality of life exceedingly, grasping all shapes through which they could express their knowledge of themselves and of the world around them, piercing below the surface to the heart which throbbed within each image of the fancy, they converted all they touched to essential realism. Men and women rose beneath their wand of art from dusty stores of erudition, from mists of faery land and fiction. Heywood, here as elsewhere, finely conscious of the playwright's function, unfolds a map before us of the ground they traversed, in these lines:

> To give content to this most curious age,
> The gods themselves we 've brought down to the stage,
> And figured them in planets; made even Hell
> Deliver up the furies, by no spell
> Saving the Muse's rapture. Further we
> Have trafficked by their help: no history
> We 've left unrifled: our pens have been dipped,
> As well in opening each hid manuscript,
> As tracts more vulgar, whether read or sung
> In our domestic or more foreign tongue.
> Of fairy elves, nymphs of the sea and land,
> The lawns and groves, no number can be scanned
> Which we 've not given feet to; nay, 't is known
> That when our chronicles have barren grown
> Of story, we have all invention stretched,
> Dived low as to the centre, and then reached
> Unto the *Primum Mobile* above,
> Nor scaped things intermediate, for your love.

A noble boast; and not more nobly boasted than nobly executed; as they who have surveyed the English Drama from Lyly to Ford will acknowledge.

VII

The variety of matter handled by the playwrights cannot be said to have affected their principles of treatment. All themes, however diverse, were subjected to the romantic

style. The same exuberance of life, the same vehement
passions, the same sacrifice of rule and method to salience of
presentation, mark all the products of our stage and give our
drama a real unity of tone. In the delineation of character,
we find less of feebleness than of extravagance; in the
texture of plots, there is rather superfluity of incident and
incoherence of design than languor. The art of that epoch
suffered from rapidity of execution, excess of fancy, inventive
waywardness. To represent exciting scenes by energetic
action, to clothe audacious ideas in vivid language, to imitate
the broader aspects of emotion, to quicken the dullest
apprehension by violent contrasts and sensational effects, was
the aim which authors and actors pursued in common. Nor
was the public so critical or so exacting as to refine the
drama by a demand for careful workmanship. What the
playwright hastily concocted, was greedily devoured and
soon forgotten. The dramatists employed distinguished
talents in pouring forth a dozen plays instead of perfecting
one masterpiece. The audience amused themselves with

> Indicting and arraigning every day
> Something they call a play.

Thus it was only, as it were, by accident, by some lucky
adjustment of a subject to the special ability of a writer, or
by the emergence of a genius whose most careless work was
masterly, that flawless specimens of the romantic style came
into existence. The theatres were open at all seasons,
competing with each other for a public bent on novelty.
These conditions of the stage in London stimulated the
fertility, but spoiled the quality of our Drama. The ceremonial festivals at which the Attic poets twice a year
produced their studied plays before a cultivated people,
encouraged the production of pure monuments of meditated
art. The audience of courtiers and academicians for whom
Racine and Molière laboured, tolerated only ripe and polished
handiwork. But English stagewrights lacked these incentives
to elaborate performance. Many dramas of their manufacture,
though they have the glow of life, the stuff of excellence,

must be reckoned among half-achievements. Many must be said to justify Ben Jonson's scornful invective : 'husks, draff to drink and swill '—'scraps, out of every dish thrown forth, and raked into the common tub.' The historian of English literature cannot afford, however, to neglect even 'things so prostitute.' Their very multitude impresses the imagination. Their mediocrity helps to explain the rhythm of dramatic art from a Shakspere's transcendent inspiration through the meritorious labours of a Massinger, down to the patchwork pieces of collaborating handicraftsmen. And in the sequel I shall hope to show that though the conditions of the London theatre were adverse to the highest perfection of art, they were helpful to its freedom.

VIII

In the Romantic Drama, men of the present age are struck by want of artistic modulation and gradation, strangely combined with vigorous conception and masterly reading of the inmost depths of nature. The design of a tragedy is often almost puerile in its simplicity. Even Othello falls into Iago's trap so stupidly as to refrigerate our feeling. The transitions from good to bad, from vice to virtue, from hate to love, in the same characters are palpably abrupt, almost to our sense impossible. What Goethe calls the *Motiviren* of a situation was neglected ; but the situation itself was powerfully presented. Bellafront, in Dekker's most celebrated comedy, begins as a bold and beautiful bad woman. Love at first sight alters her whole temper, and she becomes a modest lady. Hipolyto, the man who wrought this change in her, reflecting on her loveliness, turns round, and tempts the very woman whom his earlier persuasions had saved from evil. Under both aspects, each of these characters is drawn with admirable force. They maintain their individuality, although the motives of these complex moral revolutions receive no sufficient development at the artist's hands. Probably Dekker relied upon the sympathies of an audience, themselves capable of passionate conversion ; probably, he felt in his

own heart divisions leading to like violent issues. He did
not then appeal to such as read his drama at the present day,
to scrutinising scholars and critical historians, but to men
and women, still more fitted for sudden spiritual transforma-
tion, still more trembling on the border-line of good and
evil, than are the folk for whom Revival Meetings and
Salvation Armies shout their choruses and beat their drums
in England now. The psychological excitements of to-day
are but a feeble reflex from the stirrings of that epoch. We
have to measure the operation of that drama, not by our
blunted sensibilities, but by a far more sensitive, if grosser,
instrument of taste. The final significance of the whole
problem of Elizabethan literature lies in one point; the
people, at that fortunate epoch, vibrated to Shakspere's
delicacy, no less than to the rougher touch of men who had
in them the crudest substance of Shaksperian art. Instead
of making the allowances of our 'world-wearied flesh' and
thought-tormented minds for them, we must confess that
they threw open souls more fresh to simpler influences.

Nothing is more common in the plays of Massinger and
Fletcher than for tyrants to be softened by the beauty of
intended victims, for the tenderest strains of chivalrous
affection to flow from lips which utter curses and revilings,
for passionate love to take the place of implacable vengeance
or brutal cruelty. Are we to say that these reversions from
one temper to its opposite are unnatural? They are unnatural now. Were they unnatural then? Probably not.
The critic therefore must defer to nature as it then existed,
nor let his sense of truth be governed by the evidence of
nature as it now is moulded, for a moment haply, into forms
more firmly set.

The dramatists were well acquainted with fixed types of
character, and used these with a crudity which seems no less
to shock our apprehension of reality. No sooner have we
excused them for sudden and unexplained conversions, than
we find ourselves compelled to meet the contrary charge, and
defend them from the crime of well-nigh diabolical consistency.
They show us bad men stubborn in perversity, whom

innocence and beauty and eloquence have no power to charm. Such are Heywood's Tarquin, Fletcher's Rollo. The Flamineo and Bosola of Webster are villains of yet darker dye, ruffians whom only Italy could breed, courtiers refined in arts of wickedness, scholars perverted by their studies to defiant atheism, high-livers tainted with the basest vices, who, broken in repute, deprived of occupation, sell themselves to great men to subserve their pleasures and accomplish their revenge. In such men, the very refuse of humanity, there is no faith, no hope, no charity. Some fiend seems to have sat for their portraits. They are helpless in the chains of crime; their ill-deeds binding them to the bad masters whom they serve, and their seared consciences allowing them to execute with coldness devilish designs.

In order to explain such personages and to realise their action, it was necessary to exhibit horrors incredibly fantastic. Beaumont and Fletcher twice brought the agonies of death by poison on the stage. Webster paints a prince murdered by means of an envenomed helmet, a duchess strangled in her chamber, a sovereign lady poisoned by the kisses given to her husband's portrait. Ford adds the terror of incestuous passion to the death-scene of a sister murdered by a brother's hand. In Massinger's 'Virgin Martyr' a maiden is insulted in her honour and driven to the stake. Marston's Antonio stabs an innocent boy who trusts and loves him. Hoffmann places on his victim's head a crown of red-hot iron. A human sacrifice, a father who kills his son and mutilates himself, a girl whose hands and tongue have been cut off, together with a score or so of murders, are exhibited upon the theatre in 'Titus Andronicus.' It is needless to multiply such details. The grossness of passion in that age, whether displayed in brutal and unbridled lust, or in hate, cruelty, and torture, was more than we can understand. The savagery of human nature moved by spasms; its settled barbarisms, no less than its revulsions and revolts, are now almost unintelligible. To harmonise and interpret such humanity in a work of sublime art taxed all the powers of

even Shakspere. He did this once with supreme tragic
beauty in ' King Lear.' But if the world should rise against
' King Lear,' and cry, ' It is too terrible ! '—would not the
world be justified ?

IX

Insanity was a tragic motive, used frequently by the
romantic playwrights as an instrument for stirring pity and
inspiring dread. To understand it, and to employ it successfully, was, however, given to few. The mad humours depicted
in Fletcher's ' Pilgrim ' and in Webster's Masque of Lunatics
are fantastic appeals to the vulgar apprehension, rather than
scientific studies. But the interspaces between sanity and
frenzy, the vacillations of the mind upon a brink of horror,
the yieldings of the reason to the fret of passions, have been
seized with masterly correctness—by Massinger in Sir Giles
Overreach, by Fletcher in the love-lunes of ' The Noble
Gentleman,' by Ford in Palador's dejection, by Kyd or his
coadjutor in crazy Hieronymo, by Marston in Andrugio and
the disguised Antonio, and lastly, most effectively, by Webster
in his picture of the Duchess. There is nothing more impressive than the consciousness of tottering reason in this
lady, outraged by the company of maniacs and cut-throats.
She argues with herself whether she be really mad or not :

> O that it were possible
> To hold some two days' conference with the dead !
> From them I should learn somewhat I am sure
> I never shall know here. I 'll tell you a miracle :
> I am not mad yet to my cause of sorrow ;
> The heavens o'er my head seem made of molten brass,
> The earth of flaming sulphur ; yet I am not mad.
> I am acquainted with sad misery,
> As the tanned galley-slave is with his oar :
> Necessity makes me suffer constantly,
> And custom makes it easy.

Extravagant passions, the love of love, the hate of hate, the
spasms of indulged revenge, drive men to the verge of

delirium. This state of exaltation, when the whole nature quivers beneath the weight of overpowering repulsion or desire, was admirably rendered even by men who could not seize the accent of pronounced insanity. Ferdinand, in the same tragedy by Webster, kills his sister from excess of jealousy and avarice. When he sees her corpse, his fancy, set on flame already by the fury of his hate, becomes a hell, which burns the image of her calm pale forehead, fixed eyes, and womanhood undone in years of beauty, on his reeling brain. ' Cover her face : mine eyes dazzle : she died young.' There is no place for repentance in his soul ; he flies from the room a raving and incurable lunatic. Milder and more pathetic forms of distraction, resulting from loss, ill-treatment, slighted love, are handled no less skilfully. The settled melancholy of poor Penthea in Ford's ' Broken Heart ' is not less touching than the sorrows of Ophelia. For realistic studies of madhouses we may go to Middleton and Dekker ; for the lunacy of witchcraft to Rowley ; for the ludicrous aspects of idiocy to Jonson's Troubleall. To taste the sublime of terror we must turn the pages of ' King Lear,' or watch Lady Macbeth in her somnambulism. It is clear that all the types of mental aberration, from the fixed conditions of dementia and monomania through temporary delirium to crack-brained imbecility, were familiar objects to our drama-tists. They formed common and striking ingredients in the rough life of that epoch.

X

Emerging from the Middle Ages, the men of the sixteenth century carried with them a heavy burden of still haunting spiritual horrors. As Queen Elizabeth's Prayer Book was illustrated upon the margin with a Danse Macabre, so these playwrights etched their scenes with sinister imaginings of death. They gazed with dread and fascination on the unfamiliar grave. The other world had for them intense reality ; and they invested it with terrors of various and

vivid kinds.   Sometimes it is described as a place of soli
tude—

> Of endless parting
> With all we can call ours, with all our sweetness,
> With youth, strength, pleasure, people, time, nay reason!
> For in the silent grave no conversation,
> No joyful tread of friends, no voice of lovers,
> No careful father's counsel; nothing 's heard,
> Nor nothing is, but all oblivion,
> Dust, and an endless darkness.

Again, it is peopled with hideous shapes and fiends that
plagued the wicked.   ' 'T is full of fearful shadows,' says the
king in ' Thierry and Theodoret.'   Claudio, in his agony,
exclaims :

> Ay, but to die and go we know not where ;
> To lie in cold obstruction and to rot ;
> This sensible warm motion to become
> A kneaded clod, and the delighted spirit
> To bathe in fiery floods, or to reside
> In thrilling regions of thick-ribbed ice ;
> To be imprisoned in the viewless winds
> And blown with restless violence about
> The pendent world ; or to be worse than worst
> Of those that lawless and incertain thoughts
> Imagine howling : 't is too horrible !
> The weariest and most loathed worldly life
> That age, ache, penury and imprisonment
> Can lay on nature, is a paradise
> To what we fear of death.

Hamlet, meddling with the casuistry of suicide, is still more
terror-striking by one simple word :

> To die—to sleep ;—
> To sleep ! perchance to dream : ay, there 's the rub ;
> For in that sleep of death what dreams may come,
> When we have shuffled off this mortal coil,
> Must give us pause.

The medieval pre-occupation with the world beyond this
world, surviving in the Renaissance, led these musicians to

play upon the organ stops of death in plangent minor keys.
Instead of dread, they sometimes use the tone of weariness:

> All life is but a wandering to find home ;
> When we are gone, we 're there.   Happy were man,
> Could here his voyage end; he should not then
> Answer, how well or ill he steered his soul
> By heaven's or by hell's compass.

Milder contemplations, when death seems not merely acceptable as an escape from life, but in itself desirable, relieve the
sternness of the picture :

> 'T is of all sleeps the sweetest:
> Children begin it to us, strong men seek it,
> And kings from height of all their painted glory
> Fall like spent exhalations to this centre.

Why should the soul of man dread death ?

> These fears
> Feeling but once the fires of noble thought
> Fly like the shapes of clouds we form to nothing.

What, after all, is it to die ?

> 'T is less than to be born ; a lasting sleep ;
> A quiet resting from all jealousy ;
> A thing we all pursue ; I know, besides,
> It is but giving over of a game
> That must be lost.

Memnon, in the ' Mad Lover's Tragedy,' reasoning upon his
hopeless passion for the princess, argues thus :

> I do her wrong, much wrong : she 's young and blessèd,
> Sweet as the spring, and as his blossoms tender;
> And I a nipping north-wind, my head hung
> With hails and frosty icicles : are the souls so too
> When we depart hence, lame, and old, and loveless ?
> No, sure 't is ever youth there ; time and death
> Follow our flesh no more ; and that forced opinion
> That spirits have no sexes, I believe not.

Where, asks his friend, may pure love hope for its accomplishment ?

> Below, Siphax,
> Below us, in the other world, Elysium,
> Where 's no more dying, no despairing, mourning,
> Where all desires are full, deserts down-loaden,
> There, Siphax, there, where loves are ever living.

In the same strain of exalted feeling, but with a touch of even sweeter pathos, Caratach comforts his little nephew Hengo, at the hour of death. The boy is shuddering on the brink of that dark river: ' Whither must we go when we are dead ? '

> Why, to the blessedest place, boy ! Ever sweetness
> And happiness dwells there.
> No ill men,
> That live by violence and strong oppression,
> Come thither. 'T is for those the gods love—good ones.

Webster, contrasting the death of those who die in peace with that of tyrants and bad livers, makes a prince exclaim :

> O thou soft, natural death, that art joint twin
> To sweetest slumber ! No rough-bearded comet
> Stares on thy mild departure: the dull owl
> Beats not against thy casement ; the hoarse wolf
> Scents not thy carrion ; pity winds thy corse,
> Whilst horror waits on princes.

Dekker too, in his most melodious verse, has said :

> An innocent to die ; what is it less
> But to add angels to heaven's happiness ?

It will be observed that the purely theological note is never sounded in any of these lyrical outpourings on the theme of death. The pagan tone which marks them all takes strongest pitch, where it is well in keeping with dramatic character, in the last words of Petronius condemned to suicide by Nero :

> It is indeed the last and end of ills !
> The gods, before they would let us taste death's joys,
> Placed us i' the toil and sorrows of this world,

Because we should perceive the amends and thank them.
Death, the grim knave, but leads you to the door
Where, entered once, all curious pleasures come
To meet and welcome you.
A troop of beauteous ladies, from whose eyes
Love thousand arrows, thousand graces shoots,
Puts forth their fair hands to you and invites
To their green arbours and close-shadowed walks,
Whence banished is the roughness of our years !
Only the west wind blows ; it 's ever spring
And ever summer.   There the laden boughs
Offer their tempting burdens to your hand,
Doubtful your eye or taste inviting more.
There every man his own desires enjoys ;
Fair Lucrece lies by lusty Tarquin's side,
And woos him now again to ravish her.
Nor us, though Roman, Lais will refuse ;
To Corinth any man may go. . . .
Mingled with that fair company, shall we
On banks of violets and of hyacinths
Of loves devising sit, and gently sport ;
And all the while melodious music hear,
And poets' songs that music far exceed,
The old Anacreon crowned with smiling flowers,
And amorous Sapho on her Lesbian lute
Beauty's sweet scars and Cupid's godhead sing.

After this rapturous foretaste of Elysium, he turns to his friend :

Hither you must, and leave your purchased houses,
Your new-made garden and your black-browed wife,
And of the trees thou hast so quaintly set,
Not one but the displeasant cypress shall
Go with thee.

To his mistress :

Each best day of our life at first doth go,
To them succeeds diseasèd age and woe ;
Now die your pleasures, and the days you pray
Your rhymes and loves and jests will take away.
Therefore, my sweet, yet thou wilt go with me,
And not live here to what thou wouldst not see.

She not unnaturally shrinks from suicide.   Her lover urges:

> Yet know you not that any being dead
> Repented them, and would have lived again ?
> They then their errors saw and foolish prayers ;
> But you are blinded in the love of life.
> Death is but sweet to them that do approach it.
> To me, as one that taken with Delphic rage,
> When the divining God his breast doth fill,
> He sees what others cannot standing by,
> It seems a beauteous and pleasant thing.

Nero's meditations upon death, in the same tragedy, conjure up a companion picture of Tartarus :

> O must I die, must now my senses close?
> For ever die, and ne'er return again,
> Never more see the sun, nor heaven, nor earth ?
> Whither go I ?   What shall I be anon ?
> What horrid journey wanderest thou, my soul,
> Under the earth in dark, damp, dusky vaults ?

Phlegethon and Styx toss their hoarse waves before him ; the Furies shake their whips and twisted snakes :

> And my own furies far more mad than they,
> My mother and those troops of slaughtered friends.

XI

The eternal nature of both happiness and misery, the presence of heaven or hell within the soul of man, irrespective of creeds and dogmas, were pictured with the force of men who felt the spiritual reality of life keenly. Marlowe makes Faustus ask the devil Mephistophilis where hell is :

> Why this is hell, nor am I out of it:
> Think'st thou that I, who saw the face of God,
> And tasted the eternal joys of heaven,
> Am not tormented with ten thousand hells
> In being deprived of everlasting life ?

Dreadful was the path to death for those who died in sin. Webster's Flamineo cries to his murderous enemies :

> Oh, the way 's dark and horrid !   I cannot see.
> Shall I have no company ?

They reply :

> Yes, thy sins
> Do run before thee, to fetch fire from hell
> To light thee thither.

With the same ghastly energy his sister utters a like thought of terror :

> My soul, like to a ship in a black storm,
> Is driven, I know not whither.

Yet the dauntless courage and strong nerves of these ' glorious villains ' sustained them to the last :

> We cease to grieve, cease to be fortune's slaves,
> Yea, cease to die, by dying.

So they speak, when the game of life has been played out ; and then, like travellers,

> Go to discover countries yet unknown.

Ask of such men, what is life ?

> It is a tale told by an idiot,
> Full of sound and fury, signifying nothing.

Ask, what are men ?

> We are merely the stars' tennis balls,
> Struck and bandied which way please them.
>   To be man
> Is but to be the exercise of cares
> In several shapes ; as miseries do grow
> They alter as men's forms ; but none know how.

' The world's a tedious theatre,' says one.   Another cries :

> Can man by no means creep out of himself,
> And leave the slough of viperous grief behind ?

It is a pleasure to collect these utterances on life and death, so pointed and so passionate, so pregnant with deep thought and poignant with heartfelt emotion. It must, however, be remembered, that they are dramatic sayings, put into the lips of scenic personages. To take them as the outcry from their authors' own experience would be uncritical. Yet the frequency of their occurrence indicates one well-marked quality of our drama. That is the sombre cast of Melancholy, deep Teutonic meditative Melancholy, which drapes it with a tragic pall. When Marston invites his audience to a performance of ' Antonio's Revenge,' he not only relies upon this mood in the spectators, but he paints it with the exultation of one to whom it is familiar and dear. Listen to the muffled discords of the opening lines, and to the emergence of the spirit-shaking melody !

> The rawish dank of clumsy winter ramps
> The fluent summer's vein; and drizzling sleet
> Chilleth the wan bleak cheek of the numbed earth ;
> Whilst snarling gusts nibble the juiceless leaves
> From the naked shuddering branch, and pills the skin
> From off the soft and delicate aspects.
> O now, methinks, a sullen tragic scene
> Would suit the time with pleasing congruence !
> .   .   .   .   Therefore, we proclaim,
> If any spirit breathes within this round
> Uncapable of weighty passion—
> As from his birth being hugged in the arms
> And nuzzled 'twixt the breasts of happiness—
> Who winks and shuts his apprehension up
> From common sense of what men were and are,
> Who would not know what man must be—let such
> Hurry amain from our black-visaged shows :
> We shall affright their eyes.   But if a breast
> Nailed to the earth with grief, if any heart
> Pierced through with anguish, pant within this ring,
> If there be any blood whose heat is choked
> And stifled with true sense of misery,
> If aught of these strains fill this consort up,
> They arrive most welcome.

' Nothing 's so dainty-sweet as lovely Melancholy,' exclaims
Beaumont in the Ode which tells of :

> Folded arms and fixèd eyes,
> A sigh that piercing mortifies,
> A look that 's fastened on the ground,
> A tongue chained up without a sound :
> Fountain heads and pathless groves,
> Places which pale passion loves :
> Moonlight walks where all the fowls
> Are warmly housed, save bats and owls.

This habitual Melancholy assumed many shapes. Fantastic
in Vendice apostrophising his dead lady's skull :

> Does the silkworm expend her yellow labours
> For thee ?   For thee does she undo herself ? . . .
> Thou mayst lie chaste now ! it were fine, methinks,
> To have thee seen at revels, forgetful feasts,
> And unclean brothels.

Tender in Palador's bewilderment :

> Parthenophil is lost, and I would see him !
> For he is like to something I remember
> A great while since, a long long time ago.

Exquisite in the Dirge for Chrysostom :

> Sleep, poor youth, sleep in peace,
>   Relieved from love and mortal care ;
> Whilst we, that pine in life's disease,
>   Uncertain-blessed, less happy are.

Close to this melancholy, is religion. Though rarely touched
on by our playwrights, the cardinal points of Christian doctrine
were present to their minds ; and when they struck that
chord of piety, it was with a direct and manly hand :

> The best of men
> That e'er wore earth about him was a sufferer ;
> A soft, meek, patient, humble, tranquil spirit ;
> The first true gentleman that ever breathed.

This is no conventional portrait of the Founder of our faith.
Nor are these solemn words, in which an injured husband
absolves his penitent and dying wife, spoken from the lips
merely :

> As freely from the low depths of my soul
> As my Redeemer hath forgiven His death,
> I pardon thee.
> Even as I hope for pardon at that day
> When the great Judge of heaven in scarlet sits,
> So be thou pardoned.

XII

If the anguish of the world was painted forcibly in all its
strength and ugliness by our old dramatists, the beauty and
the peace, the calm of quiet places, the loveliness of nature
and the dignity of soul which make man's life worth living,
were no less faithfully delineated. If they doted upon the
grave, spending night-hours in sombre contemplations, they
could throw the windows of the heart wide open upon bright
May mornings, hear the lark's song, and feel the freshness
and the joy of simple things. It was the chief triumph of the
Romantic style to make these transitions from grave to gay,
from earnest to sprightly, without effort and without discord.
The multiform existence men enjoy upon this planet received
a full reflection in our theatre; nor was one of its many
aspects neglected for another. Those artists verily believed
that ' the world's a stage ; ' and they made their art a micro-
cosm of the universe. It was given to all of them, in greater
or less degree, to weave the wonder-web of human joys and
pains, to sound the depths and search the heights of nature,
modulating with unconscious felicity from key to key, blending bright hues and sad in harmony upon their arras-work.
Shakspere's pre-eminence consists chiefly in this, that he did
supremely well what all were doing. His touch on life was
so unerringly true that the most diverse objects took shape
and place together naturally in his atmosphere of art ; even
as in the full rich sunlight of a summer afternoon the many

moving crowds, the river, bridges, buildings, parks, and domes of a great city stand distinct but harmonised.

No theatre is so rich in countless and contrasted types of womanhood. Shakspere's women have passed into a proverb. But I need not, nay seek not, to draw illustrations from his works. It is rather my object here as elsewhere, to show how the ' star-ypointing pyramid' on which the sovran poet dwells enthroned, was built by lesser men of like capacity. It has been said that the very names of Fletcher's ladies have a charm : Aspasia, Ordella, Amoret, Evadne, Viola, Euphrasia, Edith, Oriana; and their characters answer to the music of their names. They are sweet, true, gentle; enduring all things, believing all things; patient, meek, strong, innocent, unto the end. His Bonduca marks another type—the Amazon, the Queen, rebellious against Rome. Such women the old playwrights loved; and they often interwove a thread of virile boldness or bravado with the portraiture. Marston's Sophonisba, the Carthaginian bride, who meets death with a dauntless countenance; Massinger's Domitia, the Roman empress, wooing an actor to her love in words that savour of habitual command; Ford's Annabella, guilty in her passion beyond thought or language, but sublime in her endurance of disgrace and death; Marston's Insatiate Countess; Dekker's Bellafront, are all of the same stamp, masculine for good or evil, and of indomitable will. The type reaches its climax in Vittoria Corombona, whose insolence and intellectual ascendency, when she stands up to defy her judges and confound them with her beauty, blaze still upon us with the splendour of an ominous star. That the same poets could draw the softer lines of female character is proved by Mellida, by Dorothea, by Isabella, in whom the tenderness of woman mingles with heroic constancy and strength in suffering. Nor was it only from the regions of romance and story that they borrowed types so varied. Contemporary English life supplied them with Alice Arden and Anne Frankford, with Winnifrede and Susan Carter, with Lady Ager and with Mrs. Wincott—mere names, perhaps, to the majority of those who meet them here; but

women with whose passionate or pathetic histories I may
perchance acquaint my readers.

How could such characters—not to speak of Imogen or
Cleopatra, Constance or Katharine—have been represented
on the English stage ?   During the reigns of Elizabeth and
James no women acted.   Boys were trained to take their
parts ; and the youth who played Lady Macbeth or the
Duchess of Malfi shaved his beard before he placed the
coronet and curls upon his head.   Here is indeed a mystery.
With all the advantages offered to the modern dramatist by
the greatest actresses, it is but rarely that he moulds a perfect
woman for the stage.   How could Shakspere have committed
Desdemona to a boy ?   How had Fletcher the heart to shadow
forth those half-tones and those evanescent hues in his
Aspasia ?

In consequence, perhaps, of this custom, great coarseness
in the treatment of dramatic subjects was allowed.   Boys
uttered speeches which the English moral sense, even of that
age, would scarcely have tolerated in the mouths of women.
Much of the obscenity which defiles the comic drama may
possibly be attributed to this practice.[1]   Yet it is certain that
the boy-actors acquired considerable skill in rendering even
the finer shades of character.   Prince Arthur in 'King John'
and Hengo in 'Bonduca' prove that some even of the male
parts assigned to them involved a delicate perception of the
subtlest sentiments.   Often, too, when they appeared as
women, they assumed a masculine disguise, and carried on
a double part with innuendoes, hints, and half-betrayals of
their simulated sex.   The pages in 'Philaster' and 'The
Lover's Melancholy,' Viola in 'Twelfth Night,' and Jonson's
'Silent Woman,' are instances of these epicene characters,
which our ancestors delighted to contemplate.   'What an
odd double confusion it must have made,' says Charles Lamb,

---

[1] The female actors of Italy and France, where comedy was certainly
more grossly indecent, warn us to be cautious on this point.   But, taking
the greater soundness of English moral feeling into account, I think that
the attempt to introduce women into the theatrical profession would
probably have ended in an earlier suppression of the stage.

'to see a boy play a woman playing a man: we cannot disen-
tangle the perplexity without some violence to the imagination.' Yet there is no violence in the presentation. When
the boy who played Euphrasia, under the disguise of Bellario,
is wounded, and breathes out these words to Philaster—

> My life is not a thing
> Worthy your noble thoughts! 't is not a life,
> 'T is but a piece of childhood thrown away!—

who but feels the woman speaking? The poet heard her
speak; and what he heard, he has conveyed to us.

XIII

While Tragedy reveals the deeper qualities of an epoch—
the essential passions, aspirations, intuitions of a people—
Comedy displays the humours, habits, foibles, superficial
aspects of society. It is not easy to make an exhaustive
classification of the many forms of Comedy exhibited by our
Romantic Drama. Yet these may be broadly divided into
two main species: Comedies of Life and Comedies of
Imagination. The Comedies of Life subdivide into Comedies
of Character, exemplified in the best work of Jonson and
Massinger; and Comedies of Manners, abundantly illustrated
by all the minor playwrights. Shakspere can hardly be said
to have produced a Comedy of Character, in the sense in
which we give this name to Jonson's 'Alchemist' or Molière's
'Tartufe;' for though no dramatist peopled the comic stage
with a greater number of finely discriminated and perfectly
realised types of character, yet we cannot say that any of his
so-called comedies were written to exemplify a leading moral
quality. Nor again, with the single exception of the 'Merry
Wives of Windsor,' did he give the world a Comedy of
Manners in the strict sense of that phrase. Where Shakspere
ruled supreme was, in the Comedy of the Imagination. This,
in truth, was his invention; as it is the rarest and most
characteristic flower of the Romantic Drama.

To call 'The Merchant of Venice,' 'The Tempest,' 'As You Like It,' and 'Measure for Measure' by the name we give to plays of Terence, Molière, Jonson, is clearly a mistake in criticism. The Shaksperian Comedies of the Imagination carry us into a world of pure Romance, where men and women move in the ethereal atmosphere of fancy. They have lost none of their reality as human beings. But their vices and their follies exact a milder censure than in actual life; their actions and their passions have a grace and charm beyond the lot of common mortals. Strictly speaking, the Romantic Tragedy and the Romantic Comedy of Shakspere present the same material, the same philosophy, the same conception of existence, under different lights and with a different tone of sympathy.[1] How Shakspere meant his Comedies to be interpreted may be gathered from the induction to 'The Taming of the Shrew,' from the title of 'A Midsummer Night's Dream,' from the magic of Prospero, and from the woodland solitudes of Arden. In these creations he avoids the ordinary ways of social life, chooses fantastic fables, or touches tales of Italy with an enchanter's wand. Lyly in his Court Comedies had preceded Shakspere on this path of art, and Fletcher followed him, although at a wide interval. After defining Shakspere's Comedy as the Comedy of pure Imagination and Romantic incident, in which the master's unrivalled character-drawing was displayed with no less strength, but to less awful purpose, than in his Tragedy; we may divide the comedies of Fletcher into two main classes, describing the one class by the name of Romantic Lustspiel, or Play of Fanciful Amusement, the other by that of Romantic Comedy of Intrigue. In the former of these species, represented by 'The Pilgrim,' 'The Sea Voyage,' and 'The Island Princess,' Fletcher handles romantic incident with something of Shaksperian grace. In the latter, includ-

---

[1] Mercutio, for example, in *Romeo and Juliet* is a comic character, and Angelo in *Measure for Measure* is deeply tragic. The part of Shylock is a tragic episode within a comedy; the part of Imogen is hardly less tragic than that of Cordelia, except in the conclusion of the plot. See Professor Ward's *History* for some excellent critical observations upon this point.

ing 'The Wild-Goose Chace,' 'The Spanish Curate,' and
'The Chances,' he follows the French and Spanish manner.
The remote scenes in which Fletcher laid the action of his
plays, the fluency of thought, fertility of invention, and exquisite poetic ease with which he wrought and carried out
his complicated plots, raise both types of comedy above a
common level, and give them the right to rank at no immeasurable distance below Shakspere's. Perusing these
light and airy improvisations, our fancy is continually
charmed and our attention fascinated. But when we reflect
upon their characters, we are forced to regard these men and
women as the figures of a pantomime, the creatures of a
poet's reverie, who, doing right or wrong, are moved by
springs of wayward impulse, and who feel no moral responsi-
bilities like those of daily life. It is just here that Fletcher's
inferiority to Shakspere in the Comedy of the Imagination is
most strongly felt. While his Romantic Lustspiel reveals
the outward show of things, and plays upon the superficies
of human nature, Shakspere's unfolds the very soul of man
made magically perfect, and his imagination freed from all
impediments to its aërial flight. Sir Thomas Browne has
said, ' We are somewhat more than ourselves in our sleep ;'
and these words might be applied to Shakspere's comedies.
There we move in a land of dreams, peopled by shapes
brighter and more beautiful than those of this gross earth,
lighted by larger suns that shine through softer air.

Besides Comedies of Imagination and Romantic Intrigue,
the fancy of the minor dramatists ran riot in many other
hybrid species. They interwove the Italian Pastoral with
classic legend or with transcripts from English rural life,
invented graceful allegories like Dekker's 'Fortunatus,' or
Day's 'Parliament of Bees,' and adapted motives of the
Masque at Court to the legitimate Drama. It would not
serve a useful purpose to pursue this analysis further. It is
enough to indicate how large a part Imagination and Romantic
Fancy played in English comic art.

What is now known as Farce was not a common form of
Comedy in the Elizabethan age. The custom of the theatre

demanded five-act pieces: and though many plots are
essentially farcical, the method of conducting them necessitated by so large a scale of treatment altered their dramatic
quality. 'Gammer Gurton's Needle' and Ben Jonson's
'Bartholomew Fair' may be mentioned, however, as strictly
farcical compositions. The 'Silent Woman,' again, is rather
a Titanic Farce than a true Comedy of Character or
Manners.

In plays belonging to the Comedy of Manners we gain
faithful studies of daily life in London. Their realism makes
them valuable; but the majority are coarse, and not a little
tedious to read. The stock personages resemble those of
Latin Comedy—a jealous husband, a wilful wife, a stupid
country squire, a parasite, a humorous serving man, a supple
courtier, a simple girl, an apish Frenchman, a whining
Puritan, a woman of the town, a gallant, a swaggering bully, a
conceited coxcomb. The playwrights, when engaged upon such
pieces, sought success by movement, broad fun, lively dialogue,
good-humoured satire, and roughly outlined silhouettes of
character. They threw them off rapidly, and took no care to
preserve them for posterity. Marston in his preface to the
'Fawne' apologises for its publication : 'If any shall wonder
why I print a comedy, whose life rests much in the actor's
voice, let such know that I cannot avoid publishing.'
He here alludes to the booksellers' practice of having plays
taken down by shorthand, and so presenting them for sale in
a pirated and garbled state. Marston makes a similar
defence for the 'Malcontent : ' 'Only one thing affects me,
to think that scenes invented merely to be spoken should be
inforcively published to be read.' So truly did 'the life of
these things consist in action,' that passages were often left
for the extempore declamation of the actors. Sometimes the
whole conduct of the piece depended on their powers of
improvisation. They were then provided with programmes
of the acts and scenes, and of the entrances and exits of the
several persons. These programmes received the name of
'Platt' or chart, from which we probably derive the word
'plot.' They were hung up on the screen-work of the stage

for reference and study. In Italy such outlines of comedies were called ' Scenario.'

In reading the ordinary Comedy of Manners, all these circumstances must be taken into consideration. We must remember that the effect of such plays, even where written, depended on the actors, who were trained more strictly to their business then than now. The old custom of maintaining jesters in castles and at Court bred a class of men whose profession it was to entertain an audience with mimicry, ludicrous tricks, and sharp sayings. Continued through centuries, the skill of these jesters reached a high degree of excellence, through the tradition of buffoonery established and through the emulation which impelled each Fool of eminence to surpass his predecessors. The celebrity of Tarleton, Green, Summer, Kempe and Robert Wilson proves that the comic playwrights could rely upon an able band of interpreters. It may even be asserted that the popular talents of these jesters proved an obstacle to the development of higher Comedy in England, by accustoming the public taste to jigs and merriments, solo pieces and inventions of the clown, instead of encouraging a demand for seriously studied art.

Dekker and Massinger, Middleton and Shirley, claim notice among the minor playwrights who dignified the Comedy of Manners by solid and thoughtful workmanship. But it was from Jonson that this species received the most masterly handling. His comedies in their way, as truly as those of Shakspere, are the productions of indubitable and peculiar genius. He never wrote at random. He never sought to please the populace by exhibitions of mere shallow merriment ; nor did he always succeed in riveting their attention by the ponderous stage-antics of his ' learned sock.' Those who would not worship his Muse were treated by him with contempt. He pursued his own designs, penning satiric dramas on his fellow-craftsmen, and pouring scorn upon

> The loathèd stage
> And the more loathsome age,
> Where pride and impudence in faction knit
> Usurp the chair of wit.

Jonson was a moralist and a philosopher, conveying through the medium of his comedy the results of mature studies and of patient inquiries into human nature. The end of poetry, in his opinion, was 'to inform men in the best reason of living;' and he wrote systematically, deducing characters from fixed conceptions of specific attributes, building up plots with all the massive machinery of learning and potent intellectual materials at his command. Unlike the poets of Imaginative Comedy, he adhered to scenes of common human experience; and, deviating from the traditions of the school he had adopted, he portrayed unusual and exaggerated eccentricities ('Volpone' and 'The Alchemist'), instead of the broader and more general aspects of humanity. Therefore the name of Humour, which recurs so often in his work, may be taken as the keynote to his conception of character.

XIV

Criticism has to separate the transient from the permanent; to attempt at least to estimate the true relations of the subject which it treats. Therefore, in this preliminary survey of Elizabethan Drama, we are led to ask some questions of more general import than those which have as yet concerned us. What were the causes of its eminent success? Why did it sink so soon into oblivion? What formative influence has it exercised over our literature and over that of other nations —the modern German and the recent French, for instance? What place shall we assign to it among the lastingly important products of the human genius? In other words: Were these plays, the majority of which seem to most of us so dull and dead now, at any time endowed with life and power over men? Did they educate the English people, and help to make this nation what it is?

These are the weightiest questions belonging to the subject; more grave than the settling of dates or dubious readings; less easy to resolve than inquiries into the antiquities of theatres. To some of them I gave a partial answer when I tried to show how our Drama embodied the spirit of

the sixteenth century in England ; for if it did this, as undoubtedly it did, then upon this account alone we have to
place it on the list of world-important products. Epics that
condense successive epochs for us in monumental poems,
Dramas that present the spirit of past periods in a series of
lively shadow-pictures, will always rank among the most
valuable and permanently interesting achievements of literature. But it is not enough to feel certain that the playwrights
worked in close dependence on the spirit of their age, and
gave its thoughts and passions utterance. It is not enough
to demonstrate their value for students bent on seizing points
of local colour, or for historians engaged in penetrating the
past workings of the human mind. We want, further, to
estimate their capacity for expressing, their influence in
forming, national character. In order to do this, we must
resume some points already partly entertained.

XV

Three things may never be forgotten in the criticism of
our Drama. First, it grew up beneath the patronage of the
whole nation ; the public to which these playwrights appealed
was the English people, from Elizabeth upon the throne
down to the lowest ragamuffin of the streets ; in the same
wooden theatres met lords and ladies, citizens and prentices,
common porters and working men, soldiers, sailors, pick-
pockets, and country folk. Secondly, the English during the
period of its development exhibited no aptitude in any marked
degree for any other of the arts. Thirdly, it was hampered
in its freedom neither by the scholastic pedantry of literary
men, nor by the political or ecclesiastical restraints of Government. These points are so important that I shall enlarge
upon each separately.

XVI

The Drama, more than any other form of art, requires a
national public. Unless it live in sympathy with the whole

people at a certain moment of intensified vitality, it cannot flourish or become more than a merely literary product. That complete sympathy between the playwrights and the nation which existed in England was wanting in Italy, France, and Spain. Italy had no common sense of nationality, no centre of national existence. Each little state worked for its own interests, maintained its own traditions and its own political diplomacy. Among them all, no single Athens, with indubitable intellectual pre-eminence, arose to make a focus for Italian arts and sciences. Florence more nearly fulfilled this part than any other town of the peninsula. But Florence was not an imperial city, like Athens in the age of Pericles; and Florence had no power to create for Italy that public which is necessary to the full perfection of the Drama. A strong national spirit animated France and Spain These two countries, next to England, produced the finest dramatic literatures of modern times. Yet in Spain the galling fetters of Court etiquette and of ecclesiastical intolerance checked the evolution of the popular genius; while in France, between the poet and the people intervened academies and aristocracy. It is not worth our while to speak of Germany. At the close of the last century some German poets strove to found a theatre. But Goethe complained bitterly that the nation had no central point, no brain, no heart, to which he could appeal.[1]

XVII

While the artistic energies of Italy were principally employed in giving figurative form to ideas, England had no native or imported art. Architecture had just ceased to exist as an original growth in our island. Instead of seeking plastic expression for their perception of the beautiful, our artists studied poetical form. They laboured to present an image to the mind, and knew not how to captivate the senses.

[1] For further development of this theme, see the Essay on 'Euripides' in my *Studies of Greek Poets*, and the chapter on 'Italian Drama' in my *Renaissance in Italy*, vol. v.

Holbein, our only great naturalised painter, produced little else but portraits. Torrigiano, a second-rate sculptor, visited these barbarous shores to make his fortune, and decamped again. No foreign masters settled here and founded schools ; for the fairest promise could not lure a Florentine beyond Paris ; England was to men of Southern race what Siberia is to us, and Paris like S. Petersburg. Thus the power of the English intellect was driven in upon itself for nutriment. Poets had to find the world of beauty in their thoughts, in the study of mankind, in dreams of the imagination. This gave a human depth and rich intensity to their dramatic writing. It encouraged the playwrights to penetrate the deepest and the subtlest labyrinths of passion, and forced them to express themselves through language, for want of any other medium. But it also impressed a certain homeliness, a well-marked stamp of insularity, upon their work.

A contemporary critic compares the ' genius ' of the English race with French ' openness of mind and flexibility of intelligence,' defining genius for his purpose as ' mainly an affair of energy.' The literature of the Elizabethan age, he tells us, is a ' literature of genius,' complaining of the poverty of its results, and pointing to the power and fecundity of the French ' literature of intelligence ' in the ' great century ' of the Grand Monarque. We may welcome the wholesome rebuke to national vanity contained in these remarks ; and may note the circumspection with which Mr. M. Arnold guards himself against doing obvious injustice to the English type of literary excellence.[1] Yet there remains the stubborn

---

[1] It seems to me a critical mistake to call genius ' mainly an affair of energy.' The genius of such a poet as Shakspere implies certainly more creative energy than his critics and admirers have. But we rate this genius so highly as we do for far other qualities ; for finer moral and intellectual penetration than is given to merely energetic personalities, for sensibility to the rarest natural influences, for a diviner intelligence of secrets and a more god-like openness of mind to the world's utmost loveliness than fell to the lot of, for example, Voltaire. It is for these high gifts, not for its energy, that we value the genius of Shakspere. And if we turn to science ; is it for energy that we value Newton or Darwin ? Surely we value Whewell for energy ; but Newton or Darwin for exceptionally potent sympathy with truths implicit in things subject to the human mind. Energy, indeed, is needed to pursue these truths

fact that a 'literature of genius' is rarer and more luminous, though less imitable and less adapted to average utilities, than a 'literature of intelligence.' The question really is, which sort of literature the world would the more willingly let die, in the comfortable assurance that by industry and self-control it could at any time recover it. Most men, I think, would answer this question by saying that a literature 'of genius,' evolved under conditions so exceptional as that of England in the sixteenth century, is more irrecoverable and less likely to be reproduced, even though more wayward, insular, and incoherent, than a literature of 'openness of mind;' and that therefore this literature is quite incalculably more valuable. All nations, including even the English, have recently made considerable progress in the acquisition of a sound prose style, in the vulgarisation of philosophical thought, and in the polite treatment of a variety of useful topics. But which of all the nations has produced a literature of genius?

Our Drama remains the monument of peculiar mental power; eccentric and unequal; full of poetry and thought, but deficient in neatness and moderation; with more of matter than of polish, of Pan than of Apollo; rough where the French is smooth, fiery where the French glitters, rude where the French is elegant; sublime, imaginative, passionate, where Gallic art is graceful, prosaic, rhetorical, and superficial.

It would be difficult for an impartial critic to accuse Elizabethan literature of inherent barrenness and poor results. The civil wars, indeed, suspended the æsthetical development of Englishmen. A sect averse to arts and letters triumphed, and were followed by a dissolute half-foreign reign. Political and religious interests, more grave than those of art, consigned the dramatists and poets of the sixteenth century to oblivion for a time. A new taste in literature succeeded, ran its course, and dwindled in a cen-

---

to their last hiding-place, and to produce them for the common mind of man. But energy alone is the mere muscle of genius, the thews and sinews of an organism differentiated by its delicacy and its power of divination.

tury to decadence, after powerfully influencing the development
of English thought and style. But the spirit of the Elizabethan age has revived in this age of Victoria. The memory
of those poets, like the memory of youth and spring, is now
an element of beauty in the mental life of a people too
much given to worldly interests. The blossoms, too, of that
spring-time of poetry, unlike the pleasures of youth or the
flowers of May, are imperishable.

We need only peruse the Fourth Book of the 'Golden
Treasury,' and take mental stock of the four or five great
living poets of our race, in order to perceive in how deep and
true a sense English poetry, by far the richest, most varied,
sweetest, and most powerful vein of poetry in modern Europe,
is still sympathetic to the poetry of the sixteenth century. I
care to say nothing here about the influence of Elizabethan
English Literature over the recent Literatures of Germany,
France, and other nations.

XVIII

The English Drama enjoyed singular advantages of
freedom from cramping restraints, whether imposed by
educated opinion or by a cautious Government. The playwrights and the public were unfastidious and uncritical.
While the wits of Italy apologised for making use of their
mother tongue, absorbed their energies in scholarship, bowed
to the verdict of coteries, and set the height of style in studied
imitation of the Romans, our poets wrote 'as love dictates,'
consulted no authority but nature, and appealed to no standard but popular approbation. Literature sprang up in
England when the labour of restoring the classics had
already been achieved, and when the superstitious veneration
for antiquity had begun to abate. Men of learning were not
the national poets of England, as they were of Italy; nor
did the universities give laws of taste to the people. Our
poets were not scholars in the strict sense of that term;
or if scholars, they were renegades from Alma Mater,
preferring London to Oxford or Cambridge, the theatre to

the lecture-room, Bandello and Spanish Comedies to Seneca and treatises on the Poetics. There existed no tyrannous Academy, like that before whose verdict Corneille had to bow, when Richelieu condemned the 'Cid' for violating rules of art.

On the other hand, the dramatists were almost equally unfettered by authority. To write what they chose so long as they did not blaspheme against religion, libel the Government, or grossly corrupt public morality, was the privilege secured to them by royal letters patent. This liberty would have been impossible in any one of the small jealous states of Italy. It would have been impossible in any country where the Holy Office held sway, or where the Church was independent of the State.

It might be urged that though exemption from political and ecclesiastical interference was an advantage to our theatre, some subordination to learned taste would have been salutary. This argument cannot, however, be maintained in the face of what is known about the influence of academies upon the Drama in Italy and France. Certainly, the form of English plays leaves much to be desired upon the score of art and careful workmanship. But this imperfection is the defect of a quality so valuable that, while we regret and censure it, we are bound to remain satisfied. The lively irregularities of a Dekker or a Heywood are more acceptable than the lifeless correctness of a Trissino or a Sperone. It was, moreover, from the matrix of this untutored art that jewels like 'Hamlet' and 'Vittoria Corombona,' 'The Broken Heart,' and 'The Maid's Tragedy,' emerged in all their conspicuous lustre.

Great monuments of art must be judged by their own ideal, and not by that of diverse, if no less commanding, excellence. The men who supplied the London theatres in that age understood their trade. The art of writing plays was not acquired in the study, but fostered by the intellectual conditions of the time. It grew gradually from small beginnings to great results. Successive masters developed this art, each taking from his predecessors what they had to teach. The playwrights formed a tradition. They acquired technical dexterity in their use of words and rhythms, ornaments of style, and modes of exposition. They learned how to handle subjects dramatically, studied the modes of entrances and exits, the introduction of underplots, the heightening of action to a climax, the creation of striking situations for their leading characters. It may be observed that in all branches of intellectual industry, wherever technical discovery is demanded as a condition of success, a school comes into being. Men of the highest genius have first to practise their art as a handicraft, before they breathe into its forms the breath of their own spiritual life. This was eminently the case with Italian painting. Young artists were articled to Ghirlandajo at Florence, to Perugino at Perugia, to Squarcione at Padua. In the workshops of those masters the pupils earned how to mix colours and compose the ground for fresco, how to strain canvases and prepare surfaces; they studied design, perspective, drawing from the model; became acquainted with conventional methods of treating secular and religious subjects. Something of the same sort was true in the case of our Drama. Playwrights began life as journey-workmen, doing the odd jobs of a company, or serving an employer like Henslowe. In this apprenticeship they grew familiar with the technical elements of their art, and were able to employ these at a later period according to the dictates of their own peculiar taste. Thus dramatic composition in the sixteenth century was a trade, but a trade which, like that of Sculpture in Athens, of Painting in Italy, of Music in Germany, allowed men of creative genius to detach themselves from the ranks of creditable handicraftsmen. Shakspere stands where Michelangelo and Pheidias stand, above all rivals; but he owed his dexterity to training. Had he been a solitary worker, exploring the rules and methods of dramatic art by study of classical masterpieces and reflection upon æsthetical treatises, it is inconceivable that his plays would have exhibited that facility of style and that unlimited command of theatrical resources which left his hands at liberty to mould the stuff of human nature into luminous form. Power over the machinery of art and familiarity with technical processes, which, unless completely mastered, are a hindrance to inventive genius; this is what a Shakspere, a Michelangelo, a Pheidias, must ever owe to the labours of predecessors and contemporaries.

In estimating the Drama as a whole, we are thus bound to give its just weight to unencumbered freedom of development; for this freedom formed, if not a school of playwrights, a tradition of playwriting which was essentially natural and yet in a strict sense methodical. That much imperfect, crude, untutored work was due to this same freedom may be conceded; but this drawback should not be allowed to outweigh so singular advantages. Perhaps the real artistic excellence of that dramatic literature would be made more manifest if some impartial critic should select the best plays of the period from the rubbish, and present these in one series to the reader. It would then be seen how admirable was the skill displayed by a large number of craftsmen, how various were their sources of inspiration, and yet how remarkable is the unity of tone pervading works so diverse.

XIX

We are led by these observations to consider another point affecting the art of the English dramatists. During the short period in which they flourished, there prevailed in our island what may be called, for want of an exacter phrase, clairvoyance in dramatic matters. Of all the playwrights of that time, whatever were their feelings, and however they differed in degree of ability, not one but had a special tact, facility, and force of touch upon the Drama. Weak, uncertain, and affected in other branches of literature—in satire, epigram, complimentary epistle, even narrative—these men showed strength, firmness, and directness when they had to write a scene. To explain this fact would be more difficult than to find parallels and illustrations from other nations and from other ages. The ancient Greeks and the Italians of the

Renaissance possessed clairvoyance in the plastic arts. The present age is clairvoyant in science and the application of science to purposes of utility. At each great epoch of the world's history the mind of man has penetrated more deeply than at others into some particular subject, has interrogated Nature in its own way, solving for one period of time intuitively and with ease problems which, before and after, it has been unable with pains to apprehend in that same manner.

In the days of our dramatic supremacy, the nature of man became in its entirety the subject of representative poetry; and the apocalypse of man was more complete than at any other moment of the world's history. Shakspere and his greater contemporaries reveal human passions, thoughts, aspirations, sentiments, and motives of action with evidence so absolute, with so obvious an absence of any intervenient medium, that the creations even of Sophocles, of Calderon, of Corneille, when compared with these, seem to represent abstract conceptions or animated forms rather than the inner truths of life.

In order to estimate the force of this dramatic insight, we might compare the stories on which our dramatists founded their tragedies with the tragedies themselves—'Romeo and Juliet' or 'Othello' with the novels of Da Porto or Cinthio, 'The Duchess of Malfi' with Bandello's prose, 'Arden of Feversham' with Holinshed's Chronicle. It would then be evident that, taking the mere outline of a plot, they filled this in with human life of poignant intensity, 'piercing' (to use those words of Milton) 'dead things with inbreathed sense.' The tales from which the playwrights drew their tragedies contained incident in plenty but feeble silhouettes of character, enough of rhetoric but no passion of poetry, enough moralising but little of world-wisdom. The dramatists knew how to use the framework, while they changed the spirit of these pieces; animating them with salient portraiture of men and women studied from the life, adorning them with unpremeditated song, and making them the lesson-books of practical philosophy.

The clairvoyance of our playwrights enabled them to understand the true nature of their art; to separate the epic, idyllic, or didactic mode of treatment from the dramatic. They felt that the essential duty of the Drama is that it should not moralise, but that it should exhibit character in action. Therefore, they made action the main point; and it was their incommunicable gift, the gift of a great moment, that nothing which they touched was failing in the attribute of active energy.

Furthermore, this clairvoyance gave them insight into things beyond their own experience. Shakspere painted much that he had never seen; and it was true to nature. As the skilled anatomist will reconstruct from scattered bones an animal long since extinct, so from one trait of character he reasoned out the complex of a man or woman. He made that man or woman stand before us, not as the embodiment of one selected quality, but as a living and incalculable organism. This power, in a greater or a less degree, was shared by his contemporaries. They owed it to that intuition into human character which was the virtue of their age. Familiar with the idea of man, they never found themselves at fault when man, the subject of their art, appeared before them in an antiquated or a foreign mode. This explains the vivid treatment which all phases of past history received from them. The heroes of Greece and Rome, of the Bible and Norse Sagas, of Chivalrous Romance and Southern Fiction, were equally real in their eyes with men of their own age and kindred; because they neglected accidental points of difference, and understood what man has been and man must be.

Whatever material was presented to them for manipulation, the truth at which they aimed was always psychological. A Roman or an Ancient Briton, a Greek or an Italian, was for them simply a man. They cared not to take him upon any other terms. Thus they divested their art of frivolous preoccupations concerning local colour, costume, upholstery, and all the insignificances which are apt to intervene between us and the true truth of a past event. If they lack knowledge of special customs, geographical relations, or political circumstance, their judgments on the passions, aims, duties, and home-instincts of humanity are keen and searching.

XX

This brings me not unnaturally to consider a question of great moment: What was the moral teaching of our dramatists? Speaking broadly, we may answer—unexceptionable. That is to say, their tone is manly and wholesome; the moral sense is not offended by doubtful hints, or debilitated by vice made interesting—the sentimentalism of more modern fiction. What is bad, is recognised as bad, and receives no extenuation. It cannot, however, be denied that there are exceptions to this healthiness of tone. Some of Fletcher's, Ford's, and Massinger's plays are founded upon subjects radically corrupt; while the touch of these latter dramatists on questions of conduct and taste is often insecure and casuistical. The student who peruses the whole of Beaumont and Fletcher's works will hardly recommend them for family reading, and will probably be inclined to feel with Leigh Hunt that he has suffered some outrage to his own sense of right and wrong, of cleanliness and decency.

It is not needful to observe that almost every play of that epoch contains much that is coarse in sentiment and gross in language. The comedies, especially, abound in undisguised indelicacy. But, for the most part, these ribald scenes and clownish jokes are excrescences upon the piece itself; and though they are justly disagreeable to a modern taste, they convey no lessons of wantonness. If Spungius and Hircius, Rutilio and Annabella, Bellafront and Malefort, were to contend for the prize of impurity with the heroes and heroines of modern French fiction, they would assuredly have small chance of success.

The theatres of London were the resort of profligate and noisy persons, causing constant annoyance to their neighbourhoods. Therefore, as will be set forth in a separate essay of this volume, the Corporation resisted their establishment within the City bounds, and reluctantly tolerated them in the suburbs. Puritan divines denounced their teaching from the pulpit; while a succession of books and pamphlets taxed them with corrupting manners. But though it was manifest that playhouses encouraged loose living in the persons who frequented them, and though the social influence of plays upon the youth of London was at least questionable, neither the last Tudor nor the first Stuart attempted to suppress them on this account. Besides enjoying theatrical representations with keen relish herself, Elizabeth seems to have understood their utility as means of popular education. To institute a censorship of plays, to restrain unlicensed companies from acting, to forbid the exercise of this art upon Sundays, to make the use of blasphemous oaths in dramatic compositions penal, and to punish the publication of seditious or scandalous libels, were the utmost measures taken by successive Governments in regulating the morals of the theatre. For the rest, they trusted, not without good reason, to the wholesome instincts of the people, with whom the playwrights lived and wrote in closest sympathy. It was only when the tone of a profligate Court began to make itself felt on the public stage, that a distinct tendency to deterioration became evident.

XXI

Whatever view may be taken about the morality of the Elizabethan Drama, one thing is certain. It formed a school of popular instruction, a rallying-point of patriotism. The praises of civil and religious liberty, the celebration of national glories, reached all ears from the theatres. Here the people learned to love their Queen and to hate slavery. They saw before their eyes the deeds of patriots and heroes vividly enacted. They grew familiar with the history of England. The horrors of bad government and civil strife, the baneful influence of Court favourites, the corruptions of a priestly rule and the iniquities of despotism, were written plainly in large characters for all to read. Poets, orators, and scholars poured forth learning, eloquence, and imagery to express to

Englishmen the greatness of their past, the splendour of their destiny. No national epic could have been so potent in the formation of a noble consciousness as those dramatic scenes which reproduced the triumphs of Crecy and Agincourt, the wars of York and Lancaster, the struggle of the Reformation, and the Defeat of the Armada. If the ballad of 'Chevy Chase' stirred Sir Philip Sidney like the blast of a trumpet, how must the dying words of Gaunt have thrilled an English audience? Rarely did one of our dramatists mention any island without some passionate praise of England. The coldest kindled at this theme : [1]

> Look on England,
> The Empress of the European isles ;
> When did she flourish so, as when she was
> The mistress of the ocëan, her navies
> Putting a girdle round about the world ?
> When the Iberian quaked, her worthies named ;
> And the fair flower de luce grew pale, set by
> The red rose and the white ?

It was indeed no idle boast of Heywood's, when he contended that the pageantry of heroism and patriotism, displayed before a people on the stage, bred virtue and inflamed the soul to emulation.

It cannot be doubted that the stage exercised wide-reaching influence over the development of English character at a moment when the nation was susceptible to such impressions. Reading the plays of Marlowe, Shakspere, Jonson, Heywood, Chapman, Dekker, Beaumont, we are fain to cry with Milton: 'Methinks I see in my mind a noble and puissant nation rousing herself like a strong man after sleep, and shaking her invincible locks : methinks I see her like an eagle mewing her mighty youth, and kindling her undazzled eyes at the full mid-day beam ; purging and unscaling her long-abused sight at the fountain itself of heavenly radiance : while the whole noise of timorous and flocking birds, with those also that love the twilight, flutter about amazed at what she

---

[1] Massinger's *Maid of Honour.*

means, and in their envious gabble would prognosticate a year of sects and schisms.'

Even the Puritans may have felt grateful to the playhouse when they came to exchange their character of private sanctimoniousness for one of public resistance to tyranny. Then they found in the people a nobility of spirit and a deeply rooted zeal for freedom, which had been brought to consciousness in no small measure by the stage. These obligations remained, however, unrecognised; and perhaps it is even only now that we are beginning to acknowledge them. The Drama had done its work before the Civil Wars began. Its vigour was exhausted; every day it became less pure, more subservient to the pleasures of a luxurious Court. When it revived with Charles II. it had changed its character. The function of the theatre in England had been great and beneficial; it had helped to cherish a strong sense of national honour, to popularise the new ideas and liberal culture which permeated Europe; it had evolved an original and stable type of art, developed the resources of our language, and enriched the world with inexhaustible funds of poetry. Now it was dead, and only the faint shadow of its former self survived.

> Strong were our sires, and as they fought they writ,
> Conquering with force of arms and dint of wit:
> Theirs was the giant race before the Flood;
> And thus, when Charles returned, our empire stood.
> Like Janus he the stubborn soil manured,
> With rules of husbandry the rankness cured;
> Tamed us to manners, when the stage was rude;
> And boisterous English wit with art indued.
> Our age was cultivated thus at length;
> But what we gained in skill, we lost in strength:
> Our builders were with want of genius cursed;
> The second temple was not like the first.

Thus wrote Dryden to Congreve on his ' Double Dealer,' mingling false compliment with sound criticism.

XXII

One point, incidentally dropped in the foregoing paragraph, remains for consideration. What are the obligations of the English language to the Drama? Heywood, in the Apology to which I have already alluded, adduces, among other arguments in favour of the stage, that through its means English had been raised 'from the most rude and unpolished tongue' to 'a most perfect and composed language.' Each playwright, he adds, attempted to discover fresh beauties of rhythm and expression, and to leave the dialect more pliable and fertile for his successors.

During the half-century in which the Drama flourished, English became a language capable of conveying exquisite, profound, and varied thought. The elements of which it is composed were fused into one vital whole. And though we dare not attribute this advance to the Drama alone, yet if we compare the poetry of that age with contemporary prose, it will be clear that, while both started nearly on a par, the style of the prosaists declined in perspicuity and rhythm, while that of the playwrights became versatile, melodious, and dignified. Even the prose writing of the stage was among the best then going. Lyly, first of English authors, produced prose of scrupulous refinements ; Nash used a prose of incomparable epigrammatic pungency ; while some of Shakspere's prose is modern in its clearness. A similar comparison between the verse of the Drama and that of translations from the Latin or of satire and elegy—Phaer's Virgil, Marston's 'Scourge of Villany,' or Donne's epistles for example—will lead to not dissimilar results. The dramatic poetry of the period is superior to all but its lyrics.[1]

It is not difficult to understand why this should be. The capabilities of the English language were exercised in every department by dramatic composition. For the purposes of

---

[1] These remarks must of course be taken in a general sense. It would be easy to adduce Sidney's *Defence of Poetry* as an example of pure prose, Fairfax's *Tasso* as a specimen of pure translation, and the *Faery Queen* as a masterpiece of lucid narrative in verse.

conversation, it had to assume epigrammatic terseness. In description of scenery, and in the eloquent outpouring of passion, it suggested pictures to the mind and clothed gradations of emotion with appropriate words. At one time the sustained periods of oratory were needed; at another, the swiftest and most airy play of fancy had to be conveyed in passages of lyric lightness. Different characters demanded different tones of diction, yet every utterance conformed to uniformity of style and rhythm. Throughout all changes, the writer was obliged to remain clear and intelligible to his audience.

In handling the language of the theatre, each author developed some specific quality. The fluent grace of Heywood, the sweet sentiment of Dekker, Marston's pregnant sentences, the dream-like charm of Fletcher's melody, Marlowe's mighty line, Webster's sombreness of pathos and heart-quaking bursts of rage, Jonson's gravity, Massinger's smooth-sliding eloquence, Ford's adamantine declamation, and the style of Shakspere, which embraces all—as some great organ holds all instruments within its many stops— these remain as monuments of composition for succeeding ages. Who shall estimate what benefits those men conferred upon the English speech? Our ancestors accustomed their ears to that variety of music, impregnated their intellects with all those divers modes of thought. Besides, the vocabulary was nearly doubled. Shakspere is said to have some 15,000, while the Old Testament contains under 6,000 words. The dramatists collected floating idioms, together with the technical phraseology of trades and professions, the learned nomenclature of the schools, the racy proverbs of the country, the ceremonious expressions of the Court and Council-chamber, and gave them all a place in literature. Instead of being satisfied with the meagre and artificial diction of the Popian age, we may now return to those 'pure wells of English undefiled,' and from their inexhaustible springs refresh our language when it seems to fail.

Nor must it finally be forgotten that the Drama, in its effort after self-emancipation, created the great pride of

English poetry—blank verse. Further occasion will be
granted me for dwelling upon this point in detail. It is
enough here to remark that when Milton used blank verse
for the Epic, he received it from the Drama, and that the
blank verse of the present century is consciously affiliated to
that of the Elizabethan age.

XXIII

To conclude a panegyric, rather than criticism, of the
English Drama, it would be well to give some history of
opinion regarding so great a treasure of our literature during
the past three centuries.

Not very long ago Shakspere himself was half-forgotten.
By degrees admirers disinterred his plays, and wrote of him
as though he had been born like Pallas from the brain of
Jupiter. Garrick reformed, and acted some of his chief
parts. Johnson paid surly homage to his genius; but of
Shakspere's contemporaries this critic said that 'they were
sought after because they were scarce, and would not have
been scarce had they been much esteemed.' Malone and
Steevens, about the same time, made it known that other
playwrights of great merit flourished with Shakspere in the
days of his pre-eminence. The bookseller Dodsley published
twelve volumes of old plays. Gifford spent pains upon the
text of some of them, and Scott used their defunct reputation
for a mask to headings of his chapters. They became the
shibboleth of a coterie. Coleridge and Hazlitt lectured on
them. Charles Lamb made selections, which he enriched
with notes of purest gold of criticism. The 'Retrospective
Review' printed meritorious notices of the more obscure
authors. After those early days, Alexander Dyce, Hartley
Coleridge, J. O. Halliwell, Thomas Wright, and many others,
began to edit the scattered works of eminent dramatists with
antiquarian zeal and critical ability; while J. P. Collier
illustrated by his industry and learning the theatrical annals
of the sixteenth and seventeenth centuries. Continuing this
pious tradition, a host of eloquent and genial writers have

risen to vindicate the honours of that Drama in our times. I have attempted in the preface to this volume to recognise the luminous and solid labours of contemporary scholars in this field. It cannot now be said that the English Drama has not received its due meed of attention from literary men. But it may still be said that it is not sufficiently known to the reading public.

For the close of this exordium and prelude to more detailed studies, I will borrow words from a prose writer in whom the spirit of old English rhetoric lived again with singular and torrid splendour. De Quincey writes about our Drama : ' No literature, not excepting even that of Athens, has ever presented such a multiform theatre, such a carnival display, mask and antimask, of impassioned life—breathing, moving, acting, suffering, laughing :

> Quicquid agunt homines : votum, timor, ira, voluptas,
> Gaudia, discursus :

all this, but far more truly and more adequately than was or could be effected in that field of composition which the gloomy satirist contemplated, whatsoever in fact our medieval ancestors exhibited in the "Dance of Death," drunk with tears and laughter, may here be reviewed, scenically draped, and gorgeously coloured. What other national Drama can pretend to any competition with this ? '

CHAPTER III

MIRACLE PLAYS

1. Emergence of the Drama from the Mystery—Ecclesiastical Con-
demnation of Theatres and Players—Obscure Survival of Mimes
from Pagan Times — Their Place in Medieval Society. — II.
Hroswitha—Liturgical Drama.—III. Transition to the Mystery or
Miracle Play—Ludi—Italian *Sacre Rappresentazioni*—Spanish *Auto*
—French *Mystère*—English Miracle.—IV. Passage of the Miracle
from the Clergy to the People—From Latin to the Vulgar Tongue—
Gradual Emergence of Secular Drama.—V. Three English Cycles
—Origin of the Chester Plays—Of the Coventry Plays—Differences
between the Three Sets—Other Places famous for Sacred Plays.—
VI. Methods of Representation — Pageant — Procession — Italian,
French, and Spanish Peculiarities—The Guilds—Cost of the Show—
Concourse of People—Stage Effects and Properties.—VII. Relation
of the Miracle to Medieval Art—Materialistic Realism—Place in the
Cathedral—Effect upon the Audience.—VIII. Dramatic Elements
in the Miracles—Tragedy—Pathos—Melodrama—Herod and the
Devil.—IX. Realistic Comedy—Joseph—Noah's Wife—The Nativity
—Pastoral Interludes.—X. Transcripts from Common Life—Satire
—The Woman taken in Adultery—Mixture of the Sacred and the
Grotesque.—XI. The Art of the Miracles and the Art of Italian
Sacri Monti.

N.B.—The text of the Widkirk or Towneley Miracles will be found
in the Surtees Society's Publications, 1836. That of the Coventry and
Chester Plays in the Old Shakespeare Society's Publications, 1841, 1843.

I

THE gradual emergence of our national Drama from the
Miracle, the Morality, and the Interlude has been clearly
defined and often described. I do not now propose to attempt
a learned discussion of this process. That has been ably done
already by Markland, Sharp, Wright, Collier, and others,
whose labours have been briefly condensed by Ward in his
History. But, as a preface to any criticism on the English

Drama, some notice must be taken of those medieval forms of
art which are no less important in their bearings upon the
accomplished work of Shakspere's age than are the
Romanesque mosaics or the sculpture of the Pisan school
upon the mature products of the Italian Renaissance. Art,
like Nature, takes no sudden leaps, *nihil agit per saltum*;
and the connection between the Miracles and Shakspere's
Drama is unbroken, though the æsthetic interval between
them seems almost infinite.

A drama on Christ's Passion, called the Χριστὸς πάσχων,
ascribed to Gregory of Nazianzus in the fourth century, is still
extant. This play, as its name denotes, conformed to the
spirit of Greek tragedy, and professed to exhibit the sufferings
of Christ upon the cross, as those of Prometheus upon Caucasus
had been displayed before an Attic audience. But it was
impossible in the decadence of Greek literature, in the age
which witnessed the fierce strife of Arians and Athanasians,
and the Pagan revival attempted by Julian, to treat that
central fact of Christian history with literary freedom.
Gregory's Passion-play is a series of monologues rather than
a drama, a lucubration of the study rather than a piece
adapted to the stage. Its scholastic origin is betrayed by the
author's ingenuity in using passages and lines extracted from
Athenian tragedies; and his work at the present day owes its
value chiefly to the centos from Euripides which it contains.
Moreover, at this epoch the theatre was becoming an
abomination to the Church. The bloody shows of Rome, the
shameless profligacy of Byzantium, justified ecclesiastics in
denouncing both amphitheatre and circus as places given over
to the devil. From the point of view of art, again, the true
spirit of dramatic poetry had expired in those orgies of lust
and cruelty.

With the decline of classic culture and the triumph of
dogmatic Christianity, the Drama, which had long ceased to
be a fine art, fell into the hands of an obscure and despised
class. It is impossible to believe that the race of players
expired in Europe. Indeed, we have sufficient evidence that
during the earlier Middle Ages such folk kept alive in the

people a kind of natural paganism, against which the Church waged ineffectual war. The stigma attaching to the playwright's and the actor's professions even in the golden age of the Renaissance may be ascribed to monastic and ecclesiastical denunciations, fulminated against strolling mimes and dancers, buffoons and posture-makers, ' thymelici, scurræ, et mimi,' in successive councils and by several bishops. Undoubtedly, these social pariahs, the degenerate continuators of a noble craft, by the very fact that they were excommunicated and tabooed, denied the Sacraments and grudgingly consigned at death to holy ground, lapsed more and more into profanity, indecency, and ribaldry. While excluded from an honoured status in the commonwealth, they yet were welcomed at seasons of debauch and jollity. The position which they held was prominent if not respectable, as the purveyors of amusement, instruments of pleasure, and creatures of fashionable caprice. Among the Northern races circumstances favoured the amelioration of their lot. The bard and the skald held high rank in Teutonic society ; and it was natural that a portion of this credit should fall upon the player and buffoon. With the advance of time, we find several species of their craft established as indispensable members of medieval society. It must, moreover, be remembered that all through the Middle Ages, in spite of prevalent orthodoxy and the commanding power of the Church, a spirit survived from the old heathen past, antagonistic to the principles of Christian morality, which we may describe as naturalism or as paganism according to our liking. This spirit was at home in the castles of the nobles and in the companies of wandering students. It invaded the monasteries, and, in the person of Golias, took up its place beside the Abbot's chair. The ' Carmina Vagorum ' and some of the satires ascribed to Walter Mapes sufficiently illustrate the genius of these pagans in the Middle Ages. The *joculatores*, whom the Church had banned, became in course of time *jongleurs* and jugglers. To them we owe the *fabliaux*. Meanwhile the *ministeriales*, or house-servants of the aristocracy, took the fairer name of minstrels. Lyric poetry

rose, in the new dialects of the Romance nations, to a place
of honour through the genius of troubadours and *trouvères*,
who were recognised as lineal descendants from *mimi* and
histriones. Taillefer himself, who led the van on Senlac
field, tossing his sword into the air and singing Roland, is
thus described by Guy of Amiens in verses which retain the
old prejudice against the class of players:

> Histrio, cor audax nimium quem nobilitabat . . .
> Incisor-ferri mimus cognomine dictus.

Rhapsodes, again, who recited the *Chansons de Geste*, so
popular among the Franks and Normans, laid the foundations
of imaginative literature in their Songs of Roland and
Charlemagne. Descendants from the *citharistæ* of base
Latin, these left the name of jester in our English speech.
Thus it is hardly too much to say that the despised race of
players in the Middle Ages helped to sow the seeds of modern
lyrical and epical poetry, of social and political satire, of novel
and romance. They contributed little, in the earlier age at
least, to the development of the Drama. The part they
played in this creation at a later period was, however, of considerable moment. This will be manifest when we come to
the point at which the clergy began to lose their hold upon
the presentation of Mysteries and Miracles.

II

Meanwhile another species of dramatic art had been
attempted in the cloister during the tenth century. Hroswitha,
a Benedictine nun of Gandersheim, wrote six comedies in
Latin for the entertainment of her sisterhood. Inspired with
the excellent notion of not letting the devil keep the good
tunes to himself, she took Terence for her model, and
dramatised the legendary history of Christian Saints and
Confessors. It is needful to pay this passing tribute to
Hroswitha, if only for the singularity of her endeavour. But
it would be uncritical in the highest sense of the word to

regard her, any more than the Greek author of the Χριστὸς
πάσχων, as a founder or precursor of the modern stage.
The real origins of our drama have to be sought elsewhere.

Recent investigations have thrown a flood of new light on
what is known as the Liturgical Drama. It has been pointed
out that the Office of the Mass is itself essentially dramatic,
and that from very early times it became a custom to supplement the liturgy with scenic representations. The descent of
the angel Gabriel at the Feast of the Annunciation, the procession of the Magi at Epiphany, the birth of Christ at Christmas,
the Resurrection from the tomb at Eastertide, may be mentioned among the more obvious and common of these
shows invented by the clergy to illustrate the chief events of
Christian history, and to enforce the principal dogmas of the
faith upon an unlettered laity by means of acting. The
parish priest, aided by the good folk of the village, managed
these theatrical displays, of which the scene was usually the
church, and the occasion service time on festivals. This
appears from a somewhat ribald episode in the old novel of
'Howleglas,' which narrates the pranks played by the rogue
upon the priest, his master for the time. 'In the mean
season, while Howleglas was parish clerk, at Easter they
should play the Resurrection of our Lord : and for because
the men were not learned and could not read, the priest took
his leman, and put her in the grave for an Angel : and this
seeing, Howleglas took to him three of the simplest persons
that were in the town, that played the three Maries ; and the
parson played Christ, with a banner in his hand.' The lives
of the Saints were treated after the same fashion ; and since
it was needful to instruct the people through their senses,
dramatic shows on all the more important feast days formed
a regular part of the Divine service. From the Church this
custom spread by a natural transition to the chapels of religious confraternities and the trade-halls of the guilds, who
celebrated their patron saints with scenic shows and pageants.
To what extent words were used on these occasions, and at
what date dialogue was introduced, is doubtful. Yet this is a
matter of purely antiquarian interest. The passage from

dumb show, through simple recitation of such phrases as the
Angel's ' Ave Maria gratia plena,' to a more dramatic form of
representation, was inevitable ; while our copious collections
of Latin hymns, lauds, litanies, and Passion monologues
prove that appropriate choral accompaniments were never
wanting. The chief point to be borne in mind is that from
an early period of the Middle Ages the Church accustomed
men to acting in connection with her services ; and that,
while the clergy took care to keep this adjunct to the liturgy
in their control, the people participated, and thus became
familiarised with drama as a form of art. When we reflect
that the Scripture and the legends of the Saints formed
almost the whole intellectual treasure of the laity, we shall
better understand the importance of the religious Drama
which thus came into existence. It was not, as it now might
be, a thing apart from life, reserved for pious contemplation.
It gave artistic shape to all reflections upon life ; presented
human destinies in their widest scope and their most striking
details; incorporated medieval science, ethics, history, cosmography, and politics; bringing abstractions vividly before the
eyes and ears of folk who could not read.

III

The transition from the liturgical drama and the ecclesi-
tical pageant to the Miracle or Mystery was simple. Exactly
at what date plays setting forth the Scripture history and
legends of the Saints in words intended to be spoken were
first composed, we do not know. But from the extant specimens of such plays in the chief languages of Europe, it seems
clear that they were already widely diffused before the middle
of the thirteenth century ; and it is probable that the festival
of Corpus Christi, instituted in 1264 by Urban IV., gave an
impulse to their performance. The text was written by
monks, and in the first instance almost certainly in Latin.
The common name for them was *Ludus*. Thus we read in
the Friulian Chronicles that a *Ludus Christi*, embracing the
principal events from the Passion to the Second Advent, was

acted at Cividale in the Marches of Treviso in 1298. Our
Coventry Miracles are called *Ludus Coventriæ*. As early as
1110 a ' Ludus de S. Katharina ' was represented at Dunstaple
by Geoffrey, Abbot of S. Albans.

As these sacred dramas became more popular, the vernacular was substituted for Latin in their composition, their
scope was enlarged until it embraced the whole of Christian
history, and the artistic form assumed a different shape and
name in different countries. In France a distinction was
drawn between the *Mystère* and the *Miracle* ; the former
being adapted from Scripture, the latter from the legend of a
saint. One of the very earliest religious dramas in a modern
language is the *Mystère de la Résurrection*, ascribed to the
twelfth century. In Italy the generic name for such plays in
the vulgar tongue was *Sacra Rappresentazione* ; while subordinate titles like *Divozione, Misterio, Miracolo, Figura,
Passione, Festa,* and so forth, indicated the specific nature of
the subject in each particular case. Italy, it may be said in
passing, developed the religious drama on a somewhat different
method from the rest of Europe. The part played in its
creation by private confraternities was more important than
that of the Church, and, with the exception of the Friulian
Ludus already mentioned, we are not aware of any very early
plays in Italy exactly corresponding to those of the North.
In Spain the name of *Auto* became consecrated to the sacred
Drama. In England, after the use of *Ludus* had gone out of
fashion, that of *Miracle* obtained. William Fitz-Stephen,
writing about the end of the twelfth century, describes the
plays of London as ' repræsentationes miraculorum quæ sancti
confessores operati sunt, seu repræsentationes passionum
quibus claruit constantia martyrum.' Matthew Paris, half a
century later, says that Geoffrey's 'Ludus de S. Katharina '
was of the sort which ' miracula vulgariter appellamus.'
Wright, in his edition of the Chester Plays, quotes from a
medieval Latin tale a similar phrase, 'spectacula quæ miracula
appellare consuevimus.' This name of Miracle was never lost
in England. Langland in ' Piers Ploughman ' speaks of
Miracles, and Chaucer of Plays of Miracles.

Not only did the name thus vary, while the substance of
the thing was much the same throughout Europe, but the
mode of treatment differed considerably. In France, although
both Mysteries and Miracles ran to an inordinate length,
counting many thousands of lines, and requiring more than
one day for their presentation, they were confined to certain
episodes and portions of the Sacred History. In Italy this
limitation of the subject was even more marked ; while none
of the *Sacre Rappresentazioni* exceed the proportions of a
moderate modern play. The distinctive point about the
English Miracle, as we possess it, is that it incorporated into
one cycle of plays the whole history of the world from the
Creation to the Last Judgment ; successive episodes being
selected to illustrate God's dealings with the human race in
the Fall, the Deluge, the Antitypes of Christ, our Lord's
birth, life, and death, His Resurrection, Ascension, and Second
Advent. This needs to be specially noted ; for it is a characteristic of the Sacred Drama in our island.

IV

The Miracles and Mysteries remained for a long while in
the hands of the clergy. They were composed by monks,
and acted in churches, monasteries, or on meadows con-
veniently situated near religious houses. Yet we have seen
already that, side by side with these ecclesiastical players,
there existed a class of popular and profane actors ; and also
that the laity were pressed into the service of the Liturgical
Drama. It was therefore natural that in course of time
laymen should encroach upon this function of the clergy.
According to an uncertain tradition, it was as early as 1268
that the trading companies began to play in England ; and
we know that in 1258 the performances of strolling actors
had been prohibited in monasteries. We may also assume
that about this date English was beginning to supplant Latin
and Norman French in the Miracles. By the year 1398,
when the Brothers of the Passion founded a sort of permanent
theatre in Paris for the representation of their Mysteries, it

is clear that the religious drama had already for a long space of time passed out of the hands of the clergy in France. In England at the same date a similar change had certainly taken place. The Guilds in the great towns were now performing Cyclical Miracles upon their own account, employing the craftsmen of their several trades, or else engaging the services of professionals, called 'players of price.' [1] So much matter of a comic and satirical nature, alien to the original purpose of edification, had been mixed up with the performance, that the Church at this epoch was rather anxious to restrain than to encourage the participation of the clergy. Chaucer's portrait of the Jolly Absolon—

> Sometime to show his lightnesse and maistrie
> He plaieth Herode on a skaffold hie—

gives a hint of abuses to which the ancient custom had become liable. After much moralising and preaching against the practice, it was finally forbidden to the clergy in the first half of the sixteenth century by Wolsey and Bonner.

After this fashion, the English Miracle sprang from the Liturgical Drama, substituted Norman French for Latin, and English for Norman French, outgrew ecclesiastical control, and engrafted on its solemn art the feats of skill and humours of the strolling players. Originally instituted as a means of education by the clergy, it preserved the religious character impressed upon it to the last ; but in its passage from the cloister to the market-place, and by its substitution of the mother tongue for a learned language, it became emphatically popular and national. The elements of independent comedy and pathos, of satire and of allegory, the free artistic handling of historic characters, the customs of the stage, and the spectacular contrivances, with which it familiarised the nation, contained the germ of what was afterwards our drama. When the Middle Ages melted into the Renaissance, the substantial fabric of the Christian Miracle fell to pieces;

---

[1] The speech of the *Tertius Vexillator*, which closes the Prologue of the Coventry Play, seems to point to a performance by strolling players, as the insertion of *N* in lieu of the place where the Miracle was to be shown indicates that it was not performed at Coventry alone.

but those portions of the structure which had previously been
held for accidents and excrescences were then found adequate
to the creation of a new and self-sufficing art. Dogma disappeared. The mythology and history of Christian faith
retreated once more to the church, the pulpit, and the study.
Humanity was liberated ; and our playwrights dealt with
man as the material of their emancipated art. This evolution
corresponds exactly to the passage which society effected from
the vast and comprehensive systems of medieval feudalism
into the minor but more highly organised, more structurally
complicated, modern States.

V

The three Cycles of ' Miracles ' which have come down to
us are known severally as those of Widkirk, Chester, and
Coventry, from the places where they were performed.   They
are composed in English, with embedded fragments of Latin
and of French, betraying their descent from older originals
written in those languages.   We must in truth regard these
vast collections as the accretions of many previous essays in
religious drama, the mature form assumed by a long series of
literary experiments.   In spite of their colossal rudeness, they
are clearly no primitive works of art, but the final outcome
of a slowly developed evolution.   Like the architectural
monuments of the Middle Ages, no single author claims them
for his own.   They are the work of numberless unknown
collaborators contributing to one harmonious whole.   In
point of style and diction, the Widkirk plays bear traces of
the oldest origin, and are ascribed by scholars to the reign of
Henry VI.   Those of Chester, in their present form, are
certainly more recent.   We learn from the Banes, or proclamation which introduced them to the public, that they
were first exhibited during the mayoralty of Sir John Arnway
in 1268.   Another proclamation, dated 24 Henry VIII.,
ascribes their composition to Sir Henry Frances, a monk of
Chester, who obtained from Pope Clement (Clement V., 1305–
1314 ?) one thousand days of pardon for ' every person

resorting in peaceable manner with good devotion to hear and see the said plays from time to time.' A note to one of our MSS. of the Chester Miracles further informs us that Ralph Higden, compiler of the 'Polycronicon,' 'was thrice at Rome before he could obtain leave of the Pope to have them in the English tongue.' Since Higden died in 1363 or 1373, we are left to suppose that for nearly a century after their first production they continued to be acted in Latin, or perhaps more probably in French. There were many reasons why the Papal Curia should regard the use of English in these popular performances with jealousy. Langland, Wickliff, and the Lollards, satirists of manners, poets eager for ecclesiastical reforms, bold democratic sectaries, were proving in the fourteenth century that England was no passive handmaid of the Church of Rome. But Higden won his point, if we may trust this tradition; and the English redaction of the Miracles, upon this supposition, can be referred to some time near the middle of the fourteenth century. It should, however, be observed that the whole of this constructive criticism rests upon the very frailest basis. The Banes, published in 1600, ascribes the authorship to 'one Don Rendall, monk of Chester Abbey;' and a note appended to the proclamation of 1515 gives it to 'Randall Higgenett, a monk of Chester Abbey,' naming 1327 as the date of the first version. This confusion of Higden and Higgenett, Ralph and Randal, excites suspicion; and all that remains tolerably certain is that the plays were instituted at the end of the thirteenth, and produced in English some time in the fourteenth century. They continued to be regularly acted at Whitsuntide until 1577, and were revived in 1600, which is the date of our extant version.

The Coventry Miracles have descended to us in a MS. of 1468, entitled 'Ludus Coventriæ, sive Ludus Corporis Christi.' In form and style they are less archaic than those of Widkirk and even of Chester, while certain passages in the plays themselves enable us to assign their composition, in part at all events, to the reign of Henry VII. They were played at the festival of Corpus Christi by the Grey Friars of Coventry.

The Widkirk plays consist of thirty pieces, the Chester of twenty-four, the Coventry of forty-two. All of them embrace the history of man's creation, fall, and redemption, stories from the Old Testament, the life of Christ, the Harrowing of Hell, and the Judgment of the world. The Apocryphal Gospels as well as the New Testament are largely drawn upon. They dispose of the same matter in different ways, use different metrical structures, and exhibit many other points of divergence. For example, the Coventry Miracles contain an Assumption of the Virgin, and the Chester a Coming of Antichrist, which are not to be found in either of the corresponding cycles. Alliterative verse is used in combination with short rhyming lines, modelled upon French originals. A form of stanza, imitated from Latin hymnology, gives singular richness by its thrice-repeated rhymes to many scenes in the Chester plays. Of this structure I will here extract a specimen from the speech of Regina Damnata in the Chester Doomsday :

> Alas! alas! now am I lorn!
> Alas! with teen now am I torn!
> Alas! that I was woman born,
>   This bitter bale to abide!
> I made my moan even and morn,
> For fear to come Jesu beforn,
> That crowned for me was with thorn,
>   And thrust into the side.
> Alas! that I was woman wrought!
> Alas! why God made me of naught,
> And with His precious blood me bought,
>   To work against His will?
> Of lechery I never wrought,
> But ever to that sin I sought,
> That of that sin in deed and thought
>   Yet had I never my fill.
> Fie on pearls! fie on pride!
> Fie on gown! fie on guyde! [1]
> Fie on hue! fie on hide! [2]
>   These harrow me to hell.

---

[1] *Guyde -?*   [2] *Hide—skin.*

Against this chance I may not chide,
This bitter bale I must abide,
With wo and teen I suffer this tide,
   No living tongue may tell.
I that so seemly was in sight,
Where is my bleye [1] that was so bright?
Where is the baron, where is the knight,
   For me to leadge [2] the law?
Where in the world is any wight,
That for my fairness now will fight,
Or from this death I am to dight [3]
   That dare me hence to draw?

The Coventry Plays make use of this same stanza, but are more partial to quatrains of alternating rhymes in verses of different lengths and measures. Speaking broadly, the construction of both Cycles shows a highly developed prosody, a familiarity with complicated metrical resources on the part of their compilers. The Widkirk, Chester, and Coventry plays abound in local references, and illustrate the dialects of their several districts.

Besides these three places, we know for certain that Miracles were commonly performed at Wymondham, York, Newcastle, Manningtree, and Tewkesbury. One William Melton of York in 1426 was termed 'a professor of holy pageantry,' which seems to prove that the actors in these dramas, and probably the monkish scribes who wrote them, formed a recognised class of artists. The city of Bristol exhibited a ' Shipwrights' Play,' most likely in dumb show, upon the Ark of Noah, before Henry VII. Cornwall had its so-called Guary Miracles, which were religious spectacles of a like nature. There is no reason to suppose that any district of England was unprovided with the means of producing them, though some towns, like Coventry and Chester, took a special pride in presenting them with more than common splendour.

[1] *Bleye*—complexion.   [2] *Leadge*—wrest.
[3] *Dight*—assume.

VI

The Miracles were exhibited on wooden scaffolds, either stationary in churches or moved about the streets on wheels. The Latin name for these erections was *pagina*, which has been correctly derived from the same root as *pegma*, and which merged into the English *pageant*. From the stage directions to the plays it appears that in some cases the scaffold contained several rooms or stories, and this was no doubt usual when the structure was set up in a church or on a meadow. The movable carts on which the players performed in towns like Chester consisted of two rooms, a lower, in which they dressed, and an upper, open to the air, in which they acted. These carts were drawn in order round the town, stopping at fixed points for recitation, so that when one pageant was finished, another arrived to continue the show before the same group of spectators. From the processional character communicated in this way to the Miracle, the name *processus* as well as *pagina* was sometimes given to each act in the Drama. For scenes involving movement, actors in the streets were associated with the actors on the stage. Messengers rode up on horseback, and Herod or the Devil leapt from the cart to rage about among the people.

It is interesting to compare these English customs of the religious Drama with those of other countries. In Italy we know that the *Divozioni*, when shown in church, were performed upon a wooden scaffold raised across the nave and divided into several departments, with a central space for the chief action, smaller side-rooms for subordinate scenes, a gallery for the celestial personages, and a sunken pit for Satan and his crew. The *Edifizi*, or movable towers, exhibited by the chief guilds of Florence on S. John's Day, corresponded in all essential respects to the pageants of Chester, except that they were undoubtedly adorned with greater richness of artistic details. This Florentine procession set forth the whole of Christian history from the Fall of

Lucifer to the Last Judgment; but the show was strictly pantomimic, being presented in tableaux without speech. In France, before the establishment of a regular religious theatre in 1402, Mysteries were performed, after a like fashion, either processionally in the streets or on temporary scaffolds erected for the purpose in a consecrated building. In Spain the exhibition of the *Autos* took place in churches, until this practice was forbidden in 1565. Yet the highly elaborated form of art developed from them with such magnificence by Calderon retained the nature of a sacred show. Late on into the seventeenth century the *Auto* was presented on an open square in daylight, with accompaniment of flambeaux and candles. It must have been a spectacle of singular and curious magnificence : the wide piazza in the white glare of a Southern noontide, crowded with Court, clergy, and people ; the sumptuous scene of Calderon displayed; God, saints and angels, heathen deities and metaphysical abstractions, elements of nature and deadly sins, brought into harmony and moulded to one type of art by the artist's plastic touch. Altar candles flared and guttered round the stage in the fierce heat of the meridian sun, symbolising, as it were, the blending of diverse lights, the open life of man on earth, and the dim religious mysteries of the sanctuary, the night of pagan myths and the noon of Christian faith, which genius had assembled and combined upon that hieroglyphic of the world, the theatre.

As in Florence, so in Chester, special portions of the sacred spectacle were consigned by old tradition to each guild. Thus ' the good simple water-leaders and drawers of Dee ' had the superintendence of the Deluge and the Ark appropriately left to them. The tanners, not perhaps without ironical reference to their trade, exhibited the Fall of Lucifer ; and the cooks set forth the Harrowing of Hell. When the time drew near, proclamation in the town was made, warning the several companies to be ready with their pageants. At Coventry this proclamation was spoken by three Vexillatores or banner-bearers in speeches which described the argument of each pageant. At Chester it was termed the Banes or

Banns. Our copy of these Banes, dated in 1600, is interesting for the apologetic tone in which it comments on the Miracles to be exhibited. After mentioning that they were written by one Don Rendall, the prologue proceeds :

> This monk, monk-like, in Scriptures well seen,
> In stories travailed with the best sort,
> In pageants set forth apparently to all een
> The Old and New Testament with lively comfort,
> Intermingling therewith, only to make sport,
> Some things not warranted by any writ,
> Which to glad the hearers he would men to take it.

It then compliments the monkish author on his good digestion of the matter into twenty-four plays, and on his boldness in bringing the sacred lore forth ' in a common English tongue,' and finally begs the audience not to judge the antique style of the performance too harshly :

> As all that shall see them shall most welcome be,
> So all that hear them we most humbly pray
> Not to compare this matter or story
> With the age or time wherein we presently stay,
> But in the time of ignorance wherein we did stray.

And again :

> Go back, I say, to the first time again;
> Then shall you find the fine wit at this day abounding,
> At that day and age had very small being.

Considering that Shakspere's plays were being brought upon the London stage in 1600, this recommendation to the audience was hardly superfluous.

The expenses incurred by the city at these times of festivity were doubtless considerable. Guild vied with guild in bringing pageants forth with proper magnificence. It has been estimated that each show cost at least 15*l.* In addition to the payment of the players, there were various disbursements for apparel and stage properties, carpentry, gilding, upholstery, and painting. We read of such items as the following :

Paid to the players for rehearsal—Imprimis to God, ii*s.* viii*d.*
Item to Pilate his wife, ii*s.*
Paid to Fauston for cock-crowing, iii*d.*
Paid for mending Hell, ii*d.*
Item for painting of Hell-mouth, iii*d.*
Item for setting World on fire, v*d.*

Yet town and trades were amply repaid by the concourse
which the plays drew. Lasting several days and filling the
hostelries with guests from all the country side, each celebration served the purpose of a fair. Dugdale, the antiquary,
in his notice of the Coventry Miracles, writes as follows : ' I
have been told by some old people, who in their younger days
were eye-witnesses of these pageants so acted, that the yearly
confluence of people to see that show was extraordinary great,
and yielded no small advantage to this city.' Gentles and
yeomanry filled the neighbouring country houses and farm-
steads with friends for the occasion. Thousands of people ;
the motley crowd of medieval days ; monks, palmers, merchants in their various costumes, servants of noble families
with badges on their shoulders, hawkers of pardons and relics,
pedlars, artificers, grooms, foresters, hinds from the farm and
shepherds from the fells ; all known by special qualities of
dress and bearing ; crowded the streets and thronged the
taverns. Comely women, like Chaucer's Wife of Bath, made
it their business to be present at some favourable point of
view. The windows and the wooden galleries were hung
with carpets. Girls leaned from latticed casements, and old
men bent upon their crutches in the doorways. In these circumstances, it is not to be wondered at that Whitsuntide or
Easter, when the Miracles were played, became a season of
debauch and merry-making. A preacher of the fourteenth
century inveighs against them in no measured words on this
account. ' To gather men together to buy their victuals the
dearer, and to stir men to gluttony and to pride and boast,
they play these Miracles, and to hold fellowship of gluttony
and lechery in such days of Miracles playing, they beseen
them before to more greedily beguiling of their neighbours,
in buying and in selling ; and so this playing of Miracles

nowadays is very witness of hideous covetousness, that is
maumetry.'[1]   Similar complaints were made against the
Brethren of the Passion in Paris. The Hotel of Burgundy,
where they performed, was called 'that sewer and house of
Satan, whose actors, with shocking abuse, term themselves
the Brothers of the Passion of Jesus Christ. That place is
the scene of a thousand scandalous assignations. It is the
bane of virtue, the destroyer of modesty, the ruin of poor
families. Long before the play begins, it is thronged with
workmen, who pass their time in uncouth jests, with cards
and dice, gormandising and drinking, from the which spring
many quarrels and assaults.'

I do not seek to describe with any minuteness the stage
properties and dresses used in Miracles; yet a few details
may be given, fit to place the reader at the proper point of
view for thinking of them. The man who played God, wore
a wig with gilded hair and had his face gilt. Special apology
is made at Chester for the non-appearance of this personage
on one occasion; and the reason assigned is, that this gilding
'disfigured the man.' How well founded the excuse was,
can be gathered from a contemporary account of shows at
Florence, where it is briefly said that the boy who played the
Genius of the Golden Age, with body gilded for the purpose,
died after the performance. Christ wore a long sheepskin,
such as early frescoes and mosaics assign to the Good
Shepherd. The Devil appeared in orthodox costume of
horns and tail, with a fiery red beard to signify the place of
flames in which he dwelt. Judas Iscariot had also a wig of
this colour; and it was common among German painters—
witness the 'Last Supper' by Holbein at Basel—to give this
colour, eminently disagreeable in a Jew, to the arch-traitor.
How Paradise was represented, we may perhaps imagine to
ourselves from the elaborate accounts furnished by Vasari of
the *Nuvole* at Florence. These were frames of wood and iron
wires, shaped like aureoles and covered with white wool, with
sconces at their sides for candles. The celestial personages
sat enshrined within these structures. Hell-mouth was a

[1] *Reliquiæ Antiquæ*, ii. 54, modernised.

vast pair of gaping jaws, armed with fangs, like a shark's open swallow. Such representations of the place of torment may be seen in the ' Biblia Pauperum ' and ' Speculum Humanæ Salvationis' and other books illustrated with early woodcuts, all of which throw light upon the disposition of these medieval scenes. Dragons, with eyes of polished steel ; scaly whales ; asses that spoke ; a serpent to tempt Eve, with female face and swingeing tail ; added bizarre variety to the mere commonplace crowd of kings in gorgeous raiment, flaming Herods, mailed soldiers, and hideous uncouth ministers of torture. In the Coventry Miracles, Death once appeared upon the stage in all the horror of worm-eaten flesh and snake-enwrithed ribs, as is manifest from the speech upon his exit. Adam and Eve before the Fall, it may be said in passing, were naked ; and we have the right to assume that in the Doomsday some at any rate of the dead rose naked from their graves.

VII

Reading the Miracle Plays of Widkirk, Chester, and Coventry, is not much better than trying to derive some notion of a great master's etchings from a volume of illustrative letter-press without the plates. The Miracles were shows, pageants, spectacles presented to the eye ; the words written to explain their tableaux and give motion to their figures, were in some sense the least part of them. Modern students should take this fact into account. Even the dramas of the greatest poets, Sophocles or Shakspere, suffer when we read them in the lifeless silence of our chamber. If this be so, how little can we really judge the artistic effect of a Miracle from the libretto which was merely meant to illustrate a grand spectacular effect ! After making due allowance for this inevitable drawback, after taking the rudeness of the times into account, the undeveloped state of language and the playwright's simple craft, we shall be rather impressed with the colossal majesty and massive strength of structure in these antique plays, than with their uncouth

details. Each Miracle, viewed in its entirety, displays the
vigour and the large proportions of a Gothic church. It is
with the master builder's skill that we must compare the
writer's talent. Judging by standards of accomplished beauty,
we feel that workmen and not artists in the highest sense of
the word carved the statues on the front of Wells Cathedral
and penned the dialogues of Chester. Art, except in architecture, hardly existed among the nations who produced the
Mysteries and at the epoch of their composition. The
æsthetic creations of medieval ingenuity, traceries in stone
and beaten metal, illuminated windows, wrought wood-work
upon canopy and stall, must always be regarded as subordinate to the Cathedral, not as having any independent end as
works of art. The same is true of those vast compositions
which presented sacred history in shows beneath Cathedral
arches to the Christian laity. Poetry is here the handmaid
of religious teaching, the submissive drudge of dogma. Language in the Miracles barely clothes the ideas which were meant
to be conveyed by figured forms; meagrely supplies the motives
necessary for the proper presentation of an action. Clumsy
phrases, quaint literalism, tedious homilies clog the dramatic
evolution. As in the case of medieval sculpture, so here the
most spontaneous and natural effects are grotesque. In the
treatment of sublime and solemn themes we may also trace a
certain ponderous force, a dignity analogous to that of fresco
and mosaic. Subjects which in themselves are vast, imaginative, and capable of only a suggestive handling, such as the
Parliaments of Heaven and Hell, Creation, Judgment, and
the Resurrection from the dead, when conceived with positive
belief and represented with the crudest realism, acquire a
simple grandeur. Remote from the conditions of our daily
life, these mysteries express themselves in fittest form by
bare uncompromising symbols. For this reason, there are
not a few among contemporary artists who will prefer a
colossal Christ in mosaic on the tribune of a Romanesque
basilica to a Christ by Raphael in transfigured ecstasy, a Last
Judgment sculptured by an unnamed artist on some Gothic
portal to the fleshly luxuriance of Rubens' or the poised

symmetry of Cornelius' design. It is rare indeed to find instances of emancipated art so satisfactory in such high themes as the ' Creation of Adam ' by Michelangelo, or the ' Christ before Pilate ' of Tintoretto.

The literal translation of spiritual truths into corporeal equivalents, which distinguished the medieval religious sense —that positive and materialising habit of mind which developed the belief in wonder-working relics, the Corpus Christi miracle, the sensuous God of the Host—lent a certain quaint sublimity to the dramatic presentment of mysteries beyond the scope of plastic art. But the same qualities degenerated into unconditioned grossness, when the playwright had to touch such topics as the Immaculate Conception of our Lord. It is with a sense of wonder bordering upon disgust that we read the parts assigned to the Holy Ghost and to Joseph in this episode. The same material coarseness of imagination mars the æsthetical effect of many passages, which might, according to our present canons of taste, have been more profitably left to such pantomimic presentation as a purely figurative art affords. But this was not the instinct of those times. The sacredness of the subject-matter banished all thought of profanity. The end of edification justified the plainest realism of presentment. What was believed to have actually taken place in the scheme of man's redemption, that could lawfully and with all reverence, however comically and grotesquely, be exhibited.

Scenery and action rendered the bare poetry of the Miracle-play imposing ; and we have every reason to believe that both were adequate to their purpose. For we must remember that the people who performed these plays were the same folk who filled the casements of our churches with stained glass, hung the chapel walls with tapestries, carved the statues, and gilt the shrines. They knew what was needed to bring their pageants into harmony with edifices, not then as now vacant and whitewashed, swept by depredators of the Reformation period, garnished by churchwardens of the eighteenth century, scrubbed and scraped and desolated by self-styled restorers ; but glowing with deep and solemn hues cast

from clerestory windows, enriched with frescoes, furnished with
the multitudinous embellishments of art expended on each
detail of the structure by the loving prodigality of pious
hands. Little indeed is left to us in England of that earlier
architectural magnificence, when the Cathedral or the
Abbey Church was a poem without speech, perfected in
every part with beauty, a piece of stationary music sounding
from symphonious instruments, a storied illustration of the
spiritual life of Christendom, conveying through the medium
of forms and colours what the mind had not yet learned to
frame in rhythmic words. When a Miracle was shown in
such a building, it completed and enlivened the whole scene.
The religion which appealed from every portion of the edifice
to the intellect through the senses now found ultimate expression in dramatic action. The wooden scaffold, richly
gilt and painted, curtained with embroidered arras, and
occupied by actors in their parti-coloured raiment, shone like
a jewelled casket in the midst of altar-shrines and tabernacles,
statues and fretted arches, mellow with subtly tinted ara-
besques. The character of the spectacle was determined,
not by the poetic genius of the monk who wrote the words of
the play, but by the unison of forms and colours which prevailed throughout the edifice. What the whole building
strove to express in stationary and substantial art, started for
some hours into life upon the stage.

The Passion Plays of Ammergau enable us at the present
time to understand the effect produced by Miracles upon a
medieval audience. Multitudes of men and women derived
their liveliest conceptions of sacred history from those
pageants. In countless breasts those scenes excited profound emotions of awe, terror, sympathy, and admiration.
Nor was this influence, so powerful in stimulating religious
sentiment, without its direct bearing on the arts. Painters
of church walls, stainers of choir windows, craftsmen in metal,
stone, and wood, received impressions which they afterwards
translated into form upon the Chapter House of Salisbury,
the front of Lincoln, over the west porch of Reims, in the
choir stalls and the panels of a hundred churches. The

origins of art in medieval Europe reveal a common impulse
and a common method, which the study of subsequent
divergences renders doubly interesting and suggestive.
Between the bas-reliefs of the Pisani at Orvieto, from which
Michelangelo's frescoes of the Creation descend in a direct
line, and the rude work of those English stone-cutters, before
whom a female Eve and a male Adam in the Miracles stood
naked and were not ashamed, we may trace a close resemblance, proving how the same ideas took similar form in divers
nations. Plastic art and the religious drama acted and
reacted, each upon the other, through the period of medieval
incubation. Thus it is not too much to affirm that the
Mysteries contributed in an essential degree to the development of figurative art in Europe. How and in what specific
details Miracles aided the evolution of the modern theatre in
England, must now be briefly investigated.

VIII

The dramatic elements of the Miracles may sufficiently,
for present purposes, be classified under the following titles :
Tragic, Pathetic, Melodramatic, Idyllic, Comic, Realistic, and
Satiric. By reviewing these with due brevity we shall be able
to estimate on what foundations in this medieval work of art
the playwrights of the coming period built. But first it
should be plainly stated that the regular drama cannot be
regarded either as the exact successor in time, or as the immediate offspring of religious plays. Those plays continued
to be acted until quite late in the sixteenth century, at an
epoch when English tragedy and comedy were fully shaped ;
nor is it reasonable to suppose that the people would have
abandoned the custom of performing them except for changes
in religious feeling wrought by the Reformation, and for
changes in æsthetic taste effected by the Revival of Learning.
Contact with Italian culture, the study of classical literature,
and the larger instinct of humanity developed by the
Renaissance, determined both the form and spirit of our

drama. Still the medieval Miracle bequeathed to the Elizabethan playwright certain well-defined dramatic characters
and situations, a popular species of comedy, a plebeian type of
melodrama, and, what is far more important, a widely diffused
intelligence of dramatic customs and conventions in the
nation. The English people had been educated by their
medieval pageants for the modern stage. The Miracles
supplied those antecedent conditions which rendered a
national theatre possible, and saved it from becoming what it
mostly was in Italy, a plaything of the Court and study. The
vast dogmatic fabric of the Miracle was abandoned, like so
many Abbey Churches, to decay and ruin. The religious
spirit which had animated medieval art, was superseded by a
new enthusiasm for humanity and nature. But the comprehensive and colossal lines on which that elder ruder work of
art had been designed, were continued in the younger and
more artificial. The dramatic education of the people was
prolonged without intermission from the one period into the
other.

Of tragedy, in the highest and truest sense of the word, we
find but little in the Miracles. Many of the situations,
especially the Crucifixion and the Last Judgment, are indeed
eminently tragic. But the writer has been content to leave
them undeveloped, trusting to the effect of the bare motives
and their presentation through the pageant. Having to deal
with matter of such paramount importance to every Christian
soul, he could hardly have used a more consciously artistic
method. In the Chester plays, however, the tragic opportunities of Doomsday are seized upon with some skill. We
are introduced to pairs of representative personages standing
upon either side of Christ's throne and pleading at His
judgment bar. An emperor, a king, a queen, a pope, a judge,
and a merchant appear among the damned; a pope, a king,
an emperor, a queen, among the saved. Devils answer to
angels. And over all the voice of Christ is heard, arraigning
the wicked for their ill deeds done on earth, welcoming the
good into the bliss of His society in heaven. The playwright's
talent is chiefly exhibited in the elaborate but clear-cut

portraiture of the bad folk, each of whom is made too late
repentant, uttering his own accusation with groans and
unavailing tears. We have before us such a scene as the
painter of the Last Judgment represented on the Campo
Santo walls at Pisa.

Pathos emerges into more artistic clearness, chiefly, I
think, because the situations whence it sprang put less of strain
upon the writer's religious preconceptions. In the old Italian
Divozioni no pathetic motive was more tragically wrought
than Mary's lamentation at the foot of the Cross.[1] And this is
managed with considerable, though far inferior, effect by the
author of the Coventry Mysteries. As in the Italian ' Corrotto,'
Mary Magdalen brings the news :

Maria Magdalen

I would fain tell, Lady, an I might for weeping,
    For sooth, Lady, to the Jews He is sold ;
With cords they have Him bound and have Him in keeping,
    They Him beat spiteously, and have Him fast in hold.

Maria Virgo

Ah ! ah ! ah ! how mine heart is cold !
    Ah ! heart hard as stone, how mayst thou last ?
When these sorrowful tidings are thee told,
    So would to God, heart, that thou mightest brast.

Ah ! Jesu ! Jesu ! Jesu ! Jesu !
    Why should ye suffer this tribulation and adversity ?
How may they find in their hearts you to pursue,
    That never trespassed in no manner degree ?

For never thing but that was good thought ye.
    Wherefore then should ye suffer this great pain ?
I suppose verily it is for the trespass of me,
    And I wist that mine heart should cleave on twain.

The Magdalen herself is introduced, upon a previous
occasion, for the first time to the audience before the feet

---

[1] See my *Renaissance in Italy*, vol. iv. p. 293, and the translation
of Jacopone's *Corrotto* in the Appendix.

of Christ, uttering a prayer, which strikes me in its simplicity
as eminently pathetic :

> As a cursed creature closed all in care,
>   And as a wicked wretch all wrapped in woe,
> Of bliss was never no berde [1] so base,
>   As I myself that here now go.
> Alas! alas! I shall forfare,[2]
>   For the great sins that I have do ;
> Less that my Lord God some deal spare,
>   And His great mercy receive me to.
>   Mary Magdalen is my name,
>   Now will I go to Christ Jesu ;
>   For He is the Lord of all virtue ;
>   And for some grace I think to sue,
>   For of myself I have great shame.
>
> Ah! mercy! Lord! and salve my sin ;
>   Maidens flower, thou wash me free ;
> There was no woman of man his kin
>   So full of sin in no country.
> I have befouled be fryth [3] and fen,
>   And sought sin in many a city ;
> But Thou me borrow,[4] Lord, I shall brenne,[5]
>   With black fiends aye bowne [6] to be.
>   Wherefore, King of Grace,
>   With this ointment that is so soot,[7]
>   Let me anoint Thine holy foot,
>   And for my bales thus win some boot,
>   And mercy, Lord, for my trespass.

Later on in the same Miracle, a part of striking interest
is assigned to Magdalen, when she goes alone to the grave
of Christ, and relates her sorrows to the gardener, who turns
and looks upon her uttering the one word ' MARIA ! '

The scene in which pathos is most highly wrought with a
deliberate dramatic purpose, is the sacrifice of Isaac in the
Chester Plays :

[1] *Berde*—damsel.   [5] *Brenne*—burn.
[2] *Forfare*—perish.   [6] *Bowne*—ready.
[3] *Fryth*—wood.   [7] *Soot*—sweet.
[4] *Borrow* or *Borwe*—ransom.

Isaac

Father, tell me, or I go,
Whether I shall be harmed or no.

Abraham

Ah, dear God, that me is woe!
Thou breaks my heart in sunder.

Isaac

Father, tell me of this case,
Why you your sword drawn has,
And bears it naked in this place;
Thereof I have great wonder.

Abraham

Isaac, son, peace, I thee pray;
Thou breaks my heart in tway.

Isaac

I pray you, father, lean [1] nothing from me,
But tell me what you think.

Abraham

Ah, Isaac, Isaac! I must thee kill!

Isaac

Alas! father, is that your will,
Your own child for to spill
Upon this hill's brink?
If I have trespassed in any degree,
With a yard you may beat me;
Put up your sword, if your will be,
For I am but a child.

Abraham

O my dear son, I am sorry
To do to thee this great annoy.
God's commandment do must I;
His works are ever full mild.

---

[1] *Lean*—conceal.

Isaac

Would God my mother were here with me !
She would kneel down upon her knee,
Praying you, father, if it may be,
For to save my life.

Abraham

O comely creature, but I thee kill,
I grieve my God, and that full ill.

Abraham then explains how God has commanded him to
slay his son ; and Isaac, when he fully comprehends, is ready
for the sacrifice :

Isaac

But yet you must do God's bidding.
Father, tell my mother for nothing.

[*Here* ABRAHAM *wrings his hands, and saith :*]

Abraham

For sorrow I may my hands wring ;
Thy mother I cannot please.
Ho ! Isaac, Isaac, blessed must thou be !
Almost my wit I lose for thee ;
The blood of thy body so free
I am full loth to shed.

[*Here* ISAAC *asketh his father blessing on his knees, and saith :*]

Isaac

Father, seeing you must needs do so,
Let it pass lightly, and over go ;
Kneeling on my knees two,
Your blessing on me spread.
Father, I pray you hide my een,
That I see not the sword so keen :
Your stroke, father, would I not see,
Lest I against it grill.

The scene is prolonged for several speeches, Abraham's
determination being almost overcome and his will weakened

by the boy's meekness. At last, Isaac is bound upon the altar :

> Father, greet well my brethren young,
> And pray my mother of her blessing;
> I come no more under her wing;
> Farewell for ever and aye !
> But, father, I cry you mercy
> For all that ever I have trespassed to thee,
> Forgiven, father, that it may be
> Until doom's day.

Then Abraham kisses his son and binds a scarf about his head. Isaac kneels, and, while Abraham is getting his sword ready for the stroke, he says :

> I pray you, father, turn down my face
> A little, while you have space,
> For I am full sore adread.

At this turn of the action, the Angel appears and shows Abraham the ram in the thicket, while the Expositor, who in the Chester Miracle comments on situations involving doctrine, explains to the audience how Isaac is a type of Christ.

Melodrama of a ranting and roaring type, as distinguished from tragedy or pathos, had a very prominent and popular place assigned to it in the character of Herod. The Shaksperian expression ' to out-Herod Herod ' indicates the extravagance with which this part was played in order to please the groundlings and make sport. A large sword formed part of his necessary equipage, which he is ordered in the stage directions to ' cast up ' and ' cast down.' He was also attended by a boy wielding a bladder tied to a stick, whose duty was probably to stir him up and prevent his rage from flagging. In the Coventry Miracle this melodramatic element is elaborated with real force in the banquet scene which follows the Massacre of the Innocents. Herod appears throned and feasting among his knights, boasting truculently of his empire, and listening to their savage jests upon the slaughtered children. Then Death enters unperceived, except by the spectators, and strikes Herod down in the midst of his riot; whereupon the Devil springs upon the stage, and carries off the King with two of his Knights to Hell.

If Herod supplied melodrama, the Devil furnished abundance of low comedy and grotesque humour. His first appearance as Lucifer in the Parliament of Heaven shows him a proud rebellious Seraph. While the angels are singing Sanctus to God upon His throne, he suddenly starts forth and interrupts their chorus: [1]

> To whose worship sing ye this song ?
> To worship God or reverence me ?
> But ye me worship, ye do me wrong;
> For I am the worthiest that ever may be.

On this note Lucifer continues, not without dignity, defying God, menacing the loyal angels, and drawing to his side the rebels. But when the word, expelling him from heaven, is spoken, his form changes, and his language takes a baser tone. His companions rush grovelling and cursing one another to the mouth of hell, howling, ' Out harrow!' and ' Ho! Ho!' [2]—the cries with which, when devils came upon the stage, they always advertised their entrance. When Satan reappears, he has lost all his former state and beauty. He is henceforth the hideous, deformed, and obscene fiend of medieval fancy. One of his speeches may suffice for a specimen. After the Fall, God curses him again in the shape of the serpent, and he answers: [3]

> At Thy bidding, foul I fall ;
> I creep home to my stinking stall;
> Hell-pit and heaven-hall
>   Shall do Thy bidding boon.
> I fall down here a foul freke ; [4]
> For this fall I gin to quake ;
> With a fart my breech I break ;
>   My sorrow cometh full soon.

It was customary for the Devil to disappear thus with an unclean gesture. In addition to Satan, Beelzebub and

---

[1] Coventry Plays. [2] Chester Plays.
[3] Coventry Plays. [4] *Freke* -fellow.

Belial are personified; and in the Widkirk Plays a subordinate fiend named Tutivillus, who was destined to play a popular part in the Moralities, appears upon the scene of Doomsday.

IX

Another kind of comedy, less fantastically grotesque, but far grosser to our modern apprehension, arose from the relations between Joseph and his wife, the Virgin Mother of our Lord. The real object of those monkish playwrights was to bring the miraculous and immaculate conception of Christ into clear relief. But they wrote as though they wanted to insist on what is coarse and disagreeable in the situation. Joseph is depicted as superfluously old, unwilling to wed, and conscious of marital incapacity. Mary professes her intention of leading a religious life in celibacy. Wedlock is thrust upon the pair by an unmistakable sign from heaven that they are appointed unto matrimony. Listen to Joseph before he is dragged forth to offer up his wand:

> Benedicite! I cannot understand
>   What our Prince of Priests doth mean,
> That every man should come and bring with him a wand.
>   Able to be married; that is not I; so mote I then!
>   I have been maiden ever, and ever more will ben;
> I changed not yet of all my long life;
>   And now to be married, some man would wen
> It is a strange thing an old man to take a young wife!

Soon after the wedding, Joseph leaves his bride; and when he returns, he finds to his dismay that she has conceived a child:

> That seemeth evil, I am afraid,
>   Thy womb too high doth stand.
> I dread me sore I am betrayed,
>   Some other man thee had in hand
>   Hence sith that I went.

Mary tells him the truth. But he can naturally not believe her.

> God's child! Thou liest, ifay!
> God did never jape so with may.

> Alas! alas! my name is shent!
> All men may me now despise,
> And say, ' Old cuckold, thy bow is bent
> Newly now after the French guise!'

Mary repeats her story of the angel. This rouses Joseph's wrath.

> An angel! Alas, alas! Fie for shame!
> Ye sin now in that ye do say,
> To putten an angel in so great blame.
> Alas, alas! let be, do way!
> It was some boy began this game,
> That clothed was clean and gay;
> And ye give him now an angel's name—
> Alas, alas, and well away!

After Joseph has been satisfied by the descent of Gabriel from heaven confirming Mary's narrative, the situation is not dropped. It seemed necessary to the monkish scribe that he should drive the doctrine of the Incarnation home into the thickest skull by further evidence. Therefore he devised a scene in which Mary is arraigned for incontinence before the Bishop's Court by two detractors or false witnesses. Of their foul language and scurrilous insinuations no special account need here be taken, except it be to point out that they dwell on Joseph's age, and make merry with the common fate of old men married to young brides. The suit is decided by the ordeal of a potent drink of which Mary and Joseph both partake without injury, while the false witnesses, who are also obliged to taste the cup, fall down astonied and distraught:

> Out, out, alas! What aileth my skull?
> Ah, mine head with fire methinketh is brent!
> Mercy, good Mary! I do me repent
> Of my cursed and false language.

To our notions, Noah's wife was a better butt than Mary's husband for this comic badinage. And in the Chester Pageant of the Deluge this personage is made to furnish forth much fun. Early in the scene, she declares her intention of

not entering the Ark at all. At any rate, nothing shall
induce her to do so until she has made merry with her
gossips, and taken a good sup of wine. Then, if she may
bring them with her, she will think about it. All the beasts
and fowls have been already packed away, when this dialogue
between the patriarch and his wife opens :

Noye

Wife, come in : why stands thou there ?
Thou art ever froward, I dare well swear.
Come in, on God's name ! Half time it were.
For fear lest that we drown.

Noye's Wife

Yea, sir, set up your sail,
And row forth with evil hail,
For withouten fail
    I will not out of this town ;
But I have my gossips everyone,
One foot further I will not gone :
They shall not drown, by Saint John,
    An I may save their life.
They loven me full well, by Christ !
But thou let them into thy chest,
Els row now where thy list,
    And get thee a new wife !

Noye

Sem, son, lo ! thy mother is wrawe ;
By God, such another I do not know.

Sem

Father, I shall fetch her in, I trow,
    Withouten any fail.
Mother, my father after thee send,
And bids thee into yonder ship wend.
Look up and see the wind ;
    For we be ready to sail.

Noye's Wife

Sem, go again to him, I say ;
I will not come therein to-day.

Noye

Come in, wife, in twenty devils' way !
Or else stand there all day.

Cam

Shall we all fetch her in ?

Noye

Yea, sons, in Christ's blessing and mine !
I would you hied you betime ;
For of this flood I am in doubt.

The Good Gossippes' Song

The flood comes flitting in full fast,
On every side that spreads full far ;
For fear of drowning I am aghast ;
Good gossips, let us draw nere.
And let us drink or we depart,
For oft times we have done so ;
For at a draught thou drinks a quart,
And so will I do or I go.
Here is a pottel full of Malmsey good and strong ;
It will rejoice both heart and tongue.
Though Noye think us never so long,
Here we will drink alike.

At length, after much further beseeching on the part of Noah and his sons, and bargaining upon her side, Noah's wife with all her gossips is bundled into the Ark, and the Deluge begins in good earnest.

The Nativity gave occasion for blending comic and idyllic motives in a very graceful combination. The pure and beautiful narrative of S. Luke's Gospel, with its romantic suggestion of the shepherd folk awaked by angels on the hills of Bethlehem to gaze upon Christ's star, touched the imagination of all Christendom. It brought heaven into contact with the simplest form of rural industry ; invested pastoral life with sacred poetry ; and dedicated the Divine Infant in His cradle of the manger to the sympathy of those rude watchers on the fells and uplands. Therefore we find that the *Presepio* of Umbrian devotion, the Pifferari of Rome and Naples, the musette-players of France, the Christmas music of Bach and Handel, the Noels and the carols of all Northern nations, have yielded a continuous succession of the rarest and most quaintly touching passages in Christian art. In the first rank with these productions we may reckon the pastoral scenes in our religious drama. Two of these deserve especial comment. The first is a celebrated episode in the Widkirk Miracles, which forms a comedy of rustic life complete in all its parts, and turns upon the jovial humours of one shepherd Mak, who steals a sheep from his companions, and conceals it in his cottage as the new-born baby of his wife. This little piece, detached from the action of the Miracle, rightly deserves the name of interlude, and proves that independent comedy had a very early existence in England. Still and Udall, the first writers of regular comedy in our language, had little more to do than to develop similar motives and work upon the lines of this original. The Chester Plays contain a piece of less dramatic importance, but equally interesting for its realistic delineation of rural habits. The name of the comic characters in this Nativity are Harvey, Tudd, and Trowle, who occupy the night, before the shining of the angel, with rude jokes and vauntings of their pastoral craft. Their discussion of Gabriel's message, 'Gloria in excelsis,' &c. is marked by a racy sense of what such seely shepherds may have gathered from an angel's song. Quoth one:

> What song was this, say ye,
> That they sang to us all three?
> Expounded shall it be,
>   Or we hence pass.
> For I am eldest of degree,
> And also best, as seemes me.
> It was glore glare with a glee;
>   It was neither more nor less.

Trowle, who is the comic personage *par excellence*, replies:

> Nay, it was glori, glory, glorious!
> Methought that note ran over the house.
> A seemly man he was and curious;
>   But soon away he was.

Another shepherd answers Trowle :

> Nay, it was glory, glory, with a glo!
> And much of celsis was thereto :
> As ever I have rest or roo,
>   Much he spake of glass.

It may parenthetically be observed that the painters and
glaziers of Chester presented this pageant. Therefore the
allusion in the last line to their trade may have been meant
to move mirth. After bandying their conjectures to and fro,
the shepherds rise and wend their way to the stable in Bethlehem, where they find Christ new-born, and worship Him
with various simple prayers and offerings :

> Hail, King of heaven so high !
> Born in a crib !
> Mankind unto Thee
> Thou hast made fully.
> Hail, King ! born in a maiden's bower !
> Prophets did tell, Thou shouldst bear succour.
> Thus clerks doth say.
> Lo, I bring Thee a bell.
> I pray Thee save me from hell,
> So that I may with Thee dwell
> And serve Thee for aye.

When it comes to the turn of Trowle, that incorrigible jester,
he has no gift to make but ' a pair of my wife's old hose.'
But this crude note, no sooner than struck, is resolved in a
really charming quartette of boys, who approach the infant,
each with a gift suitable to his own poor estate.

The First Boy

> Now, Lord, for to give Thee have I nothing;
> Neither gold, silver, brooch, nor ring,
> Nor no rich robes meet for a king,
>   That have I here in store.
> But that it lacks a stoppel,
> Take Thee here my fair bottle,
> For it will hold a good pottle:
>   In faith I can give Thee no more.

The Third Boy

O noble child of Thee !
Alas, what have I for Thee
  Save only my pipe ?
Else truely nothing.
Were I in the rocks or in . . . . . .
  I could make this pipe,
That all the woods should ring
And quiver, as it were.

The Fourth Boy

Now, Child, although Thou be comen from God,
And be God Thyself in Thy manhood,
Yet I know that in Thy childhood
  Thou wilt for sweet meat look ;
To pull down apples, pears, and plums ;
Old Joseph shall not need to hurt his thumbs,
Because Thou hast not plenty of crumbs ;
  I give Thee here my nut-hook.

X

Passages of realistic delineation may be culled pretty copiously from all the Miracles. The eldest, those of Widkirk, for example, introduce a dialogue between Cain and his Garçon, curiously illustrative of vulgar boorish life. An episode of dicers in the Crucifixion of the same series forms a short interlude detached from the chief action. In the Chester Plays the dishonest alewife, who abides with the Devils, after Hell has been harrowed and Michael has sung Te Deum, and who is welcomed with effusion by Satan and his crew, supplies the motive of what is practically a brief comic farce. A more distinct satiric aim is traceable in some parts of the Coventry Plays—for instance, in the monologue of the 'Great Duke of Hell,' who comes upon the stage in the fashionable costume of a Court gallant, and reads a homily upon the modern modes of sinning : [1] also in the curious interpolated pageant of the Assumption, which abounds

---

[1] Pageant 25.

in allusions to reformers and heretics, and is written in a
harsh, coarse, controversial style, combined with much vulgarity of abuse. The introduction to the 14th Pageant of the
Coventry series is a satire, the point of which has, I think,
been missed by both Halliwell in his edition of these plays
and Collier in his commentary on them. The Bishop's
Court is about to be opened for the trial of Mary accused of
incontinence. An usher enters, and makes proclamation :

> Avoid, sirs, and let my lord the Bishop come,
>   And sit in the court the laws for to do ;
> And I shall go in this place them for to summon ;
>   Those that be in my book, the court ye must come to.

He then reads out a list of names, obviously meant to indicate
parishioners over whom the Bishop's Court had jurisdiction
for sins of the flesh. They run in pairs mostly, men and
women, as thus :

> Cook Crane and Davy Drydust,
> Lucy Liar and Lettice Littletrust,
> Miles the Miller and Colle Crakecrust,
>   Both Bett the Baker and Robin Reed.

Lastly, having summoned these evil livers, he bids them put
money in their purse, lest their cause fare ill in the Bishop's
Court—a warning similar to that we find in Mapes's rhymes
upon the Roman Curia :

> And look ye ring well in your purse,
> For else your cause may speed the worse.

Both Halliwell and Collier interpret this passage to mean
that entrance fees were paid at exhibitions of the pageants.
This, however, is inconsistent with the whole tenor of the
proclamation, and is quite in contradiction with the last words
of the usher :

> Though that ye sling God's curse
> Even at mine head, fast come away :

where it is clear that the fellow is not inviting spectators to a

show, but making believe to summon unwilling folk before
the justice.

I shall close these remarks with yet another scene of
dramatic realism, chosen from the Coventry Plays. It occurs
in the Pageant of the Woman taken in Adultery. A Scribe
and a Pharisee are consulting how they may entrap Christ,
and bring Him to confusion. A third person, who is styled
Accusator, suggests that they should present Him with the
puzzling case of a woman detected in the act of sin :

> A fair young quean here by doth dwell,
>> Both fresh and gay upon to look ;
> And a tall man with her doth mell :
>> The way into her chamber right even he took.

> Let us there now go straight thither ;
>> The way full even I shall you lead ;
> And we shall take them both together,
>> While that they do that sinful deed.

The Pharisee and Scribe assent. The Accuser leads them to
the house. They break open the door, and the tall man
comes rushing out, pursued by the three witnesses. The
stage direction runs as follows :

[*Hic juvenis quidam extra currit in diploide, caligis non ligatis,
et braccas in manu tenens, et dicit* ACCUSATOR]

Accusator

> Stow that harlot, some earthly wight !
> That in advowtry here is found !

Juvenis

> If any man stow me this night,
>> I shall him give a deadly wound.
> If any man my way doth stop,
>> Or we depart dead shall I be ;
> I shall this dagger put in his crop;
>> I shall him kill or he shall me !

Pharisee

> Great God his curse may go with thee !
> With such a shrew will I not mell.

Juvenis

That same blessing I give you three,
    And queath you all to the devil of hell.

[*Turning to the audience, and showing them in what
    a plight he stands.*]

In faith I was so sore afraid
    Of yon three shrews, the sooth to say,
My breech be not yet well up tied,
    I had such haste to run away :
They shall never catch me in such affray—
    I am full glad that I am gone.
Adieu, adieu ! a twenty devils' way !
    And God his curse have ye every one !

What follows, when the Scribe, the Pharisee, and the Accuser
drag the woman forth, is too foul-mouthed for quotation. It
proves that the monkish author of the text shrank from
nothing which could make his point clear, or could furnish
sport to the spectators. The scene acquires dignity as it
proceeds. Christ writes in silence with His finger on the
sand, while the three witnesses utter voluble invective, ply
Him with citations from the law of Moses, and taunt Him
with inability to answer. At last He lifts His head and
speaks :

Jesus

Look which of you that never sin wrought,
    But is of life cleaner than she,
Cast at her stones and spare her nought,
    Clean out of sin if that ye be.

[*Hic* JESUS *iterum se inclinans scribet in terra, et omnes accusa-
tcres quasi confusi separatim in tribus locis se disjungent.*]

Pharisee

Alas, alas ! I am ashamed.
I am afeard that I shall die.
All mine sins even properly named
    Yon prophet did write before mine eye.
If that my fellows that did espy,
    They will tell it both·far and wide ;
My sinful living if they out cry
    I wot never where mine head to hide !

The same effect is produced on the other witnesses by Christ's mystic writing in the sand. They slink away, abashed or silenced, while the woman makes confession and receives absolution :

> When man is contrite, and hath won grace,
> God will not keep old wrath in mind ;
> But better love to them He has,
> Very contrite when He them find.

Some reflections are forced upon the mind by the mixture of comedy with sacred things in these old plays, and by their gross material realism. In order to comprehend what strikes a modern student as profanity, we must place ourselves at the medieval point of view. The Northern races who adopted Christianity delighted in grotesqueness. The broad hilarity of their Yule rites and festivals added mirth to Christmas. To separate the indulgence of this taste for humour from religion would have been impossible ; because religion was the fullest expression of their life, absorbing all their intellectual energies. The Cathedral, which embodied the highest spiritual aspirations in a monumental work of art, admitted grotesquery in details and flung wide its gate at certain seasons to buffoonery. Grinning gargoils, monstrous Lombard centaurs, mermaids clasped with men, indecent miserere stalls, festivals of Fools and Asses, burlesque Masses performed by boy-bishops, travesties of holiest rites did not offend, as it would seem, the sense of men who reared the spire of Salisbury, who carved the portals of Chartres, who glazed the chancel windows of Le Mans, who struck the unison of arch and curve and column, and could span in thought the vacant air with aisles more bowery than forest glades. We, in this later age of colder piety and half-extinguished art, explore the relics of the past, scrutinise and ponder, classify and criticise. It is hardly given to us to understand the harmony of parts apparently so diverse. It shocks our taste to dwell on coarseness and religion blent in one consistent whole. We forget that the artists we admire—our masters in design how unapproachably beyond the reach of modern genius !—lived their whole lives out in what they wrought. For those folk, so simple in their mental state, so positive in their belief, it was both right and natural that the ludicrous and even the unclean should find a place in art and in religious mysteries.

XI

As a last word on the subject of Miracle Plays, I may suggest that those who are curious to form an adequate conception of the pageants as they were performed should pay a visit to the Sacro Monte at Varallo. There, on the broad flat summit of a rocky hill some thousand feet above the valley of the Sesia, is a sanctuary surrounded with numberless chapels embowered in chestnut woods. Each chapel contains a scene from sacred history, expressed by figures of life size, vividly painted, and accompanied with simple scenery in fresco on the walls. The whole series sets forth the life of Christ with special reference to the Passion. Architecture, plastic groups, and wall-paintings date alike from a period in the middle of the sixteenth century, and are the work of no mean craftsmen. The great Gaudenzio Ferrari plied his brush there together with painters of Luini's school. But the method of treatment, particularly in episodes of vehement emotion, such as the Massacre of the Innocents, the Flagellation, and the Crucifixion, indicates antique tradition. Designed for the people who crowd this festival in summer time on pilgrimage from all the neighbouring hill country and cities of the plain, they are no finished masterpieces of Renaissance art, but simply realistic pageants bringing facts with rude dramatic force before the eyes. It seems to me impossible to approach the Miracles, as they were probably exhibited in Coventry and Chester, more closely than on this Holy Mountain, where the popular art of the sixteenth century is still in close relation with the religious sentiments of a rustic population.

CHAPTER IV

MORAL PLAYS

I. Development of Minor Religious Plays from the Cyclical Miracle—Intermediate Forms between Miracle and Drama—Allegory and Personification.—II. Allegories in the Miracle—Detached from the Miracle—Medieval *Contrasti, Dialogi,* and *Disputationes*—Emergence of the Morality—Its essentially Transitional Character.—III. Stock Personages in Moral Plays—Devil and Vice—The Vice and the Clown—IV. Stock Argument—Protestant and Catholic—' Mundus et Infans.'—V. The ' Castle of Perseverance '—' Lusty Juventus '—' Youth.'—VI. ' Hick Scorner '—A real Person introduced—' New Custom '—' Trial of Treasure '—' Like will to Like.'—VII. ' Everyman '—The Allegorical Importance of this Piece.—VIII. Moral Plays with an Attempt at Plot—' Marriage of Wit and Wisdom '—' Marriage of Wit and Science '— ' The Four Elements '—' Microcosmus.'—IX. Advance in Dramatic Quality—' The Nice Wanton '—' The Disobedient Child.'—X. How Moral Plays were Acted—Passage from the old Play of ' Sir Thomas More.'—XI. Hybrids between Moral Plays and Drama—' King Johan '—Mixture of History and Allegory—The Vice in ' Appius and Virginia '—In ' Cambyses.'

(N.B.—The majority of the Plays discussed in this chapter will be found in Hazlitt's *Dodsley*, vols. i. ii. iii. iv. v. vi.)

I

THE examples already given of humorous passages occurring in the Miracles suffice to prove that comedy was ready to detach itself from the religious drama, and to assert its independence. But other causes had to operate, and a whole phase of evolution had to be accomplished before the emancipation of tragedy, that far more highly organised artistic form, could be effected. In proportion as the Miracles passed more and more into the hands of laymen, and characters like Herod or Pilate acquired greater prominence, the transition from the Cyclical Mystery to an intermediate type, out of

which the serious drama of History and Tragedy ultimately
emerged, was rendered gradually possible.   Sacred plays
with titles like the following, 'Godly Queen Esther,' 'King
Darius,' 'The Conversion of Saul,' 'Mary Magdalen,' show
the tendency to select some episode of Biblical history for
separate treatment, and, while maintaining the conventional
structure of the Miracle, to concentrate interest on some
single personage.   In the Cyclical Miracle, the human race
itself had been the protagonist, and the action was commensurate with the whole scheme of man's salvation.   In these
minor Miracles one man or woman emerged into distinctness,
and the dramatic action was determined by the character and
deeds of the selected hero.

It was not possible, however, for the art to free itself upon
these simple lines.   Instruction had been the chief end of the
sacred play, and to this purpose the drama still clung in its
passage toward liberty.   Allegory and personification supplied
the necessary intermediate form.   We have only to remember
what a commanding part was played by Allegory through the
fourteenth and fifteenth centuries all over Europe—in the
Divine Comedy of Dante, in Giotto's painting and Orcagna's
sculpture, in the French Romance of the Rose, in the
mysticism of the German Parzival, in the Vision of our
English Ploughman—in order to comprehend the reasons
why this step was inevitable, and why the type determined
by it for the drama was not then without attraction.   Three
centuries of militant and triumphant humanism, of developed
art, and of advancing science have rendered allegory irksome
to the modern mind.   We recognise its essential imperfection,
and are hardly able to do justice to such merits as it undoubtedly possessed for people not yet accustomed to distinguish thought from figured modes of presentation.   It is our
duty, if we care to understand the last phase of medieval
culture, to throw ourselves back into the mental condition of
men who demanded that abstractions should be clothed for
them by art in visible shapes—men penetrated in good
earnest with the Realism of the Schools, and to whom the
genders of the Latin Grammar suggested sexes —men who

delighted in the ingenuity and grotesquery of what to us is little better than a system of illustrated conundrums; for whom a Prudence with two faces or a Charity crowned with flames seemed no less natural than Gabriel kneeling with his lily at the Virgin's footstool—men who naturally thought their deepest thoughts out into tangibilities by means of allegorical mythology.

II

The Miracles in England had already brought personifications upon the stage. In the Coventry Plays, Justice, Mercy, Truth, and Peace hold conference with the three Persons of the Trinity. Death strikes Herod down among his knights. Contemplation acts the part of hierophant, explaining mysteries of faith. Medieval literature, moreover, abounded in debates and dialogues between abstractions. From the Latin poems attributed to Walter Mapes in England, we might quote a 'Disputatio inter Corpus et Animam,' and a 'Dialogus inter Aquam et Vinum.' The Italian Contrasti, some of which, like the 'Commedia dell' Anima,' are undoubtedly of great antiquity, bring the scheme of human destiny before us under the form of personified abstractions conversing and disputing. To take a further step; to detach the element of allegory already extant in the Miracles from the framework in which it was embedded, and to combine this dramatic element with the moral disputations of scholastic literature, was both natural and easy. This step was taken at a comparatively early period. Moral plays, extant in MS., have been ascribed to the reign of Henry VI. In the reign of Henry VII. they were both popular and fashionable, and they kept their vogue through that of his successor, increasing in complexity. The artistic type which resulted from this process made no unreasonable demands upon the imagination of a laity imbued with allegorical conceptions, and accustomed by the plastic arts to figurative renderings of abstract notions. Yet the defect adherent to all allegory in poetic art renders these figures ineffective. Intended for the stage, they strike us as being even more ineffective than they might have been in a poem meant to be perused. This defect may be plainly stated. According to the allegorical method, persons are created to stand for qualities, which qualities in all living human beings are blent with other and modifying moral ingredients. Being qualities isolated by a process of abstraction and incarnated by a process of reflective art, brought into æsthetical existence in order to symbolise and present single facets of character, they cannot delude us into taking them for personalities. They fail to attain concrete reality or to convey forcible lessons in human ethics. How cold and lifeless, for example, are the struggles of Juventus between Pity and Abominable Living, matched with the real conflict of a young man trained in piety, but tempted by a woman !

It was thus that the Morality came into existence : an intermediate form of dramatic art which had less vogue in England than in France, and which preserves at this time only a faint antiquarian interest. To touch lightly upon its main features will serve the purpose of a work which aims at literary criticism rather than at scientific history. The chief point to be insisted on is the emergence through Moralities of true dramatic types of character into distinctness. The Morality must, for our present purpose, be regarded as the schoolmaster which brought our drama to self-consciousness. It has the aridity and mortal dullness proper to merely trans- itional and abortive products. The growth of a brief moment in the evolution of the modern mind, representing the passage from medievalism to the Renaissance, from Catholic to humanistic art, this species bore within itself the certainty of short duration, and suffered all the disabilities and awkwardnesses of a temporary makeshift. We might com- pare it to one of those imperfect organisms which have long since perished in the struggle for existence, but which interest the physiologist both as indicating an effort after development upon a line which proved to be the weaker, and also as con- taining within itself evidences of the structure which finally succeeded. This comparison, even though it be not scientifically correct, will serve to explain the nature of the Morality, which can hardly be said to lie in the direct line of evolution between the Miracle and the legitimate Drama, but rather to be an abortive side-effort, which was destined to bear barren fruit.

III

Let us pass the actors in a prefatory review. From their names we shall learn something of the drama which they constituted. Perseverance, Science, Mundus, Wit, Free-will, the Five Senses reduced to one spokesman, Sensual Appetite, Imagination, a Taverner, Luxuria, Conscience, Innocency, Mischief, Nought, Nowadays, Abominable Living, Ignorance, Irksomeness, Tutivillus, the Seven Vices, Anima, Garçio (figuring Young England), Humanum Genus, Pity, Everyman, Honest Recreation—such are some of the strange actors in these moral shows. Abstract terms are personified and quaintly jumbled up with more familiar characters emergent from the people of the times. An effort is clearly being made to realise dramatic types, which after trial in this shape of metaphysical entities, will take their place as men and women animated by controlling humours, when the stage becomes a mirror of man's actual life. For the present period the stage has ceased to be the mirror of God's dealings with the human race in the scheme of creation, redemption, and judgment. It has not yet accustomed itself to reflect true men and women as they have been, are, and will be for all time. This intermediate dramatic form is satisfied with bodying forth the figments of the mind. It reflects logical generalities in the mirror of its art, investing these with outward form and allegorical impersonation.

Prominent among this motley company of abstract characters moved the Devil, leaping upon the stage dressed like a bear, and shouting 'Ho! Ho!' and 'Out Harrow!' His frequent but not inseparable comrade was the Vice— that tricksy incarnation of the wickedness which takes all shapes, and whose fantastic feats secure a kind of sympathy.

The Vice was unknown in the English Miracles, and played no marked part in the French Moralities. He appears to have been a native growth, peculiar to the transitional epoch of our moral interludes. By gradual deterioration or amelioration, he passed at length into the Fool or Clown of Shakspere's Comedy. But at the moment of which we are now treating the Vice was a more considerable personage. He represented that element of evil which is inseparable from human nature. Viewed from one side he was eminently comic; and his pranks cast a gleam of merriment across the dullness of the scenes through which he hovered with the lightness of a Harlequin. Like Harlequin, he wore a vizor and carried a lathe sword. It was part of his business to belabour the Devil with this sword; but when the piece was over, after stirring the laughter of the people by his jests, and heaping mischief upon mischief in the heart of man, nothing was left for the Vice but to dance down to Hell upon the Devil's back. The names of the Vice are as various as the characters which he assumed, and as the nature of the play required. At root he remains invariably the same—a flippant and persistent elf of evil, natural to man. Here are some of his titles, taken from the scenes in which he figures: Iniquity, Hypocrisy, Infidelity, Hardydardy, Nichol Newfangle, Inclination, Ambidexter, Sin, Desire, Haphazard. The names, it will be noticed, vary according as the play is more or less allegorical, and according to the special complexion of human frailty which the author sought to represent.

The part of the Vice was by far the most original feature of the Moralities, and left a lasting impression upon the memory of English folk long after it had disappeared from the stage. The Clown in 'Twelfth Night' sings:

> I am gone, sir;
>   And anon, sir,
> I'll be with you again
>   In a trice,
>   Like to the old Vice,
> Your need to sustain
> Who, with dagger or lath

In his rage and his wrath,
Cries Ah, ha! to the Devil:
Like a mad lad,
Pare thy nails, dad;
    Adieu, goodman drivel.

Ben Jonson, who preserved so much of old stage learning
and tradition in the introductions to his comedies, brings
Satan and the impish demon Pug, together with Iniquity,
into the first scene of 'The Devil is an Ass.' Satan opens
the play with 'Hoh, hoh, hoh, hoh, hoh, hoh, hoh, hoh, hoh,
hoh!' Pug begs to be sent up to earth to try his budding
devilhood on human kind:

    O chief;
    You do not know, dear chief! what there is in me!
    Prove me but for a fortnight, for a week,
    And lend me but a Vice, to carry with me!

'What Vice?' answers Satan.

    Why, any: Fraud,
    Or Covetousness, or Lady Vanity,
    Or Old Iniquity.

Iniquity is forthwith summoned, and comes leaping on the
stage in his Harlequin's costume:

    What is he calls upon me, and would seem to lack a Vice?
    Ere his words be half spoken, I am with him in a trice;
    Here, there, and everywhere, as the cat is with the mice:
    True *Vetus Iniquitas*. Lack'st thou cards, friend, or dice?
    I will teach thee to cheat, child, to cog, lie, and swagger,
    And ever and anon to be drawing forth thy dagger.

And so forth, rattling along in a measure suited to his antic
dance. Satan, however, tells Pug that the Vice is half a
century too old:

    Art thou the spirit thou seem'st? So poor, to choose
    This for a Vice, to advance the cause of Hell,
    Now, as vice stands this present year? Remember
    What number it is, six hundred and sixteen.
    Had it but been five hundred, though some sixty

> Above; that 's fifty years agone, and six,
> When every great man had his Vice stand beside him,
> In his long coat, shaking his wooden dagger,
> I could consent that then this your grave choice
> Might have done that, with his lord chief, the which
> Most of his chamber can do now.

The Vice, in fact, is out of date, discredited, no better than a Court fool, fit only to play clowns' pranks at sheriffs' dinners.

> We must therefore aim
> At extraordinary subtle ones now,
> When we do send to keep us up in credit:
> Not Old Iniquities.

In the induction to 'The Staple of News' two cronies are introduced as critics of the comedy. After sitting through the first act, Gossip Mirth says to Gossip Tattle:

> But they have no fool in this play, I am afraid, gossip.

Gossip Tattle remembers the good old times of her youth, when the Vice and Devil shook the stage together:

> My husband, Timothy Tattle—God rest his poor soul!—was wont to say there was no play without a fool and a Devil in 't; he was for the Devil still, God bless him! The Devil for his money, would he say. I would fain see the Devil.

Gossip Mirth caps these reminiscences with her own recollection of a certain Devil:

> As fine a gentleman of his inches as ever I saw trusted to the stage, or anywhere else; and loved the Commonwealth as well as ever a patriot of them all: he would carry away the Vice on his back, quick to hell, in every play where he came, and reform abuses.

These passages prove sufficiently that the salt of the Moralities existed for the common folk in the diabolic characters, and that these characters were confounded with the parts of clown and fool, sinking gradually into insignificance with the advance of the Drama as a work of pure art.

IV

'Lusty Juventus,' one of the best and most popular of
the Moralities, is styled, 'An enterlude, lively describing the
frailty of youth: of nature prone to vice: by grace and good
counsel trainable to virtue.' Such, in truth, is the argument
of all these plays. In the delineation of man's vicious
companions the author had some scope for the exhibition of
coarse scenes of humour and characters drawn from common
life. Of this opportunity he availed himself liberally. The
virtuous company of abstract qualities, who save the hero at
the close, are employed to deliver dry homilies upon duty, the
means of salvation, and the fundamental doctrines of religion.
Inasmuch as the Moralities were composed during the
uncertain reigns of the first three Tudors, they reflect the
conflict of opinion between Protestantism and the elder faith.
Some favour the Reformation, and abound in bitter satire on
the Roman priesthood; others, hardly less satirical, uphold
Catholic tradition. The dramatic talent of the playwright is
shown in the greater or less ability with which he transforms
his allegorical beings into lifelike personages; and, as may
readily be conceived, he succeeds best with the bad folk.
Hypocrisy plays a fair monk's part; Sensuality and Abominable Living are women of the town; Freewill is a turbulent
ruffler; Imagination a giddy-pated pleasure-seeker.

One of our earliest printed Moral Plays, 'Mundus et
Infans,' or 'The World and the Child,' issued from the press
of Wynkyn de Worde in 1522. Mundus, not unlike God in
the Miracles, prologises on his own great power and majesty.
A child comes to him naked and newly born, asking for
clothes and for a name. Mundus calls him Wanton, and
bids him return when fourteen years are over. The child
spends his boyhood in pastime; and having come again to
Mundus, gets the name of Lust and Liking. Love and
pleasure fill his thoughts now, and he declares himself to be
'as fresh as flowers in May.' On reaching the age of twenty-
one he is styled Manhood, dubbed knight, and consigned to

the fellowship of the Seven Deadly Sins. But at this period of his career, Conscience, attired apparently like a monk, accosts him in the street, and begs to be informed of his condition :

Conscience

Why, good sir knight, what is your name ?

Manhood

Manhood, mighty in mirth and game :
All power of pride have I ta'en :
I am as gentle as jay on tree.

Conscience

Sir, though the world have you to manhood brought,
To maintain manner ye were never taught.
No, conscience clear ye know right nought,
And this longeth to a knight.

Manhood

Conscience ! What the devil, man, is he ?

Conscience

Sir, a teacher of the spirituality.

Manhood

Spirituality ! What the devil may that be ?

Conscience

Sir ! all that be leaders in to light.

Then follows a long debate, in which Conscience declares to Manhood that, though the Seven Sins be great and puissant monarchs, holding their might from Mundus, yet is it no part of Manhood's duty to consort with them. Manhood is persuaded, and resolves to take the good advice of Conscience. But no sooner has he come to this determination, than Folly, who plays the part of Vice, enters with unseemly jests, and seduces Manhood. A dialogue reveals the birth and haunts of Folly :

Manhood

But hark, fellow, by thy faith where wast thou born?

Folly

By my faith, in England have I dwelt yore,
And all my ancestors me before.
But, sir, in London is my chief dwelling.

Manhood

In London! Where, if a man thee sought?

Folly

Sir, in Holborn I was forth brought,
And with the courtiers I am betaught.
To Westminster I used to wend.

Manhood

Hark, fellow, why dost thou to Westminster draw?

Folly

For I am a servant of the law.
Covetous is mine own fellow.
We twain plead for the king;
And poor men that come from upland,
We will take their matter in hand;
Be it right or be it wrong,
Their thrift with us shall wend.

It next appears that Folly is acquainted with all the taverns and houses of ill fame; and what is more, with all the monasteries.

Manhood

I pray thee yet tell me more of thine adventures.

Folly

In faith, even straight to all the friars;
And with them I dwelt many years,
And they crowned me king.

Manhood

I pray thee, fellow, whither wendest thou though?

Folly

Sir, all England to and fro :
In to abbeys and in to nunneries also ;
And alway Folly doth fellows find.

Manhood

Now hark, fellow, I pray thee tell me thy name.

Folly

I wis I hight both Folly and Shame.

Manhood takes Folly into his service ; and living riotously
in this bad company, is brought at last to misery.   In his
last state he is called Age, and repents him of his evil living :

Alas ! my lewdness hath me lost.
Where is my body so proud and prest ?
I cough and rout, my body will brest,
Age doth follow me so.
I stare and stagger as I stand,
I groan glysly upon the ground.
Alas ! Death, why lettest thou me live so long ?
I wander as a wight in woe
And care,
For I have done ill.
Now wend I will
My self to spill,
I care not whither nor where.

Perseverance now appears, like a *Deus ex machina*, and
reminds Age of the good counsels he received from Conscience.   Age despairs, and says he has deserved the name of
Shame.   But Perseverance christens him Repentance, and
cheers him with the examples of Mary Magdalen, Saul the
persecutor, and Peter who denied his Lord.   The play ends
with a well-digested diatribe upon the articles of faith and
means provided in the Sacraments for salvation.

It will be seen that 'Mundus et Infans' is a dry ' Rhaps-
ody of Life's Progress ' which the modern reader may enliven
for himself with marginal illustrations borrowed from the

allegorical mosaics upon the pavement of the Sienese Duomo. In those fresh and charming studies for the Seven Ages of Man, Infantia goes forth, a winged and naked Cupid, among flowers to play ; Pueritia takes his walks abroad, attired in a short jacket, through a pleasaunce ; Adolescentia wears the habit of a gallant bent on amorous delights, treading the same primrose path of pleasure ; Juventus carries a hawk upon his wrist, but just in front of him the road seems winding upwards to a hill ; Virilitas wears the long robes of a jurist, and holds a book in his left hand ; Senectus is yet hale, but shrunken in his long straight skirts, and bears a staff to stay his feet ; Decrepitas totters upon crutches over a bare space of ground toward an open tomb.

V

The 'Castle of Perseverance,' supposed to belong to the reign of Henry VI., was a moral play of the same type as 'Mundus et Infans.' Indeed, it may be said, once and for all, that the motives of these shows were few, and that the same theme passed muster under several titles. This proves the antiquity of the species, and gives us the right to believe that the specimens we now possess in MS. and print were survivals from still earlier originals. 'Lusty Juventus' goes a step farther in dramatic interest. The scene opens with a pretty lyric sung by the chief actor, Youth, the refrain of which is so freshly and joyously repeated that we might fancy it the echo of a bird's voice in spring :

> In an arbour green asleep where as I lay,
> The birds sang sweet in the midst of the day ;
> I dreamed fast of mirth and play :
>   In youth is pleasure, in youth is pleasure.

> Methought I walked still to and fro,
> And from her company I could not go ;
> But when I waked, it was not so :
>   In youth is pleasure, in youth is pleasure.

Therefore my heart is surely pight
Of her alone to have a sight,
Which is my joy and heart's delight :
    In youth is pleasure, in youth is pleasure.

Good Counsel surprises Juventus in the midst of a soliloquy
describing the amusements in which the young gentleman
delights. Juventus turns to him with :

Well met, father, well met !
Did you hear any minstrels play,
As you came hitherward upon your way ?
An if you did, I pray you wise me thither;
For I am going to seek them, and, in faith, I know not whither.

Good Counsel and a third interlocutor, Knowledge, who enters
after a short space, find Juventus shamefully ignorant of the
rudiments of religious education. Is he bound, he asks, as
well as the clergy, to know and keep God's law ? They take
him seriously to task, quoting chapter and verse from
Ephesians and Galatians to prove their points, and having
primed the youth with good doctrine, leave him well disposed
to walk in the right path. Juventus has in truth become a
model Puritan, furnished with Protestant principles, and imbued with a proper hatred for the Papacy. But the Devil suddenly jumps up. 'Ho, ho !' quoth he. 'This will not do !
The old folk were loyal in my service ; but these young people
who are growing up, scorn tradition and rule their lives as
" Scripture teacheth them." ' So he calls Hypocrisy, his
dear son, who has been busy manufacturing relics, beads,
copes, creeds, crowns, and pardons for the Pope. Hypocrisy
undertakes to mould Juventus after the Devil's own wish.
Accordingly he gets him introduced to Abominable Living, a
loose serving woman, who plays the wanton while her
masters are at morning sermon. Juventus takes kindly to
her company, swears like a trooper, and proves his manhood on her lips. A song appropriate to this situation is
introduced :

Why should not youth fulfil his own mind,
As the course of nature doth him bind ?
Is not everything ordained to do his kind ?
    Report me to you, report me to you.

Do not the flowers spring fresh and gay,
Pleasant and sweet in the month of May ?
But when their time cometh, they fade away.
    Report me to you, report me to you.

Be not the trees in winter bare ?
Like unto their kind, such they are ;
And when they spring, their fruits declare.
    Report me to you, report me to you.

What should youth do with the fruits of age,
But live in pleasure in his passage ?
For when age cometh, his lusts will swage.
    Report me to you, report me to you.

Why should not youth fulfil his own mind,
As the course of nature doth him bind ?
Is not everything ordained to do his kind ?
    Report me to you, report me to you.

Juventus now goes off the stage, to pass his time in mirth
and solace with Abominable Living ; for whom, it may be
parenthetically said, he is far too charming a companion.
From dicing, drinking, and wenching, his former tutors
rescue him with some pains, renew their instructions in
Divinity, and bring him to remorse. God's Merciful Promises
appears in the form of a preacher, and bids him take heart.
Juventus repents, reconciles himself to God, and ends the
play with a homily upon the duty of avoiding Satan and the
Pope, and clinging steadfastly to Christ's Gospel. The whole
piece, with the exception of its pretty lyrics, the satiric part
of Hypocrisy, and the realistic scenes with Abominable
Living, may well be styled, in the words of Hawkins and the
learned Dr. Percy, · a supplement to the pulpit.' Before
leaving it, however, I will extract a part of the speech in
which Hypocrisy describes to his father, the Devil, the shams

which he has foisted on the world in the name of religion.
His list runs off like Leporello's in ' Don Giovanni,' and must
have been effective in the mouth of a good buffo-singer :

> I set up great idolatry
> With all kind of filthy sodometry,
> To give mankind a fall ;
> And I brought up such superstition,
> Under the name of holiness and religion,
>   That deceived almost all :
> As holy cardinals, holy popes,
> Holy vestments, holy copes,
>   Holy hermits and friars ;
> Holy priests, holy bishops,
> Holy monks, holy abbots,
>   Yea, and all obstinate liars :
> Holy pardons, holy beads,
> Holy saints, holy images,
>   With holy, holy blood ;
> Holy stocks, holy stones,
> Holy clouts, holy bones,
>   Yea, and holy holy wood :
> Holy skins, holy bulls,
> Holy rochets and cowls,
>   Holy crouches and staves ;
> Holy hoods, holy caps,
> Holy mitres, holy hats,
>   Ah, good holy, holy knaves :
> Holy days, holy fastings,
> Holy twitching, holy tastings,
>   Holy visions and sights ;
> Holy wax, holy lead,
> Holy water, holy bread,
>   To drive away sprights :
> Holy fire, holy palm,
> Holy oil, holy cream
>   And holy ashes also ;
> Holy brooches, holy rings,
> Holy kneeling, holy censings,
>   And a hundred trim-trams mo :
> Holy crosses, holy bells,
> Holy relics, holy jewels,
>   Of mine own invention ;

> Holy candles, holy tapers,
> Holy parchments, holy papers—
>   Had you not a holy son ?

More delicate in literary quality, and perhaps elder in date of composition, than ' Lusty Juventus,' is the Interlude of ' Youth,' a Moral Play upon the same theme.   Charity takes the part of good genius, contending for the soul of Youth with Riot the Vice, Lady Lechery the Courtesan, and Pride, their boon companion.   To dwell upon the texture of the plot, and to show how Humility helps Charity to rescue Youth from Riot, is not needful, for this Interlude has little pretension to dramatic development.   Its charm consists in a certain limpid purity of language and clear presentation of simple pictures.   Youth's own description of himself, when he makes his first entrance, is very pretty :

> Aback, fellows, and give me room ;
> Or I shall make you to avoid soon !
> I am goodly of person ;
> I am peerless wherever I come.
> My name is Youth, I tell thee,
> I flourish as the vine tree :
> Who may be likened unto me,
> In my youth and jollity ?
> My hair is royal and bushed thick ;
> My body pliant as a hazel-stick ;
> Mine arms be both big and strong,
> My fingers be both fair and long ;
> My chest big as a tun ;
> My legs be full light for to run,
> To hop and dance and make merry.
> By the mass, I reck not a cherry
> Whatsoever I do !
> I am the heir of all my father's land,
> And it is come into my hand :
> I care for no mo.

Charity admonishes Youth for his self-complacency.

> You had need to ask God mercy :
> Why did you so praise your body ?

Youth

Why, knave, what is that to thee ?
Wilt thou let me to praise my body ?
Why should I not praise it, an it be goodly ?
I will not let for thee.

Charity warns Youth that his beautiful body will wither and
go down into the grave, and he himself be burned in hell.
Were it not better to make sure of heaven :

Where thou shalt see a glorious sight
Of angels singing, and saints bright,
Before the face of God ?

But all is to little purpose, for Youth tells Charity with blunt
irreverence that God is not likely to take such dreary guests
as he into His company :

Nay, nay, I warrant thee,
He hath no place for me ;
Weenest thou He will have such fools
To sit on His gay stools ?
Nay, I warrant thee, nay !

Riot is much more to Youth's mind than Charity ; and Riot
puts the old proverb about wild oats so pithily before him as
to make short work with Charity's arguments.

Hark, Youth, for God avow,
He would have thee a saint now ;
But, Youth, I shall you tell—
A young saint, an old devil :
Therefore I hold thee a fool,
An thou follow his school.

All the same, in spite of his bluster and recalcitration, when
the time comes for the piece to end, Youth yields to Charity
and suffers himself to be converted by Humility without a
struggle. The authors of Moralities had not advanced beyond
the point of personification and dramatic collocation. To
take the further step, and to display the reciprocal interaction
of persons, was beyond them.

VI

In 'Hick Scorner,' a real personage, though divided by the thinnest partition wall from allegory, enlivens the usual exhibition of abstract qualities. The piece opens with a dialogue between Pity, Contemplation, and Perseverance, attired like Doctors of Divinity. They discourse at length upon the low state of public morality. Pity is then left alone, to bear the brunt of the two comic characters, Freewill and Imagination, who come upon the stage swaggering like black-guards. The conversation of these good fellows brings the humours of the town before us in language which, if racy, hardly bears transcription. Hick Scorner, a traveller from foreign parts, breaks in upon their colloquy, and is welcomed as a boon companion by the jolly pair. Hick has been every-where and seen everything. The ship which brought him back to England, bore the vices, weathering a storm in which the virtues with their godly crew foundered. He scoffs at all things human and divine, and, after quarrelling awhile with Freewill and Imagination, makes the matter up, and puts Pity in the stocks. Then he disappears. This is all we hear of the person who gives his name to the play. Pity's two friends return, liberate him from the stocks, and help him to convert Freewill and Imagination ; a job which the trio carry through with truly undramatic celerity. The construction of this play is radically bad. It falls flat between an allegory and a farce ; nor does it display that analysis of life which lends a scientific interest to some of the weightier Moralities. Yet, in the development of the English drama, it takes a place of mark ; for all the characters are well touched, with pungency of portraiture and verisimilitude. Hick himself, though so occasional a personage, shows the author's effort after artistic emancipation.

A set of woodcuts appended to this play in Wynkyn de Worde's edition exemplify the figures which the actors cut upon the stage. Pity is a mild old man ; as fits the character of God's eternal Mercy. Contemplation carries a sword, to use in shrewd passes with the Evil One. Hick walks delicately, waving his hands to and fro, like one who jests upon the surface of the world. Freewill bears a staff, and is a gallant of the town. Imagination distinguishes himself from his friend and master less by costume than by an airy motion of his legs, betokening inconstancy and lightness. Perseverance is armed at all points in plate mail, rests his right hand on a trenchant blade, and carries in his left a banner, striding forth alert for action. Gazing at these wood-cuts, we understand what allegory was for the English people, and how after two centuries the 'Pilgrim's Progress' came into existence.

'New Custom' claims some passing notice in connection with 'Lusty Juventus' and 'Hick Scorner.' To judge by its style, it is considerably later in date, and may be ascribed perhaps to the first decade of Elizabeth's reign. In substance it is neither more nor less than a tract in favour of the Reformation, furnished with dramatic forms, but composed in so wooden a manner that one can hardly conceive it to have been often acted. The names of the persons are, how-ever, interesting. Perverse Doctrine and Ignorance are two old Popish priests ; New Custom and Light of the Gospel, two ministers of the reformed faith. Cruelty and Avarice, who gloat with delight over their memories of the Marian persecution, are described as rufflers—that is, bullies. Hypo-crisy is an old woman. There is no Vice. One sentence put into the mouth of Perverse Doctrine deserves quotation :

For since these Genevan doctors came so fast into this land,
Since that time it was never merry with England.

'The Trial of Treasure' is another Moral Play which bears the impress of the Reformation, and may be attributed to the same period as 'New Custom.' Its aim, however, is ethical and not religious edification ; and the chief point to notice is the quaint mixture of moral saws from classic sources jumbled up with sentences from the Epistles. The Vice takes a prominent part, under the name of Inclination ; but in spite of his crude horse-play with Lust, Greedy-gut,

and Elation, there is little to move laughter in the piece.
Ulpian Fulwell's 'Like will to Like' may be placed in the
same class as the 'Trial of Treasure.' The Vice is called
Nichol Newfangle; his companions are Tom Tosspot,
Cuthbert Cutpurse, Ralph Roister, Pierce Pickpurse, Hance
a serving man, Hankin Hangman, Philip Fleming, Tom
Collier—names which sufficiently indicate the author's
endeavour to substitute comedy for allegory. Indeed, the
allegorical setting of this piece is merely conventional, and
the moralising made to order.

VII

Far more perfect in design, and very full of interest to
modern readers, is the ancient piece called 'Everyman.' That
it was not so popular as ' Lusty Juventus ' or 'Hick Scorner'
can be readily conceived, because its lesson is grim and
dreadful. We may bring ourselves into relation with the
motive of this play by studying the woodcuts in Queen
Elizabeth's Prayer Book or any one of the Dances of Death
ascribed to Holbein. The frontispiece to 'Everyman' recalls
one of those remorseless meditations on the grave. A fine
gentleman of the Court of Henry VII. is walking with his
hat upon his head and a chain around his neck among the
flowers of a meadow. Death, the skeleton, half-clothed in a
loose shroud, and holding in his arm the cover of a sepulchre,
beckons to this gallant from a churchyard full of bones and
crosses. Life is thus brought into abrupt collision with the
' cold *Hic jacets* of the dead ' and him who rules there.
Collier, who thinks this play may be as old as the reign of
Edward IV., terms it ' one of the most perfect allegories ever
formed ; ' nor is this praise extravagant, for the texture of the
plot is both simple and strong, in strict keeping with its
stern and serious theme. God opens the play with a monologue in which He sets forth the sacrifice of Christ, and
upbraids mankind for their ingratitude. Worldly riches
cumber them ; they pay no heed to piety ; justice must be

done upon them, and each soul shall be reminded of his latter end.   Therefore he calls Death to Him : [1]

> Where art thou, Death, thou mighty messenger ?

Death answers :

> Almighty God, I am here at your will.

He is then sent forth to go in search of Everyman, and tell him to prepare for a long pilgrimage.   Death finds this representative of the whole human race disporting himself in careless wise, and suddenly arrests him :

> Everyman, stand still !   Whither art thou going
> Thus gaily ?

When Everyman hears the message, he begs a respite, and offers Death gold ; but all the favour he can find is the permission to take with him such friends as shall be willing to bear him company.   Fellowship proffers his readiness to do anything for Everyman : but when he hears of Death and that long pilgrimage, he shakes his head.   If you had asked me to drink or dice or kill a man with you, I would have done it—but this, no !   Kindred passes by, hears Everyman's request, and says the same as Fellowship, but with even less sympathy.   Then Everyman betakes him to his Goods ; but these are so close packed away in bags and boxes that they cannot stir.   Far from being disposed to help him, Gold only mocks at his distress, rejoices in it, and chuckles at the thought of staying in the world to corrupt more souls of men. At length Everyman remembers his Good Deeds.   'My Good Deeds, where be you ? '   She (for Good Deeds is a female character) replies :

> Here I lie, cold in the ground ;
> Thy sins have me so sore bound
> That I cannot stir.

---

[1] In the Coventry Miracles, Mors says : 'I am Death, God's messenger.'

She, however, is the only one of Everyman's acquaintances who yields him any service. She bids him have recourse to Knowledge, and Knowledge introduces him to Confession. Confession shrives him, and releases Good Deeds from her dungeon. Then Everyman makes ready for his journey, taking with him Strength, Discretion, Beauty, and Five Wits. When they reach the churchyard, Everyman begins to faint; and each of these false friends forsakes him. Good Deeds alone has no horror of the grave, but descends with him to abide God's judgment. The piece ends with an Angel's song, welcoming the soul of Everyman, which has been parted from the body and made fit for heaven.

The Moral Play of 'Everyman' has an interesting parallel in William Bullein's 'Dialogue both pleasant and pitiful, wherein is a goodly Regiment against the Fever Pestilence.' This tract, printed in 1564, and again in 1573, illustrates the influence which the Drama at that early period exercised over style. It is conceived in the manner of the Moralities, and its descriptive passages enable us to understand how they affected the imaginations of their audience. The dialogue introduces a citizen, with his wife and serving-man, flying from London during a visitation of the plague. Death meets them on their journey. The wife deserts her husband, 'for poverty and death will part good fellowship.' The servant runs away, and the citizen is left alone to parley with the awful apparition. He tries to bribe Death with money, and to soften him with prayers. But Death is obdurate; the man's hour has come; he must away from wife and children; no matter whether he leave his debts unpaid, his business in confusion. 'For,' says Death, 'I have commission to strike you with this black dart called the pestilence; my master hath so commanded me: and as for gold, I take no thought of it, I love it not; no treasure can keep me back the twinkling of an eye from you; you are my subject, and I am your lord.' Before executing his commission, the Angel of the Lord holds discourse with his victim upon the meaning of the three darts, plague, famine, and war, he carries in his hand. His speech ends with a solemn passage, worthy to be quoted side by side with Ralegh's famous apostrophe to 'eloquent, just, and mighty Death.' It runs as follows: 'I overthrow the dancer, and stop the breath of the singer, and trip the runner in his race. I break wedlock, and make many widows. I do sit in judgment with the judge, and undo the life of the prisoner, and at length kill the judge also himself. I do summon the great Bishops, and cut them through the rochets. I utterly banish the beauty of all courtiers, and end the miseries of the poor. I will never leave off until all flesh be utterly destroyed. I am the greatest cross and scourge of God.' [1]

VIII

A whole group of the Moral Plays are devoted to subjects capable of more dramatic development, involving the outlines of a love-plot and a regular *dénouement*. Of these it may suffice to mention the 'Marriage of Wit and Wisdom' and the 'Marriage of Wit and Science,' the latter of which exists in two separate forms. Wit is the son of Severity and Indulgence. The characters of the father and the mother are sharply contrasted and brought into bold relief by a few strong touches in the opening scene. They send Wit forth to court the maiden Wisdom, giving him Good Nurture for a guardian. But Idleness, the Vice, intrudes; and assuming many disguises, leads him astray. He first lures him under the name of Honest Recreation to Dame Wantonness, by whom Wit is besotted and befooled. Then he causes him, in the pursuit of tedious study, to be entrapped by Irksomeness, who always lurks in wait for Wisdom's suitors. The lady, however, rescues her knight, and gives him a sword with which he puts Irksomeness to flight. Wit has not yet learned by experience to walk straight forward to his end. Fancy, therefore, is able to decoy him into prison. Here Good Nurture discovers and releases him; and at last he is wedded

[1] I am indebted to Mr. A. H. Bullen for the above extracts from this rare 'Dialogue,' which he communicated to me while the proof-sheets of this book were passing through the press. It is to be hoped that before long he will edit a reprint of the whole tract.

to Wisdom, the virgin, who has waited for him all this while
in desert places. The allegory of this play is clear; its language
has some delicacy, and the comic scenes are entertaining.

The plot of ' Wit and Science ' is conducted on the same
lines. Wit goes through similar adventures, and finally weds
Science. It contains a curious comic scene, in which Idleness
teaches the child Ignorance to spell, purposely making the
lesson difficult. This corresponds to a passage in the ' Marriage of Wit and Wisdom,' where Idleness mocks Search by
pretending to follow what he says, repeating all his words after
him with ludicrous misinterpretations.

The ' Four Elements ' introduces a different species of
allegory. Nature undertakes to instruct Humanity in the
physical sciences, and gives him Studious Desire as a companion. Humanity takes kindly to her tedious homilies
until the Vice, named Sensual Appetite, appears upon the
scene. He then plunges into a whirl of vulgar dissipation with
the Vice and Ignorance and a Taverner, not, however, wholly
intermitting his studies in cosmography and such like matters.
There is, however, no cohesion between the several parts of
the action ; and we may assume, I think, that in the piece,
as we possess it, the mirth-making scenes, which bring the
Vice and his comic crew into play, have overgrown the allegory to its ultimate confusion. Some interest attaches still to
the 'Four Elements,' because the type of allegory first displayed in it held the stage all through the golden period of
art, in Masques and learned shows. Long after the publication of Shakspere's plays in 1637, Thomas Nabbes brought
out a ' Moral Masque ' styled ' Microcosmus,' in which Physander, or the natural man, is married to Bellanima, and
receives for his attendants the Four Complexions and a Good
and Evil Genius. Lured astray by the Evil Genius, he forsakes
his chaste wife, and takes up his abode with the Five Senses
in the house of Sensuality, a Courtesan. Bellanima tries in
vain to reclaim him, until at last he is flung forth, weak,
jaded, and good for nothing, from the halls of Sensuality.
Then Bellanima and the Good Genius conduct him in sorry
plight to Temperance, who cures him of his sickness, while

Reason fortifies his soul against the attacks of Remorse and
Despair and the Furies, whom the Evil Genius has summoned
to accuse him at the bar of Conscience. At the end of the
piece, which is a formal play divided into five acts, Bellanima
and Physander ascend to Elysium.

I have given this rapid sketch of ‘Microcosmus’ in order
to show how the motives of the Moral Plays were combined
and treated by the later Elizabethan authors. In the interval
between the date of the ‘Four Elements’ and ‘Mundus et
Infans’ and that of ‘Microcosmus,’ they assumed a classical
complexion, and a more elaborate form. But they remained at
root the same. It would be easy to illustrate this point from
many subsequent products of our stage—from the ‘Misogonus’
of Rychards, of which we have a MS. dated 1577; from
Woodes’ ‘Conflict of Conscience,’ printed in 1581; from the
anonymous ‘Contention between Liberality and Prodigality,’
printed in 1602; and from such later works of literary
ingenuity as Randolph’s ‘Muses’ Looking Glass,’ and Brewer’s
excellent ‘Lingua.’ But enough has been already said to
indicate the comparative vitality of the species; and it is
probable that I shall have to draw particular attention at a
later stage of these studies to some at least of the works which
I have named.

IX

Already, in the early period of which I am at present
treating, efforts were made to disengage the Moral Play from
its allegorical setting, and to present the pith of its motives
in a form of proper Comedy. The ‘Nice Wanton,’ for
example, introduces us to a family consisting of Barnabas,
Delilah, and Ismael, and their mother Xantippe. Xantippe
spares the rod, and lets her children grow up as they
list. Iniquity, who supports the chief action of the piece,
seduces Delilah to wantonness, and Ismael to roguery. Both
come to miserable deaths. Xantippe is on the point of dying of
shame, when her son Barnabas, after rating his mother soundly
for her weak indulgence, reminds her of God’s mercy, and

saves her from despair. The 'Disobedient Child' presents a son, who scorns his father's good advice, marries a wanton wife, spends his substance in divers pleasures with her, and returns home penniless. Unlike the father in the Parable of the Prodigal Son, this stern parent contents himself with reminding the lad that he had told him so beforehand, and sends him about his business with a small dole. The Devil utters a long soliloquy in the middle of the play, but does not influence its action. A third piece, named 'Jack Juggler,' said to be written 'for children to play,' deserves mention for the curiosity of its being modelled on the 'Amphitryon' of Plautus, which it follows *longissimo sane intervallo!* It is really nothing more than a merry interlude between a scape-grace page called Jenkin Careaway, and Jack Juggler, which latter is our old friend the Vice. The other characters have slight importance.

X

Having examined some of the Moralities in detail, it will be interesting to inquire into the mode of their performance. During the heyday of their popularity, it appears that they were acted by roving companies on holidays and at hock-tide festivals in the halls of noblemen and gentry, as well as on the open squares of towns. They acquired the subordinate name of Interlude from the custom of having them exhibited in the intervals of banquets or the interspace of other pastimes. A Messenger announced the show in the case of public representations, and explained the argument in a prologue. Not unfrequently a Doctor, surviving from the Expositor of the Miracles, interpreted its allegory as the action proceeded.

It may also be remarked that noblemen, whose households were maintained upon a princely scale, kept their own companies of actors. We hear of the 'Players of the King's Interludes' so early as the reign of Henry VII.; and the books of the Percy family contain curious information respecting payments made to the Lord Northumberland's

Servants. The Lords Ferrers, Clinton, Oxford, and Buckingham, are known to have kept private actors at the beginning
of the sixteenth century. In those great baronial establishments, musicians, minstrels, and chapel choristers had long
formed a separate department; and when the acting of
Interludes became fashionable, the players were attached to
this section of the household. Cities also began to entertain
companies for the occasional representation of Pageants,
Masques, and Plays. Thus a dramatic profession was
gradually formed, which only waited for a favourable opportunity to render itself independent of patronage, and to
develop a national theatre by competition and free appeal to
public favour.

For the further illustration of these details, we are
fortunate in having ready to our hand a lively episode in the
History Play of ' Sir Thomas More.' It may be premised
that the strolling companies consisted of four or at the outside
five persons. The leading actor played the part of Vice and
undertook stage management. There was a boy for the
female characters; and the remaining two or three divided
the other parts between them. Sir Thomas More, in the
play in question, has invited the Lord Mayor and Aldermen
with their respective ladies to a banquet. The feast is
spread; but no further entertainment has been furnished,
and the guests are presently expected. At this moment a
Player is announced. More greets him with :

Welcome, good friend; what is your will with me ?

Player

My lord, my fellows and myself
Are come to tender you our willing service,
So please you to command us.

More

What ! for a play, you mean ?
Whom do ye serve ?

Player

My Lord Cardinal's grace.

More

My Lord Cardinal's players !   Now, trust me, welcome !
You happen hither in a lucky time.
To pleasure me, and benefit yourselves.
The Mayor of London and some Aldermen,
His lady and their wives, are my kind guests
This night at supper.   Now, to have a play
Before the banquet will be excellent.
I prithee, tell me, what plays have ye ?

Player

Divers, my lord : ' The Cradle of Security,'
' Hit the Nail o' th' Head,' ' Impatient Poverty,'
' The Play of Four P's,' ' Dives and Lazarus,'
' Lusty Juventus,' and ' The Marriage of Wit and Wisdom.'

So the player runs through his repertory.   The name of the
last hits More's mood, and he rejoins :

' The Marriage of Wit and Wisdom ! '   That, my lads
I 'll none but that !   The theme is very good,
And may maintain a liberal argument.
We 'll see how Master-poet plays his part,
And whether Wit or Wisdom grace his art.
Go, make him drink, and all his fellows too.
How many are ye ?

Player

Four men and a boy.

More

But one boy ?   Then I see,
There 's but few women in the play.

Player

Three, my lord ; Dame Science, Lady Vanity,
And Wisdom—she herself.

More

And one boy play them all ?   By 'r Lady, he 's loaden !
Well, my good fellows, get ye strait together,
And make ye ready with what haste ye may.
Provide their supper 'gainst the play be done,

Else we shall stay our guests here overlong.
Make haste, I pray ye.

Player

We will, my lord.

The Chancellor now tells his wife that the Lord Cardinal's Players have luckily turned up. She approves of their engagement. They both receive their guests, and seat them for the Interlude. At this point the chief player, dressed as the Vice, appears, and begs for a few minutes' respite. More addresses him:

More. How now! What 's the matter?

Vice. We would desire your honour but to stay a little. One of my fellows is but run to Oagles for a long beard for young Wit, and he 'll be here presently.

More. A long beard for young Wit! Why, man, he may be without a beard till he comes to marriage, for wit goes not all by the hair. When comes Wit in?

Vice. In the second scene, next to the Prologue, my lord.

More. Why, play on till that scene comes, and by that time Wit's beard will be grown, or else the fellow returned with it. And what part playest thou?

Vice. Inclination, the Vice, my lord.

More. Grammercy! Now I may take the Vice if I list; and wherefore hast thou that bridle in thy hand?

Vice. I must be bridled anon, my lord.

They exchange a few words about the purpose of the play; and then the scene opens. It is the first act of 'Lusty Juventus,' adapted with retrenchments. Inclination and Lady Vanity are in the course of seducing Wit, when the Vice suddenly pulls up with:

Is Luggins yet come with the beard?

Enter another Player

No, faith, he is not come: alas! what shall we do?

The Vice, who is the driver of the team, expresses the dislocation of the whole company by this unforeseen accident:

Forsooth, we can go no further till our fellow Luggins come ; for he plays Good Counsel, and now he should enter, to admonish Wit that this is Lady Vanity and not Lady Wisdom.

More throws himself into the breach, and from his place before the stage undertakes to play the part of Good Counsel, which he does excellently well in default of Luggins. When Luggins at length appears with the beard, the Vice turns to his lordship :

Oh, my lord, he is come.   Now we shall go forward.

But the Chancellor thinks it is about time to conduct his guests to the banquet chamber.   So the scene breaks up, and the players are left to altercate about this hitch in their arrangements.   They pay due compliments to More's ready wit :

Do ye hear, fellows ?   Would not my lord make a rare player ? Oh, he would uphold a company beyond all.   Ho ! better than Mason among the King's Players !   Did ye mark how extemprically he fell to the matter, and spake Luggins's part almost as it is in the very book set down ?

While they are so discoursing, a serving man enters with the news that More is called to Court, and that he bids the players take eight angels, and, after they have supped, retire. The fellow doles the money out short of twenty shillings, taking his discount, as the way of flunkeys was, and is.   Wit begins to grumble :

This, Luggins, is your negligence ;
Wanting Wit's beard brought things into dislike ;
For otherwise the play had been all seen,
Where now some curious citizen disgraced it,
And discommending it, all is dismissed.

They count their money, and find wherein it fails.   But Wit mends the whole matter ; for when the Chancellor sweeps by to Court, he bids his lordship notice that two of the eight angels have been somehow dropped in the rushes.   More calls his servant to account, rights the players, and goes forth on affairs of State.

This scene, which in some of its incidents reminds us roughly of Hamlet's interview with the Players, was no doubt intended to mark the character of More, and bring his humour and good nature into relief. But it serves our present purpose of vividly presenting the circumstances under which a strolling company of actors may have oftentimes in noble houses found the opportunity to play some more or less mangled version of a popular Morality.

XI

Before taking final leave of the Moral Plays, it will be necessary to notice three pieces which may be described as hybrids between this species and the serious drama of the future. The first of these is 'King Johan,' by John Bale the controversialist. Written certainly before Mary's accession to the throne of England, this play is the earliest extant specimen of the History, which was reserved for such high treatment at the hands of Marlowe and Shakspere. King John plays the chief part, and the legend of his death by poison is followed. But the interesting feature of the performance is that personifications, including the Nobility, the Clergy, Civil Order, the Commonalty, Verity and Imperial Majesty, are introduced in dialogue with real historical beings. The Vice too, under the name of Sedition, plays his usual pranks, while Dissimulation hatches the plot of the king's murder. 'King Johan' must be read less as a history-drama than as a pamphlet against Papal encroachment and ecclesiastical corruption. But it has some vigorous and some tolerably amusing scenes, and contains the following very curious old wassail song :

> Wassail, wassail, out of the milk pail ;
> Wassail, wassail, as white as my nail ;
> Wassail, wassail, in snow, frost, and hail
> Wassail, wassail, with partridge and rail ;
> Wassail, wassail, that much doth avail ;
> Wassail, wassail, that never will fail.

Besides this piece, John Bale wrote a Moral Play in seven parts, with the title of 'God's Merciful Promises,' and two sacred plays on 'The Temptation of our Lord' and 'John Baptist,' both of which are survivals from the elder Miracles These are in print. Others of the same description by his hand remain in MS.

The anonymous tragedy of 'Appius and Virginia' is a dramatised version of the Roman legend which had previously. been handled by Chaucer in his 'Doctor of Physic's Tale.' A leading part is assigned to the Vice, Haphazard; and allegorical personages, Conscience, Rumour, Comfort, Reward, Memory, and Doctrine, are intermingled with the mortal personages. The same hybrid character distinguishes Preston's 'Cambyses.' Here, the Vice is styled Ambidexter; and a crowd of abstractions jostle with clowns and courtiers —Huff and Ruff, Hob and Lob, Smirdis and Sisamnes, Praxaspes and the Queen. Neither of these clumsy attempts at tragedy invites a close analysis. It is enough to have mentioned them as intermediate growths between the Moral Play and the emancipated drama.

CHAPTER V

THE RISE OF COMEDY

I. Specific Nature of the Interlude—John Heywood—The Farce of 'Johan the Husband'—'The Pardoner and the Friar.'—II. Heywood's Life and Character.—III. Analysis of 'The Four P's'—Chaucerian Qualities of Heywood's Talent.—IV. Nicholas Udall and 'Ralph Roister Doister'—Its Debt to Latin Comedy.—V. John Still—Was He the Author of 'Gammer Gurton's Needle'?—Farcical Character of this Piece—Diccon the Bedlam.—VI. Reasons for the Early Development of Comedy.

N.B. The three pieces reviewed in this chapter will be found in Hazlitt's *Dodsley*, vols. i. and iii.

I

THE passage from Moral Plays to Comedy had been virtually effected in such pieces as 'Calisto and Meliboea' and 'The Disobedient Child,' both of which are wrought without the aid of allegories. In dealing with the origins of the Drama, it would, however, be impossible to omit one specifically English form of comedy, which appeared contemporaneously with the later Moralities, and to which the name of Interlude has been attached. The Interlude, in this restricted sense of the term, was the creation of John Heywood, a genial writer in whom the spirit of Chaucer seems to have lived again. In some of his productions, as 'The Play of the Weather' and 'The Play of Love,' he adhered to the type of the Morality. Others are simple dialogues, corresponding in form to the Latin Disputationes, of which mention has been made above. But three considerable pieces, 'The Merry Play between Johan the Husband, Tyb his Wife, and Sir John the Priest, 'The Four P's,' and 'The Merry Play between the Pardoner and the Friar, the Curate and Neighbour Pratt,' detach themselves from any previous species, and constitute a class apart. The first is a simple farce, in which a henpecked husband sits by fasting, while his wife and the jovial parish priest make a good meal on the pie which was provided for the dinner of the family. It contains abundance of broad humour, and plenty of coarse satire on the equivocal position occupied by the parson in Johan's household. The third has no plot of any kind. Its point consists in the rivalry between a Pardoner and a Friar, who try to preach each other down in church, vaunting their own spiritual wares with voluble and noisy rhetoric. The speeches are so managed that when the Pardoner has begun a sentence, it is immediately intercepted by the Friar, with a perpetual crescendo of mutual interruptions and confusing misconstructions, till the competition ends in a downright bout at fisticuffs. Then the Curate interferes, protesting that his church shall not be made the theatre of such a scandal. He calls Pratt to his assistance; and each of them tackles one of the antagonists. But Pratt and the Curate find themselves too hardly matched; and at length they send both Pardoner and Friar to the devil with the honours of the fray pretty equally divided. It may be incidentally mentioned that Heywood has incorporated some fifty lines of Chaucer's 'Pardoner's Prologue' almost verbatim in the exordium of his Pardoner —a proof, if any proof were needed, of the close link between his art and that of the father of English poetry.

II

John Heywood was a Londoner, and a choir boy of the Chapel Royal.[1] When his voice broke, he proceeded in due course to Oxford, and studied at Broadgate Hall, now Pem-

---

[1] I take this on the faith of Mr. Julian Sharman's Introduction to his edition of *The Proverbs of John Heywood* (London: George Bell, 1874). Heywood is there stated to have held a place among the Children of the Chapel in 1515. It is not altogether easy, however, to bring this detail into harmony with the little that we know about his early life, especially with the circumstance that he owned land at North Mims.

broke College. Sir John More befriended him, and took a kindly interest, we hear, in the composition of his first work, a collection of epigrams. Early in his life Heywood obtained a fixed place at Court in connection with the exhibition of Interludes and Plays. It is probably due to this fact that he has been reckoned among the King's jesters; and if he was not actually a Yorick of the Tudor Court, there is no doubt that he played a merry part there, and acquired considerable wealth by the exercise of his wit. After Henry's death he fell under suspicion of disaffection to the Government, and only escaped, says Sir John Harrington, 'the jerk of the six-stringed whip' by special exercise of Edward's favour. Heywood was a staunch Catholic, and his offence seems to have been a too sturdy denial of the royal supremacy in spiritual affairs. When Mary came to the throne, he was recalled to Court, where he exercised his dramatic talents for the Queen's amusement, and lived on terms of freedom with her nobility. After Mary's death, being a professed enemy of the Reformed Church, Heywood left England, and died about the year 1565 at Mechlin. One of his sons, Jasper Heywood, played a part of some importance in the history of our drama, as we shall see when the attempted classical revival comes to be discussed.

The vicissitudes of Heywood's life are not without their interest in connection with his Interludes. During the religious changes of four reigns, he continued faithful to the creed of his youth. Yet, though he suffered disgrace and exile for the Catholic faith, he showed himself a merciless satirist of Catholic corruptions. Though he was a professional jester, gaining his livelihood and taking his position in society as a recognised mirth-maker, he allowed no considerations of personal profit to cloud his conscience. He remained an Englishman to the backbone, loyal to his party and his religious convictions, outspoken in his condemnation of the superstitions which disgraced the Church of his adoption. This manliness of attitude, this freedom from time-service, this fearless exposure of the weak points in a creed to which he sacrificed his worldly interests, give a dignity to Heywood's character, and prepossess us strongly in favour of his writings. Their tone, like that of the man, is homely, masculine, downright, and English, in the shrewdness of the wit, the soundness of the sense, and the jovial mirth which pervades each scene.

III

The 'Four P's,' which I propose to examine more closely, is an excellent comic dialogue. More than this it cannot claim to be; for it has no intrigue, and aims at the exhibition of characters by contrast and collocation, not by action. Its motive is a witty situation, and its *dénouement* is a single humorous saying. Thus this Interlude has not the proportions of a play, although its dialogue exhibits far more life, variety, and spirit than many later and more elaborate creations of the English stage. It is written in pure vernacular, terse and racy if rude, and undefiled by classical pedantry or Italianising affectation. Heywood, here as elsewhere, reminds us of Chaucer without his singing robes. As Charles Lamb called his namesake Thomas Heywood a prose Shakspere, so might we style John Heywood a prose Chaucer. The humour which enchants us in the 'Canterbury Tales,' and which we claim as specifically English, emerges in Heywood's dialogue, less concentrated and blent with neither pathos nor poetic fancy, yet still indubitably of the genuine sort.

The Four P's are four representative personages, well known to the audience of Heywood's day. They are the Palmer, the Pardoner, the Poticary, and the Pedlar. The Palmer might be described as a professional pilgrim. He made it his business to travel on foot all through his life from shrine to shrine, subsisting upon alms, visiting all lands in Europe and beyond the seas where saints were buried, praying at their tombs, seeking remission for his sins through their intercessions and entrance into Paradise by the indulgence granted to pilgrims at these holy places.[1] His

---

[1] Dante defines a Palmer thus in the *Vita Nuova* : ' Chiamansi *Palmieri* inquanto vanno oltra mare, laonde molte volte recano la

wanderings only ended with his death. Pardoners are described in an old English author as 'certain fellows that carried about the Pope's Indulgences, and sold them to such as would buy them.'[1] Since this was a very profitable trade, it behoved the purchasers of their wares, which, besides Indulgences, were generally relics of saints, rosaries, and amulets, to see that their credentials were in order ; for, even supposing, if that were possible, that a Pardoner could be an honest man, and his genuine merchandise be worth the money paid for it, who could be sure that impostors, deriving no countenance from the Roman Curia, were not abroad? Therefore all Pardoners displayed Bulls and spiritual passports from the Popes, which, if duly executed and authenticated, empowered them to sell salvation at so much the groat. The difficulty of testing these credentials put wary folk in much perplexity. Ariosto has used this motive in a humorous scene of one of his best comedies, where a would-be purchaser of pardon insists on taking the friar's Bull to his parish priest for verification.[2] Chaucer alludes to the custom of Pardoners exhibiting their Bulls, in the exordium of his 'Pardoner's Tale,' and Heywood in the Interlude of 'The Pardoner and the Friar' makes merry for many pages with the same motive.[3] The sale of Indulgences, as is well known, brought large profits to the Papal exchequer; and when the extravagance of Leo X. plunged him into deep financial difficulties, his eagerness to stimulate this source of revenue drove Germany into the schism of the Reformation. While S. Peter's was being built with commissions upon pardons, Luther was taunting the laity with 'buying such cheap rubbish at so dear a price.'

---

palma : *Peregrini,* inquanto vanno alla casa di Galizia ; *Romei* inquanto vanno a Roma.' In England a distinction was drawn between Palmers and Pilgrims. 'The pilgrim had some home or dwelling-place ; but the palmer had none. The pilgrim travelled to some certain designed place or places; but the palmer to all. The pilgrim went at his own charges ; but the palmer professed wilful poverty, and went upon alms,' &c. See Note 2 to p. 331 of Hazlitt's *Dodsley,* vol. i.

[1] Hazlitt's *Dodsley,* i. 343, Note 2.
[2] *Scolastica,* Act iv. Scene 4.
[3] See Hazlitt's *Dodsley,* vol. i. pp. 212–223.

Chaucer's portrait of the Pardoner forms so good a frontispiece to Heywood's Interlude, that a quotation from it may be here acceptable:

> This pardoner hadde heer as yelwe as wex,
> But smothe it heng, as doth a strike of flex;
> By unces hynge his lokkes that he hadde,
> And therewith he his schuldres overspradde.
> Ful thinne it lay, by culpons on and oon;
> But hood, for jolitee, ne werede he noon.
>   *   *   *   *   *
> A voys he hadde as smal as eny goot.
> No berd ne hadde he, ne nevere scholde have,
> As smothe it was as it were late i-schave.
>   *   *   *   *   *
> But trewely to tellen atte laste,
> He was in churche a noble ecclesiaste.
> Wel cowde he rede a lessoun or a storye,
> But altherbest he sang an offertorie.

The Poticary, or Apothecary, and the Pedlar require no special introduction to a modern audience. Both are much the same in our days as in those of Queen Mary—the Pedlar with his pack stuffed full of gauds and gear for women; the Poticary taking life as a philosopher inclined to materialism.

The scene opens with a monologue of the Palmer. He recites a long list of the shrines which he has visited:

> I am a Palmer, as ye see,
> Which of my life much part have spent
> In many a fair and far country:
> As Pilgrims do, of good intent.
> At Jerusalem have I been
> Before Christ's blessed sepulchre:
> The Mount of Calvary have I seen,
> A holy place, you may be sure.
> To Jehosaphat and Olivet
> On foot, God wot, I went right bare:
> Many a salt tear did I sweat,
> Before my carcase could come there.
> Yet have I been at Rome also,
> And gone the stations all a-row;
> S. Peter's shrine and many mo,
> Than, if I told all, ye do know.

Beginning with the holiest places, Jerusalem and Rome, he runs through the whole bede roll of inferior oracles, until he comes to:

> Our Lady that standeth in the oak.

While he is still vaunting the extent of his excursions, as a modern globe-trotter might do, the Pardoner breaks in upon him:

> And when ye have gone as far as ye can,
> For all your labour and ghostly intent,
> Ye will come home as wise as ye went.

This ruffles the Palmer's pride and self-esteem. Is the fame of his achievement nothing? Is the palm for which he has been travailing, of no avail? The Pardoner says: Nay, your object was a worthy one; the saving of your soul is a great matter; it is not for a man of my trade to cheapen his own wares. But consider the thing calmly:

> Now mark in this what wit ye have,
> To seek so far, and help so nigh!
> Even here at home is remedy;
> For at your door myself doth dwell,
> Who could have saved your soul as well
> As all your wide wandering shall do,
> Though ye went thrice to Jericho.

This is the very argument which the Pardoning Friar in Ariosto's 'Scolastica' uses to Don Bartolo. That conscience-burdened jurisconsult was minded to make a pilgrimage to Compostella for his soul's peace. The Friar told him he was little better than a fool. By laying out on pardons considerably less than his journey money, he might stay at home and be saved at ease. The Palmer in our Interlude makes much the same reply to the Pardoner as Don Bartolo made to the Friar:

> Right seldom is it seen, or never,
> That truth and pardoners dwell together.
> For be your pardons never so great,

Yet them to enlarge ye will not let
With such lies that ofttimes, Christ wot,
Ye seem to have that ye have not.
Wherefore I went myself to the self thing
In every place, and without saying
Had as much pardon there assuredly,
As ye can promise me here doubtfully.

The Palmer preferred the real article—pardons at the shrine, however toilfully obtained, to pardons signed and sealed by Papal licences. He was in the position of an invalid who travels to drink the waters at the spring, instead of taking them corked and bottled in his sick-room. In spite of brands upon the cork and labels on the bottle, those mineral waters are so often manufactured! This metaphor will hold good for the whole business of pardoning. Special virtue emanated from the bodies of martyrs, relics of confessors, tombs of saints, the person of the Pope himself in Rome. These were the salutiferous fountains, where gout and leprosy of soul were cured. At first it was reckoned indispensable to drink those spiritual waters at the source. But the princes of the Church, like the possessors of the Carlsbad or S. Moritz springs, soon perceived what means of profit lay within their grasp. To draw off the virtues of the saints, to tap the apostolic spring of grace perennially flowing from S. Peter's chair, to cork them up in flasks and phials at Rome, and to label them with Papal Bulls, was easy and convenient. Everybody profited by the transaction. The waters of salvation were brought to the sick soul's door by agents who returned a handsome profit to the owners, after pocketing a fair commission for themselves. But who could be certain that the bottled Carlsbad, or the S. Moritz, warranted to stimulate a drooping faith, were genuine? There lay the difficulty. And until the world was satisfied upon this point, which in plain truth it could never be, hardier invalids, like our Palmer, preferred to travel to the holy wells themselves.

The Pardoner, in his turn, is not unreasonably nettled by the Palmer's sneers. If it be a question of truth or untruth, says he, your traveller's tales are at least as likely to be spurious as my Indulgences:

> I say yet again my pardons are such,
> That if there were a thousand souls on heap,
> I would bring them to heaven as good cheap
> As ye have brought yourself on pilgrimage
> In the least quarter of your voyage,—
> Which is far aside heaven, by God!
> There your labour and pardon is odd.
> With small cost and without any pain,
> These pardons bring them to heaven plain:
> Give me but a penny or two pence,
> And as soon as the soul departeth hence,
> In half an hour, or three-quarters at the most,
> The soul is in heaven with the Holy Ghost.

No sooner has the sleek charlatan made this astonishing assertion, than a third personage, starting up at his elbow, puts a word in very quietly.

> Send ye any souls to heaven by water?

This is the Poticary, who, observing that the Pardoner and Palmer are disputing which of them sends souls the quickest and the safest way to heaven, puts in a word for his own profession. Few folk came into the world without a midwife: few go out of it without a Poticary. Thieves, indeed, are hanged. But, quoth he:

> Whom have ye known die honestly,
> Without help of the Poticary?

The contention, like a fugue or canon, has now three voices in full cry, pursuing the same theme; when a fourth joins in. This is the Pedlar. His entrance occasions a pause and a momentary diversion; for he has to show his wares: and his wares suggest a somewhat unedifying but humorous debate on women. After this excursion into a region of discourse where tongues of men are wont to wag, the three disputants return to their original contention; and the Pedlar undertakes to play the part of umpire. Having no

experience in spiritual things, he suggests that each of the
plaintiffs should make trial of his skill in a matter, of which
all alike are masters, and he is eminently qualified to judge.
Let them tell lies against each other.

> Now have I found one mastery,
> That ye can do indifferently ;
> And is neither selling nor buying,
> But even on very lying.
> And all ye three can lie as well
> As can the falsest devil in hell.
> And though, afore, ye heard me grudge
> In greater matters to be your judge,
> Yet in lying I can some skill,
> And if I shall be judge, I will.

The two competitors assent to the fairness of this proposal.
But before they proceed to trial, Heywood contrives to introduce a burlesque scene, which serves to bring the Pardoner
and Poticary into strong contrast. As the Pedlar had exhibited
the contents of his pack—points, pin-cases, gloves, laces,
thimbles, and so forth ; so now the Pardoner undoes his
wallet and produces the relics it contains. The pursy rogue,
who thrives on superstition and half believes his own impos-
tures, brings to sight

> Of All Hallows' the blessed jawbone . . .
> The great toe of the Trinity . . .
> The bees that stang Eve under the forbidden tree . . .
> A buttock-bone of Pentecost . . .

and many more absurdities, on which the Poticary, as a man
of sense and science, passes caustic sceptical remarks. When
the toe, for instance, is held up to admiration, he observes :

> I pray you turn that relic about !
> Either the Trinity had the gout,
> Or else, because it is three toes in one,
> God made it as much as three toes alone.

The Pardoner, too merry to be much offended, points out that
this relic would be handy for a man with the toothache. He

might roll it in his mouth. But the Poticary, with the
scepticism which has always marked the medical profession,
prefers his own drugs to these unsavoury panaceas. This
gives him an opportunity of displaying his medicine chest,
which he does with comical bravado, winding up with an
attempt to bribe the judge by the offer of a box of mar-
malade.

The Pedlar protests his incorruptibility, and the plaintiffs
fall to their contention in good earnest. The Poticary is within
an ace of winning the cause by assault. His first shot is a
fair one ; for, turning to the Pedlar, he exclaims :

> Forsooth, ye be an honest man !

This wakes the fugue up, and the trial is carried briskly on
upon the theme suggested by the obviously false imputation
of honesty to the Pedlar. Arguments on all three sides are
subtly pleaded ; but the umpire expresses his inability to decide
the suit in this way. Each of the contending parties must
tell some tale :

> And which of you telleth most marvel,
> And most unlikest to be true,
> Shall most prevail, whatever ensue.

The Poticary starts with an extraordinary cure he made ;
too gross in details for discussion.[1]

The Pardoner takes up with the far better tale of how he
saved the soul

> Of one departed within this seven year,
> A friend of mine, and likewise I
> To her again was as friendly.

The poor woman had died suddenly without ghostly comfort
or viaticum of any sort. Her sad case weighed heavily upon
the Pardoner's conscience ; and bethinking him how many
souls he had saved in his day, the least he could do was to

---

[1] The humour of this cure is of an American type. Its point consists
in a comical exaggeration of the effect produced by common causes
playing on the sense of space.

go to Purgatory and look after her.   When he arrived there,
he was right welcome ; bnt he could not find his friend :

> Then feared I much it was not well ;
> Alas ! thought I, she is in hell ;
> For with her life I was so acquainted,
> That sure I thought she was not sainted.

So after scattering a few pardons, and helping out a kindly
soul who blessed him when he chanced to sneeze, the Pardoner proceeded on his journey to hell-gate.   The porter, as
it happened, was an old acquaintance :

> He knew me well, and I at last
> Remembered him since long time past :
> For, as good hap would have it chance,
> This devil and I were of old acquaintance ;
> For oft, in the play of ' Corpus Christi,'
> He hath played the devil at Coventry.

By the help of this opportune friend at court, the Pardoner
received a safe-conduct from head-quarters, and was introduced
at a favourable moment to the great Duke of Hell.   It was
the anniversary of Lucifer's fall from heaven, and the devils
were keeping high tide and festival :

> This devil and I walked arm in arm
> So far till he had brought me thither,
> Where all the devils of hell together
> Stood in array in such apparel
> As for that day there meetly fell :—
> Their horns well gilt, their claws full clean,
> Their tails well kempt, and, as I ween,
> With sothery butter their bodies anointed :
> I never saw devils so well appointed !
> The master-devil sat in his jacket,
> And all the souls were playing at racket :
> None other rackets they had in hand
> Save every soul a good firebrand ;
> Wherewith they played so prettily
> That Lucifer laughed merrily,
> And all the residue of the fiends
> Did laugh thereat full well like friends,

The Pardoner looked around for his friend, but could not find
her, and durst not yet ask after her.   An usher then brought
him into the presence of Lucifer, who received him
graciously :

> By Saint Anthony
> He smiled on me well-favouredly,
> Bending his brows as broad as barn-doors,
> Shaking his ears as rugged as burrs,
> Rolling his eyes as round as two bushels,
> Flashing the fire out of his nostrils,
> Gnashing his teeth so vaingloriously
> That methought time to fall to flattery.

Neither low obeisance nor seasonable panegyric did the
Pardoner spare ; and after some preliminary colloquy, he
ventured to unfold the object of his visit :

> I am a Pardoner,
> And over souls as controller
> Throughout the earth my power doth stand,
> Where many a soul lieth on my hand,
> That speed in matters as I use them,
> As I receive them or refuse them.

Such being the authority of his office, he proposes to exchange
the soul of any wight alive the devil chooses for that of his
friend.   Lucifer agrees :

> Ho, ho ! quoth the devil, we are well pleased !
> What is his name thou wouldst have eased ?
> Nay, quoth I, be it good or evil,
> My coming is for a she devil.
> What call'st her, quoth he, thou whoreson ?
> Forsooth, quoth I, Margery Corson.

This demure and casual introduction of the woman's name
strikes one as highly comic, after so much preparation ; and
the immediate effect produced is no less dramatic.   Lucifer
forgets all about the bargain, and swears that not a devil in
hell shall withhold her :

> And if thou wouldest have twenty mo,
> Wer 't not for justice, they should go !

> For all we devils within this den
> Have more to do with two women
> Than with all the charge we have beside.

He therefore begs the Pardoner, by good-will and fellowship, to leave the men to their sins, and to apply all his pardons in future to womankind, in order that hell at least may be rid of the sex. Margery had been drafted into the kitchen, and there the Pardoner found her, spitting the meat, basting and roasting it.

> But when she saw this brought to pass,
> To tell the joy wherein she was,
> And of all the devils, for joy how they
> Did roar at her delivery,
> And how the chains in hell did ring,
> And how all the souls therein did sing,
> And how we were brought to the gate,
> And how we took our leave thereat,
> Be sure lack of time suffereth not
> To rehearse the twentieth part of that !

The gratification afforded by the Pardoner's story almost distracts attention from its lie. The Pedlar comments on the danger of the journey. The Palmer takes it seriously ; but one point, he says, perplexes him. He cannot understand why women have such bad characters in hell. He has wandered over earth and sea, and visited every town in Christendom :

> And this I would ye should understand,
> I have seen women five hundred thousand ;
> And oft with them have long time tarried,
> Yet in all places where I have been,
> Of all the women that I have seen,
> I never saw or knew in my conscience
> Any one woman out of patience.

Thus quietly, and with this force of earnest asseveration, does the largest and most palpable lie leap out of the Palmer's lips. The plaintiffs and the judge are unanimous :

> *Poticary*
> By the mass, there is a great lie !

Pardoner

I never heard a greater, by our Lady!

Pedlar

A greater! Nay, know ye any so great?

It only remains for the Pedlar to pass judgment, and to assign the prize of victory to the Palmer. This he does at some length, discoursing with comical details upon the composition of woman's character, and demonstrating how shrewishness, whatever other qualities may co-exist, is a fixed element in every member of the female sex. The Interlude concludes with a sound and wholesome homily from the stout-hearted old author, put into the Pedlar's mouth, whereby he expounds his own views about the right use of pilgrimage and pardons, and lectures the materialistic apothecary upon the necessity of saving virtues. Thus the fun of the piece is turned to good doctrine at its close.

I have indulged myself in a detailed analysis of Heywood's Interlude, and in copious quotations, partly because of its intrinsic excellence, but more especially because it is unique as a dramatic composition of the purest English style, unmodified by erudite or foreign elements. It presents the England of the pre-Renaissance and pre-Reformation period with singular vivacity and freshness; the merry England which had still a spark of Chaucer's spirit left, an echo of his lark-like morning song. The Drama was not destined to expand precisely on the lines laid down by Heywood. Indeed, a very few years made his Interlude almost as archaic to the men of Elizabeth's reign as it is to us. Italian and classical influences were already at work in the elaboration of a different type of art. Still the vigour of this piece is so superabundant, that to neglect it would be to leave out of account the chief factor—native dramatic faculty—which rendered our playwrights in the modern style superior to those of Italy or France.

IV

Two formal comedies of an early date may be fitly included in this study. These are 'Ralph Roister Doister' and 'Gammer Gurton's Needle.' Heywood's 'Four P's' was written, in all probability, soon after the year 1530. 'Roister Doister' had been produced to the public before 1550. 'Gammer Gurton' was acted at Cambridge in 1566. These dates bring three epoch-making compositions in the comic art almost within the compass of a quarter of a century. No serious dramatic essays, tragedies, or histories, of like artistic excellence existed at that period.

To combine a skilfully constructed fable with Heywood's character-delineation was all that comedy required to bring it to maturity. This union Nicholas Udall effected in his 'Ralph Roister Doister.' The author of this, the first regular comedy in the English language, was born about 1505 in Hampshire. He was a Protestant throughout his life, and won some scholarly distinction by translating portions of the Paraphrase of the New Testament by Erasmus. While a student at Oxford, Udall enjoyed Leland's intimacy. Bale praised him for his learning and accomplishments. For some time he held the head mastership of Eton College, which he had to resign on a charge, not fully proved, of conniving at a robbery of College plate. He died in 1556, having been for a few years before his death head master of Westminster School. This sketch of Udall's biography prepares us for the taste, propriety of treatment, and just proportions which we find in his dramatic work. 'Ralph Roister Doister,' however unpromising its title may be, is the composition of a scholar, who has studied Terence and Plautus to good purpose. From the Latin playwrights Udall learned how to construct a plot, and to digest the matter of his fable into five acts. The same models of style gave him that ease of movement and simplicity of diction which make his work, in spite of superficial archaisms, classical. In 'Roister Doister' we emerge from medieval grotesquery and allegory into the clear

light of actual life, into an agreeable atmosphere of urbanity
and natural delineation. Udall avoided the error of imitating
his Roman master too closely. He neither borrowed his
fable nor his persons, as was the wont of the Italian comedians, straight from Plautus. His play is founded, indeed,
upon the 'Miles Gloriosus'; but it is free from that un-
pleasant taint of unreality which mars the *Commedia erudita*
of the Florentines. The antique plot has been accommodated
to a simple episode of English life among people of the comfortable middle class. The hero, Ralph Doister, is a braggart
and a coward; well to do, but foolish in his use of wealth;
boastful before proof, but timid in the hour of trial; ridicu-
lously vain of his appearance, with a trick of dangling after
any woman whom chance throws in his way. A parasite and
boon companion, called Matthew Merigreek, turns him round
his finger by alternate flatteries and bullyings. This character
Udall owed to the Latin theatre; but he combined the popular
qualities of the Vice with the conventional attributes of the
classic parasite, contriving at the same time to create a real
personage, who would have been at home in ordinary English
households. The name Merigreek seems to point to Juvenal's
'Græculus Esuriens'; it has also something in common with
the abstract titles of the Vice in the Moralities. This clever
knave discovers that Ralph is in love with a widow, Dame
Custance, who is betrothed to the merchant Gawin Goodluck.
While Goodluck is away upon a voyage, Ralph and Merigreek
pester the widow with love-letters, tokens, serenades, and
visits. Her opinion of Ralph is that he is a contemptible
coxcomb, not worth an honest woman's notice. She therefore
treats his wooing as a joke; but finding that she cannot
shake him off, makes the best fun she can out of the circumstances. This gives a colour of familiarity to his attentions;
and a servant of Goodluck's appearing suddenly upon the scene
while Ralph's courtship is in full progress, arouses his master's
jealousy. Dame Custance is now placed in a difficult position,
from which she is finally extricated by the testimony of an
old friend, who was acquainted with her behaviour in the
matter, and also by the cowardly admissions of the simpleton

Ralph. Thus this slight story contains the principal elements of a comedy—ridiculous as well as serious characters; laughable incidents; temporary misunderstandings; a perplexity in the fourth act; and a happy adjustment of all difficulties by the self-exposure of the mischief-making braggart. The conduct of the piece is spirited and easy. The author's art, though refined by scholarship, is homely. Between 'Ralph Roister Doister' and 'The Merry Wives of Windsor' there is, in point of construction and conception, no immeasurable distance, although the one play is the work of mediocrity, the other of genius.

V

'Gammer Gurton's Needle' has been hitherto ascribed, on slender but not improbable grounds of inference, to John Still. He was a native of Lincolnshire, who received his education at Christ's College, Cambridge. After enjoying a canonry at Westminster and the masterships of S. John's and Trinity at Cambridge, he was promoted to the Bishopric of Bath and Wells in 1592. His effigy may still be seen beneath its canopy in Wells Cathedral. A grim Puritan divine, with pointed beard and long stiff painted robes, lies face-upward on the monument. This is the author of the first elaborately executed farce in our language. 'Gammer Gurton's Needle' is a humorous and vulgar picture of the lowest rustic manners, dashed in with coarse bold strokes in telling realistic style. Its chief merit as a play is the crescendo of its interest, ending in a burlesque *dénouement*. Unlike 'Ralph Roister Doister,' it has no plot, properly so called, and owes nothing to the Latin stage. We may rather regard it as a regular development from one of the comic scenes interpolated in the Miracles. Gammer Gurton loses her needle; and Diccon the Bedlam, who is peeping and prying about the cottage, accuses Dame Chat, the alewife, of stealing it. This sets all the village by the ears. One by one the various authorities, parson, baily, constables, are drawn into the medley. Heads are broken; ancient feuds are exacerbated; the confusion seems hopeless, when the needle is found sticking in the breeches of Hodge, the Gammer's farm-servant. Diccon the Bedlam, who raised and controlled the storm, may be compared to the Vice of the Moralities, inasmuch as all the action turns upon him. But he has nothing in common with abstractions. He is a vigorously executed portrait of a personage familiar enough in England at that epoch. After the dissolution of the monasteries, no provision was made for the poor folk who used to live upon their doles. A crowd of idle and dissolute beggars were turned loose upon the land, to live upon their wits. The cleverer of these affected madness, and got the name of Bedlam Beggars, Abraham Men, and Poor Toms. Shakspere has described them in ' King Lear ' :

> The country gives me proof and precedent,
> Of bedlam beggars who, with roaring voices,
> Strike in their numbed and mortified bare arms,
> Pins, wooden pricks, nails, sprigs of rosemary,
> And with this horrible object from low farms,
> Poor pelting villages, sheepcotes, and mills,
> Sometimes with lunatic bans, sometimes with prayers,
> Enforce their charity.

Dekker in one of his tracts introduces us to the confraternity of wandering rogues in the following curious passage : ' Of all the mad rascals, that are of this wing, the Abraham Man is the most fantastic. The fellow that sat half-naked at table to-day, from the girdle upwards, is the best Abraham Man that ever came to my house, and the notablest villain. He swears he hath been in Bedlam, and will talk frantically of purpose. You see pins stuck in sundry places of his naked flesh, especially in his arms, which pain he gladly puts himself to (being indeed no torment at all, his skin is either so dead with some foul disease or so hardened with weather) only to make you believe he is out of his wits. He calls himself by the name of Poor Tom, and coming near anybody cries out, " Poor Tom is a-cold ! " ' These vagrants wandered up and down the country, roosting in hedge-rows, creeping into barns, extorting bacon from farm-servants by intimidation, amusing the company in rural inns by their mad jests, stealing and bullying, working upon superstition, pity, terror, or the love of the ridiculous in all from whom they could obtain a livelihood. How Shakspere used this character to heighten the tragedy of 'Lear,' requires no comment. Still employed the same character in working out a purely farcical intrigue. His Diccon is simply a clever and amusing vagabond.

It is worthy of notice that 'Gammer Gurton's Needle' was played at Christ's College, with the sanction of the authorities, in 1566. We might wonder how grave scholars could appreciate the buffoonery of this coarse art, which has neither the intrigue of Latin comedy nor the polish of classic style to recommend it. Yet, if the intellectual conditions of the time are taken into account, our wonder will rather be that 'Roister Doister' should have been written than that 'Gammer Gurton' should have been enjoyed. The fine arts had no place in England. Literature hardly existed, and the study of the classics was as yet confined to a few scholars. Formal logic and the philosophy of the schoolmen occupied the graver thoughts of academical students. When those learned men abandoned themselves to mirth, they relished obscenity and grossness with the same gusto as the cheese and ale and onions of their supper table. Nor let it be forgotten that the urbane Pope of the House of Medici, the pupil of Poliziano, the patron of Raphael, could turn from Beroaldo's 'Tacitus' and Bembo's courtly elegiacs, to split his sides with laughing at Bibbiena's ribaldries. Allowing for the differences between Italy and England, the 'Calandria' is hardly more refined than 'Gammer Gurton's Needle.' Beneath its classical veneer and smooth Italian varnish, it hides as coarse a view of human nature and a nastier fable.

VI

There are many reasons why Comedy should have preceded Tragedy in the evolution of our Drama. The comic scenes, which formed a regular department of the Miracle, allowed themselves to be detached from the whole scheme.

From the first they were extraneous to the sacred subject-matter of those Pageants; and after passing through the intermediate stage of the Morality, they readily blent with Latin models (as in the case of ' Roister Doister '), and no less readily settled into the form of the five-act farce (as in the case of ' Gammer Gurton '). Comedy attracts an uninstructed audience more powerfully than Tragedy. Of this we have plenty of evidence in our own days; when 'the better vulgar' crowd the Music Halls, and gather to Burlesques, but barely lounge at fashion's beck to a Shaksperian Revival. Comedy of the average type can be more easily invented than Tragedy. It appeals to a commoner intelligence. It deals with more familiar motives. Lastly, but by no means least, it makes far slighter demands upon the capacity of actors. Passing over into caricature, it is not only tolerable, but oftentimes enhanced in effect. Whereas Tragedy, hyperbolised—Herod out-Heroding Herod, Ercles' and Cambyses' vein—becomes supremely ridiculous to those very sympathies which Tragedy appeals to. Among the Northern nations grotesqueness was indigenous. They found buffoonery ready to their hand. For the statelier and sterner forms of dramatic art, models were needed. What the Teutonic genius originated in the serious style, was epical; connected with the minstrel's rather than the jongleur's skill. Comedy, again, was better fitted than Tragedy to fill up the spaces of a banquet or to crown a revel. The jongleurs and jugglers, who descended from the Roman histriones, had their proper place in medieval society; and these jesters were essentially mimes. Comedy belonged of right to them. Every daïs in the hall of manor-house or castle had from immemorial time furnished forth a comic stage. The Court-fools were public characters. Sumner, Will Kempe, Tarleton, and Wilson were as well known to our ancestors of the sixteenth century as Garrick and the Kembles to our great-grandfathers. The occasional and extemporaneous jesting of these men passed by degrees into settled types of presentation. They wrote, or had written for them, Merriments, which they enriched with sallies of the choicest gag, illustrated with movements of the most fantastic humour. When formal plays came into fashion by the labour of the learned, these professional comedians struck the key-note of character, and took a prominent part in all performances. From what we know about private or semi-private theatricals in our own days, we are able furthermore to comprehend how anxiously young gentlemen at College, or fashionable members of an Inn of Court, would imitate the gestures of a Tarleton ; how pliantly the scholar-playwright would adapt his leading comic motive to the humours of a Kempe. It was thus through many co-operating circumstances that Comedy took the start of Tragedy upon the English stage. The graver portions of the Miracles, the heavier parts of the Moral Plays, meanwhile, developed a school of acting which made Tragedy possible. The public by these antecedents were educated to tolerate a serious style of art. But the playwright's genius—adequate to a first-rate Interlude like the 'Four P's,' to a first-rate Comedy of manners like ' Roister Doister,' to a first-rate screaming farce like ' Gammer Gurton '—was still unequal to the task of a true tragic piece.

CHAPTER VI

THE RISE OF TRAGEDY

I. Classical Influence in England—The Revival of Learning—English Humanism—Ascham's ' Schoolmaster '—Italian Examples.—II. The Italian Drama—Paramount Authority of Seneca—Character of Seneca's Plays. — III. English Translations of Seneca—English Translations of Italian Plays.—IV. English Adaptations of the Latin Tragedy—Lord Brooke—Samuel Daniel—Translations from the French—Latin Tragedies—False Dramatic Theory.—V. 'Gorboduc' —Sir Philip Sidney's Eulogy of it—Lives of Sackville and Norton— General Character of this Tragedy—Its Argument—Distribution of Material—Chorus—Dumb Show—The Actors—Use of Blank Verse.— VI. 'The Misfortunes of Arthur'—Thomas Hughes and Francis Bacon—The Plot—Its Adaptation to the Græco-Roman Style of Tragedy—Part of Guenevora—The Ghost—Advance on 'Gorboduc' in Dramatic Force and Versification.—VII. Failure of this Pseudo-Classical Attempt—What it effected for English Tragedy.

N.B. The two chief tragedies discussed in this chapter will be found in the old Shakespeare Society's Publications, 1847, and in Hazlitt's *Dodsley*, vol. iv.

I

THE history of our Tragic Drama is closely connected with that of an attempt to fix the rules of antique composition on the playwright's art in England.   Up to the present point we have been dealing with those religious pageants, which the English shared in common with other European nations during the Middle Ages, and with a thoroughly native out-growth from them in our Moral Plays and Comedies.   The debt, already indicated, of ' Jack Juggler ' to the ' Amphi-tryon ' of Plautus, and that of ' Roister Doister ' to the ' Miles Gloriosus,' together with a very early English version of the ' Andria ' of Terence, prove, however, that classical studies were beginning to affect our theatre even in the period of its origins. To trace the further and far more pronounced influence of these studies on tragic poetry, will be the object of this chapter. I shall have to show in what way, when men of culture turned their attention to the stage, a determined effort was made to impose the canons of classical art, as they were then received in Southern Europe, on our playwrights; how the genius of the people proved too strong for the control of critics and ' courtly makers ; ' how the romantic drama triumphed over the pseudo-classic type of comedy and tragedy ; and how England, by these means, was delivered from a danger which threatened her theatre with a failure like to that of the Italian.

The Revival of Learning may be said to have begun in Italy early in the fourteenth century, when Petrarch, by his study of Cicero, and Boccaccio, by his exploration of Greek literature, prepared the way for discoverers of MSS. like Poggio and Filelfo, for founders of libraries like Nicholas V. and Cosimo de' Medici, for critics and translators like Lorenzo Valla, for poets like Poliziano, for editors like Aldus Manutius, and for writers on philosophy like Ficino and Cristofero Landino. A new type of education sprang up in the universities and schools of Italy, supplanting the medieval curriculum of Grammar, Rhetoric, and Logic by a wider and more genial study of the Greek and Latin authors. This education, reduced to a system by Vittorino da Feltre at Mantua, and developed in detail by wandering professors, who attracted scholars from all countries to their lectures in the universities of Padua and Bologna, Florence and Siena, rapidly spread over Europe. Grocin (1442–1519) and Linacre (1460–1524) transplanted the study of Greek from Italy to Oxford, whence it spread to Cambridge. The royal family and the great nobles of England, vying with the aristocracy of Mantua and Milan, instituted humanistic tutors for their sons and daughters. The children of Henry VIII., the Prince Edward and the Princesses Mary and Elizabeth, grew up accomplished in both ancient languages. Lady Jane Grey preferred the perusal of Plato's 'Phædo' in her study to a hunting party in her father's park. Queen Elizabeth at Windsor turned

from consultations with Cecil on the affairs of France and
Spain to read Demosthenes with Ascham. Sir Thomas More
at Westminster, Dean Colet at S. Paul's, Sir John Cheke at
Cambridge, and the illustrious foreign friends of these men,
among whom the first place must be given to Erasmus,
formed as brilliant a group of classical scholars, at the opening of the sixteenth century, as could be matched in Europe.
Meanwhile large sums were being spent on educational
foundations ; by Wolsey at Christ Church, by Edward VI. in
the establishment of grammar schools, by Colet in his
endowment of S. Paul's, and by numerous benefactors to
whom we owe our present system of high class public education. A race of excellent teachers sprang into notice, among
whom it may suffice to mention Nicholas Udall, Roger
Ascham, William Camden, Elmer the tutor of Lady Jane
Grey, and Cheke the lecturer on Greek at Cambridge.
English gentlemen, at this epoch, were scholars no less than
soldiers, men of whom the type is brilliantly represented by
Sir Walter Raleigh and Sir Philip Sidney. English gentle-
women shared the studies of their brothers ; and if a Lady
Jane Grey was rare, a Countess of Pembroke and a Princess
Mary may be taken as the leaders of a numerous class.[1]

Of the humanistic culture which prevailed in England, we
possess a vigorous and vivid picture in the ' Schoolmaster ' of
Ascham. Imported from Italy, where it had flourished for at
least a century before it struck its first roots in our soil, this
culture retained a marked Italian character. But in the
middle of the sixteenth century Italian scholarship had
already begun to decay. Learning, exclaimed Paolo Giovio,
is fled beyond the Alps. The more masculine branches of
erudition were neglected for academical frivolities. The study
of Greek languished. It seemed as though the Italians were
satiated and exhausted with the efforts and enthusiasms of
two centuries. In the North, curiosity was still keen. The

---

[1] See the note on female education by Nicholas Udall in his preface
to Erasmus' *Paraphrase of S. John*, translated together with him by the
Princess Mary and the Rev. F. Malet, D.D. It will be found in Prof.
Arber's Introductions to *Ralph Roister Doister*, p. 4.

speculative freedom of the Reformation movement kept the minds of men alert to studies which taxed intellectual energy. And though the methods of education, both in public schools and in private tuition, were borrowed from the practice of Italian professors, no class of professional rhetoricians corresponding to the Humanists corrupted English morals, no learned bodies like the academies of the South dictated laws to taste, or imposed puerilities on erudition. Society in general was far simpler; the Court purer; manners less artificial; religion more influential in controlling conduct. Sidney furnished a living illustration of Ascham's precepts; and no one who should compare the life of Sidney with that of a contemporary Italian of his class, would fail to appreciate the specifically English nature of this typical gentleman.

Still, though English culture was now independent, though English scholars held the keys of ancient learning and unlocked its treasures for themselves, though English thinkers drew their own philosophy from original sources, while the character of an accomplished Englishman differed from that of an Italian by superior manliness, simplicity, sincerity, and moral soundness; yet the example of Italy was felt in all departments of study, in every branch of intellectual activity. Three centuries ahead of us in mental training; with Dante, Petrarch, Boccaccio, Ariosto, and Tasso already on their list of classics; boasting a multifarious literature of novels, essays, comedies, pastorals, tragedies, and lyrics; with their great histories of Guicciardini and Machiavelli; with their political philosophy and metaphysical speculations; the Italians—as it was inevitable—swayed English taste, and moved the poets of England to imitation. Surrey and Wyat introduced the sonnet and blank verse from Italy into England. Spenser wrote the 'Faery Queen' under the influence of the Italian romantic epics. Raleigh could confer no higher praise on this great poem than to say that Petrarch's ghost, no less than Homer's, was moved thereby to weeping for his laurels. Sidney copied the Italians in his lyrics, and followed Sannazzaro in the 'Arcadia.' The bookstalls of London were flooded with translations of loose Italian novels, to such an extent that Ascham trembled for the morals of his countrymen.[1] Harrington's Ariosto, Fairfax's Tasso, Hoby's Cortigiano, proved that the finer products of Italian literature were not neglected. This absorbing interest in the creations of Italian genius was kept alive and stimulated by the almost universal habit of sending youths of good condition on an Italian journey. It was thought that residence for some months in the chief Italian capitals was necessary to complete a young man's education; and though jealous moralists might shake their heads, averring that English lads exchanged in Italy their learning for lewd living, their religious principles for atheism, their patriotism for Machiavellian subtleties, their simplicity for affectations in dress and manners, and their manliness for vices hitherto unknown in England, yet the custom continued to prevail, until at last, in the reign of the first Stuart, the English Court competed for the prize of immorality with the Courts of petty Southern princes.

II

Trained in classical studies, and addicted to Italian models, it was natural enough that those men of letters who sought to acclimatise the lyric poetry of the Italians, who translated their novels, and adopted the style of their romance, should not neglect the tragic drama. This had long ago established itself as a branch of the higher literature in Italy. Mussato in the first years of the fourteenth century, with his Latin tragedy on the history of Eccelino da Romano; Trissino in 1515, with his Italian 'Sofonisba;' Rucellai at the same epoch, with 'Rosmunda;' Speron Sperone, Cinthio Giraldi, Lodovico Dolce, Luigi Alamanni, Giannandrea dell'Anguillara Lodovico Martelli, in the next two decades, with their 'Canace,' 'Orbecche,' 'Giocasta,' 'Antigone,' 'Edippo,' 'Tullia;' all these Italian poets wrote, printed, and performed tragedies with vast applause upon the private and the courtly theatres

[1] See *Schoolmaster*, ed. Mayor, pp. 81. 82.

of Italy. That England should remain without such compositions, struck the 'courtly makers' as a paradox. The English had their own dramatic traditions, their companies of players, their interludes in the vernacular, their masques and morris-dances and pageants; in a word, all the apparatus necessary. It only remained for men of polite culture to engraft the roses of the classic and Italian styles upon this native briar. Reckoning after this fashion, but reckoning without their host, the public, as the sequel proved, courtiers and students at the Inns of Court began to pen tragedies. Under Italian guidance, they took the classics for their models. The authority of Italian playwrights, incompetent in such affairs, enslaved these well-intentioned persons to a classic of the silver age; to Seneca, instead of the great Attic authors. Every tragic scene which the Italians of the Renaissance set forth upon the boards of Rome or Florence or Ferrara, was a transcript from Seneca. Following this lead, our English scholars went to school with Seneca beneath the ferule of Italian ushers.

Seneca's collected works include eight complete tragedies, two fragments of tragic plays, and one complete piece in the same style, but posterior to the author. The eight dramas are: 'Hercules Furens,' 'Thyestes,' 'Phædra,' 'Œdipus,' the 'Troades,' 'Medea,' 'Agamemnon,' and 'Hercules upon Mount Œta.' The fragments of an Œdipus at Colonus and a Phœnissæ have been pieced together to make up a 'Thebais.' The later play, belonging to Seneca's tradition, is a tragedy upon the subject of Octavia. With the exception of the last, all these so-called dramas are a rhetorician's reproduction of Greek tragedies. Sophocles and Euripides, familiar to that rhetorician's learned audience, have been laid under contribution. But he has invented for himself a sphere of treatment, apart from the real drama, and apart from translation. It was Seneca's method to rehandle the world-worn matter of the Greek tragedians in the form of a dramatic commentary. Instead of placing characters upon the stage in conflict, he used his persons as mere mouthpieces for declamation and appropriate reflection. Instead

of developing the fable by action, he expanded the part of
the Messenger, and gave the rein to his descriptive faculty.
For a Roman audience, in the age of Nero, this new species
of dramatic poetry furnished a fresh kind of literary pleasure.
They had the old situations of Greek tragedy presented to
them indirectly, in long monologues adorned with sophistical
embroidery, in laboured descriptions, where the art of the
narrator brought events familiar to all students of Greek plays
and Græco-Roman painting forth in a new vehicle of polished
verse. Rhetoric and the idyll, philosophical analysis and
plastic art, forensic eloquence and scholastic disputation, were
skilfully applied to touch at a dramatic point the intellectual
sense of men and women trained by education and the habits
of imperial Roman life to all these forms. It is more than
doubtful whether the pseudo-tragedies produced upon this
plan were intended for scenical representation. We have
rather reason to believe that they found utterance in those
fashionable recitations, of which the Satirists have left sufficient notices. Roman ladies and gentlemen assembled at
each other's houses, in each other's gardens, in clubs and
coteries, to applaud a Statius declaiming his hexameters, or
the school of Seneca reciting their master's studies from the
Attic drama. An audience which could appreciate whole
books of the 'Pharsalia' or the 'Thebais' at a sitting, may
have gladly enough accepted one of Seneca's orations in two
hundred iambics. A tragedy recited was anyhow less tedious
than a declaimed epic.

Such, however, being the nature of Seneca's tragedies—
regarding them, as we are bound to do, in the light of a
decadent, pedantic, reproductive period of art—ascribing their
originality and merit to the author's sympathy with very
special intellectual conditions of his age—it follows that we
must condemn them as pernicious models for incipient literature. Pernicious undoubtedly they were in their effect upon
the Italian theatre. At its very outset the authority of
Seneca stifled tragedy and set tragedians on an utterly false
scent. The society of Italy in the sixteenth century had
certain points in common with that of Neronian Rome.

There was the same taste for pedantic studies, the same appreciation of forensic oratory, the same tendency to verbal criticism, the same confinement of the higher literature to coteries. Meeting, then, with a congenial soil and atmosphere, Seneca's mannerism took root and flourished in Italy. It is not a little amusing to find Giraldi openly expressing his opinion that Seneca had improved upon the Greek tragedians, and to notice how playwrights thought they were obeying Aristotle, when they made servile copies of the Corduban's dramatic commentaries.[1]

III

Between the years 1559 and 1566, five English authors applied themselves to the task of translating Seneca. The 'Troades,' 'Thyestes,' and 'Hercules Furens' were done by Jasper Heywood; the 'Œdipus' by Alexander Nevyle; the 'Medea,' 'Agamemnon,' 'Phædra,' and 'Hercules on Œta' by John Studley; the 'Octavia' by Thomas Nuce; and the 'Thebais' by Thomas Newton. These ten plays, collected and printed together in 1581, remain a monument of English poets' zeal in studying the Roman pedagogue. In all of these versions rhymed measures were used; and the translators allowed themselves considerable latitude of treatment, adding here and there, and altering according to their fancy.

The impulse thus given, was soon felt in the production of a great variety of classical or classical-Italian plays. Only two of these call for special notice. But before I proceed to their consideration, it will be well to pass this chapter in the literary history of our Drama in rapid review, and to notice some of its more prominent personalities.

George Gascoigne was a gentleman by birth and education, a member of Gray's Inn, and the author of many excellent works in prose and verse. In the year 1566, the society of which he was a member performed two of his dramatic essays in their hall of Gray's Inn. These were a translation of

---

[1] Scaliger's and Malherbe's opinions might be quoted to prove that this strange preference of Seneca was not confined to Italy.

Ariosto's ' Suppositi,' and a version of Lodovico Dolce's ' Giocasta.' The first of these plays has special interest, since it
was the earliest known comedy in English prose. The
' Jocasta ' has hitherto been accepted by historians of our
Drama, following Collier's authority, as a free transcript from
the ' Phœnissæ' of Euripides. This it is in substance. But
critics have generally omitted to notice that before the ' Phœnissæ ' came into the hands of Gascoigne, it had passed
through those of Dolce.[1] There is no reason to suppose
that Gascoigne was a learned poet ; and the merit of
having adapted a tragedy from the Greek must, I think, be
denied him. If Collier had paid attention to his own quotations from ' Jocasta,' the point would have been clear. He
extracts the speech of a person named Bailo at the opening of
the first act. Bailo is the Italian translation of the Greek
word Paidagogos ; and what this Bailo says in English, is a
tolerably close rendering of Dolce's addition to the tutor's part
in the ' Phœnissæ ' of Euripides. Again, in the speech of the
Messenger, Gascoigne follows Dolce, where Dolce has departed
from Euripides. My excuse for insisting upon so insignificant
a matter, must be that this ' Jocasta ' is the only early English
play for which a Greek source has been claimed. The truth
appears to be that, like the rest of the classical dramas of that
period, it had an Italian derivation.[2]

IV

The study of Seneca made itself apparent in two tragedies
by Fulke Grevile, Lord Brooke. These are ' Alaham ' and
' Mustapha ; '—Oriental fables treated in the strictest pseudo-
classic style, with conscientious observance of the unities and
other rules for depriving tragedy of movement. A ghost of
one of the old kings of Ormus prologises in ' Alaham.' A
Chorus of Good and Evil Spirits, Furies and Vices, comments
on the action. In ' Mustapha ' the Chorus varies : at one

[1] See *Teatro Antico Italiano*, vol. vi., for Dolce's *Giocasta*.
[2] It ought in this connection to be noted that the *Plutus* of Aristophanes is said to have been performed in Greek before Queen Elizabeth.

time it consists of Pashas and Cadis; then of Mohammedan Priests; again of Time and Eternity; lastly, of Converts to Mohammedanism. These plays, though printed in Brooke's works as late as 1633, were certainly composed at a much earlier period. It is curious that both are written in elaborate rhymed structure. They had no influence over the development of the English Drama, and must be regarded in the light of ponderous literary studies.

Upon the close of the century, Samuel Daniel, the sweet lyrist of Delia, set himself in opposition to the current of popular taste; and blaming 'the idle fictions' and 'gross follies' with which men abused their leisure hours, produced two tragedies, 'Philotas' and 'Cleopatra,' to serve as patterns of a purer style. Both, in the opinion of impartial critics, are apparent failures. They resemble a dilettante's disquisitions upon tragic fables rather than tragedies for action. Daniel, in his determination not to violate the unities, confines himself to the last hours of Cleopatra's life; and rather than disturb the ceremonious decorum of his art, he introduces a Messenger who relates in polished phrases how she died. A better instance could not be chosen than this 'Cleopatra,' to prove the impotence in England of the pseudo-classic style. Daniel's tragedy bore points of strong resemblance to the work of contemporary French playwrights. But it hardly needed the fierce light from Cleopatra's dying hours in Shakspere's play to pale its ineffectual fires. Where Italian and French poets attained to moderate success in their imitation of antique art, English dramatists invariably failed. Their failure was due in no small measure, doubtless, to the fact that their attempt revealed an undramatic turn of mind. In the age of Elizabeth and James the born playwright felt instinctively, felt truly, that the path of Shakspere and the people was the only path to walk in. Daniel's 'Cleopatra' met with the lukewarm approval of a lettered audience. His 'Philotas' was badly received, not on account of its artistic faults apparently, but because the audience recognised in its catastrophe allusions to the fate of Essex.

Daniel, in sympathy with the French authors whom

probably he had in view, adhered to rhyme. The Countess of
Pembroke, who translated Garnier's ' Antony ' into English
as early as 1590, made some use of blank verse—a somewhat
noticeable fact, since Marlowe's 'Tamburlaine,' which heralded
the triumph of that metre, was first printed in the same year.
Another tragedy of Garnier's, the ' Cornelia,' was translated
by Thomas Kyd, and dedicated in 1594 to the Countess of
Sussex. It is also in blank verse, of vigorous quality. It
would serve no purpose to enlarge upon these essays in translation, or to do more than mention Brandon's 'Virtuous
Octavia.' They are only interesting as indicating a continuous revolt among the literary folk in England against the
prevalent and overwhelming influence of the romantic or the
native English drama. Doomed to failure, buried beneath
the *magna moles* of the work of mightier poets, the historian
of literature regards them only as exceptions and abortions,
indicating by their very failure the organic strength and
soundness of the growth which they attempted to displace.

The same judgment may be passed on numerous tragedies
in the Latin tongue, and performed at Universities before a
courtly audience. The titles and dates of these productions
are in some cases curious. Thus we find a ' Jephtha ' by
George Christopherson, dedicated in 1546 to Henry VIII.
It preceded George Buchanan's ' Jephtha ' by eight years. A
'Dido,' by John Rightwise, was exhibited in King's College
Chapel at Cambridge in 1564 before Queen Elizabeth.
Another ' Dido,' by William Gager, entertained a Polish
prince in Christ Church Hall at Oxford in 1583. An ' Ajax
Flagellifer,' adapted probably from Sophocles, was written
and got up for Queen Elizabeth's amusement at Cambridge
in 1564. For some reason, its performance had then to be
abandoned; but it was played at Oxford in 1605. The
'Roxana ' of William Alabaster, which was acted in Trinity
College Hall, at Cambridge, about 1592, and printed in 1632,
deserves notice for the praise conferred upon its author by
Fuller; also for an anecdote which relates that during one of
its performances a gentlewoman went mad on hearing the
words *sequar, sequar,* uttered in a tone of tragic horror. The

following titles, chosen pretty much at random—'Adrastus Parentans,' 'Machiavellus,' 'Lælia,' 'Leander,' 'Fatum Vortigerni,' 'Æmilia,' 'Sapientia Salomonis'—prove that the Latin playwrights went far and wide afield for subjects. Should any student have the patience to search our libraries for the MSS. of these compositions, many of which are known to be still extant, it is probable that he would find the influence of Seneca ascendant in them. What the scholars of the sixteenth century seem to have understood by classical dramatic theory, was a deduction from the practice of the Roman rhetorician, with the further application of imperfectly apprehended canons of unity derived from Italian commentaries on Aristotle's 'Poetics.' Gian Giorgio Trissino has more than any single man to answer for the growth of that quaint formalism which imposed himself on the Italian theatre, and found illustrious expression in the work of Racine and his followers. A more intelligent and sympathetic study of the Attic tragedians on the part of the Italian humanists might have saved modern Europe from a mass of errors which crept into that pedantic system. Unluckily, Seneca ranked first in the appreciation of the critics, partly because he was easier to read, but chiefly because he was easier to imitate. Even Milton, both in his practice as the author of 'Samson Agonistes' and in his judgment of the Attic stage, shows that he was infected with the same original misapprehension of Greek art. The following verses from 'Paradise Regained,' sublime and beautiful as they may be, betray a want of insight into the essence of the drama as a fable put in action :

> Thence what the lofty grave tragedians taught,
> In Chorus or Iambic, teachers best
> Of moral prudence, with delight received,
> In brief sententious precepts, while they treat
> Of fate, and chance, and change in human life,
> High actions and high passions best describing.

The qualities on which Milton here insists gave weight and dignity indeed to the Attic drama. They may be even singled out for admiration also in the monologues of Seneca. But the romantic, as opposed to the classical, school of dramatists, were right in their perception that not ethical wisdom and not description, but action, was the one thing needful to their art. They saw that the Drama, as it differs from didactic poetry, must present human life in all possible fullness, vigour, and variety; must portray and develop character; must delineate the conflict of personalities and passions, the collision of human wills with circumstance; must combine events into a single movement with a climax and catastrophe. Finally, they knew well that in a drama the doing is the whole matter. Reflection upon action is extraneous to the essence of a play. It forms, no doubt, an ornament of meditated art. But the object of tragedy is not to teach by precept. If he teaches, the tragic playwright teaches by example. With this just instinct the romantic poets applied all their energies to action, allowing the conclusions, moral and sententious, to be drawn by the spectators of that action. Working thus upon a sound method, in spite of formal differences, due for the most part to the altered conditions of the theatre itself in modern times, they shared the spirit of the Greeks more fully than the pseudo-classics. Of 'brief sententious precepts,' capable of isolation from the dramatic context, Æschylus has hardly any, Sophocles but few. Euripides, the least to be commended of the Attic tragedians, abounds in them. Seneca's plays are made up of such passages. It might almost be laid down that in proportion as a dramatist lends himself to the compilation of ethical anthologies, in that very measure is he an inferior master of his craft.

V

These remarks have led by a circuitous and discursive path to the two English tragedies which, emanating from the school of Seneca in England, still deserve particular attention. They are 'Ferrex and Porrex,' or, as the play is also called, 'Gorboduc,' and 'The Misfortunes of Arthur.' Though intended to be strictly classical, and written by Senecasters of the purest water, both are founded upon ancient English fables. This fact is not without significance. It indicates that even in the limbo of pseudo-classic imitation, the national spirit was alive and stirring. The tragedies in question are therefore connected by no unimportant link with the more vital art of the romantic Drama.

'Gorboduc' has long been famous as the first tragedy written in our tongue. Sir Philip Sidney in his 'Defence of Poesy' hailed it as the dawn-star of a brighter day for English literature. After blaming the playwrights of his time as bastards of the Muses, 'paper-blurrers,' churls 'with servile wits, who think it enough if they can be rewarded of the printer,' he passes a sweeping censure on their dramatic compositions, charging them with neglect of rule and precedent, and showing how they violate the laws of 'honest civility and skilful poetry.' The one exception he makes, is in favour of 'Gorboduc.' 'It is full,' he says, 'of stately speeches and well-sounding phrases, climbing to the height of Seneca his style.' The only grave blot he detects in it, is non-observance of the unity of time. In this criticism, delivered by so excellent a wit as Sidney, by Sidney whom the ballad of 'Chevy Chase' stirred like the sound of the trumpet, we learn how the best intellects lay under bondage to that false ideal which I have attempted to describe. What Sidney demands of the tragic drama, is solemn diction, sonorous declamation, conformity to the unities. He knows of no model superior to Seneca. Judged by these standards, 'Gorboduc' is almost perfect. Unruffled calm, sententious maxims, lengthy speeches, ceremonious style, the action dealt with by narration : all these qualities it possesses in as full a measure as a play by Trissino himself. Alas, adds Sidney, that the unity of time was not observed! Only that was lacking to a work of absolute art in English.

'Gorboduc' was written by Thomas Norton and Thomas Sackville. Norton was a strict reformer of the bitterest sect, a polemical pamphleteer, and persecutor of the Roman Catholics. Though a barrister by profession, his inclination led him to theology. He translated Calvin's 'Institutions of the Christian Religion,' and versified the Psalms in

wretched doggrel. Sackville's career belongs to English
history. Son of Elizabeth's kinsman, Sir Richard Sackville,
the Privy Councillor and Chancellor of the Court of Augmen-
tations, he grew up in close intimacy with the Queen. As
his will informs us, he was 'in his younger years, by her
particular choice and liking, selected to a continual private
attendance upon her own person.' His youth was wild and
extravagant ; and at one period, between the years 1563 and
1566, he lost the favour of his royal cousin. Elizabeth
declared that 'she would not know him till he knew himself.'
Sackville returned to a knowledge of himself in time, however,
to secure a brilliant future. On his father's death in 1566,
he entered into the enjoyment of a vast estate. He was
created Knight of the Garter, Privy Councillor, Baron Buck-
hurst, Earl of Dorset, Chancellor of the University of Oxford,
and Lord High Treasurer of England.

In his early manhood, and while his extravagance was
moving Elizabeth's indignation, Sackville played no mean
part in English literature. To him we owe the finest portions of 'The Mirror for Magistrates,' that great collection
of poems which has been justly said to connect the work of
Lydgate with the work of Spenser. Sackville's part in it has
certainly more of Spenser's than of Lydgate's spirit ; and the
Induction, though sombre enough to justify Campbell in
calling it 'a landscape on which the sun never shines,' forms
a worthy exordium to the graver poetry of the Elizabethan
age. With the publication of that work in 1565, his literary
activity ceased. 'Gorboduc' had already been played in
1561, when Sackville was but twenty-five years of age, and
had not yet deserved the Queen's displeasure. Norton, his
collaborator in the tragedy, was four years his senior. Upon
the title-page of the first and pirated edition (1565), the first
three acts are ascribed to Norton, the fourth and fifth to
Sackville. Nor does there seem to be sufficient reason for
disputing this assignment, which was not contradicted by the
authors when the play was reprinted (with their sanction
apparently) under the title of 'Ferrex and Porrex' in 1570.
It is difficult to trace any important difference of style,

although the only pathetic passage in the drama, and some descriptions not wholly unworthy of Sackville's contribution to ' The Mirror for Magistrates,' occur in the fourth act.

Framed upon the model of Seneca, 'Gorboduc' is made up of dissertations, reflective diatribes, and lengthy choruses. The action, of which there is plenty behind the scenes, is reported by Messengers. The dialogue does not spring spontaneously from the occasion ; nor is it used to bring the characters into relief by natural collision. Each personage delivers a set oration, framed to suit his part, and then gives way to the next comer. The second scene of the first act might be used to illustrate this method. Gorboduc, having decided to divide the realm of Britain between his two sons Ferrex and Porrex, seeks the advice of his Privy Council. First of all, the King sets forth at great length his reasons for desiring a change. Then each of the three Councillors unfolds a different theory of government in measured terms. Gorboduc thanks them, replies that he adheres to his opinion, and dismisses the assembly. There is no argument, no persuasion, no contention, no pleading, in this cold debate. Our mind reverts to Marlowe's disputes between Edward II. and his barons, not to speak of Shakspere's scenes of a like order.

The plot of ' Gorboduc ' is well explained in the Argument prefixed to the first edition. ' Gorboduc, King of Britain, divided his realm in his lifetime to his sons, Ferrex and Porrex. The sons fell to division and dissension. The younger killed the elder. The mother, that more dearly loved the elder, for revenge killed the younger. The people, moved with the cruelty of the fact, rose in rebellion and slew both father and mother. The nobility assembled and most terribly destroyed the rebels. And afterwards, for want of issue of the Prince, whereby the succession of the crown became uncertain, they fell to civil war, in which both they and many of their issues were slain, and the land for a long time almost desolate and miserably wasted.' This programme is fertile in surprising incidents, rife with horrors, replete with all the circumstances of a sanguinary history. Its defect is superfluity of motives. The murder of the King and Queen by their rebellious subjects should properly have closed the play. By curtailing the conclusion, Gorboduc would have taken his proper place as the tragic protagonist, and would have closely resembled a hero of the Attic stage who perishes through his own error. The error of Gorboduc, what Aristotle styles the ἁμαρτία of the hero, was his rash and inconsiderate division of the realm for which he was responsible as monarch. Though an error, it was not ignoble. It had in it an element of greatness, blended with the folly which brought forth bitter fruits. Those fruits were discord between the Princes, the murder of the elder by the younger, and the Queen's act of unnatural vengeance on her fratricidal son. She in her death was justly punished, while Gorboduc perished in the general ruin he had brought by ill-considered generosity upon his kingdom. Up to this point, therefore, the plot has tragic unity. The civil wars, which followed on the King's death, may interest the philosophical historian, but do not concern the dramatist.

The authors of 'Gorboduc' can hardly be censured for drawing out the plot beyond its due dramatic limits, for the very simple reason that they did not attempt to treat it dramatically at all. Having caught this wild beast of a subject, they tamed it down, and cut its claws by a variety of shrewd devices. Though blood flows in rivers, not a drop is spilt upon the stage. We only hear of murders and wars in brief allusions, formal announcements, and obscure hints dropped by the Chorus. The division of the play into acts is characteristically regular, and corresponds exactly to the movement of the fable. In the first act Gorboduc declares his intention of partitioning his kingdom, and Videna, the Queen, expresses her disapprobation. In the second act Ferrex and Porrex are incited by their several confidants to make war, each upon the other. In the third act, while Gorboduc is asking the gods whether they are not satisfied with Troy's destruction, a Messenger informs him that Ferrex has died by his brother's hand. In the fourth act Videna lashes herself up to vengeance in a monologue of eighty-one lines, goes off the stage, and after a short interval her murder of Porrex is announced. In the fifth act a conversation between privy councillors and noblemen informs us that Gorboduc and Videna have been assassinated by their subjects, that the rebels have been crushed, and that a Civil War of Succession is in progress. The speeches average some fifty lines.

Each act is concluded with a Chorus, spoken by 'four ancient and sage men of Britain,' into whose mouths some of the best poetry of the play is put. They comment on the situations, and draw forth the moral, as thus :

> Blood asketh blood, and death must death requite ;
> Jove by his just and everlasting doom
> Justly hath ever so requited it.
> This times before record, and times to come
> Shall find it true ; and so doth present proof
> Present before our eyes for our behoof.
> O happy wight that suffers not the snare
> Of murderous mind to tangle him in blood !
> And happy he that can in time beware
> By others' harms, and turn it to his good !
> But woe to him that, fearing not to offend,
> Doth serve his lust, and will not see the end !

In order to acquaint the audience beforehand with the motive of each act, Dumb Shows were devised, which digested the meaning of the play in five successive scenes of metaphorical pantomime. The first act, for instance, was ushered in by stringed music, 'during which came in upon the stage six wild men, clothed in leaves.' One of these ' bare on his back a faggot of small sticks, which they all, both severally and together, essayed with all their strengths to break, but it could not be broken by them.' At last, one of the wild men pulled out a stick, and broke it. He was followed by the rest, and the whole faggot fell to pieces. This Dumb Show was meant to signify that 'a State knit in unity doth continue strong against all force, but being divided is easily destroyed.' We are not surprised to find that the Dumb Shows in ' Gorboduc ' required a commentary. Standing by themselves, they were little better than allegorical charades, and did not serve to elucidate the action. The custom of prefacing the acts of a play with Dumb Shows, which prevailed widely in the first period of our Drama, had, however, its excellent uses. These pageants were not always allegorical. They frequently set forth the pith of the action in a series of tableaux, appealing vividly to the spectator's eyesight, and preparing him to follow the dialogue with a clearer intelligence and a more composed mind. They enriched the simple theatre of the sixteenth century with exhibitions corresponding to the Masque which then enjoyed great popularity in England. In the case of serious plays like ' Gorboduc,' they relieved the dull solemnity of the performance, and gave frivolous spectators something to look forward to in the intervals of those dreary scenes.

'Gorboduc,' as we have seen, was written by a learned lawyer and a lettered courtier. It was performed at White-hall before the Queen's Majesty by Gentlemen of the Inner Temple on January 17, 1561. Authors and actors, alike, were men of birth and culture, striving to please a royal mistress, famous for her erudition. These circumstances account in no small measure for the character of the tragedy. With the example of Seneca and the Italians before their eyes, they did not aim at presenting a play as we now under-stand that word. Marlowe and Shakspere had not yet taught them what a play might be. They chose a tragic story, rich in serious moral lessons. Omitting the action, they uttered grave reflections on the benefits of strong government, the horrors of division in a realm, and the disorders introduced by violence of passion into human life. The fable, with its terrible episodes, catastrophes, and scenes of bloodshed, lurked like a lurid background in the imagination of the spectators. Those grave debating personages on the stage supplied their minds with food for thought and meditation. That very little scope was left for histrionic action, mattered not. We may even doubt whether the Gentlemen of the Inner Temple could have done justice to Cordelia or King Lear, supposing that Norton and Sackville had been able to treat their similar subject with a Shakspere's genius for the drama.

What gives its chief interest to ' Gorboduc,' has not yet been mentioned. Not only is this the first regular tragedy

in English. It is also the first play written in Blank Verse.
Surrey adapted the metre from the *Versi Sciolti* of the
Italians, and used it in his translation of the second and
fourth Books of the ' Æneid.' Norton and Sackville brought
it into dramatic literature—tame as yet in cadence and monotonous in structure ; but with so fateful and august a future,
that this humble cradle of its birth commands our reverence.
The peroration to Videna's invective against her son Porrex
will show how Sackville used blank verse :

> Murderer, I thee renounce ! Thou art not mine.
> Never, O wretch, this womb conceivèd thee,
> Nor never bode I painful throes for thee !
> Changeling to me thou art, and not my child,
> Nor to no wight that spark of pity knew :
> Ruthless, unkind, monster of nature's work,
> Thou never sucked the milk of woman's breast,
> But from thy birth the cruel tiger's teats
> Have nursèd thee ; nor yet of flesh and blood
> Formed is thy heart, but of hard iron wrought ;
> And wild and desert woods bred thee to life !

Surrey, in his version of Dido's address to Æneas, had already
written :

> Faithless, forsworn ! no goddess was thy dam !
> Nor Dardanus beginner of thy race !
> But of hard rocks Mount Caucase monstruous
> Bred thee, and teats of tigers gave thee suck.

Marcella's apostrophe to Videna, upbraiding her for the
murder of Porrex, combines declamation and description in
verses which are not deficient in dramatic vigour :

> O queen of adamant, O marble breast !
> If not the favour of his comely face,
> If not his princely cheer and countenance,
> His valiant active arms, his manly breast,
> If not his fair and seemly personage,
> His noble limbs in such proportion cast
> As would have rapt a silly woman's thought—
> If this mote not have moved thy bloody heart,
> And that most cruel hand the wretched weapon

> Even to let fall, and kissed him in the face,
> With tears for ruth to reave such one by death,
> Should nature yet consent to slay her son ?
> O mother, thou to murder thus thy child !
> Even Jove with justice must with lightning flames
> From heaven send down some strange revenge on thee !

Then her memory reverts to the young bravery of Porrex in the tilting-yard and battle :

> Ah, noble prince, how oft have I beheld
> Thee mounted on thy fierce and trampling steed,
> Shining in armour bright before the tilt,
> And with thy mistress' gleeve tied on thy helm,
> And charge thy staff, to please thy lady's eye,
> That bowed the headpiece of thy friendly foe !
> How oft in arms on horse to bend the mace,
> How oft in arms on foot to break the sword ;
> Which never now these eyes may see again !

VI

The 'Misfortunes of Arthur,' like ' Gorboduc,' was written by learned men, and acted by the members of a legal society before the Queen.   The Gentlemen of Gray's Inn produced it at Greenwich on the 8th of February, 1587.   The author of the tragedy was Thomas Hughes.   The choruses, dumb shows, argument, induction, and some extra speeches—all the setting of the play in short—are ascribed to other students of the Inn.   Among these occurs the name of Francis Bacon. The future Lord Verulam was at that time in his twenty-third year.   The subject of the ' Misfortunes of Arthur ' was well chosen.   The Arthurian legend, here presented to us, is a truly Thyestean history of a royal house devoted for its crimes of insolence to ruin.   Uther Pendragon loved Igerna, the wife of Gorlois, Duke of Cornwall, whom he afterwards slew in battle.   The fruits of their adultery were a son and daughter, twins of the same birth, Arthur and Anne.   Arthur, when he grew to man's estate, became the father of Mordred by his sister Anne.   In course of time he married Guenevora ; and in his absence, on a successful campaign against the Emperor

Lucius Tiberius, left his queen with Mordred. Mordred and
Guenevora filled up the cup of incest and adultery. On Arthur's
return, Guenevora betook her to a nunnery, and Mordred
stirred war against his father. They met in battle. Mordred
slew himself on Arthur's sword ; but, dying, struck his father
with a mortal wound. Thus ended the House of Pendragon.

This legend, hideous in its details, and far more repugnant
to our taste than the common tale of Lancelot's love, supplied
the author with a fable suited to his style of art. He had set
himself to imitate Seneca's method of dealing with a tale of
antique destiny ; and no tragedy of Thebes or Pelops' line
was ever more tremendous. At the same time he treated his
main motive as a Greek, rather than the Roman rhetorician,
might have used it. I hazard this criticism although Hughes
has not permeated the whole play with that prevailing sense
of the divine wrath, of Atè following her victim from above,
and Atasthalia confusing his reason from within, which would
have made it Æschylean. In his hands the plot is conducted
on the lines of a chronicle play. This, in itself, marks an important divergence from Seneca's habit of treatment, and suggests comparison with the Euripidean drama. Yet, on the
whole, we must classify the play with ' Gorboduc ' as an experiment in Roman tragedy.

In the first act, Guenevora resolves to take refuge in the
nunnery. The rest of the tragedy relates the conflict between
son and sire. First they debate, each with the accustomed
confidant, about engaging in this war. Arthur is restrained
by motions of relenting toward his son. Mordred dreads
his father's veterans. At length the combat opens. The
King, on whose side our sympathies are powerfully enlisted,
drives his foes before him, when Mordred rushes in, and by
his desperate suicide effects the purpose of his hate. The
decisive incident is of course narrated by a Messenger. But
Arthur survives the battle, and lives to comment in the fifth
act on his nation's overthrow. He quits the stage with this
apostrophe to fate and fortune :

> This only now I crave, O fortune, erst
> My faithful friend ! Let it be soon forgot,

Nor long in mind nor mouth, where Arthur fell.
Yea, though I conqueror die, and full of fame,
Yet let my death and 'parture rest obscure!
No grave I need, O fates! nor burial rites,
Nor stately hearse, nor tomb with haughty top;
But let my carcase lurk; yea, let my death
Be aye unknown, so that in every coast
I still be feared and looked for every hour.

In order to have invested the plot with true artistic unity,
Guenevora should have stayed, like Clytemnestra, to meet the
King, or have confronted him in the last act. But this was
not demanded by the scheme of Seneca; and a kind of
external unity, more suited to his style of art, is gained by
the introduction of the Ghost of wronged and murdered
Gorlois. He opens the first act, crying for revenge; and
closes the fifth with a prophecy of Queen Elizabeth. It was
Uther's crime of $\ddot{v}\beta\rho\iota\varsigma$ against Gorlois which set in motion
the whole series of events so fatal to his house. Therefore
the Ghost of Gorlois, like the Ghosts of Tantalus in Seneca's
'Thyestes' and of Thyestes in his 'Agamemnon,' broods
above the action, and retires at last blood-surfeited, appeased.
It may also be remarked that the bringing of Arthur back to
fight his son and die in Cornwall, the first seat of crime, was
a touch worthy of the Greek sense of fate.

The Ghost, imported from Seneca into English tragedy,
had a long and brilliant career. Lord Brook, in his 'Alaham,'
summons 'the Ghost of one of the old Kings of Ormus' from
the limbo of undated age to speak his prologue. In Jonson's
'Catiline' the Ghost of Sylla stalks abroad, 'ranging for
revenge.' Marston's Andrugio, Tourneur's Montferrers, Kyd's
Andrea—to mention at haphazard but a few of these infernal
visitants—fill the scene with hollow clamours for revenge.
Shakspere, who omitted nothing in the tragic apparatus of
his predecessors, but with inbreathed sense and swift imagination woke those dead things to organic life, employed the
Ghost, all know with what effect, in 'Hamlet' and 'Macbeth'
and 'Julius Cæsar.' It is not here the place to comment
upon Shakspere's alchemy—the touch of nature by which he

turned the coldest mechanisms of the stage to spiritual use.
Enough to notice that, in his hands, the Ghost was no longer
a phantom roaming in the cold, evoked from Erebus to hover
round the actors in a tragedy, but a spirit of like intellectual
substance with those actors, a parcel of the universe in which
all live and move and have their being.

'The Misfortunes of Arthur' shows a marked advance on
'Gorboduc.' The characters are far more fully modelled—
those of Arthur and Mordred standing forth in bold relief.
The language is less studiedly sententious. The verse flows
more harmoniously. The descriptive passages are marked
by greater vividness; and the dialogue evolves itself more
spontaneously from the situation. Many vigorous single lines
anticipate the style of Marston ; who, without Shakspere's
work before his eyes, could certainly have not produced a
better tragedy. Some of these lines are due to Seneca :

> Yea, worse than war itself is fear of war . . .
> Small griefs can speak, the great astonished stand.

Seneca had written :

> Pejor est bello timor ipse belli. . . .
> Curæ leves loquuntur, ingentes stupent.

Shakspere wrote :

> The grief that does not speak,
> Whispers the o'er-fraught heart, and bids it break.

To neglect this instance of the Shaksperian alchemy, though
unseasonable, was beyond my fortitude.

What the Greeks called Stichomuthia is common in this
tragedy. Gawin, for example, urges on Mordred the impru-
dence of resisting Arthur in the field.

> G. And fear you not so strange and uncouth war ?
> M. No, were they wars that grew from out the ground !
> G. Nor yet your sire so huge, yourself so small ?
> M. The smallest axe may fell the hugest oak.
> G. Nor that in felling him yourself may fall ?
> M. He falleth well that falling fells his foe.
> G. Nor common chance, whereto each man is thrall ?
> M. Small manhood were to turn my back to chance.

This dialogue by a stroke of tragic irony prefigures the catastrophe, which is thus described by the Messenger:

> So saying, forth he flings,
> And desperate runs on point of Arthur's sword—
> A sword, alas! prepared for no such use!
> Whereon engored, he glides till, near approached,
> With dying hand he hews his father's head.
> So through his own annoy he 'noys his liege,
> And gains by death access to daunt his sire.

From the point of view of tragic passion, the finest scene
in the play, and the highest in expression, is when Arthur
greets the dead body of his son.

> *[The breathless body of* MORDRED *in armour, as he
> fell, is brought upon the stage.*
>   *A.* A causeless foe !　When wars did call me hence,
> He was in years but young, in wit too old.
> As virtue shineth most in comeliest wights,
> When inward gifts are decked with outward grace,
> So did his wit and feature feed that hope,
> Which falsely trained me to this woeful hap.
>   *[He turns to the corpse.*
> His mind transformèd thus, I cannot choose
> But long to see what change his face sustains.
> My blood and kindred, doubled in his birth,
> Inspires a mixed and twice-descending love,
> Which drives my dying veins to wish his view.
> Unhelm his luckless head, set bare his face,
> That face which erst pleased me and mine too much!
>   *Ch.* See, worthiest king, the hope of all your realm,
> Had not his lust to rule prevented all.
>   *A.* I see, alas! I see—Hide, hide again!
> Oh, spare mine eyes!—a witness of my crimes,
> A fearful vision of my former guilt,
> A dreadful horror of a future doom,
> A present gall of mind!　O happy they,
> Whose spotless lives attain a dreadless death!
> And thou, O hapless boy!　O spite of fates!
> What might I term thee—nephew, son, or both?
> Alas! how happy should we both have been,
> If no ambitious thought had vexed thy head,
> Nor thou thus strived to reave thy father's rule,
> But stayed thy time, and not forestalled us both!

Cador, an attendant noble, compares Mordred in his fate to the ' hot-spurred ' and aspiring Phaethon. Arthur resumes his lamentation :

> What ruth, ah, rent the woeful father's heart,
> That saw himself thus made a sonless sire !
> Well, since both heavens and hell conspired in one
> To make our ends a mirror to the world,
> Both of incestuous life and wicked birth,
> Would God the fates that linked our faults alike
> Had also framed our minds of friendlier mould,
> That as our lineage had approached too near,
> So our affections had not swerved so far !

Something magnanimous in Arthur's attitude toward his dead son, something noble in his meditation on their common crime, the playing with antitheses, the covert allusion to Guenevora's guilty love, the natural and dignified movement of the dying hero's apostrophes to fate—all these points of style seem to me to indicate a study of the Greek at first hand. The ' Misfortunes of Arthur,' superior in all respects to ' Gorboduc,' has this particular superiority, that it breathes in parts the air of an Euripidean tragedy.

VII

The tragedies of what I have called the pseudo-classic school differ in very essential points from the type of the true English drama. Their authors, men of birth, culture, and position, were unable to stem the tide of popular inclination. They could not persuade play-goers to prefer the measured rhetoric of Seneca to the stirring melodrama and varied scenes of the romantic poets. It remains, however, to be asked what these workers in an unsuccessful style, permanently achieved for our dramatic literature. The answer is not far to seek. Their efforts, arguing a purer taste and a loftier ideal than that of the uncultivated English, forced principles of careful composition, gravity of diction, and harmonious construction, on the attention of contemporary playwrights. They compelled men of Marlowe's mental

calibre to consider whether mature reflection might not be
presented in the form of dramatic action. The earlier
romantic playwrights regarded the dramatisation of a tale as
all-important. The classical playwrights contended for
grave sentences and weighty matter. To the triumph of the
romantic style the classics added this element of studied
thought. Mere copies of Latin tragedy were doomed to
deserved unpopularity with the vulgar. Yet these plays had
received the approbation of the Court and critics; and the
approbation of the higher social circles is rarely without
influence. Thus, though themselves of little literary value
and of no permanent importance, they taught certain lessons
of regularity and sobriety in tragic art, by which the poets of
the romantic drama did not fail to profit. We have cause to
be thankful that no Richelieu, with a learned Academy at his
back, was at hand in England to stereotype this pseudo-classic
style; and that the Queen who patronised our theatre in
its beginnings, was very far from being a purist in dramatic
matters. Else Marlowe, like Corneille, might have been
forced to walk in the fetters which Sidney and Sackville
sought to forge, and the Shaksperian drama might never
have been England's proudest boast in literature. But, while
recording our gratitude for these mercies, we should not
refuse their due meed to the School of Seneca. It is no
slight thing moreover to have given blank verse to the
English stage; and dramatic blank verse was certainly the
discovery of Norton, Sackville, Hughes, and Gascoigne.
These followers of Seneca and the Italians familiarised the
reading public with this metre in their 'Gorboduc' (1561),
'Jocasta' (1566), and 'Misfortunes of Arthur' (1587). The
first of these works was printed at least twenty years before
the production of Marlowe's 'Tamburlaine.' The last of
them was printed three years before Marlowe sent that play
to press.

CHAPTER VII

TRIUMPH OF THE ROMANTIC DRAMA

I. Fifty-two Plays at Court—Analysis of their Subjects—The Court
follows the Taste of the People—The 'Damon and Pithias' of Edwards—'Romeo and Juliet'—'Tancred and Gismunda'—'Promos
and Cassandra.'—II. Contemporary Criticisms of the Romantic Style
—Gosson—Whetstone—Sidney.—III. Description of the English
Popular Play—The Florentine Farsa—Destinies of this Form in
England.

I

THOUGH the pseudo-classical or Italian type of Tragedy
engaged the attention of learned writers, it must not therefore
be imagined that the Court was exclusively addicted to this
kind of entertainment. From Minutes of the Revels between
1568 and 1580, Mr. Collier has published a list of fifty-two
plays; eighteen of which bear antique titles, while twenty-
one appear to have been Dramatised Romances, six Moral
Plays, and seven Comedies. None of these survive. Composed by unknown playwrights only to be acted, they perished
in thumbed MSS. together with the other properties of their
itinerant possessors, before arriving at the honours of the
press. Only Gentlemen of Gray's Inn or the Middle Temple,
amateur authors and dilettante actors could afford the luxury
of printing their performances. Only tragedies put on the
stage with the *éclat* of ' Gorboduc,' tempted publishers to acts
of piracy.

That the fifty-two plays, cited by Collier as having been
exhibited at Court during those twelve years, failed to
struggle into print, proves that the life of the popular drama
was exuberantly vigorous. Men of birth and erudition might

translate or copy Seneca, with the view of elevating English taste; and such men had a direct reason for publishing their works. But those numerous professional artists who now catered for the public—strolling players, setting up their booths in the yards of hostelries or knocking at great men's gates in seasons of festivity—actors with temporary licence from the local magistrates—superior companies with licence from the Queen—Lord Leicester's Servants, Lord Derby's Servants, the Lord Chamberlain's Servants, Lord North's Servants—these men plied their trade with no further object in view than full houses, fair receipts, and the approbation of mixed audiences. Permanent theatres were already established in more than one quarter of the suburbs; and the people had become the patrons of the stage. It was not to the interest of such professional players to produce their repertories in a printed form. A popular piece was valuable property, and was jealously guarded by the company which owned it. Moreover, it is highly probable that the rudimentary dramas of this epoch existed in single copies, from which the leading actor taught his troop, or that they were 'Plat-form' sketches filled in by extemporisation.

Though the titles of these fifty-two plays are both curious and instructive, it would serve no useful purpose to attempt to classify them. 'Orestes' and the 'History of Cynocephali;' 'Duke of Milan' and 'Murderous Michael;' 'Six Fools' and 'The History of Error:' we seem in these names to detect the classic and romantic fable, the Italian story and the domestic tragedy, the farce and the morality. But one thing may be safely assumed of the whole list; viz. that whatever was their subject-matter, they were each and all designed for popular amusement. In other words, we can feel tolerably certain that these plays, produced at Court, formed together a mixed species, observant of no literary rules, depending for effect upon the scope afforded to the actor, and for success upon appeal to the taste of uninstructed London playgoers. Such as they were, they contained in embryo the English or Romantic Drama, the Drama which Marlowe was to mould and Shakspere was to perfect.

There is plenty of proof that at this period, a period decisive for the future of the English theatre, the Court rather followed than directed the taste of the people. It was the business of the Master of the Revels, upon the occasion of Christmas or some other feast-time, to convene the players and invite them to rehearse the pieces they were ready to perform. The companies produced the budget of such plays as they were in the habit of exhibiting before the public or at great men's houses ; and from these the Master of the Revels chose what he thought suitable. The Queen herself had no fastidious appetite. All she seems to have cared for in the matter of stage-spectacles, was that the supply should be both plentiful and various. Thus, instead of hampering the evolution of the national drama in its earlier stages, the Court gave it protection and encouragement. Performances at Court confirmed and ratified the popularity which any piece had gained by open competition.

The Romantic species, with all its absurdities and extravagances, with its careless ignorance of rules and single-minded striving after natural effect, took root and acquired form before critics and scholars turned their attention seriously to the stage. A school of playwrights and of actors, dependent upon popular support, came into being. London audiences were already accustomed to the type of play which thus undisputedly assumed possession of the theatre. It was too late now for critics or for scholars to resist that growth of wilding art ; for the genius of the people had adopted it, and the Queen did not disdain it. Great poets were soon to see the opportunity it offered them ; and great actors bent their talents to the special style of histrionic art which it demanded. In spite of pedantic opposition, in spite of Sidney's noble scorn, the world was destined to rejoice in Shakspere.

Even playwrights of superior station and culture, poets aspiring to the honours of the press, were irresistibly attracted by the vogue of the Romantic Drama. Thus Richard Edwards, whose work is mentioned with applause by Puttenham, selected a subject from Valerius Maximus, and composed a

tragi-comedy upon the tale of ' Damon and Pithias' (1565 ?).
Yet, though he laid the scene at Syracuse, he brought Grim,
the Collier of Croydon, to the court of Dionysius, mixing
kings and clowns, philosophers and classic worthies, in
admired confusion. The fashionable study of Italian was
not merely fruitful of translations in the style of the 'Supposes'
and ' Jocasta.' Popular tales were dramatised in all their
details. The Novella, with its complicated episodes, was
presented in a series of loosely connected scenes. Our earliest
' Romeo and Juliet' saw the light, as appears from Arthur
Brooke's preface to his poem on this story, before 1562.
Boccaccio's tale of ' Tancred and Gismunda' was produced
upon the stage in Robert Wilmot's version in 1563. George
Whetstone made one of Cinthio's Hecatommithi the subject
of his ' Promos and Cassandra,' printed in two parts in 1578.
Cinthio had already dramatised this story in the ' Epitia;' and
Shakspere conferred immortality upon its fable by using it for
' Measure for Measure.'

II

From plays which found their way into the printer's
hands, we cannot rightly judge the products of this fertile
epoch. They are far too few in number, and with some
rare exceptions are the compositions of men distinguished by
birth and literary culture. In order to form a more exact
conception of the romantic drama in its period of incubation,
when professional actors and playwrights—the two arts being
commonly exercised by the same persons—were unconsciously
shaping the new style, we have to view it in the mirror of contemporary criticism. That criticism emanates from writers
hostile to the popular stage on several accounts. Some, like
John Northbrooke, assail it on the score of immorality.
Others, like Sidney, attack its want of art. It is chiefly with
the latter class of accusers that we are here concerned.

---

[1] This play was entered on the Stationers' Books in 1567. Collier
conjectures that it may have been the ' tragedy ' by Edwards which was
played before the Queen two years earlier than this date.

Stephen Gosson had been a writer, and probably also an actor, of plays, before the year 1579, at which date he published his 'School of Abuse.' This was a comprehensive arraignment of the theatre from the ethical point of view. His tract called forth numerous replies, to one of which, composed by Thomas Lodge, he retorted in a second pamphlet, entitled 'Plays Confuted in Five Actions.'[1] This, though its object is also mainly ethical, contains some references useful to our present purpose. Regarding the variety of sources drawn on by the playwrights at that early period, he asserts : 'I may boldly say it because I have seen it, that "The Palace of Pleasure," "The Golden Ass," "The Æthiopian History," "Amadis of France," "The Round Table," bawdy Comedies in Latin, French, Italian, and Spanish, have been ransacked to furnish the playhouses in London.' That is to say, the translations of Italian Novels published by Painter, the Chivalrous Romances of the later Middle Ages, Heliodorus, the Myth of 'Cupid and Psyche,' together with comedies in Latin and three modern languages, had already become the stock in trade of dramatist and actor. On the topic of History, he says : 'If a true History be taken in hand, it is made like our shadows, largest at the rising and falling of the sun, shortest of all at high noon. For the poets drive it most commonly unto such points as may best show the majesty of their pen in tragical speeches ; or set the hearers agog with discourses of love ; or paint a few antics to fit their own humours with scoffs and taunts ; or wring in a show to furnish forth the stage when it is too bare ; when the matter of itself comes short of this, they follow the practice of the cobbler, and set their teeth to the leather to pull it out. So was the history of Cæsar and Pompey, and the play of the Fabii at the Theatre, both amplified there where the drums might walk or the pen ruffle.' Through this critique we discern how the romantic method was applied to subjects of classical History. In another place he touches on the defects of chivalrous fable as treated by romantic playwrights :

[1] Reprinted in the Roxburghe Library, 1869, from the undated edition of possibly 1581 or 1582.

'Sometimes you shall see nothing but the adventures of an amorous knight, passing from country to country for the love of his lady, encountering many a terrible monster made of brown paper, and at his return is so wonderfully changed that he cannot be known but by some posy in his tablet, or by a broken ring or a handkerchief, or a piece of cockle shell. What,' adds the critic pertinently, ' shall you learn by that ? '

George Whetstone, when he published ' Promos and Cassandra' in 1578, prefixed to it a short discourse upon contemporary plays. It is a succinct disparagement of the romantic as compared with the classical method. Having commended the moral dignity and mature art of the ancient comic poets, he proceeds thus : [1] ' But the advised devices of ancient poets, discredited with the trifles of young, unadvised, and rash-witted writers, hath brought this commendable exercise in mislike. For at this day the Italian is so lascivious in his comedies that honest hearers are grieved at his actions : the Frenchman and Spaniard follow the Italian's humour : the German is too holy, for he presents on every common stage what preachers should pronounce in pulpits. The Englishman, in this quality, is most vain, indiscreet, and out of order. He first grounds his work on impossibilities : then in three hours runs he through the world ; marries, gets children ; makes children men, men to conquer kingdoms, murder monsters ; and bringeth gods from heaven, and fetcheth devils from hell. And (that which is worst) their ground is not so imperfect as their working indiscreet ; not weighing, so the people laugh, though they laugh them, for their follies, to scorn. Many times, to make mirth, they make a clown companion with a king ; in their grave counsels they allow the advice of fools ; they use one order of speech for all persons—a gross indecorum, for a crow will ill counterfeit the nightingale's sweet voice ; even so, affected speech doth ill become a clown. For to work a comedy kindly, grave old men should instruct ; young men should show the imperfections of youth ; strumpets

---

[1] Six old plays, published by J. Nichols, 1779, p. 3.

should be lascivious ; boys unhappy ; and clowns should be disorderly : intermingling all these actions in such sort as the grave matter may instruct, and the pleasant delight : for without this change the attention would be small, and the liking less.'

The whole case against the English Drama of that age is summed up by Sir Philip Sidney in a famous passage of his 'Defence of Poesy.' Written probably in 1583, though not printed till 1595, Sidney was most likely acquainted with what Gosson and Whetstone had already published on the subject. He certainly knew Whetstone's Preface, for he borrowed some of its phrases almost verbatim. Though long, I shall not hesitate to transcribe the whole of Sidney's criticism, bidding the reader bear in mind that the apologist for poetry wrote some years before the earliest of Shakspere's plays appeared, and when the first of Marlowe's had not yet been acted. His strictures apply therefore in the most literal sense to the romantic drama in its embryonic period.

' Our tragedies and comedies, not without cause, are cried out against, observing rules neither of honest civility nor skilful poetry. Excepting " Gorboduc " (again I say of those that I have seen), which notwithstanding, as it is full of stately speeches, and well-sounding phrases, climbing to the height of Seneca his style, and as full of notable morality, which it doth most delightfully teach, and so obtain the very end of poesy ; yet, in truth, it is very defectuous in the circumstances, which grieves me, because it might not remain as an exact model of all tragedies. For it is faulty both in place and time, the two necessary companions of all corporal actions. For where the stage should alway represent but one place ; and the uttermost time presupposed in it, should be, both by Aristotle's precept, and common reason, but one day ; there is both many days and many places inartificially imagined.

' But if it be so in " Gorboduc," how much more in all the rest ? where you shall have Asia of the one side, and Afric of the other, and so many other under kingdoms, that the player, when he comes in, must ever begin with telling where he is,

or else the tale will not be conceived. Now shall you have
three ladies walk to gather flowers, and then we must believe
the stage to be a garden. By-and-by, we hear news of ship-
wreck in the same place, then we are to blame if we accept it
not for a rock. Upon the back of that comes out a hideous
monster with fire and smoke, and then the miserable
beholders are bound to take it for a cave ; while, in the meantime, two armies fly in, represented with four swords and
bucklers, and then, what hard heart will not receive it for a
pitched field ?

'Now of time they are much more liberal ; for ordinary it
is, that two young princes fall in love ; after many traverses
she is got with child ; delivered of a fair boy ; he is lost,
groweth a man, falleth in love, and is ready to get another
child ; and all this in two hours' space ; which, how absurd
it is in sense, even sense may imagine ; and art hath taught
and all ancient examples justified, and at this day the
ordinary players in Italy will not err in. Yet will some
bring in an example of the Eunuch in Terence, that containeth
matter of two days, yet far short of twenty years. True it is,
and so was it to be played in two days, and so fitted to the
time it set forth. And though Plautus have in one place
done amiss, let us hit it with him, and not miss with him:
But they will say, How then shall we set forth a story which
contains both many places and many times ?   And do they
not know, that a tragedy is tied to the laws of poesy, and not
of history ; not bound to follow the story, but having liberty
either to feign a quite new matter, or to frame the history to
the most tragical convenience ? Again, many things may be
told, which cannot be shewed ; if they know the difference
betwixt reporting and representing. As for example, I may
speak, though I am here, of Peru, and in speech digress
from that to the description of Calicut ; but in action I cannot represent it without Pacolet's horse. And so was the
manner the ancients took by some "Nuntius," to recount
things done in former time, or other place.

'Lastly, if they will represent an history, they must not,
as Horace saith, begin " ab ovo," but they must come to the

principal point of that one action which they will represent.
By example this will be best expressed; I have a story of
young Polydorus, delivered, for safety's sake, with great
riches, by his father Priamus to Polymnestor, King of Thrace,
in the Trojan war time. He, after some years, hearing of
the overthrow of Priamus, for to make the treasure his own,
murdereth the child; the body of the child is taken up;
Hecuba, she, the same day, findeth a sleight to be revenged
most cruelly of the tyrant. Where, now, would one of our
tragedy-writers begin, but with the delivery of the child?
Then should he sail over into Thrace, and so spend I know
not how many years, and travel numbers of places. But
where doth Euripides? Even with the finding of the body;
leaving the rest to be told by the spirit of Polydorus. This
needs no farther to be enlarged; the dullest wit may
conceive it.

'But, besides these gross absurdities, how all their plays
be neither right tragedies nor right comedies, mingling
kings and clowns, not because the matter so carrieth it, but
thrust in the clown by head and shoulders to play a part in
majestical matters, with neither decency nor discretion; so
as neither the admiration and commiseration, nor the right
sportfulness, is by their mongrel tragi-comedy obtained. I
know Apuleius did somewhat so, but that is a thing recounted
with space of time, not represented in one moment: and I
know the ancients have one or two examples of tragi-
comedies as Plautus hath Amphytrio. But, if we mark them
well, we shall find, that they never, or very daintily, match
hornpipes and funerals. So falleth it out, that having indeed
no right comedy in that comical part of our tragedy, we have
nothing but scurrility, unworthy of our chaste ears; or some
extreme show of doltishness, indeed fit to lift up a loud
laughter, and nothing else: where the whole tract of a
comedy should be full of delight; as the tragedy should be
still maintained in a well-raised admiration.'

Thus critics like Sidney, trained in humanistic and
Italian studies, demanded a clear separation of tragedy from
comedy. No merriment, according to their theory, may relax

the frown of Melpomene. Thalia may not borrow the chord of pathos from her sister's lyre. It were well to banish clowns, buffoons, and jugglers altogether from the stage. Kings and rustics should not figure in the same play, unless the latter be required to act the part of Nuntius. The three main species of the Drama are properly assigned to the three sections of society; Tragedy to royal personages and the aristocracy; Comedy to the middle class; the Pastoral to hand-labourers. Action in tragedy should be narrated rather than presented. The persons can discuss events which have happened or are expected; but a Messenger must always be at hand to announce important news. If needful, the clumsiest artifices should be devised in order to prevent the audience from actually beholding a battle or a murder. Lastly, the unities of time and place are to be observed with scrupulous exactitude, in spite of every inconvenience to the author and of any damage to the subject.

These canons the Italians had already compiled from passages of Aristotle and of Horace, without verifying them by appeal to the Greek dramatic authors. They were destined to determine the practice of the great French writers of the seventeenth century, and to be accepted as incontrovertible by every European nation, until Victor Hugo with Hernani raised the standard of belligerent Romanticism on the stage of Paris.

III

Not a single one of the above-mentioned rules was obeyed in our Romantic Drama. In a dialogue between G., H., and T., quoted from Florio's 'First Fruits' by Mr. Collier, one of the interlocutors says:

G. After dinner we will go see a play.

His friend answers:

H. The plays that they play in England are not right comedies.

A third joins in the conversation:

T. Yet they do nothing else but play every day!

The second sticks to his opinion:

    H. Yea, but they are neither right comedies nor right tragedies.

The first inquires:

    G. How would you name them then?

The critic scornfully replies:

    H. Representations of histories without any decorum.

Such in truth they were. Without the decorum of deliberate obedience to classic rules, without the decorum of accomplished art, without the decorum of social distinctions properly observed, they dramatised a tale or history in scenes. Nothing in the shape of a story came amiss to the romantic playwright; and perhaps we cannot penetrate deeper into the definition of the Romantic Drama than by saying that its characteristic was to be a represented story. In this it differed from the Classic or Athenian Drama; for there, although there lay a myth or fable behind each tragedy, the play itself was written on some point or climax in the fable.[1]

A Florentine, if at this epoch he had been asked, ' How do you name them then?' might possibly have answered, 'Farsa!' For it is not a little curious that in these very years, when the romantic type of art was taking shape in England, a distinguished Florentine playwright attempted to popularise a very similar species in Tuscany. The endeavour was foredoomed to failure. Italian dramatic literature had moved too long already upon different lines; and the life which remained in it, was destined to survive in the fixed personages and the improvisatory action of the *Commedia dell' Arte*. Yet Giovanmaria Cecchi's description of the *Farsa* in his prologue to 'La Romanesca' (a play of this

---

[1] I do not mean to assert that no plays of the Romantic species are written, like the Classical, upon the point or climax of a story rather than upon the story itself. What I do mean, is that the Romantic method accepted the dramatic evolution of a story—setting forth, for instance, the whole of a man's life, or the whole of a king's reign, or the whole of a complicated fable. It is only necessary to mention *King Lear, Pericles, Henry IV., Cymbeline*. And even where the plot is far more strictly narrowed to a single point, as in *Othello*, the dramatic movement remains narrative.

species composed in 1585) would serve better than the most
elaborate description to explain the nature of the English
Romantic Drama to men who never read a line of Marlowe.
I have, therefore, translated it from the Florentine reprint of
1880.

> The Farce is a third species, newly framed
> 'Twixt tragedy and comedy. She profits
> By all the breadth and fullness of both forms,
> Shuns all their limitations. She receives
> Under her roof princes and mighty lords,
> Which comedy doth not; is hospitable,
> Like some caravanserai or lazar-house,
> To whoso lists, the vulgar and the lewd,
> Whereto Dame Tragedy hath never stooped.
> She is not tied to subjects; for she takes
> Or grave or gay, or pious or profane,
> Polished or rude, mirthful or lamentable :
> Of place she makes no question ; sets the scene
> In church, in public, nay, where'er she chooses :
> Indifferent to time, if one day's space
> Content her not, she 'll run through two or three ;
> What matters it ? Troth, she 's the pleasantest,
> The readiest, best attired, fresh country lass,
> The sweetest, comeliest, this world contains !
> One might compare her to that jovial friar
> Who laughingly conceded to his abbot
> All things he craved, always except obedience !
> Enough for her to keep propriety
> Of persons ; to be honest ; to observe
> Moderate dimensions, decency of language,
> Speaking the common speech of Christian folk,
> Born and brought up in this your native land.
> She too, as I have told you, hails all fellows—
> Sansculottes, big-wigs—men alike, as brothers.
> And if the ancients used her not, brave playwrights
> Among these modern, use her. If the Sire
> Of Those that Know wrote nothing in her favour,
> Either she was not plying then, or haply
> He broached that subject in his books now lost.
> Besides, the Stagirite spoke nothing, mark you,
> Of paper, printing, or the mariner's compass ;
> Yet, prithee say, are these things not worth using
> Because, forsooth, that great man did not know them ?

Let then who lists make Farces at his will;
And note that 't is far better thus to do,
Than to breed monsters, and to christen these
Tragedies, Comedies—lame things that need
Crutches or go-carts to get into motion!
Let Farces but be played two hundred years,
They 'll not be novelties to those, I warrant,
Who in far times to come will call us Ancients.

It would hardly be possible, I think, to plead the cause
of the Romantic Drama against the supposed canons of
Aristotle and the rules of Horace more pleasantly than thus,
or to set forth with more genial intelligence the claims of the
new style on popular acceptance. Curiously enough, the
prediction uttered by Cecchi in the last lines of his prologue
has been amply verified. We condemn the stilted tragedies
of his contemporaries, and tax their comedies with imitative
affectation. We regard the Italian playwrights, with two or
perhaps three luminous exceptions, as obsolete antiquities;
while Shakspere's masterpieces in the mingled or romantic
manner are still new; a perennial Fount of Juvenescence for
all dramatists who seek fresh inspiration, and for all the
audiences of Europe who desire a draught of nature quickened
with poetic passion.

The very faults of youthfulness which Sidney made so
manifest, were now to build the fortune of this sweetest,
prettiest country lass, for whom no name as yet was found in
England. Precisely because she, the untaught girl, the
latest born of all the Muses, pronounced herself no Muse of
Tragedy or Comedy, because she knew no rules distilled from
foreign, obsolete, and scholar-disciplined tradition, it was her
mission to become the Muse of Modern Drama. The Italian
playwright called her Farsa. This title reminds us of French
Farce, with which she can indeed afford to recognise some
slight relationship. But she travelled so far wider, climbed
so far higher, penetrated so far deeper, that to name her
Farce at any time in English, would be out of question. The
destinies of all dramatic art were in her hands. She held the
keys of Tragedy and Comedy; bid classic myth and legend

suit her turn; stretched her rod over fairyland and history; led lyric poetry, like a tamed leopard-whelp, at chariot-wheels of her fantastic progress. Critics now recognise this village-maiden Muse, as Muse of the Romantic Drama, Shakspere's Drama. Under those high-sounding titles she now enjoys a fame equal to that of her grave sisters, Attic Tragedy and Comedy. It was her fortune to give to the modern world a theatre commensurate with that of ancient Greece, adapted to the spirit of the new-born age, differing indeed in type from the antique, but not less perfect nor less potent in its bearing on the minds of men.

What a future lay before this country lass—the bride-elect of Shakspere's genius! For her there was preparing empire over the whole world of man :—over the height and breadth and depth of heaven and earth and hell; over facts of nature and fables of romance; over histories of nations and of households; over heroes of past and present times, and airy beings of all poets' brains! Hers were Greene's meadows, watered by an English stream. Hers, Heywood's moss-grown manor-houses. Peele's goddess-haunted lawns were hers, and hers the palace-bordered, paved ways of Verona. Hers was the darkness of the grave, the charnel-house of Webster. She walked the air-built loggie of Lyly's dreams, and paced the clouds of Jonson's Masques. She donned that ponderous sock, and trod the measures of Volpone. She mouthed the mighty line of Marlowe. Chapman's massy periods and Marston's pointed sentences were hers by heart. She went abroad through primrose paths with Fletcher, and learned Shirley's lambent wit. She wandered amid dark dry places of the outcast soul with Ford. 'Hamlet' was hers. 'Anthony and Cleopatra' was hers. And hers too was 'The Tempest.' Then, after many years, her children mated with famed poets in far distant lands. 'Faust' and 'Wallenstein,' 'Lucrezia Borgia' and 'Marion Delorme,' are hers.

For the present moment, when Marlowe is yet at school at Canterbury, this young-eyed, nonchalant girl, with the still unrecognised promise of such womanhood, saunters afield

with nameless playwrights and forgotten singers.   The
strait-laced Melpomene, who smiled so acidly on 'Gorboduc,'
watches her pastimes with a frown.   But our Lady of
Romance heeds not Melpomene, and flouts the honours of
that pedant-rid Parnassus.   She is abroad in dew-sprent
meadows to bring home the may.   Nature, the divine
schoolmistress, instructs her in rules of living art beneath
the oaks of Arden, by the banks of Cam and Isis.   Lap-full
of flowers, ' warbling her native wood-notes wild,' the country
lass of English art returns from those excursions to crowded
booths at Bankside or Blackfriars, to torch-lit chambers of
Whitehall and Greenwich.   You may call her a grisette.
But, once again, what destinies are hovering over her!

CHAPTER VIII

THEATRES, PLAYWRIGHTS, ACTORS AND PLAYGOERS

I. Servants of the Nobility become Players—Statutes of Edward VI.
and Mary—Statutes of Elizabeth—Licences.—II. Elizabeth's and
Leicester's Patronage of the Stage—Royal Patent of 1574—Master of
the Revels—Contest between the Corporation of London and the Privy
Council.—III. The Prosecution of this Contest—Plays Forbidden
within the City—Establishment of Theatres in the Suburbs—Hostility
of the Clergy.—IV. Acting becomes a Profession—Theatres are Mul-
tiplied—Building of the Globe and Fortune—Internal Arrangements
of Playhouses—Interest of the Court in Encouragement of Acting
Companies.—V. Public and Private Theatres—Entrance Prices—
Habits of the Audience.—VI. Absence of Scenery—Simplicity of
Stage—Wardrobe—Library of Theatres.—VII. Prices given for Plays
—Henslowe—Benefit Nights—Collaboration and Manufacture of
Plays.—VIII. Boy-Actors—Northbrooke on Plays at School—The
Choristers of Chapel Royal, Windsor, Paul's—Popularity of the Boys
at Blackfriars—Female Parts—The Education of Actors.—IX. Pay-
ment to various Classes of Actors—Sharers—Apprentices—Receipts
from Court Performances—Service of Nobility—Strolling Companies
—Comparative Dishonour of the Profession.—X. Taverns—Bad Company at Theatres—Gosson and Stubbes upon the Manners of Play-
goers—Women of the Town—Cranley's ' Amanda.'—XI. ' The Young
Gallant's Whirligig '—Jonson's Fitzdottrel at the Play.—XII. Comparison of the London and the Attic Theatres.

N.B. The authorities for this chapter are Collier's ' History of English
Dramatic Poetry to the Time of Shakespeare,' upon which it is chiefly
based; the Tracts published by the Old Shakespeare Society, 1853;
and the Collection of Documents and Tracts in the Roxburghe Library,
1869.

I

THE history of English dramatic literature cannot be rightly
understood without a survey of the theatres in which plays
were exhibited, of the actors who performed them, and of the
audience for which they were provided. In the infancy of
the stage, there existed no permanent buildings set apart for

theatrical exhibitions; nor did play-acting constitute a recognised profession. We have seen in the chapter upon Moral Plays that noblemen used to maintain a musical establishment for the service of their Chapels, and to this department of their households the actors of Interludes and Moral Plays were attached. When not required by their masters, these players strolled the country, calling themselves Servants of the magnate whose pay they took and whose badge they wore. After this fashion Companies of Actors came into existence; and the towns of England were infested by wandering bands, professing to be the Servants of the Earl of Warwick, Lord Clinton, the Earl of Derby, or some other eminent person, whose household supported the luxury of a trained set of players. Often enough, the claim of such strollers was well founded. But pretenders to a title which they could not justify were numerous; and under the name of My Lord's Players, common vagabonds and men of no condition roamed the counties. During the reign of Edward VI. it was found necessary to place the theatrical establishments of noble houses under the special control of the Privy Council. Licences were granted to the aristocracy to maintain troops of players, and their performances were limited to the residences of their masters. The political and religious disturbances of that reign had given occasion to seditious propaganda under the colourable pretext of play-acting. There were no newspapers; and next to the pulpit, the stage, rude as it was, formed the most popular and powerful engine for disseminating opinions on matters of debate. During the reign of Mary, theatrical exhibitions were submitted to even stricter control. Finding that the Protestant reaction was being worked by means of Moral Plays, the Crown endeavoured to silence secular acting in public through the length and breadth of England. Encouragement, meanwhile, was given to the revival of Miracle Plays, in the belief that these would educate the people back to their old creeds. The Court, however, still maintained a musical and dramatic establishment upon a scale of great magnificence. In salaries alone, independent of board liveries, and incidental expenses, it is

calculated that Mary spent between two and three thousand
pounds a year on this department of her household. It was
impossible, however, by any repressive measures of the Privy
Council, to check a custom which had gained so strong a
hold upon the manners of the nation. Noblemen refused to
be interfered with. The public had no mind to be deprived
of their amusements. Therefore the class of men who gained
their livelihood by acting, having the goodwill of the people
and the protection of powerful masters on their side, defied
or eluded the orders of the Crown. It would seem that Mary's
edicts had the effect of increasing clandestine performances, and driving the professors of the art of acting into
vagrancy and vagabondage. This at least is the conclusion
we may draw from the tenor of Elizabeth's first proclamations
on the subject of the stage. These are clearly regulative,
implying the intention to check disorder and to place a
prevalent national amusement under State supervision. Soon
after Elizabeth's accession it was decreed that no players
should perform without a licence from the Mayors of towns,
or from the Lord-Lieutenants of counties, or from two
Justices of the Peace resident in the neighbourhood. Companies professing to be Servants of noblemen, who could not
prove their title, were to be treated as rogues and vagrants
under the rigorous Acts in force against such persons. Plays
on matters touching religion and government were strictly
forbidden. The department of the Revels at Court was put
at once upon a more economical footing. But the theatrical
establishments of the aristocracy seem, at the same period, to
have been multiplied in numbers and considerably strengthened in efficiency.

II

It was a fortunate circumstance for the development of
our theatre that both Elizabeth herself and her favourite
Leicester were enthusiastically partial to play-acting. Had
it not been for their encouragement and patronage, the stage
could hardly have established itself upon a permanent footing

in London; and the conditions which rendered a national Drama possible in England might have been missed. The justice of this observation will be perceived when we come to consider the next and most eventful chapter in the history of the English stage. In the first years of Elizabeth's reign, Leicester, then Sir Robert Dudley, had the best company of players in his service. He took a personal interest in their welfare, as appears from a letter addressed by him in June 1559 to the Earl of Shrewsbury. The object of this letter was to obtain for them the licence to play in Yorkshire. He begins by saying that his servants, 'bringers hereof unto you, be such as are players of interludes;' expressly states that they hold 'the licence of divers of my Lords here, under their seals and hands, to play in divers shires within the realm under their authorities, as may amply appear unto your Lordship by the same licence;' and recommends them to Lord Shrewsbury as 'honest men, and such as shall play none other matters, I trust, but tolerable and convenient.' Thus it seems that, in conformity with Elizabeth's edicts, the servants of Sir Robert Dudley had armed themselves with a licence signed by several Lord-Lieutenants of counties, upon the production of which they counted on the liberty to play within the jurisdictions of the signatories.

The same players, relying on their Master's powerful support, advanced so far in their pretensions that in 1574 they obtained from Elizabeth herself a Royal Patent. This document, the first licence granted by the Crown to a dramatic company, was given at Greenwich under the Privy Seal upon May 7, to James Burbage and four partners. Addressed 'to all Justices, Mayors, Sheriffs, Bailiffs, head Constables, under Constables, and all other our officers and ministers,' it empowered Lord Leicester's servants to 'use, exercise, and occupy the art and faculty of playing Comedies, Tragedies, Interludes, Stage-plays, and such other like . . . as well for the recreation of our loving subjects, as for our solace and pleasure, when we shall think good to see them.' Elizabeth, in this paragraph, specially contemplates the double function of Lord Leicester's servants; first as caterers

for the public and then as players at Court. Up to this time
the royal establishment had no formed body of dramatic
artists, and no players with the title of Queen's Servants.
The Master of the Revels for the time being engaged the
best companies to play at Court; and among these the
Servants of Lord Leicester had been conspicuous for frequent
performance. After the date of the patent, Leicester's men,
for a time at any rate, called themselves, upon the strength of
the document, 'The Queen's Majesty's Poor Players.'

The patent next rehearses the places to which the
privilege extends : ' As well within our City of London and
Liberties of the same, as also within the liberties and
freedoms of any our Cities, Towns, Boroughs, &c. whatsoever,
as without the same, throughout our Realm of England.'
Then follow the limitations under which the privilege is
granted. All plays performed by Leicester's men must have
received the sanction of the Master of the Revels. No public
representations might take place 'in the time of Common
Prayer, or in the time of great and common Plague in our
said City of London.'

The privileges granted in this Royal Licence testified to
Elizabeth's personal approval of Burbage and his comrades,
no less than to Leicester's warm-hearted patronage. They
were ample, and seemed explicit enough to have conferred a
monopoly of acting on this company throughout the length
and breadth of England. Yet the players met with a
determined opposition when they strove to exercise their
rights, and only entered, after a sharp struggle, into a partial
enjoyment of the Queen's concession.

Eleven years earlier, Archbishop Grindall had already
raised his voice against the growing frequency of plays in
London. He termed the actors ' an idle sort of people, which
had been infamous in all good commonwealths,' and called
upon the Secretary of State to get them altogether banished
to at least three miles beyond the City bounds. A disastrous
epidemic was then raging, which furnished the Archbishop
with an excellent argument. Undoubtedly the concourse of
all kinds of people to hear plays helped to spread infection.

Upon the double grounds which Grindall had adopted in 1563, namely, the lewdness and profanity of plays, and the peril of contagion in times of sickness, the Corporation of London now determined to resist the establishment of Leicester's company within their jurisdiction.

On December 6, 1575, the Common Council drew up a memorial upon the subject of play-acting, which so curiously illustrates the feeling of the times, that it must furnish copious extracts. The preamble opens thus: 'Whereas heretofore sundry great disorders and inconveniences have been found to ensue to this City by the inordinate haunting of great multitudes of people, specially youth, to plays, interludes, and shows; namely, occasion of frays and quarrels ; evil practices of incontinence in great inns, having chambers and secret places adjoining to their open stages and galleries; inveigling and alluring of maids, specially orphans, and good citizens' children under age, to privy and unmeet contracts ; the publishing of unchaste, uncomely, and unshamefast speeches and doings; withdrawing of the Queen's Majesty's servants from Divine service on Sundays and holy days, at which times such plays were chiefly used ; unthrifty waste of the money of the poor and fond persons; sundry robberies by picking and cutting of purses ; uttering of popular, busy, and seditious matters, and many other corruptions of youth, and other enormities ; besides that also sundry slaughters and maimings of the Queen's subjects have happened by ruins of scaffolds, frames, and stages, and by engines, weapons, and powder used in plays.' So far the Recorder has recited the first of Grindall's arguments. He next takes up the second : 'And whereas in time of God's visitation by the Plague, such assemblies of the people in throng and press have been very dangerous for spreading of infection, &c.' He then proceeds to remedies and regulations, which are in substance these : 1. That all plays shall be subjected to censors appointed by the Lord Mayor and Aldermen. 2. That none but players licensed by the Council shall exhibit. 3. That the same shall be taxed for maintenance of poor and sick persons. 4. That no performance shall take place during Divine service, or in times of general sickness. 5. That though the private houses of the nobility be exempt from these restrictions, the Council shall determine what constitutes a privileged residence, and shall exercise control and censure over the plays there represented.

Among the ' Orders appointed to be executed in the City of London ' during the year 1576, one provided for the total prohibition of theatrical performances in public within the City-bounds, upon the score of their ungodliness.   This Order of the Common Council, had it taken full effect, would have nullified the Queen's Licence.   What gave further importance to the matter was, that the Justices of Middlesex made common cause with the Corporation ; and it seemed not improbable that the players would be driven far off into the country.   Leicester's servants, therefore, seeing their privileges threatened with extinction, sent up a petition (in which they styled themselves ' the Queen's Majesty's Poor Players ') to the Privy Council.   This was answered, point by point, in a Memorandum addressed by the Corporation to the same body.   The actors argued that they needed practice in public, in order that they might acquire proficiency enough to play before the Queen at Court.   Their livelihood was being taken from them.   Their dramatic performances were honest recreations, fit for holydays.   London was the proper place for theatrical exhibitions, inasmuch as disorders would certainly arise on winter evenings from persons flocking to and from the stages in the fields.   Though it was right and proper to suspend play-acting in times of the plague, it ought to be clearly defined what rate of mortality constituted a general and dangerous sickness.   Lastly, they claimed the monopoly of acting, which seemed to have been granted them.

To these pleas the Recorder responded.   It is not decent that the Queen should witness shows which had been ' commonly played in open stages before all the basest assemblies in London and Middlesex ; ' therefore, if the players need practice, they must take it in the private residences of their masters.   The art of acting is not a profession by itself, but is only tolerable as a recreation exercised by men 'using other honest and lawful arts, or retained in honest services.' Holydays are abused by such folk, who do not respect the regulation respecting service time ; and 'it may be noted how uncomely it is for youth to run straight from prayer to plays, from God's service to the Devil's.'[1] If the fields are too far off to serve their turn, ' the remedy is ill conceived to bring them into London ; ' it would be far better to put a stop to them altogether. With regard to the Plague, it were desirable, Plague or no Plague, to be quit of plays ; yet, if the point has to be considered, the right data for deciding it are these : the common rate of mortality in London is between forty and fifty per week, or more often under forty ; if then the death-rate for two or three weeks together has not exceeded fifty, it may be assumed that there is no immediate peril on the score of infection. Finally, if there must be players, a monopoly extended to one company may be regarded as a blessing. In that case let the Queen's Servants be scheduled, man by man ; for as it is, the town is infested with companies, all of which call themselves Queen's Players.

From this contention between the Players and the Corporation, it appears that the latter despaired of suppressing the Drama altogether, though they would have liked to do so. They scouted the notion that Actors could be treated like the craftsmen of a recognised trade. They had indeed to tolerate them in great men's houses. But they were resolved to drive them beyond the City bounds into the fields or country, to silence them in Plague-time, and to restrain them from performing on Sundays and holydays. It is also clear that the strong point in the actor's case was the Queen's partiality for the drama. This circumstance is confirmed by an order sent from the Privy Council, December 24, 1578, to the Lord Mayor, commanding him to suffer six companies— the Children of the Chapel Royal and S. Paul's, and the Servants of the Lord Chamberlain, Lord Warwick, Lord

---

[1] In the tract called *The Second and Third Blast of Retreat from Plays*, the author says of Holidays : ' Then all Hell breaks loose.'

Leicester, and Lord Essex—to play in London 'by reason
that they are appointed to play this Christmas before her
Majesty.'[1]

III

Open warfare on the subject of the Drama was thus
declared between the Court and the City. But it was
conducted upon terms of mutual respect and cautious
circumspection. Both parties took the tone of armed
neutrality rather than one of active hostility. The Queen's
patronage of Leicester's men, her known partiality for stage-
shows, and the privilege claimed by the nobility, rendered it
impossible for the Common Council to prosecute their case
with vigour. While protesting, they were forced to tolerate.
The Court, upon the other hand, was glad to temporise. It
formed no part of the Crown's policy to tamper with the
ancient freedom of the City; and the attitude assumed by the
burghers of London showed that the matter in debate was
one of no slight moment to them. Instead, therefore, of
fighting out the battle, both sides consented to a compromise.
Instead of defining the situation by fixed statute, it was left
indefinite. The players took the best line which was open to
them. Relying on the favour of the Court, bending to the
authority of the Corporation, they established themselves in
permanent buildings outside the strict limits of the City.
This was a conclusion of the struggle which the City can
hardly have foreseen. Hitherto plays had been acted in the
yards and galleries of inns on scaffolds erected for the purpose.
The Orders of the Common Council had been directed chiefly
against scandals thence ensuing. Now they found themselves
obliged to tolerate a far more formidable nuisance. In

---

[1] *The Second and Third Blast*, printed in 1580, 'allowed by Authority,'
and adorned with the shield of the City, forms an important manifesto
against plays and theatres from the side of the Corporation. A long
section is directed against the privilege of Noblemen to maintain players,
and their abuse of this privilege by omitting to support them and turning
them over to the public as their source of income. See Roxburghe
Library Reprint, pp. 133 *et seq.*

Shoreditch, at Blackfriars, on Bankside, in the best frequented and most accessible suburbs, the players, whom the burghers wished to extirpate, began to erect theatres. The debatable lands which these persistent servants of the public and the Court had chosen for their settlement, illustrated in geographical terms the compromise upon which their future existence depended. Those outlying districts were neither in the City nor the fields. Comprehended for certain purposes within the jurisdiction of the Mayor, they still formed no parcel of his undisputed, indefeasible domains. The suburbs savoured of the country, to which the Corporation sought to relegate play-acting. Yet they lay convenient to the public, and were handy to the gallants of the Court. It was under the tacit, if unwilling, consent of the Mayor, though not without explicit protest from distinguished inhabitants of the invaded quarters, that the first self-styled Theatres were built in 1576.

The decisive issue in this contest between the Court and players on the one hand and the Corporation on the other, resulting in the banishment of the players from the City and their erection of permanent stages, is commemorated in the following popular rhyme :

> List unto my ditty !
> Alas, the more the pity,
> From Troynovant's old city
> The Aldermen and Mayor
> Have driven each poor player !

What the ballad leaves unnoticed, because it was not then apparent, is that this expulsion of the players from the City, with their ensuing settlement in the suburbs, decided the fortunes of our Drama, and advanced it from the state of nomadism to that of urbane and accredited civility.

The year 1576, following that in which the Corporation made its unsuccessful onslaught on play-acting, may be regarded as the birth-year of the English Drama. Three theatres, at least, were then established in the purlieus of the City. The first of these was styled 'The Theatre ; ' the

second took its name, in all probability, from the plot of
ground on which it stood, and was called 'The Curtain.'[1]
Both were in Shoreditch, and both soon obtained a bad
reputation for brawling, low company, and disreputable
entertainments. In the old play of Stukeley, the hero
discharges, among his other debts, upon his marriage
morning, five marks to the Bailiff of Finsbury—

> For frays and bloodshed in the Theatre fields.

A ballad written in contempt of Marlowe records, among the
disorders of his manhood, that—

> He had also a player been
> Upon the Curtain stage,
> But brake his leg in one lewd scene
> When in his early age.

The Servants of Lord Leicester in the same year built their
theatre at Blackfriars. On hearing that Burbage had bought
up certain dwellings for this purpose, near the Lord
Chamberlain's lodgings, the respectable inhabitants of Blackfriars petitioned the Privy Council against his project. They
alleged that the concourse of 'vagrant and lewd persons'
would prove a nuisance to the neighbourhood, and in
particular that the playhouse being close to the church, 'the
noise of the drums and trumpets will greatly disturb and
hinder both the minister and the parishioners.' It is noticeable that the Lord Chamberlain did not sign this petition.
The theatre was built, and continued to enjoy a high
reputation under the name of 'The Blackfriars.' Burbage's
company, which had first been Leicester's men, soon after
their settlement at Blackfriars, were known as the Lord
Chamberlain's Servants. Later on, in the reign of James, they
called themselves the King's Servants. Their theatre, like those
of Shoreditch, was a wooden structure. After twenty years'
use it became untenantable, and in 1596 it was rebuilt,
Shakspere's name occurring at that time among the
company.[2]

---

[1] *Curtina* in base Latin means a little court.
[2] Query : Was Blackfriars rebuilt or built for the first time in 1596 ?

A sermon, preached at Paul's Cross in December 1576 or 1577, shows that the erection of these theatres had made a profound impression on the public mind. 'Look but upon the common plays in London,' exclaims the preacher, 'and see the multitude that flocketh to them and followeth them! Behold the sumptuous Theatre houses, a continual monument of London's prodigality and folly!' What, he argues, is the sense of closing them in times of sickness? 'The cause of plagues is sin; and the cause of sin are plays; therefore the cause of plagues are plays.' A triumphant syllogism, if the premisses be granted!

The voices of preachers and Puritan pamphleteers were daily raised against playhouses. Yet the Court would not abandon its amusements, and the public grew daily more attached to the Drama. Elizabeth, about this period, ratified her patronage of the Drama by selecting twelve actors from the servants of her nobles, and calling them the Queen's Players. In 1582 the contest between the Privy Council and the Corporation was renewed, and the old arguments were employed to silence the scruples of the citizens. Playgoing is an 'honest recreation,' and players must have practice in order to 'attain to the more perfection and dexterity' when they appear at Court. At the same time, the Lords of Council were desirous that the Drama should be placed under proper restrictions. Acting upon Sundays, in Lent, or during service time on holydays, was strictly forbidden—a prohibition constantly evaded in fact. Stage-plays were kept under the censorship of the Master of the Revels; and when Martin Marprelate was brought upon the stage in 1589, commissioners were appointed to assist that functionary of the Court in his labours. At this period, all acting was suspended for a season.

To the continued jealousy of the civic authorities, combined with the censorship established by the Court, we may ascribe the comparative purity of moral tone and the total absence of political or religious satire, which distinguish our early Drama. When we contrast English Interludes with French Farces, and English with Italian Comedies, we

cannot fail to be struck with the greater manliness and
innocence that mark the comic stage of London. The whole
mass of our dramatic literature reveals nothing like the
' Farce de Frère Guillebert ' or the ' Mandragola ' of Machiavelli. Perhaps, without indulging too much in national
vanity, we may attribute something also to the healthy spirit of
the English people. The public, who were the real patrons
of the Drama, kept the playwrights within decent limits; for
the public, though it did not share the Puritan horror of
dramatic exhibitions, remained in sympathy with law-abiding
and God-fearing teachers. At the same time, English people,
before the triumph of Puritan opinions, saw no reason why
theatres should not stand side by side with churches, and
both be used for purposes of intellectual advancement. The
very invectives of the preachers, humorously jealous of the
playhouse, prove how little the good folk of London dreaded
the contaminations of the stage. ' Woe is me ! ' cries one in
1586, ' the playhouses are pestered, when churches are
naked : at the one it is not possible to get a place, at the
other void seats are plenty. When the bells toll to the
Lecturer, the trumpets sound to the stages ! '

IV

Meanwhile the art and industry of acting rose into
comparative respectability, and considerable wealth was
flowing into the coffers of the Companies. ' It is a woeful
sight,' groans out the Puritan, ' to see two hundred proud
players jet in their silks, where five hundred poor people starve
in the streets ! ' as though money acquired in honest service
of the public by play-acting might not be spent upon fine
clothes, as well as money gained by selling cloth or forging
broad-swords ! ' Over-lashing in apparel,' writes Gosson, ' is
so common a fault, that the very hirelings of some of our
players, which stand at reversion of 6s. by the week, jet
under gentlemen's noses in suits of silk, exercising themselves to prating on the stage and common scoffing when
they come abroad, where they look askance over the shoulder

at every man of whom the Sunday before they begged an alms.'

Many places of public entertainment had been converted into theatres before the close of the century. Paris Garden was a circus for bear-baiting, capable of holding one thousand people, if we may trust the report of an accident which happened there one Sunday in 1582. It was fitted up and used for a playhouse, when Henslowe and Meade took it in 1613. On the Bankside in Southwark, near to London Bridge, we find a nest of such small theatres: the Hope, originally a bear-garden; the Rose, and the Swan, so called from their signs. Newington Butts was the title of a house erected for the convenience of archers and pleasurers in that suburb. On its boards 'The Jew of Malta,' the first 'Hamlet,' the 'Taming of the Shrew,' and 'Tamburlaine,' were brought out. The yard of the 'Red Bull' had long been employed for occasional performances, before the erection of permanent theatres. Late in Elizabeth's reign it was converted into a playhouse of a rough and somewhat boisterous type; though excellent playwrights, like Heywood, wrote for it. The Cockpit, or the Phœnix, in Drury Lane, was also turned into a theatre early in the reign of James. It too enjoyed no favourable reputation, being surrounded with houses of ill fame, which exposed it in 1616 to partial demolition by the prentices on Shrove Tuesday. Whitefriars and Salisbury Court could also boast their theatres. But we have reason to believe that these two houses may have occupied the same site, for Whitefriars ceased to exhibit before Salisbury Court came into notice.

I have hitherto omitted all mention of the two most famous houses in the annals of the stage, the Globe and Fortune. The Globe was first erected in 1593 by Richard Burbage, leader of the Lord Chamberlain's or King's Men. It stood on the Bankside. Street, a builder, was engaged to construct it of timber. The theatre was hexagon-shaped externally, and round within. It had two doors, one leading into the body of the house, the other into the actors' tire-room. It was open to the air with the exception of a thatched roof or 'heaven,' projecting over the stage. The audience stood in the large central place or 'yard,' which was railed off from the stage. Private boxes were provided round this yard, for such as chose to pay for them. This primitive theatre, for ever famous as the scene of Shakspere's exploits, was burned down in 1613 during the performance of a play upon the history of the reign of Henry VIII. Two small guns, it appears, were let off in the course of a pageant, and their discharge set fire to the thatched roof of the heaven. Next year, the house was rebuilt, at the cost of James and noblemen, with a tiled roof, 'in far fairer manner than before.' The Company of Burbage and Shakspere played here in the summer. In the winter they used their other theatre of Blackfriars.

The Fortune came into existence in 1599. Henslowe and Alleyn caused it to be built by Peter Street in avowed competition with the Globe. At this epoch the numerous companies of London had resolved themselves into two main rival troupes : that of Burbage and Shakspere, known as the Lord Chamberlain's or the King's Men ; and that of Henslowe and Alleyn, known as the Lord Admiral's, and afterwards as the Prince Henry's, Men. Shakspere, as dramatist, actor, and part-owner, gave the tone to the former of these companies, and supported their theatrical business with a genius which is now known to have been incomparable. But, during the period of Shakspere's management, this vast superiority was not apparent. Henslowe was a shrewd and stirring man of affairs, interested in more than one of the best London theatres, and keeping famous playwrights in his service. Alleyn was perhaps the greatest actor of the English stage. While the Lord Chamberlain's troop appealed through Shakspere to the highest faculties of the audience, and showed in their performances a certain unity of moral and artistic tone; Henslowe, on the other hand, knew well how to sustain his popularity by efficiency in theatrical details, and how to stimulate the public interest by constant variety. Consequently the two companies were not ill matched ; and to their rivalry we owe the unexampled fertility of our dramatic literature in the first decade of the seventeenth century.

The success of the Globe pushed Alleyn on to build the Fortune. It was erected in Golding Lane, Cripplegate. Up to the time of its destruction by fire in 1621, it was a square building, of lath and plaster, measuring eighty feet externally on each of its four sides. Inside, it measured fifty-five feet each way; so that about twelve feet and a half were left for boxes, galleries, and staircases in front, and tiring-rooms behind the stage. It had three tiers of boxes, rising twelve, eleven, and nine feet, one above the other. The stage was forty-three feet wide, leaving a gangway on each side into the yard, and twenty-seven feet and a half deep to the partition of the tiring-room. The 'gentlemen's and twopenny rooms,' or private boxes, had four divisions; and the tiring-rooms were furnished with windows. The stage was fenced with oak; and the roof—called ' the heaven ' or ' the shadow '— was tiled. It stood upon wooden pillars, carved square and surmounted with satyrs for capitals. From Alleyn's pocket-book we gather that the cost of the erection amounted to 520l. This sum, when added to the purchase of the lease and some adjacent buildings, he reckons at a total of 880l. The theatre was rebuilt in 1623, after a conflagration which destroyed the structure, together with the dresses, properties, and play-books of the company, in two hours. The new Fortune was probably of brick.

Thus London at the end of Elizabeth's reign had at least eleven theatres. Efforts were made, from time to time, by antagonists of the stage, to reduce this number to two, the Globe and the Fortune. But such endeavours proved unavailing; and when the Commonwealth put an end to theatres, we know that six were pulled down and destroyed between 1644 and 1656.[1] Corresponding efforts were made to check the multiplication of companies, and to confine them

[1] The Globe, April 1644; Blackfriars, August 1655; Salisbury Court March 1649; Phœnix, March 1649; Fortune, 1649; Hope 1656. These dates are given on the authority of a letter addressed by Mr. Furnivall to the *Academy*, Oct. 28, 1882.

to the two which had received Royal Licence, namely, the Lord Chamberlain's and the Lord Admiral's Men. These, as we have seen, commanded the largest share of public favour and attention. But they by no means enjoyed a monopoly of the stage. In the reign of James, it became fashionable for players to put themselves under the patronage of various members of the Royal Family. In addition to the servants of the nobility, we hear of the Queen's Servants and the Prince Palatine's Servants, not counting minor troops assembled by private adventurers. The boys attached to choirs, who took so prominent a share in theatrical performances, will receive notice in their proper place and time. From an early period they formed the nurseries of actors, and had a separate existence from that of the playing companies. It must here, however, be noted, that the Court had a direct interest in the promotion and encouragement of actors. Masques and plays formed an indispensable element of the royal equipage ; lacking which, the Court of England would have cut but a poor figure by comparison with the other Courts of Europe. The sovereign's establishment was unable to stand alone. It needed recruiting grounds and exercising grounds, schools in which the actors tried their talents on the public. Nor was the Crown disposed to check the pastimes of the people, which brought it popularity, and which supplied the gentle youth with entertainment. Therefore, the royal countenance was given, for the Court's sake and the people's sake, to private speculators. At the beginning of the seventeenth century, in England, the dramatic business of the metropolis was thus conducted by two great Companies under the King's patent, and by the Court, which needed their cooperation and assistance. Minor troops revolved around these luminaries as their centres, forming as occasion served, disbanding, and resolving their component parts into the main attractive bodies of the Globe, the Fortune, and Whitehall. When the national party, which had been hostile to playacting from the first, became politically omnipotent, theatres were swept away together with the Monarchy of England. The intimate connection between the Court and the Drama is thus established, and a certain political importance is vindicated for the Puritan tirades against the stage.

V

Of the eleven theatres above enumerated, some were called public, and some private. The latter were smaller in size, roofed all over, and frequented by a more select company. Their performances, like those of the public theatres, took place in the afternoon, but by candle-light. For night scenes, the windows were closed to exclude daylight, and some of the torches were extinguished. Blackfriars, Salisbury Court, and the Cockpit in Drury Lane (though this is not quite certain, since the Cockpit had a reputation for low company) were private houses. The Globe, Fortune, and Bull, were public. Both classes of theatres had signs. Heywood, in the fourth act of his 'English Traveller,' speaks of 'the picture of Dame Fortune before the Fortune playhouse;' and Malone asserts, on insufficient but not improbable grounds, that the sign of the Globe was a Hercules supporting the world.[1] When the play was going to begin, the actors hoisted flags and blew trumpets. Play-bills to announce the show, were also in common use; those of tragedies being printed in red letters. Performances began at three o'clock in the afternoon, and averaged about two hours in duration; so that the audience came to the theatre at a convenient time after their dinner, and got away in winter before nightfall. The piece of the day was generally closed with an address to the sovereign, recited by the actors on their knees. Then followed a kind of farce, technically called a jig, in which the Clown performed a solo. Jigs were written in rhyme, plentifully interspersed with gag and extempore action.

Entrance prices varied according to the theatre, the seat, and the kind of exhibition. First representations seem to have drawn higher sums, and so did actors of the first celebrity. For the most ordinary shows, three pennies were paid: 'one at the gate, another at the entry of the scaffold,

---

[1] Comp. *Hamlet*, act ii. sc. 2.

and a third for quiet standing.' In the larger theatres there
was a place called the 'twopenny room,' which answered to
our gallery, and was probably paid for extra after the entrance
fee, which admitted spectators to the yard or cheapest place.
Private boxes, or compartments in the 'gentlemen's rooms,'
were sold at a higher rate. The doors of these boxes shut
with locks, the keys of which were handed over to their lessees.
The lowest frequenters of the public theatres, contemptuously
alluded to as 'groundlings' and 'stinkards,' stood in the yard
beneath the open sky. In the private theatres, the yard was
called the pit, and was supplied with benches. Spectators of
the more fashionable kind, who frequented theatres to see
and be seen, sat on three-legged stools upon the stage. At
the private theatres they had the right, it seems, to do so;
but at the public houses they took this place by force, in
defiance of the hissings and hootings of the groundlings
separated from them by the barriers of the stage. For the
use of a stool they paid sixpence, which was collected after
they had taken their seats. This custom was a great
annoyance both to the actors and the audience; for the
young gallants, who affected it, showed very little consideration for either. They exchanged remarks, and chaffed the
players, peeled oranges and threw apples into the yard, puffed
tobacco from pipes lighted by their pages, and flirted with the
women in the neighbouring boxes. It was found necessary
at last to double the price of a 'tripod;' but it may be
doubted whether this served to check the practice.

Taking various circumstances into consideration, it may be
estimated that on a good night at one of the larger theatres,
prices varying from sixpence to half-a-crown were paid for a
seat.

To form an accurate and lively picture of an Elizabethan
stage-performance is not easy from the meagre references
which we now possess. Yet something of the sort might be
attempted. Let us imagine that the red-lettered play-bill of
a new tragedy has been hung out beneath the picture of Dame
Fortune. The flag is flying from the roof. The drums have
beaten, and the trumpets are sounding for the second time.

It is three o'clock upon an afternoon of summer. We pass
through the great door, ascend some steps, take our key from
the pocket of our trunk-hose, and let ourselves into our
private room upon the first or lowest tier. We find ourselves
in a low square building, open to the slanting sunlight, built
of shabby wood, not unlike a circus ; smelling of sawdust and
the breath of people. The yard below is crowded with
' sixpenny mechanics,' and prentices in greasy leathern jerkins,
servants in blue frieze with their masters' badges on their
shoulders, boys and grooms, elbowing each other for bare
standing ground and passing coarse jests on their neighbours.
A similar crowd is in the twopenny room above our heads,
except that here are a few flaunting girls. Not many women
of respectability are visible, though two or three have taken a
side-box, from which they lean forward to exchange remarks
with the gallants on the stage. Five or six young men are
already seated there before the curtain, playing cards and
cracking nuts to while away the time. A boy goes up and
down among them, offering various qualities of tobacco for
sale, and furnishing lights for the smokers. The stage itself
is strewn with rushes ; and from the jutting tiled roof of the
shadow, supported by a couple of stout wooden pillars, carved
into satyrs at the top, hangs a curtain of tawny-coloured silk.
This is drawn when the trumpets have sounded for the third
time ; and an actor in a black velvet mantle, with a crown of
bays upon his flowing wig, struts forward bowing to the
audience for attention. He is the Prologue. He has barely
broken into the jogtrot of his declamation, when a bustle is
heard behind, and a fine fellow comes shouldering past him
from the tire-room followed by a mincing page.

    ' A stool, boy ! ' cries our courtier, flinging off his cloak and
displaying a doublet of white satin and hose of blue silk. The
Prologue has to stand aside, and falters in his speech. The
groundlings hiss, groan, mew like cats, and howl out,
' Filthy ! filthy ! ' It may also happen that an apple is flung
upon the stage, to notify the people's disapproval of this
interruption. Undisturbed by these discourtesies, however,
the new comer twirls his moustachios, fingers his sword-hilt,

and nods to his acquaintance. After compliments to the gentlemen already seated, the gallant at last disposes himself in a convenient place of observation, and the Prologue ends. The first act now begins. There is nothing but the rudest scenery : a battlemented city-wall behind the stage, with a placard hung out upon it, indicating that the scene is Rome. As the play proceeds, this figure of a town makes way for some wooden rocks and a couple of trees, to signify the Hyrcanian forest. A damsel, with a close-shaved chin, wanders alone in this wood, lamenting her sad case. Suddenly a cardboard dragon is thrust from the sides upon the stage, and she takes to flight. The first act closes with a speech from an old gentleman arrayed in antique robes, whose white beard flows down upon his chest. He is the Chorus ; and it is his business to explain what has happened to the damsel, and how in the next act her son, a sprightly youth of eighteen years, will conquer kingdoms. During the course of the play, music is made use of for the recreation of the audience with songs and ditties, and much attention is bestowed upon the costly dresses of the principal performers. Meanwhile, a cut-purse has been found plying his trade in the yard. It is a diversion in the interval between the acts, to see him hoisted with many a cuff and kick to the stage. There he is tied tightly to one of the pillars, and left to linger the performance out against his will—literally pilloried—pelted and scoffed at when the audience have nothing else to do. The show concludes with a Prayer for the Queen's Majesty, uttered by the actors on their knees. After this is over, or possibly while it is still in progress, the spectators make their exit. Those who have come for rational amusement, pass criticisms on the piece, the company, and the poet's wit. Others put up the table-books, to which they have committed memoranda of choice phrases, epigrams, new-fangled oaths, and definitions fit to air at social gatherings. Young men, who have scraped acquaintance with some damsel in the galleries or boxes, conduct the fair Amanda to a supper in the private room of an adjacent tavern.

VI

It is difficult for us to realise the simplicity with which the stage was mounted in the London theatres. Scenery may be said to have been almost wholly absent. Even in Masques performed at Court, on which immense sums of money were lavished, and which employed the ingenuity of men like Inigo Jones, effect was obtained by groupings of figures in dances, by tableaux and processions, gilded chariots, temples, fountains, and the like, far more than by scene-painting. Upon the public stage such expenditure had, of course, to be avoided. Attention was concentrated on the actors, with whose movements, boldly defined against a simple background, nothing interfered. The stage on which they played was narrow, projecting into the yard, surrounded on all sides by spectators. Their action was thus brought into prominent relief, placed close before the eye, deprived of all perspective. It acquired a special kind of realism, which the vast distances and manifold artifices of our modern theatres have rendered unattainable. This was the realism of an actual event, at which the audience assisted; not the realism of a scene to which the audience is transported by the painter's skill, and in which the actor plays a somewhat subordinate part. As might be expected in a theatre of this description, the actor's wardrobe was both rich and various. John Alleyn's note-book informs us that he paid as much as 20*l*. 10*s*. for one cloak, and 16*l*. for another costume. The dresses of a playhouse formed indisputably its most valuable property. Attention being so closely and exclusively directed to the players, they were forced to be appropriately and substantially attired. Moving, as it were, upon the same plane as the audience, they had to detach themselves from their surroundings by impressive brilliancy of outfit. This want of perspective in the Elizabethan stage, and the absence of scenical appeals to the sense of sight, determined the style of dramatic composition. Our older playwrights depended upon the fancy of the audience to conjure up the scenes which they described. The

luxuriance of their diction can be attributed to the necessity
they felt for stimulating the spectators to an effort of imagination. Their disregard of place and time was justified by the
conditions of a stage which left all to the intellect. The mind
can contemplate the furthest Ind as easily as more familiar
objects; nor need it dread to traverse the longest tract of
years, the widest expanse of space, in following the sequence
of an action. It resulted from these circumstances that the
language of the dramatist and the personality of the actor
were all-important. A naked action was presented by the
player to the audience. That naked action had to be assisted
by the playwright's poetry; and much that now seems
superfluous in the descriptive passages of the Elizabethan
tragedies was needed to excite imagination.[1]

Even more valuable than the wardrobe was the library of
a theatre. Each company bought and jealously preserved the
MSS. of plays, which became its exclusive property, until
such time as the author obtained leave to print it, or some
publisher contrived to pirate it. One of the strongest charges
brought against Robert Greene was, that he had sold the
same play to two rival companies; and complaints are
frequently made that mutilated copies of a comedy had got
abroad without the owner's sanction. Shorthand writers
frequented theatres for the express purpose of taking down
the text of a new play, which they conveyed to press or sold
to a competing set of actors. This custom partly accounts
for the infamous state in which we have received many
dramas—blank verse reduced to chaos, phrases misunderstood,
and speeches clearly compressed to suit the scribe's convenience. The extraordinary indifference of playwrights must
also be taken into account. Heywood and Marston repeatedly
protest against the publication of plays which they had
written to be acted. Having placed the MS. in the hands of
the manager, and received their money for it, the authors

---

[1] It may be worth quoting a passage from Tom Coryat, who, in his
Crudities, observes that the comic theatre in Venice is 'very beggarly
and base in comparison of our stately playhouses in England; neither
can their actors compare with ours for apparel, shows, and music.'

thought it worth no more attention. Jonson was sneered at
for styling his plays ' Works ; ' and Webster got the reputation of a pedant for taking pains about the appearance of his
tragedies in print. With time, however, dramatists began to
superintend the publication of their own plays. With or
without their permission, these things reached the press.
The public bought them for sixpence, and read them with
avidity. Authors perceived that they could make a profit
from the publisher, and receive a handsome sum from the
patron to whom they inscribed their composition. It was
also to their interest to see that works which bore their name
appeared without gross blemishes.

VII

The sums paid for a play varied considerably. The Diary
of Philip Henslowe makes it clear that up to the year 1600
the highest price he ever paid was 8*l.* or 9*l.* He gave Drayton,
Dekker, and Chettle only 4*l.* for a history of Henry I. Jonson,
Porter, and Chettle received from him 6*l.* for a comedy called
' Hot Anger soon Cold.' Greene sold ' Orlando Furioso ' for
something over 7*l.* Ben Jonson raised the price of plays to
a minimum of 10*l.* In ' Histriomastix ' the poet-scholar
Chrisoganus, when asked, ' What's the lowest price ? '
answers :

> You know as well as I ; ten pound the play.

Henslowe occupied a somewhat singular position in dramatic
society. He was part-owner of the Fortune and several other
theatres. As manager and impresario, he came into business
relations with actors and authors who were not, like Shakspere, exclusively devoted to the Globe. But he also appears
to have established a kind of brokerage between the companies
and playwrights, by means of which he made much private
profit. He speculated on the necessities of authors, advancing
money to secure their services or to help them at a pinch.
Some of the needier quill-drivers, a Daborne or a Munday or
a Chettle, were thus always in his debt ; and he drove hard

bargains with them. Daborne, in one of his letters to
Henslowe, complains that the playing Company would have
given 20*l.* for his labour, which seems to prove that the
broker had some previous claim upon him. Or else we may
suppose that the Company's pay involved participation in
their profits, whereas Henslowe paid in cash and took the
risks. A passage in the 'Actors' Remonstrance' points to
the habit of securing the service of playwrights by 'annual
stipends and beneficial second-days;' and we know that it
was customary to allow the playwright a benefit upon the
second or third day, or both. Daborne stipulates with
Henslowe for 'but 12*l.* and the overplus of the second day.'
A large proportion of Elizabethan plays were the joint
production of several authors, who must have had their own
system of dividing profits. In some cases the playwrights
collaborated to save time in 'firking up' a comedy or
history. Other instances, where several names are printed
on a title-page, point to the remodelling of popular plays by
new hands. Or a poet would add prologue and epilogue to a
piece which needed some fresh attraction. For this sort of
service Henslowe generally paid 5*s.* Still, we have every
reason to believe that the practice of genuine collaboration
in the concoction of a drama was common. It does not so
much argue good fellowship among the dramatists, though
that undoubtedly existed, as their thoroughly business-like
conception of their craft. A play had to be produced for a
certain price, and they applied the principle of divided labour
to its composition, careless of posterity, seeking money profit
more than fame. When play-writing became fashionable,
poets from the universities with tedious tragedies, persons of
quality with stupid comic pieces to dispose of, had to pay the
managers to get their rubbish acted. It may here be
mentioned that in the flourishing period of the Drama,
playwrights very commonly were also actors and managers
of theatres. Marlowe and Heywood, Shakspere and Jonson,
to mention only the more prominent, served their apprenticeship as players to the stage. Cyril Tourneur took a company
across the seas to act in Flanders. Davenant in 1639

obtained letters patent for erecting what would have been the
largest theatre in London.

VIII

Considering how little the Elizabethan Drama owed to
scenery and mounting, and how wholly it depended for interpretation upon acting, the facts we know about stage-players
are not a little astonishing. First and foremost, actresses
were never seen upon the stage.[1] Beardless youths ' boyed
the greatness' of Cleopatra and Lady Macbeth. Hobble-
dehoys ' squeaked' out the pathos of Desdemona and Juliet's
passion. Sometimes the beard and broken voice were only
too apparent in these male performers of female parts. ' O,
my old friend!' says Hamlet, when he greets the players :
' thy face is valanced since I saw thee last; comest thou to
beard me in Denmark? What, my young lady and mistress!
By'r lady, your ladyship is nearer to heaven than when I saw
you last by the altitude of a chopine. Pray God, your voice,
like a piece of uncurrent gold, be not cracked within the ring.'

It appears that boys who acted female characters received
higher pay than adults. This arose, no doubt, from the
difficulty of finding lads sufficiently good-looking and well-
educated to sustain a woman's part with dignity and grace.
It was only for a short while that their capacity for representing women lasted; and during those few years they were
much sought after. When their beards grew and their voices
broke, they proceeded to the common business of the theatre.
From a ' Dialogue of Plays and Players,' written after the
Restoration, we glean a few details respecting these boy-
actors. ' Hart and Clun,' says Trueman, ' were bred up boys
at the Blackfriars, and acted women's parts. Hart was
Robinson's boy or apprentice; he acted the Duchess in the
tragedy of "The Cardinal," which was the first part that

---

[1] A strong feeling prevailed in England against actresses. In 1629 a
French company came over and played at Blackfriars. Prynne, in his
Histriomastix, terms the actresses among them, 'French women or
monsters rather.' They were not well received, but on the contrary were
' hissed, hooted, and pippin-pelted from the stage.' See Collier, i. 452.

gave him reputation.' Durfey, who had seen Hart play in
Chapman's 'Bussy d'Ambois,' calls him 'that eternally
renowned and best of actors.' He took the part in a revival
of the tragedy in 1675. The same interlocutor adds further
on : 'Amyntor was played by Stephen Hammerton, who was
at first a most noted and beautiful woman-actor, but afterwards he acted with equal grace and applause a young
lover's part.'

In the infancy of the theatre, it was customary for whole
plays to be performed by boys. At the great schools, Eton
and Westminster for instance, acting formed a part of the
ordinary course of education, combining exercise in memory
and elocution with honest recreation. When Northbrooke
published his sweeping condemnation of the stage in 1577,
he made an exception in favour of these private performances.
'I think it is lawful for a schoolmaster to practise his scholars
to play comedies, observing these and the like cautions : first,
that those comedies which they shall play be not mixed with
any ribaldry and filthy terms and words. Secondly, that
they be for learning and utterance' sake, in Latin, and very
seldom in English. Thirdly, that they use not to play
commonly and often, but very rare and seldom. Fourthly,
that they be not pranked and decked up in gorgeous and
sumptuous apparel in their play. Fifthly, that it be not
made a common exercise, publicly, for profit and gain of money,
but for learning and exercise' sake. And lastly, that their
comedies be not mixed with vain and wanton toys of love.'
Northbrooke's rules and regulations for boy-actors were
consistently violated in practice. The choristers of cathedral
and royal foundations, the Children of the Queen's Chapel, of
Windsor and of S. Paul's, became public actors, and performed upon the common stage. It also appears that great
men, who patronised the theatre, kept companies of boys as
well as adult players ; thus we hear of Leicester's boys in
1577. The custom of combining the duties of the choir and
the theatre dated from the earliest times of Mysteries and
Miracles The Children of Paul's petitioned Richard II. in
1378 against the performance of sacred pageants by lewd and

ignorant people, which interfered with their monopoly. The same choir, numbering thirty-eight boys, exhibited a Latin play before Henry VIII. in 1528, when Luther was brought upon the stage and satirised. It is clear from many sources that the theatrical establishments of royal and noble persons were attached to their chapels ; and we have already seen that the exhibition of Miracles was at first in the hands of the clergy. This helps to explain what seems to us the anomaly of choristers being avowedly dedicated to the stage, and of religious foundations being used as nurseries for actors. Elizabeth, in 1586, gave letters patent to Thomas Gyles, then Master of the Children of Paul's, empowering him to enlist and press into his service likely lads. In this, and in subsequent patents down to the year 1626, when Puritan opinions were gaining strength, and when the scandals of the public stage had grown notorious, the employment of the choristers of Paul's and of the Chapel Royal in dramatic business was always specially contemplated. The singing-room at S. Paul's became a theatre, where the public gained admittance upon payment. So far from exhibiting harmless comedies for educational exercise, these children uttered seditious matter during the Martin Marprelate controversy, and had to be silenced for some years after 1589. The Children of the Chapel Royal, recruited under similar privileges, and with the same avowed object of providing the Queen with suitable actors, took the name of Children of her Majesty's Revels. They played at Blackfriars, when this theatre was not used by the King's Servants, and had the monopoly of some of the best dramas of the period, including two or three of Jonson's. At last, in 1626, acting came to be thought inconsistent with a chorister's duties in church. A warrant granted to Nathaniel Giles in that year, provides that the boys enlisted by him for the Chapel Royal shall not be employed as comedians, ' for that it is not fit or decent that such as should sing the praises of God Almighty, should be trained or employed in such lascivious and profane exercises.' [1]

[1] All the treatises against the stage dwell on the impropriety of boys disguising as women, and learning to affect the manners and passions

A list of the boys who acted in 'Cynthia's Revels' shows
that several lived to be distinguished members of their
profession. On one of them, Salathiel Pavy, who died in
early youth, Jonson wrote the beautiful elegy beginning:

> Weep with me, all you that read
>   This little story;
> And know, for whom a tear you shed,
>   Death's self is sorry.
> 'T was a child, that so did thrive
>   In grace and feature,
> As Heaven and nature seemed to strive
>   Which owned the creature.
> Years he numbered scarce thirteen,
>   When fates turned cruel;
> Yet three filled zodiacs had he been
>   The stage's jewel.

Jonson specially commends young Pavy for his just representation of old men! The Children of Blackfriars were
very popular, and had their partisans among the poets and
the public, who preferred them to any company of adult
actors. In a tract attributed to Thomas Middleton (date
1604), they are mentioned as 'a nest of boys able to ravish a
man.' Shakspere thinks it worth while to run them down in
' Hamlet; ' where Rosencrantz is made to speak of ' an aery
of children, little eyasses,' who ' are now the fashion, berattle
the common stages,' and carry away ' Hercules and his load
too '—an allusion, perhaps, to the sign of the Globe Theatre.
The Children of Paul's were not less in request. Their
singing-room had the advantage of cleanliness and a select
audience. A personage in 'Jack Drum's Entertainment'
(date 1601) is made to say:

> I like the audience that frequenteth there
> With much applause. A man shall not be choked
> With the stench of garlic, nor be pasted
> To the barmy jacket of a beer-brewer.

---

of the female sex (see *Third Blast*, p. 147; Gosson's *Plays Confuted*,
pp. 195-197; *Short Treatise*, p. 243). But none hint at any very scandalous inconveniences resulting therefrom.

It is difficult to conceive how complex and passionate action can have been adequately represented by these boy-players of the age of thirteen. The conjecture might perhaps be hazarded, that plays expressly written for them—those of Jonson for example—took a certain fixity of type and hardness of outline from the exigencies under which the poet worked. Compared with Shakspere's art, that of Jonson is certainly distinguished by formality. Instead of persons, he presents incarnate types and humours. Has this to do with the fact that while Shakspere wrote for his own company of men, Jonson knew that he was writing for boys? From this point of view, it would be interesting to collect and analyse the plays which were composed for boy actors by the boys' poets.

However this may be, it cannot be questioned that the dramatic training of young men furnished the English theatre with an admirable body of players. Professionals like Nat Field, who had been reared among the Children of Blackfriars, were acquainted from the cradle with the business of their craft. After a like fashion, the Court and domestic fools of a previous age had founded a tradition of broad comic acting, which rose by degrees above buffoonery, retaining its raciness of homespun humour, and rendering the clowns of Shakspere possible. Pursuing the same train of thought, we are led to note how the musical ability of choristers, accustomed to sing anthems and madrigals, encouraged the poets to introduce those lyrics into plays which form so effective an element in their scenes. On all sides, the more we study its conditions, the better we perceive how workmanlike and businesslike a thing our Drama was. It had nothing amateurish about it. And though we may attribute some of its short-comings to this cause, we must also reckon it among the most serious advantages possessed by our theatre in the Elizabethan age.

IX

Actors were usually partners in the business of a theatre. They were classified as sharers, three-fourths sharers, one-half sharers, and hired men. This system of payment

connected the pecuniary interests of the performers directly
with those of the theatre, and relieved the manager of much
personal responsibility. Henslowe's Diary informs us that
15*l.* was paid by an actor for a whole share in bad times, and
9*l.* for half a share in more favourable circumstances. How
the profits were divided, we do not exactly know. Henslowe,
who took care as a capitalist to secure the lion's share in all
his ventures, pocketed the large sum of 4*l.* after one performance of ' The Jew of Malta,' and on another occasion, when
' Woman Hard to Please ' was played, he netted 6*l.* 7*s.* 8*d.*
Besides his share, a celebrated actor might also receive a
salary. Nat Field took 6*s.* a week in addition to his portion
of the profits. Hired men were under the control of the
proprietors or lessees of the theatre. They worked at fixed
wages, and had no direct interest in the business. Lads of
ten entered into articled engagements. Their masters, usually
actors, sometimes managers of theatres, taught them their
trade and pocketed their earnings. Hart, we have already
heard, was Robinson's apprentice. Beeston, a famous
player at the Cockpit, had for his apprentices Burt, Mohun,
and Shatterel, who went on playing after the Restoration.
Henslowe records the purchase of a boy from William
Augustine for 8*l.* Augustine must have trained the boy,
holding under indentures the right to use him for his own
profit.

Performances at Court were a source of considerable gain
to acting companies. After 1574, 10*l.* was the regular sum
paid by her Majesty for a performance. Like rewards were
given by noblemen and gentry, at whose houses the players
attended. This we gather from a poor comedy called
' Histriomastix,' which contains a curiously realistic altercation between the Usher and Steward of a great house and a
company of actors on the tramp, about the payment of a
play :

> Ten pounds a play, or no point Comedy !

To perform without licence from the local authorities, or
without the badge of some known magnate, was strictly

forbidden by statutes.   These regulations, however, were
commonly avoided, and players took what name they pleased :

But whose men are we all this while ?

exclaims a clownish actor in 'Histriomastix,' who does not
know that he is being passed off as a member of Sir Oliver
Owlet's company.

Large London troops not unfrequently dispersed in time
of plague.   They would then tramp 'upon the hard hoof from
village to village,' receiving small pay unless they chanced
upon some hospitable noble's house in holiday, but carefully
distinguished from the 'roguish players' who travelled
without licence.   The Induction to Shakspere's 'Taming of
the Shrew' furnishes a pretty instance of such acquaintance
as might well subsist between a lord and an actor.   On this
point it must be added that James I. in 1603 put an end to
the noblemen's privilege of licensing players as their servants.
Henceforward, companies endeavoured to obtain patents from
the Crown or licences from royal personages.   All others
strolling the country were liable to arrest as 'wandering
rogues.'   In London the regular actors gave tone to
Bohemian society.   Taverns frequented by the best of them,
the Mermaid and the Triple Tun for example, were sought
out by men of fashion.   Young fellows, who wished to cut a
figure in society, aped the manners of these artists and repeated their jokes.   Play-going citizens pursued them with
tiresome but profitable adulation.   To be an actor's Ingle, or
intimate and crony, was the ambition of many a foolish
saddler or cordwainer's prentice.

It is certain that acting reached a very high pitch of
excellence in the days of Burbage and Alleyn, Summer and
Tarlton.   Shakspere could not have written for inferior players
those parts which at the present time tax histrionic talent
beyond its faculty.   As the absence of theatrical machinery
helped playwrights to be poets, so the capacity of actors
stimulated literary genius to the creation of characters, which
the author knew beforehand would be finely and intelligently
rendered.   Yet, in spite of the elevation which the play-

wright's and the actor's arts attained at the beginning of the seventeenth century, a permanent and persistent dishonour attached to the stage. This was due to the local surroundings of the theatres in London, to the habits of a largely popular audience, and to the old religious abhorrence which gathered virulence together with the spread of Puritan opinions.[1]

X

In the origins of the stage, theatres were closely con-nected with houses of public entertainment—inns, hostelries, places of debauch, and brothels. The Corporation forced companies to seek permanent establishment in suburbs, where the Court and City alike sought questionable recrea-tion. What a tavern was in those days, may be gathered from the gross outspoken dialogues of ' The Prodigal Son ;' a play cast back on us from Germany without the benefit of censure.[2] Such taverns were the first homes of the public drama. When theatres came into existence, drinking-shops of the old sort and houses of ill-fame sprang up around them. They formed a nucleus for what was vile, adventurous, and hazardous in the floating population. This explains and justifies the opposition of the civic dignitaries. The actual habits of the audience in a London theatre may be imagined from more or less graphic accounts given by contemporary satirists. Gosson, in ' The School of Abuse,' writes as follows :

' In our assemblies at plays in London, you shall see such heaving and shoving, such itching and shouldering to sit by women ; such care for their garments, that they be not trod on ; such eyes to their laps, that no chips light in them ; such pillows to their backs, that they take no hurt ; such masking in their ears, I know not what ; such giving them pippins, to pass the time ; such playing at foot-saunt without

---

[1] Jonson in the *Poetaster* satirises all this system in the person of Histrio.

[2] *School of Shakspere*, vol. ii.

cards ; such ticking, such toying, such smiling, such winking, and such manning them home when the sports are ended, that it is a right comedy to mark their behaviour, to watch their conceits, as the cat for the mouse, and as good as a course at the game itself to dog them a little, or follow aloof by the print of their feet, and so discover by slot where the deer taketh soil.'

Stubbes, in his ' Anatomy of Abuses,' may be quoted to like purpose : ' But mark the flocking and running to Theatres and Curtains, daily and hourly, night and day, time and tide, to see Plays and Interludes, where such wanton gestures, such bawdy speeches, such laughing and fleering, such kissing and bussing, such clipping and culling, such winking and glancing of wanton eyes and the like is used as is wonderful to behold. Then these goodly pageants being ended, every mate sorts to his mate, every one brings another homeward of their way very friendly, and in their secret conclaves covertly they play the sodomites or worse.'

The private rooms in neighbouring taverns, where girls were taken for seduction, or young men led astray by wanton women, had been specially denounced under the Orders of the Common Council.[1] Gosson, in his ' Plays Confuted in Five Actions,' says : ' It is the fashion of youths to go first into the yard, and to carry their eye through every gallery ; then, like unto ravens, where they spy carrion thither they fly, and press as near to the fairest as they can. Instead of pomegranates, they give them pippins ; they dally with their garments to pass the time ; they minister talk upon all occasions ; and either bring them home to their houses on small acquaintance, or slip into taverns when the play is done.' Players are accused by Prynne of being go-betweens, and playhouses of being the purlieus of corruption. ' Our common strumpets and adulteresses, after our stage-plays are ended, are oftentimes prostituted near our playhouses, if not in them. Our theatres, if they are not bawdy-houses, as they may easily be, since many players, if

[1] See above, p. 217.

reports be true, are common panders, yet they are cousin-
germans, at leastwise neighbours to them.'   In 'The Actors'
Remonstrance,' 1643, this abuse of the player's vocation is
ingenuously admitted : ' We have left off for our own parts,
and so have commanded our servants to forget that ancient
custom which formerly rendered men of our quality infamous,
namely the inveigling in young gentlemen, merchants' factors,
and prentices to spend their patrimonies and masters' estates
upon us and our harlots in taverns. . . . We shall for the
future promise never to admit into our sixpenny rooms those
unwholesome enticing harlots that sit there merely to be
taken up by apprentices or lawyers' clerks.'[1]   Young men
came to find their partners for the evening there, as some do
now at Music-halls.   Cockaine, in a prologue, certifies :

> If perfumed wantons do, for eighteenpence,
> Expect an angel, and alone go hence,
> We shall be glad.

Women of loose life frequented them, as they do contemporary
places of public recreation.   A personage in one of Glap-
thorne's comedies makes protest :

>   We are
> Gentlemen, ladies ; and no city foremen,
> That never dare be venturous on a beauty,
> Unless when wenches take them up at plays,
> To entice them to the next licentious tavern,
> To spend a supper on them.

Girls of good character scarce dared to enter a play-house.
From ballads of the period we learn what was the peril to
their reputations :

> Thither our city damsels speed,
>   Leaving their mistress' work undone,
> To meet some gallant, who indeed
>   Doth only seek, when they are won,
>   Away from them eftsoons to run :
> When they are served, they are content
> To scorn their seely instrument.

---

[1] Roxburghe Library, issue for 1869, pp. 260, 265.

Another ballad-writer lays it down that a modest wife should eschew theatres : [1]

> I would not have her go to plays,
>   To see lewd actors in their parts,
> And cause the men upon her gaze,
>   As they would sigh out all their hearts :
> Methinks a wife it ill becomes
> To haunt their prologue trump and drums.

This aspect of theatres, considered as the snares of prentices, the gins where women lost and sold their characters, has been vividly delineated in the ' Amanda,' of Thomas Cranley (date 1635). The author is addressing a woman of the town :

> The places thou dost usually frequent
>   Is to some playhouse in an afternoon,
> And for no other meaning and intent
>   But to get company to sup with soon ;
>   More changeable and wavering than the moon,
> And with thy wanton looks attracting to thee
> The amorous spectators for to woo thee.

> Thither thou com'st in several forms and shapes
>   To make thee still a stranger to the place,
> And train new lovers, like young birds, to scrapes,
>   And by thy habit so to change thy face :
>   At this time plain, to-morrow all in lace :
> Now in the richest colours may be had ;
> The next day all in mourning, black and sad.

> In a stuff waistcoat and a petticoat,
>   Like to a chamber-maid thou com'st to-day :
> The next day after thou dost change thy note ;
>   Then like a country wench thou com'st in grey,
>   And sittest like a stranger at the play :
> To-morrow after that, thou com'st again
> In the neat habit of a citizen.

---

[1] In support of this extract see the curious story about a citizen's wife and the players Richard Burbage and William Shakspere, quoted from *The Barrister's Diary* by Collier, i. 319. *The Actors' Remonstrance* is eloquent upon the subject of amours between handsome young players and women partial to the theatre.

The next day rushing in thy silken weeds,
    Embroidered, laced, perfumed, in glittering show;
So that thy look an admiration breeds,
    Rich like a lady and attended so,
As brave as any countess dost thou go.
Thus Proteus-like strange shapes thou venturest on,
And changes hue with the cameleon.

XI

A poem published by the old Shakespeare Society graphically depicts the habits of a young man about town, and his humours at the theatre. It was written by Francis Lenton, and printed under the title of ' The Young Gallant's Whirligig ' in 1629. The lad has been sent up to study law at one of the Inns of Court. But the money which his parents provide for the purchase of books, he spends on 'fencing, dancing, and other sports.'

No, no, good man, he reads not Littleton,
But Don Quix-Zot, or else the Knight of the Sun.
Instead of Perkins' pedlar's French, he says
He better loves Ben Jonson's book of plays,
But that therein of wit he finds such plenty
That he scarce understands a jest of twenty.

As the terms fly past, his father sends him more money to defray the expenses of his studies and his call to the bar. This he lays out upon fine clothes :

This golden ass, in this hard iron age,
Aspireth now to sit upon the stage;
Looks round about, then views his glorious self,
Throws money here and there, swearing Hang pelf !

He gets entangled in love-affairs, treats penny-a-lining poets to pots of ale for sonnets, which he sends to his mistress, and frequents the cheaper playhouses in search of new adventures :

Your theatres he daily doth frequent,
Except the intermitted time of Lent,

Treasuring up within his memory
The amorous toys of every comedy
With deep delight; whereas, he doth appear
Within God's temple scarcely once a year,
And that poor once more tedious to his mind
Than a year's travail to a toiling hind.

This gives the satirist occasion for a diatribe against the
stage :

Plays are the nurseries of vice, the bawd
That through the senses steals our hearts abroad ;
Tainting our ears with obscene bawdery,
Lascivious words, and wanton ribaldry ;
Charming the casements of our souls, the eyes,
To gaze upon bewitching vanities,
Beholding base loose actions, mimic gesture
By a poor boy clad in a princely vesture.
These are the only tempting baits of hell,
Which draw more youth unto the damnèd cell
Of furious lust, than all the devil could do
Since he obtainèd his first overthrow.
Here Idleness, mixed with a wandering mind,
Shall such variety of objects find
That ten to one his will may break the fence
Of reason, and embrace concupiscence.
Or, if this miss, there is another gin,
Close-linked unto this taper-house of sin,
That will entice you unto Bacchus' feasts,
'Mongst gallants that have been his ancient guests,
There to carouse it till the welkin roar,
Drinking full bowls until their bed's the floor.

The gallant's father dies ; and he inherits the paternal lands.
Then he plunges into new extravagance ; buys coach and
horses ; maintains mistresses ; decks himself out in silks and
satins and Bristol diamonds, bought by him for Oriental
gems. His former haunts are abandoned for more fashionable
places of resort :

The Cockpit heretofore would serve his wit,
But now upon the Friars' stage he 'll sit :
It must be so, though this expensive fool
Should pay an angel for a paltry stool.

As might be expected, our gallant's whirligig runs round to ruin. His costly wardrobe has to be sold :

> His silken garments, and his satin robe,
> That hath so often visited the Globe,
> And all his spangled, rare, perfumed attires,
> Which once so glistered in the torchy Friars,
> Must to the broker's to compound his debt,
> Or else be pawnèd to procure him meat.

I have only selected those lines from the satire which illustrate the manners of the theatre. With regard to the habit of carrying fine clothes to the stage, for exhibition and effect, a parallel passage might be quoted from Ben Jonson's ' The Devil is an Ass ' (Act I. sc. 3). One of the personages in the play, Fabian Fitzdottrel, a squire of Norfolk, is speaking :

> Here is a cloak cost fifty pound, wife,
> Which I can sell for thirty, when I have seen
> All London in 't, and London has seen me.
> To-day I go to the Blackfriars playhouse,
> Sit in the view, salute all my acquaintance,
> Rise up between the acts, let fall my cloak,
> Publish a handsome man and a rich suit ;
> As that 's a special end why we go thither,
> All that pretend to stand for 't on the stage ;
> The ladies ask, Who's that ? for they do come
> To see us, love, as we do to see them.

That 50l., though an extravagant, was no extraordinary price for a cloak, is certain from the items paid out of the privy purse for masquing dresses.[1] In one bill the wife of Charles I. discharged 1,630l. for embroidery alone. No wonder the old dramatists so frequently exclaim that gentlemen and city madams carried farms and acres on their backs, and stowed estates away in their wardrobes.

It is not to be imagined—putting these direct witnesses aside—that the theatres of Elizabethan were much purer than the theatres of Victorian London. Customs in that epoch

---

[1] See details in the following chapter on Masques.

were far more strongly marked; manners coarser; vice more open and avowed. Therefore we may well believe that City scruples, Court restrictions, and Puritan prejudices were in a measure justified. It is also certain that an appreciable social stigma—the stigma under which his sonnets show that Shakspere smarted, the stigma of which Jonson bluntly speaks in his 'Hawthornden Conversations'—attached to poets who wrote for the stage, and to players who interpreted their works.[1] When the Puritans took the upper hand, scruples, restrictions, and prejudices became persecution, prohibition, and crusade. The theatre was then summarily and abruptly put an end to.

XII

These were the conditions under which our Drama came to its perfection. This was the theatre for which Shakspere wrote, where Shakspere acted, where Shakspere gained a livelihood and saved a competence. In slums and suburbs, purlieus and base quarters of the town, stood those wooden sheds which echoed to the verses of the greatest poet of the modern world. Disdainfully protected by the Court, watched with disfavour by the City, denounced by Puritans and preachers, patronised by prentices and mechanics, the Muse of England took her station on the public boards beneath a misty London daylight, or paced, half-shrouded in tobacco smoke, between the murky torches of the private stage. Compare her destiny with that of her Athenian elder sister. In the theatre of Dionysos, scooped for a god's worship from the marble flanks of the Acropolis, ringed with sculptured thrones of priests and archons, entertained at public cost, honoured in its solemn ceremonials with crowns and prizes worthy of the noblest names, the Muse of the dramatic art in Athens dwelt a Queen confessed. To serve her rites with costly liturgies, conferred distinction on the foremost citizens. To attend her high-tides, was the privilege and pleasure of a

[1] This fact is proved by the curious character of the Player drawn in *The Rich Cabinet*, 1616, republished in Roxburghe Library, 1869, p. 228.

congregated nation. To compete for her rewards was the
glory of warriors, ambassadors, men of birth and fashion,
princes—of Æschylus, of Sophocles, of Agathon, of Dionysius.
Religion, national enthusiasm, public expenditure, private
ambition, combined with the highest genius in art and literature to dignify, consecrate, enrich, immortalise the clients of
the Attic stage. For scenery, there were the sea and mountains,
the Parthenon and Propylæa, over-arched with skies of Hellas.
For audience, the people of Athens, 'ever delicately marching
through most pellucid air.' It is not to be wondered that a
monumental splendour and sublimity distinguishes what still
survives of Attic tragedy and comedy. It is not to be
wondered that the works of our Elizabethan playwrights
should be incomplete and fragmentary, grandiose by accident,
perfect only in portions, imposing in their mass and multitude
more than in single masterpieces. The marvel rather is that
on such a theatre as that of London, Shakspere should have
risen like a sun, to give light to the heavens of modern poetry.
The marvel is that round him should be gathered such a constel-
lation—planets of Marlowe's, Jonson's, Webster's, Fletcher's
magnitude, each ruling his own luminous house of fame. In the
history of literature, the Elizabethan Drama is indeed a paradox
and problem. Nothing so great and noble has emerged elsewhere from such dishonour. Those who seek to harmonise this
paradox, to solve this problem, find their answer in the fact
that England's spirit, at that epoch, penetrated and possessed
the stage. The fact itself is scarcely explicable. Yet the fact
remains. At some decisive moments of world history, art,
probably without the artist's consciousness, gives self-expression to a nation. One of these moments was the age of
Elizabeth and James. One of these elect nations was England.
The art whereby we English found expression, was the
Drama.

CHAPTER IX

MASQUES AT COURT

Definition of the Masque—Its Courtly Character—Its Partial Influence over the Regular Drama.—II. Its Italian Origin.—III. Masques at Rome in 1474—At Ferrara in 1502—Morris Dances—At Urbino in 1513—Triumphal Cars.—IV. Florentine Trionfi—Machinery and Engines—The Marriage Festivals of Florence in 1565—Play and Masques of Cupid and Psyche—The Masque of Dreams—Marriage Festival of Bianca Capello in 1579.—V. Reception of Henri III. at Venice in 1574—His Passage from Murano to San Niccolò on Lido. —VI. The Masque transported to England—At the Court of Henry VIII. and Elizabeth—Development in the Reign of James I.— Specific Character of the English Masque—The Share of Poetry in its Success.—VII. Ben Jonson and Inigo Jones—Italian and English Artists—The Cost of Masques.—VIII. Prose Descriptions of Masques —Jonson's Libretti—His Quarrels with Jones—Architect *versus* Poet.— IX. Royal Performers—Professionals in the Anti-Masque.—X. Variety of Jonson's Masques—Their Names—Their Subjects—Their Lyric Poetry.—XI. Feeling for Pastoral Beauty—Pan's Anniversary.— XII. The Masque of Beauty—Prince Henry's Barriers—Masque of Oberon.—XIII. Royal and Noble Actors—Lady Arabella Stuart— Prince Henry—Duke Charles—The Earl and Countess of Essex— Tragic Irony and Pathos of the Masques at Court.—XIV. Effect of Masques upon the Drama—Use of them by Shakspere and Fletcher —By Marston and Tourneur—Their great Popularity—Milton's Partiality for Masques—The ' Arcades ' and ' Comus.'

I

THE Masque in England was a dramatic species, occupying a middle place between a Pageant and a Play. It combined dancing and music with lyric poetry and declamation, in a spectacle characterised by magnificence of presentation. It made but little demand on histrionic talent. The persons who performed a Masque had only to be noble in appearance,

richly dressed, and dignified in movement. The real authors
and actors were the poet, who planned the motive ; the
mechanist, who prepared the architectural surroundings,
shifted the scenes, and devised the complicated engines requisite for bringing cars upon the stage or lowering a goddess
from the heavens ; the scene-painter ; the milliner ; the
leader of the band ; the teacher of the ballet. In the hands
of these collaborating artists, the performers were little more
than animated puppets. They played their parts sufficiently,
provided their costumes were splendid and their carriage
stately. Therefore the Masque became a favourite amusement with wealthy amateurs and courtiers aiming at effect.
Since it implied a large expenditure on costly dresses, jewels,
gilding, candlelights, and music, it was an indulgence which
only the rich could afford. For its proper performance, a
whole regiment of various craftsmen, each excellent in his
degree and faculty, had to be employed. We are thus prepared to understand why the Masque was emphatically a
branch of Court parade, in which royal personages and the
queens of fashion trod the daïs of Greenwich or Whitehall in
gala dress on festival occasions. The principal actors posed
upon this private stage as Olympian deities or Personifications of the Virtues, surrounded by a crowd of ballet-dancers,
singers, lutists, and buffoons. All the elements of scenic
pomp—the Pageant, the Triumph, the Morris-dance, the
Tournament, the Pastoral, the Allegorical Procession—were
pressed into the service of this medley. And to make a perfect Masque after the English fashion, accomplished actors
from the open stage and musicians had to lend their aid, who
played the comic parts and sang the lyrics written for them
by a poet capable of mastering and controlling the spirit of a
hybrid so peculiar.

On public theatres there was but little scope for Masques.
Yet the species influenced our dramatic style in many important points. Shows which mimicked Masques at Court were
often introduced into the regular drama, both as motives in
the plot, and also for spectacular effect. To what an extent
they imposed upon imagination, appears in the language of

the poets. Marston uses this striking simile in one of his
tragic plays :

> Night, like a Masque, is entered heaven's great hall
> With thousand torches ushering her way.

Milton, in his 'Ode on the Nativity,' describes the descent of
Peace to earth, in a stanza which paints a common episode of
such performances :

> But he, her fears to cease,
> Sent down the meek-eyed Peace ;
> She, crowned with olive green, came softly sliding
> Down through the turning sphere,
> His ready harbinger,
> With turtle wing the amorous clouds dividing ;
> And, waving wide her myrtle wand,
> She strikes an universal peace through sea and land.

II

The Masque came to England from Italy. In the first
historical mention made of it, Hall writes : ' On the Day of
Epiphany at night, the king with eleven other were disguised
after the manner of Italy, called a Mask, a thing not seen
before in England.' The date was 1512–13. The king was
Henry VIII. Up to this time we read in the Court records
of pageants, morices, disguisings, interludes, plays, revels.
The Masque was recognised as a new thing, combining and absorbing other previous State-shows. After the same date, the
terms of 'maskelyn' and 'masculers' occur in 'Records of
the Revels,' pointing clearly to ' Maschera ' and 'Mascherati,'
possibly pronounced in dialect by the Italian servants of the
king.[1] Thus there is no doubt at all about the Italian origin
of the Masque. Marlowe puts these lines into the mouth of
Gaveston, when that favourite looks forward to his life at
Court :

> I must have wanton poets, pleasant wits,
> Musicians, that with touching of a string

---

[1] Compare the Florentine *Mandragola* for *Mandragora*.

May draw the pliant king which way I please :
Music and poetry is his delight ;
Therefore I 'll have Italian masks by night,
Sweet speeches, comedies, and pleasing shows ;
And in the day, when he shall walk abroad,
Like sylvan nymphs my pages shall be clad ;
My men, like satyrs grazing on the lawns,
Shall with their goat-feet dance the antic hay.

The point is so clear, and at the same time so important
for the comprehension of the subject, that a digression on the
Triumphs and Ballets of the Italians may be allowed to
serve as introduction to Ben Jonson, Chapman, Fletcher,
Beaumont, and Milton.

III

The first great festival bearing on the history of Masques
in Italy, was that provided for Leonora of Aragon, the daughter
of King Ferdinand of Naples, when she passed through Rome
in 1474 to mate with Ercole d' Este. A nephew of Pope
Sixtus IV., the Cardinal Pietro Riario, converted the Piazza
de' Santi Apostoli into a temporary palace for her use. The
square was roofed with curtains, and partitioned into rooms
communicating with the Cardinal's own residence. These
were hung with tapestries of silk and velvet, and furnished
with the costliest utensils. The servants of the Cardinal's
household were dressed in liveries of satin and embroidery.
The seneschal changed his costume four times in the course
of the banquets. Nymphs and centaurs, singers and buffoons,
drank wine from golden goblets at side tables. The air was
refreshed with perfumed fountains and cooled by punkahs.
Cooks and confectioners vied, one with another, in producing
fantastic dishes. It is recorded that the histories of Perseus,
Atalanta, and Hercules, wrought in pastry, gilt and sugared,
adorned the boards at which the Papal, Royal, and Ducal
guests assembled. To entertain their eyes and ears, shows
from classical and Biblical history were provided, of which the
following extract from Corio will give sufficient details : ' After

the banquet there came upon the daïs some eight men, with other eight attired like nymphs, who were their loves. Among these came Hercules leading his Deianira by the hand, Jason with Medea, Theseus and Phædra, each man accompanied by his mistress and dressed according to their characters. When they had all entered, fifes and many other instruments began to sound, and they to dance and dally with their nymphs; in the which while leaped forth certain others in the shape of Centaurs, bearing targets in the one hand, and in the other clubs, who would have robbed Hercules and his companions of their Nymphs. Thence arose a combat between Hercules and the Centaurs, at the end of which the hero drove them from the daïs. There was besides a representation of Bacchus and Ariadne, with many other spectacles of the greatest rarity and most inestimable cost.' These shows in Rome, when a Cardinal, the favourite and nephew of a Pope, turned his palace and the adjacent piazza into a scene of revel for the entertainment of a royal bride, marked an epoch in the evolution of the Masque. But the echo of those picturesque rejoicings sounds too faintly across four centuries to captivate the ears of our imagination. We only gather from the notices of Italian annalists that artistic genius played its part upon that transitory stage in the Eternal City.

The Venetian Diary of Sanudo gives a detailed history of the festivities which followed the marriage of Lucrezia Borgia to Alfonso d' Este at Ferrara in 1502. The chief feature in the entertainments was the recitation of five plays of Plautus in Latin upon five successive nights. These gems of classical literature were set in a rich framework of Renaissance arabesque; masques and ballets being interpolated between each scene. It is noticeable that the name Moresco, whence our Morris-dance, was already used for these interludes. They were throughout accompanied by music. One hundred and ten actors formed the troop, who, on the first night, saluted the Ducal party in their dresses of taffety and camlet, cut after the Moorish fashion. It will suffice to indicate the motives of the rarer or more striking dances. On one occasion ten men appeared upon the stage, with long hair, in flesh-coloured

tights, to represent nudity. Each held a cornucopia, con·
taining four torches filled with turpentine, which flamed.
A damsel went before them in alarm, pursued by a dragon.
The dragon was vanquished and driven off the stage by a
knight. His squire caught up the damsel, and the whole troop
moved away, surrounded by the savage men shaking flames
from their torches. The next ballet was of maniacs, who
danced with frantic gestures. On another evening there
appeared a Masque of Cupid, who shot arrows and sang
madrigals. He was attended by ten actors cased in tin and
covered with lighted candles; they carried looking-glasses on
their heads, and in their hands were paper lanterns also filled
with tapers. Again, upon the fifth evening, six men of the
wild woods drew forth a globe upon the stage, out of which,
when it was opened, emerged the four Cardinal Virtues, singing appropriate songs. Ballets of armed men in the antique
habit, of German lansknechts, of Moors, of hunters, of husband-
men, of goats, and of gladiators fighting with darts and daggers,
filled up other intervals in the Plautine comedies.

It is clear, from the foregoing summary, that the shows
at Ferrara in 1502 contained in embryo the chief constituents
of the Masque as it was afterwards developed. The same may
be said about the first exhibition of Bibbiena's 'Calandria.'
The poet, Castiglione, has left an interesting account of this
performance, which took place at Urbino in 1513. The
Comedy was divided into five acts. Consequently, there were
four interludes, here also called Moresche. The first was on
the tale of Jason, who yoked a couple of fire-breathing bulls to
his plough, and sowed the dragon's teeth. Then from traps
in the stage emerged a double band of antique warriors, who
danced a wild Pyrrhic, and slew each other. The second was
a Masque of Venus, drawn along in her car by a couple of
doves, and surrounded by a bevy of Cupids tossing flame from
lighted tapers. They set fire to a door, out of which there
leaped eight gallant fellows, all in flames, careering round
the stage in a fantastic figure. The third was a Masque of
Neptune. His chariot was drawn by sea-horses, with eight
huge monsters of the deep surrounding it and gambolling

grotesquely to the sound of music. The fourth was a Masque of Juno, seated on a fiery car, drawn by peacocks. Her attendants were birds of different sorts, eagles, ostriches, sea-mews and party-coloured parrots. This oddly selected troupe executed a sword-dance, says Castiglione, with indescribable, nay incredible, grace! When the Comedy ended, Love entered and explained the allegory of the interludes in a con-cluding epilogue. The whole performance terminated with a piece of concerted music from behind the scenes, ' the invisible music of four viols, accompanying as many voices, who sang, to a beautiful air, a stanza of invocation to Love.'

IV

The special point about these ballets at Urbino was the introduction of chariots, which gave a processional character to the Masques, and made them equivalent to Triumphs. Each interlude had its Car, attended by a choir of dancers. To enlarge upon the Carri and Trionfi of Florentine Carnivals during the Medicean rule, is hardly necessary. I have already elsewhere copiously illustrated them; and those who are curious in such matters, may study Signorelli's Triumph of Cupid, or old engravings of Petrarch's Trionfi, in order to obtain some notion of their arrangement. Yet it is worth alluding here to the Triumph of Bacchus and Ariadne designed by Lorenzo the Magnificent about the year 1485; to the Triumph of Death devised by Piero di Cosimo in 1512; and to the Pageant of the Golden Age which greeted Leo X. in 1513.[1] These processional shows exercised a distinct influence over the form assumed by the Masque. Nowhere did they take richer and more complicated shapes of beauty than in Florence. The inventions ascribed by Vasari to Filippo Brunelleschi, by means of which vast aureoles were raised aloft into the air, with saints and goddesses enthroned amid cherubic creatures, clouds and candles, must also be reckoned among the most important contributions to the apparatus of the Masque.[2] The Florentines called them *Ingegni*, and we

---

[1] *Renaissance in Italy*, vol. iv. pp. 389–398.   [2] *Ibid.* p. 318.

find them largely used in London under the Italian influence
of Inigo Jones. The rare artistic genius of the Florentines
amused itself on all occasions with such shows; combining
architecture, sculpture, painting, and music, with tableaux
expressed by living actors. Thus Vasari, in his life of
Francesco Rustici, describes the recreations of a private club
of artists, called the Compagnia della Cazzuola. Once a
year they met for a sumptuous banquet, which was followed
by a Comedy and Masque. Phineus and the Harpies; the
dispute of theologians upon the Trinity, with an incomparable
heaven of angels; Tantalus in hell; Mars, surrounded with
mangled human limbs; Mars and Venus, caught naked in
the net by Vulcan and exposed to the laughter of all the
gods; were among the motives of these bizarre entertainments, each worked out with varied and capricious inventions
of gardens, wildernesses, fireworks, monsters, emblematical
figures and allegories.

The climax of Florentine ingenuity in the production of
costly and artistic spectacles was reached in two entertainments designed to celebrate the two weddings of Francesco
dei Medici, Grand Duke of Tuscany. Of each of these we
possess the fullest possible accounts, written by contemporaries
with a wealth of detail which enables the historian to view
them once again in the pallid light of the imagination.[1] In
the year 1515 Francesco married his first wife, Joan of
Austria. After making a triumphal entry into Florence, the
Queen, as she is always styled, was conducted to the palace
on the Ducal Square. The hall, constructed for the
meetings of the Great Council in the days of the Republic,
had been turned into a theatre. At one end was the stage,
concealed from view by a drop-scene painted with a hunt.
In front of this stage were seats provided for the gentlemen
of the Court and city. Further back, on a raised daïs,
covered with the finest carpets, stood the thrones of the
princely couple, with chairs for ambassadors and German

---

[1] See *Descrizione dell' Entrata, del Convito Reale, e del Canto
de' Sogni*. Firenze. Giunti, 1566, *Feste nelle Nozze*, &c. Giunti,
1579.

nobles of the Queen's retinue. Behind, and on a higher plane, swept a semicircular tribune in six tiers. This was filled with noble ladies, whose dresses of a hundred hues and sparkling jewels blent with the sober tones of frescoes on the walls around them. The hall was lighted by candles set on branches issuing from masks, and so arranged as to present the figures of Imperial, Papal, Royal, and Grand-Ducal crowns—alluding to three Emperors of the Austrian Dynasty, three Medicean Pontiffs, a Queen whom the Medici had given to France, and the five Dukes of their line who had reigned in Italy. Overhead, ran the level Florentine ceiling, carved out of solid oak, embossed with armorial emblems, heavy with gold, rich with vermilion and ultramarine. It seemed impossible that the stage should rival or surpass the hall in radiance of effect. When the curtain rose, the scene represented the Piazza of Sta. Trinità in Florence, viewed in perspective through a triumphal arch flanked by the river-gods of Danube and Arno. Giorgio Vasari was responsible for these decorations, and for the engines which now introduced the Masque. That, together with the play embedded in it after the Italian fashion, had been arranged from the Myth of Psyche, by Messer Giovambattista Cino. Out of a heaven of clouds, which opened to the sound of music, Venus appeared in her gilded chariot drawn by swans. Three Graces, naked save for their veils of yellow hair, were grouped around her. The Four Seasons appropriately clad, with wings of butterflies upon their shoulders (as Raphael has imaged forth the Hours in his Farnesina frescoes), followed in her train. While they descended to the stage, Cupid issued from the background. He was naked, as the poets have described him; and his wide wings fluttered in the wind of perfumes. Hope and Fear and Grief and Gladness bore his bow and quiver, net and torches, scattering inextinguishable flame. Thus the Masque began. To follow it through all its scenes would weary curiosity. Else I might tell how all the Legend of Psyche was set forth; how pleasant groves appeared; how Hades threw wide his iron portals, and the three-headed Cerberus howled, and the Furies shook their twisted whips;

and how the show was closed with Hymen on the summit of
the Heliconian Mount.

This Comedy of 'Psyche' was recited at Florence on
S. Stephen's Day. On the second of February in the same
winter, a second Masque of even greater rarity and beauty
was exhibited. It is called 'Il Canto de' Sogni,' or the
Music-Masque of Dreams. 'The soul or conceit of the
Masque,' as our ancestors would have expressed it, was both
subtle and imaginative. The poet conceived all human life,
with its various passions, accidents, and humours, as a Dream,
beneath the empire of the great god Morpheus. Love,
Beauty, Glory, Wealth, Ambition, Madness passed before his
vision as the shapes which vex a sick man's slumbers. And,
as he viewed them, so he brought them on the stage,
making the pomp of that arch-ducal theatre subserve the
lesson that:

We are such stuff
As dreams are made of; and our little life
Is rounded with a sleep.

The thought was ingenious. The execution was gorgeous
and varied beyond all power of description. One hundred and
sixty-eight performers took part in the Masque; some on
horseback, and some seated in cars. It was set forth in a
series of processions; a central chariot in each division of the
show being designed with appropriate emblems and paintings,
crowded with figures picturesquely grouped together, attended
by outriders, and accompanied by the performers of concerted
music. Love, Fame, Plutus, Bellona, and Madness,
surrounded by their several genii and ministers, sat enthroned
upon the chariots. Their qualities were indicated by marked
and unmistakable allegory. All the personages who composed their several trains, however else they may have been
attired, wore bat's wings on their shoulders; to symbolise the
dreams that fly abroad through brains of sleeping folk by
night. The Triumph of Love displayed the usual myths of
Hope and Fear; but the car was followed by a band, which
detached itself in quaintness from the common elements of
Masquerade. The leader of this band was Narcissus, dressed

in blue velvet embroidered with the flowers that bear his name. The beautiful young men who waited on him, called *i belli*, wore doublets of silver tissue worked with all the blossoms of the spring, and breeches of blue velvet sewn in gold and silver with narcissus flowers. When Madness appeared, her company were Bacchantes and Satyrs, pair by pair, twined with ivy and vine branches. The whole procession moved across the scene in studied groups, preceded and divided from each other by detached allegories—Mercury and Diana, Witches and Priestesses, Phantasy and Silence, Night and Dawning. Classical mythology was racked to furnish forth the several emblems of these personifications—their attendant beasts of elephants and dolphins, tortoises and tigers, unicorns and falcons. Blooming youth and wrinkled age, the grisly ugliness of witches and the lucid beauty of Olympian gods, human forms and bestial monsters, were blent together, interchanged, contrasted and combined in the slow-moving panorama.

When the Duke of Florence made his second marriage with Bianca Capello in 1579, these Triumphs were repeated on a scale of similar magnificence, and in very much the same artistic fashion. The descriptive work published upon that occasion is valuable, since it is illustrated with engravings in outline, which, though they do no more than suggest the leading motives of the shows, enable us to form some conception of their general effect. We learn how the high-piled chariots were adorned with statues, set with flaming cressets, and drawn by birds or beasts; how the allegorical personages towered on high above them, grouped with subordinate genii. Monsters of the deep wallowing in mimic oceans, huge sea-shouldering whales, Tritons blowing horns, gilded conchs crowded with naked nymphs and Cupids waving torches, a vast four-headed dragon vomiting flames, a galley preceded by sea-horses, seem to have formed the main attractions of this entertainment. By what means these bulky erections moved along upon their gilded wheels, does not appear. But Florence, from of old, was well furnished with mechanical contrivances; and the artistic genius of the people enabled them to conceal what must have been grotesque in presenta-, tion, under forms of ever fresh invention.

V

Before quitting Italy for the grey metropolis of the North, with its clouded skies and colder festivals, let us shift the scenes from Florence to Venice, and see what the Republic of S. Mark could furnish, when her Doge and Senators gave entertainment to a king. Henry, Duke of Anjou, was the last male scion of the House of Valois, by Henry the Second's marriage with Caterina de' Medici, the daughter of Lorenzo, Duke of Urbino. During early manhood this prince had distinguished himself in the Huguenot wars, and had been elected King of Poland. The death of his brother, Charles IX., made him King of France. In 1574 he was hastening from Warsaw back to his ancestral throne—back to the French palace, where a monk's knife was destined, after a few years, to terminate the craziest career which ever closed a brilliant dynasty in sanguine gloom. At this moment fortune seemed to smile upon his youth and twofold crown. Cynical physiognomists might perhaps have cast no favourable horoscope for the slim and delicate young man, of pale complexion, with a few black hairs upon the sallow chin, who stepped from his carriage at Malghera on to the shores of the lagoon. But sixty Senators of Venice, arrayed in crimson, at the place of embarkation, thought less of Henry's tarnished character and dubious blood than of the fact that he was King of Poland, King of France, Italian by his mother, and now guest of the Republic. Cap in hand, they attended him to his state-barge.[1] There they divided his followers between them, and embarked upon their several galleys. The splendid flotilla, on an afternoon of July, spread canopies of silks and satins on the mirror of that waveless lake. Saluted by the roar of cannon from the islands, this noble convoy oared its passage to Murano. There the palace of Barto-

[1] There is a picture of mediocre performance in the Ducal Palace representing this embarkation at Malghera.

lommeo Capello had been hung with cloth of gold and
embossed leather to receive the King. Sixty halberdiers,
attired in the French colours of orange slashed with blue,
were drawn up at the water staircase. Eighteen trumpeters
and twelve drummers, in the same livery, sounded a military
welcome. Forty of the noblest youths of Venice, habited in
doublets of shot silk, attended as a royal body-guard. The
King passed through this gorgeous train; his sober suit of
mourning and the pale face above the ruffles round his neck
showing dark against that painted background. That night
he spent upon the island. Next day, the Doge and all the
State of Venice waited on him with a galley manned by four
hundred oarsmen, dressed in the colours of the House of
France. High on the poop, beneath a canopy of cloth of gold
he took his station. At his right hand sat the Dukes of
Mantua, Nevers, Ferrara, and the Cardinal Legate of San Sisto.
At his left, the Doge and the Ambassadors. Fourteen galleys
followed with the Senators of Venice, trailing their robes of
purple silk on Oriental carpets. The aristocracy and gentry
of Venice brought up the rear, lashing the waters with the
oars of a thousand glittering gondolas. Through the summer
afternoon they swept, round San Pietro di Castello to Sant'
Elena, and from Sant' Elena to San Niccolo on Lido. At
every point the guns from battlement and bastion thundered
salutes, and the church towers showered their tocsins on the
startled air. Between Venice and Lido the lagoon swarmed
with boats. The whole city seemed to be afloat that day.
Each of the great Guilds had mounted a brigantine with
emblematic pomp and quaint magnificence. That of
the Silk-weavers was one heaven-pointing pyramid of
costly stuffs and banners waving to the wind; that of the
Goldsmiths glittered with chased plate and jewels; that of
the Mercers, manned by a crew in purple and yellow liveries,
burned like a pyre of crimson cloth upon the waves; the
Mirror-makers hung their masts and gunwale thick with
glasses, which flashed back sunlight, as the galley moved, in
dazzling lightnings; the Swordsmiths bristled at every point
with arms and instruments of war. Upon each of these

brigantines and on the gondolas around them were stationed
players upon instruments of music, trumpeters and drummers
and blowers of the Turkish horn, whose wild barbaric din
commingled with the rush of oars and the roar of that vast
multitude.

So the procession swept away toward Lido, where the art
of Venice was to add a crowning consecration to this pomp.
On the shore Palladio had built an arch of triumph leading
to a temple. Tintoretto, Paolo Veronese, and Antonio
Aliense, the three famous painters of the day, had lavished on
this ephemeral masterpiece their matchless colours married to
august design. The Patriarch of Venice waited at the temple
porch to greet the King of France, who, after praying at the
altar, was conducted once more to the sea. This time he
entered the state-barge of the Republic.[1] The Bucentaur
conducted him from Lido, past the Riva, past San Giorgio,
past the Ducal Palace, past the Campanile, down the Grand
Canal. It was late in the evening when he reached the
Palazzo Foscari, which, together with adjacent houses of
the Giustiniani, had been placed at his disposal. The costliest tapestries, embroideries of silk and satin, hangings of
velvet and stamped leather, draped the chambers, which were
filled with choicest furniture and pictures. A table was daily
spread there for five hundred persons. Every night the
palaces were illuminated with lamps and torches ; and every
night the waterways beneath resounded to the strains of
singing choirs and stringed orchestras. Regattas, mock-fights
between the Nicolotti and Castellani, banquets in the Great
Hall of the Ducal Palace, visits to the Arsenal, visits to the
Fuggers of Augsburg in the Fondaco dei Tedeschi, visits to
the glass-works, a musical drama in the Palace, a dress ball
in the room where Tintoretto's ' Paradise ' now hangs,
followed in bewildering succession. When Henry left his
lodgings, the Bucentaur transported him to the piazza. The
pavement was carpeted with crimson cloth ; the windows
hung with blue and orange draperies; the capitals and cor-

---

[1] It is said that Tintoretto contrived to get on board the galley disguised as a groom, and to make a portrait of the King in transit.

nices festooned with laurel wreaths and ivy. At the entrance
of the Sala del Gran Consiglio, two hundred ladies of the
Golden Book stood waiting for him in their white silk robes
of state, with ropes of pearls around their throats and twisted
in their yellow hair.[1] Venice, through those days of festival,
exhibited the scene of one vast Masque—the most imperially
mounted and played on the most splendid theatre that earth
can show. It is satisfactory to read that Henry, in the midst
of all this regal pomp and official parade, found time to
enjoy the pleasures which the city offers to more ordinary
mortals. Attended by one or another of the forty noble youths
who kept him company, he disguised himself and took the
humours of the town, buying a jewelled sceptre in one shop
of the Rialto, and sighing at the feet of an accomplished
courtesan, the famous Veronica Franco. Michelet is, perhaps,
justified in saying that the last Valois left in Venice such
remnants of virility as he brought with him from Poland.
On his return to France, Henry affected the habits and
costume of a woman, and sacrificed his kingdom's interests to
the detested Epernon. Fifteen years of civil warfare, ruined
finances, unpopularity, bad health, and eccentric pleasures,
diversified by the melodramatic murder of the Guise in his
own bedroom, brought this hero of the Venetian Masque to
death by the hand of an assassin at Saint Cloud.

VI

Transported from Italy to England, the Masque, as will
be readily imagined, was shorn of much of its artistic splendour.
The Courts of Henry and Elizabeth could boast no architects
like Giorgio Vasari and Palladio, no painters like Pontormo
and Bronzino, Tintoret and Veronese. English music had not
reached the perfection of Italian art, either in the excellence
of stringed instruments or the practised skill of vocalists.
Instead of the Cars and Triumphs of Florentine Carnivals, in
lieu of the Processions of S. John's Day, and the Venetian

---

[1] As we may see them painted by Gentile Bellini in his picture of
the Miracle of Santa Croce.

festivals of Marriage with the Adriatic, the traditions of scenical parade in England were restricted to City Pageants and the shows of Miracle plays, mummings at Christmas and disguisings at Shrovetide. Climate, scenery, and architecture were alike less favourable to theatrical display on the banks of the Thames than on the shores of Arno or the waves of the Lagoons. It must further be observed that the Italian artists who visited our island, whether sculptors or painters, architects or musicians, were men of the second or third rank. Those only who found no employment at home, or who had special reasons for abandoning their country, exiled themselves to England. In this respect, the English Court was even less fortunate than the French. Cellini and Andrea del Sarto, Primaticcio and Rosso, settled for a time in Paris ; Lionardo da Vinci died at Amboise. But Torrigiani was the most notable Italian who took up his abode in London.

Under these conditions, the Masque received no adequate treatment in England during the reigns of our Tudor sovereigns. Elizabeth was too economical to spend the large sums requisite for a really magnificent Masque at Court, when a simple play could be acted at so much less expense. On one occasion, indeed, she sent a sumptuous embassy of Masquers from London to Edinburgh, as a compliment to James on his accession to the throne of Scotland. Nor was she displeased by the costly pageants prepared for her amusement at Kenilworth. But the sums which a subject and a favourite, like Leicester, could afford for his sovereign's entertainment, the Queen herself was unwilling to expend upon the ordinary pleasures of the Court.

The accession of James I. marked an epoch in the development of the Masque. This king and his son Charles I. were both of them inordinately fond of pageants, and willing to disburse considerable sums of money yearly on such trifles. Whitehall, during these reigns, vied with the Ducal Palaces of Florence, Urbino, and Ferrara, in the pomp and beauty of its Masques. The Drama had attained full growth ; and what the English Masque might still lack upon the side of pictorial art, was fully compensated by poetical invention. The distinctive features of the Masque in Italy, as we have seen, were these. It had been used either as a kind of ballet-interlude, to relieve the graver attractions of a formal comedy, or it had assimilated the type of processional pageantry upon occasions of public rejoicing. In neither case had the poet played a very prominent part in its production. To raise the libretto to the dignity of literature, to compose words for Masques which should retain substantial value as poetry, was reserved for playwrights of our race. The English Masque was characterised by dramatic movement and lyrical loveliness far superior to anything of the kind which had appeared in Italy. In the hands of Ben Jonson, Francis Beaumont, John Fletcher, Thomas Heywood, and George Chapman, it assumed a new form, consonant with the marked bias of the national genius at that epoch to the theatre. The Masques of these eminent poets can still be read with satisfaction. They appeal to our literary sense by the beauty of their songs and by the ingenuity of their dramatic motives.

VII

Two great artists combined to fix the type of the English Masque. These were Ben Jonson, who applied his vast erudition, knowledge of theatrical effect, and vein of lyric inspiration to the libretto; and Inigo Jones, the disciple of Palladio and architect of Whitehall, who contributed the mechanism and stage scenery needed for bodying forth the poet's fancy to the eye. They were assisted by an Italian composer, Alfonso Ferrabosco, who wrote the music; and by an English choreograph, Thomas Giles, who arranged the dances and decided the costumes. The Court establishment of musicians at this epoch numbered some fifty-eight persons, twelve of whom were certainly Italians. Money was not spared either by the Royal Family or by the courtiers on these ceremonial occasions. At Christmas and Shrovetide it was customary for the King and the Queen, each of them, to present a Masque. The Inns of Court vied in prodigality with the Crown, when circumstances prompted them to a magnificent

display.   Noblemen, again, were in the habit of subscrib-
ing at their own expense to furnish forth a complimentary
pageant on the occasion of a distinguished marriage or the
arrival of illustrious guests in England.

The payments made for the Queen's Masque at Christmas
1610–11 enable us to estimate the cost of these performances
in detail.   The total amounted to 720*l.* ; of which Jonson and
Inigo Jones received 40*l.* apiece, the ballet-master 50*l.*, and
five boy-actors 2*l.* each.   When the ' Hue and Cry after Cupid '
was presented at the wedding of Lord Haddington in 1608 by
twelve English and Scottish lords, it was computed that this
would stand them in about 300*l.* a man.   Chapman's
'Memorable Masque,' played at Whitehall in 1613, by the
Middle Temple and Lincoln's Inn, cost the latter Society alone
upwards of 1,000*l.*   Jonson's ' Masque of Blackness ' in 1609,
cost the Court 3,000*l.* ; Daniel's ' Masque of Tethys ' in 1611,
may be reckoned at 1,600*l.* ; Jonson's ' Oberon ' in 1611, at
1,000*l.* ; Daniel's ' Hymen's Triumph ' in 1613, at 3,000*l.* ; the
Queen's Masque in 1637, at 1,550*l.*   ' The Triumph of Peace,'
designed by Shirley and Inigo Jones, and presented by the
Inns of Court in procession to Whitehall in 1634, was one of
the most expensive and magnificent.   1,000*l.* was spent on music
alone ; and on the costumes of the horsemen the vast sum of
10,000*l.*   The total paid by the Inns on this occasion was
estimated at over 20,000*l.*   Having a fixed musical establishment, which even in the time of Elizabeth cost over 600*l.* a year
in salaries, the Court was able to mount a Masque at a somewhat
cheaper rate than private adventurers, such as companies of
noblemen or Gentlemen of Lincoln's Inn.   The average
disbursements during the reigns of the first Stuarts may be
estimated at about 1,400*l.* for each Masque.   Of this, perhaps
400*l.* was spent on dresses, and 1,000*l.* on the apparatus.
When we take into account the difference between the value of
money at that time and this, and multiply in round numbers
by four, we obtain very considerable amounts expended by the
Court and gentlemen of England upon pageantry.

VIII

It was part of the poet's duty to prepare for publication a detailed account of the whole Masque; describing the scenes, costumes, and dances; introducing the libretto he had written for the actors, and paying tribute to his several collaborators. The names of the principal performers, if they were royal or noble persons, were printed in their proper places. The little book, we may imagine, was prized as a souvenir by those who had taken part in so august and so ephemeral a pageant. It also found numerous purchasers among those who had assisted at the representation, or such as were curious to read of what they had not been fortunate enough to witness. A solemn Masque at Court was an event of public importance. Grave personages, like Sir Francis Bacon, took interest in the arrangement of the shows; and all the town was eager to be present at their exhibition. Bacon, it will be remembered, wrote an essay upon Masques, which, coming from his pen, is curious, though it furnishes but little useful information. He also accepted Beaumont's dedication of the 'Masque of Thamesis and Rhine,' of which he himself is said to have been 'the chief contriver.'

To this custom of printing the description of Court Masques, we owe the preservation of more than thirty pieces by Ben Jonson, not to mention those of Marston, Beaumont, Heywood, Chapman, Daniel, Campion, Ford, Shirley, and other poets of less note. All these were composed after James's accession to the throne of England, at which time Jonson's connection with the Court and aristocracy commenced. From that date forward, he preferred this form of invention to play-writing. No wedding or tilting match, no reception of a foreign prince, or Shrovetide festival, was considered perfect without something from the Laureate's pen.

Jonson threw his whole spirit into the work. His Masques are not only infinitely varied, witty, tasteful, and ingenious; but vast erudition is exhibited in the notes with which the poet has enriched them. The 'Masque of Queens,' for example, contains a well-digested and exhaustive dissertation upon witchcraft in antiquity. Jonson chafed at the precedence in popular esteem which was very naturally given to the architect, scene-painter, and ballet-master, upon these occasions. He thought that the poet, whose invention was the soul of such splendid trifles, deserved the lion's share of fame. And certainly, were it not for Jonson's lyrics, we should pay them slight attention now. In his prefaces he was, however, careful to assign what he considered their due share of credit to his several collaborators. Having described the landscape scene devised for his 'Masque of Blackness' in long and detailed paragraphs, he adds : 'So much for the bodily part, which was of Master Inigo Jones's design and act.' Again, in the Masque of Queens he says : 'The device of their attire was Master Jones's, with the invention and architecture of the whole scene and machine.' The master of the dances, Thomas Giles ; the composer of the music, 'my excellent friend, Alfonso Ferrabosco ; ' and the principal soloist, 'that most excellent tenor voice and exact singer, her Majesty's servant, Master John Allin ; ' received compliments upon appropriate occasions. But the poet always reserved for himself the chief honours of each piece. His lofty introduction to the 'Hymenæi' opens thus : 'It is a noble and just advantage that the things subjected to understanding have of those which are objected to sense ; that the one sort are but momentary, and merely taking ; the other impressing and lasting : else the glory of all these solemnities had perished like a blaze, and gone out, in the beholders' eyes. So short-lived are the bodies of all things, in comparison of their souls.'

Master Inigo Jones was no less imperious and intolerant of rivalry than Master Benjamin Jonson. He by no means relished this assignment of the merely bodily and transient part to him, whereas the poet claimed an immortality of art and learning. 'Well-languaged Daniel' showed him properer respect. 'In these things,' runs the preface to the 'Masque of Tethys,' ' wherein the only life consists in show, the art and invention of the architect gives the greatest grace, and is of the most importance, ours ' (i.e. the poet's) ' the least part, and of least note in the time of the performance thereof.' Chapman, Jonson's rival in poetry and erudition, placed his own name below Jones's on the title-page of their ' Memorable Masque,' adding : ' Invented and fashioned, with the ground and special structure of the whole work, by our kingdom's most artful and ingenious Architect, Inigo Jones ; supplied, applied, digested, and written by George Chapman.' Thus both Daniel and Chapman acknowledged themselves to be the mere expositors in words of the great builder's thought; while Jonson treated the builder as the lackey waiting on his Muse. They humbly regarded their own work as the necessary illustration of fair spectacles which passed away and were forgotten with the pleasure they afforded. He proudly expected the suffrage of posterity, when all the torches of Whitehall should be extinguished, the royal actors dead and buried, the groves and cars and temples of the mechanician turned to dust. In this clash of opinions, Jonson, conscious of his own poetical achievement, was indubitably right. Had Inigo Jones left us no Banqueting Hall to grace the shore of Thames, his fame would now have vanished with the fairy world evoked by him on winter nights ' upon that memorable scene.' But even if the Tragedies and Comedies and Underwoods had perished, Jonson would still occupy an honourable place among our poets on the strength of his Masques, Entertainments, Barriers, and Marriage Triumphs alone. So true is it that while the present life of such things throbbed in their bodily present-ment to the senses, their indestructible soul was in the poet's words.

Discord ensued between these two irascible artists, whom we must regard as the main founders and supporters of the Masque in England. Jones managed to supplant Jonson in the favour of the Court. Jonson retaliated by sneering at the architect's ' twice-conceived, thrice-paid-for imagery,' and by lampooning him in a comedy. The ' Tale of a Tub ' originally contained a satirical portrait of Inigo Jones under the name of Vitruvius Hoop. This part was struck out by the Master of the Revels ; ' exception being taken against it by the Surveyor of the King's Works, as a personal injury to him.'

IX

Too much time has been spent, perhaps, upon the history of this insignificant and uninteresting quarrel between Jones and Jonson. It serves, however, to explain the conditions under which Masques were produced at Court, and the state of contemporary opinion on this topic. Before proceeding to survey the work of Jonson, I must repeat that the Masque itself was presented by royal and noble personages. On their performances the architect lavished his costliest inventions. But this magnificence required some foil. An Antimasque was consequently furnished ; and for this, some grotesque or comic motive had to be selected. For the Antimasque, actors from the public theatres were hired. We consequently find that, while the Masque assumes the form of a Triumph or Ballet, the Antimasque is more strictly and energetically dramatic. The latter gave scope to dialogue and action; the former to processions, dances, and accompaniments of music. In the Antimasque, Hecate led the revels of witches round her cauldron. In the Masque, queens attended Anne of Denmark in her passage across the stage, on chariots of gold and jewels ; lutes and viols sounded ; Prince Henry and Duke Charles stepped the high measures of the galliard or coranto. To combine the contrasted motives of the Masque and Antimasque into one coherent scheme, was the poet's pride. And it is just here that Jonson showed his mastery. The antithesis of scenical effect enlivened the whole exhibition, and enabled him to vary his caprices.

At the same time Jonson's robust and logical intellect saved him from merely setting one show against another. There is always method in the madness of his fancy, which makes some of his Masques true gems of solid and ingenious workmanship. It may be parenthetically noticed that this antithesis survives in the Italian Ballo and the English pantomime of the present day. The latter may, indeed, be fairly regarded as a lineal descendant from the Masque, with additions from the Ballo and clown's jig of our ancestors.

X

The very names of Jonson's Masques reveal their strangeness and variety. There is a Masque of Blackness, answered by a Masque of Beauty; a Welsh Masque, and an Irish Masque; a Masque of Queens, and a Masque of Owls; a Masque of Christmas, and a Masque of Lethe; a Masque of Augurs, and a Masque of Time. Neptune and Love had each his Triumph. Pan gave his title to a pastoral Masque, and Hymen to a Masque of Marriage. In one extravaganza of the poet's fancy the Golden Age was restored to earth; in another the Fortunate Isles were visited; a third revealed the wonders of a world discovered in the moon; a fourth was called 'The Vision of Delight.' Sometimes this capricious Muse assumes a loftier tone, and rescues Love from Ignorance and Folly, or reconciles the wanton boy with Virtue. Sometimes she stoops to rustic mirth; camps with gipsies on their roadside bivouac; dances with woodland nymphs and shepherds round Pan's altar; sports with young Satyrs in the brake; or leads the fairies in a ring round Oberon their prince. Sometimes she dons Bellona's casque of war, and sounds the clarion for tilts and barriers. But when her mood is serious, the Antimasque is sure to raise a smile; and when she deigns to wanton, the scene is closed with ceremonious hymns and compliments to Majesty.

These Masques, in the perusal, stripped of their 'apparelling,' as Jonson aptly styled the apparatus, make severe demands on the imagination. It is still possible, however, to read them with pleasure; especially if the student brings a scholar's memory to the task. He will wonder at the fullness and extent of learning employed on these fantastic toys, no less than at the ease with which the poet moves beneath its ponderous weight. Jonson is nowhere seen to more advantage than when he reproduces erudition in some form of lyric beauty. His best song, 'Drink to me only with thine eyes,' is a close paraphrase from Philostratus; yet who can deny the delicacy of its beauty, or the originality which places it in the first rank of English lyrics? The same faculty for alchemising a scholar's knowledge into poetry is displayed at large in the Antimasque of Witches; 'Macbeth' suggested the motive, and the whole range of classical literature furnished the details. But the motive is handled in a style so masterly, and the details are applied with such artistic freedom, that we rise from the perusal of those wild incantation scenes with a keen sense only of the poet's command of weird and ghastly imagery. The Masque of Hymen combines the erudition of Roman bridals with the epithalamial hymns of Catullus, in choruses and scenes and speeches of 'linked sweetness long drawn out.' 'The Masque of Augurs' converts the pious rites of ancient Rome into a modern pageant. The 'Hue and Cry after Cupid' dramatises an Idyll of Moschus in verse that has the sharp-cut clearness of a Greek intaglio. The induction to 'Neptune's Triumph' turns several fragments from the Attic playwrights to account in a controversy between the poet and the cook upon their several arts. 'The Masque of Oberon' is introduced by a dialogue of Satyrs, Sylvans, and Silenus, starting from Virgil's sixth Eclogue, and interweaving the mythology of Pan and Bacchus with that of Northern fairyland in a work of chastened art which can be only paralleled from Landor's poetry.

Such are the dainty delights which Jonson, 'at his full tables,' has provided for the lover of literature. It is true that a scholar's appetite must be brought to the repast; else some 'fastidious stomachs,' as he phrases it, may prefer to 'enjoy at home their clean empty trenchers.' But no one who has a true sense of verse will fail to be rewarded by a cursory perusal of those lyrics, upon which even Milton deigned to found his pastoral style. In support of this somewhat bold assertion, I must beg my reader's leave to go astray awhile at random through these paths of poetry. Imagine, then, that Venus has descended with her Graces from the heavens. She complains that Cupid has run away from home. None of the Graces know what has become of him. Then his mother turns to the ladies of the Court assembled in the hall

before her.   Perhaps, the truant is hidden in their laps or
nestling in their bosoms.   She bids the Graces cry him.
This they do in nine responsive stanzas :

> Beauties, have you seen this toy,
> Called Love, a little boy,
> Almost naked, wanton, blind ;
> Cruel now, and then as kind ?
> If he be amongst ye, say !
> He is Venus' runaway.

So the one voice sings; and a second voice takes up the
chaunt :

> He hath marks about him plenty ;
> You shall know him among twenty.
> All his body is a fire,
> And his breath a flame entire,
> That, being shot, like lightning, in,
> Wounds the heart, but not the skin.

The Masque, from which I have borrowed these two
stanzas, concludes with an Epithalamion.   It is not equal to
Spenser's sublime hymns in lyric rapture, nor yet in warmth
and wealth of imagery to Herrick's ; but it is composed of
stuff like this :

> Love's commonwealth consists of toys ;
> His council are those antic boys,
> Games, Laughter, Sports, Delights,
> That triumph with him on these nights :
> To whom we must give way,
> For now their reign begins, and lasts till day.
> They sweeten Hymen's war,
> And, in that jar,
> Make all, that married be,
> Perfection see.
> Shine, Hesperus, shine forth, thou wishèd star !

On rare occasions, Jonson's lyric touch reminds us of the
style of very modern singers.   Here is a stanza from ' The
Fortunate Isles,' which has an air of Wordsworth :

> The winds are sweet, and gently blow;
> But Zephyrus, no breath they know,
>   The father of the flowers :
> By him the virgin violets live,
> And every plant doth odours give
>   As fresh as are the hours.

The complicated choric passages in this Masque, written
for three men's voices, with question and answer, echo and
antiphony, melting into harmony or unison upon the close,
must have been singularly sweet to hear. But, alas! their
music, whether by Ferrabosco or by Harry Lawes, is lost.
We only know, through Madrigals composed about that time
by Gibbons, how pure the outline of their cadence may have
been.

XI

Jonson, stout and rugged as he was undoubtedly, Dryas-
dust as some conceive him, had yet an exquisite sense of rural
beauty. This he showed in the fine fragment of his ' Sad
Shepherd.' But the Masques abound in passages of no less
delicacy. ' Pan's Anniversary ' opens with a trio of Nymphs,
carrying prickles, or open wicker baskets, and strewing several
sorts of flowers before the altar of the god. Each sings, as
she performs her task. The third carries a basket of violets,
which she showers upon the ground to these verses :

> Drop, drop your violets! Change your hues,
> Now red, now pale, as lovers use!
> And in your death go out as well
> As when you lived, unto the smell!
> That from your odour all may say :
> This is the shepherd's holyday!

There is no crabbed erudition here ; but rather a faint
evanescent scent of Shelley's lines upon the violet. When
the Nymphs have done singing, an old shepherd addresses
them :

> Well done, my pretty ones! rain roses still,
> Until the last be dropped: then hence, and fill

Your fragrant prickles for a second shower.
Bring corn-flag, tulips, and Adonis' flower,
Fair ox-eye, goldy-locks, and columbine,
Pinks, goulands, king-cups, and sweet sops-in-wine,
Blue harebells, pagles, pansies, calaminth,
Flower-gentle, and the fair-haired hyacinth;
Bring rich carnations, flower-de-luces, lilies,
The checked, and purple-ringèd daffodillies,
Bright crown imperial, king-spear, hollyhocks,
Sweet Venus-navel, and soft lady-smocks;
Bring too some branches forth of Daphne's hair,
And gladdest myrtle for these posts to wear,
With spikenard weaved and marjoram between,
And starred with yellow-golds and meadows-queen,
That when the altar, as it ought, is dressed,
More odour come not from the phœnix nest,
The breath thereof Panchaia may envy,
The colours China, and the light the sky !

It may well be wondered, when the poet has sent his Shepherd
with this flourish off the stage, whether he could himself
have pointed out each herb amid that prodigality of quaint-
named blossoms in some actual garden at one same and
certain season of the year. The effect, however, is rich ; and
those who care to reconstruct old English flower-beds in their
imagination, may learn from Gerard's Herbal what goldy-
locks and goulands, sops-in-wine and pagles, lady-smocks and
calaminth and purple-ringed daffodillies really were.

XII

In the Masque of Beauty, Jonson sounds a higher lyric
note than this. To judge by the description he has furnished
of the show, the 'bodily presentment' must have been
magnificent and exquisite. Harmonia was seated on a throne,
adorned with painted statues, and approached by six steps,
which were 'covered with a multitude of Cupids (chosen out
of the best and most ingenious youths of the kingdom, both
noble and others) that were the torch-bearers.' Around the
throne were 'curious and elegant arbours appointed.' Behind

it spread ' a grove of grown trees laden with golden fruit,
which other little Cupids plucked, and threw at each other,
whilst on the ground leverets picked up the bruised apples,
and left them half eaten.' Into this pleasance, on a floating
island, came the Masquers; and when they had 'danced
forth a most curious dance, full of excellent device and change,'
they stood in the figure of a diamond, 'and so, standing still,
were by the musicians with a second song, sung by a loud
tenor, celebrated : '

> So Beauty on the waters stood,
> When Love had severed earth from flood !
> So when he parted air from fire,
> He did with concord all inspire !
> And then a motion he them taught,
> That elder than himself was thought ;
> Which thought was, yet, the child of earth,
> For Love is older than his birth.

In the libretto of 'Prince Henry's Barriers,' Jonson
attacks history, and summons Merlin from his grave within
the lake to marshal forth the glories of Plantagenets and
Tudors. Henry, on the day preceding this trial of arms,
had been created Prince of Wales with extraordinary pomp.
He was a youth of singular beauty and athletic grace, an
adept in chivalrous sports, and a pursuivant of love, though
only in his fifteenth year. To greet him on this great
occasion with the muster-roll of England's potent Edwards
and heroic Henrys, was a compliment no less instructive than
effective. First come the builders-up of English greatness ;
then the Crusaders ; next the Black Prince :

> That Mars of men,
> The black prince Edward, 'gainst the French who then
> At Cressy field had no more years than you.

After him, the hero of Agincourt :

> Yet rests the other thunderbolt of war,
> Harry the Fifth, to whom in face you are
> So like, as fate would have you so in worth,
> Illustrious prince !

Lastly, Elizabeth, before whose auspices fled shattered the
Invincible Armada :
> That covered all the main,
> As if whole islands had broke loose, and swam,
> Or half of Norway with her fir-trees came
> To join the continent.

The young prince, so lately consecrated heir of England,
must have had churl's blood in his veins if he blushed and
thrilled not to the martial music of these verses. He could
not know to what a timeless death his adolescence was
devoted. Nor could any of the Court then present have
predicted how the splendours of the House of Stuart would be
merged in two grim revolutions. Strangely enough, as
though the poet were also prophet, Jonson reserves the last
lines of his panegyric for a princess of the Stuart line—
Elizabeth, the wife of the Elector Palatine, from whom the
Empress-Queen of England at our epoch draws her blood.
Of her he says :
> She shall be
> Mother of nations !

In this prediction lurks a deep poetic irony. While intending
a compliment, the Laureate wrote a motto for America and
Canada, for Australia and New Zealand, for the Colonies of
Africa and China, for the South-Sea Islands, and the Empire
of the Eastern Indies.

Young Henry proved himself not unworthy of these royal
honours. Upon the morrow of the Masque, he held the
lists together with his chosen champions against their
chivalrous assailants. That day, he gave and received thirty-
two pushes of pikes, and about three hundred and sixty
strokes of swords. Allowing for the fact that this was a toy-
tournament, in which a Prince of Wales was no doubt well
regarded, we may still repeat Sir George Cornwallis's
comment on his prowess with national pride : ' the which is
scarce credible in so young years, enough to assure the
world that Great Britain's brave Henry aspired to immortality.' On the evening of the day following these Barriers,

the Prince appeared as Oberon among his fairies in a new
and still more splendid entertainment. They danced until
the night was well-nigh spent, when Phosphor, rising, bade
them all, like duteous fays, speed home to bed :

> To rest, to rest !   The herald of the day,
> Bright Phosphorus, commands you hence !   Obey
> The moon is pale, and spent; and wingèd night
> Makes headlong haste to fly the morning's sight,
> Who now is rising from her blushing wars,
> And with her rosy hand puts back the stars :
> Of which myself the last, her harbinger,
> But stay to warn you that you not defer
> Your parting longer !   Then do I give way,
> As Night hath done, and so must you, to Day.

This warning from the morning star may well be taken as
a warning for the modern scribe, sitting late into the night
with Jonson, who feels the exploration of the beauties scattered
through those Masques to be an infinite quest.

XIII

Thus far, I have confined attention to the scenic splendour
of our Masques ; to the flowers of lyric poetry adorning them ;
and to the deep subsoil of learning, from which those radiant
blossoms sprang. But there is a dark and ominous shadow
cast by history upon their brightness. The last word spoken
must concern the actors, must disclose the tragic irony of
their appearance on that courtly stage. Let us recall the
English beauties who attended Anne of Denmark—Belanna,
as her Laureate styled the Queen—in her triumphal progress
through the Masque of Beauty. Countesses of Arundel and
Derby, of Bedford and Montgomery; Ladies Guilford,
Petre, Winsor, Winter, Clifford, Neville, Hatton, Chichester,
and Walsingham. Many of these women had sad tales to tell
in days of coming troubles. But the saddest tale of all was
that of the Lady Arabella Stuart. Heiress of the House of
Lennox, she was watched with jealousy alike by Tudor and

by Stuart sovereigns. To prevent her marriage, was the policy of Scotch and English Courts. Yet she held a dazzling place, so near the throne, in both; and love makes pastime for himself with courtiers' hearts. Her intimacy with a cousin, Esmé Stuart, was forbidden. The suit of a Percy was frosted in the bud. The King of France thought of her for a moment, but rejected her 'on better judgment making,' as too distant from the crown of England. Then, it seems, her feelings were engaged for William Seymour, grandson of the Earl of Hertford. State interference in this matter compromised her woman's fame. She was imprisoned at Lambeth; he was committed to the Tower. They both escaped, and took their flight to Flanders. But the Lady Arabella was captured at Calais, and brought back to London. She had played her part at Whitehall in the 'Masque of Beauty,' in 1608. She died in the Tower, a raving lunatic, in 1615.

Turn to 'Prince Henry's Barriers,' and the Masque of Oberon. In these, the heir apparent shone before his people and the Court in 1610. He was a youth heroic, beautiful, and brave, a nation's darling. From her lethargy of age he roused the Dame of Chivalry, brought Merlin from his grave, and unsphered Arthur from the skies. The poet hailed him as a second Harry, fit for Agincourt in form and feature. Scholars dubbed him Mœliades, Lord of the Isles, and out of this mysterious name made anagrams—A Deo Miles. None then could know that he was the Marcellus of a kingdom. But round him, as he danced among his fairies, floated shades of Death and Hades.

> Egregium forma juvenem et fulgentibus armis,
> Sed frons læta parum, et dejecto lumine vultus.

Scatter lilies and roses! Henry will have died before three years are over, and the poets will be shedding tears for Mœliades in Hawthornden and London.

And the little Duke Charles, who danced so bravely with the fairies in his brother's festival; the Prince Charles, who, when he came from Spain, led forth the revels of 'Time

Vindicated;' what shall be said of him? The Prince's
Masque of 1623 was followed by a very different pageant at
Whitehall in 1649. And what had passed between those
dates—what death-throes of a dynasty, divisions of a nation!

> He nothing common did or mean
> Upon that memorable scene,
> But with his keener eye
> The axe's edge did try;
> Nor called the gods, with vulgar spite,
> To vindicate his helpless right;
> But bowed his comely head
> Down as upon a bed.

Pass, once again, to the Masque of Hymen. Through those
epithalamial hymns which sounded in the ears of Essex and
his bride in 1616, who does not hear the mutterings of destiny
and dire disgrace? The Lady Frances Howard was in her
fourteenth year. The heir of Elizabeth's and the nation's
darling, the young Earl of Essex, was hardly fifteen. Jonson,
in his marriage chorus for these children, sang:

> And wildest Cupid waking hovers
> With adoration 'twixt the lovers.

The girl-wife lived to seek a dishonourable divorce, and to wed
the Earl of Somerset, that Carr who made his fortunate
début in James's favour on the morning of 'Prince Henry's
Barriers.' Tried and condemned for the murder of Sir
Thomas Overbury, the lives of this guilty couple were spared
by the King's terror of detection. They ended their days in
separation, the objects of universal horror. The boy-husband
of Jonson's hymeneal pageant was destined to lead the armies
of the Parliament against his sovereign, and to sink at last
before the power and popularity of Cromwell.

With the advance of years, the tragic irony of these
Masques at Court deepens. The last great entertainment
of this kind, of which we have any detailed information, was
a Masque presented by Charles and Henrietta Maria at
Shrovetide 1640. The usual sum of 1,400l. had been granted

for the mounting of the piece ; and an additional sum of 120*l*. was expended on the King's costume. What the subject was, or who wrote the libretto, is not known. But we may believe that Whitehall presented to the outer eye on this, as on so many previous occasions, a pageant of undimmed magnificence, a scene of undisturbed security. The Monarchy of England, indeed, was tottering already to its fall; the foundations of society were crumbling. Yet, as usual, the hall was crowded with noble men and noble women, exchanging compliments beneath the torches, dancing brawls or galliards as though there were no Pym and Hampden in existence. Those brilliant and bejewelled cavaliers, innocent as yet of civil strife, unstained with fratricidal slaughter, were soon to part, with anger in their breasts and everlasting farewell on their lips, for adverse camps. Gazing in fancy on the women at their side, that voice which De Quincey heard in vision thrills our ears : ' These are English ladies from the unhappy times of Charles I. These are the wives and daughters of those who met in peace, and sat at the same tables, and were allied by marriage or by blood ; and yet, after a certain day in August 1642, never smiled upon each other again, nor met but on the field of battle ; and at Marston Moor, at Newbury, or at Naseby, cut asunder all ties of love by the cruel sabre, and washed away in blood the memory of ancient friendship.'

XIV

It remains to note the effects of Masques at Court upon the Drama. Like everything which formed a prominent part of the national life, the Masque was adopted and incorporated into the popular art of the theatres. Shakspere in ' The Tempest ' has left us an example of its most judicious intro-duction, as a brief interlude, in the conduct of a serious play. A similarly successful instance might be cited from Fletcher's 'False One,' where the Masque of Nilus forms a splendid and agreeable episode. The Bridal Masque in his ' Maid's Tragedy ' is not less beautiful and rightly placed. Cupid's

Masque in ' A Wife for a Month ' presents the mere silhouette
or sketch in outline of a courtly pageant. On the public
stage, it was of course necessary that the Masque, exhibited
within a play, should be simple in its theme and capable of
quick despatch. Webster used a Masque of Madmen with
terrible effect at the climax of his Duchess' tragedy. Marston,
Tourneur, and other playwrights of the melodrama, as they
abused Ghosts for purposes of stage-effect, so did they stretch
this motive of the Masque within the Drama beyond just
limits. It became the customary device in their hands for
disposing of a tyrant.

From the dramatists themselves we learn how City folk
and petty gentry crowded to Whitehall on masquing nights.[1]
Men forgave their debts, and women sold their honour, to
obtain a seat. To have a friend at Court among the Ushers
or the Porters was the heart's wish of those aspiring citizens
who panted to gaze on royalty and aristocracy performing
actors' parts upon the stage of a palace. The ante-rooms and
galleries of Whitehall became on those occasions a scene of
indescribable debauchery and riot. ' The masques and plays
at Whitehall,' writes Sir Edward Peyton in his ' Divine
Catastrophe of the Stuarts,' ' were used only for incentives to
lust ; therefore the courtiers invited the citizens' wives to
those shows on purpose to defile them in such sort. There is
not a lobby nor chamber (if it could speak) but would verify
it.' The passages cited from Fletcher and Jonson in a note
appended by Dyce to this paragraph, fully corroborate the
Puritan's assertion.

Jonson told Drummond at Hawthornden, that ' next
himself, only Fletcher and Chapman could make a Masque.'
Jonson did not live to welcome Milton's Muse, or he might
have added that a fourth Masque-maker had arisen, who
combined the art of Fletcher with his own in a new style of
incomparably higher poetry. It is clear from indications

---

[1] See, in particular, the Induction to Fletcher's *Four Plays in One*,
the opening of his *Humorous Lieutenant*, the *Maid's Tragedy* (act i. sc. 2),
A Wife for a Month (act ii. sc. 4), and the introduction to Jonson's *Love
Restored*.

scattered through Milton's works, that the Masques which in
his boyhood reached their height of splendour, had powerfully
affected his imagination. Both the songs and the discourse
of his 'Arcades' reveal, to my mind at least, a careful study
on the youthful poet's part of Jonson's work; and I find the
influence of Fletcher no less manifest in the lyrics of ' Comus.'
The meditative music of the Genius' speech, the incomparable
touches of nature-painting scattered through the ' Arcades,'
and the heightened dignity of language which raises this
little piece into the region of classical art, place Milton already
above his masters. But his immeasurable superiority becomes
only unmistakable in ' Comus.' This exquisite composition,
in which poetry of the loftiest is blent with philosophy of the
purest and the sweetest, bears upon its title-page the name
of Masque. But except in the antithetical treatment of the
Spirit and the Genius of sensual pleasure ; except in the lyrics
scattered with a hand not over-liberal through its scenes ;
' Comus ' challenges no comparison in any ponderable qualities
of craftsmanship with those sturdy works of art in which
James's Laureate strove with James's architect for fashionable
laurels. In the history of English literature, ' Comus ' remains
to show how the scenic elements of the Masque, touching the
fancy of a great poet, became converted into flawless poetry
beneath his hand. Nominally a Masque, it has really nothing
in common with entertainments which demanded 'bodily
presentment' and 'apparelling' upon the stage. Yet it
would probably have never issued from the poet's brain but
for shows at Court. Masque and Antimasque, sweeping before
his sense, had left their impress upon Milton's fancy. The
memories of those fair scenes, whether actually witnessed, or
studied in a printed page, dwelt in his mind, emerging later
to evoke that fairy fabric of romantic allegory which he called
the Masque of Comus. Had the 'Midsummer's Night's
Dream' been composed by Shakspere for courtly theatricals,
or the ' Faithful Shepherdess ' by Fletcher for like purpose,
this name might with equal propriety have been given to
those two pieces.

CHAPTER X

ENGLISH HISTORY

I. The Chronicle Play is a peculiarly English Form—Its Difference from
other Historical Dramas—Supplies the Place of the Epic—Treatment
of National Annals by the Playwrights.—II. Shakspere's Chronicles
—Four Groups of non-Shaksperian Plays on English History.—
III. Legendary Subjects—'Locrine'—'The History of King Leir.'—
IV. Shakspere's Doubtful Plays—Principles of Criticism—'The Birth
of Merlin.'—V. Chronicle-Plays Proper—'Troublesome Reign of
King John'—'True Tragedy of Richard III.'—'Famous Victories of
Henry V.'—'Contention of the Two Famous Houses.'—VI. 'Ed-
ward III.'—The Problem of its Authorship—Based on a Novella and
on History—The Superior Development of Situations.—VII. Mar-
lowe's 'Edward II.'—Peele's 'Edward I.'—Heywood's 'Edward IV.'—
Rowley's Play on Henry VIII.—VIII. The Ground covered by the
Chronicle Plays—Their Utility—Heywood's 'Apology' quoted.—IX.
Biographies of Political Persons and Popular Heroes—'Sir Thomas
More'—'Lord Cromwell'—'Sir John Oldcastle'—Schlegel's Opinion
criticised—'Sir Thomas Wyatt'—Ford's 'Perkin Warbeck'—Last
Plays of this Species.—X. English Adventurers—'Fair Maid of the
West'—'The Shirley Brothers'—'Sir Thomas Stukeley'—His Life
—Dramatised in 'The Famous History' &c.—'Battle of Alcazar.'—
XI. Apocryphal Heroes—'Fair Em'—'Blind Beggar of Bethnal
Green'—Two Plays on the Robin Hood Legend—English Partiality
for Outlaws—Life in Sherwood—'George a Greene'—Jonson's 'Sad
Shepherd'--Popularity in England of Princes who have shared the
People's Sports and Pastimes.

N.B.   The Historical Plays discussed in this chapter will be found as
follows : 'Locrine,' 'The Birth of Merlin,' 'Lord Cromwell,' in the
Tauchnitz edition of Shakespeare's 'Doubtful Plays;' 'King Leir,'
'Troublesome Reign of King John,' 'True Tragedy of Richard III.,'
'Famous Victories of Henry V.,' 'Contention of the Two Houses,' in W.
C. Hazlitt's 'Shakespeare's Library;' 'Edward III.' in Delius' 'Pseudo-
Shakspere'sche Dramen;' Marlowe's, Peele's, Heywood's Chronicles in
Dyce's editions of Marlowe and Peele and Pearson's reprint of Heywood;
Rowley's 'When You See Me, You know Me,' in Karl Elze's reprint;
'Sir Thomas More,' in the Old Shakespeare Society's Publications;
'Sir Thomas Wyatt,' in Dyce's 'Webster,' and 'Perkin Warbeck' in
Gifford's 'Ford;' 'The Famous History of Sir Thomas Stukeley' in

Simpson's ' School of Shakspere,' and ' The Battle of Alcazar ' in Dyce's
' Peele ; ' ' Fair Em ' in Delius ; ' The Blind Beggar ' and ' The Shirley
Brothers ' in Bullen's ' Day ; ' ' Dick of Devonshire ' in Bullen's ' Old
Plays ; ' the two plays on ' Robert, Earl of Huntingdon,' in Hazlitt's
' Dodsley,' vol. viii. ; ' George a Greene ' in Dyce's ' Greene.'

I

THE Chronicle Play is peculiar to English literature. The
lost tragedy by Phrynichus, entitled ' The Capture of Miletus,'
which is said to have cost the poet a considerable fine from
the Athenian people, and the triumphal pageant of ' The
Persæ,' in which Æschylus sang the pæan of the Greek race
over conquered Asia, cannot be reckoned in the same class as
the Chronicles of Shakspere and his predecessors. Nor do
the few obscure plays produced by Italian authors upon
events in their national history, whether we take into account
Mussato's ' Eccelinis ' or the popular Representation of
' Lautrec,' deserve this title. Coleridge has remarked that
our Chronicle Play occupies an intermediate place between the
Epic and the Drama. It is not, like the ' Wallenstein ' of
Schiller or Victor Hugo's ' Roi s'amuse,' an episode selected
from the national annals, and dramatised because of its
peculiar tragic or satiric fitness. Its characteristic quality is
the dramatic presentation in a single action of the leading
events of a reign. The Chronicle Plays, which in the
Elizabethan age probably covered the whole field of English
history, had for their object the scenic exposition of our
annals to the nation. If we possessed that series intact, we
should see unrolled before us, as in a gigantic and unequal
epic, the succession of events and vicissitudes from mythic
Brute to the defeat of the Armada.

English literature possesses no national epic. The legends
of Arthur formed, it is true, a semi-epical body of romance.
But these legends were not purely English in their origin ;
nor were they digested into the ' Mort d'Arthur,' by Sir
Thomas Malory, until a comparatively late period. When
our language attained the proper flexibility for poetical
composition, the age of the heroic Epic had passed away.

The great events of our annals, whether mythical or historical, instead of being sung by rhapsodists, were acted by tragedians, in accordance with the prevalent dramatic impulse. But the epical instinct was satisfied by the peculiar form which the Chronicle Play assumed. The authors of these works combined fidelity to facts and observance of chronology with their effort after a certain artistic unity of effect. They fixed attention on tragic calamities and conflicting passions, endeavouring, so far as in them lay, to bring the characters of men in action into striking prominence. As the scientific historian seeks to investigate the laws which underlie a nation's growth, regarding men as agents in the process of evolution ; so, by a converse method, our dramatists fixed their eyes upon the personal elements of history, and kept out of sight those complex influences which narrow the sphere of individual activity. The one process presents us with the philosophy of history, the other with its poetry. Neither mode of treatment is dishonest, though the whole truth is not to be found in either result : for the history of the world, as Hegel remarked, has a double aspect ; and the highest aim of the historian is to place the heroes who seem to resume the spirit of their several epochs, in proper relation to the world-spirit. As was right and necessary, the authors of our Chronicle Plays made history subservient to art, and character more potent than circumstance. Yet they abstained from violating the general outlines of the annals which they dramatised. They introduced no figmentary matter of importance, and rarely deviated from tradition to enhance effect. Their chief licence consisted in altering the relative proportion of events, in concentrating the action of many years within the space of a few hours, and in heightening for tragic purposes the intellectual and moral stature of commanding personages. Episodical incidents were freely invented ; but always with the object of enforcing and colouring the fact as they received it from the annalists. Only here and there, as in Peele's dastardly libel on the good Queen Eleanor, do we find a deliberate attempt to falsify history for a purpose of the moment. I do not of course mean to assert that any of our dramatists were conscientious in the scientific sense of the word, and that they did not share the common prejudices of their age. What I wish to insist upon is that they approached the historical drama from the epical point of view, and that their main object was the scenic reproduction of history rather than the employment of historical material for any further-reaching purpose.

II

Were it not for Shakspere's Chronicle Plays, it might be hardly needful to dwell at considerable length upon this species. But these masterpieces are so unique in their kind, combining as they do fidelity to the main sources at the dramatist's command with perfect artistic freedom in a harmony unparalleled, that it behoves us to consider the crude work of his predecessors. In the best plays of Shakspere's historical series, the heroes of English annals are glorified, but not metamorphosed. That grasp of character which enabled him to create a Hamlet and a Lady Macbeth, was here employed in resuscitating real men and women from their graves. He translated them to the sphere of poetry without altering their personal characteristics. Only, instead of flesh and blood, he gave in his scenes portraits of them, such as Titian or Rubens might have painted, by dwelling on their salient qualities, flattering without sycophancy, and revealing the dark places of the soul without animosity.

I propose to arrange the non-Shaksperian plays on English history in four groups. The first consists of dramas founded on mythical events. The second is the body of Chronicle Plays, properly so called. The third is a set of biographical dramas, bringing English worthies·or famous characters upon the stage. The fourth group deals with semi-legendary heroes dear to the English people, or with pleasant episodes in the traditionary lives of their princes.

III

We have seen that the earliest tragedies of the pseudo·
classic school were founded on the legendary history of
England—'Gorboduc' and 'The Misfortunes of Arthur.'
A proper third to these two stilted plays may be found in
'Locrine;' the subject of which is the death of Brutus, first
king of Britain, with the subsequent adventures of his three
sons. This drama, a piece of passable but wooden workmanship, has long been included in the list of Shakspere's
Doubtful Plays. There is, however, no shadow of reason for
supposing that Shakspere had a hand in it.[1] 'Locrine'
is written throughout in a level style of vulgar and pedestrian
bombast, tumid with the metaphors and classical mythology
which Greene made fashionable, and which Marlowe transfigured. Humber, described as 'King of the Scythians,'
wanders fasting through North English deserts, and soliloquises :

> Ne'er came sweet Ceres, ne'er came Venus here;
> Triptolemus, the god of husbandmen,
> Ne'er sowed his seed in this foul wilderness.
> The hunger-bitten dogs of Acheron,
> Chased from the nine-fold Pyriphlegethon,
> Have set their footsteps in this damnèd ground.

All the characters, Britons and Scythians, with the exception
of the comic personages, who are not totally devoid of merit,
talk this fine language. Such interest as the play possesses,
is due to the fact that it constitutes a hybrid between the
type of 'Gorboduc' and the new romantic drama. The
subject is treated romantically; but the author has freely
indulged his pseudo-classic partiality for ghosts. He introduces each act with a dumb show, which is explained by Até
'in black, with a burning torch in one hand, and a bloody

---

[1] It was printed in 1595, as 'newly set forth, overseen and corrected
by W. S.' On this foundation the editor of the folio Shakspere, 1664,
included it in his collection. The best passages of the play, act iv. sc. 4,
for example, are very much in the manner of Greene.

sword in the other.' He makes two heroes, on the point of
suicide, declaim Latin hexameters, and puts Latin mottoes
like ' Regit omnia numen ' or ' In pœnam sectatur et umbra,'
into the mouth of his spectres. There are no less than five
suicides altogether in the action, the poet being apparently
unable to make his personages kill each other.

' The History of King Leir and his Three Daughters ' takes
higher rank than 'Locrine.' The unknown writer of the piece
deals in the sober spirit of an honest craftsman with the old
English legend, which gave to Shakspere material for the
most terrific of all extant masterpieces. The style is plain
and sturdy ; free from the intolerable pedantries and pet-
tinesses of Greene's mythologising school. There is considerable power in the characterisation of the three sisters, and no
little pathos in the situation of Leir and Perillus. Leir,
Gonorill, Ragan, Cordella, and Perillus, indeed, only awaited
the magic-working hand of Shakspere to become the Lear,
Goneril, Regan, Cordelia, and Kent of his tremendous tragedy.
Yet it must not be thought that the master owed anything
considerable to this old play ; for these characters, together
with the main situations of the drama, were clearly given in
the prose story. What he has added, in the episode of
Gloucester and his sons, in the Fool's part, and in the tragic
close, is Shakspere's own invention. The playwright of
' King Leir,' adhering to the letter of his text, left Cordella
happy with her father at the drama's ending. We shall never
know what moved Shakspere to drop that pall of darkness
upon the mystery of inscrutable woe at the very moment when
there dawned a brighter day for Lear united to his blameless
daughter. For once, it would appear, he chose to sound the
deepest depths of the world's suffering, a depth deeper than
that of Æschylean or Sophoclean tragedy, deeper than the
tragedy of ' Othello,' deeper than Malebolge or Caina, a stony
black despairing depth of voiceless and inexplicable agony.

IV

The third play of this group brings us once more face to
face with the problem of inferior works doubtfully or falsely
attributed to Shakspere. In dealing with these so-called
Doubtful Plays, we are 'wandering about in worlds not
realised,' with no sure clue to guide us, tantalised by suspicious
tradition. We know that before Shakspere began his great
series of authentic and undisputed dramas, he spent some
years of strenuous activity as a journeyman for the Company
of Players he had joined. At this period he was certainly
employed in revising earlier compositions for the stage, and
was probably engaged as a collaborator with unknown poets
in the preparation of new plays.   That fairly competent
writers for the theatre, men capable of plain dramatic handiwork, and not devoid of skill to imitate the manner of
superior masters, abounded in London at this epoch, cannot
be doubted. Shakspere, moreover, as is clearly proved by the
gradual emergence of his final style, by his slow self-disen-
tanglement from rhyme, and by his lingering love of
prettinesses and conceits, did not start as a dramatist with a
manner so fixed and unmistakable as that of Marlowe. When,
therefore, there is any scintilla of external evidence in favour
of his authorship, we are bound to weigh the question, and
not to discard a work because it seems to us palpably
unworthy. There is always the possibility that he may have
had a hand in it, either as a restorer or as a collaborator;
or, again, that it may have been a trial essay in some vein of
work abandoned by him 'upon better judgment making.'
These possibilities or probabilities fall into three or four main
categories. We have to ask ourselves : Is the doubtful play
in question a work of considerable merit retouched by the
master's hand ? If so, it may be classified with the Second
or Third Parts of ' Henry VI.' Is it an old piece entirely
rewritten and rehandled ? If so, it will take rank with
' Romeo and Juliet.' Is it one on which Shakspere engrafted
fresh scenes of incontestable mastery and beauty ? If so, it

finds its analogue in ' Pericles.' Is it one in which he wrought
with a collaborator ? If so, we may compare it with ' The
Two Noble Kinsmen,' or perhaps with ' Henry VIII.'
There remains the further possibility of trial-work or prentice-
labour in a style rejected by the mature artist. Some would
explain the difficulties of ' Henry VIII.' upon this theory,
ascribing the parts on which Fletcher seems to have been
engaged, to Shakspere's own experiments in an afterwards
abandoned manner. ' Arden of Feversham,' if we accept this
fine play as Shaksperian, would stand upon nearly the same
ground, as an early effort.

Such are some of the preliminary questions which the
critic has to ask himself. Yet having weighed them in the
balance of his judgment, he must face another set of difficulties.
These arise from the tribe of imitators. It is comparatively
easy for men of talent in a fertile literary age to ape the men
of genius. Therefore, when we detect some note which has in
it the master's accent, but lacks the full clear ring of his
authentic utterance, we are forced to choose between two
hypotheses. Either the passage in question is the product
of his immaturity or weakness ; or else it is the parrot
utterance of a clever disciple. In this perplexity a sound
critic, if he arrives at any conclusion whatsoever, will do so
by trusting his sense of what the master would have felt and
thought, quite as much as by analysing language and rhythm
—will ask himself whether the real Shakspere conceived
character thus, or treated a situation in this way. He will
be cautious in drawing inferences from similarity, which is
not genuine identity, of style. He will form his final judgment from a survey of the whole work in dispute, not from a
comparison of single passages. In some cases he will rise
from the perusal of a doubtful play, as Swinburne rose from
the study of ' Edward III.,' with the conviction that he has
before him the vigorous performance of no mean man, who,
having sat at the feet of two great masters, has managed to
reproduce their manner, with only a moderate portion of their
spirit. The fine anonymous ' Tragedy of Nero,' for example,
shows such enthusiastic study of both Marston and Fletcher

that the ascription of certain passages to either poet would be reasonable, were not the whole work cast in the mould of a mind differing from both.

There remains a further source of hesitation and perplexity, which has to be taken into calculation. This is the mangled condition in which plays, during the whole Elizabethan period, were apt to issue from the press—piratically seized upon by publishers who had no access to the author's MS., but took on trust a shorthand writer's notes. Many instances of deformed versification, mutilated scenes, and confused grammar, can be explained by the simple hypothesis of piracy ; and it is therefore dangerous to reject a misshapen piece of work, in the face of any external evidence, on the mere score of imperfection or unworthiness. I might cite the first issue of Shakspere's ' Henry V.' or our sole text of Marlowe's ' Massacre at Paris,' as instances of what I wish to indicate.

From this digression I return to ' The Birth of Merlin.' It was printed in 1662 by the bookseller Kirkman, a most untrustworthy caterer and angler for the public, with an ascription to William Shakespear and William Rowley. Little indeed is known about this Rowley's life. But if he collaborated with Shakspere, it must have been in the full maturity of that poet's powers. Nothing in the plan or style of the play reminds us of the adult Shakspere. If therefore we attach any value to Kirkman's title-page, we must suppose that Rowley retouched an early piece in which Shakspere was known to have had some hand ; or that Shakspere received this piece of Rowley's for his theatre with approval. There are Shaksperian qualities in ' The Birth of Merlin ; ' but these can be accounted for by referring it to the post-Shaksperian epoch, when the master's manner had helped to create a current style.

The play is by no means despicable, though far too long, crowded with irrelevant dramatic stuff, and confused in action. The intricacy of the warp, and the intellectual vivacity of the woof woven over it, are not altogether unlike the early work of Shakspere. The cast of some soliloquies, with interjected philosophical reflections, the contorted phrasing and occasional pregnancy of thought, taken in combination with the absence of Greene's mythological jargon, and with a notable superfluity of motives and situations—the very parbreak of a youthful poet's indigestion—mark it out as, at the least, post-Shaksperian. It belongs, indeed, in my opinion, to the category of plays sufficiently imitative of the master's style to have suggested the legend of his part-authorship.

'The Birth of Merlin' is the second play founded on the Arthurian cycle. It combines the tale of Uther Pendragon's wanderings and loves with the story of Merlin's diabolical parentage. Under the form of a Court-gallant, the devil begets a child on a peasant-girl. When he is born, this son, who enters the world in full maturity and with more than a man's wisdom, consigns his father to a prison in a rock, and addresses himself to the State affairs of Britain. These supernatural and romantic elements are, however, subordinated to a medley of farce ; and the ill-constructed drama leaves no clear impression on the mind.

Having touched upon the style of this play in the foregoing remarks, I must proceed to quote some specimens. Here is a speech in rhyming couplets :

O my good Sister, I beseech you hear me :
This world is but a masque, catching weak eyes,
With what is not ourselves, but our disguise,
A vizard that falls off, the dance being done,
And leaves death's glass for all to look upon.
Our best happiness here lasts but a night,
Whose burning tapers make false ware seem right ;
Who knows not this, and will not now provide
Some better shift before his shame be spied,
And knowing this vain world at last will leave him,
Shake off these robes that help but to deceive him ?

Prince Uther, in his love-lunes, exclaims :

O, you immortal powers,
Why has poor man so many entrances
For sorrow to creep in at, when our sense
Is much too weak to hold his happiness ?
O, say I was born deaf : and let your silence
Confirm in me the knowing my defect.

> At least be charitable to conceal my sin ;
> For hearing is no less in me, dear brother.

A Hermit refuses to drink healths at a wedding feast :

> Temperate minds
> Covet that health to drink, which nature gives
> In every spring to man.   He that doth hold
> His body but a tenement at will,
> Bestows no cost but to repair what 's ill.

The following soliloquy, with its curious blending of
redundant blank verse and rhyme, has a passable vein of
thought :

> Noble and virtuous !   Could I dream of marriage,
> I should affect thee, Edwin !   O, my soul,
> Here 's something tells me that these best of creatures,
> These models of the world, weak man and woman,
> Should have their souls, their making, life and being,
> To some more excellent use.   If what the sense
> Calls pleasure were our ends, we might justly blame
> Great nature's wisdom, who reared a building
> Of so much art and beauty, to entertain
> A guest so far incertain, so imperfect.
> If only speech distinguish us from beasts,
> Who know no inequality of birth or place,
> But still to fly from goodness—oh, how base
> Were life at such a rate !   No, no, that Power
> That gave to man his being, speech, and wisdom,
> Gave it for thankfulness.   To Him alone
> That made me thus, may I thence truly know
> I'll pay to Him, not man, the debt I owe.

V

The list of Chronicle Plays, properly so called, is headed
by Bale's 'King Johan,' of which brief notice has been already
taken.   'The Troublesome Reign of King John,' in two parts,
deals with the same period of our history.   It is, to all
appearances, a piece of work posterior to Marlowe's 'Tamburlaine,' written in sustained but very rough blank verse,
converting the prose chronicle bluntly into scenes, and

Indulging in but rare occasional diversions. A ribald episode in rhyme, introduced into the first part, and containing a coarse satire on monastic institutions, may be regarded as a farcical interlude rather than an integral portion of the play. When Shakspere set his hand to ' King John,' he found the bastard's part blocked out with swaggering vigour in the elder Chronicle, the formless germ of Hubert's character, and a bare suggestion of the King's contrivance for his nephew's murder. In the evolution of our theatrical literature, it is singularly interesting to notice the gradual development of this historical drama in its three stages. Bale's performance marks the emergence of the subject, still encumbered with the allegorical personifications and didactic purposes of the Morality. ' The Troublesome Reign ' exhibits a dull specimen of solid play-carpentry in the earliest and crudest age of blank-verse composition. ' King John ' is a masterpiece belonging to the second period of Shakspere's maturity.

' The True Tragedy of Richard III.' bears signs of an elder origin and a more complex composition than ' The Troublesome Reign.' In form it contains remnants of old rhyming structure, decayed verses of fourteen feet, and clumsy prose, pieced and patched with blank verse of very lumbering rhythm. The play, as we possess it, must have undergone several processes of botching and bungling before it settled down into the printed copy of 1594. Some traces of the pseudo-classic style are discernible in the Induction, which introduces Truth and Poetry, ushered upon the stage by the ghost of Clarence crying aloud : *O cito, cito, vindicta !* Setting apart the curiosity of this obsolete conglomerate, the Chronicle has no points of literary interest. It cannot be said to have helped Shakspere in the production of his ' Richard III.,' which, as Mr. Swinburne observes, is a study in the manner of Marlowe. A still more singular dramatic work upon the life of Richard is Dr. Legge's ' Richardus Tertius,' a Latin Chronicle Play, in two parts, not modelled upon Seneca, but closely following the English plan of such performances in regular iambics.

'The Famous Victories of Henry V.' is another piece of uncouth but honest old English upholstery. It presents internal evidences of composition at a later period than ' The True Tragedy of Richard III.' and may be classed upon a somewhat higher level than ' The Troublesome Reign of King John.' When we have said that Shakspere built upon its ground-plan in his Chronicle of 'Henry V.' all that can or need be spoken in its commendation has been uttered. The romance of Prince Hal's youth, the episode of his imprisonment in the Fleet, the incident of his abstracting the crown from his father's pillow, his change of character, and his bluff wooing of the French Princess, are touched with artless and sturdy straightforwardness by the stage-carpenter of plays who made it. But of poetry or passion there is dearth throughout.

The first and second parts of ' The Contention of the Two Famous Houses of York and Lancaster' are obviously the originals on which the Second and Third Parts of ' Henry VI.' are based. But they are more than this alone implies. We have in these two plays work in the process of formation; new stuff patched upon old, and materials re-moulded. It is an open question whether Shakspere himself is responsible for the part of Richard and for the scenes of Jack Cade's insurrection in the elder plays; or whether, as I think more probable, we may ascribe Richard to a poet of eminent tragic power, possibly to Marlowe, and leave Jack Cade in the rough draft to some unknown craftsman who was not incapable of such a sketch. Taken together with ' Henry VI.' these Chronicles present an interesting but insoluble problem to the critic. It is impossible to analyse their successive and interpenetrative strata of style, or to name their several authors with any approach to certainty.

VI

' Edward III.' presents a different but hardly less perplexing riddle. This anonymous play, founded on Bandello's story of the Countess of Salisbury and Holinshed's digest of

Froissart, was printed in 1596, after it had already enjoyed some popularity upon the stage. No one thought of attributing it to Shakspere until the critic, Edward Capell, did so in 1760. There is, therefore, in this case no spark of external evidence in favour of Shaksperian origin. The Chronicle is not, like the three parts of 'Henry VI.,' a composite conglomerated piece of patchwork, but the finished production of one author, or at most of two authors in collaboration. It displays unity of style sufficient to justify us in believing that it was written off as we possess it; and this style is of a high order, considering the date of publication. It is indeed so good that we are forced to think of Shakspere and of Marlowe, of Shakspere in his period of lyrism, or of Shakspere following the track of Marlowe. Our critical cock-boat, in a word, is afloat upon a sea, without compass, now blown by gales from Marlowe's genius, now by a finer breath from Shakspere's early Muse. We are left to wonder whether the wind be not wafted from some spurious quarter of imitative inspiration, or whether it peradventure be an authentic blast from either of those mighty ones. The first two acts are separated from the last three not only by subject, but also by slight differences of manner. The play, indeed, is defective in artistic unity; for the first part is a dramatised love tale, the second a dramatised chronicle of Cressy, Poitiers, and Calais. The working of the former part is more poetical and masterly. In the latter, the author has crowded incidents together; and though he touches some points with a vigorous hand, he misses the true heroic ring, the chivalry of his surpassing theme. On the supposition of a single authorship by some unknown but not ignoble follower of Marlowe and Shakspere, these discrepancies are explicable; for the love tale of the Countess was ready-made for dramatisation by even a feeble hand in the glowing scenes of the Italian *Novella*, while the Chronicle demanded the full powers of a mature and mighty master for its condensation and theatrical expression. Those critics, on the contrary, who would fain detect the veritable Shakspere in Acts I. and II. have something plausible to say. Suppose he wrote these acts, and turned the copy over to some journeyman to finish? This would not have been inconsistent with the practice of contemporary playwrights, and would tally well with what Greene spitefully recorded of the method of Johannes Factotum. The date of publication must also be taken into account. This was the year 1596, after the piece had been 'sundry times played about the City of London.' Now Shakspere's 'Richard III.,' a work decidedly written in the style of Marlowe, was not printed until 1597; and the Sonnets—though this is unimportant, since they had been handed about in MS.—were not published until 1609. It is not absolutely impossible that Shakspere might have taken part in the composition of a Chronicle so good as 'Edward III.' at an epoch when he certainly had not yet entered into full possession of his style.

Still there remains the fact that we have no spark of external evidence to support the Shaksperian hypothesis; and I think that the arguments so ably and elaborately supported by Mr. Swinburne in his essay on 'Edward III.' reduce its probability to almost zero. But in this case, we are thrown back upon the supposition that before 1596 there was a playwright equal to the production of so excellent a piece; that is to say, a playwright superior to Greene, Peele, Nash, and Lodge; to all in fact but the two masters Shakspere and Marlowe; and one moreover who had deliberately chosen for his model the Shaksperian style of lyrism in its passage through the influence of Marlowe. That such a supposition is not only maintainable, but also in accordance with the anonymity of the play, is obvious. Only we must remember what effect its adoption will have upon the problem of other doubtful plays—of 'Arden of Feversham' for instance. We shall hardly be justified in reasoning that no one but Shakspere existed capable of the production of that drama, when we have conceded a nameless author of 'Edward III.;' for the point on which I am inclined to differ with Mr. Swinburne, is in rating 'Edward III.' considerably higher than he does. Not merely, in my opinion, have we here to deal with a mocking-bird who makes a clever imitation of the callow

nightingale, but also with a playwright who in his way of
attacking situations, seizing on turning-points and hinges in
the action (as for instance when Edward unfolds himself to
Warwick, and Warwick to the Countess; when the sight of
the Black Prince sways Edward's resolution to one side, and
the sight of his mistress to the other), was more than merely
aping the method of a genuine dramatic poet. Yet, considering the extraordinary richness of the Elizabethan age, the
carelessness of playwrights for their work, and the injuries of
accident and time to which the literature of that epoch has
been exposed, is it not safer to postulate a score of unknown
talents than to ascribe doubtful compositions without external
evidence to one or another of the leading and acknowledged
masters?

Having dwelt at this length on the problem of 'Edward III.'
I shall transcribe what seems to me the best, and is assuredly
the most Shaksperian, scene in the play. Any competent
reader will perceive that he is in the company of no ordinary
poet such as a Greene or a Peele, and also that the inspiration,
if borrowed, is not in this place Marlowe's:

> *Countess.* Sorry I am to see my liege so sad:
> What may thy subject do, to drive from thee
> Thy gloomy consort, sullen melancholy?
> *Edward.* Ah, lady, I am blunt, and cannot strew
> The flowers of solace in a ground of shame:—
> Since I came hither, Countess, I am wronged.
> *Coun.* Now, God forbid, that any in my house
> Should think my sovereign wrong! Thrice gentle king,
> Acquaint me with your cause of discontent.
> *Edw.* How near then shall I be to remedy?
> *Coun.* As near, my liege, as all my woman's power
> Can pawn itself to buy thy remedy.
> *Edw.* If thou speak'st true, then have I my redress
> Engage thy power to redeem my joys,
> And I am joyful, Countess; else, I die.
> *Coun.* I will, my liege.
> *Edw.* Swear, Countess, that thou wilt.
> *Coun.* By heaven, I will.
> *Edw.* Then take thyself a little way aside;
> And tell thyself a king doth dote on thee:

Say, that within thy power it doth lie,
To make him happy ; and that thou hast sworn
To give me all the joy within thy power :
Do this, and tell me when I shall be happy.

Coun. All this is done, my thrice dread sovereign :
That power of love, that I have power to give,
Thou hast with all devout obedience ;
Employ me how thou wilt in proof thereof.

Edw. Thou hear'st me say that I do dote on thee.

Coun. If on my beauty, take it if thou canst ;
Though little, I do prize it ten times less :
If on my virtue, take it if thou canst ;
For virtue's store by giving doth augment :
Be it on what it will, that I can give
And thou canst take away, inherit it.

Edw. It is thy beauty that I would enjoy.

Coun. O, were it painted, I would wipe it off,
And dispossess myself, to give it thee :
But, sovereign, it is soldered to my life ;
Take one, and both ; for, like an humble shadow,
It haunts the sunshine of my summer's life.

Edw. But thou mayst lend it me, to sport withal

Coun. As easy may my intellectual soul
Be lent away, and yet my body live,
As lend my body, palace to my soul,
Away from her, and yet retain my soul.
My body is her bower, her court, her abbey,
And she an angel, pure, divine, unspotted ;
If I should lend her house, my lord, to thee,
I kill my poor soul, and my poor soul me.

Edw. Didst thou not swear to give me what I would ?

Coun. I did, my liege ; so what you would, I could.

Edw. I wish no more of thee than thou mayst give :
Nor beg I do not, but I rather buy,
That is, thy love ; and, for that love of thine,
In rich exchange, I tender to thee mine.

Coun. But that your lips were sacred, O my lord
You would profane the holy name of love :
That love you offer me, you cannot give ;
For Cæsar owes that tribute to his queen ;
That love you beg of me, I cannot give ;
For Sarah owes that duty to her lord.
He that doth clip or counterfeit your stamp,

Shall die, my lord; and will your sacred self
Commit high treason 'gainst the King of Heaven,
To stamp His image in forbidden metal,
Forgetting your allegiance and your oath ?
In violating marriage sacred law,
You break a greater honour than yourself:
To be a king, is of a younger house
Than to be married; your progenitor,
Sole-reigning Adam on the universe,
By God was honoured for a married man,
But not by Him anointed for a king.[1]
It is a penalty, to break your statutes,
Though not enacted by your highness' hand:
How much more, to infringe the holy act
Made by the mouth of God, sealed with His hand ?
I know, my sovereign in my husband's love,
Who now doth loyal service in his wars,
Doth but to try the wife of Salisbury,
Whether she 'll hear a wanton tale or no ;
Lest being therein guilty by my stay,
From that, not from my liege, I turn away.

[*Exit* COUNTESS

    Edw. Whether is her beauty by her words divine ;
Or are her words sweet chaplains to her beauty ?
Like as the wind doth beautify a sail,
And as a sail becomes the unseen wind,
So do her words her beauty, beauty words.
O that I were a honey-gathering bee,
To bear the comb of virtue from his flower ;
And not a poison-sucking envious spider,
To turn the vice I take to deadly venom !
Religion is austere, and beauty gentle ;
Too strict a guardian for so fair a ward.
O that she were, as is the air, to me !
Why, so she is; for, when I would embrace her,
This do I, and catch nothing but myself.
I must enjoy her ; for I cannot beat
With reason and reproof fond love away.

A high conception of this poet's power of rhetorical
dramatisation will be formed by the reader, who, continuing
the perusal of the original text, observes how the situation

---

[1] These lines read like Heywood.

is prolonged by the entrance of Warwick at this moment, by the King's ensuing debate with his subject, and Warwick's unwilling execution of the odious commission to persuade his daughter. Dialogue follows dialogue in an uninterrupted scene, unfolding a succession of emotions skilfully conducted to a doubtful issue. Then comes an interpose, in which the King's preoccupation with his passion is strikingly exhibited, leading up to the final conflict between him and the Countess, preluded by the master-touch whereby the young Prince is made to sway King Edward's inclination.

VII

The remaining Chronicle Plays, of which I propose to make a brief enumeration, offer no critical difficulties regarding authorship. While this department of the drama still laboured in the thraldom of clumsy stage-carpentry, Marlowe's touch transfigured it by the production of 'Edward II.' His play may have been written as early as 1590; but it was only entered on the Stationers' Books in 1593, and printed in 1598. More will be said in the proper place about this epoch-making Chronicle. Peele gave the public a drama on the life of 'Edward I.' in 1593, which, though it cannot be compared with Marlowe's, marks a considerable advance upon such work as 'The Troublesome Reign' and 'The Famous Victories.' Following a scurrilous ballad on Queen Eleanor, and yielding to the popular . prejudice against Spaniards, he stained an otherwise meritorious composition with a gross and unhistorical libel on the wife of Longshanks. In the same decade, Thomas Heywood issued from the press his two parts of the Chronicle of 'Edward IV.,' a principal feature in which plays was the episode of Jane Shore. In 1605 the same author sent to the press his play upon the reign of Mary and the accession of Elizabeth. It had been acted several years before, and bore the curious title of, 'If You know not Me, You know Nobody.' Next year, the second part of this Chronicle, dealing with Sir Thomas Gresham's building of the Royal Exchange and the Defeat of the Armada, appeared. The proper occasion for estimating Heywood's capacity as an author of Chronicle Plays, will occur in the examination of his essentially English art Much in the same style, but marked by inferior dramatic power, is the double Chronicle Play by Samuel Rowley, entitled, 'When You see Me, You know Me.' It was printed in 1605, but was probably well known upon the stage before that date. As Heywood treated some of the events of Elizabeth's reign, so Rowley in this formless production touched upon those of Henry VIII. But he could not or dared not address himself seriously to the real history of a period so recent and so full of perilous matter. The best scenes in his superficial work are comic—Henry's meeting with the thief Black Will, his imprisonment in the Counter, and the vicarious birching of his whipping-boy Ned Browne. Plays of this description, which bring English princes on the stage in merry moments, were highly popular, as will be seen when we discuss the fourth section mentioned at the opening of this chapter.

VIII

Adding to these inferior Chronicles the great Shaksperian group, it will be seen that what remains to us of this species includes plays on the reigns of King John, Edward I., Edward II., Edward III., Richard II., Henry IV., Henry V., Henry VI., Edward IV., Richard III., Henry VIII., Mary and Elizabeth—an almost continuous series of studies in English history from 1199 to 1588—embracing in round figures four centuries, from the accession of John to the Defeat of the Armada. The gaps in the list of sovereigns are supplemented by Greene's 'James IV. of Scotland' and Ford's 'Perkin Warbeck,' which deal with events of the reign of Henry VII., and by Decker and Webster's 'Sir Thomas Wyatt,' which forms a sequel to the reign of Edward VI. Very unequal in artistic capacity, rising to the highest in Shakspere and Marlowe, sinking to the lowest in Rowley and the author of 'The Troublesome Reign,' these dramatists of our old annals performed no petty service for

the nation, at a moment when the English were growing to
full consciousness of their high destiny. 'Gildon,' to quote
some words from Mr. Halliwell's Introduction to 'The First
Part of the Contention,' 'tells us of a tradition, that Shakespeare, in a conversation with Ben Jonson, said that, "finding
the nation generally very ignorant of history, he wrote plays
in order to instruct the people in that particular." ' This
states, while it distorts, a truth. We know quite well that
Shakspere did not make, but found the Chronicle Play in
full existence. Yet he and his humbler fellow-workers
together undertook the instruction of the people in their
history. Nash, in 'Pierce Penniless,' enables us to form a
conception of the effect produced by even such wooden work
as 'The Famous Victories of Henry V.' upon a public
audience. 'Tell them,' he writes, 'what a glorious thing it
is to have Henry the Fifth represented on the stage, leading
the French king prisoner, and forcing both him and the
Dolphin swear fealty.' And again, referring probably to the
rough draught of the First Part of 'Henry VI.,' now lost:
'How would it have joyed brave Talbot (the terror of the
French) to think that after he had lain two hundred year in
his tomb, he should triumph again on the stage, and have
his bones now embalmed with the tears of ten thousand spectators at least, at several times, who, in the tragedian that represents his person, imagine they behold him fresh bleeding?'
    Heywood, penning his 'Apology for Actors' twenty years
later, and in the maturity of the stage, touches more directly
upon the utility of these performances. 'Plays have made
the ignorant more apprehensive, taught the unlearned the
knowledge of many famous histories, instructed such as
cannot read in the discovery of all our English chronicles;
and what man have you now of that weak capacity that
cannot discourse of any notable thing recorded even from
William the Conqueror, nay from the landing of Brute, until
this day? being possessed of their true use, for or because
plays are writ with this aim, and carried with this method, to
teach their subjects obedience to their king, to show the
people the untimely ends of such as have moved tumults,

commotions, and insurrections, to present them with the flourishing estate of such as live in obedience, exhorting them to allegiance, dehorting them from all traitorous and felonious stratagems.'

IX

The third group of plays on subjects drawn from English history includes those which dramatise the biographies of eminent political characters or popular heroes. The earliest in date of these is ' Sir Thomas More,' which was probably first acted about 1590. This is a pleasant composition, suggesting to our mind the style of Heywood in the making. It deals with More in his private rather than his public capacity, drawing a homely but effective picture of the people's idol; the wise and merry Englishman ; the good-hearted frank stout gentleman, who left the highest office in the realm no richer than he entered it, and who laid his life down cheerfully for conscience' sake. Very inferior, both as a play and as a picture of English character and manners, is ' The Life and Death of Thomas Lord Cromwell.' Nothing need be said, indeed, about this lifeless and scamped piece of journey-work, except to point out how, no less than ' Sir Thomas More,' it proves the freedom of the English theatre, in spite of censorship. More was beheaded in 1535, and Cromwell in 1540, at the command of Henry VIII. Yet about fifty years after these events, in the reign of his daughter Elizabeth, these two victims of Henry's policy were exhibited as heroes on the stage of London. In ' Sir John Oldcastle,' a play by Drayton Wilson and Chettle, we possess the first part of a similar work, rather superior in dramatic quality. It deals with the life of Lord Cobham, the Lollard martyr, who was burned in 1417. But for its false ascription to Shakspere, and for the confusion between its hero and Sir John Falstaff in the First Part of ' Henry IV.,' we could well afford to consign ' Sir John Oldcastle ' to oblivion.

The names at least of ' Lord Cromwell ' and ' Sir John Oldcastle ' must remain as danger-signals upon the quick-sands of oracular criticism. Schlegel fathered ' Oldcastle,' the authors of which Malone had already ascertained, on Shakspere. And, as though he wished to prove that owls are not more purblind in the daylight than a German in the noon of unmistakable internal evidence, he proceeded to ascribe 'Cromwell' to the same hand. Concerning both plays, the one correctly referred on good external grounds to three inferior craftsmen, the other excluded by its style no less than by its prologue's sneer at Shakspere from even the limbo of Doubtful Plays, Schlegel wrote with magisterial self-confidence, they ' are not only unquestionably Shakspere's, but in my opinion they deserve to be classed among his best and maturest works.' 'Humanum est errare;' yet if something can be said in favour of erring with Plato, all critics will pray to be delivered from erring after like fashion with Schlegel !

Place might here be found for a rude and half-articulate show, rather than play, upon Wat Tyler's insurrection. It is entitled 'The Life and Death of Jack Straw,' and may be referred to an early period of the Drama. In its bearing upon Shakspere's handling of Jack Cade, this piece has a certain archæological interest. But not one of its four acts, however much they may have entertained the groundlings, will arrest a literary student's attention.

Two extant plays of a later period belong to this class. They are ' Sir Thomas Wyatt ' and ' Perkin Warbeck.' ' Sir Thomas Wyatt ' is a selection of scenes from an earlier Chronicle in two parts, written by Chettle, Heywood, Dekker, Smith, and Webster in collaboration, upon the tragical history of Lady Jane Grey. In its present form it bears the names of Dekker and Webster on the title-page; and the hands of both poets may perhaps be traced in it. When Guildford and Lady Jane, after her proclamation as Queen, are lodged by Northumberland in the Tower, they exchange these reflections :

> *Guildford.* The Tower will be a place of ample state :
> Some lodgings in it will, like dead men's sculls,
> Remember us of frailty.
> *Jane.* We are led

With pomp to prison.   O prophetic soul !
Lo, we ascend into our chairs of state,
Like several coffins, in some funeral pomp,
Descending to their graves !

This is somewhat in Webster's manner, though certainly
not in his best. The following couplet may possibly be
assigned to Dekker :

An innocent to die, what is it less
But to add angels to heaven's happiness ?

Yet the whole texture of the play seems rather to belong to
another workman, perhaps to Chettle ; and in one speech I
am inclined to trace the touch of Heywood :

O, at the general sessions, when all souls
Stand at the bar of justice, and hold up
Their new-immortalisèd hands, O, then
Let the remembrance of their tragic ends
Be razed out of the bead-roll of my sins !
Whene'er the black book of my crime 's unclasped,
Let not these scarlet letters be found there ;
Of all the rest only that page be clear !

Let, however, the beacon of Schlegel warn a diffident
critic off the perilous shoals of such assignments ! The
strongest part of the play, as we possess it, is the character of
Wyatt. His portrait is drawn and sustained with spirit.
Resisting Northumberland and Suffolk in their attempt to
enthrone Lady Jane, declaring Mary's right by lawful
succession, but protesting against her cruelty toward the
innocent and unwilling pretender, then breaking the bond of
loyalty and obedience in indignation at the baseness of her
Spanish match—he is shown in all the changes of his action
as a fearless, high-spirited, tender-hearted, but hot-headed
English gentleman. He disappears, however, from the
scene ; and the tragedy concludes with the execution of Lady
Jane Grey and Guildford in the Tower. If Dekker and
Webster arranged this History out of the materials of the
elder Chronicle, they attempted the impossible task of

converting what had been an episode, the part of Wyatt, into a complete play; and had to fall back upon the original catastrophe for their climax. Imperfect, however, as it is, 'Sir Thomas Wyatt' deserves honourable mention as the best of these early biographical studies from recent English history.

Ford's 'Perkin Warbeck' takes a place apart, and ought hardly to be treated in this connection. It belongs to the period when dramatic composition had become critical, and the playwright reflected on his art. In his Dedication, Ford says that he was attracted to the subject by 'a perfection in the story.' The Prologue, after touching upon the neglect which had recently fallen upon 'studies of this nature,' proceeds as follows:

> We can say
> He shows a History, couched in a Play!
> A history of noble mention, known,
> Famous, and true; most noble, 'cause our own;
> Not forged from Italy, from France, from Spain,
> But chronicled at home.

This is not the place to demonstrate with what careful skill Ford wrought the materials derived from Bacon's 'History of Henry VII.' into an elaborate drama. His play might be styled the apotheosis of a pretender; for he has contrived to maintain the princely dignity of Warbeck throughout, showing him more kingly in his dubious fortunes than either the crafty Tudor or the easy-going Stuart. The curtain drops at last upon the courageous death of the adventurer, dauntless in overthrow, professing to be convinced of his own right upon the scaffold:

> Our ends, and Warwick's head,
> Innocent Warwick's head (for we are prologue
> But to his tragedy) conclude the wonder
> Of Henry's fears; and then the glorious race
> Of fourteen kings, Plantagenets, determines
> In this last issue male; Heaven be obeyed!

I have dealt only with extant plays on minor characters in English history. But it appears from various sources that many more were known to the Elizabethan public. It is enough to mention a play of ' Buckingham ' (1593), Chettle's ' Cardinal Wolsey ' (1601–2), Middleton's tragedy of 'Randal, Earl of Chester' (1602), a ' Duchess of Suffolk,' a ' Duke Humphrey,' an ' Earl of Gloucester,' a ' Hotspur,' the fragment of Jonson's ' Mortimer,' and the play of ' Gowry,' which was represented in the reign of James I. What these history plays really were, and whether any of them were identical, in part at least, with extant works, cannot be ascertained, unless, as is possible, the MSS. of some of them exist.

X

Closely connected with these biography plays are a small set founded upon the marvellous adventures of English worthies. In an age which produced men like Drake, Hawkins, Cavendish, Frobisher, and Raleigh, half heroes and half pirates, explorers of hitherto untravelled oceans, and harriers of Spain on shore and sea, it was natural that a dubious undergrowth of speculators and adventurers should spring up. The Queen herself not only tolerated buccaneering expeditions of a mixed military and commercial nature ; but she also went the length of risking her own money upon undertakings hardly differing from piracy. The best spirits of the age were bent on schemes of glory and aggrandisement. Even Sir Philip Sidney dreamed of winning new realms with his sword for England, wresting colonies from Philip, and returning from fabled El Dorado burdened with laurels and gold. Political ambition and the greed for wealth went hand in hand with the chivalrous passion for adventure and the restlessness engendered in an old sea-roving race by the discovery of continents beyond the ocean. The glittering dross which Frobisher brought back from North America, the bullion of the Aztecs and the Incas which was dooming Spain to beggary and famine, the brilliant exploits of Cortez and Pizarro, those paladins of pioneering bravery, combined to stir a 'sacred thirst for gold,' an 'unbounded lust of honour,' in English breasts. As alchemy preceded chemistry, as astrology prepared the way for astronomy, so the filibustering spirit of this epoch was destined to inaugurate the solid work of colonisation, exploration, and commerce, which has been performed in the last three centuries by England. Its first-fruits were the crippling blows inflicted upon Spain in piratical descents on the West Indies and in the ruin of the Invincible Armada. Its final result was the formation of Greater Britain and the conquest of India by the Anglo-Saxon race, solid achievements of wealth-extending industry and chivalrous audacity beyond the wildest dreams of Elizabeth's freebooters.

That the drama of the period should reflect an impulse, which agitated the whole nation, was inevitable. Our chief surprise is to find that the plays which deal with this aspect of English life, are so poor. In explanation of their inferiority, we may call into account the difficulty of dramatising tales of maritime adventure and of representing Oriental magnificence. The subject-matter offered no central point, except in episodes, to the playwright; and the stage of that epoch was deficient in spectacular resources. By far the best portions of the plays which deal with the biographies of Stukeley, Spencer, and the Shirley brothers, are their introductions, when the scene is laid in England. We are afterwards carried to the Courts of the Sophy and the Sultan, to Indian islands, Turkish dungeons, the palaces of European princes, the wilds of Tartary, and battle-fields of Africa or Persia. But however the shifting of these scenes may have amused the fancy of a London audience, they offered no opportunities to the dramatic artist. He was forced back upon a mere medley of disjointed pageants, through which the bold English buccaneer moved, with an arrogance peculiar to his age and nation. Heywood, perhaps, succeeded best in this species with a play in two parts, called ' The Fair Maid of the West.' It is in reality the dramatised version of a contemporary legend of real life, the hero of which is Captain Spencer, and the heroine a girl who follows his adventures. Rowley, Day, and Wilkins sink below mediocrity in their hastily written and unhistorical version of the famous travels of the three brothers, Anthony, Thomas, and Robert Shirley, who sought divers fortunes in Persia, Spain, and Turkey. Much might here be said in commendation of an anonymous piece, entitled ' Dick of Devonshire,' which its recent editor, Mr. A. H. Bullen, is inclined to ascribe, on evidence of style, to Thomas Heywood. This play sets forth with vigour and simplicity the doughty deeds and unassuming courage of the English soldier, Richard Pike, who won his freedom from captivity in Spain by challenging and defeating three champions in a duel before the Spanish army. The arm he used on this occasion was the quarter-staff, ' my own country's weapon,' as he styles it. A romantic fable is somewhat inartificially combined with Dick's adventures ; but the real interest of the comedy centres in the fresh and homely portrait of its hero. Heywood's patriotism glows in the following spirited panegyric of Sir Francis Drake :

> That glory of his country and Spain's terror,
> That wonder of the land and the sea's minion,
> Drake of eternal memory.

More than a merely passing notice may be taken of one popular hero, who earliest engaged the attention of our dramatists, and whose authentic history, reclaimed by Mr. Richard Simpson, furnishes all the ingredients of a sixteenth-century romance. Sir Thomas Stukeley's chequered career is so characteristic of the period in which he played his part, that I may be excused for borrowing some details regarding it from Fuller's ' Worthies ' and from the careful records of his last biographer.

Thomas Stukeley, or Stucley, born about the year 1520, was the third son of a Devonshire knight. There is a dim tradition to the effect that his real father was Henry VIII. but of this no evidence is forthcoming, beyond the somewhat unaccountable acceptance he received at foreign courts, and the extraordinary insolence of the style he used. Entering the service of the Duke of Suffolk, and following the party of the Lord Protector, he was forced by Somerset's downfall to take refuge in France, where he fought in the campaigns of

Henry II. against Charles V. Henry gave him a strong letter of recommendation to the English Court, relying upon which Stukeley returned to London in 1552. He then disclosed to the Privy Council a French plan for seizing Calais, and using that port as the basis for an invasion of England. There is good reason to believe that Stukeley's information was genuine; but, be that as it may, he was consigned to the Tower for his pains. On his liberation, being unable to return to France, he joined the Imperial army, and served for some time under Philibert of Savoy. Twice, at this period of his career, he addressed letters to Queen Mary in a style which takes his personal importance for granted, and lends some colour to the fable of his royal illegitimacy. In the autumn of 1554, Mary granted him free entrance into England and security from arrest during the space of six months. Accordingly, we soon find Stukeley back again in London, where he married his first wife, Anne, the granddaughter and heiress of Sir Thomas Curtis. Shortly after this marriage, being now furnished with funds, he engaged for the first time in piracy. What he did or failed to do, is far from clear. But during the course of the next reign, his reputation as a freebooter stood continually in the way of his advancement. It should also be said that he remained a Catholic, which may have been one reason why his peccadilloes on the high seas were not more readily overlooked. He held, however, a commission in the first years of Elizabeth's reign as captain in the Berwick garrison, gaining the goodwill of the soldiers, to whom he always showed a royal generosity. In 1563, he planned his expedition to Florida, concerning which so many anecdotes are told. Elizabeth favoured the scheme, and engaged money in the venture. 'Lusty Stukeley,' as his contemporaries loved to call him, aimed at nothing less than sovereignty. 'I had rather be king of a molehill than subject to a mountain,' was one of his favourite speeches. And when the Queen asked 'whether he would remember her when he was settled in his kingdom; "yes," saith he "and write unto you also." "And what style wilt thou use?" "To my loving sister, as one prince writes to another." ' If

Stukeley started to found a colony and rule a kingdom, he returned a pirate. His Florida expedition ended in nothing but marauding exploits, which infuriated the Spanish Crown, involved the English Government in diplomatic difficulties, and brought the Captain loss of credit and but little pecuniary gain. A new chapter in our hero's romance opens with his semi-official mission to Ireland in 1564. The distracted state of that island made it the fit scene for the operations of an adventurer. Sir Henry Sidney took him up, and used him in negotiations with O'Neil. Meanwhile Stukeley, looking about for a permanent settlement, entered into treaty with Sir Nicholas Bagnall for the purchase of his Irish estates and the reversion of his post as Marshal. The Queen would not hear of conferring important office on a man who had discredited her Government by piracy. Stukeley, however, adhered to his plan of an Irish career, and next attempted to establish himself as Seneschal of Wexford. He had already bought the estates and office of Captain Heron, when he was dislodged, accused of treason, and imprisoned in Dublin Castle. He was a Catholic, and was probably concerned in a Popish plot for making Philip king of Ireland. Having lain seventeen weeks in prison, Stukeley was released on parole ; and seeing that all hopes of a national career were over, he threw himself boldly, as a Catholic and traitor, into the arms of Philip. ' Out of Ireland,' wrote Cecil in 1583, ' ran away one Thomas Stukeley, a defamed person almost through all Christendom, and a faithless beast rather than a man, fleeing first out of England for notable piracies, and out of Ireland for treacheries not pardonable.' In 1570, he set foot on Spanish soil, was honourably entertained by the King, and began at once to form a scheme for the conquest of Ireland. Philip paid almost unaccountable attention at first to the projects of the English ' rake-hell.' Closer inquiry into the matter made him, however, relinquish the undertaking as too hazardous. But, in the meantime, Stukeley enjoyed high favour and substantial privileges. He swaggered about the Spanish Court in fine clothes, airing his self-assumed title of the Duke of Ireland, and preparing himself for knighthood in the Order

of Calatrava, which Philip graciously bestowed upon him.
The Irish plan came to an end without, it seems, seriously
impairing Stukeley's credit at the Spanish Court. Yet his
restless spirit could not brook an idle life of compliment and
ceremony. Passing through Flanders, and intriguing on the
way, he reached Rome in 1571, where Pius V. gave him a
splendid reception. Afterwards, he fought with bravery in
the battle of Lepanto. In spite of the comparative insignificance of his birth, the ill success of his political projects, and
his want of estate, Stukeley had now created for himself a
position of some importance both at Madrid and Rome.
Whether he really passed for a royal bastard, or whether he
owed his elevation to address, audacity, and the prestige of
towering self-confidence, it is impossible to say. I do not
think it needed more than daring and ambition, combined
with a reputation for military capacity and some specific
touch on European politics, to launch a man like Stukeley.
The age of the Condottieri was still remembered; and the
age of intriguing diplomatists was at its height. Uniting the
character of Condottiere and political projector, and working
Ireland as his speciality, he climbed the ladder of distinction
by personal ability and hardihood. There was a place in
sixteenth-century society for such adventurers; but how they
contrived to support their station on the slender doles of
patrons and the meagre pay of war-captains, we find it
difficult to comprehend. Gregory XIII. treated Stukeley
with even more consideration than his Papal predecessor or
the King of Spain. He was seriously bitten with the Irish
project, and was thought to entertain a notion of making his
own son king of that island. Stukeley, as a good Catholic, an
English rebel, an experienced pirate and captain of adventure,
a schemer who had lived in Ireland, and who understood its
people and its parties, seemed exactly the right instrument
for the Pope's plan of conquest. Gregory conferred upon his
favourite many sounding titles—Baron of Ross and Idron,
Viscount of the Morough and Kenshlagh, Earl of Wexford and
Catherlough, and Marquess of Leinster. Then, adding the
commission of General in his army, he sent Stukeley to join

the Portuguese King Sebastian's expedition against Morocco. What followed is matter of history. Stukeley breathed his last in the ill-conducted and fatal battle of Alcazar in 1578.

By no means all the foregoing details were known to Stukeley's dramatic biographers; nor did these concern themselves with the political aspects of their hero's career. The rebel disappears. The traitor to his queen and country is forgotten. Only the bold Englishman, climbing to the height of an adventurous ambition, and dying chivalrously in conflict with the Moors, survives. The first play on this subject is entitled 'The Famous History of the Life and Death of Captain Thomas Stukeley.' It was printed in 1605, and was the work of an unknown author. The first scenes are presented in a round clear English style of portraiture. The old Devonshire knight, on a visit to his son's chambers in the Temple, finding swords and bucklers there in lieu of law-books—the scapegrace hero's meeting with his father—the part of the page between them—the wooing and wedding of the rich heiress, Mistress Anne Curtis—Stukeley's quarrel at the marriage feast with her former suitor Herbert, and the payment of his bachelor debts with the bride's dowry money —and afterwards his exit on a filibustering excursion before three days of the honeymoon are over—all these details form a pleasing bustling introduction to a pageant of adventures, which had subsequently to be helped out hobbling on the crutches of a chorus. There is one striking piece of braggadocio in the desert of dull business, which concludes this history. Stukeley has undertaken a mission from Philip to the Pope of Rome. He sets forth on his journey, and is followed by an envoy bearing a gift of five thousand ducats, upon which a percentage has been discounted. The interview between Valdes, the King's Commissioner, and the English donatee must have brought down the gallery:

> *Stukeley.* How many ducats did the king assign?
> *Valdes.* Five thousand.
> *Stu'k.* Are they all within these bags?
> *Val.* Well near.
> *Stuk.* How near?

Val. Perhaps some twenty want.

[*The bags are set on the table.*

Stuk. Why should there want a marmady, a mite ?
Doth the king know that any ducats lack ?

Val. He doth, and saw the bags would hold more,
And sealed them with his signet, as you see.

Stuk. Valdes, return them ; I will have none of them ;
And tell thy master, the great King of Spain,
I honour him, but scorn his niggardise,

[*Casts the bags down.*

And spurn abridgèd bounty with my foot.
Abate base twenty from five thousand ducats !
I 'll give five thousand ducats to my boy !
If I had promised Philip all the world,
Or any kingdom, England sole excepted,
I would have perished or performed my word,
And not reserved one cottage to myself,
Nor so much ground as would have made my grave.

Peele, if Peele was the author of the 'Battle of Alcazar,' has
given a distinguished place to Stukeley in the last act of that
play, dramatising the circumstances of his death, and con-
densing the legend of his life in a long dying speech. That
the 'rake-hell,' as Cecil styled him, was a favourite of the
public, is proved by the frequency of ballads and pamphlets
touching on his story, no less than by a casual reference
which shows he was a hero of the stage :

Bid theatres and proud tragedians,
Bid Mahomet, Hoo, and mighty Tamburlain,
King Charlemagne, Tom Stukeley, and the rest
Adieu.

XI

The plays of the fourth group, dealing with legendary
heroes and the apocryphal history of England, are for the
most part poor. It is, for instance, hardly needful to mention
such feeble performances as 'Fair Em,' in which an unknown
author of Greene's epoch exhibited William the Conqueror in
love at the Danish Court; or Day's and Chettle's worthless

'Blind Beggar of Bethnal Green,' founded on the mythical adventures of Lord Mumford and his daughter. Three pieces drawn from the history of Robin Hood deserve more attention. These are Anthony Munday's 'Downfall of Robert Earl of Huntingdon;' 'The Death of Robert Earl of Huntingdon,' written by the same author with Henry Chettle's assistance; and the anonymous 'George a Greene, Pinner of Wakefield,' attributed on somewhat slender evidence to Robert Greene. Taken together, these three dramas form a fairly comprehensive digest of the legend of England's most popular medieval hero.

Whether the famous outlaw was a myth, as Mr. Thomas Wright has been at pains to prove, or whether he had a real historical existence, does not concern the present study. What is certain is, that Robin Hood, the ideal English robber, was a very different personage from a Greek Klepht or an Italian bandit. He represented all the virtues of the national character, and some of its absurdities. He was an 'unfortunate nobleman,' deprived of his rights by unjust relatives and a tyrannous usurper, whose only fault in his more prosperous days had been over-liberality, or love of generous living. Driven from his home, he gathered jolly mates around him in Sherwood Forest, chasing the deer, and doing simple justice 'under the greenwood tree.' He lived, as Stow relates, 'by spoils and thefts; but he spared the poor and plundered the rich. He suffered no woman to be oppressed, violated, or otherwise molested. Poor men's goods he spared abundantly, relieving them with that which he got by theft from abbeys and the houses of rich carles.' Though he made free perforce with the king's venison, he remained a loyal subject; and while wandering beyond the pale of society, he and his merry men observed unwritten laws of natural justice, charity, and mercy. His sweetheart, the daughter of an earl, became Maid Marian, and dwelt a virgin huntress in his company, until such time as marriage rites could be performed. The Anglo-Saxon features of this legendary character, law-abiding in outlawry, loyal in resistance to authority, respecting Judge Lynch in the desert, gentle to

women, hospitable to the homeless, generous to the needy,
organising vigilance committees to restrain indecency and outrage, unembittered by injustice, hopeful and self-helpful in
adversity, exulting in the freedom of field, fell, and forest,
are unmistakable and firmly traced.   Robin Hood, as his
myth presents him to us, had probably no real existence.
But the spirit of the people which created him, has since
expressed itself in many a Western ranch and Rocky Mountain canyon.

Nothing illustrates the wholesome and cheerful tone of
English popular literature more strongly than the three
Robin Hood plays which I have mentioned.   In the first of
these, the Earl of Huntingdon is expelled from his fiefs and
outlawed.   He forms his republic and gives laws to his
followers.   Little John declares the articles :

> First, no man must presume to call our master
> By name of Earl, Lord, Baron, Knight, or Squire;
> But simply by the name of Robin Hood.
> Next, 't is agreed, if thereto she agree,
> That fair Matilda henceforth change her name,
> And while it is the chance of Robin Hood
> To live in Sherwood a poor outlaw's life,
> She by Maid Marian's name be only called.
> Thirdly, no yeoman, following Robin Hood
> In Sherwood, shall use widow, wife, or maid ;
> But by true labour lustful thoughts expel.
> Fourthly, no passenger with whom ye meet
> Shall ye let pass, till he with Robin feast ;
> Except a post, a carrier, or such folk
> As use with food to serve the market towns.
> Fifthly, you never shall the poor man wrong,
> Nor spare a priest, a usurer, or a clerk.
> Lastly, you shall defend with all your power
> Maids, widows, orphans, and distressèd men.

To this constitution, democratic in its essence, with a touch
of chivalry and of chivalrous hatred for the lettered and
moneyed classes, everyone agrees.   Robin turns to Marian,
and draws a seductive picture of woodland joys and pastimes :

Marian, thou seest, though courtly pleasures want,
Yet country sport in Sherwood is not scant :
For the soul-ravishing, delicious sound
Of instrumental music we have found,
The wingèd quiristers with divers notes
Sent from their quaint recording pretty throats,
On every branch that compasseth our bower,
Without command contenting us each hour :
For arras-hangings and rich tapestry,
We have sweet nature's best embroidery :
For thy steel glass, wherein thou wont'st to look,
Thy crystal eyes gaze in a crystal brook :
At court a flower or two did deck thy head ;
Now with whole garlands is it circlèd ;
For what we want in wealth, we have in flowers,
And what we lose in hall, we find in bowers.

He only omits what the song in 'As You Like It' dwells upon in passing—'winter and rough weather.' The hero's portrait is completed in the speech of a private enemy, who eventually procures his death by poison :

I hate thy cousin, Earl of Huntingdon,
Because so many love him as there do,
And I myself am lovèd of so few.
Nay, I have other reasons for my hate :
He is a fool, and will be reconciled
To any foe he hath ; he is too mild
Too honest for this world, fitter for heaven.
He will not kill these greedy cormorants,
Nor strip base peasants of the wealth they have.
He does abuse a thief's name and an outlaw's,
And is, indeed, no outlaw nor no thief :
He is unworthy of such reverend names.
Besides, he keeps a paltry whimling girl,
And will not bed, forsooth, before he bride.
I 'll stand to 't, he abuses maidenhead,
That will not take it being offerèd,
Hinders the commonwealth of able men !
Another thing I hate him for again :
He says his prayers, fasts eves, gives alms, does good '
For these and such like crimes swears Doncaster
To work the speedy death of Robin Hood.

The second part opens with the death of Robin, and proceeds with the romantic history of Marian. She is pursued by King John, who woos her with lawless violence till she finds relief in death. The play becomes a chronicle of minor events in John's reign. He is drawn as a detestable tyrant, cruel and lustful. By far the most powerful episode of the piece is the description of Lady Bruce and her son starved to death in Windsor Castle.

'George a Greene' interweaves an incident in the Robin Hood legend with the valorous exploits of another popular hero. The Pinner of Wakefield by his personal strength and influence quells the rebellion of Lord Kendal, forces Sir Gilbert Mannering to eat the traitor's seal, and entraps James, King of Scotland, who has crossed the Border on a foray. The Pinner's fame reaches to Sherwood Forest; and Robin Hood, putting himself at the head of his merry men, goes forth to visit the Yorkshire champion at Wakefield. George beats the merry men at their own weapons, and fraternises with Robin. King Edward of England and James of Scotland join the fun in disguise, carouse with shoemakers, and after making known their royal personages, wind the play up with a general jollification.

Before quitting the dramatised versions of Robin Hood's legend, I ought here to mention the fragment of Ben Jonson's 'Sad Shepherd.' Whether the imperfect state in which that play has come down to us be due to the accident of death, intervening before the poet had versified further than the opening of the third act, or else to the carelessness of those who undertook the charge of editing his manuscripts, cannot be determined. But students will agree that few of the many losses which English Dramatic Literature has sustained, are comparable to that of 'The Sad Shepherd.' This last offspring of Jonson's Muse promised to be one of the most interesting and entertaining, as it certainly would have been the most complete and regular, of English Pastorals. Lacking it, our Drama may be said to miss a mature and purely national masterpiece, in the pastoral style. Fletcher's 'Faithful Shepherdess,' however beautiful, is still an echo from Italian literature. Jonson in his ' Sad Shepherd' interwove romantic fable with the myth of an English hero, who, though he was localised as an outlaw in Sherwood, may probably have been a rustic deity, surviving from the dim antiquity of Northern paganism.

History is, so to speak, nowhere in plays of this description. Their authors sought to dramatise the doughty deeds of common folk, and to exhibit English kings and princes mixing with simple people, sharing their sports, making love to their daughters, receiving hospitality from humble entertainers. Greene's ' Friar Bacon,' of which some notice will be taken in the proper place, represents this species fairly ; so do the opening scenes of ' The Famous Victories of Henry V.' Heywood worked the same vein in his ' Edward IV. ; ' while Shakspere, laying his golden touch on all that lesser men made popular, bequeathed to us the highest picture of this kind in his portrait of Prince Hal. That the portrait has been proved mythical, when tested by the touchstone of State documents, does not signify. It owes its force, its permanent artistic value, to the animating sentiment, a sentiment akin, though different, to that which runs through Robin Hood's conception.

The English working classes, loyal to the Crown, in spite of civil wars and treasons, have always loved to pat their princes on the back, to hob and nob with nobles, and if possible with scions of the royal race. Heirs apparent, who understood the secret of this popularity, have not unwillingly infused a grain of Bohemianism into their conduct. We may regard this partiality for madcap princes as a settled factor in the English Constitution. Based on a sound foundation— upon the touch of nature which makes all men kin—the willingness of royalty to sign its debt to vulgar sympathies, the pleasure of the folk to see that debt acknowledged—this sowing of wild oats in common by the people and their beardless rulers constitutes a bond of sentiment more forcible than statutes. It eliminates the moneyed aristocracy, depreciates the courtier, exposes the squirearchy to ridicule, effaces the shams of etiquette and caste. It brings the extremes of society, those who in their several stations risk the most and suffer most from the encroachments of the intermediate classes, into fellowship. Meanwhile, in England, the law-abiding instinct has been ever hitherto respected, in legend no less than in fact. Prince Hal and Bluff Harry go to prison for their scapegrace tricks, and bear the Justice no ill-will. We might, perhaps, attribute something in the failure of the Stuarts to their non-recognition of this English idiosyncrasy, and something also in the popularity of the present royal family to their perception of the same. Be this as it may, the dramatists of the great epoch, with their keen sense of national characteristics, seized upon the point, and left us a gallery of pictures in the style I have attempted to describe.

In order to complete this study, it would have been admissible to catalogue those plays which glorify the several guilds, trades, and popular crafts of England—to show how the City and Corporation, the King's Jesters, prominent Clowns like Tarlton, the Prentices of London, the Shoe-makers, Thieves, and Jolly Beggars, all of them representing English life under one or more distinctive aspects, received due meed of dramatic celebration. To carry out such analysis in detail might be curious, but hardly interesting. Opportunity, moreover, will be offered for resuming these points in the course of further inquiries.

CHAPTER XI

DOMESTIC TRAGEDY

N.B. Of the Tragedies discussed in this chapter, the text of 'A Warning to Fair Women ' will be found in Simpson's 'School of Shakspere,' vol. ii.; that of 'A Yorkshire Tragedy,' in Tauchnitz's edition of 'Six Doubtful Plays of William Shakespeare; ' that of 'Arden of Feversham ' in Delius' 'Pseudo-Shakspere'sche Dramen; ' that of 'A Woman Killed with Kindness,' in Collier's 'Dodsley,' vol. vii.; that of 'The Witch of Edmonton ' in Gifford's 'Ford,' vol. ii.

I

THE Induction to a play, first published, without name of author, in 1599, is a dialogue between History, Tragedy, and

Comedy, the three species at that epoch recognised in English Drama. History enters at one door of the stage, bearing a banner and beating on a drum. Tragedy issues from the opposite door, carrying a whip in one hand, and in the other a knife. While these august rivals dispute the theatre, Comedy advances from the back, rasping a fiddle's strings. Tragedy calls on both her sisters to have done :

> This brawling sheepskin is intolerable!
> I 'll cut your fiddle strings,
> If you stand scraping thus to anger me

The place is hers :

> I must have passions that must move the soul;
> Make the heart heavy and throb within the bosom ;
> Extorting tears out of the strictest eyes :
> To rack a thought, and strain it to its form,
> Until I rap the senses from their course,
> This is my office !

History, feeling perchance her own affinity to Tragedy, is not unwilling to retire. But Comedy replies with taunts :

> How some damned tyrant to obtain a crown
> Stabs, hangs, imprisons, smothers, cutteth throats ?
> And then a Chorus, too, comes howling in,
> And tells us of the worrying of a cat :
> Then, too, a filthy whining ghost,
> Lapt in some foul sheet or a leather pilch,
> Comes screaming like a pig half sticked,
> And cries Vindicta !—Revenge, Revenge !—
> With that a little rosin flasheth forth,
> Like smoke out of a tobacco pipe, or a boy's squib.
> Then comes in two or three more like to drovers,
> With tailors' bodkins, stabbing one another !
> Is not this trim ?   Is not here goodly things,
> That you should be so much accounted of ?

Tragedy is not to be daunted with sneers or criticisms. She lays about her roundly with her whip, while History, who plays the part of mediator, calls attention to the hangings of the theatre :

Look, Comedy! I marked it not till now!
The stage is hung with black, and I perceive
The auditors prepared for Tragedy.

This is the Induction to 'A Warning for Fair Women,' the
second extant example of a peculiar species, which may best
be described as Domestic Tragedies. The plays of this class
were all founded upon recent tragical events in real life.
Tales of thrilling horror, like those which De Quincey
narrated in his appendix to the essay on 'Murder considered
as a Fine Art,' supplied the dramatists with themes for
sombre realistic treatment. As in the History Play they
followed English Chronicles with patient fidelity; so in the
Domestic Tragedy they adhered to the minutest details of
some well-known crime. Fancy found but little scope, and
poetical ornament was rigidly excluded. The imagination
exercised itself in giving life to character, in analysing
passion, laying bare the springs of hateful impulses, and
yielding the most faithful picture of bare fact upon the stage.
The result is that these grim and naked tragedies are doubly
valuable, first for their portraiture of manners, and secondly
as powerful life-studies in dramatic art. The auxiliary
fascination of romance, the charm of myth, the pathos of
virtue in distress, the glamour of distant lands and old heroic
histories, are lacking here. The playwright stands face to
face with sordid appetites and prosaic brutalities, the common
stuff of violence and bloodshed, lust and covetousness. Yet
such is his method of treatment in the best works of this
species which have been preserved to us, that we learn from
these domestic tragedies better perhaps than from any other
essays of the earlier period what great dramatic gifts were
common in that age.

That plays founded on these subjects of contemporary
crime were popular throughout the flourishing age of the
Drama, is abundantly proved by their dates and titles,
preserved in several records. All classes of society seem to
have enjoyed them; for among the earliest of which we have
any mention are 'Murderous Michael' and 'The Cruelty of a

Stepmother,' performed at Court in 1578. In 1592, the first domestic tragedy, which exists in print, was published. This was called ' The lamentable and true tragedy of Master Arden of Feversham in Kent, who was most wickedly murdered by the means of his disloyal and wanton wife, who for the love she bare to one Mosbie, hired two desperate ruffians, Black Will and Shagbag, to kill him.' In 1598, appeared ' Black Bateman of the North,' a narrative in two parts, enacted by Chettle, Wilson, Drayton, and Dekker. The next year, 1599, was fertile in plays of this description. Dekker and Chettle worked together upon a ' Stepmother's Tragedy ; ' Day and Haughton on ' The Tragedy of Merry ' and ' Cox of Collumpton ; ' Jonson and Dekker on the murder of ' Page of Plymouth ; ' while ' Beech's Tragedy ' was acted by one of Henslowe's companies. At the same time, the second extant tragedy, ' A Warning for Fair Women,' ' containing the most tragical and lamentable murther of Master George Sanders of London, Merchant, nigh Shooter's Hill, consented unto by his own wife, acted by M. Brown, Mistress Drury, and Trusty Roger, agents therein,' was printed for William Apsley. ' Two Tragedies in One,' by Robert Yarrington, issued from the press in 1601. This curious piece, which we fortunately still possess, interweaves two separate tales of horror, the one being the murder of Master Beech by Thomas Merry, the other an Italian version of the ' Babes in the Wood.' ' Baxter's Tragedy ' and ' Cartwright ' followed in 1602 ; ' The Fair Maid of Bristol ' in 1605 ; and the ' Yorkshire Tragedy ' in 1608. The last two are extant ; the former in a black letter quarto, the other among Shakspere's Doubtful Plays. In 1624 appeared two tragedies, the loss of which is deeply to be regretted. One of these was called ' The Bristol Merchant,' and was written by Ford and Dekker. The other bears this dreadful title : ' A Late Murther of the Son upon the Mother.' It was composed by Ford in collaboration with Webster, the two most sinister and sombre spirits of our drama, Saturn in conjunction with Mars. After this date, the pure domestic tragedy seems to have gone out of fashion. A lost play by George Chapman, entitled ' The Yorkshire

Gentlewoman and her Son,' was, however, entered on the Stationers' Books in 1660 ; and we still possess a piece by Rowley, Ford, and Dekker, entitled ' The Witch of Edmonton,' which combines the tragedy of Mother Sawyer, burned in 1621, with a wife-murder by one Francis Thorney. It was acted in 1623, but not printed until 1658. To this list I will add Heywood's ' Woman Killed with Kindness,' a masterpiece in its way, first acted so early as 1603 and printed in 1607, but whether founded on an actual history or not, remains uncertain.

The sources chiefly drawn on by our playwrights in the composition of these tragedies, were Stow's and Holinshed's Chronicles, supplemented by special tracts and pamphlets devoted to a fuller exposition of the crimes in question. The author of ' Arden of Feversham' followed Holinshed ; the author of ' The Yorkshire Tragedy' worked on Stow ; the author of ' A Warning for Fair Women ' took for his text a detailed narrative of Sanders' murder, which appeared in 1573.[1] It will be noticed that the most prolific writer in this kind was Dekker, and that Ford on three occasions devoted his great talents to the task. Shakspere, if we could trust the title-page of the first quarto of the ' Yorkshire Tragedy,' may have made at least one experiment in domestic drama. Neither Jonson nor Chapman nor yet Webster disdained the species ; and it is probable that if the works of these men had come down to us, our dramatic literature would have been enriched with highly instructive objects of study. For a note of the domestic drama is that here even great artists laid aside their pall of tragic state, descending to a simple style, befitting the grim realism of their subject. This consideration should make us cautious in rejecting a tradition which ascribes to Shakspere one of these homely plays. The same consideration will perhaps enable us to understand how Jonson may have made those powerful additions to Kyd's ' Spanish Tragedy' which puzzled Lamb.

[1] *A Brief Discourse of the late Murther of Master George Sanders, &c.*

II

I propose to examine five domestic tragedies, beginning with the earliest and ending with the latest.[1] These are 'Arden of Feversham,' 'A Warning for Fair Women,' 'A Yorkshire Tragedy,' 'The Witch of Edmonton,' and 'A Woman Killed with Kindness.' The first two were published anonymously, but have been ascribed upon internal evidence by no mean judges to Shakspere. Edward Jacob, in his reprint of 'Arden' in 1770, was the first to suggest that the play was Shakspere's. Tieck, who translated it in 1823, adopted this view, and Goethe is said to have supported it. Mr. Swinburne in his recent 'Study of Shakespeare' pleads eloquently in favour of the Shaksperian authorship. Yet there is absolutely no external evidence to rest upon; and so far as internal evidence from style must be considered, neither the diction, though vigorous, nor the versification, though far from despicable, can be closely paralleled with Shakspere's in his youth and prime. The most substantial ground on which we might assign this play to Shakspere, is the dramatic skill, the tragic force, displayed in it. Was there any other playwright capable of producing work so masterly before the date of 1592? We may at once eliminate Marlowe, whose marked style nowhere shows itself in scene, soliloquy, or dialogue. Greene, Peele, and all their school, are out of question. Neither Heywood nor Dekker, both of them young men of twenty-two, are admissible upon the score of any similarity between their earliest extant work and this. Middleton is equally improbable. There remains Robert Yarrington, of whom we know nothing except that he wrote one domestic tragedy; and to whom it might be indeed convenient, but far too fanciful, to ascribe the three domestic

---

[1] By earliest and latest, I mean in date of publication, which is, however, no exact guide to date of composition. *Arden of Feversham*, for instance, has all the signs of more mature workmanship than *A Warning*.

plays which puzzle us.[1] 'Either,' says Mr. Swinburne, summing up the case upon this point: 'Either this play is the young Shakespeare's first tragic masterpiece, or there was a writer unknown to us then alive and at work for the stage who excelled him as a tragic dramatist not less—to say the very least—than he was excelled by Marlowe as a narrative and tragic poet.' The argument is strongly stated; and those who agree with Mr. Swinburne in rating 'Arden of Feversham' among 'tragic masterpieces,' must admit the full force of it. After repeated study of the play, I am myself inclined to set only a slightly lower value on it than he does. Yet how dangerous it is to build on arguments of exclusion, to assign to Shakspere unclaimed work chiefly because we judge it masterly, when we remember the wealth of dramatic ability in that fertile age, I have already pointed out![2]

[1] That is to say, of course, *Arden*, *A Warning*, and *A Yorkshire Tragedy*. With regard to *A Yorkshire Tragedy*, it formed part of *Four Tragedies in One*, while Yarrington's known play on Beech's murder is part of *Two Tragedies in One*. With regard to *Arden* and *A Warning*, although there is a vast difference in the power of these two dramas, the method of dealing with the prose text in each is strikingly similar, and is in keeping with the method of Yarrington's acknowledged piece. I have been both surprised and pleased to find this hazardous suggestion with regard to Yarrington confirmed in a private communication made to me by Mr. A. H. Bullen. He tells me that at one time he was inclined to ascribe *Arden* and *A Warning* to the author of *Two Tragedies in One*. About *A Yorkshire Tragedy* he says nothing; and indeed, except upon Fluellen's argument of an M in Monmouth and in Macedon, there is no ground to group this with the other three.

[2] It may be well to try and state briefly the conditions under which, if we incline to the Shaksperian hypothesis, we have to construct it. (1) There is no external proof in its favour; but there is the difficulty of assigning the play to any known writer for the stage, combined with the fact that it is the work of a first-rate dramatist. (2) We know that Shakspere was the 'Johannes Factotum' of the Globe Company, turning his hand to the most various jobs. (3) The unrivalled power which he finally acquired over both character and metre was slowly developed after many tentative efforts. (4) What marks his earlier manner is a certain shadowiness of character-drawing (e.g. in *A Midsummer Night's Dream*) combined with humour, romantic luxuriance of fancy, euphuistic conceits, and a partiality for rhymed verse. (5) What marks *Arden of Feversham* is considerable grasp of character; absence of humour, fancy, euphuism; baldness of blank verse, sparely relieved by decorative or impassioned rhetoric. (6) But the Domestic Tragedy was a well-defined species, aiming, as the Epilogue to *Arden* states, at 'nakedness' and 'simple truth' without 'filèd points' and 'glozing stuff.' Shakspere may there-

Cautious critics, whatever may be their personal bias of
opinion, must be content to leave 'Arden of Feversham'
among anonymous productions until such time, if such time
ever come, when light may be thrown upon its authorship
from documents.   Less can be urged in favour of 'A Warning
for Fair Women.'   It was indeed first published as having
'been lately divers times acted by the Right Honourable the
Lord Chamberlain his Servants,' that is by Shakspere's
Company; and Mr. Collier in his 'History of the Stage' goes
so far as to exclaim that either Shakspere or the Devil set his
hand to certain passages.   No true critic who rejects 'Arden'
on internal evidence, will, however, ascribe 'A Warning' on the
ground of style to Shakspere.   Should he follow Mr. Collier's
opinion in the later case, he would be forced à fortiori
to credit Shakspere with the former play; for 'Arden' is the
ripe production of a dramatic artist, while 'A Warning' is
hardly better than a piece of solid and sturdy journey-work.
This tragedy may, therefore, be relegated to the limbo of
ἀδέσποτα—things masterless, without an author's or an
owner's name.

The case is somewhat different with 'A Yorkshire

fore have deliberately suppressed his own early manner when he was
called upon to produce a Domestic Tragedy for the use of his company.
It is also possible that he had a previous version to rehandle; for we
know that a play called *Murderous Michael* was shown at Court in 1578.
(7) As regards the solid character-drawing which marks the piece, this
was practically supplied to the dramatist by Holinshed; and the careful
use made of Holinshed is remarkably similar to that which Shakspere
made of his materials.   (8) We might therefore plead that the species of
the play excluded the young Shakspere's poetry and fancy, binding him
down to a severe and naked style; while the copious text on which he
had to work, drew forth his latent powers of character-delineation.
(9) There are many detached passages which forcibly recall the style of
Shakspere.   Some of these will be noted in the analysis of the play given
in this chapter.   See below, pp. 356, 360, 363-365.   (10) Lastly, the
hypothesis might further be strengthened by recourse to the always
convenient theory of piratical publication.   This could be used to
explain the halting versification of some scenes.   But it is not very
applicable to *Arden of Feversham*, which came to press perfect at least
in all its parts, and not compressed in any of its numerous incidents.
It is certainly of the full length.   Oldys says: 'They have the play in
manuscript at Canterbury.'   If the MS. is extant, a comparison with
the printed text might go far to set this point at rest.

Tragedy.' This short play formed one of 'Four Tragedies in One,' acted together in the same performance at the Globe. It alone of these four pieces was selected for publication, and was printed with the name of Shakspere. But the collectors of Shakspere's dramatic works did not include it in the first folio; and we are met with the further difficulty that it was produced at the very height of Shakspere's power and fame, when 'Macbeth' and 'King Lear' had already issued from his hands. Calverley's murder of his children took place in 1604; the play was published with Shakspere's name in 1608; 'Antony and Cleopatra' may be referred with tolerable certainty to the same year. That is to say, between the date of the crime and the date of the play four years elapsed, during which Shakspere gave to the world his ripest, most inimitable masterpieces. Is it then conceivable that this crude and violent piece of work, however powerful we judge it—and powerful it most indubitably is, beyond the special powers of a Heywood or a Dekker—can have been a twin-birth of the Master's brain with 'Julius Cæsar' or with any one of the authentic compositions of his third period?[1] Have we not rather reason to reject it, and to explain the publisher Pavier's attribution, by the fact that it attracted great attention on the stage for which Shakspere worked, and which he helped to manage? Judging merely by internal evidence, there is, I think, rather less than no reason to suppose that Shakspere did more than pass it with approval for his acting company. A slight but highly suspicious point is the insertion, at the very climax, of a couplet from Nash's 'Pierce Penniless' into the hero's desperate ravings:

> Divines and dying men may talk of hell,
> But in my heart its several torments dwell.

[1] The peculiar power displayed in the short and stabbing dagger-thrusts of Calverley's furious utterance cannot, I think, be paralleled by anything in Shakspere's known writing; nor, on the other hand, has Shakspere ever drawn a female character so colourless and tame as that of Mrs. Calverley. Neither the force of Calverley nor the feebleness of his wife is Shaksperian. Mr. A. H. Bullen queries, while these sheets are going through the press, whether it was perchance the work of Tourneur. The suggestion is ingenious. But it seems idle to indulge speculation of this kind on no solid basis.

This rings upon my ear even more falsely than the line from
Shakspere's Sonnets introduced into ' Edward III. ' :

Lilies that fester smell far worse than weeds.

Were the style of the whole drama, in either of these cases,
strongly marked as Shakspere's, or were the dramatic power as
unmistakable as it is in 'Arden of Feversham,' then these lapses
into petty larceny and repetition would not be significant.
But ' A Yorkshire Tragedy ' has nothing in language or in
character-drawing suggestive of Shakspere. The one-sided
force of Calverley's portrait points to a different hand.
Therefore this line of argument cannot be maintained, and
the ' Yorkshire Tragedy ' must be left to share the fate of
' Arden ' and ' A Warning.'

The two remaining tragedies upon my list of five, present
no such difficult problems as to authorship. ' A Woman
Killed with Kindness' is Heywood's uncontested property.
' The Witch of Edmonton ' was printed as ' a Tragi-Comedy
by divers well-esteemed poets, William Rowley, Thomas
Dekker, John Ford, &c.' The ' &c.' is amusing. Though
Rowley's name takes the first place, a perusal of the piece
will prove that Ford and Dekker, collaborators on a second
occasion in domestic tragedy, were responsible for some of
the best parts of the drama.[1] They, at any rate, worked out
the tale of Frank, Winnifrede, and Susan. I am diffident of
expressing an opinion that the whole of Mother Sawyer's tale
belongs to Rowley.[2] Yet this appears to me highly probable. It serves, moreover, to explain the want of connection
between the two threads of dramatic interest, and the
publisher Blackmore's ascription of the Witch to Rowley.

Were I writing for professed students of English dramatic
literature, I should hardly venture to enter into the detailed exposition of plays so well known as these five. Still
they are not easily accessible to general readers ; and the

[1] Their *Bristol Merchant* appeared in 1624 ; *The Witch of Edmonton*
was acted, according to Gifford, in 1623.

[2] The comic parts have, in my opinion, more affinity to Rowley's
work in *The Birth of Merlin* than to Dekker's in *The Virgin Martyr*.

importance of the group in illustration of old English habits,
no less than as forming a distinct species of Elizabethan art,
is so great, that I shall not hesitate to deal with them at
large. The characteristic feature of domestic tragedy, as I
have already pointed out, is realism. These plays are studies
from contemporary life, unidealised, unvarnished with poetry
or fancy ; they are this too in a truer sense than any play-
work of the period, except perhaps some comedies of
bourgeois manners. But this realism which gives the
ground tone to their art is varied. 'A Warning for Fair
Women' might be compared to a photograph from the nude
model. 'A Yorkshire Tragedy' is the same model treated in
a rough sketch by a swift fierce master's hand, defining form
and character with brusque chiaroscuro. 'Arden of Feversham' adds colour and composition to the study. It is a
picture, elaborated with scientific calculation of effect. The
painter relied on nature, trusted to the force inherent in his
motive. But he interpreted nature, passed the motive through
his brain, and produced a work explanatory of his artist's
reading of a tragic episode in human life. All this he contrived to do without over-passing the limits of the strictest,
the most self-denying realism. 'A Woman Killed with
Kindness' is also a picture, realistic in its *mise en scène* and
details, realistic in its character-drawing, but tinctured with a
touch of special pleading. The painter did not stand outside
his subject here. He added something of his own emotion,
and invited his audience to share the pathos which he felt.
Here, then, we are upon the verge of idealistic art ; and this
infusion of idealism renders the work more ethically dubious,
akin to sentimentalism, tainted with casuistical transaction.
'The Witch of Edmonton,' in its composition of two diverse
plots, strays further from the path of bare sincerity. There
is no question here of photographic nudity, of passionate life-
study, of stern interpretation, or of tear-provoking simplicity.
The one part, the part of the witch, is unconsciously didactic·
The other part, the part of the murderous husband between
his two wives, is romantic. Yet both didactic and romantic
elements are worked upon a ground of sombre realism. The

artists have drawn their several effects from crude uncoloured homely circumstances. No more than their predecessors, did Rowley, Ford, and Dekker seek effect by rhetoric or by poetical embroidery.

We might compare these five stages in domestic tragedy to the several qualities of realism exhibited by a newspaper report, a scene from one of Zola's stories, a novel by Tourguénieff, a tale like 'Manon Lescaut,' and a piece of Eugène Sue's. These comparisons in criticism do not lead to very much of solid value. They serve their purpose if they remind the student that what we discern as generically realistic contains many species and gradations.

III

In 'A Warning for Fair Women,' the handsome young Irishman, Captain Browne, meeting with Master George Sanders and his wife, Mistress Anne, at some civic entertainment, falls in love with the latter at first sight. He notes a certain Widow Drury in her company, on whom he fixes with a *roué's* instinct as a proper go-between. This she is by nature and profession. In their first interview the plan for courting Mistress Sanders is agreed upon; Widow Drury's servant, Trusty Roger, is taken into confidence, and Browne goes off to improve acquaintance with his lady-love. He begins by walking past her house, where she is sitting in the wooden porch awaiting her husband's return from the Exchange. Browne's suit does not prosper; and when he takes his leave, Anne exclaims:

> These errand-making gallants are good men,
> That cannot pass, and see a woman sit,
> Of any sort, alone at any door,
> But they will find a 'scuse to stand and prate.

The captain returns to Widow Drury, informs her of his ill-success, and begs her to use some speedy means for coaxing Mistress Sanders to his wishes. The widow, who combines petty surgery and fortune-telling with her other oblique trade,

happens to find the merchant's wife in a momentary fit of
pique against her husband. She soothes her down, flatters
her, and playing with her hand, exclaims, ' How is this ? You
are destined to be a widow ere long ! '—

> A widow, said I ? Yea, and make a change,
> Not for the worse, but for the better far.
> A gentleman, my girl, must be the next,
> A gallant fellow, one that is beloved,
> Of great estates.

With this she draws a seductive picture of her future wealth
and honours. But Anne replies :

> Yet had I rather be as now I am ;
> If God were pleasèd that it should be so.

' Ay,' takes up the temptress :

> Ay, marry, now you speak like a good Christian :
> ' If God were pleased.' Oh, but He hath decreed
> It shall be otherwise ; and to repine
> Against His providence, you know 't is sin.

Then gradually she suggests the form and feature of Browne
to the credulous woman's recollection, pretending to read the
signs of him by palmistry :

> Briefly, it is your fortune, Mistress Sanders ;
> And there 's no remedy but you must have him.

Meanwhile, the widow urges, Anne need not be too forward.
The stars will bring about her marriage in good season. For
the present let her only use Browne with common courtesy :

> As one for whom
> You were created in your birth a wife.

The plot is set, and the first part terminates.

Tragedy now makes her entrance upon the stage. She
tells the audience they have as yet only beheld

> The fatal entrance to our bloody scene.

A Dumb Show, which supplies a good example of the employment of this device not only to explain but also to advance the

action, is introduced. Allegorical figures of Lust and Chastity appear, attending Mistress Sanders, who is led forth by Browne, while Widow Drury thrusts Chastity aside, and Trusty Roger follows at her heels. We have to suppose that Browne has made use of his opportunities, and by the aid of Drury has succeeded in seducing Anne. The lovers have determined to anticipate the slowly-working stars, and to remove Sanders. At the beginning of the second part Browne attempts the murder, and is interrupted. The third part, introduced in like manner with Dumb Show and Tragedy, is occupied with the murder itself. Browne, attended by Trusty Roger, falls upon the merchant and his servant, John Beane, in a wood near Shooter's Hill, effects his purpose, and leaves the servant for dead upon the ground.[1] But Beane, though wounded to the death, has strength to crawl away. He meets with a country fellow and his daughter, the latter of whom is Beane's own sweetheart. They rescue and take him to their cottage, where he lies in sick bed till the time arrives for giving evidence against the murderer. Browne sends Roger back to Mistress Anne with a handkerchief dipped in her husband's blood, and makes his own way to the Court. Conscience now strikes both guilty lovers. Anne, when she sees her husband's blood, turns round upon herself and her accomplices :

> Oh, show not me that ensign of despair !
> But hide it, burn it, bury it in the earth. . . .
> What tell you me ? Is not my husband slain ?
> Are not we guilty of his cruel death ?
> Oh, my dear husband, I will follow thee !
> Give me a knife, a sword, or anything,
> Wherewith I may do justice on myself—
> Justice for murder, justice for the death
> Of my dear husband, my betrothèd love !

And so forth through an animated scene of self-reproach and desperation. Browne is hardly less unmanned. He flies, heedless of the blood upon his white satin doublet and blue

---

[1] Mr. A. H. Bullen points out to me the similarity between the treatment of this scene in the wood with a parallel scene in *Arden of Feversham.*

silk breeches, to the buttery of the Court, where he draws ale,
and excuses the stains upon his clothes by saying he had
lately shot a hare. Then he hastens to Mistress Anne; but
as he approaches her house, he is met by the little son of his
victim playing in the street. In order to show how the
author of this tragedy worked the motives supplied by his
text, I will transcribe this incident from the prose 'Brief
Discourse,' and place the scene beside it. 'He was so
abashed afterward at the sight of one of Master Sanders'
little young children, as he had much ado to forbear from
swounding in the street.'

Enter BROWN *and* ROGER. BROWN *spies the boy.*

    Roger. How now, Captain?
Why stop you on the sudden? Why go you not?
What makes you look so ghastly towards the house?
    Brown. Is not the foremost of those pretty boys
One of George Sanders' sons?
    R. Yes, 't is the youngest.
    Br. Both young'st and eld'st are now made fatherless
By my unlucky hand. I prithee, go
And take him from the door; the sight of him
Strikes such a terror to my guilty conscience
As I have not the heart to look that way,
Nor stir my foot until he be removed.
Methinks in him I see his father's wounds
Fresh bleeding in my sight; nay, he doth stand
Like to an angel with a fiery sword
To bar mine entrance at that fatal door.
I prithee step, and take him quickly thence.

When Browne comes face to face with Anne, she spurns him
from her:

    Ah, bid me feed on poison and be fat;
    Or look upon the basilisk and live;
    Or surfeit daily and be still in health;
    Or leap into the sea and not be drowned:
    All these are even as possible as this,
    That I should be re-comforted by him
    That is the author of my whole lament.

Her lover tries to soften her:

> Why, Mistress Anne, I love you dearly;
> And but for your incomparable beauty,
> My soul had never dreamed of Sanders' death.

But she will have none of him; and the scene suddenly changes to the Council Chamber, where three lords are taking evidence in the matter of the murder. Piece by piece it is unravelled; but the assassin, meanwhile, has taken refuge in a house at Rochester. He, a captain, ruffling in silks, goes to a butcher of the name of Browne, and claims cousinship. The butcher is flattered:

> I love you for your name-sake, and trust me, sir,
> Am proud that such a one as you will call me cousin,
> Though I am sure we are no kin at all.

These bye-scenes, it may be said in passing—the scene before Anne's house-door, the scene in the Court-buttery, the scene of Joan and her father driving their cow home, the scene of the carpenters at Newgate—are the salt of the play. It is their blunt unvarnished portraiture of manners which gives value to a sufficiently prosaic piece of work. In the butcher's house Browne is arrested. Confronted with Beane, who is brought bleeding on the stage, he mutters to himself: [1]

> I gave him fifteen wounds,
> Which now be fifteen mouths that do accuse me;
> In every wound there is a bloody tongue,
> Which will all speak, although he hold his peace.

It is hardly needful to pursue the slow, relentless exploration of the crime further. Not a jot or tittle of the 'Brief Discourse' is spared, from Browne's conviction and hanging, through the confession of Widow Drury and Trusty Roger, to the final repentance of Anne Sanders, and their several executions. One bye-scene may, however, be dwelt upon. Anne Sanders was hoping to the last to save her life. Browne

---

[1] This is one of the passages which are adduced to support the hypothesis of Shaksperian authorship.

had died, manfully denying her complicity. His words upon
the scaffold prove him to have been no utter scoundrel :

Have I not made a covenant with her   [*Aside.*
That, for the love that I ever bare to her,
I will not sell her life by my confession ?
And shall I now confess it ? I am a villain.
I will never do it. Shall it be said Browne proved
A recreant ? And yet I have a soul.
Well : God the rest reveal ;
I will confess my sins, but this conceal.
Upon my death she 's guiltless of the fact !   [*Aloud.*
Well, much ado I had to bring it out.   [*Aside.*
My conscience scarce would let me utter it :
I am glad 't is past.

Widow Drury also promised to shield her. But, lying in her
cell in Newgate, she overheard a man in the street outside,
who ' happened to speak loud of the gallows that was set up,
and of the greatness and strongness of the same, saying it
would hold them both or more.' This is how the playwright
dramatised the motive :

Enter two Carpenters under Newgate.

Will. Tom Peart, my old companion ? Well met.

Tom. Good morrow, Will Crow, good morrow ; how dost ? I
have not seen thee a great while.

Will. Well, I thank God ; how dost thou ? Where hast thou
been this morning, so early ?

Tom. Faith, I have been up ever since three a clock.

Will. About what, man ?

Tom. Why, to make work for the hangman ; I and another
have been setting up a gallows.

Will. O, for Mistress Drewry ; must she die to-day ?

Tom. Nay, I know not that ; but when she does, I am sure
there is a gallows big enough to hold them both.

Will. Both whom ? Her man and her ?

Tom. Her man and her, and Mistress Sanders too ; 't is a
swinger, ifaith. But come, I'll give thee a pot this morning, for I
promise thee I am passing dry, after my work.

Will. Content, Tom, and I have another for thee ; and afterward I 'll go see the execution.

Their conversation, a faint echo from the vulgar workaday world piercing the prison walls, determines the catastrophe, by stirring Mistress Anne's fears, and bringing her to conference with Widow Drury, who declares her intention of making a clean breast of the whole business. Anne thereupon gives up the game, and dies in a penitent mood.

Little, on the score of art, can be claimed for this tragedy. The only figure which stands out with distinctness from the canvas is George Browne. Him we readily invest with brawny form and lawless appetites. We see him swaggering, an English bravo, in his suit of white and blue. On the scaffold we are touched by his feeling for the woman, to win whom he committed murder in this world, and to save whose life he leaves it with a lie upon his lips. Widow Drury has also, in the first part at least of the action, a definite and recognisable personality. She is not unskilfully portrayed as the human reptile, squatting in slums and ill-famed haunts of vice, whose secret nature only emerges into the light of day to work mischief. But though the play is a poor specimen of dramatic art, its bare, indifferent presentation of a squalid crime may have been ethically more effective and more drastic as a purge to a burdened memory than a tragedy better qualified by moving terror and pity to purify the emotions of the audience. Lust and murder, the self-loathing which follows guilt, the pitiful uselessness of bloodshed, the sordid end of evil-doers, are unmasked with surgical brutality. We readily conceive that what apologists for plays were fond of urging in their defence, namely, that they wrought upon the conscience of criminals in the audience, may have been true of such a play as this. One of the magistrates engaged in trying Browne tells a story to this effect :

> A woman that had made away her husband,
> And sitting to behold a tragedy,
> At Lynn, a town in Norfolk,
> Acted by players travelling that way—
> Wherein a woman that had murdered hers
> Was ever haunted with her husband's ghost,
> The passion written by a feeling pen,

And acted by a good tragedian—
She was so moved with the sight thereof
As she cried out, 'the play was made by her,'
And openly confessed her husband's murder.

Shakspere, in the first draught of 'Hamlet,' inserted a prose
tale to the same effect; and in the finished tragedy immor-
talised the motive in those famous lines:

> I have heard
> That guilty creatures sitting at a play,
> Have by the very cunning of the scene
> Been struck so to the soul, that presently
> They have proclaimed their malefactions;
> For murder, though it have no tongue, will speak
> With most miraculous organ.

IV

'This lurid little play' is the phrase by which Mr. Swinburne characterises 'A Yorkshire Tragedy.' No better words
could be chosen to convey its specific quality. Like the asp,
it is short, ash-coloured, poison-fanged, blunt-headed, abrupt
in movement, hissing and wriggling through the sands of
human misery. Having dealt with it, we are fain to drop it,
as we should a venomous thing, so concentrated is the loathing and repulsion it excites.

'Walter Calverley, of Calverley in Yorkshire, Esquire,
murdered two of his young children, stabbed his wife into
the body with full purpose to have murdered her, and in-
stantly went from his house to have slain his youngest child
at nurse, but was prevented. For which fact, at his trial at
York, he stood mute, and was judged to be pressed to death.'
This passage from Stow's Chronicle fully expresses the argument. All that the author did was to introduce a few subordinate characters, among whom we may reckon Calverley's
colourless and over-patient wife; and to explain the motives
of the crime. The play exists in and for the murderer, or
rather for the devil who inspires him; for Calverley is drawn
as acting under diabolical possession. He has lost his fortune

by gambling and loose living in town. His lands are mort-
gaged. His brother lies in prison at the University for a
debt contracted at his request. He returns to Yorkshire in a
frenzy of despair and anger; the game of life has been played
out; his children are beggars, his wife an insufferable encum-
brance; a calenture of murderous delirium seizes him, and
he wreaks his rage in a tornado of madness. The action
hurls along at such furious speed, the dialogue is so hurried
and choked with spasms, that no notion of the play can be
gained except by rapid perusal at one sitting. We rise with
the same kind of impression as that left upon our sight by a
flash of lightning revealing some grim object in a night of
pitchy darkness. The mental retina has been all but seared
and blinded; yet the scene discovered in that second shall
not be forgotten.

Quotation is to little purpose in a case like this. Yet I
must support my criticism with some extracts, selected to
show in what particulars the realism of this piece differs from
that of the last. The husband enters to the wife. It is his
first appearance, and these are his first words:

> Pox o' the last throw! It made five hundred angels
> Vanish from my sight. I'm damned, I'm damned;
> The angels have forsook me. Nay, it is
> Certainly true; for he that has no coin
> Is damned in this world; he is gone, he is gone.

The wife approaches. He turns round on her:

> O! most punishment of all, I have a wife!

She pleads with him:

> I do entreat you, as you love your soul,
> Tell me the cause of this your discontent.

He curses:

> A vengeance strip thee naked! thou art the cause,
> The effect, the quality, the property; thou, thou, thou!

Then he flings from the room, but reappears a moment after,
muttering. His beggary and the beggary of his unloved

family have taken hold upon his mind. 'Base, slavish, abject, filthy poverty!' 'Money, money, money!' 'Bastards, bastards, bastards!' This reiteration of the same words, and this renewal of the same exasperating thoughts, seems meant to indicate the man's insanity. His whole action is a paroxysm. When his wife speaks, he interrupts her:

> Have done, thou harlot,
> Whom, though for fashion-sake I married,
> I never could abide. Think'st thou thy words
> Shall kill my pleasures? Fall off to thy friends;
> Thou and thy bastards beg; I will not bate
> A whit in humour.

Let her, if she wants to keep whole bones in her body, turn her dowry into cash for him to squander:

> Let it be done;
> I was never made to be a looker-on,
> A bawd to dice; I 'll shake the drabs myself,
> And make them yield; I say, look it be done.

She goes to do his bidding:

> Speedily, speedily!
> I hate the very hour I chose a wife:
> A trouble, trouble! Three children, like three evils,
> Hang on me. Fie, fie, fie! Strumpet and bastards!
> Strumpet and bastards!

Perhaps this is enough. This serves, at least, to show how the crude portrait of a God-abandoned ruffian was dashed in. What follows is after the same fashion. Stroke upon stroke, the artist stabs the metal plate on which he etches, drowning it in aquafortis till it froths. Prose takes the place of blank verse in cooler moments of the victim's passion:

O thou confused man! Thy pleasant sins have undone thee; thy damnation has beggared thee. That Heaven should say we must not sin, and yet made women! give our senses way to find pleasure, which being found, confounds us! Why should we know those things so much misuse us? O, would virtue had been forbidden! We should then have proved all virtuous; for 't is our blood to love what we are forbidden. . . . 'T is done; I have done't

i' faith : terrible, horrible misery! How well was I left! Very
well, very well. My lands showed like a full moon round me;
but now the moon 's in the last quarter—waning, waning; and I
am mad to think that moon was mine; mine and my father's, and
my forefathers'; generations, generations! Down goes the house
of us; down, down it sinks. Now is the name a beggar; begs in
me. That name which hundreds of years has made this shire
famous, in me and my posterity runs out. In my seed five are
made miserable besides myself: my riot is now my brother's
gaoler, my wife's sighing, my three boys' penury, and mine own
confusion.

The only redeeming point in the whole ghastly picture is
that, tortured still with appetites and longings, writhing on
damnation's rack, this doomed man has yet a thought, if not
a tear, to spare his wife's, his brother's, his sons' ruin. But
he is caught, like a scotched asp, in the devil's fork. And
when chance, at this climax, offers one of his children to his
sight, the fury starts up, fanged to strike :

> My eldest beggar!
> Thou shalt not live to ask an usurer's bread,
> To cry at a great man's gate, or follow,
> *Good your honour*, by a coach; no, nor your brother;
> 'T is charity to brain you.

And brain them both he does. First, the boy playing with
his ' top and scourge.' Next, the child in a nurse's arms :

> Whore, give me that boy! . . .
> Are you gossiping, you prating, sturdy quean?
> I 'll break your clamour with your neck! Downstairs,
> Tumble, tumble headlong. So :
> The surest way to charm a woman's tongue,
> Is—break her neck : a politician did it.

Here enters the wife, and snatches up the youngest child :

> Strumpet, let go the boy, let go the beggar.

To her ' sweet husband,' ' dear husband,' ' good my husband,'
it is only ' harlot,' ' bastard,' ' brat,' until he stabs his boy,
and wounds the mother in the breast. A servant hastens in
at the noise. ' Base slave, my vassal!' Down goes the

groom, trampled on, bruised, gored with riding spurs. The devil is up in the man, and off he rides upon a saddled horse to find his last child, feverish for further bloodshed. On the way his nag falls, over-driven, stormed into stupidity. The officers are after him, and he is caught. In the clutch of justice, the devil in the man is still unquelled. He snorts out curses. But they bring him home, and confront him with his wounded wife:

> *W.* O my sweet husband, my dear distressed husband,
> Now my soul bleeds.
> *H.* How now? kind to me? Did I not wound thee?
> Left thee for dead?
> *W.* Tut! far, far greater wounds did my breast feel;
> Unkindness strikes a deeper wound than steel.
> You have been still unkind to me.
> *H.* Faith, and so I think I have.
> I did my murders roughly out of hand,
> Desperate and sudden; but thou hast devised
> A fine way now to kill me; thou hast given mine eyes
> Seven wounds apiece. Now glides the devil from me,
> Departs at every joint, heaves up my nails:
> O catch him, torments that were ne'er invented;
> Bind him one thousand more, you blessèd angels,
> In that pit bottomless! Let him not rise
> To make men act unnatural tragedies;
> To spread into a father, and in fury
> Make him his children's executioner.
> *W.* O, my repentant husband!
> *H.* O, my dear soul, whom I too much have wronged!

This exudation of the devil from the madman's skin, departing by the passages of joints and nails, is forcibly conceived. It must have appealed to an audience who believed in diabolical possession, and knew fiends' customary exits. Yet something is missed in the expression; something which we find, however, further on, when the two dead children are produced:

> But you are playing in the angels' laps,
> And will not look at me.

Then the wretch, delivered of his demon, outcast from mercy, is led forth in silence to his punishment.

V

What shall here be written about 'Arden of Feversham'?
This play preceded the two with which I have just dealt by
some years.   Yet it combined their characteristics in a style
of far more ruthlessly deliberate power, holding Calverley's
passion in subjection, preserving but transfiguring with
conscious art the frigid truth of villainy in Captain Browne
and Mistress Anne.   There is not one character in the play
which is not either detestable or despicable.   And yet the
total impression is by no means one of unmixed loathing
The execution is too workmanly and vigorous; the peculiar
type of bourgeois tragedy has been too successfully realised for
us to withhold our admiration.

The tale of murder and adultery on which 'Arden of
Feversham' was founded, is written at considerable length in
Holinshed, and the play follows that narrative with scrupulous
fidelity.   The last lines of the epilogue are these:

> Gentlemen, we hope you 'll pardon this naked tragedy,
> Wherein no filèd points are foisted in
> To make it gracious to the ear or eye;
> For simple truth is gracious enough,
> And needs no other points of glozing stuff.

A naked tragedy it is in all truth, and faithful down to the
least detail suggested by the text.   Yet it is not naked with
the anatomical bareness, as of some flayed figure, which we
notice in the 'Yorkshire Tragedy;' nor does it follow the
narrative with the prosaic servility of 'A Warning for Fair
Women.'   As Shakspere dealt in his Roman tragedies
with North's Plutarch, so the author of 'Arden' deals with
Holinshed.   He recasts each motive, retouches each sentence,
revivifies each character, by exercise of the imagination which
penetrates below the surface, divines the inner essence, and
reproduces in brief space the soul's life of the subject.   All
this is done, however, in due keeping with the style peculiar
to domestic tragedy.   'No filèd points' of finished rhetoric, no

' points of glozing ' poetry, are foisted into the bare stuff of
crime and passion ; nor is the simple impression of the tragedy
marred by matter meant to please the groundlings' ears.
Possibly the Epilogue's appeal to gentlemen may signify that
the play was not intended for the common stage. But, so far
as I am aware, we know nothing about the circumstances of
its production and performance.

' This Arden,' writes Holinshed, ' was a man of a tall and
comely personage, and matched in marriage with a gentlewoman, young, tall, and well-favoured of shape and countenance, who chancing to fall in familiarity with one Mosbie, a
tailor by occupation, a black swart man, servant to the Lord
North, it happened this Mosbie, upon some mistaking, to fall
out with her ; but she, being desirous to be in favour with
him again, sent him a pair of silver dice by one Adam Foule,
dwelling at the Flower-de-luce in Feversham. After which
he resorted to her again, and oftentimes lay in Arden's house ;
and although (as it was said) Arden perceived right well their
mutual familiarity to be much greater than their honesty, yet
because he would not offend her, and so lose the benefit he
hoped to gain at some of her friends' hands in bearing with
her lewdness, which he might have lost if he should have
fallen out with her, he was contented to wink at her filthy
disorder, and both permitted and also invited Mosbie very
often to lodge in his house. And thus it continued a good
space before any practice was begun by them against Master
Arden. She at length, inflamed in love with Mosbie and
loathing her husband, wished, and after practised the means
how to hasten his end.'

Thomas Arden, or more properly Arderne, was a Kentish
gentleman. His wife is said to have been a daughter of Sir
Edward North, created Baron in 1554. Her name, as is
natural, does not occur in published or MS. pedigrees of the
Earls of Guilford ; but if she was Sir Edward's daughter, she
was also sister to Sir Thomas North, the translator of
Plutarch. Thomas Mosbie, or Morsby as the name should be
written, began life as a tailor, entered the service of Sir
Edward North, and rose to the stewardship of his household.

The references in the tragedy to Alice's noble birth and powerful relatives, and to Mosbie's former occupation, are frequent. Mosbie gives Arden the *coup de grâce* with a 'pressing iron of fourteen pounds' weight,' which he carried at his girdle. This was an implement of his trade. When Arden draws Mosbie's sword from the scabbard and wrests it from him, he taunts the tailor thus:

> So, sirrah, you may not wear a sword!
> The statute makes against artificers.
> I warrant that, I do! Now use your bodkin,
> Your Spanish needle, and your pressing iron!
> For *this* shall go with me; and mark my words,
> You goodman botcher!

In the tragedy Arden is drawn from the first as a man aware of his wife's adultery:

> Love-letters passed 'twixt Mosbie and my wife,
> And they have privy meetings in the town:
> Nay, on his finger did I spie the ring,
> Which at our marriage-day the priest put on.

The indignity of the situation stings him to the quick:

> Ay, but to dote on such an one as he,
> Is monstrous, Franklin, and intolerable!

Yet he puts up with it, because he cannot do without his wife:

> For dear I hold her love, as dear as heaven.

He knows that the pair have resolved to murder him, put poison in his milk, set cut-throats on him. Still he entreats Mosbie to take up lodging in his house, and leaves him there when he goes to London. He sees Alice with her arms round the man's neck, and hears them call him cuckold. Yet he makes all smooth, and persists in pressing Mosbie, apparently against his wife's will, to sup and play with him. The dramatist's conception of his character is, that uxoriousness has blinded him:

> He whom the devil drives, must go perforce.
> Poor gentleman! how soon he is bewitched!

Furthermore, following the Chronicle, he makes avarice a main point of the portrait. Alice says:

> My saving husband hoards up bags of gold,
> To make my children rich.

A certain Greene, whom he has defrauded of some abbey lands by obtaining a Chancery grant of them, exclaims:

> Desire of wealth is endless in his mind,
> And he is greedy, gaping still for gain;
> Nor cares he though young gentlemen do beg,
> So he may scrape and hoard up in his pouch.

One Reede, deprived by him unjustly of a plot of ground, meets and curses him not long before the murder:

> That plot of ground which thou detain'st from me,
> I speak it in an agony of spirit,
> Be ruinous and fatal unto thee!
> Either there be butchered by thy dearest friends,
> Or else be brought for men to wonder at,
> Or thou or thine miscarry in that place,
> Or there run mad and end thy cursèd days!

This avarice, combined with the doting passion for his wife, brings about his ruin. He persists in trusting Mosbie and Alice. They work on Greene's resentment. Greene hires the murderers, Black Will and Shagbag. When Arden has been killed, his dead body is flung out upon Reede's meadow. In this way the dramatist has contrived to draw the fatal net around the husband by the means of his two base qualities. It must, however, be regarded as somewhat singular that, while he followed Holinshed so closely, he dropped one motive suggested in the passage I have quoted above. 'Because he would not offend her, *and so lose the benefit he hoped to gain at some of her friends' hands in bearing with her lewdness.*' This, and this alone, makes the real Arderne's contemptible compliance intelligible. The omission of this enfeebles the dramatic Arden, and blurs the outline of his character, in which neither uxorious passion nor avarice is forcibly enough accentuated to explain his conduct. It is, of course, possible,

the North family being at that time both powerful and noble,
that the playwright felt himself precluded from insisting on a
motive which might have been construed into a *scandalum
magnatum*, and that he unwillingly abandoned what would
have enabled him to raise the dramatic interest and intensity
of Arden's character. Also he may not have chosen to paint
his victim-hero in colours so revolting that the most indulgent
of audiences must have regarded his murder, not as a martyr-
dom, but as a merited punishment. But, while avoiding this
rock, he has drifted into the most serious weakness which is
discernible in the character-drawing of the play. It is impossible to take much interest in this clay figure.

Mosbie, the lover, is more powerfully realised. We see in
him one of the basest curs an artist ever deigned to draw
with touch on touch of deepening degradation. He is a
coward even in his love, dragged forward less by passion than
by the imperious will of his paramour. When Arden wrests
his sword and brands him on the face with infamy, he only
falters :

> Ah, Master Arden, you have injured me.
> I do appeal to God, and to the world.

He is a coward in the execution of his crime, seeking to do
the trick by poisoned pictures, poison in the cup, a poisoned
crucifix, rather than by sheer steel ; and blaming Alice for
audacity when she discovers a proper instrument in Greene.
He is a traitor in thought to his mistress and accomplices.
When they are all chin-deep in stratagems and murderous
plots he considers, in a long soliloquy, how he shall secure
himself against them in the future. Greene, Michael, and the
Painter must be brought to ' pluck out each other's throat.'
The woman must be killed :

> Yet Mistress Arden lives ; but she's myself,
> And holy Church-rites make us two not one.
> But what for that ? I may not trust you, Alice !
> You have supplanted Arden for my sake,
> And will extirpen me to plant another.
> 'T is fearful sleeping in a serpent's bed ;
> And I will cleanly rid my hands of her.

When they quarrel, his unspeakable sordidness of soul bursts out :

> Go, get thee gone, a copesmate for thy hinds!
> I am too good to be thy favourite.

Alice's real retribution is that, passion-blinded, she has to feel the fangs of such a hound. When she humbles herself to beg for pardon, he returns the speech of her despair with snarls of hating irony :

> O no! I am a base artificer!
> My wings are feathered for a lowly flight.
> Mosbie? Fie, no, not for a thousand pound!
> Make love to you? Why, 't is unpardonable!
> We beggars must not breathe where gentles are.

The touch of *not for a thousand pound* is rare. Alice never for a moment thought of money. It is the churl, who expresses the extreme of scorn by hyperboles of cash. When they make peace, his last word has a sinister double meaning. She bids him come into the house. He answers :

> Ay, to the gates of death, to follow thee!

There is no redeeming touch in Mosbie. He is wounded in an unsuccessful attack on Arden. Alice cannot bear the sight :

> Sweet Mosbie, hide thy arm, it kills my heart.

Listen to his sneering response :

> Ay, Mistress Arden, *this* is *your* favour.

The murder has been accomplished. His only thought is for his own safety :

> Tell me, sweet Alice, how shall I escape?
> Until to-morrow, sweet Alice, now farewell,
> And see you confess nothing in any case.

He is brought up together with the other criminals for sentence before the Mayor. At the sight and voice of Alice he bursts into foul-mouthed abuse :

> How long shall I live in this hell of grief?
> Convey me from the presence of that strumpet.

The last recorded utterance of his egotism is:

> Fie upon women!

By the side of Mosbie, Captain Browne and even Calverley are honest fellows.

The subordinate characters are scarcely less intolerable; but the dramatist has contrived to indicate various shades of dastardy and villainy in painting this uninviting gallery of scoundrels. There is not one but is an actual or potential murderer—Michael, Greene, Black Will, Shagbag, and the Painter Clarke. Michael says:

> For I will rid mine elder brother away,
> And then the farm of Bocton is mine own.

The Painter boasts of his skill in preparing poisons, and unctuously approves of Alice's resolve. Her love for Mosbie is enough to justify her in his mind:

> Let it suffice, I know you love him well,
> And fain would have your husband made away:
> Wherein, trust me, you show a noble mind,
> That rather than you 'll live with him you hate,
> You 'll venture life, and die with him you love.
> The like will I do for my Susan's sake.

Greene speaks to much the same effect, when he accepts Alice's challenge to despatch her husband. Black Will is the very Cambyses of cut-throats, revelling in bloodshed for its own delicious sake:[1]

> My fingers itch to be at the peasant! Ah, that I might be set a-work thus through the year, and that murder would grow to an occupation, that a man might without danger of law!

Shagbag is not so fluent of speech; but some of his condensed utterances reveal an even more dogged delight in cruelty:

> I cannot paint my valour out with words:
> But give me place and opportunity,

---

[1] There is a Shaksperian touch in this quotation, *that murder would grow to an occupation,* &c. This is humorous in the genuine vein.

> Such mercy as the starven lioness,
> When she is dry-sucked of her eager young,
> Shows to the prey that next encounters her,
> On Arden so much pity would I take.

His form of registering a vow to be revenged on one who has
played false with him, is characteristic :

> And let me never draw a sword again,
> Nor prosper in the twilight, cock-shut light,
> When I would fleece the wealthy passenger,
> But lie and languish in a loathsome den,
> Hated, and spit at by the goers-by,
> And in that death may die unpitied,
> If I the next time that I meet the slave,
> Cut not the nose from off the coward's face,
> And trample on it for his villany.

It must not, however, be understood that the playwright has
contrived to humanise either of these cut-throats in the finer
sense of the word. They remain stage-murderers, painted
from the outside, rather than portrayed with personal and
psychological differences.

One scene, in which the two ruffians bully ' murderous
Michael ' into abject subjection and submission to their will—
a bullying blent of English schoolboy and Italian bravo—is
effective :

> You deal too mildly with the peasant ;
> [BLACK WILL *says this in a loud aside to his confederate* SHAGBAG.
>   Thus it is :   [*Now speaks to* MICHAEL.
> 'T is known to us that you love Mosbie's sister ;
> We know besides that you have ta'en your oath,
> To further Mosbie to your mistress' bed,
> And kill your master for his sister's sake.
> Now, sir, a poorer coward than yourself
> Was never fostered in the coast of Kent.
> How comes it then that such a knave as you
> Dare swear a matter of such consequence ?

One sees the brawny swashbuckler swaggering up with
moustachios bristling and fist on dagger, close to the

country clown. Their breaths mingle. Then he comes to
threats :

> Tush, give me leave, there is no more but this
>   [*Spoken as above in a loud aside to* SHAGBAG, *after*
>   *which he addresses himself again to* MICHAEL.
> Sith thou hast sworn, we dare discover all ;
> And haddest thou, or shouldst thou utter it,
> We have devised a complot under hand,
> Whatever shall betide to any of *us*,
> To send *thee* roundly to the pit of hell.
> And therefore thus : I am the very man,
> Marked in my birth-hour by the destinies,
> To give an end to Arden's life on earth ;
> Thou but a member, but to whet the knife,
> Whose edge must search the closet of his breast,
> Thy office is but to appoint the place,
> And train thy master to his tragedy ;
> Mine to perform it, when occasion serves,
> Then be not nice, but here devise with us,
> How, and what way, we may conclude his death.

The rising of the style to rhetoric, the braggadocio allusion to
the destinies, the relegation of Michael to a second place in
the action, and the hectoring truculence of the bravo's self-
glorification, are sufficient to lay flat a meaner knave than
Michael is. He goes down at the bully's blow : but being a
coward to the core, he is overstrung and unnerved by the
attack. Having promised to do Black Will's bidding and
leave his master's lodging unlocked at night, he gives way,
just at the fatal moment, to a fit of spiritual horror. ' Even
physical fear,' as Mr. Swinburne writes, ' becomes tragic, and
cowardice itself no physical infirmity, but rather a terrible
passion,' in the Michael of this shuddering soliloquy :

> Conflicting thoughts, encampèd in my breast,
> Awake me with the echo of their strokes ;
> And I, a judge to censure either side,
> Can give to neither wishèd victory.
> My master's kindness pleads to me for life,
> With just demand, and I must grant it him.
> My mistress she hath forced me with an oath,
> For Susan's sake, the which I may not break,

For that is nearer than a master's love.
That grim-faced fellow, pitiless Black Will,
And Shakebag, stern in bloody stratagem—
Two rougher villains never lived in Kent—
Have sworn my death if I infringe my vow;
A dreadful thing to be considered of.
Methinks I see them with their bolstered hair,
Staring and grinning in thy gentle face,
And in their ruthless hands their daggers drawn,
Insulting o'er thee with a peck of oaths,
Whilst thou submissive, pleading for relief,
Art mangled by their ireful instruments!
Methinks I hear them ask where Michael is,
And pitiless Black Will cries: ' Stab the slave,
The peasant will detect the tragedy!'
The wrinkles in his foul death-threatening face
Gape open wide like graves to swallow men.
My death to him is but a merriment,
And he will murder me to make him sport.
He comes, he comes; ah, Master Franklin, help!
Call up the neighbours, or we are but dead!

Such, then, are the minor characters; Lord Cheyne,
Bradshaw (an innocent straw, whirled down to death on fate's
eddy), Richard Reede, and Arden's shadow, the prologising and
epilogising Franklin, are but episodical. But the real strength
of the play does not lie in the ignoble Mosbie or the pitiful
Arden, in the swaggering cut-throats or their sordid accomplices. What gives value to the piece is the portrait of Mistress
Alice—the adulterous gentlewoman, the bourgeois Clytemnestra, the Lady Macbeth of county family connections. She
detaches herself after a far more impressive fashion from the
reptile swarm around her. It is not that she is ethically
estimable. Far from it. But she is morally superior to all
the men around her—pluckier, more thoroughly possessed by
passion. Her fixed will carries the bloody business through;
and when she falls, she falls not utterly ignoble.

The author's method of unveiling, developing, and
variously displaying this unscrupulous and passion-ridden
woman's character, demands minute analysis. Unlike all the
playwrights of his time, with the exception of Shakspere and

Marlowe, he plunges into the action without the aid of dumb show or chorus, and without an awkwardly explanatory first scene. The actors themselves, in natural, self-revealing dialogue, expose the strains of character and passion out of which the plot is spun by their continuous movement to one point—the murder on which everything converges. Before Alice appears, Arden's opening conversation with his friend, Franklin, has informed us that he considers her a faithless wife, and that his heart is divided between shame, hatred, and a clinging love. She enters in the early morning light, and the first words he utters display her guilt as in a shadow-picture cast by her own dreaming fancy on his consciousness :

> This night, sweet Alice, thou hast killed my heart :
> I heard thee call on Mosbie in thy sleep.

And not only this :

> Ay, but you started up, and suddenly,
> Instead of him, caught me about the neck.

Our mind reverts for a moment to the scene in which honest Iago rouses Othello's suspicion of Cassio by the use of precisely the same motive. The next point is communicated in her own soliloquy :

> Ere noon he means to take horse, and away :
> Sweet news is this !   Oh, that some airy spirit
> Would, in the shape and likeness of a horse,
> Gallop with Arden 'cross the ocëan,
> And throw him from his back into the waves !
> Sweet Mosbie is the man that hath my heart ;
> And he usurps it, having nought but this,
> That I am tied to him by marriage.
> Love is a god, and marriage is but words,
> And therefore Mosbie's title is the rest.

Her passion already involves the desire for Arden's death, and meddles with casuistical excuses. News reaches her of Mosbie's arrival in the town. This spark sets the smouldering fire in her ablaze.

> As surely shall he die,
> As I abhor him, and love only thee !

We now know that Arden's murder is chiefly a question of
time; and when the servant Michael enters, we are not
surprised to find her working on his appetite, and luring him
to do the deed. The scene has not been interrupted, except
by entrances and exits of minor persons, when Mosbie in his
turn appears—with faint speeches and a hang-dog countenance.
He has the air of a man who, having had his way, would fain
drop a dangerous love adventure. But the woman will not
let him go thus:

> Did we not both
> Decree to murder Arden in the night?
> The heavens can witness, and the world can tell,
> Before I saw that falsehood look of thine,
> 'Fore I was tangled with thy 'ticing speech,
> Arden to me was dearer than my soul!
> And shall be still! Base peasant, get thee gone,
> And boast not of thy conquest over me,
> Gotten by witchcraft and mere sorcery!
> For what hast thou to countenance my love,
> Being descended of a noble house,
> And matched already with a gentleman,
> Whose servant thou mayst be? And so, farewell.

Had Mosbie found her irresolute, the tragedy would here have
ended. But the fire that sparkles from her heats his chillier
blood, and wakes what little manhood lingers in him. He
reiterates his former vows, and enters at once into Alice's
schemes for despatching Arden by the shortest way. The
next scene, which serves to illustrate her temper, is when
Arden suspects the poison in his broth, and she turns railing
round on him:

> There's nothing I can do, can please your taste;
> You were best to say I would have poisoned you.

This teaches us to know the woman well. She has the
courage of her criminality so fully that she dares suggest it,
holding in her hands the poisoned bowl, and knowing that
her husband has detected her. When Mosbie and she are
alone together, this is her comment on the incident:

> This powder was too gross and palpable.

Her lover's qualms have returned.   Has he not sworn to leave
her ?   Were it not better to desist ?

> Tush, Mosbie, oaths are words, and words are wind,
> And wind is mutable.

She will not let him go : but she feels now that the weight of
the affair is on her hands, and that he must be dragged along by
her superior energy.   Therefore, in the next decisive scene,
she works on Greene's cupidity and thirst for vengeance, as
she had previously worked on Michael's and the Painter's lust.
Mosbie dreads her desperate audacity, as indeed he has good
reason to do ; for a further point in her character, its reckless-
ness, is disclosed when she makes him take up his abode in
her house, Arden being absent :

> Mosbie, you know who 's master of my heart,
> As well may be the master of the house.

These lines end the first act.   The second act brings other
agents into play, but adds nothing to our conception of Alice.
In the third act occurs the finest scene of the whole drama.
Twice have the assassins hired by Greene—Black Will and
Shagbag—failed in their attempts on Arden.   The strain of
expectation makes Alice waver for one moment.   In an interval
of this yielding to better impulses, she comes on Mosbie.   The
scene is laid in a room of her own house, and she holds a
prayer-book in her hands :

> *Alice.* It is not love, that loves to murder love,
> *Mosbie.* How mean you that ?
> *A.* Thou know'st how dearly Arden loved me.
> *M.* And then ?
> *A.* And then—conceal the rest, for 't is too bad,
> Lest that my words be carried with the wind,
> And published in the world to both our shames.
> I pray thee, Mosbie, let our spring time wither,
> Our harvest else will yield but loathsome weeds.
> Forget, I pray thee, what hath passed betwixt us,
> For now I blush, and tremble at the thoughts.
> *M.* What, are you changed ?
> *A.* Ay, to my former happy life again :
> From title of an odious strumpet's name,

> To honest Arden's wife! not Arden's honest wife!
> Ha, Mosbie, 't is thou hast rifled me of that,
> And made me slanderous to all my kin :
> Even in my forehead is thy name engraven—
> A mean artificer ;—that low-born name !
> I was bewitched !—Woe worth the hapless hour,
> And all the causes that enchanted me !

Never again, until the very last scenes of the tragedy, shall we hear such words of angry conscience and repentance fall from this woman's lips.   Mosbie, who just before her entrance had been planning how to rid himself of her, now foams a torrent of abuses out :

> Nay, if thou ban, let me breathe curses forth ;
> And if you stand so nicely on your fame,
> Let me repent the credit I have lost.

And so on through twenty-three more lines, each one of which falls like a lash upon her shoulders.   Instead of confirming her in the repentant mood, his brutality drives her good angel away, and brings her back submissive to his lure :

> Nay, here me speak, Mosbie, a word or two :
> I 'll bite my tongue if it speak bitterly.
> Look on me, Mosbie, or I 'll kill myself ;
> Nothing shall hide me from thy stormy look.
> If thou cry war, there is no peace for me ;
> I will do penance for offending thee,
> And burn this prayer-book, where I here use
> The holy word that had converted me.
> See, Mosbie, I will tear away the leaves,
> And all the leaves, and in this golden cover
> Shall thy sweet phrases and thy letters dwell,
> And thereon will I chiefly meditate,
> And hold no other sect, but such devotion.
> Wilt thou not look ?   Is all thy love o'erwhelmed ?
> Wilt thou not hear ?   What malice stops thine ears ?
> Why speak'st thou not ?   What silence ties thy tongue ?
> Thou hast been sighted, as the eagle is,
> And heard as quickly as the fearful hare,
> And spoke as smoothly as an orator,
> When I have bid thee hear or see or speak :
> And art thou sensible in none of these ?

> Weigh all my good turns with this little fault,
> And I deserve not Mosbie's muddy looks.
> A fence of trouble is not thickened, still;
> Be clear again, I 'll no more trouble thee.

Ugly as Mrs. Arden has been painted, this terrible altercation scene—more terrible even than that in which Ottima and Sebald, in Browning's 'Pippa Passes,' confront each other after the murder of her husband—has the effect of raising her a little in our estimation. The tigress-woman, spiteful in her penitence, becomes gentle in the renewal of her love; and this love, unhallowed, bloody as it is, explains her future conduct. She is in the clutch of Venus Libitina henceforth till the hour of her death. Rising at one later moment almost into poetry, she excuses Arden's murder thus:

> Nay, he must leave to live, that we may love,
> May live, may love; for what is life but love?
> And love shall last as long as life remains,
> And life shall end, before my love depart.

Could the selfishness of passion, identifying itself with existence, brushing away the life that stands between anticipation and fruition like a fly, be more condensed than in these monosyllables? But the demon which rules her finds even readier utterance in crudity and coarseness. Arden becomes for her 'my husband Hornsby.' She exposes him to the disgrace of looking at her locked in Mosbie's arms; and hoping him upon the point of death, flings this aside to scorn him:

> Ay, with a sugared kiss let them untwine!

When at the end he is caught in her last trap, throttled with the towel in his own arm-chair, struck down by Mosbie's pressing iron, stabbed by Shagbag's knife, she snatches up the dagger:

> What groan'st thou? Nay, then give *me* the weapon!
> Take this for hindering Mosbie's love and mine.

What did Lady Macbeth say? 'Give *me* the dagger!' But no sooner has he fallen on the rushes in his blood—blood that ' cleaves to the ground, and will not out,' blood that ' with my nails I 'll scrape away,' blood that ' here remains ' to sicken her, what though ' I blush not at my husband's death '—in this horrid moment she springs up once more in revolt, a tigress, at the throat of Mosbie :

'T was thou that made me murder him.

Through the hurry and confusion of the closing scenes her high-strung courage begins to fail. ' Here is nought but fear ! ' Yet the cowardice of others brings her to herself again. A servant says that while they dragged the body to the field it snowed—' our footsteps will be spied.'

Peace, fool ! the snow will cover them again.

Against the neighbours who come crowding in, she bears a bold front, rapping excuses out, fencing desperately with their rapiers of proof. Then they force her to look upon Arden's corpse, and she dissolves in penitence as passionate as was her fierce desire :

Arden, sweet husband ! what shall I say ?
The more I sound his name, the more it bleeds ;
This blood condemns me, and in gushing forth
Speaks as it falls, and asks me, why I did it !
Forgive me, Arden, I repent me now,
And, would my death save thine, thou shouldst not die.
Rise up, sweet Arden, and enjoy thy love,
And frown not on me, when we meet in heaven.
In heaven I 'll love thee, though on earth I did not.

From this mood she does not return. In the condemnation scene she tries to shield Bradshaw, falsely implicated in the crime ; responds quietly to Mosbie's insults, and disappears from sight with these words :

Let my death make amends for all my sin.

Those who give ' Arden of Feversham ' to Shakspere— which I am loth in the absence of any external evidence to do—have some warranty for their opinion in this character

of Alice. Speaking of 'Edward III.' Mr. Ward suggests that
'Shakspere's gallery of female characters . . . seems incomplete without the addition of the Countess of Salisbury.'
Personally, I could well spare the Countess from the sisterhood of Imogen and Desdemona. And though Alice is not
needed in that gallery, I should be more inclined to recognise
in her, with Mr. Swinburne, the 'eldest born of that group
to which Lady Macbeth and Dionyza belong by right of
weird sisterhood.'

'Arden of Feversham' is marked by something terribly
impressive in the slow, unerring tread of assassination, baulked,
but persevering, marching like a fate to its accomplishment.
Arden's knowledge of his wife's infidelity and murderous
designs, his neglect of signs, words, omens, warning dreams,
increases the tragic effect. He is like a fascinated man, the
victim of Greek Atè, sliding open-eyed on the descent to hell.
If anything could be said in commendation of the bye-scenes
in 'A Warning for Fair Women,' much more and much
higher praise must be bestowed on the successive episodes
which lead up to the climax of *this* tragedy. There are no
bye-scenes—none that are not really needed by the exposition.
And how naturally is each presented—the chance meeting of
Greene and Bradshaw with Black Will and Shagbag on the
road to Gravesend; the Walk in Paul's, and the prentice
letting down his shutter upon Black Will's head; the night
in Aldersgate, when Arden and Franklin are summoned from
the house-porch to their beds by Michael, and the murderers
brawl outside; the quarrel and ambush on Rainham Down;
the cheery passage of Lord Cheiny and his men; the fog at
the ferry; the curse delivered by Dick Reede; Arden's dream,
and Franklin's interrupted story; the skirmish on the
heath; and lastly, the elaborate scene in Arden's parlour
(where, they say, the arms of North may still be seen in
painted glass upon the windows), the game at backgammon,
and the sudden inrush of the murderers upon the captured
man !

VI

In the prologue to 'A Woman Killed with Kindness,' Heywood makes the players say:

> Our Muse—
> Our poet's dull and earthy Muse—is bent
> Upon a barren subject, a bare scene.

These modest words strike the keynote to a tragedy, which, while it is a masterpiece of realism, contrasts agreeably with the three preceding plays. Here, instead of the police-court daylight of 'A Warning for Fair Women,' instead of the lurid glare of 'A Yorkshire Tragedy,' instead of the furnace flame of 'Arden,' we have to light us on our way the soft illumination, as of summer lightning, shed by a tenderhearted Christian artist's sympathy. The play is steeped in feeling, touched with gentle yieldings to emotion, resolutions of cruelty into love-penitence, reconciliations of the wronged and wronging, which diffuse a mellow radiance over the homely subject, the unadorned scene.

The story may be briefly told. Mr. Frankford, a country gentleman of good birth and fortune, marries the sister of Sir Francis Acton, a lady of rare accomplishments, famed throughout the county for her skill in music. A day or two after the wedding he receives into his household, on the footing of familiar friend or housemate, a young man of broken means, but of agreeable manners, called Wendoll. They live together happily till Wendoll, trusted to the full by Frankford, takes advantage of his absence to seduce the wife. Nicholas, an old servant of the family, has always disliked the interloper. With the instinct of a faithful dog, he watches Wendoll closely, discovers the intrigue, and informs Frankford of his dishonour. Frankford obtains ocular proof of his wife's guilt, and punishes her by sending her to live alone, but at ease, in a manor that belongs to him. There she pines away, and dies at last, after a reconciliation with her husband and her relatives. There is an underplot, or rather second tale, connected by slight but sufficient threads with

the main action. I do not think it has been remarked that this
subordinate drama is derived from Illicini's Sienese Novella of
the courteous Salimbeni (see ' Renaissance in Italy,' vol. v.
p. 99). Such, however, is the case. But Heywood, with his
rare knowledge and feeling for the details of English life,
re-cast the Italian motive and clothed it in a garb of homely
realism, so that it passes now for a finished picture of Elizabethan society. Whether Mrs. Frankford's tragedy had a
basis of fact, or whether, like the underplot, it was adopted—
as I think most probable—from romance, or invented by the
poet, we do not know.

The chief interest of the play centres in the pure, con-
fiding, open-hearted character of Frankford. His blithe
contentment during the first weeks of marriage, and the
generosity with which he shares his home with Wendoll,
form a touching prelude to the suspicions, indignantly
repelled at first, which grow upon him after he has weighed
the tale of his wife's infidelity related by Nicholas :

> Thou hast killed me with a weapon, whose sharp point
> Hath pricked quite through and through my shivering heart:
> Drops of cold sweat sit dangling on my hairs ;
> And I am plunged into strange agonies !
> What didst thou say ? If any word that touched
> His credit or her reputation,
> It is as hard to enter my belief,
> As Dives into heaven.

Nicholas only repeats that he has nothing to gain, everything
perhaps to lose, by the disclosure. Yet, ' I saw, and I have
said.' This saps the husband's confidence.

> 'T is probable : though blunt, yet he is honest.
> Though I durst pawn my life, and on their faith
> Hazard the dear salvation of my soul,
> Yet in my trust I may be too secure.
> May this be true ? O, may it ? Can it be ?
> Is it by any wonder possible ?
> Man, woman, what thing mortal can we trust,
> When friends and bosom wives prove so unjust ?

Frankford, still doubtful, resolves to learn the truth, if possible, by actual discovery. Here is interposed an admirable,

if somewhat artificial scene, in which the husband and wife, with Wendoll and another gentleman, play at cards. Their dialogue is a long *double entendre*, skilfully revealing the tortures of a jealous mind which puts misinterpretations upon every casual word. When they rise from the card-table, Frankford instructs his servant to prepare duplicate keys for all the bedrooms. He then causes a message to be delivered, calling him from home on a dark and stormy evening, and sets out with Nicholas, intending to return at midnight, unnoticed and unexpected. His hesitation on the threshold of his wife's chamber is one of the finest turning points in the dramatic presentation:

> A general silence hath surprised the house;
> And this is the last door. Astonishment,
> Fear, and amazement beat upon my heart,
> Even as a madman beats upon a drum.
> O keep my eyes, you heavens, before I enter,
> From any sight that may transfix my soul:
> Or, if there be so black a spectacle,
> O strike mine eyes stark blind; or if not so,
> Lend me such patience to digest my grief,
> That I may keep this white and virgin hand
> From any violent outrage or red murder!

At last he summons up courage to enter, but draws back immediately:

> Oh me unhappy! I have found them lying
> Close in each other's arms, and fast asleep.
> But that I would not damn two precious souls,
> Bought with my Saviour's blood, and send them, laden
> With all their scarlet sins upon their backs,
> Unto a fearful judgment, their two lives
> Had met upon my rapier!

Then, with a passionate stretching forth of his desire toward the impossible, which reveals the whole depth of his tenderness, he cries:

> O God! O God! that it were possible
> To undo things done; to call back yesterday!
> That Time could turn up his swift sandy glass,
> To untell the days, and to redeem these hours!

> Or that the sun
> Could, rising from the West, draw his coach backward ;
> Take from the account of time so many minutes,
> Till he had all these seasons called again,
> These minutes, and these actions done in them,
> Even from her first offence ; that I might take her
> As spotless as an angel in my arms !
> But oh ! I talk of things impossible,
> And cast beyond the moon.   God give me patience,
> For I will in and wake them.

Wendoll rushes from the room in his night-dress ; and
Frankford, pursuing him with drawn sword, is stopped by a
woman servant :

> I thank thee, maid ; thou, like an angel's hand,
> Hast stayed me from a bloody sacrifice.

It is quite consistent with Frankford's character, with his
Christianity, with the prayer he uttered before entering the
bedroom, and with his subsequent action, that he should
spare the adulterer.   Heywood has, however, saved this
mercifulness from contemptibility by showing him for one
moment in the act to strike.   The immediately ensuing
scene between Frankford and his conscience-stricken wife, is
deeply touching.   She grovels on the ground, crying, swoon-
ing.   He seems to stand looking down on her :

> Spare thou thy tears, for I will weep for thee :
> And keep thy countenance, for I 'll blush for thee.
> Now, I protest, I think, 't is I am tainted ;
> For I am most ashamed ; and 't is more hard
> For me to look upon thy guilty face,
> Than on the sun's clear brow.

Then he asks, what can she urge in her defence.   Nothing,
she replies ; and she expects, as she deserves, nothing but
instant death ; only let him kill her without mutilation.   Then
he bids her rise :

> *Fr.* My God, with patience arm me !   Rise, nay rise ;
> And I 'll debate with thee.   Was it for want
> Thou play'dst the strumpet ?   Wast thou not supplied

With every pleasure, fashion, and new toy,
Nay even beyond my calling?
    Mrs. F. I was.
    Fr. Was it then disability in me?
Or in thine eye seemed he a properer man?
    Mrs. F. O, no.
    Fr. Did not I lodge thee in my bosom?
Wear thee in my heart?
    Mrs. F. You did.
    Fr. I did indeed; witness my tears, I did.
Go, bring my infants hither. O Nan, O Nan;
If neither fear of shame, regard of honour,
The blemish of my house, nor my dear love
Could have withheld thee from so lewd a fact,
Yet for these infants, these young harmless souls,
On whose white brows thy shame is charactered,
And grows in greatness as they wax in years:—
Look but on them, and melt away in tears.

This scene exactly suits the genius of Heywood. Its
passion is simple and homefelt. Its tenderness is human
and manly. Each question asked by Frankford is such as a
wronged husband has the right to ask. Each answer given
by the wife is broken in mere monosyllables, more eloquent
than protestation. We feel the truth of the whole situation
poignantly, because no word is strained or far-fetched, because
Frankford in his justice avoids rhetoric, and in his mercy
shows no sentimental weakness; finally because, in the very
depth of his grief, he still can call his wife by her pet name.
He then leaves the room:

Stand up, stand up, I will do nothing rashly:
I will retire a while into my study,
And thou shalt hear thy sentence presently.

When he returns, it is to pronounce the verdict of exile from
her home, himself, her children:

So, farewell, Nan; for we will henceforth be
As we had never seen, ne'er more shall see.

One of the most delicate touches which round off the
character of Frankford, is his anxiety to clear the house of

everything that may remind him of his wife, when she is gone.
He searches it :

> O, sir, to see that nothing may be left
> That ever was my wife's : I loved her dearly,
> And when I do but think of her unkindness,
> My thoughts are all in hell; to avoid which torment,
> I would not have a bodkin or a cuff,
> A bracelet, necklace, or rebato-wire,
> Nor anything that ever was called hers
> Left me, by which I might remember her.

His servant spies her lute, flung in a corner :

> Her lute ?   O God ! upon this instrument
> Her fingers have ran quick division,
> Sweeter than that which now divides our hearts.
> These frets have made me pleasant, that have now
> Frets of my heart-strings made.   O Master Cranwell,
> Oft hath she made this melancholy wood,
> Now mute and dumb for her disastrous chance,
> Speak sweetly many a note, sound many a strain
> To her own ravishing voice !—
> Post with it after her.   Now nothing 's left.

Even the conceits and play on words in this passage are not
frigid ; so natural and so intense is the emotion which
penetrates the speaker's mood.   Nicholas is sent with the
lute after Mrs. Frankford, who is now on her way to the
manor house appointed for her exile.   When she looks on it,
she says :

> I know the lute ; oft have I sung to thee ;
> We both are out of tune, both out of time.

Then she bids it be dashed to pieces against the carriage
wheels :

> Go, break this lute upon my coach's wheel,
> As the last music that I e'er shall make ;
> Not as my husband's gift, but my farewell
> To all earth's joys.

Music, it will be remembered, was one of the poor lady's chief

accomplishments. During the gaiety of her marriage morning, a light-hearted guest had said :

Her own hand
Can teach all strings to speak in their best grace,
From the shrill'st treble to the hoarsest bass.

Mrs. Frankford is no Guinevere ; nor, again, like Alice in
' Arden of Feversham,' is she steeled and blinded by an overwhelming passion. Heywood fails to realise her character
completely, drawing, as elsewhere in his portraits of women,
a dim and vacillating picture. She changes too suddenly
from love for her newly wedded husband to a weak compliance with Wendoll ; she falls rather through helplessness
than any explicable emotion :

What shall I say ?
My soul is wandering, and hath lost her way.
Oh, Master Wendoll, oh !

This is how she meets and yields to his solicitations. It is
only after the intrigue has been carried on for some while,
and when Frankford has discovered her in the act, that she
shows signs of a deeply troubled conscience. Then, with no
less suddenness, she changes round to the remorse which
preys upon her life. In order to preserve the respect and
sympathy which he claims for her at last, Heywood ought to
have better *motivirt* her fault.

Wendoll is drawn more powerfully, yet not with wholly
satisfactory firmness. It is as though, in both these guilty
characters, Heywood had wished to prove how much of misery
and crime may spring from weakness and inconsequence.
Viewed in this light, his art, though it lacks something of
dramatic impressiveness, is realistic in a subtler sense than
many harder and more brilliant studies. Some of the finest
poetry in the play is put into Wendoll's mouth ; both when
he wavers between the sense of duty to his benefactor and
the love which invades him like a rising tide, swallowing the
landmarks set to warn him off that perilous ground ; and also
when he urges his suit at last on Mrs. Frankford. The

following soliloquy paints the combat of his passion and his conscience :

> I am a villain if I apprehend
> But such a thought; then to attempt the deed—
> Slave, thou art damned without redemption !
> I 'll drive away this passion with a song—
> A song ! Ha, ha ! a song ! as if, fond man,
> Thy eyes could swim in laughter, when thy soul
> Lies drenched and drownèd in red tears of blood !
> I 'll pray, and see if God within my heart
> Plant better thoughts. Why, prayers are meditations:
> And when I meditate (O God, forgive me !)
> It is on her divine perfections !
> I will forget her : I will arm myself
> Not to entertain a thought of love to her :
> And when I come by chance into her presence,
> I 'll hale these balls until my eye-strings crack
> From being pulled and drawn to look that way !

In the seduction scene, after Mrs. Frankford has enu-merated all the reasons which make his suit peculiarly odious, he answers :

> O speak no more !
> For more than this I know, and have recorded
> Within the red-leaved table of my heart.
> Fair, and of all beloved, I was not fearful
> Bluntly to give my life into your hand ;
> And one hazard all my earthly means.
> Go, tell your husband : he will turn me off,
> And then I am undone. I care not, I ;
> 'T was for your sake. Perchance in rage he 'll kill me :
> I care not, 't was for you. Say I incur
> The general name of villain through the world,
> Of traitor to my friend—I care not, I.
> Beggary, shame, death, scandal, and reproach,
> For you I hazard all : why, what care I ?
> For you I 'll love, and in your love I 'll die.

Then, playing the seducer's last card :

> I will be secret, lady, close as night ;
> And not the light of one small glorious star
> Shall shine here in my forehead, to bewray
> That act of night.

This brings her to his wishes. After she has fallen, Heywood
makes her say that she yielded first ' for want of wit ; ' and
we have to construct her character upon this basis. Wendoll,
when the conflict with his better impulse is once over, sinks
into the mere dead sea of adultery, and flies, a conscience-
burdened but not desperate man, to seek new fortunes in
distant lands. He disappears, in fact, from sight, as the
mischief-maker in such cases is wont to do.

Tastes may differ as to the moral wholesomeness of the
sentiment evolved in the last act. Some perhaps will feel
in it a touch too much of ' Frou Frou ' for their hearty liking.
None, however, can deny its dramatic beauty, or resist its
artless claim upon our sympathy. Mrs. Frankford is dying.
Her brother and his friends are round her. Her husband,
yielding to her death-bed prayer, has broken his resolve, and
enters her chamber with this salutation : ' How do you,
woman ? ' The reserve, indicated in these cold words, has to
be broken by her supplication :

> Oh, good man,
> And father to my children, pardon me !
> Pardon, oh pardon me ! My fault so heinous is
> That if you in this world forgive it not,
> Heaven will not clear it in the world to come.
> Faintness hath so usurped upon my knees,
> That kneel I cannot, but on my heart's knees
> My prostrate soul lies thrown down at your feet,
> To beg your gracious pardon.   Pardon, O pardon me !

Then Frankford's heart melts :

> As freely from the low depth of my soul
> As my Redeemer hath forgiven His death,
> I pardon thee.   I will shed tears for thee ;
> Pray with thee ; and, in mere pity of thy weak estate,
> I 'll wish to die with thee.
> Even as I hope for pardon at that day,
> When the great Judge of heaven in scarlet sits,
> So be thou pardoned.
> My wife, the mother to my pretty babes !
> Both those lost names I do restore thee back,
> And with this kiss I wed thee once again :

Though thou art wounded in thy honoured name,
And with that grief upon thy death-bed liest,
Honest in heart, upon my soul, thou diest.

It is difficult to say anything about such words as these,
except that they are true, true to good human nature, true to
the Christianity which all profess and few exhibit. Heywood's realistic method deserves to be well studied by those
who believe that realism is of necessity hard, ugly, and
vicious.

VII

I have said that 'The Witch of Edmonton' breaks up
into two stories, united by a thread so slender as to be hardly
perceptible. With the tale of country life which engages our
interest in this intricate old play, the witch, though she
gives her name to the whole work, has nothing to do. Sir
Arthur Clarington is a wealthy knight, living on his estate
near Edmonton. In his household are Winnifrede, a maid,
and Frank Thorney, the son of a poor gentleman. Before
the opening of the first act, Winnifrede has been seduced by
her master, and afterwards by her fellow-servant. She conceals from Frank her former connection with Sir Arthur, and
induces him to marry her. Clarington, who sees his own
advantage in this match, promises to supply the young couple
with money. They are married; and Winnifrede begins at
once to retrieve the errors of her past by honest conduct.
Her subsequent action engages the sympathy which at the
first we are unwilling to accord her. Levity and deceit have
placed her in a false position; but she gradually wins her
way by simple faithfulness and suffering into respect. It is
necessary that the marriage should be concealed; for old
Thorney is of gentle birth, and would ill brook his son's unthrifty act of justice to a girl of doubtful character. Indeed,
he is already in treaty with a wealthy yeoman, Carter, for
the union of his son to the farmer's well-dowered daughter,
Susan. Accordingly Frank places his wife with her uncle,
near Waltham Abbey, and returning to his father's home,

finds himself involved in a tangle of falsehood and prevarication. He denies his marriage with Winnifrede, of which a rumour has reached old Thorney's ears, and produces a letter from his evil genius Sir Arthur Clarington, attesting that he is still a bachelor. Then the Squire unfolds his plan for freeing the estate from debt by means of Susan's dowry, and offers to resettle it upon his son. Frank has not force of character to resist the pressure of circumstance. To give himself the lie and make a clean breast to his father is now the only way of extricating himself. But he chooses what seems, at the moment, the easier course of drifting down the current :

> On every side I am distracted ;
> Am waded deeper into mischief
> Than virtue can avoid ; but on I must :
> Fate leads me ; I will follow.

Susan takes kindly to the young man as her lover ; Carter presses on the match with rustic joviality ; the dowry is paid down ; and Frank sees himself engaged beyond recovery :

> In vain he flees whom destiny pursues.

Ford, to whom we certainly owe the draught of this character, has made young Thorney one of those weak men who lay their crimes to the account of fate, forgetting that ' Man is his own star ; ' *nos te, nos facimus, Fortuna, deam.*

Married to Susan, who is a loving loyal wife, one of the purest women in the long gallery of female characters painted by our dramatists, Frank finds his life intolerable. He really loves Winnifrede, whom he knows to be waiting for him at her uncle's home. She has to learn the truth of his disloyal conduct from his lips ; a disclosure which she accepts with humility, remembering her own fault. Frank's ' second adulterous marriage ' is in truth only a little more criminal in the sight of Heaven than that lie with which Winnifrede first wedded him :

> You had
> The conquest of my maiden-love.

Only she is now reluctant to accept Frank's proposal that they should escape together 'with the dowry of his sin,' and live their lives out in a foreign country.

Winnifrede assumes the habit of a page, in order to attend her husband on a journey. Whither he is bound, we are not told ; and, indeed, the whole of this part of the drama is so ill-explained as to raise a suspicion whether two plays have not been curtailed and fused into one piece. Susan walks with them, meaning to bid Frank farewell a little further on his way ; and now follows a very touching scene between the two women, the real wife disguised in man's dress, and the deceived Susan, who loves with all her heart and strives to engage the interest of the supposed lad :

> I know you were commended to my husband
> By a noble knight.

This simple opening has such a painful irony, considering how Clarington had actually commended Winnifrede to Frank, that it stings her like a snake's fang :

> *Susan.* How now ?   What ail'st thou, lad ?
> *Win.* Something hit mine eye (it makes it water still),
> Even as you said ' commended to my husband.'
> Some dor I think it was.   I was, forsooth,
> Commended to him by Sir Arthur Clarington.

While they thus converse together, Susan in every artless word revealing more and more of her sweet woman's nature, Thorney joins them. The scene is continued in a dialogue between him and Susan. She is loth to part, and makes excuses always for following a little further. He grows ever more and more impatient, feeling the situation intolerable. At last she points to a certain clump of trees upon the hill's brow, where she will say farewell :

> That I may bring you through one pasture more
> Up to yon knot of trees ; amongst whose shadows
> I 'll vanish from you, they shall teach me how.

Winnifrede has passed ahead with the horses ; and having reached that knot of trees, Frank's rising irritation suddenly

turns to a murderous impulse. He will cut the bond which
unites him to Susan; she is too clinging, too loving; her
kindness cloys and maddens him. So he draws his knife;
but before he plunges it into her breast, he tells her the
whole story of his former marriage, brutally. Then he stabs
her the first time. What follows is far from simple. I will
transcribe the dialogue, since it raises the question so often
forced upon us by the later work of the dramatists, whether
such rhetorical embroidery of a poignant situation is pathetic
or involves a bathos:

> *Frank.* I was before wedded to another; have her still.
> I do not lay the sin unto your charge;
> 'T is all my own: your marriage was my theft;
> For I espoused your dowry, and I have it:
> I did not purpose to have added murder.
> The devil did not prompt me—till this minute [1]—
> You might have safe returned; now you cannot.
> You have dogged your own death.   [*Stabs her.*
> *Sus.* And I deserve it;
> I am glad my fate was so intelligent:
> 'T was some good spirit's motion. Die? Oh, 't was time!
> How many years might I have slept in sin,
> The sin of my most hatred, too, adultery!
> *Fr.* Nay, sure 't was likely that the most was past;
> For I meant never to return to you
> After this parting.
> *Sus.* Why, then I thank you more:
> You have done lovingly, leaving yourself,
> That you would thus bestow me on another.
> Thou art my husband, Death, and I embrace thee
> With all the love I have. Forget the stain
> Of my unwitting sin; and then I come
> A crystal virgin to thee: my soul's purity

[1] The old copy, says Gifford, punctuates this line thus:
> 'The devil did not prompt me: till this minute
> You might have safe returned.

In fact, the devil, in the shape of Mother Sawyer's black dog, had just
rubbed up against him, enticing him by contagion to the crime. I see
here a point of doubt in the construction of the drama, which confirms
the view I have already expressed that *The Witch of Edmonton* is really
two separate plays, pieced together by an afterthought.

Shall, with bold wings, ascend the doors of Mercy;
For innocence is ever her companion.
  Fr. Not yet mortal ? I would not linger you,
Or leave you a tongue to blab.   [*Stabs her again.*
  Sus. Now, Heaven reward you ne'er the worse for me !
I did not think that Death had been so sweet,
Nor I so apt to love him. I could ne'er die better,
Had I stayed forty years for preparation ;
For I 'm in charity with all the world.
Let me for once be thine example, Heaven ;
Do to this man, as I him free forgive ;
And may he better die, and better live !   [*Dies.*

Having completed this dastardly murder, Frank wounds
his own body and contrives to tie himself to a tree, where he
calls aloud for help. His father and old Carter enter to his
cry ; he charges the crime on two former suitors of Carter's
daughter, Somerton and Warbeck, and is taken back to
Carter's house to have his wounds cured. Winnifrede, who
knows nothing of his guilt in this last fact, follows him still
dressed like a page, and in his sick-bed he is waited on by
her and Susan's sister, Katharine, another fair type of
womanhood. The prolonged dialogue, which constitutes the
beauty of this play, rises nowhere to a higher point of Euripidean realism than in a scene where Frank is discovered con-
science-smitten, feverish, and haunted by delirious fancies,
between Katharine and Winnifrede. The ghost of Susan
stands at his bedside. He cannot distinguish phantoms from
realities. For a while he strives to maintain the fiction of
Susan's murder by Somerton and Warbeck. At the last he
breaks down, and reveals the truth to Winnifrede. Meantime,
the two women surround him with gentle ministrations and
consolatory words, going about their work with heavy hearts
indeed, but bent on helpful service, until the point when
Katharine discovers a bloody knife in Frank's coat pocket,
jumps at once to the conclusion of his guilt, and hurries out
to warn her father. The play runs fast to its conclusion now.
Frank is, of course, executed, and, of course, goes manfully,
repentant, to his death. Very touching scenes are written in

this part for old Thorney and for Winnifrede, who grows continually upon our sympathy :

> *Thor.* Daughter, be comforted.
> *Win.* Comfort and I
> Are too far separated to be joined
> But in eternity ; I share too much
> Of him that 's going thither.
> *War.* Poor woman, 't was not thy fault.
> *Win.* My fault was lust, my punishment was shame.

Frank is led by :

> Thou much-wronged woman, I must sigh for thee,
> As he that 's only loath to leave the world
> For that he leaves thee in it unprovided,
> Unfriended.

Winnifrede responds :

> Might our souls together
> Climb to the height of their eternity,
> And there enjoy what earth denied us, happiness !

Students of the text will judge how far such passages as these are marred by elaborate expansion in Ford's frigidly rhetorical manner. For my own part, I can bear the exhibition of the playwright's conscious art, because I recognise its dramatic effectiveness.

I said that Frank Thorney's romance is joined to the second story of this drama by a slender thread. That thread I have omitted in my exposition. His sudden impulse to murder Susan is supposed to proceed from a spell cast on him by Mother Sawyer, the Witch of Edmonton, whose familiar spirit, in the shape of a black dog, appears upon the stage at the moment of his crime, and again reappears before the discovery of the bloody knife. But the playwrights bungled their work sadly in the opening of the third act, where the witch's malice might have been motived and brought into play. They took no pains to connect her with Frank Thorney, and suffered her to wreak her spite upon a crowd of minor personages. I cannot, indeed, avoid the sus-

picion that we either possess 'The Witch of Edmonton' in
a mutilated form, or that its authors hastily patched two
separate compositions together with slight attention to unity.

This want of cohesion is no drawback to the force and
pathos of Mother Sawyer's portrait; perhaps the best picture
of a witch transmitted to us from an age which believed firmly
in witchcraft, but drawn by men whose humanity was livelier
than their superstition. From the works of our Elizabethan
Dramatists we might select studies of witch life more imaginative, more ghastly, more grotesque : Middleton's Hecate and
Stadlin, Marston's Erichtho, Jonson's Maudlin, Shakspere's
weird sisters and Sycorax. None of these, however, are so true
to common life; touched with so fine a sense of natural justice.
The outcast wretchedness which drove old crones to be what
their cursed neighbours fancied them, is painted here with
truly dreadful realism. We see the witch in making, watch
the persecutions which convert her from a village pariah to a
potent servant of the devil, peruse her arguments in self-
defence, and follow her amid the jeers and hootings of the
rabble to her faggot-grave. Mother Sawyer first appears upon
the stage gathering sticks :

> And why on me ?   Why should the envious world
> Throw all their scandalous malice upon me ?
> Cause I am poor, deformed, and ignorant,
> And like a bow buckled and bent together
> By some more strong in mischief than myself,
> Must I for that be made a common sink
> For all the filth and rubbish of men's tongues
> To fall and run into ?   Some call me witch ;
> And being ignorant of myself, they go
> About to teach me how to be one ; urging
> That my bad tongue, by their bad usage made so,
> Forspeaks their cattle, doth bewitch their corn,
> Themselves, their servants, and their babes at nurse.
> This they enforce upon me ; and in part
> Make me to credit it.

Beaten before our eyes by a brutal peasant, she falls to
cursing, and stretches out her heart's desire toward the unknown power 'more strong in mischiefs than herself:'

What is the name? Where, and by what art learned,
What spells, what charms or invocations,
May the thing called Familiar be purchased?

The village rabble fall upon her, lash her with their leathern
belts, and din the name of witch into her ears, until the name
becomes a part of her:

I have heard old beldams
Talk of familiars in the shape of mice,
Rats, ferrets, weasels, and I wot not what,
That have appeared, and sucked, some say, their blood;
But by what means they came acquainted with them,
I now am ignorant. Would some power, good or bad,
Instruct me which way I might be revenged
Upon this churl, I 'd go out of myself,
And give this fury leave to dwell within
This ruined cottage, ready to fall with age!
Abjure all goodness, be at hate with prayer,
And study curses, imprecations,
Blasphemous speeches, oaths, detested oaths,
Or anything that 's ill: so I might work
Revenge upon this miser, this black cur,
That barks and bites, and sucks the very blood
Of me, and of my credit. 'T is all one
To be a witch, as to be counted one.
Vengeance, shame, ruin light upon that canker!

As the devil himself, later on in the play, observes:

Thou never art so distant
From an evil spirit, but that thy oaths,
Curses and blasphemies pull him to thine elbow.

This Mother Sawyer now experiences; for the familiar she
has been invoking, starts up beside her in the form of a black
dog:

Ho! have I found thee cursing? Now thou art
Mine own.

From him she learns the formula by which he may be
summoned, seals their compact by letting him suck blood
from her veins, and proceeds to use him against her enemies.

Whoever wrote the part of Mother Sawyer—Dekker or Rowley; for we cannot attribute it to Ford—took care to exhibit her from several points of view. Interrogated by two magistrates, she stands for her defence upon the blunt democracy of evil.

> I am none—no witch.
> None but base curs so bark at me; I am none.
> Or would I were! if every poor woman
> Be trod on thus by slaves, reviled, kicked, beaten,
> As I am daily, she to be revenged
> Had need turn witch.
>   Men in gay clothes,
> Whose backs are laden with titles and honours,
> Are within far more crookèd than I am,
> And if I be a witch, more witch-like.
> A witch! who is not?
> What are your painted things in princes' courts,
> Upon whose eyelids lust sits, blowing fires
> To burn men's souls in sensual hot desires?
> Have you not city-witches, who can turn
> Their husbands' wares, whole standing shops of wares,
> To sumptuous tables, gardens of stolen sin?
> Reverence once
> Had wont to wait on age; now an old woman,
> Ill-favoured grown with years, if she be poor,
> Must be called bawd or witch. Such, so abused,
> Are the coarse witches; t' other are the fine,
> Spun for the devil's own wearing.

So she rages on. Termagant wives, covetous attorneys, usurers, seducers, these are the true witches; not hate-hardened, miserable beldams.[1] Folengo and Michelet have not laid bare with satire or philosophy more searching the common elements of human evil, out of which witchcraft sprang like a venomous and obscene toadstool.

After this outburst against the hypocrisies of a society with which she is at open war, the wretched creature takes solace with her familiar in a scene grotesquely ghastly:

[1] This fierce apology of Mother Sawyer might be paralleled from that grim satire with which Folengo in his Maccaronic epic of *Baldus* draws the Court of the Sorceress Smirna Gulfora from all classes of society. See *Renaissance in Italy*, vol. v. pp. 348-350.

I am dried up
With cursing and with madness; and have yet
No blood to moisten these sweet lips of thine.
Stand on thy hind legs up—kiss me, my Tommy,
And rub away some wrinkles on my brow,
By making my old ribs to shrug for joy
Of thy fine tricks.

The effects of her damned traffic with the fiend are obvious in murder, suicide, domestic ruin. But as time goes on, her power wanes, and the familiar deserts her. She calls upon him, famished, in her isolation:

Still wronged by every slave? and not a dog
Barks in his dame's defence? I am called witch,
Yet am myself bewitched from doing harm.
Have I given up myself to thy black lust
Thus to be scorned? Not see me in three days!
I 'm lost without my Tomalin; prithee come;
Revenge to me is sweeter far than life:
Thou art my raven, on whose coal-black wings
Revenge comes flying to me. O my best love!
I am on fire, even in the midst of ice,
Raking my blood up, till my shrunk knees feel
Thy curled head leaning on them! Come, then, my darling;
If in the air thou hoverest, fall upon me
In some dark cloud; and as I oft have seen
Dragons and serpents in the elements,
Appear thou now so to me. Art thou i' the sea?
Muster up all the monsters from the deep,
And be the ugliest of them; so that my bulch
Show but his swarth cheek to me, let earth cleave,
And break from hell, I care not! could I run
Like a swift powder-mine beneath the world,
Up would I blow it all, to find thee out,
Though I lay ruined in it. Not yet come!
I must then fall to my old prayer.

The dog appears at last, but changed in hue from black to white—the sign, he mockingly assures her, of her coming trial and death. We do not see her again till she is brought out for execution, with the rabble raging round her:

Cannot a poor old woman have your leave
To die without vexation?
                              Is every devil mine?
Would I had one now whom I might command
To tear you all to pieces!
Have I scarce breath enough to say my prayers,
And would you force me to spend that in bawling?

The part, from beginning to ending, is terribly sustained.
Not one single ray of human sympathy or kindness falls upon
the abject creature. She is alone in her misery and sin,
abandoned to the black delirium of God-forsaken anguish.
To paint a witch as she is here painted—midway between an
oppressed old woman and a redoubtable agent of hell—and to
incorporate this double personality in the character of a
common village harridan, required firm belief in sorcery, that
curse-begotten curse of social life, which flung back on human
nature its own malice in the form of diabolical malignity.

The attention I have paid to these five domestic tragedies
may seem to be out of due proportion to the scheme of my
work. I think, however, that I am justified by their exceptional
importance. Works of finer fibre and more imaginative
quality illustrate in a less striking degree the command of
dramatic effect which marked our theatre in its earliest as in
its latest development.

CHAPTER XII

TRAGEDY OF BLOOD

I. The Tough Fibres of a London Audience—Craving for Strong Sensa-
tion—Specific Note of English Melodrama—Its Lyrical and Pathetic
Relief.—II. Thomas Kyd—'Hieronymo' and 'The Spanish Tragedy'
—Analysis of the Story—Stock Ingredients of a Tragedy of Blood—
The Ghost—The Villain—The Romantic Lovers—Suicide, Murder,
Insanity.—III. 'Soliman and Perseda'—The Induction to this Play
—'The Tragedy of Hoffmann.'—IV. Marlowe's use of this Form—
'The Jew of Malta'—'Titus Andronicus'—'Lust's Dominion'
—Points of Resemblance between 'Hamlet' and 'The Spanish
Tragedy'—Use made by Marston, Webster, and Tourneur of the
Species.—V. The Additions to 'The Spanish Tragedy'—Did
Jonson make them?—Quotation from the Scene of Hieronymo
in the Garden.

N.B. All the Tragedies discussed in this chapter will be found in
Hazlitt's *Dodsley.*

I

THE sympathies of the London audience on which our playwrights worked might be compared to the chords of a
warrior's harp, strung with twisted iron and bulls' sinews,
vibrating mightily, but needing a stout stroke to make them
thrill. This serves to explain that conception of Tragedy
which no poet of the epoch expressed more passionately than
Marston in his prologue to 'Antonio's Revenge,' and which
early took possession of the stage. The reserve of the Greek
Drama, the postponement of physical to spiritual anguish,
the tuning of moral discord to dignified and solemn moods of
sustained suffering, was unknown in England. Playwrights
used every conceivable means to stir the passion and excite
the feeling of their audience. They glutted them with
horrors; cudgelled their horny fibres into sensitiveness.

Hence arose a special kind of play, which may be styled the
Tragedy of Blood, existing, as it seems to do, solely in and
for bloodshed. The action of these tragedies was a prolonged
tempest. Blows fell like hail-stones; swords flashed like
lightning; threats roared like thunder; poison was poured
out like rain. As a relief to such crude elements of terror,
the poet strove to play on finer sympathies by means of
pathetic interludes and 'lyrical interbreathings'—by the
exhibition of a mother's agony or a child's trust in his
murderer, by dialogues in which friend pleads with friend for
priority in death or danger, by images leading the mind away
from actual horrors to ideal sources of despair, by the
soliloquies of a crazed spirit, by dirges and songs of 'old,
unhappy, far-off things,' by crescendos of accumulated passion,
by the solemn beauty of religious resignation. This variety
of effect characterises the Tragedies of Blood. These lyrical
and imaginative elements idealise their sanguinary melodrama.

II

Thomas Kyd—if 'Hieronymo' and 'The Spanish Tragedy'
are correctly ascribed to him—may be called the founder of
this species.[1] About his life we know absolutely nothing,
although it may be plausibly conjectured that he received a
fair academical education. He makes free use of classical
mythology in the style of Greene, and interrupts his English
declamation with Latin verses. For many years Kyd occupied
a prominent place among the London dramatists. His two
epoch-making plays were ridiculed by Shakspere and Jonson,
proving their popularity with the common folk long after the
date (earlier than 1588) of their original production. Jonson
in his lines on Shakspere gave to Kyd the epithet of 'sporting,'
apparently with the view of scoring a bad pun, rather than
with any reference to the playwright's specific style.

'Hieronymo' and 'The Spanish Tragedy' are practically

---

[1] I have adhered throughout to the spelling *Hieronymo*, though the
first part of the play in the 4to of 1605 is called *Ieronimo*.

speaking one play in two parts. Andrea, a nobleman of Spain, is sent to claim tribute from the King of Portugal. During this embassy a Portuguese, Balthazar, defies him to single combat. When the duel takes place, Andrea falls ; but he is avenged by his friend Horatio, son of Hieronymo, Marshal of Spain. During life Andrea had enjoyed the love of a lady, Bellimperia, whose brother, Lorenzo, is a Court villain of the darkest dye. After Andrea's death, Horatio makes Balthazar his captive, and brings him back to Spain, where he, Horatio, pledges his troth to Bellimperia, and is beloved by her instead of the slain Andrea. Lorenzo, however, chooses that she shall be married to Balthazar. He therefore murders Horatio, and hangs him to a tree in his father's garden. Old Hieronymo discovers the corpse, is half crazed by grief, and devotes the rest of his life to vengeance on the assassins. With this object in view, he presents a play at Court, in which he and Bellimperia, Lorenzo and Balthazar, act several parts. The kings of Spain and Portugal assist at the performance. At the close of the tragic piece, Hieronymo and Bellimperia stab the two traitors in good earnest, and afterwards put an end to their own lives upon the stage.

This outline of ' The Spanish Tragedy ' will give a fair notion of the stock ingredients of a Tragedy of Blood. There is a ghost in it—the ghost of Andrea—crying out, ' Revenge ! Vindicta ! ' as it stalks about the stage. There is a noble and courageous lover, young Horatio, traitorously murdered. There is a generous open-hearted gentleman, old Hieronymo, forced to work out his plot of vengeance by craft, and crazy with intolerable wrongs. There is a consummate villain, Lorenzo, who uses paid assassins, broken courtiers, needy men-at-arms, as instruments in schemes of secret malice. There is a beautiful and injured lady, Bellimperia, whose part is one romantic tissue of love, passion, pathos, and unmerited suffering. There is a play within the play, used to facilitate the bloody climax. There are scenes of extravagant insanity, relieved by scenes of euphuistic love-making in sequestered gardens ; scenes of martial conflict, followed by pompous shows at Court; kings, generals, clowns, cutthroats, chamberlains, jostling together in a masquerade medley, a carnival of swiftly moving puppets. There are, at least, five murders, two suicides, two judicial executions, and one death in duel. The principal personage, Hieronymo, bites out his tongue and flings it on the stage; stabs his enemy with a stiletto, and pierces his own heart. Few of the characters survive to bury the dead, and these few are of secondary importance in the action.

III

A contemporary and anonymous tragedy, ' Soliman and Perseda,' illustrates the same melodramatic qualities of unfortunate love and wholesale bloodshed. It hardly deserves notice, except as showing how the Tragedy of Blood took form. I may also mention that it was selected by Kyd for the play within the play presented by his hero Hieronymo. The Induction to this piece is curious. Love, Death, and Fortune dispute among themselves which takes the leading part in tragedies of human life. They agree to watch the action of the drama ; and at the end, Death sums his triumphs up, proving himself indisputably victor :

> Alack ! Love and Fortune play in Comedies !
> For powerful Death best fitteth Tragedies.

Love retires, beaten, but unsubdued :

> I go, yet Love shall never yield to Death !

One more of the earlier melodramas, written to glut the audience with bloodshed, deserves mention. This was the work of Henry Chettle, produced before the year 1598, and styled ' The Tragedy of Hoffmann ; or, a Revenge for a Father.' The scene is laid on the shores of the Baltic. The hero is son to Admiral Hoffmann, who had been executed unjustly for piracy, by having a crown of red-hot iron forced upon his head. The son hangs up his father's corpse as a memento of revenge, and by various devices murders in succession six or seven of the enemies who were instrumental in his death. At the end he, too, dies by imposition of the fiery crown. This grisly drama of retributive cruelty, enacted in a remote region of the Northern seas, combining the most violent incidents of torture and assassination, has no beauty of language, no force of character, no ingenuity of plot, to excuse its violation of artistic decencies. It relies upon fantastic horror for effect.

IV

Enough has been said to indicate a species which took firm possession of the stage. Marlowe, finding it already popular, raised it to higher rank by the transfiguring magic of his genius. 'The Jew of Malta' marks a decided step in advance upon the plays which I have noticed. Two dramas of superior merit, clearly emanating from the school of Marlowe, may also be reckoned among the Tragedies of Blood in this second period of elaboration. These are 'Titus Andronicus,' which, on the faith of an old anecdote, we may perhaps infer to have been the work of an amateur, dressed for the theatre by Shakspere; and 'Lust's Dominion; or, The Lascivious Queen,' a play ascribed to Marlowe, but now believed to have been written by Dekker, Haughton, and Day. Both in 'Titus Andronicus' and in 'Lust's Dominion,' Marlowe's sanguinary Jew is imitated. Barabas, Aaron, and Eleazar are of the same kindred. I shall have occasion to study Barabas closely in another chapter of this book. Aaron, since he rests beneath the ægis of Shakspere's name, may here be left untouched.[1] But Eleazar, and the play of 'Lust's

---

[1] Aaron seems to me as inferior to Barabas in poetic and dramatic pith, as he exceeds him in brutality. But the play of *Titus Andronicus* is interesting, independently of this villain's character, for its systematic blending, and in some sense heightening, of all the elements which constitute a Tragedy of Blood. We have a human sacrifice and the murder of a son by his father in the first act; in the second, a murder and the rape and mutilation of a woman; in the third, two executions and the mutilation of the hero; in the fourth, a murder; in the fifth, six murders, a judicial death by torture, and a banquet set before a queen of her two dead sons' flesh. The hyperbolical pathos of Lavinia's part, the magnificent lunacy of Titus (so like to that of Hieronymo in quality),

Dominion,' in which he takes the leading part, demand some words of passing comment. This is strictly a Tragedy of Blood; yet the motive, as its title implies, is lawless appetite leading to death in various forms. The Queen Mother of Spain loves Eleazar, the Moor, with savage passion. King Fernando loves Maria, the Moor's wife. Cardinal Mendoza loves the Queen. Each of these personages sacrifices duty, natural affection, humanity itself, to ungovernable desire. Eleazar alone remains cold and calculating, using their weakness to attain his own ambitious ends. Pretending love to the Queen, he forces her to kill her son Philip, and then schemes her murder. In order to checkmate the Cardinal, he betrays his young wife to Fernando, albeit she is ' chaste as the white moon.' His designs, at the last, prove unavailing, and he dies in stubborn contumacy. Ambition was his devil; the strength of intellect, the physical courage, possessed by him in no common measure, he concentrated on the end of climbing to a throne through blood. The direct imitation of Marlowe is obvious in the large conception, broad handling, and exaggerated execution of this character, no less than in the florid imagery and sounding versification which distinguish the style adopted by the authors of the play. It is, in fact, a creditable, though extremely disagreeable, piece of imitative craftsmanship.

The Tragedy of Blood, passing successively through the stages marked by Kyd and Marlowe, became a stock species. It would not be correct to assign any of Shakspere's undoubted dramas to this class. Yet Shakspere did not disdain to spiritualise what his predecessors had so grossly and materialistically rough-hewn. 'Hamlet,' as it has been often pointed out, is built upon the lines suggested by 'The Spanish Tragedy,' and uses for its poetry, philosophy, and passion, motives pre-existing in the English melodrama.

Three considerable playwrights of the later age devoted their talents to the Tragedy of Blood. These were Marston,

and the romantic lyrism which relieves and stimulates imagination, belong to the very essence of the species. So also does the lust of Tamora and the frantic devilishness of her paramour.

Webster, and Tourneur. Ghosts, Court villains, paid assassins, lustful princes, romantic lovers, injured and revengeful victims, make up the personages of their drama; and the stage is drenched with blood. There is one standing personage in these later melodramas, which had from the earliest been sketched firmly enough by Kyd in ' Hieronymo.' That is the desperate instrument of perfidy and murder. When Lorenzo, the arch-villain of ' The Spanish Tragedy,' needs an agent, he bethinks him of a certain Lazarotto :

> I have a lad in pickle of this stamp,
> A melancholy discontented courtier,
> Whose famished jaws look like the chap of death ;
> Upon whose eyebrow hangs damnation ;
> Whose hands are washed in rape and murders bold ;
> Him with a golden bait will I allure,
> For courtiers will do anything for gold.

In the hands of Webster the rough sketch of Lazarotto became the finished pictures of Flamineo and Bosola. Tourneur transformed the ' melancholy discontented courtier ' into Vendice. Marston played various tunes on the same jangled lute. All three of them had recourse to Kyd's fantastic incident of Masques, disguising murder. But it was reserved alone for Webster to stamp the Tragedy of Blood with a high spiritual and artistic genius. The thing, when he touched it, unlocked springs of sombre dramatic terror and wayward picturesque effect beyond the reach of vulgar workmen.

V

I shall close this brief study with a return to ' The Spanish Tragedy.' From Henslowe's Diary we learn that Ben Jonson received divers sums in 1601 and 1602 for additions to this play. These additions, ' the very salt of the old play,' in Lamb's often quoted words, are so unlike Jonson's style that few students of our Drama would disagree with Lamb in wishing he could ascribe them to ' some more potent spirit,' perhaps to Webster. Still there is no external reason for assigning them to any known writer of the time, or for rejecting the plain evidence of Henslowe's Diary.[1] Jonson certainly produced nothing so poignant and far-searching in his acknowledged tragedies. Yet we may perhaps refer this circumstance to self-restraint and absolute adherence to dramatic theory. Jonson was a doctrinaire, we know, and his mature canons of art were opposed to the Romantic method. But we need not, therefore, determine that so powerful a writer could not have worked upon occasion in a style which he deliberately afterwards rejected in obedience to formed opinions.

One dialogue between Hieronymo, crazed by finding the dead body of his son suspended to the tree in his own garden, and a painter introduced for the sole purpose of discoursing with him, might be selected to illustrate the mingled extravagance and truth to nature which is characteristic of English melodrama. There is here a leonine hunger, blent with pathetic tenderheartedness, a brooding upon 'things done long ago and ill done,' an alternation between lunacy and the dull moodiness of reasonable woe, which brings the maddened old man vividly before us. The picture is only less terrible than that of Lear—less terrible because more artificially fantastic. The doubt regarding its composition renders it furthermore so curious that I do not hesitate to quote the passage at full length.

HIERONYMO *is discovered in his garden. First enters to him his wife* ISABELLA. *Then a servant,* PEDRO, *who introduces the* PAINTER.

Isa. Dear Hieronymo, come in a doors,
O seek not means so to increase thy sorrow.
    Hier. Indeed, Isabella, we do nothing here;
I do not cry, ask Pedro and Jaques:
Not I, indeed; we are very merry, very merry.

----

[1] Henslowe, under the dates Sept. 25, 1601, and June 24, 1602, lent Jonson sums of money for *additions* and *new additions* to *Hieronymo.* In the year 1602 the play was printed in 4to as being ' enlarged with new additions of the Painter's part and others.' The agreement of dates between Henslowe's memoranda and the publication of the enlarged play is too important to escape notice.

Isa. How ? Be merry here, be merry here ?
Is not this the place, and this the very tree,
Where my Horatio died, where he was murdered ?
    Hier. Was—do not say what : let her weep it out.
This was the tree, I set it of a kernel ;
And when our hot Spain could not let it grow,
But that the infant and the human sap
Began to wither, duly twice a morning
Would I be sprinkling it with fountain water :
At last it grew and grew, and bore and bore :
Till at length it grew a gallows, and did bear our son.
It bore thy fruit and mine.   O wicked, wicked plant.
See who knocks there.   *[One knocks within at the door.*
    Ped. It is a painter, sir.
    Hier. Bid him come in, and paint some comfort,
For surely there 's none lives but painted comfort.
Let him come in, one knows not what may chance.
God's will [it was] that I should set this tree ! but even so
Master's ungrateful servants rear from nought,
And then they hate them that did bring them up.

The PAINTER *enters.*

    Pain. God bless you, sir.
    Hier. Wherefore, why, thou scornful villain ?
How, where, or by what means should I be blessed ?
    Isa. What wouldst thou have, good fellow ?
    Pain. Justice, madam.
    Hier. O ambitious beggar, wouldst thou have that
That lives not in the world ?
Why, all the undelved mines cannot buy
An ounce of justice, 't is a jewel so inestimable.
I tell thee, God hath engrossed all justice in His hands,
And there is none but what comes from Him.   [son !
    Pain. O, then I see that God must right me for my murdered
    Hier. How ?   Was thy son murdered ?
    Pain. Ay, sir, no man did hold a son so dear.
    Hier. What ! not as thine ?   That 's a lie
As massy as the earth : I had a son,
Whose least unvalued hair did weigh
A thousand of thy sons ; and he was murdered.
    Pain. Alas ! sir, I had no more but he.
    Hier. Nor I, nor I ; but this same one of mine
Was worth a legion.   But all is one.

Pedro, Jaques, go in a doors. Isabella, go ;
And this good fellow here and I
Will range this hideous orchard up and down,
Like two she lions, 'reaved of their young.
Go in a doors, I say. [*Exeunt. The* PAINTER *and he sit down.*
Come, let 's talk wisely now.
Was thy son murdered ?

 Pain. Ay, sir.

 Hier. So was mine.

How dost thou take it ? Art thou not sometime mad ?
Is there no tricks that come before thine eyes ?

 Pain. O Lord ! yes, sir.

 Hier. Art a painter ? Canst paint me a tear, a wound ?
A groan or a sigh ? Canst paint me such a tree as this ?

 Pain. Sir, I am sure you have heard of my painting ;
My name 's Bazardo.

 Hier. Bazardo ! 'fore God, an excellent fellow ! Look you, sir.
Do you see ? I 'd have you paint me in my gallery, in your oil-
colours matted, and draw me five years younger than I am : do
you see, sir. Let five years go, let them go—my wife Isabella
standing by me, with a speaking look to my son Horatio, which
should intend to this, or some such like purpose : ' God bless thee !
my sweet son ; ' and my hand leaning upon his head thus, sir ; do
you see ? May it be done ?

 Pain. Very well, sir.

 Hier. Nay, I pray, mark me, sir.
Then, sir, would I have you paint me this tree, this very tree :
Canst paint a doleful cry ?

 Pain. Seemingly, sir.

 Hier. Nay, it should cry ; but all is one.
Well, sir, paint me a youth run through and through ;
With villains' swords hanging upon this tree.
Canst thou draw a murderer ?

 Pain. I 'll warrant you, sir ; I have the pattern of the most
notorious villains that ever lived in all Spain.

 Hier. O let them be worse, worse ; stretch thine art,
And let their beards be of Judas's own colour,
And let their eyebrows jut over : in any case observe that.

 Then, sir, after some violent noise, bring me forth in my shirt,
and my gown under my arm, with my torch in my hand, and my
sword reared up thus, and with these words, ' What noise is this ?
Who calls Hieronymo ? ' May it be done ?

 Pain. Yea, sir.

 Hier. Well, sir, then bring me forth—bring me through alley and alley, still with a distracted countenance going along, and let my hair heave up my night cap. Let the clouds scowl; make the moon dark, the stars extinct, the winds blowing, the bells tolling, the owls shrieking, the toads croaking, the minutes jarring, and the clock striking twelve. And then at last, sir, starting, behold a man hanging, and tottering, and tottering, as you know the wind will wave a man, and with a trice to cut him down. And looking upon him by advantage of my torch, find it to be my son Horatio. There you may show a passion; there you may show a passion. Draw me like old Priam of Troy, crying, 'The house is a-fire, the house is a-fire,' and the torch over my head; make me curse, make me rave, make me cry, make me mad, make me well again; make me curse hell, invocate, and in the end leave me in a trance, and so forth.

Pain. And is this the end?

Hier. O no, there is no end; the end is death and madness.
And I am never better than when I am mad.
Then methinks, I am a brave fellow;
Then I do wonders; but reason abuseth me;
And there 's the torment, there 's the hell.
At last, sir, bring to me one of the murderers;
Were he as strong as Hector,
Thus would I tear and drag him up and down.

　　　　　　　　　　　　　[He beats the PAINTER *in.*

After all has been said and suggested, impenetrable mystery hangs over the authorship of this scene. Henslowe's Diary and certain allusions to 'The Spanish Tragedy' in Jonson's comedies, point to Ben Jonson as the writer. But it is almost impossible to conceive that Ben Jonson, if he had composed this scene to order while yet a prentice in the playwright's craft, should have afterwards abandoned a style which he commanded with such gust and passion. How came he to exchange it for that scholastic mannerism which, except for the romantic passages of 'The Case is Altered,' we discern as second nature in his genius? Had Shakspere a hand in these additions? Or was he, perhaps, thinking of Hieronymo's hyperbolical retort upon the Painter, when he penned for 'Hamlet':

　　　　I loved Ophelia; forty thousand brothers
　　　　Could not with all their quantity of love
　　　　Make up my sum?

Had the author of 'Titus Andronicus' anything to do with them? Or, in the lunacies of Titus, did he simply imitate and dilute the concentrated frenzy of Hieronymo? Such queries and surmises are idle. But they have at least the effect of keeping vividly before our minds the extraordinary potency of scenes which tempt us to ever new unprofitable guess-work.

CHAPTER XIII

JOHN LYLY

I

In the year 1579 a book appeared in London which was destined to make an epoch in English literary history, and to win for its author fame and fashion almost unparalleled among his contemporaries. This book bore the title of 'Euphues, the Anatomy of Wit.' It was written by John Lyly, a member of Magdalen College, Oxford, Master of Arts, then in his twenty-seventh year. In the spring following, a sequel, called 'Euphues, his England,' issued from the press. The two parts formed one work, conceived and executed after the Italian style of moral dissertation and romantic story. 'Euphues' is, in fact, a collection of essays, tales, letters, and meditative disquisitions, 'sowed,' to use the author's own words, 'here and there like strawberries, not in heaps like hops.' In planning this book Lyly had a clearly didactic intention. It was his purpose to set forth opinions regarding the formation of character by training and experience; to criticise social conduct; to express his views upon love and friendship, religion and philosophy; to discuss the then so favourite topic of foreign travel; and to convey this miscellaneous instruction in a form agreeable to his readers.

The story, with which Lyly interwove his weightier discourses, may be briefly told. The book opens with a minute description of the hero's character and person. Euphues, who is meant to embody the qualities denoted by his Greek name, is an Athenian youth of good fortune, comely presence, and quick parts, somewhat too much given to pleasure. He comes to Naples, where he makes acquaintance with an old man named Eubulus, and a young man called Philautus. Eubulus gives him abundance of good counsel, both as regards the conduct of his life in general and the special dangers he will have to meet in Naples. Euphues receives it kindly, but prefers to buy wisdom by experience, arguing that it ill beseems a young man to rule himself by the precepts of the aged, before he has tasted of life for himself. With Philautus he strikes up a romantic friendship. This new comrade brings him into the society of Lucilla, a Neapolitan lady, to whom Philautus is already paying his addresses with her father's sanction. In their first interview, Lucilla and Euphues fall in love, each with the other. Euphues tries to conceal his passion from his friend by pretending to admire another woman, Livia; but, in the absence of Philautus, he declares his love to Lucilla, and receives the confession of hers in return. Lucilla, when urged by her father to accept her former suitor, openly avows her new fancy for Euphues. This leads to a rupture between the two friends. But it soon appears that the fickle fair has thrown over Euphues for a fresh adorer, named Curio. Euphues falls into a fever of fury, shame, and disappointed passion. He and Philautus shake hands again, consoling themselves with the reflection that friendship is more stable and more durable than love. Then they separate—Euphues returns to study moral and physical philosophy at Athens; Philautus remains to cure himself, as best he can, at Naples. Euphues, in his own university, applies himself with zeal to serious learning, and is soon so strengthened against passion that he writes 'a cooling card for Philautus and all fond lovers.' This he sends his friend, together with a discourse upon the education of young men, a refutation of atheism, and other products of his fruitful brain—in short, epistolary essays. These terminate the first part of the book. In the second, Lyly brings Euphues and Philautus to England. He describes the discourse they held on shipboard, to keep off sea-sickness and *ennui*; their landing, and their visit to Fidus, an old bee-master of Kent. Fidus has a long-winded love story, tale within tale, of his own to tell. After hearing this the friends reach London, where Philautus falls in and out of love two or three times, and at last is married to a lady whom he calls his Violet. Euphues leaves him happily settled in England, and concludes with a neatly worded panegyric of Elizabeth and her Court, entitled ' Euphues' Glass for Europe.'

II

Such is the slender thread of narrative on which Lyly strung his multitudinous reflections—some commonplace, some wise, some whimsical, some quaint, but all relating to the inexhaustibly attractive themes of love and conduct. The story lacks definite outline and strong colouring, but it was of a kind which won acceptance in that age. The popularity of Greene's novels and Sidney's ' Arcadia ' is not less inexplicable to a modern reader than the fascination exercised by 'Euphues.' The thought—except, perhaps, in one tractate upon education, entitled ' Euphues and his Ephœbus'—is rarely pregnant or profound. Yet Lyly's facile handling of grave topics, his casuistry of motives and criticism of life, exactly suited the audience he had in view. He tells us that he meant his ' Euphues ' for gentlewomen in their hours of recreation. 'I am content that your dogs lie in your laps, so "Euphues" may be in your hands; that when you shall be weary in reading of the one, you may be ready to sport with the other.' And again : ' "Euphues" had rather lie shut in a lady's casket than open in a scholar's study.' In days when there were no circulating libraries and magazines, 'Euphues' passed for pleasant and instructive reading. The ladies, for whom it was written, had few books except romances of the Round Table and the Twelve Peers ; and these, though stimulating to the imagination, failed to exercise the wit and understanding. The loves of Lancelot and Tristram were antiquated and immoral. The doughty deeds of Paladins suited a soldier's rather than a damsel's fancy. Lyly supplied matter light enough to entertain an idle moment, yet sensible and wholesome. He presented in an English dress the miscellaneous literature of the Italians, combining Alberti's ethical disquisitions with Sannazzaro's narratives, but avoiding the licentiousness which made Painter's translations from the *Novellieri* an object of just suspicion. Furthermore, he popularised some already celebrated writings of a meritorious but affected Spanish author, and succeeded in presenting all this miscellaneous matter in a piquant form, which passed for originality of style. The love tales of Euphues, Philautus, and Fidus, served for polite fiction. The discourses on marriage, education, politics, and manners conveyed some such diluted philosophy as ladies of the present day imbibe from magazines and newspapers. The inartistic blending of these divers elements in a prolix languidly conducted romance, did not offend against the taste of Lyly's age.

III

The success of this book was sudden and astounding. Two editions of the first part were exhausted in 1579, a third in 1580, a fourth in 1581. Between that date and 1636 it was nine times reprinted. The second part enjoyed a similar run of luck. How greedily its pages were devoured, is proved by the extreme rarity of the earliest editions. After 1636 this gale of popularity suddenly dropped. The ‘Euphues’ of ‘eloquent and witty John Lyly,’ as Meres styled its author; the ‘Euphues,’ which Webbe had praised for ‘singular eloquence and brave composition of apt words and sentences,’ for ‘fit phrases, pithy sentences, gallant tropes, flowing speech, plain sense’; the ‘Euphues,’ which won for Lyly from John Eliot the epithet of ‘raffineur de l’Anglais’; the ‘Euphues,’ which, in the words of Edward Blount, had taught our nation a new English, and so enthralled society that ‘that Beauty in Court which could not parley Euphuism, was as little regarded as she which now there speaks not French’; this ‘Euphues,’ the delight of ladies and the school of poets, passed suddenly out of fashion, and became a byword for false taste and obsolete absurdity. Historians of literature joined in condemning without reading it. Sir Walter Scott essayed a parody, which proved his ignorance of the original. At length, in 1868, nearly three centuries after its first appearance and sudden triumph, nearly two centuries and a half after its last issue and no less sudden loss of popularity, English students received a scholarly reprint from the hands of Professor Arber.

Those who peruse this volume will be inclined to moralise on fashion; to wonder how a work so signally devoid of vivid interest excited such enthusiasm, or became the object of such vehement abuse. The truth is that, besides the novelty of his performance, on which I have already dwelt, Lyly owed his great success to what we recognise as the defects of his style. When literary popularity is based on faults accepted by the bad taste of an epoch for transcendent merits, it is foredoomed to a decline as rapid as its uprise, and to reaction as powerful as the forces which promoted it. Euphues entranced society in the sixteenth century, because our literature, in common with that of Italy and Spain and France, was passing through a phase of affectation, for which Euphuism was the national expression. It corresponded to something in the manners and the modes of thinking which prevailed in Europe at that period. It was the English type

of an all but universal disease. There would have been
Euphuism, in some form or other, without Euphues ; just as
the so-called æsthetic movement of to-day might have
dispensed with its Bunthorne, and yet have flourished.
Lyly had the fortune to become the hero of his epoch's'
follies, to fix the form of fashionable affectation, and to find
the phrases he had coined in his study, current on the lips
of gentlemen and ladies.

Euphuism not only coloured the manners of polite society,
but it also penetrated literature. We trace it, or something
very like it, in the serious work of Sidney and of Shakspere ;
in the satires of Nash and the conceits of Donne; in the
theological lucubrations of Puritan divines and the philosophical rhapsodies of Sir Thomas Browne. The specific
affectations of the Court might be satirised by Shakspere or
by Jonson; yet neither Jonson nor Shakspere was free from
mannerisms, of which Lyly's style was only symptomatic.
Sidney is praised for avoiding its salient blemishes ; but
Sidney revelled in conceits and dissertations on romantic topics,
which a modern student scarcely thinks it worth his while
to separate from Euphuism. Perched on the pinnacle of
history and criticism, at the distance of three centuries, we
are able to confound Lyly with his censors, and to perceive
clearly that the purest among his contemporaries were tarred
with the same pitch. It is only the mediocrity of his genius,
combined with his good or evil luck in producing an eponymous work of fiction, which renders him conspicuous. He
helped to ' fish the murex up,' and dyed the courtly wardrobe
with its purple. This gives Euphuism real importance, and
forces us to ask ourselves exactly what it was.

IV

The medieval mind delighted in allegories, symbolism,
scholastic distinctions. Science was unknown. Men ascribed
strange potencies to plants and minerals and living creatures.
The Bestiaries of the convents set forth a system of zoology,
invented for edification. No one cared to ascertain what a

thing really was. It sufficed to discover some supposed virtue in the thing, or to extract from it some spiritual lesson. When the Revival of Learning began in Italy, students transferred their attention from theology and scholastic logic to classical literature; but they could not shake off the medieval modes of thinking. The critical faculty was still dormant. Every ancient author had equal value in their eyes. A habit was formed of citing the Greeks and Romans upon all occasions, parading a facile knowledge of their books, and quoting anecdotes from antique history without regard for aptness of application. The quibbling of the schoolmen was transferred to scholarship and literature. To idle exercise in logic succeeded empty exercise in rhetoric. At the same time, a few great writers founded modern literature. Petrarch and Boccaccio were by no means free from medieval mannerisms. But each, in his own line, stood in a direct relation to real life, and formed a style of dignity and grace. The imitation of the ancients became gradually more intelligent; and at the opening of the sixteenth century Italy could boast a literature in Latin and the vulgar tongue, eminent for variety, admirable for artistic purity and beauty. At this point a retrograde impulse made itself felt. The Academies began to imitate the faults without the saving graces of their predecessors. Petrarch had shunned commonplace by periphrasis and metaphor. The Petrarchisti prided themselves on that 'wonderful art which adorns each thing by words appropriate to others.' When they praised a woman, they called 'her head fine gold or roof of gold; her eyes, suns, stars, sapphires, nest and home of love; her cheeks, now snow and roses, now milk and fire; rubies, her lips; pearls, her teeth; her throat and breast, now ivory, now alabaster.'[1] Purity of form, propriety of diction, truth to nature, sincerity of presentation, were sacrificed to the manufacture of conceits. The poet who produced the quaintest verbal conundrums passed for the best wit. Prose style was infected with antithesis. To be sententious about nothing, copious in mythological allusion, curious in learning,

[1] Speron Sperone. See my *Renaissance in Italy*, vol. v. p. 255.

covered poverty of thought and excused vulgarity of feeling.
Writers, who scorned the pedantry of academicians, and
sought to take the world by storm—men of Aretino's stamp,
Doni, Albicante, Franco, Vergerio—played upon these literary
vices. No book, says Doni in his ' Marmi,' has a chance of
success, if it appears in modest style with a plain indication of
its subject. You must coin attractive titles, ' The Pumpkin,'
or ' The Cobbler's Caprices,' or ' The Hospital of Fools,' or
' The Synagogue of Ignoramuses,' to carry off your ethical
discourses. If you want to sell an invective, you must invent
for it some bizarre superscription, as, for instance : ' The
Earthquake of Doni, the Florentine, with the Ruin of a Great
Bestial Colossus, the Antichrist of our Age.' [1] Then folk
will read you. Aretino, who thoroughly understood the
public, proved his originality by creating a new manner, brassy
and meretricious. Antithesis followed antithesis ; forced
metaphors, outrageous similes, hyperbolical periphrases,
monstrous images, made up a style of clap-trap only to be
pardoned by the author's ruffianly power. The manner
spread like wild-fire. Campanella in his prison punned upon
his surname and peculiarly shaped skull, rejoicing in the
sobriquet of ' Settimontano Squilla,' or the ' Seven-hilled
Bell.' Bruno uttered his philosophy in a jargon of conceits,
strained allegories, and allusive metaphors, which is all but
incomprehensible. One of his metaphysical works, dedicated
to Sir Philip Sidney, bears this title : ' Lo Spaccio della
Bestia Trionfante.' Another is styled : ' Gli Eroici Furori.'
It had become impossible for sage or theologian, satirist or
pedant, essayist or versifier, to express himself with classical
propriety or natural directness. Marini, an indubitable poet,
consecrated this aberration of taste in his ' Adone,' the marvel
of the age, the despair of less authentic bards.

It was precisely at this point of its development that Italian
literature exercised the widest and deepest influence in Europe.
The French, the Spaniards, and the English rushed with
the enthusiasm of beginners into imitation of Italian vices.
An affectation, drawn from many diverse sources, from

[1] See *Renaissance in Italy*, vol. v. pp. 95, 96.

medieval puerility and humanistic pedantry, from the sentimentalism of the Petrarchisti and the cynical audacities of
Aretino, from the languors of Marini and Doni's impudent
bids for popularity—an affectation bred in the premature decay
of the renascence, invaded every country where Italian culture
penetrated. The masterpieces of pure literature, the antique
classics, the poems of Petrarch and Ariosto, the histories of
Guicciardini and Machiavelli, received due studious attention.
But while these were studied, the mannerisms of feebler men,
the faults of contemporaries, were copied. It was easier to
catch the trick of an Aretino or a Marini than to emulate the
style of a Tasso or a Castiglione. Still, what in Italy had
been to some extent a sign of decadence and exhaustion,
became, when it was carried to barbarian shores, a petulant
parade of youthful vigour. The effete literature of Florence
and Venice generated this curious hybrid, which was enthusiastically cultivated on the virgin soils of France and Spain and
England. It there produced new rarities and delicacies of
divinest flavour ; monstrosities also, outdoing in extravagance
the strangest of Italian species. Where the national genius
displayed a robust natural growth, as in England for example,
literature was only superficially affected—in the prose of Lyly,
the elegies of Donne, the slender Euphuistic thread that runs in
iron through Marlowe, in silver through Shakspere, in bronze
through Bacon, in more or less inferior metal through every
writer of that age. Teutonic and Celtic qualities absorbed while
they assimilated, dominated while they suffered, that intrusive
Southern element of style. Yet the emphasis added to spontaneous expression by its foreign accent was so marked that
no historian can venture to neglect it. The romantic art of
the modern world did not spring, like that of Greece, from an
ungarnered field of flowers. Troubled by reminiscences of the
past and by reciprocal influences from one another, the literatures of modern Europe came into existence with composite
dialects, obeyed confused canons of taste, exhibited their adolescent vigour with affected graces, showed themselves senile
in their cradles.

In France the post-Italian affectation ran its course

through two marked phases, from Du Bellay and Du Bartas
to the Précieuses of the Hôtel Rambouillet. In Spain it engendered the poetic diction of Calderon, who called the birds
in heaven 'winged harps of gold'; and it expired in that
estilo culto of Gongora, which required a new system of
punctuation to render its constructions intelligible, and a
glossary to explain its metaphors and mythological allusions.
Of all parts of Europe, Spain perhaps produced the most
extravagant specimens of this preposterous mannerism. In
England it first appeared as Euphuism, passing on into the
metaphysical conceits of Cowley, and the splendid pedantries
of Sir Thomas Browne.[1]

This affectation, which I have attempted to trace to its
source in Italy, took somewhat different form in each country
and in every writer. But its elementary conditions were the
same. From the Middle Ages survived a love of allegory and
symbolism, the habit of scholastic hair-splitting, and the
romantic sentiment which we associate with chivalry.
Humanism introduced the uncritical partiality for classical
examples and citations, the abuse of mythology, and the
sententious prolixity which characterise this literary phase
in all its manifestations. The Petrarchisti gave currency to
a peculiar conceited style, definable as the persistent effort to
express one thing in terms of another, combined with a patient
seeking after finished form. The Venetian school of Aretino

---

[1] It has been my object in the foregoing paragraphs to describe in
general the origins of that literary affectation, which appears under many
forms and species in Italy, Spain, France, and England, upon the close of
the Renaissance—species known to us apart, and designated by the
names of eminent or fashionable writers; of Petrarch and Marini,
Montemayor and Gongora, Ronsard and Du Bartas, Lyly and Cowley.
I have dwelt upon the generic rather than the specific characteristics of
this *lues literaria*, because I think Euphuism may fairly claim to be a
separate type. But I must also here profess my belief in the very close
dependence of Lyly's style and matter upon the work of the Spanish
author Guevara, without whom, as Dr. Landmann has abundantly
proved, Euphuism would certainly not have crystallised into its well-
known and characteristic form. In some important respects the species
Euphuism, strictly so called, is immediately derived from Guevara's
purer and weightier mannerism. See Dr. Landmann's *Euphuismus*,
Giessen, 1881, and his article in the New Shakspere Society's *Transac-
tions*, 1880-2.

and his followers set the fashion of *bizarrerie* in titles, effect by antithesis, verbal glare and glitter. Marini, preceded by the author of the ' Pastor Fido,' brought the specific note of the new literary style—its effort to be rich and rare, at the expense of taste, by far-fetched imagery, surprises, striking metaphors, and unexpected ingenuity in language—into the domain of poetry. In his work it dropped much of its medieval and pedantic apparatus. It shone before the entranced eyes of Europe as an iridescent marvel, on which the intellect and fancy fed with inexhaustible delight. The unexplored riches of modern literatures, exulting in their luxuriance, and envying the fame of Greece and Rome, tempted writers to extravagant experiments in language. Imagination itself was young, and ran riot in the prodigality of unexhausted forces.

Euphuism, after this preamble, may be defined as a literary style used by Lyly in his prose works, and adopted into the language of polite society. It is characterised by a superficial tendency to allegory; by the abuse of easy classical erudition; by a striving after effect in puns, conceits, and plays on words; by antithesis of thought and diction, carried to a wearisome extent, and enforced by alliterative and parisonic use of language; and, finally, by sententious prolixity in the display of commonplace reflections. Lyly's euphuism is further and emphatically distinguished by the reckless employment of an unreal natural history for purposes of illustration. This constitutes what may be termed the keynote of his affectation. He seems to have derived it in the first place from Pliny; but also from the Bestiaries and Lapidaries of the Middle Ages, with indiscriminate reference to Herodotus and Mandeville, and an idle exercise of his inventive fancy. To animals, plants, stones, &c. he attributes the most absurd properties and far-fetched virtues, applying these to point his morals and adorn his tales. ' Let the falling out of friends,' he writes, ' be the renewing of affection, that in this we may resemble the bones of the lion, which lying still and not moved begin to rot, but being stricken one against another, break out like fire and wax green.' Page after page of his prose

runs on after this fashion; empty, vague, prolix, decorated
with preposterous examples. It would be a nice task for idle
antiquarian research to discover whether there are or are not
sources in medieval erudition for such statements as the
following :

'As the fire-stone in Liguria, though it be quenched with
milk, yet again it is kindled with water, or as the roots of
Anchusa, though it be hardened with water, yet it is made
soft with oil.'

'As the precious stone Sandrasta hath nothing in outward appearance but that which seemeth black, but being
broken poureth forth beams like the sun.'

'As by basil the scorpion is engendered, and by the means
of the same herb destroyed . . . or as the salamander which
being a long space nourished in the fire, at the last quencheth
it.'

'I lived, as the elephant doth by air, with the sight of my
lady.'

'Like the river in Arabia, which turneth gold to dross, and
dirt to silver.'

'As the dogs of Egypt drink water by snatches, and so
quench their thirst, and not hinder their running.'

The more sensible readers of Lyly's works seem to have
felt the tediousness of this fabulous natural history no less
than we do, though certainly the list of Vulgar Errors concerning the fauna and flora of distant lands was then a larger
one than it is now. Drayton, publishing his poems in 1627,
upon the eve of 'Euphues'' extinction, says of Sir Philip
Sidney that he

> Did first reduce
> Our tongue from Lyly's writing then in use ;
> Talking of stones, stars, plants, of fishes, flies,
> Playing with words and idle similes ;
> As the English apes and very zanies be
> Of everything which they do hear and see,
> So imitating his ridiculous tricks,
> They spake and writ, all like mere lunatics.

V

Soon after the publication of ' Euphues,' Lyly attached himself to the Court. In 1582 he was in the service of Lord Burleigh, as appears from a letter of apology written in the summer of that year. In 1590 he addressed a petition to the Queen, setting forth his claims to notice, and adding, that ten years had elapsed since ' I was entertained, your Majesty's servant, by your own gracious favour.' Lyly's avowed object in following the Court was to gain the place of Master of the Revels. He states in his petition that the reversion of that office had been almost promised him. With this aim in view he began to compose comedies, methodically and elaborately flattering the Queen with studied compliment and allegory. But notwithstanding his efforts to please Elizabeth, in spite of lamentable appeals for recognition, he never succeeded in obtaining the coveted post of honour and emolument. It was his doom :

> To lose good nights that might be better spent,
> To waste long days in pensive discontent,
> To speed to-day, to be put back to-morrow,
> To feed on hope, and pine with fear and sorrow.

That his plays were admired, that he was 'graced and rewarded' with fair speeches, was the utmost he could compass. His last petition, dated 1593, gives forth a wailing note of hope deferred and disappointment. 'Thirteen years your Highness' servant; but yet nothing! Twenty friends, that though they say they will be sure, I find them sure to be slow! A thousand hopes; but all nothing! A hundred promises; but yet nothing! Thus casting up the inventory of my friends, hopes, promises, and times, the *summa totalis* amounteth to just nothing. . . . . The last and the least, that if I be born to have nothing, I may have a protection to pay nothing; which suit is like his that having followed the Court ten years, for recompense of his service committed a robbery, and took it out in a pardon.' Lyly survived this

petition some years, and died in the first decade of the seven
teenth century.

The inventor of Euphuism spoke from the heart and
plainly on his own affairs. His dramatic work is also comparatively free from euphuistic affectation. The soliloquies
and monologues, indeed, are often tainted with the author's
mannerism. Antitheses and classical allusions abound. All
the characters, from the highest to the lowest, use the same
refined language, and seem to have enjoyed a polite education.
But the dialogue is for the most part free in style, and terse
even to bareness. The lyrics are as neat and delicate as
French songs. Some of the scenes suggest antique sculpture
or the subjects of engraved gems. After making due allowance
for the alloy of conceits, which mingles with the finer ore
of his production, Lyly's style deserves to be called Attic.

In ' Euphues ' he had given signal proof of his originality.
His Comedies were no less new creations. Nothing of the
same sort had previously been known in England. They
combined the qualities of the Masque and the Drama, interwove classical fable with allegory, and made the whole work
of art subservient to compliment. We cannot call them
Comedies of character, of intrigue, or of manners. They
are devoid of plot, and deficient in dramatic movement. But
the succession of their scenes is brilliant, their dialogue
sparkling, their allegory interesting. The title under which
they were published in Blount's edition of 1632 sufficiently
describes them. There they are termed Court Comedies.
The curious rarity of their invention is well, though euphuisti-
cally, characterised in the same editor's panegyric on the
author : ' The spring is at hand, and therefore I present you
a Lily growing in a Grove of Laurels. For this poet sat
at the sun's table. Apollo gave him a wreath of his own
bays, without snatching. The lyre he played on had no
borrowed strings.'

VI

Of the eight comedies ascribed to Lyly,[1] six were first
exhibited before the Queen's Majesty by the children of her
choir and the children of Paul's. Of these six, four were
founded upon classical fables; but the fables only served to
veil allusions to the Queen. Each piece forms a studied
panegyric of her virtue, beauty, chastity, and wisdom. In
' Endimion' her loftiness and unapproachable virginity are
celebrated. Spenser had already styled her Cynthia. So
Lyly's allegory was transparent, and Leicester was easily
identified with Endimion. ' What thing,' cries Endimion to
his friend Eumenides, ' what thing, my mistress excepted,
being in the pride of her beauty and latter minute of her age,
then waxeth young again ? Tell me, Eumenides, what is he
that having a mistress of ripe years and infinite virtues, great
honours and unspeakable beauty, but would wish that she
might grow tender again ? getting youth by years and never-
decaying beauty by time ; whose fair face neither the summer's
blaze can scorch, nor the winter's blast chap, nor the
numbering of years breed altering of colours. Such is my
sweet Cynthia—whom time cannot touch, because she is
divine ; nor will offend, because she is delicate.' Tellus, who
loves Endimion, and to whom he has been privately contracted—the earthly mistress, abandoned for his celestial lady
—persuades a witch to charm him into a deep sleep upon a
bank of lunary. There he slumbers forty years, till his friend
Eumenides discovers from an oracle in Thessaly that
Cynthia's kiss will bring him back to life. The great queen

---

[1] It is certain, I think, that the *Maid's Metamorphosis* was not
Lyly's work. It bears marks of imitation of his style. But the lyrics
are not in his manner ; and the subject is handled with far greater
dramatic freedom than is usual with Lyly. The rhymed couplets in
which a large portion is composed show the craftsmanship of a different
school. We must assign it to a younger playwright, working upon
Lyly's lines for the boy-actors of S. Paul's. This comedy was printed
anonymously in 1600, the year of Lyly's death, and has been reprinted
by Mr. A. H. Bullen.

of the night, hearing this among her ladies, deigns to visit
Endimion, and finds him grown in his long sleep from
comely youth to grizzled age. Cynthia stoops above the bed
of lunary, and speaks :

Cynthia. Although my mouth hath been heretofore as untouched as my thoughts, yet now to recover thy life, though to
restore thy youth it be impossible, I will do that to Endimion
which yet never mortal man could boast of heretofore, nor shall ever
hope for hereafter. (*She kisseth him.*)

Eumenides. Madam, he beginneth to stir.

Cynth. Soft, Eumenides ; stand still.

Eum. Ah, I see his eyes almost open.

Cynth. I command thee once again, stir not:
I will stand behind him.

Eum. Endimion, Endimion ! art thou deaf or dumb ? Or hath
this long sleep taken away thy memory ? Ah ! my sweet
Endimion, seest thou not Eumenides, who for thy safety hath
been careless of his own content ? Speak, Endimion, Endimion,
Endimion !

Endimion. Endimion ? I call to mind such a name.

Eum. Hast thou forgotten thyself, Endimion ? Then do I not
marvel thou rememberest not thy friend !

Still Endimion will not be stirred from his dead lethargy.
Eumenides then points to Cynthia, and the queen speaks :

Cynth. Endimion, speak, sweet Endimion, knowest thou not
Cynthia ?

End. O heavens, whom do I behold, fair Cynthia, divine
Cynthia ?

Cynth. I am Cynthia, and thou Endimion.

End. Endimion ? What do I here ? What, a grey beard ?
Withered body ? Decayed limbs ? And all in one night ?

Eum. One night ? Thou hast slept here forty years, by what
enchantress as yet it is not known ; and behold, the twig to which
thou layedst thy head, is now become a tree ! Callest thou not
Eumenides to remembrance ?

End. Thy name I do remember by the sound ; but thy favour
I do not yet call to mind. Only divine Cynthia, to whom time,
fortune, death, and destiny are subject, I see and remember ; and
in all humility I regard and reverence.

Thus Endimion returns to consciousness; and when the charm has been removed, and his youth has been miraculously restored, the handsome shepherd concludes the play with this courtly speech: ' The time was, madam, and is, and ever shall be, that I honoured your highness above all the world; but to stretch it so far as to call it love, I never durst.' He therefore resolves to consecrate the whole of his life to the contemplation of Cynthia's perfections.

Lyly warns his audience in the prologue that this play is but 'a tale of the Man in the Moon,' and specially requests them not ' apply pastimes,' or, in other words, to affix real names to his fancied characters.[1] Yet this has since been done for him; and it is highly probable that Tellus was meant for Leicester's wife Lady Sheffield, and Dipsas the witch for the Countess of Shrewsbury.[2] It is not impossible that the poet's career at Court was injured by the application of his somewhat too transparent allegory.

'Endimion' has no dramatic interest; it is nothing but a censer of exquisitely chased silver, full of incense, to be tossed before Elizabeth upon her throne, with Leicester and her ladies at her side. Yet the compliment is never gross. The theme of purity in a divine or royal maiden is one of the most delicate that art can touch. Lyly has treated it with quaint and courtly grace. The placidity of the piece seems well suited to those childish actors, whose tender years and boyish voices were more in harmony with Lyly's studied diction and tranquil fancy than with the terrible passion and heroic utterance of a Marlowe or a Shakspere. Hazlitt has praised the comedy with uncritical extravagance; he seems to have read it with the eyes of Keats, exclaiming: 'Happy Endimion! faithful Eumenides! divine Cynthia! Who would not wish to pass his life in such a sleep—a long, long sleep, dreaming of some fair heavenly goddess, with the moon shining over his face and the trees growing silently

---

[1] This use of the verb ' to apply ' and of the noun ' application ' is common enough in our dramatic authors. Numerous examples might be adduced from Ben Jonson.

[2] See Mr. Halpin's essay in the Old Shakespeare Society's publications.

over his head ? ' This rapture is appropriate enough to the myth of Endymion upon Mount Latmos, as we see it sculptured on the bas-reliefs of old sarcophagi, where the shepherd is a youth for ever sleeping and for ever young, and the moon steps nightly from her dragon-car to kiss her dearest. But it does not better Lyly's comedy to pretend that he dreamed of Endymion as Keats dreamed, or to fancy that these scenes were presented with classical accuracy. In reading it, we must picture to our mind a large low room in the palace of Greenwich. The time is ' New Year's Day at night.' The actors are the ' children of Paul's.' Candles light the stage, in front of which are drawn silk curtains. Elizabeth, in all her bravery of ruffs and farthingales, with chains and orders round her neck, and the sharp smile on her mouth, is seated beneath a canopy of state. Lords, ladies, and ambassadors watch her face, as courtiers watch a queen. On the stage lies no Hellenic shepherd in the bloom of youth, but a boy attired in sylvan style to represent an aged man with flowing beard. Cynthia—not the solitary maiden goddess, led by Cupid, wafting her long raiment to the breeze of night; but a queen among her ladies, a boy disguised to personate Elizabeth herself—bends over him. And Endymion's dream, when he awakes, has been no fair romance of love revealed in slumber, but a vision of treason, envy, ingratitude, assassination, threatening his sovereign.

VII

'Midas' is another Court Comedy on a classical story, treated with even more obvious reference to public events. Hazlitt, who often praises the right things for wrong reasons, talks of being transported to ' the scene of action, to ancient Greece and Asia Minor.' Lyly, according to this critic, succeeded in preserving ' the manners, the images, the traditions '—as though anybody knew what the traditions and manners of prehistoric Phrygia may have been ! Local colour is just what Lyly has not got, or sought to get, in ' Midas.' His shepherds, who fancy that ' the very reeds bow down as though they listened to their talk,' are shepherds of the poet's fancy, gazing at reeds that might grow and rustle on an English just as well as on a Mysian common. The courtiers, kings, and clowns, nay, the very gods, talk like English people; and this is their chief merit, for the English of their speech is pure and undefiled. Lyly, in truth, is never classical by imitation of the classics, but by a certain simplicity of conception and purity of outline, which remind us of antique workmanship. In this comedy Midas is an unmistakable Philip II. The Lesbos upon which he tries to lay his hand is England. The gift, which brings a curse, conferred on him by Bacchus, is the wealth of the West Indies, flowing into Spain and paralysing her activity. The touch that turns all things to gold, 'the gold that thou dost think a god,' is Philip's vain and ruinous reliance on his riches. The ass's ears, which Midas cannot lose till he leaves Lesbos, are his arrogance and folly. Whenever Midas speaks, we read allusions to cruelties in the Low Countries, to the Armada, to Spanish plots in England, to Philip's aggressive policy in Europe.—'I have written my laws in blood, and made my gods of gold. Have I not made the sea to groan under the number of my ships; and have they not perished, that there was not two left to make a number? Have I not enticed the subjects of my neighbour princes to destroy their natural kings? To what kingdom have I not pretended claim? A bridge of gold did I mean to make in that island where all my navy could not make a breach. Have not all treasons been discovered by miracle, not counsel? Is not the country walled with huge waves?'

For the sake of proving Lyly's political allusions, I have singled out, perhaps, the prosiest passage in this comedy. But the malice of making Philip utter a short summary of his own crimes before the throne of his triumphant sister-in-law is so crudely and effectively direct, that the quotation yields a savour above the choicest flowers of Euphuism.

In ' Sapho and Phao ' the poet shows a queen enthralled by love for a poor ferryman. Venus made Phao so fair that all who saw him doted on his beauty. Sapho, the virgin queen of Sicily, gazed and sighed. Venus herself, by Cupid's spite, was entangled in the snare which she had spread for Sapho. Here, again, the allegory is not hard to read; and the end of the comedy must have been flatteringly grateful to Elizabeth. Sapho is released by Cupid from the pangs in which she had a goddess for companion. Phao is left to languish for her in hopeless and respectful longing. His last words to his royal mistress—'O Sapho, thou hast Cupid in thine arms, I in my heart; thou kissest him for sport, I must curse him for spite: yet will I not curse him, Sapho, whom thou kissest. This shall be my resolution: wherever I wander, to be as I were ever kneeling before Sapho; my loyalty unspotted, though unrewarded '—this declaration of everlasting service embodied the essence of that passionate homage and romantic adoration, that chivalrous self-devotion and Platonic constancy, that blind enchantment and enthusiastic worship, with which, as with a phantom and vain show of happiness, the Queen consoled her solitude. Some of the pictures in this play are daintily conceited. Nothing in the Dresden china style of antiquated compliment is prettier than the first meeting of Sapho with Phao on the ferry-boat, unless it is their conversation when he brings narcotic herbs to soothe her into sleep:

Sapho. What herbs have you brought, Phao?

Phao. Such as will make you sleep, madam, though they cannot make me slumber.

S. Why, how can you cure me when you cannot remedy yourself?

P. Yes, madam; the causes are contrary. For it is only a dryness in your brains that keepeth you from rest. But——

S. But what?

P. Nothing—but mine is not so.

S. Nay, then I despair of help, if our disease be not all one.

P. I would our diseases were all one.

S. It goes hard with the patient when the physician is desperate.

P. Yet Medea made the ever-waking dragon to snort, when she, poor soul, could not wink.

S. Medea was in love, and nothing could cause her rest but Jason.

P. Indeed I know no herb to make lovers sleep, but heartsease ; which because it groweth so high, I cannot reach for.

S. For whom ?

P. For such as love.

S. It stoopeth very low, and I can never stoop to it, that——

P. That what ?

S. That I may gather it : but why do you sigh so, Phao ?

P. It is mine use, madam.

S. It will do you harm, and me too : for I never hear one sigh, but I must sigh also.

P. It were best then that your ladyship give me leave to be gone : for I can but sigh.

S. Nay, stay, for now I begin to sigh, I shall not leave though you begone. But what do you think best for your sighing, to take it away ?

P. Yew, madam.

S. Me ?

P. No, madam ; yew of the tree.

S. Then will I love yew the better. And indeed it would make me sleep too ; therefore all other simples set aside, I will simply use only yew.

P. Do, madam ; for I think nothing in the world so good as yew.

S. Farewell for this time.

The outrageous plays on words and stiff mannerism—as of box hedges in an antiquated pleasance cut into quaint shapes —which characterise the dialogue, do not to my sense at least, deprive it of a very piquant charm.

The song of the love-sick queen is a fair, though not a perfect, specimen of Lyly's lyric. Sapho, finding herself alone, exclaims :

Ah, impatient disease of love, and goddess of love thrice unpitiful ! The eagle is never stricken with thunder, nor the olive with lightning ; and may great ladies be plagued with love ? O Venus, have I not strawed thine altars with sweet roses ? kept thy swans in clear rivers ? fed thy sparrows with ripe corn, and harboured thy doves in fair house ?

Sleep will not visit her, and she lays her curse on Cupid in these rhymes :

O cruel Love ! on thee I lay
My curse, which shall strike blind the day ;

Never may sleep with velvet hand
Charm thine eyes with sacred wand;
Thy jailors shall be hopes and fears;
Thy prison-mates, groans, sighs, and tears;
Thy play to wear out weary times,
Fantastic passions, vows and rhymes.

VIII

Lyly takes the same liberties with the story of Sappho that he took with the legend of Endymion. He chose to see in her a love-sick sovereign, whose history might be pointed so as to flatter the Queen of England. Beyond her name she has nothing in common with the Lesbian poetess. In 'Alexander and Campaspe' he again touches on Greek history—showing how noble a thing it was for the conqueror of the world to prefer the toils of sovereignty to the delights of love. Alexander, after taking Thebes, becomes enamoured of his captive, the beautiful Campaspe. He makes Apelles paint her portrait; and Apelles loves her with a warmth that conquers in her soul the love of Alexander. The king, discovering their mutual passion, generously betroths the lady to the painter, consoles himself with Hephæstion's friendship, and marches off with drum and fife to subdue Asia. The moral must have been consoling to Elizabeth, who always faltered between passion and her crown. This comedy, though it is nothing but a dramatised anecdote, is, I think, the best of Lyly's. He has caught something of Plutarch's spirit, sympathising, as the English of that age could do, with the martial greatness of Alexander, the audacity of Alcibiades, the strong resolves of Epameinondas or Timoleon. In the dialogues between Alexander and Diogenes, Lyly was able to bring his own fencing style into appropriate play. Careless, as usual, of Greek local colouring, these combats of wit express the well-known episode with terse and vivid fancy. There is something akin to Shakspere's 'Timon' in the following:

Diog. Who calleth?

Alex. Alexander; how happened it that you would not come out of your tub to my palace?

D. Because it was as far from my tub to your palace, as from your palace to my tub.

A. Why then, dost thou owe no reverence to kings?

D. No.

A. Why so?

D. Because they be no gods.

A. They be gods of the earth.

D. Yea, gods of earth.

A. Plato is not of thy mind.

D. I am glad of it.

A. Why?

D. Because I would have none of Diogenes' mind but Diogenes.

A. If Alexander have anything that may pleasure Diogenes, let me know, and take it.

D. Then take not from me that you cannot give me, the light of the world.

A. What dost thou want?

D. Nothing that you have.

A. I have the world at command.

D. And I in contempt.

A. Thou shalt live no longer than I will.

D. But I shall die whether you will or not.

A. How should one learn to be content?

D. Unlearn to covet.

A. Hephæstion! Were I not Alexander, I would wish to be Diogenes.

Between Apelles and Campaspe there is a pretty conceited dialogue on love. Apelles is showing the pictures in his studio :

Camp. What counterfeit is this, Apelles?

Apelles. This is Venus, the goddess of love.

C. What, be there also loving goddesses?

A. This is she that hath power to command the very affections of the heart.

C. How is she hired—by prayer, by sacrifice, or bribes?

A. By prayer, sacrifice, and bribes.

C. What prayer?

A. Vows irrevocable.

C. What sacrifice?

A. Hearts ever sighing, never dissembling.

C. What bribes?

A. Roses and kisses; but were you never in love?

C. No, nor love in me.

A. Then have you injured many.

C. How so ?

A. Because you have been loved of many.

C. Flattered perchance of some.

A. It is not possible that a face so fair and a wit so sharp, both without comparison, should not be apt to love.

C. If you begin to tip your tongue with cunning, I pray you dip your pencil in colours ; and fall to that you must do, not to that you would do.

The lyrics in the play are also among Lyly's best. Apelles' song, 'Cupid and my Campaspe played,' is too well known to need a word of commendation. But this upon the notes of birds deserves to be recovered from the somewhat tedious scene in which it lies embedded :

> What bird so sings, yet so does wail ?
> Oh, 't is the ravished nightingale !
> Jug, jug, jug, jug, tereu, she cries ;
> And still her woes at midnight rise.
> Brave prick-song !   Who is 't now we hear ?
> None but the lark, so shrill and clear ;
> How at heaven's gates she claps her wings,
> The morn not waking till she sings !
> Hark, hark, with what a pretty throat
> Poor Robin red-breast tunes his note !
> Hark how the jolly cuckoos sing
> Cuckoo, to welcome in the spring—
> Cuckoo, to welcome in the spring !

IX

'Gallathea' deserves to be classed with its author's complimentary Court Comedies. The scene is laid in Lincolnshire. The plot turns upon the yearly sacrifice of a virgin to the sea-monster Agar, in whom we may discern the Ægir, or great wave of the river Humber. Diana and her nymphs, Neptune and Venus, Tityrus and Melibœus, with augurs, alchemists, and English clowns, make up the motley list of personages. To discuss this play in detail would be superfluous. But I cannot refrain from calling attention to

the pretty underplot of Phyllida and Gallathea, two girls
disguised in male attire.   Each thinks the other is what she
pretends to be, and falls in love with her companion as a boy.
The double confusion is sustained with art and delicacy,
considering the difficulty of the motive; and occasion is given
for a succession of dialogues in Lyly's quaintest style.[1]   His
peculiar charm of treatment might also be illustrated by the
scene in which Diana catches Cupid, cuts his wings, burns
his arrows, and exposes him bound to the resentment of her
nymphs.[2]   In clear simplicity and perfect outline, this
picture resembles an intaglio cut to illustrate some passage of
Anacreon.   The proclamation to the nymphs, who have been
hurt by Cupid, is written in three graceful lyric stanzas, sung
by solo voices and chorus : [3]

> O yes ! O yes ! has any lost
> A heart which many a sigh hath cost ?
> Is any cozened of a tear,
> Which, as a pearl, disdain doth wear ?
> Here stands the thief ! let her but come
> Hither, and lay on him her doom.

The sentiment of virginity, which forms the moral element
in 'Gallathea,' refers to Elizabeth ; and the same motive is
worked up in 'Love's Metamorphosis.'   Cupid again runs
wild, and makes mischief among the nymphs of Ceres.
Ceres in this play assumes the same attitude as Diana in the
former.   The pastoral subject once more furnishes the author
with subjects for idyllically classical episodes.   Among these,
the scene of the nymphs adorning a rustic altar on their
harvest holyday might be chosen for quotation.[4]   Ben Jonson
deigned to imitate it in 'Pan's Anniversary,' as in his 'Hue
and Cry after Cupid' he borrowed the motive of Diana's
proclamation from 'Gallathea.'

Two Comedies by Lyly remain to be briefly mentioned.
One, called 'Mother Bombie,' is a tedious love-farce representing English manners.   It scarcely deserves to be remembered, but for a pretty song introduced by way of a duet :

---

[1] Act ii. sc. 1, iii. 2, iv. 4, v. 3.   [2] Act iii. sc. 4.
[3] Act iv. sc. 2.   [4] Act i. sc. 2.

O Cupid! Monarch over kings!
Wherefore hast thou feet and wings?
Is it to show how swift thou art,
When thou wouldst wound a tender heart?
Thy wings being clipped, and feet held still,
Thy bow so many could not kill.

It is all one in Venus' wanton school
Who highest sits, the wise man or the fool!
     Fools in love's college
     Have far more knowledge
     To read a woman over,
     Than a neat prating lover.
     Nay, 't is confessed
     That fools please women best!

'The Woman in the Moon' was Lyly's first dramatic
essay, as we read in the Prologue:

Remember all is but a poet's dream,
The first he had in Phœbus' holy bower,
But not the last, unless the first displease.

Unlike his other Comedies, it is written throughout in
blank verse, and is free from euphuistic mannerism. These
peculiarities induce a doubt as to whether it was really Lyly's
composition. But since the play was printed with his name
in 1597, three years before his death, there is no sufficient
reason to reject it from the list of his works. We must
rather suppose that he had not formed his style when he
made this earliest attempt at writing for the stage. The
allegory, if it was meant to have any reference to the Queen,
is rather satirical than complimentary. Nature forms a woman
at the entreaty of the shepherds of Utopia. She calls her
Pandora, and dowers her with exceeding beauty. The stars
in jealousy shower vices on her head. Saturn gives her
churlishness; Jupiter adds pride; Mars turns her to a vixen.
Under the rule of Sol, she marries Stesias, a shepherd of that
land. In the ascendency of Venus, she turns wanton.
Mercury fills her with cunning and falsehood. Cynthia
makes her, like herself, 'new-fangled, fickle, slothful, foolish

mad.' Stesias watches all these phases of her nature with horror, and prays to be delivered from the torment of such a wife. Pandora at length is relegated to the moon, and ordered to rule that inconstant luminary, while Cynthia haunts the woods or dwells with Pluto on the throne of Hecate. It seems singular that Lyly should have made his *début* at Court with this satire upon women and on Cynthia herself.[1]

X

As the first considerable poet who composed the imaginative pieces which we call Court Comedies, Lyly holds an important place in our dramatic history. He invented a species. Both Shakspere and Fletcher knew well how to profit by his discovery. Shakspere was just twenty when 'Alexander and Campaspe' appeared. He arrived in London, and began to work for the stage soon after this date. Lyly exercised considerable influence over his imagination and his method of production. The earlier Shaksperian Comedies abound in euphuistic dialogues, and display minute evidences of euphuistic studies. Beatrice and Benedick, Timon and Apemantus, can be traced by no uncertain method to the poet's early admiration for John Lyly. Dogberry owes something to the Watch in 'Endimion;' the fairies of 'The Merry Wives of Windsor' owe even more to a catch-song in that comedy. The confused sexes and complicated loves of Phyllida and Gallathea reappear in 'As You Like It.' Lyly's lark-note from 'Campaspe' sounds again in 'Cymbeline.' The elder playwright had styled two of his Comedies ('Sapho'

[1] Were it not for the reason given above, I should be inclined to reject *The Woman in the Moon.* If it was Lyly's first work, it must have been written before 1584 (the date of *Campaspe's* publication). This was very early in the development of dramatic blank verse. The title, again, might pass for a parody of his *Endimion* or *The Man in the Moon*; while the satire of the piece parodies his style of compliment to Elizabeth. The title-page of 1597 adds, 'as it was presented before her Highness.' Yet Edward Blount, in his edition of Lyly's *Six Court Comedies* (1632), neither included nor mentioned it. *Love's Metamorphosis* he also excluded; but in the first edition of this play (1601) it is not mentioned as having been performed before the Queen.

and ' The Woman in the Moon ') dreams. The younger gave
the world a masterpiece in the romantic style of Comedy,
when he produced his ' Midsummer Night's Dream.'

Lyly was emphatically a discoverer. He discovered
euphuism, and created a fashionable affectation, which ran
its course of more than twenty years. He discovered the
dialogue of repartee in witty prose. He discovered the
ambiguity of the sexes, as a motive of dramatic curiosity.
He discovered what effective use might be made of the
occasional lyric, as an adjunct to dramatic action. He
discovered the suggestion of dramatic dreaming. He discovered the combination of Masque and Drama, which gave
rise to the Courtly or Romantic Comedy.

Shakspere bettered Lyly's best, and used his discoveries
with such artistic freedom, such poetic supremacy, that we
are tempted to forget the quaint petitioner at Court who
' fished the murex up.' It is the duty, however, of historic
criticism to indicate origins. And in the study of Shakspere
we are bound to remember that Lyly preceded him ; just as
when we estimate the greatness of Michel Angelo in Rome,
we have to turn our eyes back upon Ghirlandajo and
Signorelli.

CHAPTER XIV

GREENE, PEELE, NASH, AND LODGE.

I

WHEN Shakspere left Stratford-upon-Avon for London, and began his career as actor and arranger of old plays for the Lord Chamberlain's Servants, a group of distinguished scholar-poets held possession of the stage. The date of this event, so memorable in modern literary history, cannot be fixed with certainty. But we may refer it with probability to the year 1585. Before 1600 Shakspere had already shown himself the greatest dramatist of the romantic school, not only by the production but also by the publication of his earlier comedies and tragedies. In that period of fifteen years, between 1585 and 1600, the men of whom I speak either died or left off writing for the theatre. They were Robert Greene, George Peele, Christopher Marlowe, Thomas Lodge, Thomas Nash, and Thomas Kyd. Greene died in 1592, Marlowe in 1593, Peele in 1597, Kyd not later than 1594. Nash produced his only extant play in 1592, and died soon after 1600. The tragedy by which Lodge is best known as a playwright, was printed in 1594. He exchanged literature for medicine, and practised as a physician until his death in 1625. Lyly, it will be remembered, died soon after 1600.

These are the playwrights with whom Ben Jonson, in his famous elegy, thought fit to compare Shakspere—not, as it seems to me, in spite, but because they were contemporaries. William Basse, writing on the same occasion, bade Spenser, Chaucer, and Beaumont lie somewhat closer, each to each, in order to make room for Shakspere in their 'threefold, fourfold tomb.' Jonson says he will not use a similar rhetorical contrivance; for Shakspere is 'a monument without a tomb,' living as long as his book lives, as long as there are men to read and praise him. Then he proceeds:

> That I not mix thee so, my brain excuses,
> I mean with great, but disproportioned Muses;
> For if I thought my judgment were of years,
> I should commit thee surely with thy peers,
> And tell how far thou didst our Lily outshine,
> Or sporting Kyd, or Marlowe's mighty line.

That he meant no disparagement to Shakspere is manifest from his immediately calling upon Æschylus, Sophocles, and Euripides, on Aristophanes, and on the tragic and comic poets of Rome, to rise and admire Shakspere's masterpieces in both kinds. To time Shakspere is no tributary, nor are his works subject to comparisons based on considerations of chronology or nationality:

> Triumph, my Britain, thou hast one to show,
> To whom all scenes of Europe homage owe.
> He was not of an age, but for all time!
> And all the Muses still were in their prime,
> When, like Apollo, he came forth to warm
> Our ears, or like a Mercury to charm

I have dwelt upon this elegy, not merely to disprove the false inference which some have drawn from it to Jonson's disadvantage, but also to show how a great contemporary poet regarded Shakspere's relation to his comrades in the dramatic art. If Shakspere is to be judged by 'years,' by chronological parallelism, says Jonson, he must be compared with that group of playwrights of whom Lyly, Marlowe, and Kyd are representatives. But Shakspere is amenable to no such jurisdiction. He belongs to the world and to all ages. The incarnation of his spirit at that precise moment is a matter of indifference.

The group of six dramatists enumerated above must further be distinguished. Marlowe stands apart, as a vastly superior genius, the true founder of Shaksperian drama, a pioneer and creator in the highest sense. Kyd is separated from the rest by the comparative insignificance of what remains to us of his work. Greene heads a little coterie of writers bound together by ties of personal comradeship, and animated by a common spirit. Greene, Peele, Nash, and Lodge attach themselves to the past rather than the future. They submit to Marlowe's unavoidable dictatorship, and receive him into their society. But they belong to a school which became doubly antiquated in their lifetime. Marlowe outshone them; and Shakspere, as they were uneasily conscious, was destined to eclipse them altogether. I propose, therefore, to treat now of these four friends, having already given a word to Kyd in isolation, while I reserve a separate study for the greatest poet of the group. This method conforms to the evolution of the Drama. But it has the disadvantage of anticipating what properly belongs to the criticism of Marlowe. He revolutionised the English stage during Greene's ascendency, and forced his predecessors to adapt their style to his inventions.

II

The men of letters who form the subject of this study were respectably born and highly educated. They prided themselves on being gentlemen and scholars, Masters of Arts

in both Universities.   Robert Greene was the son of well-to-
do citizens of Norwich, where he was born perhaps about the
year 1550.[1]   He took his Bachelor's degree at Cambridge
in 1578, and passed Master in 1583.   George Peele was a
gentleman of Devonshire, born about 1558, instructed in
the rudiments at Christ's Hospital, elected Student of Christ
Church in 1573, and admitted Bachelor of Arts in 1577.
While still at Oxford, he acquired considerable literary
reputation, and was praised by Dr. Gager—no mean judge
—for his English version of an ' Iphigeneia.'   Thomas Lodge
was the second son of Sir Thomas Lodge, Lord Mayor of
London, by his wife Anne, a daughter of Sir William Laxton.
Born in 1557, he took his degree at Oxford in 1577, and
entered the Society of Lincoln's Inn next year.   Being of a
roving nature, Lodge never settled down to literature.   After
wasting the time which ought to have been given to law
studies, he joined the expeditions of Captain Clarke and
Cavendish, visited the Canary Islands, and penned a fashionable romance in the Straits of Magellan.   On his return to
England he adopted medicine as a profession, studied at
Avignon, and established himself as a practitioner in London.
Upon his title-pages he was always careful to describe himself ' Thomas Lodge of Lincoln's Inn Gentleman.'   Greene
assumed the style of ' Magister utriusque Academiæ,' and
Peele insisted on his Master of Arts degree.   Thomas Nash,
descended from an honourable family in Herefordshire, was
born at Lowestoft in 1567.   He took his degree at Cambridge
in 1585, and after travelling in Italy, came up to London,
where we find him engaged in literary work with Greene
about the year 1587.

Unlike Lyly, these four friends did not attach themselves
to the Court.   They worked for booksellers and public
theatres, selling their compositions, and living on the produce of their pen.   They seem to have been diverted from
more serious studies and a settled career by the attractions
of Bohemian life in London.   What we know of their
biography, proves how fully some of them deserved the stigma

[1] This date is quite uncertain.

for vagrancy, loose living, and profanity, which then attached to players and playwrights. Excluded from respectable society, depending on the liberality of booksellers and managers, with no definite profession, enrolled in no acknowledged guild or corporation, they passed their time at taverns, frequented low houses of debauchery, and spent their earnings in the company of thieves and ruffians. In this general description it would not be quite safe to insert the name of Thomas Lodge, though we may presume that he shared in the amusements, and possibly also, if we ascribe biographical value to his 'Alarum against Usurers,' in the pecuniary troubles of his literary friends. But Lodge was almost too scrupulous to keep aloof from the set before the public, describing himself as ' Gentleman ' and ' of Lincoln's Inn.' From the degradation which then attached to professional literature no one did so much to elevate the playwright's calling as Shakspere. He found it sunk below contempt, not only in the estimation of Puritans, but also in fact, patent to every observer of the lives of men like Marlowe, Greene, and Peele. Styling themselves scholars, and boasting their academical degrees, they chose a theatrical career because of its lawlessness and jollity. Shakspere came from Stratford with no such pretensions, adopted the stage as a profession, and dignified it by his honest labour.[1]

III

The romance of Greene's life has been often told ; but it so exactly illustrates the conditions under which our playwrights at this epoch laboured, that I cannot omit to pass it in review. The details are gathered not only from uncontradicted statements of his literary enemies, but also from his own autobiographical writings, 'Never too Late,' ' A Groatsworth of Wit,' and ' The Repentance of Robert Greene.'

[1] Notice the curious praise bestowed upon Shakspere for respectability by Chettle in his *Kind-Harts Dreame*. He apologises for having printed some offensive passages in Greene's posthumous *Groatsworth of Wit*, and distinctly asserts Shakspere's superiority to the Bohemian playwrights. Quoted by Dyce in his edition of Marlowe (1858), p. xxix.

Laboriously pieced together from the extracts furnished by Alexander Dyce, and illustrated by gleanings from contemporary tracts, the record of Greene's brief career and miserable end may be presented with some completeness.

After taking his degree as Bachelor of Arts in 1578, Greene left England, persuaded by some college associates, to wander over Spain and Italy. 'For being at the University of Cambridge, I light amongst wags as lewd as myself, with whom I consumed the flower of my youth ; who drew me to travel into Italy and Spain, in which places I saw and practised such villany as is abominable to declare.' His early friends and comrades are described in the following sentence : ' Being then conversant with notable braggarts, boon companions, and ordinary spendthrifts, that practised sundry superficial studies, I became as a scion grafted into the same stock, whereby I did absolutely participate of their nature and qualities.' When he returned to England he took up his residence again at Cambridge, 'ruffling out in silks, in the habit of malcontent, and seeming so discontent that no place would please me to abide in, nor no vocation cause me to stay myself in.' What he had learned upon his journeys, he now applied in his own country. ' Being new-come from Italy (where I learned all the villanies under the heavens) I was drowned in pride, whoredom was my daily exercise, and gluttony with drunkenness was my only delight.' He extracted money from his father's purse ' by cunning sleights,' and worked upon his mother's fondness, ' who secretly helped me to the oil of angels.' Having taken his Master's degree, he made his way to London. At first he was received by friends as a young man of promise ; but he soon abandoned these for evil company. ' Where, after I had continued some short time and driven myself out of credit with sundry of my friends, I became an author of plays, and a penner of love pamphlets, so that I soon grew famous in that quality, that who for that trade grown so ordinary about London as Robin Greene ? Young yet in years, though old in wickedness, I began to resolve that there was nothing bad that was profitable : whereupon I grew so rooted in all mischief that I had

as great delight in wickedness as sundry hath in godliness,
and as much felicity I took in villany as others had in
honesty.' The vilest fellows were his companions; the ale-
house and the brothel were his haunts. ' After I had wholly
betaken me to the penning of plays (which was my continual
exercise), I was so far from calling upon God that I seldom
thought on God, but took such delight in swearing and
blaspheming the name of God that none could think otherwise of me than that I was the child of perdition.' He lived
upon his pen, and entertained a tribe of parasites with the
fruits of his literary labours. ' Now famoused for an arch-
playmaking poet, his purse, like the sea, sometimes swelled,
anon like the same sea fell to a low ebb; yet seldom he
wanted, his labours were so well esteemed. He had shift
of lodgings, where in every place his hostess writ up the
wofull remembrance of him, his laundress and his boy; for
they were ever his in household, besides retainers in sundry
other places. His company were lightly the lewdest persons
in the land, apt for pilfery, perjury, forgery, or any villany.
Of these he knew the cast to cog at cards, cosen at dice; by
these he learned the legerdemain of nips, foists, conycatchers,
crosbiters, lifts, high-lawyers, and all the rabble of that unclean generation of vipers.' These companions, as he says
in another place, ' came still to my lodging, and there would
continue quaffing, carousing, and surfeiting with me all day
long.'

Hitherto I have made Greene tell his own tale, breath-
lessly and disjointedly, but with palpable sincerity, in his
own words. Though it is very probable that, with a novel-
writer's tendency to the sensational in literature, he somewhat overdrew the picture of his vices, yet this picture is too
vivid to be mistaken for fiction. What Ascham and Howell
wrote about the injury to English youth from foreign travel,
finds a striking illustration in Greene's confessions. De-
moralised by bad associates at college, trained to infamy in
the slums of Florence and the base quarters of Venice, he
returned to England, the *diavolo incarnato* of the famous
proverb. It was impossible with such antecedents to follow

a sober student's career at Cambridge. Therefore he came
to London, engaged his talents in the service of the stage
and press, and plunged into Bohemian dissipations. Nothing
paints London at that period in more curious colours than
the description which Greene has given us of his associates.
Between respectable society and the company of the most
abandoned ruffians, this man of letters found no middle term
of intercourse. That intermediate region, frequented by
artists, playwrights, pamphleteers, law-students, and men
about town, which we call Bohemia in modern capitals,
did not then apparently exist. To speak more strictly, it
came into existence a short while afterwards, when Shakspere and Jonson, Beaumont and Chapman, gave tone to
literary clubs and taverns. Greene, through his own fault,
but also through the fault of a society which had not yet
developed its Bohemia, was thrown upon the basest comradeship of knaves and sharpers, pimps and strumpets. Ill
adapted to respectable society, he found his only refuge and
abiding-place in Alsatia.

In spite of the infamous life with which Greene charges
himself, he does not seem to have been a thorough-going and
contented scoundrel, but rather a weak, vain, vicious man,
who abandoned himself to evil courses. He suffered occasional pangs of remorse, and made one or two feeble efforts to
amend his ways. Once it was a sermon which stung his
conscience to the quick. At another time he married a
respectable woman, who bore him a child in wedlock. But
his old associates got hold of him. He deserted his wife,
squandered her money, and answered her unavailing efforts
to reclaim him with brutal insults. By the sister of one of
his friends—a thief, called Cutting Ball, who was afterwards
hanged at Tyburn—he had a son, whom he christened Fortunatus. His enemies in their satires turned this name into
Infortunatus, which was certainly more appropriate to the
child of such parents. Notwithstanding the intimate connections he thus formed with the rogues of London, Greene
exposed the tricks of their trade in a series of pamphlets
with startling titles, as: 'A Notable Discovery of Cozenage,'

' A Disputation between a He-Coneycatcher and a She-Coney-catcher,' &c. ; proving himself vile enough to turn informer for the sake of a profitable literary venture. We must, how-ever, bear in mind that to coin money by his pen was an absolute necessity. After working out his vein in love pamphlets and Euphuistic novels, he turned his experience in crime to account, and lastly betook himself to autobiography. The shamelessness of the man is a sufficient guarantee for the truth of his personal revelations. Vain, and desirous of keeping his name before the public, but without a character to lose, he made a cynical exposure of his vices. These con-fessions, moreover, are stamped with indubitable signs of earnestness. The accent of remorse is too sincere and strongly marked in them to justify a suspicion of deliberate fiction.

The last scene of Greene's miserable existence has been often described. He lay, penniless, deserted by his friends, consumed with the diseases of a libertine and drunkard, on a bed for which he owed his landlord money, without even the clothes which might have enabled him to leave it. A surfeit of pickled herrings and Rhenish wine is said to have been the final cause of his death. As he lay there, alone and dying, the thought of his injured wife and of his friends oppressed his conscience. In the agony of repentance he addressed a solemn warning to Peele, Nash, and Marlowe, calling upon them with all the eloquence of death to repent of their debaucheries and profanities. He prayed his wife for forgiveness, and begged her to discharge his debts : ' Doll, I charge thee, by the love of our youth and by my soul's rest, that thou wilt see this man paid ; for if he and his wife had not succoured me, I had died in the streets.' Two women visited the dying poet in this extremity. One of them was the mother of his illegitimate son, the sister of the felon Cutting Ball. The other was his landlady. She cherished affection and respect for the distinguished man of letters, and tended him during a month's sickness. When he was dead, she placed a wreath of bays upon his forehead, and buried him at her own cost.

Greene deserves almost unmitigated reprobation. He was
not only profligate, but bad-hearted, and, as we shall see, he
indulged a rancorous animosity upon his death-bed. Yet we
may believe that had his youth escaped the contamination of
Italian vices, had his abilities been recognised by society, or
had a place among men of education and good manners been
open to his choice, he might perhaps have prospered. There
are points in his dramatic and lyric work which show that
circumstance, at least as much as natural frailty, made
Greene what he came to be ; and that, with a fair share of
the world's sunshine to bask in, he might have passed for a
jovial and irritable man of letters and of pleasure. But at
that epoch the trade of literature, especially in connection
with the stage, was regarded with contempt. Gabriel Harvey
flung it in his face that he made a living by his pen. He
was almost compelled to consort with the lowest populace.

Greene's career is typical. His friend Peele fared hardly
better, sinking into deep pecuniary distress, as appears from a
lamentable appeal to Lord Burleigh, and dying of a dishonourable disease. Nash lived in extreme poverty, repented
publicly of his thriftless and wretched existence, and died
before his time. Marlowe became a byword for profanity
and atheism, and was murdered in a tavern-brawl at Deptford before reaching the age of thirty. Lodge alone, after
spending a troubled youth in many scenes of varied action,
retrieved his fortunes, joined the respectable classes, and died
decently of the plague at the ripe age of sixty-seven. The
four less fortunate members of the group barely reckoned
forty years apiece when they passed out of life, exhausted by
what Anthony Wood contemptuously styles 'that high and
loose course of living which poets generally follow.' The
pleasantest glimpse we get of them is in a pamphlet by that
genial friend of authors, Thomas Dekker. In his 'Knight's
Conjuring' he feigns to find the friends together in a Grove
of Bay-trees in Elysium. 'To this consort-room resort none
but the children of Phœbus, poets and musicians. When
these happy spirits sit asunder, their bodies are like to many
stars ; and when they join together in several troops, they

show like so many heavenly constellations.' Here, he says,
' Marlowe, Greene, and Peele, had got under the shades of a
large vine, laughing to see Nash, that was but newly come to
their college, still haunted with the sharp and satirical spirit
that followed him here upon earth.'

IV

Greene's dying exhortation to his brother-playwrights is
not only impressive by reason of its moral earnestness, but
also interesting for the light it casts upon the theatre in that
year, 1592. It opens thus : ' To those gentlemen his quondam
acquaintance, that spend their wits in making plays, R. G.
wisheth a better exercise, and wisdom to prevent his
extremities.' After calling upon Marlowe, 'famous gracer
of tragedians,' to abandon his blasphemies and atheistical
opinions, and upon Nash, ' young Juvenal, that biting satirist,'
to abate the virulence and personality of his attacks,[1] he
specially addresses Peele, ' no less deserving than the other
two, in some things rarer, in nothing inferior.' Peele, he
says, is unworthy better hap, ' sith thou dependest on so mean
a stay.' That stay was the theatre. Greene thus expounds
his meaning : ' Base-minded men all three of you, if by my
misery ye be not warned ; for unto none of you, like me,
sought those burrs to cleave—those puppets, I mean, that
speak from our mouths, those antics garnished in our colours.'
These puppets are the players, to whose neglect rather than
to his own vices he attributes his present destitution. Not
long ago they throve upon the bounty of Greene's pen, but
now they have deserted him, ' for there is an upstart crow
beautified with our feathers, that, with his " Tiger's Heart
wrapt in a Player's Hide," supposes he is as well able to
bombast out a blank verse as the best of you ; and being an
absolute Johannes-fac-totum, is in his own conceit the only
Shake-scene in the country.' In other words the playing

[1] It has been doubted whether Greene meant Nash or Lodge by
' young Juvenal.' On the whole I feel sure that Nash is intended.
But it signifies comparatively little.

companies can afford to do without Greene because one of
their own craft, Shakspere the actor, has begun to write
dramas. Having him at home and in their partnership, the
actors leave the scholar-poets to starve. Up to this point
Greene has not actually accused Shakspere of plagiarism,
since it appears from parallel passages in his works that the
' crow beautified with our feathers ' is only another metaphor
for a stage-player.[1] This, however, he proceeds to do when he
entreats his friends to ' employ your rare wits in more profitable courses, and let these apes imitate your past excellence,
and never more acquaint them with your admired inventions.'
The drift of the argument is this : ' We, gentlemen and
scholars, have founded the Drama in England, and have
hitherto held a monopoly of the theatres. Those puppets,
antics, base grooms, buckram gentlemen, peasants, painted
monsters '—for he calls the players by all these names in
succession—' have now learned not only how to act our
scenes, but how to imitate them ; and there is one among
them, Shakspere, who will drive us all to penury.' Nothing
can justify the violence of this abuse or defend the assumption
that the field of dramatic composition was only open to
graduates in arts. Nothing can excuse the spite of flinging
Shakspere's country birth and lack of culture in his face
because his overwhelming greatness had become apparent to
his rivals. The contempt poured on the actor's calling is also
inexcusable ; for we have good reason to believe that Greene
himself, Marlowe, Peele, Nash, and possibly Lodge also, had
played their parts upon the public stage. But the peculiar
circumstances of Greene's life as a playwright may be pleaded
in some extenuation of his virulence. He, first of all the
group of scholar-poets, quitted his university for London and
engaged in the Drama. Rhymed plays were then in fashion,
and these he produced with so much facility and so excellent
that he soon became the ' arch-playmaking poet.' At this
point of his career Marlowe revolutionised the stage with
' Tamburlaine.' Greene violently opposed the introduction of

---

[1] See Simpson's *School of Shakspere*, vol. ii. pp. 359, 368, 383.

blank verse, comparing its stately music to the 'fa-burden of Bow bell,' and sneering at poets 'who set the end of scholarism in an English blank verse.' He engaged Nash in the same quarrel. In a preface to Greene's 'Menaphon' the young satirist inveighed against 'idiot art-masters, that intrude themselves as the alchemists of eloquence, and think to out-brave better pens with the swelling bombast of bragging blank verse . . . the spacious volubility of a drumming deca-syllabon.' This was in 1589. Greene was defeated; and in order to maintain his position as a playwright, he found him-self compelled to adopt Marlowe's innovations, and to imitate, so far as in him lay, the mightier poet's style. Marlowe, we have every reason to believe, was a man of kindly tempera-ment, on whom it was not easy to fix a literary quarrel.[1] Therefore he soon joined the society of scholar-playwrights, and was accepted by Greene into his friendship. But no sooner had the confraternity of 'arch-playmaking poets,' 'scholar-like shepherds,' been established upon this new basis, than the star of Shakspere rose above the horizon. It was obvious to the meanest capacity, indisputable by the grossest vanity, that Shakspere was entering like a young prince into the dominions conquered by his predecessors, and that his reign would be extended far beyond the limits of their empire. Greene was an egotistical, irascible man, proud of his academical honours and jealous of his literary fame in London. Having bowed to Marlowe's superior genius, he had now the mortification of beholding a greater than Marlowe ; one, too, who was not even a scholar, who had not travelled in Italy, who studied the subjects of his plays in English versions, 'feeding on nought but the crumbs that fall from the translator's trencher.'[2] Not only his fame but his daily bread was imperilled by this intrusion into his territories. And what probably made the matter worse, was that while

[1] Soon after his tragic death, when everybody was abusing him, Nash called him 'poor deceased Kit Marlowe,' and Dyce quotes the epithet 'kind Kit Marlowe' from a MS. poem published in 1600.

[2] See Nash's introduction to Greene's *Menaphon* for this phrase and many others directed against the actor-playwright.

Greene deplored a misspent life in the service of the playgoing
public, he saw Shakspere winning golden opinions by the
sobriety of his conduct and amassing wealth by thrift and
business-like habits. No one could have written about Greene
what Chettle wrote in 1592 of Shakspere: [1] 'Myself have
seen his demeanour no less civil than he excellent in the
quality he professes; besides, divers of worship have reported
his uprightness of dealing, which argues his honesty, and his
facetious grace in writing that approves his art.'   To the
Bohemian scholar-poet, the professional dramatist, who
dignified his calling and pursued his trade with profit, became
an object of aversion. Greene's dying address to his friends
is thus a groan of disappointment and despair; a lamentation
over wasted opportunities, envenomed by envious hatred of a
rival, wiser in his deportment, more fortunate in his ascendant
star. Despicable as were the passions which inspired it, we
cannot withhold a degree of pity from the dying Titan, discomfited, undone, and superseded, who beheld the young
Apollo issue in splendour and awake the world to a new day.

V

The fame of Robert Greene during his lifetime eclipsed
that of his contemporaries. So greatly was he esteemed that
Gabriel Harvey, the remorseless enemy who attacked him in
the grave, exclaims in anger: 'Even Guiccardine's silver
History and Ariosto's golden Cantos grow out of request; and
the Countess of Pembroke's Arcadia is not green enough for
queasy stomachs; but they must have Greene's "Arcadia,"
and, I believe, most eagerly long for Greene's "Faery
Queen."' He was, in fact, the popular author of the day,
perused by gallants and Court ladies, and by waiting-women
who aped the manners of their mistresses. His friends
applauded the facility with which he turned his talents to
account. 'In a night and a day,' says Nash, 'would he have
yarked up a pamphlet as well as in seven years; and glad

[1] See Dyce's *Greene*, p. 61.

was that printer that might be so blest to pay him dear for
the very dregs of his wit.' This popularity was deservedly
short-lived. Greene did not write for immortality. His
ephemeral productions caught the taste of the moment, and
brought him quick returns of money and reputation. But
the fashion changed ; and ere long the very bulk of his works
in prose and verse, when compared with their quality, became
a reason for consigning them to oblivion. As Anthony Wood
remarks : ' He was author of several things which were pleasing to men and women of his time. They made much sport
and were valued among scholars, but since they have been
mostly sold on ballad-mongers' stalls.'

Of all his miscellaneous productions, Greene's novels had
the greatest vogue. He was an avowed imitator of Lyly,
whom he followed in his choice of subjects, treatment, and
stylistic mannerism. When Harvey called Greene ' the ape
of Euphues,' and Nash ' the ape of Greene,' Nash indignantly
retorted : ' Did I ever write of coney-catching, stuff my style
with herbs and stones, or apprentice myself to the running
of the letter ? ' He thus indirectly admits that his friend
abused alliteration, and adopted Lyly's absurd system of
metaphor. Yet Greene was by no means a mere Euphuist.
He employed the fashionable jargon in speeches, epistles, and
reflective digressions. But his narrative is clear and flowing,
and he has far more to tell than Lyly. His own experience
of life had been varied and interesting. He knew how to
reproduce it with much liveliness in the delineation of
characters, the invention of incidents, and the analysis of
passions, strong and firmly outlined, if not remarkable for
depth. The autobiographical pamphlets, ' Never Too Late,'
' Francesco's Fortunes,' ' Greene's Groatsworth,' and his
' Repentance,' are powerfully written, with direct simplicity
of language. Even now they deserve attention, both for
their revelation of the playwright's character and for the
light they throw upon the manners of Bohemians in London.
Nor must it be forgotten that Shakspere founded the
' Winter's Tale ' on Greene's ' Pandosto.'

Greene interspersed his novels with lyrics ; a custom

derived from Sannazzaro, and illustrated by Sidney. To
these songs imperfect justice, has, in my opinion, hitherto
been done. Though far from taking high rank among the
lyrics of the age—though inferior to the similar compositions
of Lodge and Barnfield—they are distinguished by a certain
sweetness, a fluent vein of fancy, and a diction at once poetical
and easy to be understood. That they exerted no slight
influence over the work of succeeding song-writers, will be
evident from a few extracts. I will first select 'Philomela's
Ode that she sung in her Arbour : '

> Sitting by a river's side,
> Where a silent stream did glide,
> Muse I did of many things
> That the mind in quiet brings.
> I gan think how some men deem
> Gold their god ; and some esteem
> Honour is the chief content
> That to man in life is lent ;
> And some others do contend
> Quiet none like to a friend ;
> Others hold there is no wealth
> Comparèd to a perfect health ;
> Some man's mind in quiet stands
> When he is lord of many lands :
> But I did sigh, and said all this
> Was but a shade of perfect bliss ;
> And in my thoughts I did approve
> Nought so sweet as is true love.
> Love twixt lovers passeth these,
> When mouth kisseth and heart agrees,
> With folded arms and lips meeting,
> Each soul another sweetly greeting ;
> For by the breath the soul fleeteth,
> And soul with soul in kissing meeteth.
> If love be so sweet a thing,
> That such happy bliss doth bring,
> Happy is love's sugared thrall ;
> But, unhappy maidens all,
> Who esteem your virgin blisses
> Sweeter than a wife's sweet kisses !
> No such quiet to the mind
> As true love with kisses kind :

But if a kiss prove unchaste,
Then is true love quite disgraced.
Though love be sweet, learn this of me,
No love sweet but honesty.

A little group of these lyrics is devoted to the loves of
Venus and Adonis, which possessed so enthralling an attraction for the poets of that age—for the young Shakspere—for
Constable and Lodge and Richard Barnfield. We may
detect a foretaste of their richer music in the following
stanzas :

In Cyprus sat fair Venus by a fount,
    Wanton Adonis toying on her knee :
She kissed the wag, her darling of account ;
    The boy gan blush ; which when his lover see,
She smiled, and told him love might challenge debt,
And he was young, and might be wanton yet.

Reason replied that beauty was a bane
    To such as feed their fancy with fond love,
That when sweet youth with lust is overta'en,
    It rues in age : this could not Adon move,
For Venus taught him still this rest to set,
That he was young, and might be wanton yet.

Infida's song, from 'Never Too Late,' upon the same
theme, is slight, but very pretty :

Sweet Adon, darest not glance thine eye—
    N'oserez-vous, mon bel ami ?—
Upon thy Venus that must die ?
    Je vous en prie, pity me ;
N'oserez-vous, mon bel, mon bel,
N'oserez-vous, mon bel ami ?

See how sad thy Venus lies,—
    N'oserez-vous, mon bel ami ?—
Love in heart, and tears in eyes ;
    Je vous en prie, pity me ;
N'oserez-vous, mon bel, mon bel,
N'oserez-vous, mon bel ami ?

Here again is a charming sketch of Love dressed like a pilgrim :

Down the valley gan he track,
Bag and bottle at his back,
In a surcoat all of grey ;
Such wear palmers on the way,
When with scrip and staff they see
Jesus' grave on Calvary . . .
Adon was not thought more fair :
Curlèd locks of amber hair,
Locks where love did sit and twine
Nets to snare the gazers' eyne.
Such a palmer ne'er was seen,
'Less Love himself had palmer been.

The Shepherd's Wife's Song praises the pleasures of a pastoral life in a series of graceful stanzas :

Ah, what is love ?   It is a pretty thing,
As sweet unto a shepherd as a king;
     And sweeter too :
For kings have cares that wait upon a crown,
And cares can make the sweetest love to frown :
     Ah then, ah then,
If country loves such sweet desires do gain,
What lady would not love a shepherd swain ?

His flocks are folded, he comes home at night,
As merry as a king in his delight ;
     And merrier too :
For kings bethink them what the state require,
Where shepherds carol careless by the fire :
     Ah then, ah then,
If country loves such sweet desires gain,
What lady would not love a shepherd swain ?

The best of Greene's lyrical verses are in Sephestia's Song to her Child, from ' Menaphon : '

Weep not, my wanton, smile upon my knee ;
When thou art old there 's grief enough for thee.
     Mother's wag, pretty boy,
     Father's sorrow, father's joy ;
     When thy father first did see
     Such a boy by him and me,

He was glad, I was woe ;
Fortune changèd made him so,
When he left his pretty boy,
Last his sorrow, first his joy.

Weep not, my wanton, smile upon my knee ;
When thou art old there's grief enough for thee.
The wanton smiled, father wept,
Mother cried, baby leapt ;
More he crowed, more we cried,
Nature could not sorrow hide ;
He must go, he must kiss
Child and mother, baby bless,
For he left his pretty boy,
Father's sorrow, father's joy.
Weep not, my wanton, smile upon my knee ;
When thou art old there's grief enough for thee.

It may be remarked that the earlier dramatists commanded rhyme and lyrical measures more effectively than prose or blank verse. In England lyrical poetry was not at that epoch dissociated from music. A sonnet ascribed to Shakspere compares Dowland upon equal terms with Spenser. Dekker places the poets and musicians together in Elysium : ' the one creates the ditty, and gives it the life and number ; the other lends it voice, and makes it speak music.' Every house had its lute and virginal or spinet. Every lover could salute his lady with a madrigal, or join in part-songs at her table. The Puritans swept music into the dusthole of oblivion, whence it has never again emerged to gladden English ears with strains of native art. But in the days of Elizabeth this change was still far distant. When therefore Greene and his contemporaries wrote Canzonets and Sonnets, they were using a well-tried and supple instrument. When they endeavoured to construct blank verse, or to build harmonious periods in prose, they were creating new forms, and could not at first exercise the unfamiliar art with ease. This accounts for the superior smoothness and metrical variety which may be noticed in the songs of Greene.

VI

In Greene's plays we can always trace the hand of the novelist. He did not aim at unity of plot, or at firm definition of character. Yet he manages to sustain attention by his power of telling a story, inventing an inexhaustible variety of motives, combining several threads of interest with facility, and so arranging his incongruous materials as to produce a pleasing general effect. He has the merit of simplicity in details, and avoids the pompous circumlocution in vogue among contemporary authors. His main stylistic defect is the employment of cheap Latin mythology in and out of season. But his scenes abound in vivid incidents, which divert criticism from the threadbare thinness of the main conception, and offer opportunities to clever actors. In spite of these good points, we feel how crude and poor a thing the drama still remained. Greene's plays, intermediate between comedy, tragedy, and history, illustrate a step in the development of the Romantic Drama, which had to be taken before Shakspere set his own and final seal upon that form of art. Stale devices of the Miracle and Morality survive, indicating the poet's lack of power to organise the mechanism of a play. The Vice and Devil still amuse the groundlings; and the principal personages introduce their parts, *more antiquo*, with a blunt description of their qualities and claims to notice. The best of Greene's work realises Cecchi's description of the *Farsa*.[1] The worst relapses into the insipid buffoonery of the old English jig and merriment.

We possess none of Greene's earlier dramatic compositions. Those which survive are posterior to Marlowe's 'Tamburlaine.' Greene uses blank verse, but in his use of it betrays the manner of the couplet. His 'Orlando' is versified from Ariosto, and contains a whole Italian stanza embedded in its English. The 'Looking-Glass for London' dramatises the history of Jonah at Nineveh, so as to point a moral for the capital of England. 'Alphonsus Prince of

[1] See above, p. 207-209.

Arragon ' is a stage-show of processions, battles, coronations,
and the like, without dramatic merit. ' James the Fourth of
Scotland ' claims a somewhat higher place. It partakes of
the history play and the novella, pretending to be borrowed
from Scotch annals, but relying for its interest upon a
romantic love-story. The induction might be mentioned as
an early instance of a very popular theatrical device. In
order to create more perfect illusion, or to enliven the pauses
between the acts with dialogue, our elder dramatists represented the real fruit of their invention as a play within a play,
feigning that the persons who first appeared upon the stage
fell asleep and saw the drama in a vision, or that it was con-
jured up by magic art before them, or that they chanced upon
some strange adventure while wandering in woody places.
The ' Taming of a Shrew,' before Shakspere touched it, was
already furnished with that humorous deception practised
upon Sly, which serves to introduce the comedy. Lyly
begged his audience to regard two of his pieces as dreams.
Peele caused the action of one of his rural medleys to grow
from a discussion between travellers belated in a forest.
Heywood in his Masque of ' Love's Mistress ' brings Midas
and Apuleius on the stage, disputing about poetry. The play
occurs as matter for their argument, and they canvass it at
intervals between the scenes. Jonson and Marston employed
similar artifices for blending criticism with the drama. Beaumont introduced the ' Knight of the Burning Pestle ' with a
humorous dialogue between a citizen and his wife who insist
upon their prentice taking part in the performance. The
introduction to Greene's ' James the Fourth ' brings Oberon
with his elves and a discontented Scot upon the stage. The
elves dance ; the Scot produces the play in order to explain
his discontent. Oberon remains as a spectator, and makes
mirth during the intervals by dances of his fairies. The
drama illustrates the miseries of states, when flatterers rule
the Court, and kings yield to lawless vice. In the portrait of
the Lady Ida, for whose love James deserts his wife and
plots her murder, Greene conceived and half expressed a true
woman's character. There is a simplicity, a perfume of

purity, in Ida, which proceeds from the poet's highest source of inspiration. Nor do the romantic adventures and pathetic trials of the queen fall far short of a melodramatic success. That this man, dissolute and vicious as he was, should have been the first of our playwrights to feel and represent the charm of maiden modesty upon the public stage, is not a little singular. Perhaps it was, in part, to this that Greene owed his popularity. Fawnia in 'Pandosto,' Margaret in 'Friar Bacon,' Sephestia in 'Menaphon,' Ida and Dorothea in 'James the Fourth,' Philomela and the Shepherd's Wife in the 'Mourning Garment,' belong to one sisterhood, in whom the innocence of country life, unselfish love, and maternity are sketched with delicate and feeling touches.

'Friar Bacon and Friar Bungay' takes its name from the famous Franciscan monk, and closely follows an old English version of his legend in one portion of the plot. The conjuring tricks and incantations of the Friar are cleverly interwoven with a romantic tale of Edward Prince of Wales's love for Margaret, the fair maid of Fresingfield; the Earl of Lincoln's honest treachery, who woos her for his lord and wins her for himself; and the history of her two suitors, Lambert and Serlsby, who, together with their sons, are parenthetically killed upon the stage. A double comic interest is sustained by Edward's Court fool Ralph, and Miles the servant of Bacon. Written by a clever story-teller, who, without a high ideal of art or deep insight into character could piece a tale together with variety of incidents, this play is decidedly interesting. The action never flags. Pretty scenes succeed each other: now pastoral at Fresingfield, now grave at Oxford, now terrible in Bacon's cell, now splendid at the Court, now humorous with Miles, the Friar's man. A jocund freshness of blithe country air blows through the piece, and its two threads of interest are properly combined in the conclusion. Edward pardons the Earl of Lincoln by giving him Margaret in marriage on the same day that he weds Eleanor of Castile. Friar Bacon forgoes his magic arts; and Miles, who is a lineal descendant of the Vice, dances off the stage upon a merry devil's back, promising to play the tapster in a certain thirsty place where 'men are marvellous dry.'

In his treatment of the magician, Greene differed widely from his friend Marlowe. Marlowe idealised the character of Faustus, using that legend for his interpretation of the criminal passion for unlawful power. Greene left Bacon as he found him in the popular romance—a necromancer, whose ambition is to circle England with a brazen wall; a conjurer with familiar spirits at his beck, the maker of the brazen head, and the possessor of a magic glass. His chief exploits are the discomfiture of various obnoxious personages, whom he spirits through the air or strikes with dumbness, and the service rendered to the Prince of Wales by suspending Margaret's marriage rites at the distance of many miles.

The language of the play, in spite of its essentially English character, is curiously defaced with superficial pedantry. The serious characters make use of classical mythology on all occasions. Young Edward describes the keeper's daughter of Fresingfield as 'sweeping like Venus through the house,' and 'shining among her cream-bowls as Pallas 'mongst her princely housewifery.' Margaret herself is no less glib with allusions to Semele and Paris and Œnone. But these flowers of rhetoric are mere excrescences upon a style of silvery simplicity. As a fair specimen of Greene's natural manner, I will quote a description of Oxford, first seen by King Henry and the Emperor riding over Magdalen Bridge:

> Trust me, Plantagenet, these Oxford schools
> Are richly seated near the river side:
> The mountains full of fat and fallow deer,
> The battling pastures lade with kine and flocks,
> The town gorgeous with high-built colleges,
> And scholars seemly in their grave attire,
> Learnèd in searching principles of art.

Writing in direct competition with Marlowe, and striving to produce 'strong lines,' Greene indulged in extravagant imagery, which, because it lacks the animating fire of

Marlowe's rapture, degenerates into mere bombast. The
Prince of Wales is wooing the keeper's daughter :

> I tell thee, Peggy, I will have thy loves:
> Edward or none shall conquer Margaret.
> In frigates bottomed with rich Sethin planks,
> Topt with the lofty firs of Lebanon,
> Stemmed and incased with burnished ivory,
> And over-laid with plates of Persian wealth,
> Like Thetis thou shalt wanton on the waves,
> And draw the dolphins to thy lovely eyes
> To dance lavoltas in the purple streams :
> Sirens, with harps and silver psalteries,
> Shall wait with music at thy frigate's stem,
> And entertain fair Margaret with their lays.

There is one good line here. ' Sirens with harps and silver
psalteries,' is pretty ; and the whole passage illustrates the
rococo of the English Renaissance which Marlowe made
fashionable.[1]

VII

Peele, though less prolific and many-sided than Greene,
early won and late retained the reputation of a better poet.
Nash, the friend of both, called him *primus verborum artifex*,
and ' an Atlas of poetry.' Campbell observes : ' We may
justly cherish the memory of Peele as the oldest genuine
dramatic poet of our language. His " David and Bethsabe "
is the earliest fountain of pathos and harmony that can be
traced in our dramatic poetry. His fancy is rich and his
feeling tender ; and his conceptions of dramatic character
have no inconsiderable mixture of solid veracity and ideal
beauty. There is no such sweetness of versification and
imagery to be found in our blank verse anterior to Shakspere.' This judgment, considering that Marlowe preceded
Shakspere, and formed the style of his immediate contem-

---

[1] See the description of Hero's buskins in *Hero and Leander*, and the
curious attire promised to the Shepherdess in ' Come, live with me.'
Marlowe's imitators loved to indulge this vein, as might be illustrated
from *Lust's Dominion*.

poraries, cannot be supported. Gifford places Peele, together
with Marlowe, at the point in our dramatic history when ' the
chaos of ignorance was breaking up : they were among the
earliest to perceive the glimmering of sense and nature, and
struggled to reach the light.' Lamb dismisses the Scriptural
play so highly praised by Campbell in one contemptuous
word, calling it ' stuff.' The truth is that Peele exercised far
less influence over the development of our Drama than either
Lyly or Greene, not to mention Marlowe. The Court
Comedies of Lyly and the romantic medleys of Greene led by
no uncertain steps to Shakspere's comedies of the imagination.
Marlowe determined the metre and fixed the form of tragedy.
Peele discovered no new vein. It is in elegant descriptions,
in graceful and ingenious employment of mythology, in
feeling for the charms of nature, in tenderness of expression
and sweetness of versification, that we find his highest poetical
qualities. These he possessed in an eminent degree, considering the age in which he lived. His best, but also his earliest,
work, the ' Arraignment of Paris,' is distinguished by a certain
sense of proportion, dignity of repose, and harmonious distribution of parts, which prove that he might have become a
correct poet in that period of bombast and exaggeration.
But his necessities forced him to follow the taste of the time ;
and the Calipolis of one of his romantic tragedies passed with
Cambyses and Tamburlaine into a by-word for extravagance.

Three of Peele's plays may be dismissed with a bare
mention. In the ' Chronicle of Edward ' he used a ballad
grossly libellous of Eleanor, the good queen. As Eleanor
was a Spaniard, it is not improbable that Peele displayed her
character in the worst light in order to court popularity at a
time when the prospect of a Spanish marriage was odious to
the English people. At any rate, ' Longshanks,' as the
Chronicle was called, became a favourite with the play-going
public, and kept the stage long after Peele and his associates
had been superseded by better playwrights. ' The Battle of
Alcazar,' like Greene's ' Alphonsus,' is a mere melodrama of
' sound and fury, signifying nothing.' The introduction of
the popular hero Thomas Stukeley, gives it a certain interest

To the student of dramatic evolution this play furnishes an excellent example of the machinery employed by our oldest writers, in order to make their scenes intelligible in the absence of proper theatrical apparatus. A Presenter appeared before each act and recited the argument, eking out his explanatory remarks with a dumb show or symbolical representation, so that the subject was analysed and exhibited in brief, and the minds of the spectators were prepared to follow the action with undisturbed attention. Fame, in the ' Battle of Alcazar,' enters the stage at the end of the fourth act. Thunder and lightning, comets and fireworks, herald her advent. The Presenter, hereupon, declares that danger menaces the kingdoms of Barbary, Morocco, and Portugal. Fame advances, and suspends three crowns upon the branches of a tree. In the hurly-burly of the tempest these are shaken down ; and as each falls, the Presenter pronounces the name of the ruined throne. It will be remembered that a Doctor or Expositor played a prominent part in the Miracles ; the Presenter is a survival of that antique functionary.[1]

Peele's ' Old Wives' Tale' deserves to be remembered because of its resemblance to ' Comus.' If Milton borrowed the conception of his Masque from this rustic comedy, he undoubtedly performed the proverbial miracle of making a silk purse out of a sow's ear. The mere outline of both pieces is the same. Two brothers, seeking a lost sister in a wood by night, find that she has fallen into the power of a sorcerer, from whom she cannot be rescued until his magic wreath has been torn off, his sword broken, and his lamp extinguished. Moreover, the instrumentality of a spirit is needed to accomplish her emancipation. So far the coincidence with ' Comus ' is manifest. But Peele takes no advantage of these romantic circumstances, either to point a moral or to lift his subject into the heavens of poetry. His heroine has actually become besotted by the wizard. The wizard is a

---

[1] Gower, in *Pericles,* presents the scenes and interprets the dumb shows. In the Second Part of *Henry IV.* Rumour is called the Presenter, but only speaks a prologue. In *Henry V.* a Chorus performs the Presenter's duty, but without dumb shows.

common conjurer. The spirit is a vulgar village ghost. In
nothing is the genius of a true poet more conspicuous than
in the intuition which enabled Milton to perceive that such
a dead thing might be pierced with 'inbreathed life' of art,
philosophy, and allegory. So far as the history of our drama
is concerned, the chief interest of the 'Old Wives' Tale' lies
in its setting.[1] Three clowns lose their way in a wood, and
come by chance upon a poor smith's cottage. There is not
room for all of them to sleep in bed; so the smith's wife
proposes to keep them waking with a merry tale. She begins
a rambling story about giants, conjurers, and princesses,
hopelessly confusing herself in the labyrinth of her narrative,
and suffering divers interruptions from her audience. Then
the real actors—the two brothers—enter, lamenting in blank
verse their sister's loss. The smith's wife hereupon suspends
her tale, and, with the clowns, hears out the piece and
comments on its incidents.

Peele's earliest essay in dramatic writing was 'The
Arraignment of Paris,' a Classical Masque or Court Comedy
in honour of Elizabeth. Printed in 1584, this 'first increase'
of his wit, as Nash calls it, can have owed nothing to Lyly.
It shows no traces of Lyly's style, and is moreover written,
not in prose, but in a variety of rhyming metres and blank
verse. The scene opens with an assembly of the rural gods
in Ida. Pan, Faun, and Sylvan have met 'to bid Queen Juno
and her feres most humble welcome hither.' Pomona joins
them with a gift of fruit, and Flora scatters flowers upon the
meadow. When the three great ladies of Olympus enter,
these rustic deities, who play the part of foresters and wood-
men, invite them to the simple pleasures of a *fête champêtre*.
Then the scene changes to a grove, where Paris and Œnone
are discoursing of their loves. He pipes, and she sings that
well-known roundelay, which has for its refrain the curse of
Cupid:

> They that do change old loves for new,
> Pray gods they change for worse.

---

[1] See above, p. 447.

In the second act, Ate's golden ball, inscribed with the fatal words *Detur pulcherrimæ*, is discovered by the goddesses, who refer their claims to Paris. Each speaks in turn, offering the shepherd gifts to sway his judgment. Juno says:

> Shepherd!
> I will reward thee with great monarchies,
> Empires and kingdoms, heaps of massy gold,
> Sceptres and diadems.

Pallas disdains these trivial bribes:

> Me list not tempt thee with decaying wealth . . .
> But if thou have a mind to fly above,
> If thou aspire to wisdom's worthiness,
> If thou desire honour of chivalry,
> To fight it out, and in the champaign field
> To shroud thee under Pallas' warlike shield,
> To prance on barbèd steeds; this honour, lo,
> Myself for guerdon shall on thee bestow.

Venus speaks of love after the wanton fashion of the sixteenth century, and reveals a stationary figure of Helen attired 'in all her bravery.' Helen sings an Italian sonnet, while attendant Cupids ' fan fresh air in her face.' Paris decides that if beauty is to have the ball, it must belong to Venus. With this verdict the rival goddesses are dissatisfied, and the shepherd is arraigned before the high court of Olympus. Mercury, sent down to summon Paris, finds him conversing with Venus, who describes the punishment of infidelity:

> In hell there is a tree,
> Where once a day do sleep the souls of false forsworn lovers,
> With open hearts; and thereabout in swarms the number hovers
> Of poor forsaken ghosts whose wings from off this tree do beat
> Round drops of fiery Phlegethon to scorch false hearts with heat.

Paris is now conducted to the council of the gods, before whom he stands and pleads:

> A mortal man amid this heavenly presence.

He denies the charge of partiality and corruption, arguing that the apple was due to pre-eminent beauty. His speech is eloquent and powerful. The gods admire his manliness,

applaud his verdict, and send him back to earth. But Juno
and Pallas being still unsatisfied, Venus lays her prize before
the male gods, and leaves them to adjudicate. Jupiter,
between the claims of justice and his fear of Juno, is perplexed. Vulcan's jealousy prevents him from supporting
Venus. Saturn takes no interest in so insignificant a contest.
At length Apollo rises, declares that women must be judged
by women, and refers the suit to Diana. This leads to the
catastrophe. In the last act Diana delivers her sentence to
the satisfaction of all. She describes England and Elizabeth
in glowing language, hyperbolical and tender, such as the old
poets used when treating of so dear a theme. The Fates, she
says, intend that day to shower upon the maiden monarch all
their choicest gifts. Let the goddesses go too, and lay the
apple at Eliza's feet. This they do with cheerful acquiescence,
and the play ends with an epilogue sung by all the actors :

> Vive diu felix votis hominumque deumque,
> Corpore mente libro doctissima candida casta.

This solution of the plot, though extravagantly flattering, is
both ingenious and felicitous ; and the whole play deserves high
praise for its artistic construction.

' David and Bethsabe,' regarded by some of Peele's critics
as his masterpiece, presents us with a curious specimen of the
Miracle Play in its most modern form. Joab, Abishai, and
Jonadab discourse in the euphuistic language of the period ;
but when we reflect that they probably wore trunk-hose and
ruffs, the inconsistency does not appear so glaring. Peele
endeavoured to invest his imagery with Oriental splendour ;
nor has he altogether failed. David's passion is expressed in
glowing hyperboles. Metaphors borrowed from the Song of
Solomon recur throughout the piece ; and when we read of
the

> Kingly bower,
> Seated in hearing of a hundred streams,

through which the mistress of the king comes ' tripping like a
roe,' bringing his ' longings tangled in her hair,' we feel that

some measure of inspiration was granted to the poet. There is imagination, though of a turbid and plethoric species, in the following apostrophe to Tamar on her shameful love :

> Fair Thamar, now dishonour hunts thy foot,
> And follows thee through every covert shade,
> Discovering thy shame and nakedness,
> Even from the valley of Jehosophat
> Up to the lofty mounts of Lebanon ;
> Where cedars, stirred with anger of the winds,
> Sounding in storms the tale of thy disgrace,
> Tremble with fury, and with murmur shake
> Earth with their feet and with their heads the heavens,
> Beating the clouds into their swiftest rack,
> To bear this wonder round about the world.

That is Cambyses' vein applied to what Mr. Ruskin calls the 'pathetic fallacy '—the greatest powers of nature in commotion, storms rushing through the length of Palestine, immemorial cedars shaken on their everlasting hills, the depths below and heights above, all agitated by the story of a woman's shame.

It is doubtful whether a dull rhyming play entitled ' Sir Clyomon and Sir Clamydes ' be Peele's. Anyhow, it does not call for comment. I prefer to quote some lines from the warlike ode addressed to Sir John Norris and Sir Francis Drake upon the eve of their disastrous expedition to Portugal. Written when the defeat of the Armada was yet fresh, it glows with the awakened spirit of the English nation, and sounds a clarion note of what would now be called Elizabethan Jingoism :

> Bid theatres and proud tragedians,
> Bid Mahomet, Scipio,[1] and mighty Tamburlane,
> King Charlemagne, Tom Stukeley, and the rest,
> Adieu. To arms, to arms, to glorious arms !
> With noble Norris, and victorious Drake,
> Under the sanguine cross brave England's badge
> To propagate religious piety,

---

[1] Is this rightly corrected ? Or should we adopt *Hoo* or *Howe*? The old copies give *Poo*, I believe.

And hew a passage with your conquering swords
By land and sea, wherever Phœbus' eye,
Th' eternal lamp of heaven, lends us light;
By golden Tagus, or the western Inde,
Or through the spacious bay of Portugal,
The wealthy ocean-main, the Tyrrhene sea,
From great Alcides' pillars branching forth
Even to the gulf that leads to lofty Rome;
There to deface the pride of Antichrist,
And pull his paper walls and popery down,—
A famous enterprise for England's strength,
To steel your swords on avarice's triple crown,
And cleanse Augeas' stalls in Italy.
To arms! my fellow soldiers! Sea and land
Lie open to the voyage you intend;
And sea or land, bold Britons, far or near,
Whatever course your matchless virtue shapes,
Whether to Europe's bounds or Asian plains,
To Afric's shore, or rich America,
Down to the shades of deep Avernus' crags,
Sail on, pursue your honours to your graves:
Heaven is a sacred covering for your heads,
And every climate virtue's tabernacle.
To arms, to arms, to honourable arms!
Hoise sails, weigh anchors up, plough up the seas
With flying keels, plough up the land with swords:
In God's name venture on; and let me say
To you, my mates, as Cæsar said to his,
Striving with Neptune's hills; 'you bear,' quoth he,
'Cæsar and Cæsar's fortune in your ships.'
You follow them whose swords successful are;
You follow Drake, by sea the scourge of Spain,
The dreadful dragon, terror to your foes,
Victorious in his return from Inde,
In all his high attempts unvanquishèd;
You follow noble Norris, whose renown
Won in the fertile fields of Belgia,
Spread by the gates of Europe to the courts
Of Christian kings and heathen potentates;
You fight for Christ and England's peerless Queen
Elizabeth, the wonder of the world,
Over whose throne the enemies of God
Have thundered erst their vain successless braves.
O, ten-times-treble happy men that fight

> Under the cross of Christ, and England's Queen,
> And follow such as Drake and Norris are !

The same spirit animates Peele's poem on the Order of the Garter.   The first knights or Founders of the Garter are thus enumerated : [1]

> Edward, Prince of Wales,
> Was first ; then Henry, Duke of Lancaster ;
> And Nicholas, Earl of Warwick, made the third ;
> Captain de Buch was next, renowned for arms ;
> Then the brave Earls of Stafford and Southampton,
> And Mortimer, a gentle, trusty lord ;
> Then Lisle, and Burghersh, Beauchamp, and Mohun,
> Grey, Courtenay, and the Hollands, worthy knights,
> Fitz-Simon, Wale, and Sir Hugh Wrottesley,
> Nele Loring, Chandos, Sir Miles Stapleton,
> Walter Pagannel, Eam, and D'Audley ; last
> Was the good knight Sir Sanchet D'Abrichecourt.

VIII

Thomas Nash claims a place of no little importance in the history of English prose.   His pamphlets, modelled upon those in vogue among Italian writers of the school of Aretine, display a trenchant wit and a directness in the use of language, which were rare in that age.   He was a born satirist, hitting hard, abstaining from rhetorical parades of erudition, sketching a caricature with firm and broad touches, and coining pithy epigrams which stung like poisoned arrows.   No writer before Nash, and few since his death, have used the English language as an instrument of pure invective with more complete mastery and originality of manner.   Returning from an Italian journey in the summer of 1588, Nash joined Greene's circle, and began to employ his pen at the dictation of the Bishops Whitgift and Bancroft in the Martin Marprelate dispute.   It was his chief literary exploit to bring the matter of ecclesiastical debate from the pulpit down into

---

[1] Piety to these knights of the French wars, among whom I count a collateral ancestor, Sir Richard Fitz-Simon, rather than admiration for the poetry of this passage, makes me print these lines.

the market-place, and to disarm a cumbrous antagonist by
ridicule and scurrilous abuse instead of argument and dissertation. Thus much in the art of controversy Nash had
learned from the Italian humanists and their successors, the
Venetian pamphleteers. But these foreign weapons he used
with the coarse vigour and grotesque humour of an Englishman. His lampoons attracted immediate intention. Their
style was imitated but not equalled by Lodge, Lyly, and
others. Nash acquired a sudden and a lasting reputation as
the first and most formidable satirist of his epoch. His
name is always coupled with some epithet like 'gallant
Juvenal,' the 'English Aretine,' and 'railing' Nash. The
friendship he formed with Greene was close, and lasted to
the end of that unhappy poet's life. Nash, it is said, assisted
at the supper which resulted in Greene's fatal illness. After
his comrade's death he was drawn into a famous word-con-
flict with Gabriel Harvey, the Cambridge pedant and friend
of Spenser, who currishly vented his spleen against the dead
man in a clumsy satire. Nash took the cudgels up, and
overwhelmed Harvey with such abuse as he alone could hurl
at an antagonist, pouring forth pamphlet after pamphlet of
the bitterest sarcasm and most voluble denunciation. Harvey
responded, as well as his more lumbering wits were able ; till
at last the See of Canterbury intervened with an order that
the tracts hitherto published by both champions should be
taken up and destroyed, and that no printer should regale
the public with any further libels from their scandalous pens.
Enough attention has been called on various occasions and
by several critics to these obsolete literary conflicts. In a
survey of the Elizabethan stage, it is not needful to revert to
them, except with the purpose of characterising an author,
who, while he was the first pamphleteer, took rank as one of
the least eminent among the many playwrights of his age.
Yet one word may still be added upon a prose tract, rather
autobiographical than controversial, in which Nash has bequeathed to us some interesting sketches of contemporary
London manners. 'Pierce Penniless, his Supplication to the
Devil,' was clearly written to relieve its author's necessities.

The introduction sets forth in grave and heartfelt terms the discouragement of a scholar driven to desperate shifts and seduced to evil courses by the neglect of patrons and the difficulty of making a livelihood out of literature. It confirms the truth of Greene's dying appeal to his Bohemian companions, and illustrates the miserable position of those academical writers, cast adrift in London without a fixed employment or a recognised profession, who were doomed, less by their own fault than by the adverse circumstances of the literary life as they pursued it, to failure, indigence, and early death. The London of Elizabeth had in fact its Grub Street no less than the London of Queen Anne. 'Pierce Penniless' is further valuable for the series of animated portraits it contains, studied from the life and representing types of character about town. To these and to the incidental defence of stage-plays, which Nash found occasion to introduce, I shall return at the proper opportunity.

Nash's fame as a dramatist rests upon three plays. The first of these, and probably the most characteristic of his genius, was never printed. It bore the title of the 'Isle of Dogs,' was possibly, but not certainly, a political satire, and cost its author an imprisonment in gaol. This punishment brought him, however, rather reputation than disgrace. Meres, in his 'Palladis Tamia,' alludes kindly to the incident: 'Dogs were the death of Euripides; but be not disconsolate, gallant young Juvenal; Linus, the son of Apollo, died the same death. Yet God forbid that so brave a wit should so basely perish! Thine are but paper dogs; neither is thy banishment, like Ovid's, eternally to converse with the barbarous Getes.' When Nash came out of prison, he took credit to himself for the past consequences of his caustic speech; whence we may infer that, if not political, the satire of his 'Isle of Dogs' concerned some persons of importance, to libel whom was not less honourable than perilous.

Nash had some share, but what share it is impossible to settle, in a dramatic adaptation of the Fourth Æneid, which appeared in 1594 under Marlowe's name. It is possible

that the MS. was left unfinished, and that Nash, a friend of
Marlowe, did no more than to edit and prepare it for the
stage. All that is original and striking in this tragedy,
especially the opening scene in Olympus, and the part
assigned to Cupid, may with certainty be ascribed to Marlowe. There remains, perhaps, a sufficiency of plain pedestrian blank verse, to establish the inferior poet's title to
collaboration. But after careful study of ' Queen Dido,' I
am inclined to think that Nash's share in it was small, and
that the play was one of Marlowe's earlier essays, thrust
aside for some uncertain reason, and brought forth when
death had added lustre to his name. It abounds in rhyming
lines and assonances, which points to an early date of composition ; but its style is distinguished throughout by traces
of Marlowe's peculiar manner.

Of what dramatic work, in conception and in versification,
Nash himself was capable, is apparent from his sole surviving
piece, ' Will Summer's Testament.' This is a Court Comedy,
or Show, without a plot, depending for its now evaporated
interest on learned quips and fashionable cranks served up
with masquerade and satire for the Queen's amusement. It
represents a bygone phase of taste, before the world had
learned to read, when word-of-mouth tirades on things in
general had their savour. The motive is a play of words
maintained upon the name of Summer. Will Summer, the
Court fool of Henry VIII., whose portrait by Holbein still
exists at Kensington, speaks prologue, and conducts the
piece. He or his ghost appears in clown's costume, and
nodding to the audience, opens with : ' I'll show you what a
scurvy prologue our play-maker has made in an old vein of
similitudes.' Summer then pulls forth and reads a pompous
parody of Euphuism in a long preposterously laboured diatribe of nonsense. This, when he has played with it for a few
paragraphs, the fool tosses carelessly aside, and speaks in his
own person to the audience. ' How say you, my masters ?
Do you not laugh at him for a coxcomb ? Why, he hath
made a prologue longer than his play ! Nay, 'tis no play
neither, but a show.' After this box-on-the-ears to Lyly

Summer, the Season, enters, holds his Court, reviews the revolutions of the year, and makes his will, reserving all the honours of the prime to Queen Elizabeth :

> Unto Eliza, that most sacred dame,
> Whom none but saints and angels ought to name.

While the Seasons in their masquing dresses pass across the stage and furnish forth appropriate entertainment, Summer, the Court fool, sits by and comments. To modern readers the fun of the show, if fun it ever had, is withered and gone by—more withered than the roses, and more wasted than the snows of yester-year. 'Ingenious, fluent, facetious Thomas Nash,' wrote genial Dekker; 'from what abundant pen flowed honey to thy friends, and mortal aconite to thy enemies!' Alas, poor Tom Nash! Little enough is left of thee, thy humour and thy satire! The men of our days cannot taste thy honey, and thy aconite has lost its venom. Dust too are the pedants and the puritans on whom it was so freely spilt. Yet something still survives from this dry *caput mortuum* of an ephemeral medley. The first lyric printed in the 'Golden Treasury,' that gift-book to all children of our time and *vade-mecum* of all lovers of old literature, is a spring song from 'Will Summer's Testament.' Nor is there wanting in its scenes a second ditty, of less general application, but sweeter still and sadder, in which the dying Summer proves that our 'young gallant Juvenal' was a real poet. Let one of its stanzas serve to vindicate this claim, and satisfy his disappointed ghost :

> Beauty is but a flower,
> Which wrinkles will devour:
> Brightness falls from the air;
> Queens have died young and fair:
> Dust hath closed Helen's eye:
> I am sick, I must die.
> Lord, have mercy on us!

IX

One more dramatist of Greene's brood must be mentioned. Thomas Lodge, Lord Mayor's son, master of arts, law student, perhaps actor, buccaneer, physician, poet of Scylla and of Rosalynde, satirist of manners, defender of the stage, exposer of money-lenders and their myrmidons—this man of multifarious ability and chequered experience, was also a playwright. In proportion to his other works, the plays of Lodge are insignificant. He aided his friend Greene in 'The Looking Glass for London,' and quarried a tragedy from Plutarch on the rivalries of Marius and Sylla. 'The Wounds of Civil War' is disappointing in execution—especially in the versification, which shows no effort to profit by Marlowe's invention, and in the comic parts, which fall below the usual level of such stuff. Lodge may indeed be credited with an honest effort to trace firm outlines of his principal male characters. Yet his reputation as an English poet will not rest upon this lifeless play, but on the charming lyrics which are scattered through his novels.

X

It is time to leave the little coterie of friends who clustered around Greene in London, and to concentrate attention upon Marlowe, himself a member of their society, but far superior in all qualities which make a dramatist and poet. In the prose romances of this group, the influence of Lyly's style is still discernible. But Greene marks a new departure in dramatic literature. The romantic play, the English Farsa, may be called in a great measure his discovery. Nash marks a no less noticeable departure in the prose of controversy and satire. Peele is a sweet versifier and an

---

[1] Lodge has found so genial and able an expositor in Mr. Gosse, that I have purposely curtailed the above notice of his interesting career and distinguished literary work. See the first essay in that charming collection, *Seventeenth Century Studies*, by G. W. Gosse.

artist gifted with a sense of proportion unusual in his age.
Lodge distinguishes himself as a rarely musical and natural
lyrist.   Marlowe, intervening at the height of Greene's
popularity, imposed his style in a measure on these contemporaries.   But none of them were able effectively to profit by
the contact of this fiery spirit.   He took the town by storm;
they adopted some of his inventions, without understanding
their importance and without assimilating the more potent
influences of his art.

CHAPTER XV

MARLOWE

I

Of the life of Christopher Marlowe very little is known. He was a shoemaker's son, born at Canterbury in 1564—two months earlier than Shakspere at Stratford—and was educated at the King's School in that town. He entered Benet College,

Cambridge, as a Pensioner, in 1581, and after taking his B.A. degree came up to seek his fortune in London, 'a boy in years, a man in genius, a god in ambition,' as Swinburne no less truly than finely writes of the young Titan of the stage. It is more than probable that Marlowe, under the influence perhaps of Francis Kett, who was a Fellow of Benet College in 1573, and was burned at Norwich in 1589 for anti-Christian heresy, had already contracted opinions which closed a clerical career against him, and which rendered any of the recognised professions distasteful. Be this as it may, he was indubitably born a poet, and nothing but the exercise of his already full-grown genius could have satisfied his nature. The most remarkable point to notice about Marlowe is that he served no apprenticeship to art, and went to school with none of the acknowledged masters of his age. His first extant tragedy shows him in possession of a new style, peculiar to himself, representative of his own temperament, and destined by its force, attractiveness, and truth to revolutionise the practice of all elder playwrights and contemporaries. The demand for plays in public theatres was sufficient at this epoch to make dramatic authorship fairly profitable. The society of the green-room and the stage, in revolt against conventions and tolerant of eccentricities in conduct and opinion, suited the wild and ardent spirit of a man who thirsted lawlessly for pleasure and forbidden things. Marlowe does not seem to have hesitated in his choice of life, but threw his lot in frankly with the libertines and reprobates, whose art he raised from insignificance to power and beauty. No sooner had his imagination given birth to the first part of 'Tamburlaine' than he became the idol of the town.[1]

Marlowe took his Master's degree in 1587, and before this date 'Tamburlaine' had been performed. The rest of his

---

[1] If we could trust the genuineness of an old ballad, *The Atheist's Tragedy*, published by Dyce at the end of his edition of Marlowe's works, we should believe that Marlowe began his theatrical career as an actor at the Curtain, where he broke his leg. But the ballad in question, printed from a MS. in the possession of the late Mr. J. P. Collier, has to be classified with other dubious materials furnished by that ingenious student, on which a cautious critic will prefer to found no theories.

short life was spent in writing tragedies for money. What he gained by his pen he is said to have squandered among the frequenters of suburban taverns. Puritans, who did their best to stigmatise the morals of the stage, described him as a blasphemer and notorious evil-liver. We cannot feel sure that their portrait of the man was substantially correct; though Greene's address to Marlowe on his death-bed makes it appear that, even among his intimate friends, he had gained a reputation for insolent atheism. His end was tragic: a rival in some love adventure stabbed him with his own dagger in a tavern at Deptford. This was in 1593, before the completion of his thirtieth year. If we assign the first part of ' Tamburlaine' to 1587, this gives a period of some six years to Marlowe's activity as an author. Within that brief space of time he successively produced the second part of 'Tamburlaine,' 'Dr. Faustus,' 'The Massacre at Paris,' 'The Jew of Malta,' and 'Edward II.' These tragedies were performed during their author's lifetime; and though it is impossible to fix their order with any certainty, internal evidence of style justifies us in assigning the two last-named plays to the later years of his life, while the two 'Tamburlaines' are undoubtedly among the earliest fruits of his genius. At his death he left an unfinished drama on the tragedy of 'Dido,' which I am inclined to refer to the beginning of his career as playwright. It shows a still imperfect command of blank verse and a hesitation between that measure and rhyme, which does not belong to the poet's maturity. In addition to these dramatic works Marlowe bequeathed to the world the fragment of a narrative poem, which stands higher in poetic quality, both of conception and execution, than any similar work of the Elizabethan age, not excepting Shakspere's 'Venus and Adonis.' I mean, of course, the 'Hero and Leander.' The translation into blank verse of the first book of Lucan's 'Pharsalia' may pass for an exercise in Marlowe's own 'licentiate iambic' metre. The rhymed translation of Ovid's 'Amores,' which an Archbishop of Canterbury and a Bishop of London thought worthy of public burning, may also be regarded as an exercise prelusive to that liberal use of

the couplet in 'Hero and Leander,' whereby Marlowe stamped
rhyming heroic verse with his own seal no less emphatically
than he had stamped unrhymed heroic verse in 'Tamburlaine.'
A few minor pieces, including the beautiful and well-known
pastoral, 'Come live with me and be my love,' complete the
tale of the young poet's contributions to our literature.

II

Marlowe has been styled, and not unjustly styled, the father
of English dramatic poetry. When we reflect on the conditions of the stage before he produced 'Tamburlaine,' and
consider the state in which he left it after the appearance of
'Edward II.,' we shall be able to estimate his true right to
this title. Art, like Nature, does not move by sudden leaps
and bounds. It required a slow elaboration of divers elements,
the formation of a public able to take interest in dramatic
exhibitions, the determination of the national taste toward
the romantic rather than the classic type of art, and all the
other circumstances which have been dwelt upon in the preceding studies, to render Marlowe's advent as decisive as it
proved. Before he began to write, various dramatic species
had been essayed with more or less success. Comedies
modelled in form upon the types of Plautus and Terence ;
tragedies conceived in the spirit of Seneca ; chronicles rudely
arranged in scenes for representation ; dramatised novels and
tales of private life ; Court comedies of compliment and
allegory ; had succeeded to the religious Miracles and ethical
Moralities. There was plenty of productive energy, plenty of
enthusiasm and activity. Theatres continued to spring up,
and acting came to rank among the recognised professions.
But this activity was still chaotic. None could say where or
whether the germ of a great national art existed. To us,
students of the past, it is indeed clear enough in what
direction lay the real life of the drama ; but this was not
apparent to contemporaries. Scholars despised the shows of
mingled bloodshed and buffoonery in which the populace
delighted. The people had no taste for dry and formal dis-

quisitions in the style of 'Gorboduc.' The blank verse of
Sackville and Hughes rang hollow; the prose of Lyly was
affected; the rhyming couplets of the popular theatre interfered with dialogue and free development of character. The
public itself was divided in its tastes and instincts; the mob
inclining to mere drolleries and merriments upon the stage,
the better vulgar to formalities and studied imitations. A
powerful body of sober citizens, by no means wholly composed
of Puritans and ascetics, regarded all forms of dramatic art
with undisguised hostility. Meanwhile, no really great poet
had arisen to stamp the tendencies of either Court or town
with the authentic seal of genius. There seemed a danger lest
the fortunes of the stage in England should be lost between
the prejudices of a literary class, the puerile and lifeless pastimes of the multitude, and the disfavour of conservative
moralists. From this peril Marlowe saved the English
drama. Amid the chaos of conflicting elements he discerned
the true and living germ of art, and set its growth beyond all
risks of accident by his achievement.

When, therefore, we style Marlowe the father and
founder of English dramatic poetry, we mean that he perceived the capacities for noble art inherent in the Romantic
Drama, and proved its adaptation to high purpose by his
practice. Out of confusion he brought order, following
the clue of his own genius through a labyrinth of dim
unmastered possibilities. Like all great craftsmen, he
worked by selection and exclusion on the whole mass of
material ready to his hand; and his instinct in this double
process is the proof of his originality. He adopted the
romantic drama in lieu of the classic, the popular instead of
the literary type. But he saw that the right formal vehicle,
blank verse, had been suggested by the school which he
rejected. Rhyme, the earlier metre of the romantic drama,
had to be abandoned. Blank verse, the metre of the pedants,
had to be accepted. To employ blank verse in the romantic
drama was the first step in his revolution. But this was
only the first step. Both form and matter had alike to be
transfigured. And it was precisely in this transfiguration of

the right dramatic metre, in this transfiguration of the right
dramatic stuff, that Marlowe showed himself a creative poet.
What we call the English, or the Elizabethan, or better
perhaps the Shaksperian Drama, came into existence by this
double process. Marlowe found the public stage abandoned
to aimless trivialities, but abounding in the rich life of the
nation, and with the sympathies of the people firmly enlisted
on the side of its romantic presentation. He introduced a
new class of heroic subjects, eminently fitted for dramatic
handling. He moulded characters, and formed a vigorous
conception of the parts they had to play. Under his touch
the dialogue moved with spirit ; men and women spoke and
acted with the energy and spontaneity of nature. He found
the blank verse of the literary school monotonous, tame,
nerveless, without life or movement. But he had the tact to
understand its vast capacities, so vastly wider than its makers
had divined, so immeasurably more elastic than the rhymes
for which he substituted its sonorous cadence. Marlowe,
first of Englishmen, perceived how noble was the instrument
he handled, how well adapted to the closest reasoning, the
sharpest epigram, the loftiest flight of poetry, the subtlest
music, and the most luxuriant debauch of fancy. Touched
by his hands the thing became an organ capable of rolling
thunders and of whispering sighs, of moving with pompous
volubility or gliding like a silvery stream, of blowing trumpet-
blasts to battle or sounding the soft secrets of a lover's heart.
I do not assert that Marlowe made it discourse music of so
many moods. But what he did with it, unlocked the secrets
of the verse, and taught successors how to play upon its
hundred stops. He found it what Greene calls a 'drumming
decasyllabon.' Each line stood alone, formed after the same
model, ending with a strongly accented monosyllable.
Marlowe varied the pauses in its rhythm ; combined the
structure of succeeding verses into periods ; altered the
incidence of accent in many divers forms and left the metre
fit to be the vehicle of Shakspere's or of Milton's thought.
Compared with either of those greatest poets, Marlowe, as a
versifier, lacks indeed variety of cadence, and palls our sense

of melody by emphatic magniloquence. The pomp of his
' mighty line ' tends to monotony ; nor was he quite sure in his
employment of the instrument which he discovered and
divined. The finest bursts of metrical music in his dramas
seem often the result of momentary inspiration rather than
the studied style of a deliberate artist.[1]

This adaptation of blank verse to the romantic drama,
this blending of classic form with popular material, and the
specific heightening of both form and matter by the application of poetic genius to the task, constitutes Marlowe's
claims to be styled the father and the founder of our stage.
We are so accustomed to Shakspere that it is not easy to
estimate the full importance of his predecessor's revolution.
Once again, therefore, let us try to bear in mind the three
cardinal points of Marlowe's originality. In the first place,
he saw that the romantic drama, the drama of the public
theatres, had a great future before it. In the second place,
he saw that the playwrights of the classic school had
discovered the right dramatic metre. In the third place, he
raised both matter and metre, the subjects of the romantic
and the verse of the classic school, to heights as yet unappre-
hended in his days. Into both he breathed the breath of
life ; heroic, poetic, artistic, vivid with the spirit of his age.
From the chaotic and conflicting elements around him he
drew forth the unity of English Drama, and produced the
thing which was to be so great, is still so perfect.

Marlowe was fully aware of his object. The few and
seemingly negligent lines which serve as prologue to ' Tamburlaine,' written probably when he was a youth of twenty-
two, set forth his purpose in plain terms :

> From jigging veins of rhyming mother-wits,
> And such conceits as clownage keeps in pay,

---

[1] These remarks on Marlowe's use of Blank Verse remain much as I
first wrote them in September 1864. Their substance I have already
published in *Cornhill* essays on ' The Drama of Elizabeth and James ' and
' Blank Verse ' (1865-6) and a *Pall Mall Gazette* article on ' Marlowe '
(1867). After nearly twenty years I do not see reason to modify in any
essential points the panegyric I then penned, and which has been far
more eloquently uttered since by Mr. Swinburne.

> We 'll lead you to the stately tent of war ;
> Where you shall hear the Scythian Tamburlaine
> Threatening the world with high astounding terms,
> And scourging kingdoms with his conquering sword.

In other words, Marlowe undertakes to wean the public from its drolleries and merriments. He advertises a metre hitherto unused upon the popular stage. He promises an entertainment in which heroic actions shall be displayed with the pomp of a new style. The puerilities of clownage are to retire into the second place. Yet the essential feature of the romantic drama, its power to fascinate and please a public audience, is not to be abandoned.

III

The importance of Blank Verse in the history of English poetry, especially dramatic poetry, is so great that Marlowe's innovations in the use of it demand a somewhat lengthy introduction, in order that their scope may be understood.

The single line, or unit, in a blank verse period is a line of normally five accents, of which the final accent falls on the last syllable, or, if that syllable be not definitely accented, is supplied by the closing pause.[1] It consists frequently, but by no means invariably, of ten syllables. It has usually, but not inevitably, a more or less discernible pause, falling after the fourth or the sixth syllable. Out of these determinations, it is possible to make or to select a typical line—the normal line of English heroic rhythm. And for this purpose we can do no better than choose the one indicated by Johnson from Milton :

> Love lights his lamp, and waves his purple wing.

Here it will be noticed we get five accents regularly falling on the second syllable of each foot, and a pause marked at the

---

[1] As the terminal syllable in the classical metres may be long or short, so the terminal syllable in blank verse may be accented or unaccented, the close of the verse sufficing. Sophocles ends a line, e.g., with ἐλαύνετε, and Shakspere one with *alacrity*. This observation might lead to further remarks upon what quantity and accent have in common, metrically speaking ; but the inquiry would be too long.

end of the fourth syllable. Such a line may be termed the ideal line of English heroic prosody; and it is our business to keep its scheme somewhere, in however shadowy a shape, present to our mind, in order to appreciate and judge the almost innumerable declensions from the type, which constitute the variety and beauty of the metre in the handling of great masters.

This line, which has become the standard metre of serious English poetry in epic, story, idyll, satire, drama, elegy, and meditative lyric, had been used from early times anterior to its application to blank verse. Chaucer and his followers employed it in the couplet and rime royal; Surrey, Wyatt, and Sidney in the sonnet; Spenser in the stanzas of the 'Faery Queen.' But in the hands of these masters, and applied to these purposes, the verse was still subservient to rhyme. Surrey, in his translation of the ' Æneid,' was the first poet who attempted to free the measure from this servitude. It is supposed that, in making his experiment, he followed Italian models. The Italian heroic verse, a line of five accents, but commonly of eleven syllables, and not distinguished by a normal pause, had undergone a similar transition from rhymed to unrhymed usage. Employed at first in the terza rima of Dante, the ottava rima of Boccaccio. the sonnet of Petrarch, it had been emancipated from rhyme by Trissino, Rucellai, and Alamanni, writers of tragic, epic, and didactic poems. Among the Italians the transformed measure acquired the name of *versi sciolti*, or verse freed from rhyme. Surrey is presumed to have imitated the example of these poets when he attempted what we call Blank Verse—verse, that is, where the rhymes are blank or vacant. We may, at any rate, affirm that Surrey's innovation rested on the same scholastic basis as that of his Italian predecessors. The humanistic tendencies of the Renaissance referred all canons of artistic method to classical precedents. The ancients did not rhyme. It seemed, therefore, right and reasonable to these students of antiquity that rhyme should be discarded. From this deliberate act of reasoning proceeded the effort to dispense with rhyme in the Italian *versi sciolti* and in English blank verse. When the effort had been made in England, and the practice of a hundred play-wrights had proved it successful, Milton theorised the system in his preface to ' Paradise Lost ' : [1]

> The measure is English Heroic Verse, without Rime, as that of Homer in Greek, and of Virgil in Latin ; Rime being no necessary Adjunct or true Ornament of Poem or good Verse, in longer Works especially, but the Invention of a barbarous Age, to set off wretched Matter and lame Meeter.

It was thus, obeying humanistic and Italian influences, that Surrey, followed by Sackville, Norton, and Hughes, first discarded rhyme in the verse of five accents. Under the same influences, Sidney and his coterie of learned poets attempted the Hexameter, the Sapphic, Asclepiad, and other unrhymed classic metres in the English tongue. The success of their experiments was slight. These Latin measures never took root in our literature ; whereas blank verse was destined to a brilliant future. The reason for this difference is obvious. Sapphics, hexameters, asclepiads, and so forth, are metres based on the principle of quantitative scansion, the effect of which can be but poorly and awkwardly imitated by means of accent. They are exotic to the English system of versification in form and structure. The heroic line, on the contrary, is native to our language ; combining, as the language itself combines, indigenous Teutonic and exotic Latin qualities. The omission of the rhyme, to which it was originally linked, does not structurally alter it—although, as will be afterwards observed, this omission very essentially affects the mode of its employment and the metrical effects of which it can be made the vehicle.

The cultivated poets who first employed this unrhymed verse, were struck with the similarity it offered to the Iambic measure of the ancients. Having studied prosody in Greek and Latin metres, they applied the classical nomenclature of quantitative scansion to English rhythms. At the same time

[1] Ascham, in *The Schoolmaster*, said all that needed to be said about the place of rhyme in English poetry and its omission, before Milton made his dictatorial remarks.

they overlooked this important circumstance, that the heroic
line fell short of the Greek senarius by one whole foot.
Hence, in the very origin of metrical criticism, a slight but
not insignificant confusion was introduced ; for terms which
are proper to a quantitative system, and rules which govern
the Greek tragic senarius, will never exactly suit another
rhythm and a shorter line constructed on the principle of
accent.   Iambs, trochees, dactyls, anapæsts, and other
classical feet, from choriambi to molossi, can indeed be found
in every language, and may be observed even in verses which
do not owe to them their melody.   These feet represent fixed
relations in the value of syllables ; the word *harmony* in
English, for example, is both by quantity and accent a dactyl.
But the detection of these feet in accentual verses does not
throw any clear light on their scansion.   It may even lead to
such misapprehensions of metrical laws as Collier made, when
he described Marlowe's lines of five accents and eleven
syllables as iambic lines closed with trochees ; or as Todd
made, when he scanned two lines of Milton as iambics with
' choriambics in the third and fourth and in the fourth and
fifth places.'   Trochees at the end of a tragic or a comic Greek
iambic, choriambics anywhere, would be wholly inadmissible ;
and thus the primal laws of classic prosody are overlooked in
the unintelligent effort to apply them to a metre which is not
quantitative but accentual.   That English verses can be
quantitative, as is proved by Tennyson's experiments in the
Alcaic and Hendecasyllabic metres, does not affect the
question.   What we have to bear in mind is that the heroic
English line, though similar in rhythm to the classical iambic,
is not a quantitative but an accentual verse, and that its
prosody cannot therefore be analysed by a strict application of
classical terms and rules.[1]

---

[1] The redundant unaccented syllable at the end of the line, so
common in blank verse, would be sufficient to prove this point.   When
the verse of five accents rhymed, a double rhyme was admissible, the
accent always falling on the penultimate syllable.   When the rhyme was
removed, the same privilege remained to blank verse ; but this privilege
was not granted to the quantitative metres of antiquity.   Euripides could
not have written :

ἐνταῦθ' ὁ χρυσός ἐστι· σημεῖον δὲ τοῦτο.

Starting with the notion that the heroic line was what an old critic has called it, 'a licentiate iambic,' the first writers of blank verse took pains to imitate the iambic rhythm as closely as possible by alternating an unaccented with an accented syllable throughout the line. This process led them to end the line with a strong monosyllable, and to isolate each verse. The metre moved tamely thus:

> O mother, thou to murder thus thy child !
> Ah noble prince, how oft have I beheld !

George Gascoigne, in his short tract, ' On the Making of Verse in English,' was quick to perceive the consequent impoverishment of rhythm. ' Surely I can lament,' he says, ' that we are fallen into such a plain and simple manner of writing that there is none other foot used but one.' Gascoigne was well aware that English prosody relied on accent; and he described this foot of whose tyranny he complained, as composed ' of two syllables, whereof the first is depressed or made short, and the second is elevate or made long.' He further pointed out that Chaucer had used greater liberties with metre; ' and whosoever do peruse and well consider his works, he shall find that although his lines are not always of one self-same number of syllables, yet, being read by one that hath understanding, the longest verse and that which hath most syllables in it will fall to the ear correspondent unto that which hath fewest syllables in it; and likewise, that which hath in it fewest syllables, shall be found yet to consist of words that have such natural sound, as may seem equal in length to a verse which hath many more syllables of lighter accents.' This passage contained the pith of the whole matter; and closer analysis of classic and Italian metres led poets to the same result; namely, that what they called ' the licentiate iambic ' could be written with far greater effect of melody and force of rhetoric by varying the unit of the rhythm, or the foot.

Here, however, intervened the great difficulty of English scansion, so long as that scansion was still referred to the quantitative theory. A Greek tragic senarius consisted of six

feet ; each foot consisted of a short syllable followed by a long ;
but in certain places of the verse, in the first, third, and fifth,
two longs might be used. Thus the normal structure of the
line was this :

$$\breve{-} \mid \smile- \mid \breve{-} \mid \smile- \mid \breve{-} \mid \smile- \mid$$

Furthermore, equivalents for both the iamb and the spondee
might be employed at fixed intervals ; and thus the tribrach,
anapæst, and dactyl were, under certain restrictions, admitted
into the verse. The one inadmissible foot was the trochee ;
and the one invariable foot was an iamb in the final place.
Now, in order to imitate an iambic line upon the accentual
system, it was necessary to make an unaccented syllable pass
for a short, and an accented syllable for a long. According to
the practice of Surrey and Sackville the imitative process
seemed easy, so long as the versifier confined himself to the
simple foot of which Gascoigne complained. He sacrificed
the native variety of the English rhythm, and did not profit
by the foreign varieties of the classical metre. This was
because he was working upon a radically false theory. But
no sooner did a poet arise who flung theory to the winds and
returned to the native liberty of English accentual versification, than variety was at once attained without the sacrifice
of melody, but at the same time the laws of classical or
quantitative prosody of the iambic had to be freely violated.
Trochees appeared in all places but the last, and chimerical
choriambi sprawled, to the purblind eyes of pedants, over two
feet. Take this line of Marlowe's for example :

See where Christ's blood streams in the firmament.

Scanned according to the nomenclature of classical prosody
this is a quinarius, with a trochee in the first place, a spondee
in the second, a trochee in the fourth, and two iambs to wind
up with. Take another line from Shakspere :

Thy knee bussing the stones,—for in such business.

There is here a trochee in the second place, while the fourth
place has what cannot properly be called an iamb or a

trochee, and the whole verse is closed with two strongly
accented syllables followed by a redundant syllable—a foot
whi3h must be quantitatively described as a spondee with a
short syllable over. It might indeed be argued that though
there is not enough accent in the words ' for in ' to make an
accentual iamb or trochee, yet they form a quantitative iamb.
But if we invoke quantity in this place we shall be met with
a palpable spondee in the last place. In fact, it is inadmissible at one moment to use quantity and at the next accent,
for the sake of adapting English to Greek scansion ; and this
illustration proves how dangerous it is to apply quantitative
terms in the analysis of an accentual scheme. Take yet
another line from Milton :

> Burned after them to the bottomless pit.

This is equally monstrous, viewed as a tragic iambic line, of
the Greek type : a trochee in the first place, an iamb in the
second, followed by two successive trochees and a final iamb.
Take still another line from Milton :

> Me, me only, just object of his ire.

The first foot is a spondee or a trochee or an iamb, according
as we choose to emphasise. The second is a trochee. The
third is a spondee. The fourth becomes an iamb by forcing
an accent on the word ' of,' but is a decided quantitative
trochee. The fifth is, both accentually and quantitatively, a
good iamb. The awkwardness and indecision of scansion
thus conducted prove its absurdity.

Such instances might be chosen from nearly every page
of every poet who has used blank verse with spirit and
variety. It is clear that the line which forms the unit of the
measure is, to say the very least, an exceedingly licentiate
iambic. So long as our nomenclature of prosody remains
what it is, we may feel obliged, when thinking of the normal
blank verse line, to describe it as an iambic, with laws and
licences different from those of the Greek tragic metre. But
this necessity should not make us forget that those laws and
licences, on which its special quality depends, are determined

by the fact that it is accentual and not quantitative ; and that, though accent may be made to do the work of quantity, it imposes different conditions on the prosody of which it forms the natural basis. A rhythm born and bred in a nation which knew nothing about quantity, a rhythm developed with variety by Chaucer before the humanistic revival, has to be studied in its origins and analysed according to its primitive structure. Instead of seeking to define its five feet by terms of quantity, it were better to classify the incidences of its accents, and to examine these in relation to the pause ; keeping meanwhile suspended in our memory the rhythm of the normal line, and testing by this standard the divergences we notice.[1] At the same time we may profitably bear in mind that the dramatic poets with whose work we have to deal, deliberately sought to adapt their versification to Greek, Latin, and Italian rules of prosody, as these had then been imperfectly analysed. On the Old English stock they grafted slips of artful growth imported from their classic and Italian studies. The developed blank verse of the Elizabethan age is, therefore, a hybrid between a native rhythm and an antique metre. Unless we grasp this fact we shall miss some of the specific beauties of a measure which, without ceasing to be native and accentual, adopted qualities of rhetoric and movement from the Attic stage, the Latin epic, and the Italian imitators of the classic style.

Since blank verse is an accentual rhythm, it lends itself with great effect to emphasis—for emphasis is only enforced accent. The facility with which it can be written, the monotony to which it is peculiarly liable in the hands of a weak versifier, justify, nay, almost necessitate, daring

---

Great advance toward a sound theory of English prosody has recently been made by classifying the numerous cadences of blank verse from the normal type. See, for instance, Dr. Abbott's *Shakespearian Grammar*. But how uncertain the method of analysis still is, may be perceived by comparing such an essay as this of Dr. Abbott's with Dr. Guest's *History of English Rhythms*, where a totally opposite theory is supported with a vast mass of erudition. Whatever may be thought of his principles, Dr. Guest deserves the truest gratitude of students for his minute investigation of the native English rhythms, out of which the metres of our Renaissance period emerged.

variations in its structure ; and these variations assist rhetorical effects.   In the absence of rhyme one line can be linked to another without injury, and periods may be formed, like those of prose, in which phrase balances phrase, and the music of language is drawn through sequences of mutually helpful verses.   The pause and stop, which are important elements in English prosody, add another element of variety, by allowing each line to be broken in more than one place, and enabling a skilful craftsman to open and close periods of rhythmic melody at several points in the structure.   Reviewing these qualities of English blank verse, we shall perceive that it is an eminently dramatic metre.   Its facility and rapid movement bring it into close relation to the speech of common life, and impose no shackling limitations upon dialogue.   At the same time the fixed element of rhythm raises it above colloquial language, and renders even abrupt transitions from the pedestrian to the impassioned style of poetry both natural and easy.   The emphasis on which it mainly relies for variety of music, gives scope to rhetoric. By shifting the incidence of accent, a playwright not only animates his verse and produces agreeable changes in the rhythm ; but he also marks the meaning of his words, and yields opportunities for subtly modulated declamation to the actor.   The same end is gained by altering the pauses, on which a very wide scale of oratorical effects can be touched. When Johnson complained that Milton's method of versification 'changes the measures of a poet to the periods of a declaimer,' he laid his finger on that quality of blank verse which is certainly a gain to the Drama, whatever may be thought about its value for the epic.   The true and only way of appreciating the melody of good blank verse is to declaim it, observing how the changes in the rhythm obey the poet's meaning, and enforce the rhetoric he had in view.   Blank verse is, in fact, the nearest of all poetical measures to prose; yet it does not sacrifice the specific note of verse, which is the maintenance of one selected rhythm, satisfying the ear by repetition, and charming it by variety within the compass of its formal limitations.

Marlowe, with the instinct of genius, observed these
advantages of the unrhymed heroic measure, and with the
faculty of a great artist he solved the problem of rendering
it the supreme instrument of tragic poetry. Instead of the
improver he may almost be called the creator of blank verse ;
for the mere omission of rhyme in the metre of his predecessors did not suffice to constitute what we now understand
by blank verse. He found the heroic line monotonous,
monosyllabic, divided into five feet of tolerably regular
alternate shorts and longs. He left it various in form and
structure, sometimes redundant by a syllable, sometimes
deficient, and animated by unexpected emphases and changes
in the pause. He found it a clumsy and mistaken imitation
of the classical iambic; he restored it to its birthright as
a native English rhythm. He found no sequence of con-
catenated lines or attempt at periods—one verse followed
another in isolation, and all were made after the same
insipid model. He grouped his lines according to the sense,
allowing the thought contained in his words to dominate
their form, and carrying the melody through several verses
linked together by rhetorical modulations. His metre did
not preserve one unalterable type, but assumed diversity of
cadences, the beauty of which depended on their adaptation
to the current of his ideas. By these means he produced the
double effect of unity and contrast ; maintained the fixed
march of his chosen rhythm ; and yet, by alteration in the
pauses, speed, and grouping of the syllables, by changes in
emphasis and accent, he made one measure represent a
thousand. His blank verse might be compared to music,
which demands regular rhythm, but, by the employment of
phrase, induces a higher kind of melody to rise above the
common and despotic beat of time. Bad writers of blank
verse, like Marlowe's predecessors, or like those who in all
periods have been deficient in plastic energy and power of
harmonious adaptation, sacrifice the poetry of expression,
the force of rhetoric, to the mechanism of their art.[1] Metre

[1] In the progress of Shakspere's versification through three broadly
marked stages, nothing is more noticeable than the changes whereby he

with them becomes a mere framework, ceases to be the
organic body of a vivifying thought. And bad critics praise
them for the very faults of tameness and monotony, which
they miscall regularity of numbers. These faults, annoying
enough to a good ear in stanzas and rhymed couplets, are
absolutely insufferable in blank verse, which relies for
melodious effect upon its elasticity and pliability of cadence,
and which is only saved from insipidity by licences interpre-
tative of the poet's sense and demanded by his rhetoric.[1]

IV

The creation of our tragic metre was not Marlowe's only
benefit conferred upon the stage. This was indeed but the
form corresponding to the new dramatic method which he
also introduced. He first taught the art of designing tragedies
on a grand scale, displaying unity of action, unity of character,
and unity of interest. Before his day plays had been pageants
or versified tales, arranged in scenes, and enlivened with
' such conceits as clownage keeps in pay.' He first produced
dramas worthy of that august title. Before his day it might
have been reckoned doubtful whether the rules and precedents
of the Latin theatre would not determine the style of tragic
composition in England as in Italy. After the appearance
of ' Tamburlaine,' it was impossible for a dramatist to attract
the public by any play which had not in it some portion of
the spirit and the pith of that decisive work. How overwhelming was the influence of Marlowe can be estimated by
counting the few plays which survive from the period before
his revolution was effected. From that great body of popular
and courtly rubbish, scornfully criticised or faintly praised
by Sidney, we possess two passable comedies, two stiff and

---

makes metre more and more obey the purposes of rhetoric, starting with
lines in which the sense is closed, advancing to lines in which the sense
is prolonged though periods, until at last the metre, though never
sacrificed, is nowhere forced upon our ear.

[1] Sufficient examples of Marlowe's versification will be given in
quotations below. I may refer my readers to three essays on Blank
Verse published in an appendix to my *Sketches and Studies in Italy*.

antiquated tragedies, a rambling romance, a fustian historic
drama in doggerel rhyme, some delicate and graceful masques
in studied prose, a pleasant pastoral, and an insufferable tale
of chivalry in rhyming couplets of fourteen syllables.   I allude,
of course, to ' Roister Doister,' ' Gammer Gurton's Needle,'
' Gorboduc,' ' The Misfortunes of Arthur,' ' Cambyses,' Lyly's
' Campaspe ' and other pieces, ' The Arraignment of Paris,' and
' Sir Clyomon and Sir Clamydes.' [1]   ' The iniquity of oblivion,'
in this case not ' blindly scattering her poppies,' has covered
up and sealed from sight unreckoned multitudes of raw,
imperfect essays—the delight of a rude age—the nebulous and
seething mass from which the planetary system of Shaksperian Drama was to issue.   Of only a very few can it be
said with any certainty that they emerged into the light of
publicity before Marlowe shook the stage.   What remains of
Greene's, Peele's, Lodge's, and Nash's work, with the exception of ' The Arraignment of Paris,' is posterior to Marlowe.
The same may be asserted, though perhaps with diffidence, of
Kyd's two tragedies.   Thus even over the inferior productions
of the sixteenth century upon its close, had passed the swift
transforming spirit of the master.   It was the central fire of
Marlowe's genius which hardened that dull and shapeless
matrix of English dramatic poetry, and rendered it capable
of crystallising flawless and light-darting gems.   When we
remember that Marlowe, born in the same year as Shakspere,
died at the early age of twenty-nine, while Shakspere's genius
was still, so far as the public was concerned, almost a poten-
tiality ; when we reflect upon the life which Marlowe had to
lead among companions of debauch in London, and further
estimate the degradation of the art he raised so high, we are
forced to place him among the most original creative poets of
the world.   His actual achievement may be judged imperfect,
unequal, immature, and limited.   Yet nothing lower than the
highest rank can be claimed for one who did so much, in a
space of time so short, and under conditions so unfavourable.
What Shakspere would have been without Marlowe, how his

---

[1] I cannot find valid reasons for assigning this last piece with
absolute certainty to Peele.

far more puissant hand and wonder-working brain would
have moulded English Drama without Marlowe, cannot even
be surmised. What alone is obvious to every student is that
Shakspere deigned from the first to tread in Marlowe's footsteps, that Shakspere at the last completed and developed to
the utmost that national embryo of art which Marlowe drew
forth from the womb of darkness, anarchy, and incoherence.

V

About Marlowe there is nothing small or trivial. His
verse is mighty ; his passion is intense ; the outlines of his
plots are large ; his characters are Titanic ; his fancy is extravagant in richness, insolence, and pomp. Marlowe could
rough-hew like a Cyclops, though he was far from being able
to finish with the subtlety and smoothness of a Praxiteles.
We may compare his noblest studies of character with marbles
blocked out by Michel Angelo, not with the polished perfection of 'La Notte' in San Lorenzo. Speaking of 'Dr. Faustus,'
Goethe said with admiration : ' How greatly it is all planned ! '
Greatly planned, and executed with a free, decisive touch,
that never hesitates and takes no heed of modulations. It is
this vastness of design and scale, this simplicity and certainty
of purpose, which strikes us first in Marlowe. He is the
sculptor-poet of Colossi, aiming at such effects alone as are
attainable in figures of a superhuman size, and careless of fine
distinctions or delicate gradations in their execution. His
characters are not so much human beings, with the complexity
of human attributes combined in living personality, as types
of humanity, the animated moulds of human lusts and
passions which include, each one of them, the possibility of
many individuals. They ' are the embodiments or the expo-
nents of single qualities and simple forces.' [1] This tendency
to dramatise ideal conceptions, to vitalise character with one

[1] So Mr. Swinburne has condensed the truth of this matter in his
Study of Shakespeare. Professor Dowden has written to like effect in
an essay on Marlowe, published in the *Fortnightly Review*, January
1870.

dominant and tyrannous motive, is very strong in Marlowe.
Were it not for his own fiery sympathy with the passions
thus idealised, and for the fervour of his conceptive faculty,
these colossal personifications might have been insipid or
frigid. As it is, they are far from deserving such epithets.
They are redeemed from the coldness of symbolic art, from
the tiresomeness of tragic humours, by their author's intensity
of conviction. Marlowe is in deadly earnest while creating
them, believes in their reality, and infuses the blood of his
own untamable heart into their veins. We feel them to be
day-dreams of their maker's deep desires; projected from his
subjectivity, not studied from the men around him ; and
rendered credible by sheer imaginative insight into the dark
mysteries of nature. A poet with a lively sense of humour
might, perhaps, have found it impossible to conceive and sustain passions on so exorbitant a scale with so little relief, so
entire an absence of mitigating qualities. But it was precisely
on the side of humour that Marlowe showed his chief
inferiority to Shakspere. That saving grace of the dramatic
poet he lacked altogether. And it may also be parenthentically
noticed as significant in this respect that Marlowe never drew
a woman's character. His Abigail is a mere puppet. Isabella,
in his 'Edward II.,' changes suddenly from almost abject
fawning on her husband to no less abject dependence on an
ambitious paramour. His Dido owes such power as the
sketch undoubtedly possesses to the poetry of the Fourth
Æneid.

VI

It is no function of sound criticism to decoct a poet's work
into its final and residual essence, deducing one motive from
the complex efforts and the casual essays of a mind placed
higher *ex hypothesi* in the creative order than the critic's
own ; or inventing a catch-word whereby some incommensurable series of achievements may be ticketed. And yet,
such is the nature of Marlowe's work, that it imperatively
indicates a leading motive, irresistibly suggests a catch-word.

This leading motive which pervades his poetry may be defined as *L'Amour de l'Impossible*—the love or lust of unattainable things; beyond the reach of physical force, of sensual faculty, of mastering will; but not beyond the scope of man's inordinate desire, man's infinite capacity for happiness, man's ever-craving thirst for beauty, power, and knowledge. This catch-word of the Impossible Amour is thrust by Marlowe himself, in the pride of his youthful insolence and lawlessness of spiritual lusts, upon the most diffident and sober of his critics. Desire for the impossible—impossible not because it transcends human appetite or capacity, but because it exhausts human faculties in the infinite pursuit—this is the region of Marlowe's sway as poet. To this impossible, because unlimited, object of desire he adds another factor, suggested by his soul's revolt against the given order of the world. He and the Titanic characters into whom he has infused his spirit— even as a workman through the glass-pipe blows life-breath into a bubble, permanent so long as the fine vitreous form endures—he and all the creatures of his fancy thirst for things beyond man's grasp, not merely because these things exhaust man's faculties in the pursuit, but also because the full fruition of them has been interdicted. Thus Marlowe's lust for the impossible, the lust he has injected like a molten fluid into all his eminent dramatic personalities, is a desire for joys conceived by the imagination, floating within the boundaries of will and sense at some fixed moment, but transcending these firm limitations, luring the spirit onward, exhausting the corporeal faculties, engaging the soul itself in a strife with God. This lust assumes the shape of thirst for power, of thirst for beauty, of thirst for knowledge. It is chiefly thirst for power which animates this poet and his brood. When knowledge, as in Faustus, seems to be the bait, that knowledge will conduce to power. But there is a carnal element in the desire itself, a sensuality which lends a grip to Belial on the heart-strings of the lust. This sometimes soars aloft in aspirations, exhales itself in longings after Helen, the world's queen of loveliness evoked from Hades; sometimes it sinks to avaricious, solitary, gluttonous delight in

gems. It resolves itself again into the thirst for power when
we find that the jewels of Barabas are hugged and gloated
over for their potency of buying states, corrupting kingdoms;
when we see that the wraith of Helen has been dragged from
Lethe to flatter a magician's vision of omnipotence.

Let us fix the nature of this leading motive by some salient
passages from Marlowe's dramas.   I take the rudest and
the crudest first.   In the 'Massacre at Paris' the Duke of
Guise should not properly have been displayed as more than
what world-history reveals to us—a formidable rival of the
House of Valois on the throne, a bloody and unscrupulous foe
of the Huguenot faction.   But the spirit of Marlowe entering
into the unwieldy carcass he has framed for this great schemer,
breathes these words :

> Oft have I levelled, and at last have learned
> That peril is the chiefest way to happiness,
> And resolution honour's fairest aim.
> What glory is there in a common good,
> That hangs for every peasant to achieve ?
> That like I best, that flies beyond my reach.

The central passion which inspires Marlowe and all the
characters of Marlowe's coinage finds utterance here.   The
Guise seeks happiness through peril ; finds honour only in
a fierce resolve ; flings common felicity to the winds ; strains
at the flying object of desire beyond his grasp.   Then he
turns to the definite point of his ambition :

> Set me to scale the high pyramides,
> And thereon set the diadem of France ;
> I'll either rend it with my nails to nought,
> Or mount the top with my aspiring wings,
> Although my downfall be the deepest hell.

Before his imagination hangs the desired thing ; it is the
crown of France. It is placed upon a pyramid beyond his
reach ; but he can soar to it on wings of will and desperate
endeavour. Wings are needed for the adventure ; no scaling
steps will serve his turn. Whether he shatter the crown to
atoms in the assault, or beat his pinions round about it in

the gust of victory, concerns not the present mood of his desire. Nor does it signify whether he seize and wear it, or tumble headlong into the abyss of ruin. The thirst, the lust of the impossible allures his soul.

This, as I have said, is the barest, nakedest exhibition of Marlowe's leading motive. He framed one character in which the desire of absolute power is paramount; this is Tamburlaine. When the shepherd-hero is confronted with the vanquished king of Persia he pours himself forth in a monologue which voices Marlowe through the puppet's lips :

> The thirst of reign and sweetness of a crown,
> That caused the eldest son of heavenly Ops
> To thrust his doting father from his chair,
> And place himself in the empyreal heaven,
> Mov'd me to manage arms against thy state.
> What better precedent than mighty Jove ?
> Nature, that fram'd us of four elements
> Warring within our breasts for regiment,
> Doth teach us all to have aspiring minds :
> Our souls, whose faculties can comprehend
> The wondrous architecture of the world,
> And measure every wandering planet's course,
> Still climbing after knowledge infinite,
> And always moving as the restless spheres,
> Will us to wear ourselves, and never rest,
> Until we reach the ripest fruit of all,
> That perfect bliss and sole felicity,
> The sweet fruition of an earthly crown.

It is Nature herself, says Tamburlaine, who placed a warfare of the elements within the frame of man ; she spurs him onward by an inborn need toward empire. It is our souls, uncircumscribed by cosmic circumstances, free to weigh planets in their courses and embrace the universe with thought, that compel men to stake their all on the most perilous of fortune's hazards. In this speech the poet, who framed Tamburlaine, identifies himself with his creation, forgets the person he has made, and utters through his mouth the poetry of his desire for the illimitable.

There was a side-blow aimed at knowledge in this diatribe
of Tamburlaine on power. See now how Faustus answers,
abyss calling to abyss from the same abysmal depth of the
creator's mind :

> Divinity, adieu !
> These metaphysics of magicians,
> And necromantic books are heavenly ;
> Lines, circles, scenes, letters, and characters ;
> Ay, these are those that Faustus most desires.
> O, what a world of profit and delight,
> Of power, of honour, and omnipotence,
> Is promis'd to the studious artisan !
> All things that move between the quiet poles
> Shall be at my command : emperors and kings
> Are but obeyèd in their several provinces ;
> But his dominion that exceeds in this,
> Stretcheth as far as doth the mind of man ;
> A sound magician is a demigod :
> Here tire, my brains, to gain a deity.

On the ordinary paths of learning, logic, philosophy, physic,
law, divinity, Faustus finds himself cramped, tied to dry rules,
confined within the circle of diurnal occupations. These things
may be done for service of man's common needs ; but there
lies—or he divines there lies—beyond the reach of all such
vulgar and trivial ways a far more hazardous path, a path
which by assiduous study and emperilment of self shall lead to
empire. He knows that the soul's welfare is engaged in the
endeavour ; but the conqueror will sway throughout his lifetime a kingdom commensurate with the mind of man. To
gain this knowledge, to possess the power that it confers,
becomes the passion of his nature. He therefore also yields,
and yields with open eyes to the allurements of impossible
desire. When he has sold his soul, the price appears a little
thing :

> Had I as many souls as there be stars,
> I 'd give them all for Mephistophilis.

Descending from the high imaginative region in which
Faustus moves, travelling back from the dim realms of Ind,
where Tamburlaine defies the Fates, reaching England under

the reign of our second Edward, we find the same chord touched in Marlowe's Mortimer. Upon the point of death, checkmated and flung like the Guise 'to deepest hell,' he still maintains the old indomitable note, the key-note of the leading motive:

> Base Fortune, now I see that in thy wheel
> There is a point, to which when men aspire
> They tumble headlong down : that point I touch'd,
> And, seeing there was no place to mount up higher,
> Why should I grieve at my declining fall ?—
> Farewell, fair queen : weep not for Mortimer,
> That scorns the world, and, as a traveller,
> Goes to discover countries yet unknown.

I have pursued the leading motive, applied the catch-word, through many examples bearing on the theme of power. It remains to select one passage in which the same lust for the impossible shall be exhibited when Marlowe turns his thought to beauty. Xenocrate, the love of Tamburlaine, is absent and unhappy. The Tartar chief is left alone to vent his passion in soliloquy. At first he dwells upon the causes of her sorrow, with such 'lyrical interbreathings' as this, evoked from the recollection of her—

> Shining face,
> Where Beauty, mother to the Muses, sits
> And comments volumes with her ivory pen.

Gradually he passes into that vein of meditation, which allows the poet's inspiration to transpire. Then Marlowe speaks, and shows in memorable lines that beauty has, no less than power, her own impossible, for which he thirsted :

> What is beauty, sayeth my sufferings, then ?
> If all the pens that ever poets held
> Had fed the feeling of their masters' thoughts,
> And every sweetness that inspired their hearts,
> Their minds and muses on admirèd themes ;
> If all the heavenly quintessence they still
> From their immortal flowers of poesy,
> Wherein, as in a mirror, we perceive
> The highest reaches of a human wit :
> If these had made one poem's period,

> And all combined in beauty's worthiness,
> Yet should there hover in their restless heads
> One thought, one grace, one wonder, at the least,
> Which into words no virtue can digest.

The impossible beauty, on which Tamburlaine here meditates, is beauty eluding the poet and the artist in their highest flight; that apple topmost on the topmost bough, which the gatherers have not overlooked, but leave perforce, because they strove in vain to reach it. It is always this beauty, inflaming the artist's rather than the lover's soul, which Marlowe celebrates. He has written no drama of love ; and even in ' Hero and Leander ' that divinest dithyramb in praise of sensual beauty, the poet moves in a hyperuranian region, from which he contemplates with eyes of equal adoration all the species of terrestrial loveliness. The tender emotions and the sentiment of love were alien to Marlowe's temper. It may even be doubted whether sexual pleasures had any very powerful attraction for his nature. To such, we think, he gave his cruder poetry-exhausted moments. When he evoked the thought of women to tempt Doctor Faustus, he touched this bass-chord of carnal desire with the hand of a poet-painter rather than a sensualist :

> Sometimes like women, or unwedded maids,
> Shadowing more beauty in their airy brows
> Than have the white breasts of the queen of love.

Yet it was in no Platonic mood that he set those mighty sails of his imagination to the breeze upon the sea of Beauty. That thirst for the impossible, when once applied to things of sense and loveliness, is a lust and longing after the abstraction of all beauties, the self of sense, the quintessence of pleasures. This is, of course, the meaning of Faustus' address to Helen, summoned from the ghosts as the last tangible reality of beauty, to give comfort to his conscience-laden soul :

> Was this the face that launched a thousand ships,
> And burnt the topless towers of Ilium ?—
> Sweet Helen, make me immortal with a kiss. [*Kisses her.*

> Her lips suck forth my soul : see, where it flies !—
> Come, Helen, come, give me my soul again.
> Here will I dwell, for heaven is in these lips,
> And all is dross that is not Helena.
>
> .   .   .   .
>
> O, thou art fairer than the evening air,
> Clad in the beauty of a thousand stars ;
> Brighter art thou than flaming Jupiter
> When he appear'd to hapless Semele ;
> More lovely than the monarch of the sky
> In wanton Arethusa's azur'd arms ;
> And none but thou shalt be my paramour !

The same triumphant sense of having conquered the
unconquerable, and enjoyed the final gust of pleasure in
things deemed impossible for men, emerges in another speech
of Faustus :

> Have I not made blind Homer sing to me
> Of Alexander's love and Œnon's death ?
> And hath not he, that built the walls of Thebes
> With ravishing sound of his melodious harp,
> Made music with my Mephistophilis ?

When Xenocrate is dying Tamburlaine pours forth a monody,
which, however misplaced on his lips, gives Marlowe scope to
sing the nuptial hymn of beauty unapproachable, withdrawn
from 'loathsome earth,' returning to her native station in
the heavens. There, and there only, says the poet, shall
the spirit mate with loveliness and be at peace in her
embrace :

> Now walk the angels on the walls of heaven,
> As sentinels to warn the immortal souls
> To entertain divine Xenocrate . . .
> The cherubins and holy seraphins,
> That sing and play before the King of kings,
> Use all their voices and their instruments
> To entertain divine Xenocrate ;
> And in this sweet and curious harmony,
> The god that tunes this music to our souls
> Holds out his hand in highest majesty
> To entertain divine Xenocrate.

Then let some holy trance convey my thoughts
Up to the palace of the empyreal heaven,
That this my life may be as short to me
As are the days of sweet Xenocrate.

In this rapturous and spiritual marriage-song, which celebrates
the assumption or apotheosis of pure beauty, the master
bends his mighty line to uses of lyric poetry, as though a
theme so far above the reach of words demanded singing.

Dwelling upon these passages, we are led to wonder what
a drama Marlowe would have written if the story of Tannhäuser had been known to him.   As in the Faust-legend the
thirst for illimitable power, so in the Tannhäuser-legend
the thirst for illimitable pleasure leads a human soul to self-
abandonment.   The imaginative region of each legend is
equally vast ; the lust in either case is equally transcendent ;
the sacrifice accomplished by both heroes to an infinite
desire is equally complete.   In his first dramatic creation,
Tamburlaine, Marlowe interwove the double strings of this
Impossible Amour.   In his second, Faustus, he developed the
theme of knowledge desired for power's sake upon earth.   In
Tannhäuser, if that had been his third creation, he might
have painted what he knew so well and felt so deeply, the
poet's thirst for beauty's self, his purchase at the soul's price
of unmeasured rapture in a goddess' arms.   He would
assuredly not have suffered this high mystic theme to
degenerate into any mere vulgarities of a sensual Venus-
berg.   Rather may we imagine that Marlowe would have
shown how the desire for beauty beyond human reach is
a form of the soul's desire for power—no trivial thirst
for pleasure, but a longing to achieve the unattainable, and
hold in human grasp the bliss reserved for gods.   But
such speculations, if not wholly idle, only serve to cast a
side-light on that conception of Marlowe's leading motive
which I have endeavoured to develop.   As it was, his third
creation, Barabas, incarnated a lower form of the same
insatiable longing.   Ambition, the desire of empire, the
adoration of beauty, the control of power by means of superhuman knowledge, yield place here to avarice.   But the

avarice of the Jew of Malta is so colossal, so tempered with a
sensuous love of rarity and beauty in the priceless gems he
hoards, so delirious in its raptures, so subservient to
ungovernable hatred and vindictive exercise of power conferred
by wealth upon its owner, that we dare not call even this
baser exhibition of the Impossible Amour ignoble. Swinburne, who cannot assuredly be arraigned for want of sympathy with Marlowe, has styled Barabas ' a mere mouthpiece
for the utterance of poetry as magnificent as any but the best
of Shakespeare's.' With this verdict we must unwillingly
concur. Considering the rapid and continual descent from
bathos unto bathos after the splendid first and second acts,
so large in outline, so vigorous in handling, so rich in verse,
through the mad abominations and hysterical melodrama of
the last three acts ; no sane critic will maintain that the ' Jew
of Malta ' was a love-child of its maker's genius. One only
hypothesis saves Marlowe's fame, and explains the patent
inequalities of his third tragedy—beginning, as it does, with
the face and torso of a Centaur, ending in the impotent and
flabby coils of a poisonous reptile. It is that stage-necessities
and press of time compelled the poet to complete in haste
as task-work what he had conceived with love, and blocked
out at his leisure. Brief indeed, we fancy, must have been
the *otia dia* of this poet.

But I must return to my main argument, and show with
what a majestic robe of imperial purple Marlowe's imagination
has draped the poor and squalid skeleton of avarice. This he
has done by drawing that 'least erected' vice within the
sphere of his illimitable lust. The opening soliloquy, when
Barabas is ' discovered in his counting-house, with heaps of
gold before him,' amply suffices to prove the point :

> So that of thus much that return was made;
> And of the third part of the Persian ships
> There was the venture summ'd and satisfied.
> As for those Samnites and the men of Uz,
> That brought my Spanish oils and wines of Greece,
> Here have I purs'd their paltry silverlings.
> Fie, what a trouble 't is to count this trash !

Well fare the Arabians, who so richly pay
The things they traffic for with wedge of gold,
Whereof a man may easily in a day
Tell that which may maintain him all his life.
The needy groom, that never finger'd groat,
Would make a miracle of thus much coin ;
But he whose steel-barr'd coffers are cramm'd full,
And all his life-time hath been tirèd,
Wearying his fingers' ends with telling it,
Would in his age be loath to labour so,
And for a pound to sweat himself to death.
Give me the merchants of the Indian mines,
That trade in metal of the purest mould ;
The wealthy Moor, that in the eastern rocks
Without control can pick his riches up,
And in his house heap pearl like pebble-stones,
Receive them free, and sell them by the weight ;
Bags of fiery opals, sapphires, amethysts,
Jacynths, hard topaz, grass-green emeralds,
Beauteous rubies, sparkling diamonds,
And seld-seen costly stones of so great price,
As one of them indifferently rated,
And of a carat of this quantity,
May serve, in peril of calamity,
To ransom great kings from captivity.
This is the ware wherein consists my wealth ;
And thus methinks should men of judgment frame
Their means of traffic from the vulgar trade,
And, as their wealth increaseth, so inclose
Infinite riches in a little room.

In the course of the tragedy, Barabas is despoiled by Christians
of the bulk of his wealth. His house has been turned into
a nunnery ; and there, in an upper chamber, lies secreted a
hoard of gems and gold, known only to himself. In order to
obtain possession of this treasure he makes his daughter
Abigail assume the veil, using her feigned conversion, as he
also uses her fictitious love-caresses, to defeat his foes. The
situation in which Abigail is thus placed by her father bears
a strong resemblance to that of the girl in Tourguénieff's tale
'Le Juif.' What Marlowe reached upon the path of powerful
imagination—a depth below all depths conceivable of

cynicism—the Russian novelist revealed as proper to the
nature of a Polish Jew. Outcast from society, degraded by
the lust of gain, a Jew will seem to sell his daughter, relying
all the while upon that purity, protected by the hatred for an
alien race, which makes a Christian's love as little moving
to her woman's instinct as the passion of a hound or horse
might be. This, it may be parenthetically said, is one of the
strongest extant instances of idealistic art corroborated and
verified by realism.

While Barabas is skulking below his daughter's window
in uncertainty and darkness, awaiting the moment when
Abigail shall disinter his money-bags, Marlowe seizes the
occasion for heightening his avarice to passion :

> Thus, like the sad-presaging raven, that tolls
> The sick man's passport in her hollow beak,
> And in the shadow of the silent night
> Doth shake contagion from her sable wings,
> Vex'd and tormented runs poor Barabas
> With fatal curses towards these Christians.
> The incertain pleasures of swift-footed time
> Have ta'en their flight, and left me in despair ;
> And of my former riches rests no more
> But bare remembrance ; like a soldier's scar,
> That has no further comfort for his maim.—
> O Thou, that with a fiery pillar ledd'st
> The sons of Israel through the dismal shades,
> Light Abraham's offspring ; and direct the hand
> Of Abigail this night ! or let the day
> Turn to eternal darkness after this !—
> No sleep can fasten on my watchful eyes,
> Nor quiet enter my distemper'd thoughts
> Till I have answer of my Abigail.

Abigail now appears upon the upper platform of the theatre.
The spectators see her at work, searching for the hidden
store. Her father is still unaware of her presence. Hovering
disquieted and sick with fear, he seems to his own fancy like
the ghosts which haunt old treasuries and guard the hoards
of buried men :

> Now I remember those old women's words,
> Who in my wealth would tell me winter's tales,

And speak of spirits and ghosts that glide by night
About the place where treasure hath been hid:
And now methinks that I am one of those;
For, whilst I live, here lives my soul's sole hope,
And, when I die, here shall my spirit walk.

When at length she flings him down the bags, it is as though
the sun had risen on the darkness of his soul:

O my girl,
My gold, my fortune, my felicity,
Strength to my soul, death to mine enemy;
Welcome the first beginner of my bliss!
O Abigail, Abigail, that I had thee here too!
Then my desires were fully satisfied:
But I will practise thy enlargement thence:
O girl! O gold! O beauty! O my bliss! [*Hugs the bags.*

He abandons himself to the transport of the moment so
wildly, that Abigail has to remind him of the peril of
discovery. Lifted into poetry by passion, Barabas wafts his
daughter a parting kiss, and calls upon the day to rise, the
lark to soar into the heavens, while his uplifted spirit floats
and sings above his gems, as the swift bird above her
younglings in the nest:

Farewell, my joy, and by my fingers take
A kiss from him that sends it from his soul.—
Now, Phœbus, ope the eye-lids of the day,
And, for the raven, wake the morning lark,
That I may hover with her in the air,
Singing o'er these, as she does o'er her young.
Hermoso placer de los dineros!

The passage in this short scene from midnight gloom and
meditations upon wandering ghosts to day-spring, joy, and
plans for future vengeance—from the black raven to the
morning lark—is so swift and so poetically true, that
Mammon for one moment walks before us clothed in light;
not sullen with the sultry splendours and material grossness
of the 'Alchemist' (though these are passionate in their own
cumbrous style), but airy and ethereal, a spiritual thing, a
bright 'unbodied joy.'

VII

In dealing with Marlowe, it is impossible to separate the poet from the dramatist, the man from his creations. His personality does not retire, like Shakspere's, behind the work of art into impenetrable mystery. Rather, like Byron, but with a truer faculty for dramatic presentation than Byron possessed, he inspires the principal characters of his tragedies with the ardour, the ambition, the audacity of his own restless genius. Tamburlaine, who defies heaven, and harnesses kings and princes of the East to his chariot, who ascends his throne upon the necks of prostrate emperors, and burns a city for his consort's funeral pyre, embodies the insolence of his creator's spirit. At the same time, in this haughty and aspiring shepherd the historic Tartar chief is firmly rendered visible. Through Tamburlaine's wild will and imperturbable reliance upon destiny, the brute instincts of savage tribes yearning after change, pursuing conquest and spreading desolation with the irresistible impulse of a herd of bisons marching to their fields of salt, emerge into self-consciousness. Marlowe has traced the portrait with a bold hand, filling its details in with broad and liberal touches:

> Of stature tall, and straightly fashionèd,
> Like his desires, lift upward and divine;
> So large of limbs, his joints so strongly knit,
> Such breadth of shoulders as might mainly bear
> Old Atlas's burden. . . . .
> Pale of complexion, wrought in him with passion,
> Thirsting with sovereignty and love of arms;
> His lofty brows in folds do figure death,
> And in their smoothness amity and life;
> About them hangs a knot of amber hair,
> Wrappèd in curls, as fierce Achilles' was,
> On which the breath of heaven delights to play,
> Making it dance in wanton majesty;
> His arms and fingers, long and sinewy,
> Betokening valour and excess of strength;
> In every part proportioned like the man
> Should make the world subdued to Tamburlaine.

This is the picture drawn of him at the beginning of his fortunes by a generous enemy. There is a magnetism in the presence of the man. A Persian captain, commissioned to overawe and trample down his pride, no sooner sees Tamburlaine than he falls a victim to his influence :

> His looks do menace heaven and dare the gods ;
> His fiery eyes are fixed upon the earth,
> As if he now desired some stratagem,
> Or meant to pierce Avernus' darksome vaults,
> To pull the triple-headed dog from hell.

Tamburlaine, on his side, favours the manly bearing of his foe, and bids him welcome with such words as bind the captain to his cause :

> Forsake thy king, and do but join with me,
> And we will triumph over all the world ;
> I hold the Fates bound fast in iron chains,
> And with my hand turn Fortune's wheel about ;
> And sooner shall the sun fall from his sphere
> Than Tamburlaine be slain or overcome.

Such confidence is contagious, imposing, as Napoleon's belief in his star imposed, and working out its own accomplishment. His most powerful opponents recognise the spell, and are cowed by it :

> Some powers divine, or else infernal, mixed
> Their angry seeds at his conception ;
> For he was never sprung of human race,
> Since with the spirit of his fearful pride
> He dares so doubtlessly resolve of rule,
> And by profession be ambitious.

With the unresisted advance of his arms, and the tumbling down of empires at his approach, the conviction of his destiny grows on Tamburlaine :

> Where'er I come the fatal Sisters sweat,
> And grisly Death, by running to and fro,
> To do their ceaseless homage to my sword.

. . . .

> Millions of souls sit on the banks of Styx,
> Waiting the back return of Charon's boat;
> Hell and Elysium swarm with ghosts of men,
> That I have sent from sundry foughten fields
> To spread my fame through hell and up to heaven.

The lust for sovereignty passes into blind, bewildering lust for blood and overthrow; from the midst of which emerges a belief in his commission from God to scourge the nations:

> I will, with engines never exercised,
> Conquer, sack, and utterly consume
> Your cities and your golden palaces;
> And, till by vision or by speech I hear
> Immortal Jove say, Cease, my Tamburlaine!
> I will persist a terror to the world,
> Making the meteors (that, like armèd men,
> Are seen to march upon the towers of heaven)
> Run tilting round about the firmament,
> And break their burning lances in the air,
> For honour of my wondrous victories.

Filled now with the notion that he is *Flagellum Dei*, he bears a scourge aloft among his ensigns and his 'coal-black colours':

> There is a God, full of revenging wrath,
> From whom the thunder and the lightning breaks,
> Whose scourge I am, and him will I obey.

If Tamburlaine were asked what God he follows, he could hardly give that God a name. It is his own Genius, the Genius of tyranny, destruction, slaughter. Yet this hyperbolical monster moves admiration rather than loathing. Marlowe has succeeded in saving his hero, amid all his 'lunes,' from caricature, by the inbreathed spirituality with which he sustains his madness at its height. The last scene he wrote for Tamburlaine is impressive in its dignity; torrid with the heat of Asia's sun descending to the caves of night through brazen heavens. There are no more kingdoms left for Tamburlaine to conquer, and the Titanic marauder feels his strength ebbing:

What daring god torments my body thus,
And seeks to conquer mighty Tamburlaine?
Shall sickness prove me now to be a man,
That have been termed the terror of the world?
Techelles and the rest, come, take your swords,
And threaten him whose hand afflicts my soul!
Come, let us march against the powers of heaven,
And set black streamers in the firmament,
To signify the slaughter of the gods.

Alas! these are but idle vaunts, and Tamburlaine is now aware of it. Even for would-be deicides death waits.

Ah, friends, what shall I do? I cannot stand.

This is the one solitary cry of weakness wrung from the death-smitten tiger. Pain racks him. His captains comfort him by saying that such pain as this must pass; it is too violent. Then he bursts into the most magnificent of all his declamations, pointing to the bony skeleton who followed like a hound upon his heels across so many battle-fields, and who, all-terrified, is lurking now to paralyse the hand which surfeited his jaws with slaughter:

Not last, Techelles? No! for I shall die.
See where my slave, the ugly monster Death,
Shaking and quivering, pale and wan for fear,
Stands aiming at me with his murdering dart,
Who flies away at every glance I give,
And when I look away, comes stealing on.
Villain, away, and hie thee to the field!
I and mine armies come to load thy back
With souls of thousand mangled carcasses.
Look, where he goes! but see, he comes again,
Because I stay! Techelles, let us march,
And weary Death with bearing souls to hell.

After this, the scene proceeds upon a graver and more tranquil note of resignation, abdication, and departure. Tamburlaine retains his stout heart and high stomach to the end, but he bows to the inevitable and divides his power among his sons. His body, the soul's subject, though it

break beneath the stress of those fierce passions, shall survive
and be his children's heritage :

> But, sons, this subject, not of force enough
> To hold the fiery spirit it contains,
> Must part, imparting his impressions
> By equal portions into both your breasts.
> My flesh, divided in your precious shapes,
> Shall still retain my spirit, though I die,
> And live in all your seeds immortally.

There is surely enough of absurdity and extravagance in
the two parts of 'Tamburlaine.' Relays of captive monarchs,
fattened on raw meat and ' pails of muscadel,' draw the hero's
chariot. A king and queen dash out their brains against the
cage in which they are confined. Virgins are ravished and
mangled, kingdoms overrun, and cities burned to satisfy a
whim. Tamburlaine kills one of his three sons because he is
a coward, and rips up the flesh of his own left arm to teach
his other sons endurance. Blood flows in rivers. Shrieks and
groans and curses mingle with heaven-defying menaces and
ranting vaunts. The action is one tissue of violence and
horror. The language is truculent bombast, tempered with
such bursts of poetry as I have prudently selected in my
specimens.[1] Yet in spite of preposterousness, more than
enough in volume and monotonous variety to justify Mine
Ancient's huffing vein of parody, the vast and powerful conception of the Tartar conqueror redeems 'Tamburlaine' from
that worst bathos, the bathos of involuntary caricature.
Marlowe knew well what he was after. He produced a
dramatic poem which intoxicated the audience of the London
play-houses with indescribable delight, and which inaugurated
a new epoch. Through the cloud-world of extravagance

---

[1] In the passage proverbial for bombast which begins :

> Holla, ye pampered jades of Asia !
> What ! can ye draw but twenty miles a day,

our imagination is still recreated by such lines as these:

> The horse that guide the golden eye of heaven,
> And blow the morning from their nostrils,
> Making their fiery gait above the clouds.

which made 'Tamburlaine' a byword, he shot one ray of light, clear still, and excellent in the undaunted spirit of the hero.

VIII

Not long before the composition of Marlowe's 'Doctor Faustus,' a prose version of the life, adventures, and dreadful death of the famous magician had appeared in Germany. It was printed in 1587 by John Speig at Frankfort. A reprint of this edition issued from the press in 1588; and in 1589 the same, with some considerable alterations and additions, was repeated. Before 1593 the tale of Faust had acquired such popularity that a continuation, entitled the 'Wagnerbuch,' was produced; and again, in 1599, another version of the story, inferior to that of Speig, was published by Moller at Hamburgh. Thus in the space of eleven years five several editions of the legend of Faust were needed to satisfy the curiosity of the German public. It may be noticed that all these works had a distinctly Protestant tendency. They were soon translated into other languages. The English received a version of the Frankfort issue of 1588 from the press of Thomas Orwin—probably in the same year. A revised edition was published in 1592; and, as early as the year 1588, a ballad on the 'Life and Death of Doctor Faustus' had been licensed by Aylmer, Bishop of London. The 'Wagnerbuch,' adapted and altered for English readers, saw the light in 1594; and thus the English were placed in full possession of the German Faustiad. Meanwhile Marlowe's tragedy, which may have been exhibited in 1589, had made the larger outlines of the legend popular upon the stage.

This legend has been rightly called a Faustiad. No epic of the Middle Ages condenses within shorter compass the spirit, sentiment, and science of that period, then drawing to its close, upon the eve of the great modern revolution. It depicts the fears and passions of the times which preluded the Renaissance; epitomises medieval knowledge; expresses the mingled reverence for learning and dread of occult lore which distinguished an age intellectually impotent, but plagued with the longing after mysteries beyond the grasp of men ; traces in hard, grim outlines the sinister religious superstition, the constitutional melancholy, the desperate revolt against intolerable mental bondage, the grotesque hysterical amusements as of some paralytic but gigantic infant, and the inordinate desire to penetrate forbidden secrets, out of which emerged the belief in magic and the ghastly realities of witchcraft, no less than the exuberant forces of the modern world· This epic is strictly Northern and Teutonic. There is no conceivable period of Italian literature in which it could have been created. The cold, remorseless revelation of Hell, accepted in its recognised eternity of torments by a soul made reckless with the ennui and stagnation of a present life too empty and too pleasureless to be endured, breathes the stoical courage, the scornful imagination of Beowulf's posterity. The purchase of knowledge, power, and enjoyment by a human spirit, conscious of its infinite capacity for all these things, but ' cabined, cribbed, confined ' within the dungeon of insuperable limitations—this purchase at the price of infinite agony and never-ending remorse, is a tragedy of aspiration, insubordination, and ultimate acceptance of inevitable doom, which has for its dim background the sublimely sombre religion of the Eddas. While the Germans were writing down their Faustiad—no casual biography of a conjuror, but the allegory of a whole past epoch of intellectual somnambulism, visited with fiery dreams—the Italians had already wrought by art, by humanism, by the energies of a diversified and highly coloured social life, deliverance for Europe. It was not their mission to enact or to compose the Faustiad—for this they had not then the requisite gifts of courage or imagination, of mental grasp upon the dreadfulness of existence or of passionate insurgence against its stern fatalities—but to contrive the conditions of thought and culture under which Faustus might wed the real Helen of resuscitated arts and letters, might deliver his soul from hell, and satisfy his thirst for power and knowledge by science.

The Faustiad precedes the Renaissance, and belongs to a superseded past. Yet, like the legends of Don Juan and

Tannhäuser, it became the property of succeeding ages,
because it expressed with mythic largeness a real experience
of humanity. The tragic conflicts of the soul set forth in
these three legends lend themselves to modern interpretation,
to the art of Goethe, Mozart, and Wagner. Marlowe, acting
the part which poets have so often played in preserving the
very form and pressure of the times in which they lived,
invested one sombre and grotesque product of the Middle Ages
with the imaginative splendour of the Renaissance. At first
sight it might appear that he was satisfied with arranging
the German text-book in scenes ; so closely has he adhered to
his original, so carelessly has he dramatised the uncouth
drolleries and childish diableries with which it is enlivened.
His tragedy is without a plot, without a female character. It
is not even divided into acts ; and the scenes, with the exception of the first three and the last two, might be transposed
without material injury to the plan. Yet the closer we
inspect it, and the more we study it, the better shall we learn
that he has given a great and tragic unity to his drama, that
he has succeeded in drawing a modern work of art from the
chaotic medieval matter. This unity is Faustus in his pro-
tracted vacillation between right and wrong, his conflict
between curiosity and conscience. 'Doctor Faustus' is more
nearly allied in form to the dramatic poems of our own days,
which present a psychological study of character to the
reader, than any other work of our old theatre. Marlowe
concentrated his energies on the delineation of the proud life
and terrible death of a man in revolt against the eternal laws
of his own nature and the world, defiant and desperate,
plagued with remorse, alternating between the gratification of
his appetites and the dread of a God whom he rejects without
denying. It is this tragic figure which he drew forth from
the substance of the German tale, and endowed with the
breath and blood of real existence. He traced the outline
with a breadth and dignity beyond the scope of the prose
legend. He filled it in with the power of a great poét, with
the intensity of life belonging to himself and to the age of
adolescent vigour. He left us a picture of the medieval rebel,

true in its minutest details to that bygone age, but animated
with his own audacious spirit, no longer mythical, but
vivified, a living personality. By the side of Faustus he
placed the sinister and melancholy Mephistophilis, a spirit
who wins souls for hell by the allurements of despair, playing
with open cards and hiding no iota of the dreadfulness of
damnation. He introduced good and bad angels, hovering
in the air, and whispering alternately their words of warning
and enticement in the ears of Faustus. The professional
magicians who lend their books to the hero, the old man who
entreats him to repent, the scholars who assuage his last
hours with their sympathy, make up the minor persons of
the drama. But each and all of these subordinate characters
are dedicated to the one main purpose of expressing the
psychological condition of Faustus from various points of
view :—the perplexities of his divided spirit, his waverings of
anguish and remorse, the flickerings of hope extinguished in
the smoke of self-abandonment to fear, the pungent pricks of
conscience soothed by transient visions of delight, the prying
curiosity which lulls his torment at one moment, the soul's
defiance yielding to despair, and from despair recovering
fresh strength to sin and suffer. To this vivisection of a
ruined man, all details in the gloomy scene contribute. Even
the pitiful distractions—pitiful in their leaden dulness and
blunt edge of drollery—with which Faustus amuses his worse
than Promethean leisure until the last hour of his contract
sound, heighten the infernal effect. The stage swarms continually with devils, running at one time at their master's
bidding on the sorriest errands, evoking at another the most
dismal shows from hell. We are entertained with processions
of the Seven Deadly Sins, and with masques of the damned
' in that vast perpetual torture-house ' below. In the absence
of the hero, Lucifer, Beelzebub, and Mephistophilis commune
together with gross irony. The whole theatre is sulphurous
with fumes of the bottomless pit. Through the smoke and
stench thereof there flashes once a Woman-Devil—

> Beautiful
> As was bright Lucifer before his fall;

but her kisses are hot as ' sops of flaming fire : ' and once again there glides the fair ghost of Helen in a vision ; ineffectual as feasts of Tantalus.

Marlowe's Faustus is a Teutonic and a medieval sceptic. There is nothing light or Latin in his attitude ; no carelessness or banter, no irony, no willingness to sneer away the ruin of his soul in epigrams. He personifies disbelief as disbelief then was ; convinced of a supernatural environment of spiritual realities ; surrounded by the terrors of a ghostly world. The Florentine indifference of Machiavelli, absorbed in actualities of human life ; the Venetian indifference of Aretino, besotted with Greek wine and wanton cynicism ; the modern indifference of free-thinkers, who have divested their minds of God and devil, heaven and hell ; were all alike alien to his nature. Faustus doubts, indeed, whether there be a hell— confounds this in his bolder moments with Elysium. Yet he sells himself, soul and body, by a formal bond, signed with the blood of his own veins, to Lucifer ; and the first questions he addresses to his familiar, concern the state of fallen spirits. His atheism has a background of terror thinly veiled by the mind's inquisitiveness. He is the sceptic of an age of nightmares ; and though these only come at intervals, they recur with fearful and accelerated force as time advances. Faustus risks the future for the sake of novel experience and present power. Discontented with the known results of former speculations, wearied with the stale *sic probo* of the schools, he flings himself into the devil's arms. This fatigue of current knowledge, this attempt to transcend its tedious limitations by a compact with the fiend, was only possible in a theological unscientific age. Modern scepticism is both more subtle and less passionate. The Faustus of our moment doubts all things ; but believes that if there be a God, He will be merciful. Irritated perhaps by the slow advance of science, he is yet aware that power and knowledge cannot be acquired by magic. If there is no God, there is no devil to help him out of his inaction. He is flung back on a tideless sea of stagnation, listlessness, and trivial pleasures.

The case was far different with the men of Marlowe's

age. The world-old identification of man's thirst for power
and knowledge with rebellion still oppressed their spirits.
The forbidden tree of Paradise still stretched its ominous
branches across their heaven. The story of Faustus is, in
this light, another version of the Fall. How the belief that
knowledge was prohibited by God to man first became a part
and parcel of the human conscience, defeats investigation.
This belief is one of the direst evils with which religion has
tormented the blind, groping spirit of our race. Man, surrounded by insoluble mysteries, seeks to fathom them.
Possessed with the idea that inquiry is impious, he pursues
it with unholy ardour. The height and depth, the strength
and weakness of his being interpenetrate : conscious of
finite power and infinite capacity, he mistakes the limitations
of the present for eternal laws. Hence spring the figments
of jealous deities, of secrets which it is a crime to fathom.
Prometheus is chained on Caucasus for bringing fire from
heaven; Ulysses roasts in hell because he set his sails
beyond the Pillars of Hercules; Roger Bacon is consigned
to perdition for studying chemistry. The first astronomers,
the first navigators, the first anatomists, are shunned and
imprisoned like maniacs, if they escape burning as atheists.

Faustus is the hero and the martyr of forbidden knowledge. The knowledge he sought was by hypothesis unholy,
and the means he took to acquire it were unlawful. It was
not science, as we understand it, or as the world even then
understood it, that he pursued, but thaumaturgy, after which
a mind, wearied with scepticism, is wont to hanker. Having
exhausted the learning of his age, impotent to carry it any
further, fatigued with the reiteration of its formulas, he loses
hold on life and on the truth. Logic, physic, law, theology,
each presents him with a crazy doubt. He has turned each
to poison by refusing to exercise them within the sphere of
practice. What remains? Nothing but the vast external
void, which his own doubts and questions fill like fiends and
phantoms. Nothing but the spirit-shaking, all-absorbing
appetite for that which lies behind the veil. 'Where the
Gods are not, ghosts abound.' This saying is true of the

distempered, ennui-haunted soul. In this region Faustus
wanders, half misdoubting, half creating the spectres which
throng round him, but gradually waking to discover that
they have awful counterparts in the real world.

It seemed, no doubt, right to the men of that century,
ready as they were to burn each other for points of doctrine,
that Lucifer should exact his bond and Faustus be damned.
At the same time, their own strong passions responded to his
arrogant intrepidity. Face to face with hell, convinced of
its reality by the fiend whom he evoked, Faustus plunged
into the abyss, partly from curiosity, partly from the lust of
power and pleasure, partly blinded by the fate which over-
takes aspirants against God. This was a picture to fascinate
men passing from the torpor of the past into the activity of
the Renaissance, remembering those nightmares, but feeling in their veins the blood of a new epoch. They hailed
Faustus as a hero, but they acquiesced in his doom ; they
had as yet no thought of sneering away God and hell. They
would as soon have cared to rescue a pirate from the gallows
as to waste pity upon Faustus. Yet Faustus had in him the
passion of that spirit which discovered America, which cir-
cumnavigated the globe, which revealed the planetary system,
which overthrew the tyranny of Rome. What makes Faustus
a tragic personage is that the passion of this noble spirit in
him was perverted. What constitutes the claim of Marlowe
to the fame of a great tragic poet in this creation, is the
firmness with which he has traced the indelible and everlasting signs of a damned conscience in this not ignoble
character. Sin and the symptoms of sin, the soul's sin
against the Holy Ghost, its agony and its ruin, are depicted
for us with a force which preachers and divines might envy.

At the opening of the play Faustus is discovered in his
study, taking stock of his acquirements, and reflecting on the
course he should adopt in future. The very first words he
speaks reveal a rebellious spirit :

> Settle thy studies, Faustus, and begin
> To sound the depth of that thou wilt profess :
> Having commenced, be a divine in show,

> Yet level at the end of every art,
> And live and die in Aristotle's works.

Shall he addict himself, then, wholly to philosophy ? What
is the end of logic ? 'To dispute well—*bene disserere !*'
That will not suffice. Pass physic in review. He has exhausted the wisdom of Galen and applied it to such good
purpose that the world rings with the report of his cures :

> Yet art thou still but Faustus, and a man.

The secret of his sin is peeping out. Faustus, ' glutted with
learning's golden gifts,' would fain be more than man. He
now takes up Justinian, and turns the leaves :

> This study fits a mercenary drudge,
> Who aims at nothing but external trash ;
> Too servile and illiteral for me.

Theology remains. He pulls the Vulgate from the shelf
and opens it. *Stipendium peccati mors est. Si peccasse
negamus, fallimur.* 'The reward of sin is death. If we
say that we have no sin, we deceive ourselves :'

> Ay, we must die an everlasting death !
> What doctrine call you this, *Che sarà, sarà,*
> What will be, shall be ?

Divinity drives him into fatalism, for he forgets the sacrifice
of Christ. All this while his fingers have been itching for
the books of magic, which remain upon the shelf ; and now
he clasps them with something of the miser's clutch on
gold :

> These metaphysics of magicians
> And necromantic books are heavenly ! . . .
> Oh, what a world of profit and delight,
> Of power, of honour, and omnipotence,
> Is promised to the studious artisan !
> All things that move between the quiet poles
> Shall be at my command ; emperors and kings
> Are but obeyèd in their several provinces ;

> But his dominion that exceeds in this,
> Stretcheth as far as doth the mind of man.

The die is cast. Power, limitless as the mind, raising man to
godhood, is the lure to which the soul of Faustus stoops. He
sends for Valdes and Cornelius, professed magicians, to aid him
in his studies; and, while he waits for them, the good and bad
angels, who dramatically objectify the double impulses of
appetite and conscience, whisper in his ear, the one dissuading,
the other encouraging his resolution.

Valdes and Cornelius inflame Faustus' fancy further with
the splendid pictures of material pomp and sensual delights
they paint; and having lent him books and instruments of
the black art, instruct him how to use them at the proper
moment. When night comes he seeks a solitary wood, and
raises Mephistophilis, who first appears under the form of a
monstrous dragon:

> I charge thee to return, and change thy shape!
> Thou art too ugly to attend on me.
> Go, and return an old Franciscan friar;
> That holy shape becomes a devil best.

The ready compliance of this black seraph inflates the vanity
of Faustus, and confirms him in his resolution. When the
diabolical friar enters, there begins that darkest colloquy,
whereby Marlowe seems bent on proving that the powers of
evil need no Jesuitry to entice a blinded soul. The magician
haughtily commands the service of his vassal. The fiend
answers he is 'servant to great Lucifer.' Faustus submits
that his conjuring had brought him hither; Mephistophilis
replies:

> That was the cause, but yet *per accidens*;
> For when we hear one rack the name of God,
> Abjure the Scriptures and his Saviour Christ,
> We fly in hope to get his glorious soul;
> Nor will we come, unless he use such means
> Whereby he is in danger to be damn'd.
> Therefore the shortest cut for conjuring
> Is stoutly to abjure all godliness,
> And pray devoutly to the prince of hell.

Enough surely to make Faustus shrink upon the verge of
perdition !   But he is so ravished with his own conceit that
he cries:

> This word damnation terrifies not me;
> For I confound hell in Elysium ;
> My ghost be with the old philosophers !

Then, as though to give his soul another chance, but really in
order to satisfy a craving curiosity, he asks again :

> But, leaving these vain trifles of men's souls,
> Tell me what is that Lucifer thy lord ?

The dialogue which follows must be transcribed at length, not
only for its own impressive dignity and beauty, but also for
the light it casts on Marlowe's dramatic conception of a sin-
blind soul, gazing on the anguish of the damned, and yet per-
sisting in its own desire :

> *Faust.* Tell me what is that Lucifer thy lord ?
> *Meph.* Arch-regent and Commander of all spirits.
> *Faust.* Was not that Lucifer an angel once ?
> *Meph.* Yes, Faustus, and most dearly lov'd of God.
> *Faust.* How comes it, then, that he is prince of devils ?
> *Meph.* O, by aspiring pride and insolence ;
> For which God threw him from the face of heaven.
> *Faust.* And what are you that live with Lucifer ?
> *Meph.* Unhappy spirits that fell with Lucifer,
> Conspir'd against our God with Lucifer,
> And are for ever damn'd with Lucifer.
> *Faust.* Where are you damn'd ?
> *Meph.*   In hell.
> *Faust.* How comes it, then, that thou art out of hell ?
> *Meph.* Why, this is hell, nor am I out of it ;
> Think'st thou that I, that saw the face of God,
> And tasted the eternal joys of heaven,
> Am not tormented with ten thousand hells
> In being depriv'd of everlasting bliss ?
> O, Faustus, leave these frivolous demands,
> Which strike a terror to my fainting soul !

The fiend's visible torment only draws this taunt from
Faustus:

> What, is great Mephistophilis so passionate
> For being deprivèd of the joys of heaven?
> Learn thou of Faustus manly fortitude,
> And scorn those joys thou never shalt possess.

Then he bids him bear a message back to Lucifer, stipulating
for the purchase of his soul, already damned by traffic in forbidden things:

> So he will spare him four and twenty years,
> Letting him live in all voluptuousness.

He bargains for the unconditional service of Mephistophilis
through this space of time; and having sent the devil on his
errand, sighs his heart's wish out in two imperishable lines:

> Had I as many souls as there be stars,
> I'd give them all for Mephistophilis.

Upon cold reflection, conscience resumes her sway for a
moment. Faustus soliloquises in his study:[1]

> Now, Faustus, must
> Thou needs be damned, and canst thou not be saved.
> What boots it, then, to think on God or heaven?
> Away with such vain fancies, and despair;
> Despair in God, and trust in Belzebub.
> Now go not back, Faustus; be resolute!
> Why waverest thou? O, something soundeth in mine ear,
> 'Abjure this magic, turn to God again!'
> Why he loves thee not;
> The god thou serv'st is thine own appetite,
> Wherein is fixed the love of Belzebub.

The two voices of the good and evil angels whisper once more
in his ears; and while he is arguing with the one and leaning
to the other, Mephistophilis re-enters, the bond is written
with the blood of Faustus, and the compact is accomplished.
The first question Faustus asks, after he has sold himself to

---

[1] Choosing between the texts of quartos 1604 and 1616, I should like
to emend the opening sentence thus:
> Now, Faustus,
> Must thou, needs be, be damned, canst not be saved.

Lucifer, concerns the state of hell. Where, to begin with, is the place of torment ?

> *Meph.* Within the bowels of these elements,
> Where we are tortur'd and remain for ever :
> Hell hath no limits, nor is circumscrib'd
> In one self-place ; but where we are is hell,
> And where hell is, there must we ever be ;
> And, to be short, when all the world dissolves,
> And every creature shall be purified,
> All places shall be hell that are not heaven.
>   *Faust.* I think hell 's a fable.
>   *Meph.* Ay, think so still, till experience change thy mind.
>   *Faust.* Why dost thou think that Faustus shall be damn'd ?
>   *Meph.* Ay, of necessity, for here 's the scroll
> In which thou hast given thy soul to Lucifer.
>   *Faust.* Ay, and body too ; and what of that ?
> Think'st thou that Faustus is so fond to imagine
> That after this life, there is any pain ?
> No, these are trifles, and mere old wives' tales.
>   *Meph.* But I am an instance to prove the contrary,
> For I tell thee I am damn'd and now in hell.
>   *Faust.* Nay, an this be hell, I'll willingly be damn'd :
> What ! sleeping, eating, walking and disputing !

Only one scene known to me in modern poetry offers any parallel to these weird dialogues between the fiend and Faustus. That is, the conversation which Malagigi holds with Astarotte in 'The Morgante Maggiore.' But Pulci is not, like Marlowe, in earnest. The Italian magician has not compromised his soul ; and the discourse glides gracefully from painful topics into a strain of courteous persiflage. Far more captivating to the imagination than Astarotte is this melancholy figure of Mephistophilis, the fallen angel, the servant of the Lord of Hell, standing at midnight in the doctor's study, dressed like a brown Capuchin, and resolving doleful problems of damnation with sinister sincerity. Marlowe's dramatic instinct drew advantage from the fiend's uncompromising candour. He used it to heighten the intrepidity of Faustus, to deepen the picture of the doomed man's spiritual arrogance.

Faustus makes ample use of his dearly purchased power. He surfeits his sense with carnal pleasure, and gluts his appetite for knowledge. Homer sings, and Amphion plays to him. He forces Mephistophilis to answer questions in astronomy and cosmography; flies in a chariot drawn by dragons round about the world; pries upon the planets, and surveys the kingdoms of the earth. Yet, when he is left alone, the snakes of conscience wake, and the two voices keep buzzing in his ear. The good angel grows faint; the evil threatens. He has reached a critical point, where he begins to regret the past: the hours of agony are frequent, and he groans aloud:

> My heart is hardened; I cannot repent;
> Scarce can I name salvation, faith, or heaven:
> Swords, poisons, halters, and envenomed steel,
> Are laid before me to despatch myself;
> And long ere this should I have done the deed,
> Had not sweet pleasure conquered deep despair.

Even his familiar mocks him, bidding him muse on Hell, since he is damned. He listens for one moment to the better voice. Alone upon the silent stage, in the darkness, he thrice invokes the holy name:

> O Christ, my Saviour, my Saviour!
> Help to save distressèd Faustus' soul!

Then suddenly emerges Lucifer with all his train:

> Christ cannot save thy soul; for He is just:
> There 's none but I have interest in the same.

Thus a devil speaks the naked truth to Faustus, who perforce must cringe before him, slinking back into obedience. Immediately afterwards he is fantastically soothed with nothing more attractive than a masque of the Seven Deadly Sins. The doomed man's only thought now is to spend the rest of his short years in a variety of fresh enjoyments. He travels far and wide; performs apish tricks in the Vatican, raises ghosts before the Emperor, plays practical jokes on clowns.

In this wild whirligig of change the horror of damnation
seizes him :

> What art thou, Faustus, but a man condemned to die?
> Thy fatal time draws to a final end.

It is this ever-recurring cry of the damned, growing more acute
as the end approaches, which makes even the buffooneries of
Doctor Faustus terrible. As the years move on this horror of
the end increases. In a scene of very great, because sober,
tragic power, Marlowe gives the victim one last chance. An
old man enters, and reminds Faustus that there is still room
for repentance :

> Yet, yet, thou hast an amiable soul,
> If sin by custom grow not into nature.

Hope seems ready to leap up in the withered heart; but
Mephistophilis is at his victim's elbow, with a dagger, the
symbol of despair :

> Thou traitor, Faustus, I arrest thy soul
> For disobedience to my sovereign lord ;
> Revolt, or I 'll in piecemeal tear thy flesh.

Faustus knows too well that the obsequious fiend, his servant,
is a tyrannous master ; for verily

> The gods are just, and of our pleasant vices
> Make instruments to plague us.

It only remains to plunge again into forbidden bliss, and, as
a crowning pleasure, Faustus demands Helen for his paramour.

The last scene is introduced by a dialogue of calm
simplicity and quiet dignity between Faustus and his former
pupils. The tender solicitude of these scholars, their love for
their old master, their respect for his attainments, the
sympathy with which they strive in vain to stanch the wound
of his spirit at this final hour, shed a soft gleam of natural
light upon the otherwise unmitigated gloom of the tragedy.
One of them would fain abide the issue of the night in company with Faustus. 'God will strengthen me,' he says ; 'I

will stay with Faustus.' But the wretched man, divining what must happen, cannot permit this sacrifice; and the scholars retire into the adjoining room to pray for him. Faustus is now alone, alone with spiritual beings—with jeering and exultant Mephistophilis, and with the angels; the good angel, who shows the celestial throne on which he might have sat and 'triumphed over Hell;' the bad angel, who reveals the 'ever-burning chair' on which 'o'er-tortured souls' may rest. As throughout the play, these angels are but Faustus's own thoughts objectified; and the contrasted thrones they now display are things of his imagination, rendered visible to the spectators.

The last hour of the hero's life unrolls itself slowly in one powerful soliloquy. The minutes are counted by sand-grains of his agony:

> O Faustus,
> Now hast thou but one bare hour to live,
> And then thou must be damned perpetually!

Starting from this contemplation, he calls upon the 'ever-moving spheres of heaven' to stand, or for the sun to rise 'and make perpetual day;' or for this hour to be

> A year, a month, a week, a natural day,
> That Faustus may repent and save his soul.

Then, by an exquisite touch of nature—the brain involuntarily summoning words employed for other purposes in happier hours—he cries aloud the line which Ovid whispered in Corinna's arms:

> O lente, lente currite, noctis equi!

But the heavens in their cycles will not be stopped to save one sinner's soul:

> The stars move still, time runs, the clock will strike,
> The devil will come, and Faustus must be damned.

We seem to see him at his study window with the night of stars above, and not a voice or footstep in the streets of

Wittenberg respondent to his agony. As he leans forth to
the darkness, cannot wings be given to his spirit's wish ?—

> O, I 'll leap up to heaven !—who pulls me down ?—
> See where Christ's blood streams in the firmament !
> One drop of blood will save me ; O my Christ !—
> Rend not my heart for naming of my Christ ;
> Yet will I call on him ; O, spare me, Lucifer !

The heated eye of his despair beholds the galaxy itself turned
into a river of red flowing blood, far, far beyond his reach ;
and though we do not see the devil, we feel him wrestling
with his soul, forbidding, mastering him. Horrid visions of
'a threatening arm, an angry brow,' distract his mind. He
calls upon the mountains and the hills to fall on him. Earth
'will not harbour him.' The 'stars that reigned at his
nativity' are deaf to his entreaty. While he is thus strug-
gling in the toils of vain desire, the half-hour strikes. This
rouses a new train of thought :

> O, if my soul must suffer for my sin,
> Impose some end to my incessant pain ;
> Let Faustus live in hell a thousand years,
> A hundred thousand, and at last be saved !

But, no, the soul is everlasting, and damnation has no limit :

> Why wert thou not a creature wanting soul ?

This reminds him of Pythagorean metempsychosis, and he
falls to envying the revolutions of imbruted spirits. There is
something maddening in the pressure of the thought of immortality upon a soul, whose endless plagues not even suicide
can lighten. Nothing is left but curses. Cursing his parents,
his birth, himself, and Lucifer, the clock strikes twelve, the
devils rush with thunder on the stage, and Faustus is dragged
down to hell.

Marlowe, it will be seen, spared his audience no iota either
of the spiritual or the physical torment of his hero. Would
it not have been more magnificent, we are inclined to wonder,
if he could have shown us Faustus in revolt against the devil

also at the end—like Dante's Farinata, holding hell in great disdain—or like Mozart's Don Juan, who, while the marble grasp of the Commendatore stiffens round his fingers, answers to the oft-repeated *Pentiti* a stubborn No? This indeed he might have done, and done with terrible effect, if the conscience of the public and the age would have permitted it. So far as we know anything at all about Marlowe, we have some right to assume that he had himself adopted the rebellious attitude of Faustus. In depicting his end thus with force so penetrative of imagination, did he mean to paint the terrors of his own remorseful soul; or, with an artist's irony, did he sacrifice the finest point of the situation to conventions and the exigencies of accepted beliefs? This we cannot now decide. But the whole handling by Marlowe of the Faust-legend inclines one rather to believe that, if it is in any true sense autobiographical, the poet was but an ill-contented and heart-sick atheist.

The Epilogue spoken by the Chorus points the moral of the tragedy in noble lines, three of which supply an epitaph for Marlowe's grave:

> Cut is the branch that might have grown full straight,
> And burnèd is Apollo's laurel-bough,
> That sometime grew within this learnèd man.
> Faustus is gone :—regard his hellish fall,
> Whose fiendful fortune may exhort the wise,
> Only to wonder at unlawful things,
> Whose deepness doth entice such forward wits
> To practise more than heavenly power permits.

Possibly Marlowe reckoned that, not having dabbled in black arts, nor having signed a compact with his blood, he would escape damnation. Possibly he was an atheist so complete, and an artist so consummate, as to be able to smile at the Acheron he luridly made visible to mortal eyes.

IX

I have said much already about the character of Barabas, in 'The Jew of Malta.' It is clear that Marlowe yielded to the traditions of the Miracles when he put this Jew upon the

stage, out-Heroding Herod in his fury. But it is also clear
that he sketched the prototype of Shylock. Barabas, down-
trodden, kicked into corners, and despoiled by the Christians,
retains the Hebrew pride of race:

> In spite of these swine-eating Christians—
> Unchosen nation, never circumcised,
> Poor villains, such as were ne'er thought upon,
> Till Titus and Vespasian conquered us—
> Am I become as wealthy as I was.
> I am not of the tribe of Levi, I,
> That can so soon forget an injury.
> We Jews can fawn like spaniels when we please;
> And when we grin we bite; yet are our looks
> As innocent and harmless as a lamb's.
> I learn'd in Florence how to kiss my hand,
> Heave up my shoulders when they call me dog,
> And duck as low as any barefoot friar;
> Hoping to see them starve upon a stall,
> Or else be gather'd for in our synagogue,
> That, when the offering basin comes to me,
> Even for charity I may spit into 't.

A Christian, the lover of his daughter greets him in the
street with: 'Whither walk'st thou, Barabas?' He answers:

> No further: 't is a custom held with us,
> That when we speak with Gentiles like to you,
> We turn into the air to purge ourselves;
> For unto us the promise doth belong.

This arrogance of race and religion is fortified by the comparison between his people and the Christian hypocrites who
persecute them:

> Thus trolls our fortune in by land and sea,
> And thus are we on every side enrich'd:
> These are the blessings promised to the Jews,
> And herein was old Abraham's happiness:
> What more may heaven do for earthly man
> Than thus to pour out plenty in their laps
> Ripping the bowels of the earth for them,
> Making the seas their servants, and the winds
> To drive their substance with successful blasts?

Who hateth me but for my happiness ?
Or who is honoured now but for his wealth ?
Rather had I, a Jew, be hated thus
Than pitied in a Christian poverty;
For I can see no fruits in all their faith,
But malice, falsehood, and excessive pride,
Which, methinks, fits not their profession.
Haply some hapless man hath conscience,
And for his conscience lives in beggary.
They say we are a scattered nation;
I cannot tell; but we have scrambled up
More wealth by far than those that brag of faith.
There's Kirriah Jairim, the great Jew of Greece,
Obed in Bairseth, Nones in Portugal,
Myself in Malta, some in Italy,
Many in France, and wealthy every one;
Ay, wealthier far than any Christian.

Up to this point Barabas is not unworthy of Shylock.
But it would be a waste of labour to prolong the comparison
of two pictures so differently executed. The one is a powerful
but rough draft. The other is a finely finished portrait.
Shylock disappears together with the storm and passion he
has stirred. And round him Shakspere grouped some of our
dearest friends—noble Bassanio, devoted Antonio, witty
Gratiano, the dignity of Portia, the tenderness of Jessica, the
merriment of Nerissa. These remain ; and over them, at last,
is shed an atmosphere of peace and music in that moonlight
act, the loveliest Shakspere ever wrote. Its beauty never dies.
Jessica still sits upon the bank, and Lorenzo whispers to her
of 'the young-eyed cherubin.' We hear the voices of Portia
and Nerissa coming through the twilight of the garden. The
music, sweeter by night than day, still lingers in our ears.
The lover's quarrel, so artfully contrived and so delightfully
concluded, still enchants our sympathy. How different is the
impression left by Marlowe's play ! Round the wolf-fanged
figure of Barabas gathers a rout of grasping tyrants and
vindictive pariahs, hypocritical friars and cut-throat slaves, the
rapacious Bellamira, the hideous Ithamore, the ruffian Pilia
Borza. It is as though Marlowe, in pure wantonness of

cynicism, had planned the vilest scheme of villany, debauchery, greed, treason, homicide, concupiscence, infernal cruelty; raking the dregs and ransacking the dunghills of humanity to justify the melodrama of his hero's cursing end.

The unrelieved cruelty of this play encourages a belief that Marlowe dramatised it from some Spanish novel; and there is one scene which, in its unconscious humour, grotesque and ghastly, forcibly reminds us of Spanish art. Barabas has been detected in one of his rogueries by two friars belonging to different religious bodies. In order to extricate himself and to involve them both in ruin, he determines to work upon their common avarice and mutual jealousy. He begins by pretending repentance, and dazzling their imaginations with a picture of his wealth:

> *Bara.* O holy friars, the burden of my sins
> Lies heavy on my soul! then, pray you, tell me,
> Is 't not too late now to turn Christian?
> I have been zealous in the Jewish faith,
> Hard-hearted to the poor, a covetous wretch,
> That would for lucre's sake have sold my soul;
> A hundred for a hundred I have ta'en;
> And now for store of wealth may I compare
> With all the Jews in Malta; but what is wealth?
> I am a Jew, and therefore am I lost.
> Would penance serve [to atone] for this my sin,
> I could afford to whip myself to death.
>   *Itha.* And so could I; but penance will not serve.
>   *Bara.* To fast, to pray, and wear a shirt of hair,
> And on my knees creep to Jerusalem.
> Cellars of wine, and sollars full of wheat,
> Warehouses stuff'd with spices and with drugs,
> Whole chests of gold in bullion and in coin,
> Besides, I know not how much weight in pearl,
> Orient and round, have I within my house;
> At Alexandria merchandise untold;
> But yesterday two ships went from this town,
> Their voyage will be worth ten thousand crowns;
> In Florence, Venice, Antwerp, London, Seville,
> Frankfort, Lubeck, Moscow, and where not,
> Have I debts owing; and, in most of these,
> Great sums of money lying in the banco;

> All this I 'll give to some religious house,
> So I may be baptis'd, and live therein.

Friar Jacopo and Friar Barnardine immediately fall to bidding one against the other for this desirable penitent. Each in turn depreciates his rival's order, and exalts the merits of his own. Barabas stimulates their several cupidities. At last the friars come to blows. He then assumes the character of peacemaker, cajoling Friar Barnardine to stay in his own house, and making an appointment with Friar Jacopo for the following night. Barnardine, as might have been expected, is strangled in the meanwhile by the Jew and his accomplice Ithamore. They prop him up upon his staff in a doorway through which the other friar will have to pass. 'So, let him lean upon his staff,' grins Ithamore; 'excellent! he stands as if he were begging of bacon.' Jacopo, in haste to keep his appointment with the wealthy convert, soon appears, and by the dim light of the moon detects his rival in the archway. At first he speaks him fair; then, getting no answer and spying the staff, he thinks an ambush has been laid for him, and knocks the body down. Barabas rushes from the house, lifts the corpse, and accuses Jacopo of the murder. There lies dead Barnardine, and over him is stretched the tell-tale staff. Barabas, with brutal sarcasm, exclaims:

> For this example I 'll remain a Jew:
> Heaven bless me! What, a friar, a murderer!
> When shall you see a Jew commit the like?

Then he drags Jacopo off to justice, with Ithamore for witness and the staff for evidence.

It is not easy to calculate the acting capabilities of plays. Tamburlaine in his 'copper-laced coat and crimson velvet breeches,' and Barabas with his huge red nose, were no less popular upon the stage than Faustus in his 'cloak and jerkin.' The great actor, Edward Alleyn, gained applause, we know, in all these characters, 'and won the attribute of peerless.' Richard Perkins, who sustained the weight of Webster's Brachiano, was also famous for his personation of the Jew.

To students the distance between Faustus and Barabas, considered from the point of view of psychological analysis, is immense. But it is conceivable that the bustle, bloodshed, and continual business of ' The Jew of Malta ' may have made this drama more attractive than the other. Heywood, in a prologue written for the Court about the year 1633, describes it as :

Writ many years agone,
And in that age thought second unto none.

X

Modern criticism will place ' The Jew of Malta ' below the fourth of Marlowe's tragedies.   This is the ' Chronicle of Edward II.,' upon which Shakspere modelled his Richard II., and which, in my opinion, offers points of superiority to the first of the Shaksperian history-plays. That species of dramatic skill which consists in protracting a tragic situation by fixing attention on the gradual consummation of a fate involved in the folly of the protagonist, by harassing our feelings with renewed demands upon their sympathy, and by showing the victim of his own insolence more noble in misfortune than when he sunned his wilfulness in noonday pride, has been brilliantly displayed by Marlowe in Edward II.   Putting Shakspere's studies from the English chronicles out of account, this is certainly the finest historical drama in our language, as it also is the first deserving of that title.

In the three tragedies by Marlowe which have been hitherto examined one personage predominates ; the rest are mainly accessory to the action. ' Tamburlaine,' ' Doctor Faustus,' and ' The Jew of Malta ' exist for and in their eponymous heroes. ' Edward II.' exhibits three characters of almost equal power in conflict and contrast ; these are Edward, Gaveston, and Mortimer—the king, besotted by his doting fondness for a minion ; the favourite, clutching at power and place, using his base influence for a realm's ruin ; the ambitious subject climbing to a crown by trading on the general hatred for this upstart, not less than on the queen's wounded

sense of self-respect. Round these leading personages are
grouped temporal and spiritual barons of a feudal epoch,
bound to the throne by allegiance, but conscious of their
power as vassals of the Crown or representatives of Rome—
stung to rebellion by the foolishness of an unkingly king.
The dialogue, in its brief, hot vehemence, suits these turbulent
passions. For the first time in a play of this description steel
grates on steel and blow responds to blow, in the quick, tense
speech of natural anger. The king and his minion, the insulted
queen, the haughty bishop, the wrathful lords, the bold
ambitious paramour, and the hired assassin clash together
through successive scenes of strife and intrigue, in which a
kingdom is twice lost and won, and lost again. How largely
it is all planned ! not deftly plotted, but traced upon the lines
of history in bold and vivid characters.

The openings of Marlowe's plays are always fine, and this
of ' Edward II.' is no exception. Gaveston appears upon the
scene ; and after some preliminary dialogue, which serves to
accentuate the minion's character, he breaks into this
soliloquy :

These are not men for me.
I must have wanton poets, pleasant wits,
Musicians, that with touching of a string
May draw the pliant king which way I please.
Music and poetry is his delight.
Therefore I'll have Italian masks by night,
Sweet speeches, comedies, and pleasing shows ;
And in the day, when he shall walk abroad,
Like sylvan nymphs my pages shall be clad,
My men, like satyrs grazing on the lawns,
Shall with their goat-feet dance the antic hay ;
Sometimes a lovely boy in Dian's shape,
With hair that gilds the water as it glides,
Crownets of pearls about his naked arms,
And in his sportful hands an olive tree,
Shall bathe him in a spring; and there, hard by,
One like Actæon, peeping through the grove,
Shall by the angry goddess be transformed,
And running in the likeness of an hart,
By yelping hounds pulled down, shall seem to die:
Such things as these best please his majesty

This monologue of Gaveston's, underlined as it is by the last verse, indicates, as in a frontispiece, the motive of the drama. Afterwards it remains to see how Edward flings away wife, crown, and people's love for the idle pleasures promised him by Gaveston.

There are two passages in ' Edward II.' where Marlowe rises to sublime poetic pitch. The one deals with what Lamb called ' the reluctant pangs of abdicating royalty ; ' the other is that death scene, which, in the words of the same critic, ' moves pity and terror beyond any scene, ancient or modern, with which I am acquainted.' The poet undertook no facile task when he essayed to show the light, lascivious Edward dignified in suffering. Yet this he has accomplished by the passionate rhetoric and thrilling verse with which he has enforced the tragic pathos of royalty eclipsed, exposed to outrage, menaced with murder. For awhile, before his fall, Edward, in the company of his friends Spencer and Baldock, takes refuge with the monks of Neath. The abbot receives the disguised fugitives :

> *Abbot.* Have you no doubt, my lord ; have you no fear:
> As silent and as careful we will be
> To keep your royal person safe with us,
> Free from suspect, and fell invasion
> Of such as have your majesty in chase,
> Yourself, and those your chosen company,
> As danger of this stormy time requires.
>   *K. Edw.* Father, thy face should harbour no deceit.
> O, hadst thou ever been a king, thy heart,
> Pierc'd deeply with sense of my distress,
> Could not but take compassion of my state !
> Stately and proud in riches and in train,
> Whilom I was, powerful and full of pomp ;
> But what is he whom rule and empery
> Have not in life or death made miserable ?

Then the king turns to his companions :

> Come, Spenser—come, Baldock—come, sit down by me,
> Make trial now of that philosophy
> That in our famous nurseries of arts
> Thou suck'dst from Plato and from Aristotle.

> Father, this life contemplative is heaven;
> O, that I might this life in quiet lead!

One of them lets fall the name of Mortimer:

> Mortimer! who talks of Mortimer?
> Who wounds me with the name of Mortimer,
> That bloody man?—Good father, on thy lap
> Lay I this head, laden with mickle care.
> O might I never ope these eyes again,
> Never again lift up this drooping head,
> O, never more lift up this dying heart!

This scene serves as prelude to the abdication scene at
Killingworth. The Earl of Leicester and the Bishop of
Winchester are in attendance, the one soothing the king's
anguish with kind words; the other stubbornly insisting on
his resignation of the crown. Edward opens the debate in a
speech of harmony so rich and varied, that in this I recognise
the master's perfected command of his own mighty line:

> Leicester, if gentle words might comfort me,
> Thy speeches long ago had eas'd my sorrow,
> For kind and loving hast thou always been.
> The griefs of private men are soon allay'd;
> But not of kings. The forest deer, being struck,
> Runs to an herb that closeth up the wounds;
> But when the imperial lion's flesh is gor'd,
> He rends and tears it with his wrathful paw,
> [And], highly scorning that the lowly earth
> Should drink his blood, mounts up to the air;
> And so it fares with me, whose dauntless mind
> Th' ambitious Mortimer would seek to curb,
> And that unnatural queen, false Isabel,
> That thus hath pent and mew'd me in a prison;
> For such outrageous passions clog my soul,
> As with the wings of rancour and disdain
> Full oft[en] am I soaring up to heaven,
> To plain me to the gods against them both.
> But when I call to mind I am a king,
> Methinks I should revenge me of my wrongs
> That Mortimer and Isabel have done.
> But what are kings, when regiment is gone,

But perfect shadows in a sunshine day ?
My nobles rule ; I bear the name of king ;
I wear the crown ; but am controlled by them,
By Mortimer, and my unconstant queen,
Who spots my nuptial bed with infamy ;
Whilst I am lodged within this cave of care,
Where Sorrow at my elbow still attends,
To company my heart with sad laments,
That bleeds within me for this strange exchange.

The Bishop submits that Edward will resign his crown to his
own son, and not to Mortimer.   'No,' he replies :

No, 't is for Mortimer, not Edward's head ;
For he 's a lamb, encompassèd by wolves,
Which in a moment will abridge his life.
But if proud Mortimer do wear this crown,
Heaven turn it to a blaze of quenchless fire !
Or, like the snaky wreath of Tisiphon,
Engirt the temples of his hateful head ;
So shall not England's vine be perishèd,
But Edward's name survive though Edward dies.

Both Leicester and the Bishop urge.   Edward vacillates
between necessity and shame.   At one moment he takes the
crown from his head ; at the next he replaces it :

Here, take my crown ; the life of Edward too :
                              [*Taking off the crown.*
Two kings in England cannot reign at once.
But stay a while ; let me be king till night,
That I may gaze upon this glittering crown ;
So shall my eyes receive their last content,
My head, the latest honour due to it,
And jointly both yield up their wishèd right.
Continue ever, thou celestial sun ;
Let never silent night possess this clime ;
Stand still, you watches of the element ;
All times and seasons, rest you at a stay,
That Edward may be still fair England's king !

Yet an answer must be given to the lords, and the inevitable
cannot be avoided :

> Heavens and earth conspire
> To make me miserable.   Here, receive my crown.
> Receive it ? no, these innocent hands of mine
> Shall not be guilty of so foul a crime ;
> He of you all that most desires my blood,
> And will be call'd the murderer of a king,
> Take it.   What, are you mov'd ? pity you me ?
> Then send for unrelenting Mortimer,
> And Isabel, whose eyes being turn'd to steel,
> Will sooner sparkle fire than shed a tear.
> Yet stay ; for, rather than I'll look on them,
> Here, here ! [*Gives the crown.*] Now, sweet God of heaven,
> Make me despise this transitory pomp,
> And sit for aye enthronisèd in heaven !
> Come, death, and with thy fingers close my eyes,
> Or, if I live, let me forget myself !

The king's last thoughts are for his son :

> Let not that Mortimer protect my son :
> More safety is there in a tiger's jaws
> Than his embracements.   Bear this to the queen,
> Wet with my tears, and dried again with sighs ;
> If with the sight thereof she be not moved,
> Return it back, and dip it in my blood.
> Commend me to my son, and bid him rule
> Better than I.   Yet how have I transgressed,
> Unless it be with too much clemency ?

Now all is over with Edward.   Dragged from place to place, starved, and taunted, we find him next at Berkeley Castle in a dungeon underneath the moat.   The aspect of the monarch, wasted with long watching and fasting in his loathsome prison, suggests too much of that Euripidean squalor which high tragedy repudiates.   Yet the kingliness with which he calls to mind his majesty of happier days, and bestows his last jewel on the cut-throat sent to murder him, ennobles the revolting details Marlowe has thought fit to accumulate.   Lightborn, the assassin, enters the dungeon with a lamp, and on the threshold recoils disgusted by its venomous stench.   The dialogue between him and his victim, famous as it is, must be transcribed at length :

K. Edw. Weep'st thou already ? list a while to me,
And then thy heart, were it as Gurney's is,
Or as Matrevis', hewn from the Caucasus,
Yet will it melt ere I have done my tale.
This dungeon where they keep me, is the sink
Wherein the filth of all the castle falls.
    Light. O villains !
    K. Edw. And there, in mire and puddle, have I stood
This ten days' space; and, lest that I should sleep,
One plays continually upon a drum;
They give me bread and water, being a king;
So that for want of sleep and sustenance,
My mind 's distempered and my body 's numbed,
And whether I have limbs or not I know not.
O, would my blood dropped out from every vein,
As doth this water, from my tattered robes !
Tell Isabel the queen I looked not thus,
When for her sake I ran at tilt in France,
And there unhorsed the Duke of Cleremont.
    L. O speak no more, my lord; this breaks my heart.
Lie on this bed and rest yourself a while.
    E. These looks of thine can harbour nought but death:
I see my tragedy written in thy brows.
Yet, stay a while; forbear thy bloody hand,
And let me see the stroke before it comes;
That even then when I shall lose my life,
My soul may be more steadfast on my God.
    L. What means your Highness to mistrust me thus ?
    E. What mean'st thou to dissemble with me thus ?
    L. These hands were never stained with innocent blood,
Nor shall they now be tainted with a king's.
    E. Forgive my thought for having such a thought.
One jewel have I left; receive thou this;
Still fear I, and I know not what 's the cause,
But every joint shakes as I give it thee.
O ! if thou harbour'st murder in thy heart,
Let this gift change thy mind, and save thy soul !
Know that I am a king: O, at that name
I feel a hell of grief ! Where is my crown ?
Gone, gone ! and do I yet remain alive ?
    L. You 're overwatched, my lord; lie down and rest.
    E. But that grief keeps me waking I should sleep;
For not these ten days have these eyelids closed.
Now, as I speak they fall; and yet with fear
Open again.   O, wherefore sitt'st thou here ?

L. If you mistrust me, I 'll begone, my lord.

E. No, no : for if thou mean'st to murder me,
Thou wilt return again ; and therefore stay.　　　*[Sleeps.*

　L. He sleeps.

　E.　　　　　　O, let me not die yet ! O, stay a while !

　L. How now, my lord ?

　E. Something still buzzeth in my ears,
And tells me, if I sleep, I never wake :
This fear it is which makes me tremble thus ;
And therefore tell me ; wherefore art thou come ?

　L. To rid thee of thy life.—Matrevis, come !

Over what follows it were well to draw the veil ; for Marlowe,
with the savagery of his age, shows Edward smothered,
sparing only one incident of that unnatural regicide.

XI

　The fifth of Marlowe's undoubted tragedies, produced in
his own lifetime, is ' The Massacre at Paris.' This play was
popular under its second title of ' The Guise,' and, like the
majority of the poet's dramatic works, was written apparently
to provide one great actor with a telling part. As we possess
it, the text bears signs not only of hasty composition but also
of negligent printing. It is chiefly interesting for its fierce
anti-papal feeling, inflamed to rabidness by the horrors of
S. Bartholomew. Yet, even from this point of view, its
passion falls far short of the concentrated rage expressed by
D'Aubigné in ' Les Tragiques.' Nor has Marlowe relieved the
forcible feebleness of its chaotic cruelties with any bursts of
poetry or ringing declamation.

　' The Tragedy of Dido, Queen of Carthage,' was left unfinished, and produced after Marlowe's death. I have already
expressed the opinion that this may have been an early essay.
In the main, it consists of translations from the second and
fourth books of the ' Æneid,' somewhat resembling the tumid
style of the lines declaimed in ' Hamlet ' by the player. But
Marlowe introduced one or two original scenes, characteristic

of his manner and of the fashion of the day.   In one of these
Jupiter is 'dallying with Idalian Ganymede,' petting his cup-
bearer back into good humour by the praise of a thousand
pretty things.   Hermes lies asleep, with folded wings, beside
them; and the picture is one that Correggio might have painted.
In another, Venus carries the boy Iulus asleep to Ida:

> Now is he fast asleep ; and in this grove,
> Amongst green brakes, I'll lay Ascanius,
> And strew him with sweet-smelling violets,
> Blushing roses, purple hyacinths ;
> These milk-white doves shall be his centronels.

In a third, Cupid, who has assumed the form of Ascanius, be-
witches an old nurse, and sets her thinking upon love.   To
tempt him away from Dido, she invites him thus :

> I have an orchard that hath store of plums,
> Brown almonds, services, ripe figs, and dates,
> Dewberries, apples, yellow oranges ;
> A garden where are beehives full of honey,
> Musk-roses, and a thousand sort of flowers ;
> And in the midst doth run a silver stream,
> Where thou shalt see the red-gilled fishes leap,
> White swans, and many lovely water-fowls.

The hyperbolical splendour of description running over into
nonsense, which Marlowe seems to have made fashionable
and which Greene and Peele but feebly imitated, is illustrated
in Dido's offers of a fleet to Æneas :

> I 'll give thee tackling made of rivelled gold,
> Wound on the barks of odoriferous trees ;
> Oars of massy ivory, full of holes,
> Through which the water shall delight to play ;
> Thy anchors shall be hewed from crystal rocks,
> Which, if thou lose, shall shine above the waves ;
> The mast whereon thy swelling sails shall hang,
> Hollow pyramides of silver plate ;
> The sails of folded lawn, where shall be wrought
> The wars of Troy,—but not Troy's overthrow.

This is in the true style of Hero's buskins ; and the blank
verse, falling in couplets, seems to cry aloud for rhymes.

Much might be said about Marlowe's treatment of Virgil's text, and the exaggerated, almost spasmodic attempt made to heighten the tragic tension of each situation. Take the apparition of Hector's ghost for an example :

> Then buckled I mine armour, drew my sword,
> And thinking to go down, came Hector's ghost,
> With ashy visage, blueish sulphur eyes,
> His arms torn from his shoulders, and his breast
> Furrowed with wounds, and, that which made me weep,
> Thongs at his heels, by which Achilles' horse
> Drew him in triumph through the Greekish camp,
> Burst from the earth, crying, ' Æneas, fly !
> Troy is a-fire, the Grecians have the town ! '

Instead of ' blueish sulphur eyes,' ' arms torn off,' and ' breast furrowed with wounds,' Virgil writes :

> Raptatus bigis ut quondam, aterque cruento
> Pulvere, perque pedes trajectus lora tumentes.

Then, as though the vision were too horrible :

> Hei mihi, qualis erat ! quantum mutatus ab illo
> Hectore !

And when he speaks again of those wounds, he tempers their disgrace :
> quæ circum plurima muros
> Accepit patrios.

Nor does Virgil's Hector ' burst from the earth,' but steals upon Æneas like a dream in the first sleep of night. Each of these points the translator misses ; and, instead, presents us with the picture of a mangled corpse, starting from the charnel, and shrieking a shrill message of sudden woe. The neglect of modulation and reserve is a main point in Elizabethan tragedy. We may surmise that even Shakspere, had he dealt with Hector's as he did with Hamlet's father's ghost, would have sought to intensify the terror of the apparition at the expense of artistic beauty.

XII

I have reviewed, perhaps at intolerable length, the authentic work of Marlowe as a dramatist. One play, which bears his name upon the title-page, and which passed till recently for his, namely, 'Lust's Dominion,' must be attributed to a feebler though imitative hand. Nor do I think we can with certainty assign to Marlowe any definite portions of the Shaksperian Histories. That he had a hand in the first draughts which went to form 'Henry VI.' can be accepted; and that his influence may be traced in 'Edward III.' is a tenable theory. But in the absence of external evidence, it would be vain to draw conjecture further, especially when we have seen that the whole manner of that epoch is saturated with the master's style.

Marlowe was great as a dramatist; but as a poet he was still greater. Even in his tragedies it is the poet, rather than the playwright, who commands our admiration. His characters are too often the mouthpieces of their maker's passionate oratory, rather than beings gifted with a complex, independent vitality. At another time I hope to study 'Hero and Leander,' in combination with 'Venus and Adonis,' 'Salmacis and Hermaphroditus,' and a few other narrative poems of this epoch; works in which our chiefest dramatists expressed their sense of beauty, unimpeded by theatrical necessities. It will then be seen into how clear and lofty a region of pure poetry Marlowe soared; and in how true a sense he deserves the name of pioneer and maker. Marlowe's contemporaries hailed in him a morning star of song, and marked him out as the young Apollo of his age. Not the dramatist, but the inspired artist, moved their panegyric when they wrote of him. Let me conclude this essay with some of their testimonies, selecting only those which seem to catch a portion of his spirit. Chapman shall speak first of the dead friend who—

> Stood
> Up to the chin in the Pierian flood,
> And drank to me half this Musæan story,
> Inscribing it to deathless memory.

Peele shall follow with his tribute to the poet's grave ·

> Unhappy in thine end,
> Marley, the Muses' darling for thy verse,
> Fit to write passions for the souls below,
> If any wretched souls in passion speak.

Drayton shall tell how—

> Marlowe, bathed in the Thespian springs,
> Had in him those brave translunary things
> That the first poets had ; his raptures were
> All air and fire, which made his verses clear ;
> For that fine madness still he did retain,
> Which rightly should possess a poet's brain.

Petowe, less renowned, less skilful, but hardly less discrimina·
ting, sings of—

> Marlo admired, whose honey-flowing vein
> No English writer can as yet attain,
> Whose name in Fame's immortal treasury
> Truth shall record to deathless memory,
> Marlo, late mortal, now framed all divine—

and hails his entrance into the heaven of poetry ; where :

> Marlo, still-admirèd Marlo 's gone
> To live with beauty in Elysium—
> Immortal beauty, who desires to hear
> His sacred poesies sweet in every ear.

These laurels, which were showered on Marlowe's hearse,
are still evergreen. The most impassioned singer of our own
day, Charles Algernon Swinburne, has scattered the roses and
lilies of high-sounding verse and luminous prose upon that
poet's tomb. One of the noblest, as he is now the eldest of
our poets, Richard Horne, has digested the romance of his untimely death into a worthy tragedy. Yet why should we use
the language of the grave in speaking about Marlowe ?

> He has outsoared the shadow of our night ;
> Envy and calumny, and hate and pain,
> And that unrest which men miscall delight,
> Can touch him not and torture not again.

His nightingales, 'the glad dear angels of the spring' of
English poetry, survive and fill our ears with music. They
are not dead, although—

> Cut is the branch that might have grown full straight,
> And burnèd is Apollo's laurel bough,
> That sometime grew within this learnèd man.

INDEX